TO MY WIFE

TO MY WIFE

WITHDRAWN

TRADE UNION DOCUMENTS

TRADE UNION DOCUMENTS

Compiled and Edited with an Introduction

by

W. MILNE-BAILEY

*Secretary of the Research and Economic Department
of the Trades Union Congress*

LONDON
G. BELL & SONS LTD.
1929

60:639

PRINTED IN GREAT BRITAIN BY ROBERT MACLEHOSE AND CO. LTD.
THE UNIVERSITY PRESS, GLASGOW.

PREFACE

TRADE UNIONISM has a large and growing literature, but hitherto there has not been available for students any collection of the original documents that are necessary if a first-hand acquaintance with the activities of this great movement is to be obtained. As Trade Unions become more powerful, and assume more and more the character of public institutions, it may be taken for granted that interest in their doings and in their organisation will continue to increase, and while enquirers will doubtless still turn to Mr. and Mrs. Webb's monumental works on Trade Unionism, this 'source-book' will, it is hoped, prove a serviceable adjunct.

Collections of documents are like anthologies, in that every reader has to bewail the omission of some item which to him seems to be of the first importance. That the present volume is full of imperfections is undeniable, but some of the more obvious can perhaps be explained.

It is clear, in the first place, that some of the documents included have only ephemeral value; others remain as of permanent importance in the annals of Trade Unionism. The inclusion of the former is deliberate, for it seems necessary that the current, and perhaps temporary, aspects of the movement should be illustrated as well as the long-time tendencies. If they were excluded, a more critical standard would be observed at the expense of losing touch with realities. If ever a new edition should be called for, a new selection of 'ephemeral' matter would probably be needed.

No documents of purely historical interest have been included. The material used either refers to present-day conditions, or is of direct and immediate value in the discussion of the problems of to-day. It must not be assumed, however, that the Union Rules and other documents included are in all cases in operation at the time of publication. Changes are constantly taking place, but the extracts given are typical of modern Trade Unionism. To emphasise the fact that my object has been to illustrate the general features of the movement, a brief introduction to each Part links up the documents into a continuous series, and suggests some of the more important sources of further information. The historical Introduction is not intended as a substitute for studying a standard history of Trade Unionism. It is, indeed, taken for granted that every serious reader of this collection will turn continually to Mr. and Mrs. Webb's *History of Trade Unionism* and *Industrial Democracy*, having, as a preliminary step, worked through Mr. Lloyd's *Trade*

Unionism and Mr. Cole's *Short History of the British Working Class Movement.* The historical Introduction may then serve to remind the reader of some of the outstanding events which have led up to the complexities, problems, and achievements of modern Trade Unionism.

Some slight references have been made to the Trade Union movements in other countries, but only in order to illustrate important differences or similarities between them and the British movement.

I have finally to make a number of acknowledgments both for the valuable help I have received in the compilation of this volume and for permission to use material. For the defects, and for all expressions of opinion, I alone am responsible, however, and neither the Trades Union Congress nor individual Unions must be held responsible for any views or interpretations contained in the Introduction or Commentaries.

To the Trades Union Congress and to the Unions and Employers' Associations whose publications and documents I have used I have to express my deepest thanks for the permission, willingly given, to include these extracts, as also to the authors and publishers of the books from which passages have been taken. The extracts from documents in this book are made with the permission of the official Controller of H.M. Stationery Office. The extracts from H. D. Henderson's *The Cotton Control Board* are used by permission of the Oxford University Press and the Carnegie Endowment for International Peace. Permission has been willingly given, also, by the following : Mr. and Mrs. Webb, for the use of extracts from their *History of Trade Unionism* and *Industrial Democracy* ; Mr. G. D. H. Cole and Messrs. Macmillan for the use of extracts from *The World of Labour* and *Self Government in Industry* ; Mr. G. D. H. Cole and Mr. W. Mellor for the use of a passage from their pamphlet *The Greater Unionism* ; Mr. R. H. Tawney and Messrs. Bell & Sons, Ltd., for the use of extracts from *The Acquisitive Society* ; Mr. W. M. Citrine and the International Federation of Trade Unions for the use of extracts from *The Trade Union Movement of Great Britain* ; Mr. W. M. Citrine and the *Manchester Guardian* for the use of an article from the *Manchester Guardian* ' Industrial Relations Supplement ' ; Mr. L. H. Green and the *Manchester Guardian* for the use of another article from the same ' Supplement ' ; Prof. H. J. Laski and the Fabian Society for the use of an extract from the Fabian Tract, *The State in the New Social Order* ; Prof. H. J. Laski and the Yale University Press for the use of passages from *Authority in the Modern State*; the *Manchester Guardian* for the use of an extract from the late Prof. Geldart's 'The Osborne Judgment and After'; the I.F.T.U. for the use of extracts from their *Year Book*; the Labour Party for the use of extracts from their publications; the Food Trades International for the use of its Constitution; the Canadian Department of Labor for an extract from its Annual Report; the Nat. Joint Council for the Building Industry for the use of its Constitution and Working Rules; the Workers' Educational Assoc. for the use of its Report on Adult Education and the Trade Unionist; the L.G.O.C. for the use of its notice on recognition of Unions; the Nat. Joint Council for the Elec. Supply Industry for the use of its Resolution on recognition of Unions; and the American Federation of Labor for the use of extracts from its Annual Reports.

Finally, I have the pleasant duty of thanking several friends for their ungrudging assistance and advice: Rt. Hon. Sidney Webb, M.P., Mr. Arthur Henderson, Jun., my colleagues at the T.U.C., and, above all, Prof. H. J. Laski, for whose generous help and encouragement I cannot adequately express my gratitude. Special thanks are due, I feel, to Messrs. G. Bell & Sons, who have shown so much more than ordinary business interest and care in the production of this book. Lastly, my deepest thanks are due to my wife for unfailing help throughout the preparation of the Documents and for the compilation of the Index.

W. M.-B.

CONTENTS

DOCUMENTS

b

PAGE

PART III.

[1] The official title is " Conference on Industrial Reorganisation and Industrial Relations." The popular name "Mond-Turner Conference" and the title " Conference between the General Council of the T.U.C. and the 'Mond' group of Employers " are also used in this book.

INTRODUCTION

TRADE UNIONS are born, not made. This is a truth that must be firmly grasped by those who wish to understand the complex structure, multifarious activities, and oft-times illogical policies of the Trade Unions of to-day. Their growth has been a spontaneous, healthy process arising out of the needs of the common people.

Those needs,—for fellowship between craftsmen, for mutual help, for improvement in the remuneration and conditions of labour, for an increasing measure of control over the circumstances of daily life,—gave rise to that voluntary organisation and that group spirit which we know as the Trade Union Movement.

The State has everywhere looked askance on the birth of voluntary associations within itself, lest they should so command the allegiance of men as to threaten the sovereignty of the State itself. Curiously enough, the association of men merely for personal gain has been looked upon more tolerantly than their organisation for benevolent, educational or religious purposes.

That such apparently laudable objects may mask a conspiracy aimed to overthrow the existing sovereign is true enough, but is there not also in this attitude of the State some recognition of the fact that group life based on those deeply-rooted needs of the spirit is likely to be far more enduring and to command a more unfaltering loyalty than is an association based on the desire for personal profit? It has been this social character and vivid group life of the Trade Unions, with the resultant conflict of loyalties, that has aroused the hostility of the State, as formerly in the case of the Church. So we find in every country, despite the differences in legal systems and political traditions, a long struggle against the attempt of the State first to suppress Unions, then to ignore them and treat them as non-existent. With admirable clarity Dicey [1] has shown how similar in fact, though different in law and political theory, has been the evolution of the 'right of association' in England and France,

---

[1] Dicey, A. V., *Law and Opinion in England*, App., Note 1, on Freedom of Association.

respectively.   In almost every country Trade Unions have had to
wage a similar fight for recognition and indeed for the right to exist.

We now see the beginnings of the third stage.   Having failed,
because of economic circumstances which mould political institutions, either to suppress or ignore Unions, the State finally decides to
assimilate them into its own organisation, and to make them part of
its own administrative machine.   How far such a process may go is
to be seen in the antithetical yet curiously parallel constitutions of
Fascist Italy and Soviet Russia.

The Corporative State, Mussolini's greatest achievement, is
assuredly one of the most interesting experiments yet made in
political mechanics, and perhaps the only thoroughgoing attempt to
reconcile the conflicting claims of group and State.

So in Russia, too.   'The Trade Unions,' say Bukharin and
Preobrazhensky, 'must develop in such a way that they will be
transformed into economic departments and instruments of the
State authority,' [1] and Russia has tried to act on this injunction.

In both cases it may seem that the 'reconciliation' of the conflicting claims is complete, if somewhat one-sided, but although at
the moment the smile is on the face of the State tiger, one may
prophesy that he will yet have indigestion.

In Britain the stages of development have been clearly marked by
the Combination Acts of 1799-1800, their repeal in 1824-25, and
the Trade Union Acts of 1871-76.   First, savage suppression of
Unions ; next, sulky admission that they must be allowed to exist,
but without legal rights ; finally, a grudging recognition that they
are organisations having some rights that are enforceable.   Much
more recently, in various Acts making provision for the protection of
workers and for social insurance, the State has to some extent
utilised the Unions by handing over to them certain administrative
functions.

A movement so fully accepted in the modern community, so
bound up in all its varied activities with the lives of millions of
workers, and so strong, with the power of a common purpose, as to
affect vitally the fortunes of a nation, must be worth the study of
every citizen interested in the economic and political institutions in
and by which he lives.   Much more is it worth the study of every
individual Trade Unionist, whose actions and thoughts help to
determine its destinies.

[1] *The A.B.C. of Communism*, Eng. ed., p. 289.   See also *The Trade
Union Movement in Soviet Russia* (International Labour Office).

The story is a fascinating one and may most conveniently be followed by considering first, what aims Trade Unions have set before themselves ; second, how they have organised to achieve those aims ; third, what methods they have followed and what functions they have tried to fulfil ; and fourth, what their status in the community and in industry has been.

But their background must be appreciated, too ; to understand the development of the Trade Union movement one must know something of the economic history of Britain during the same period, and, to some extent, of other countries as well.

The aims, structure, functions, and activities of the Unions have been continuously, though unconsciously, adapted to the changing economic circumstances of the time, and they have been regarded by Government and governing class with hatred, disdain, or respect, as those same circumstances have made the workers' movement powerful, insignificant, or invincible.

Industry in the Eighteenth Century.

The first Trade Unions appeared in Britain early in the eighteenth century.[1] The date is significant. Towards the end of the seventeenth century industry was visibly changing its form. From a system in which the worker was still not divorced from the ownership of his tools, the transformation to a system in which there were separate classes of capitalists and wage earners was rapidly taking place. There is not space here to detail the changes in industrial technique which resulted in the rise of the so-called *entrepreneur* class and produced in the later years of the century and the early nineteenth century what is loosely termed the Industrial Revolution. The first real factory in England was a silk factory near Derby, in 1718,[2] but the factory system did not extend over any wide area of industry until the end of the century. Nevertheless, throughout the whole of the period, the separation into economic classes was steadily proceeding, and Trade Unions among skilled workers flourished, though their members had as yet no sense of the solidarity of Labour

[1] Webb, *History of Trade Unionism,* ch. i. (1920 ed.). It has been claimed, however, that there was a permanent Union of hatters in 1667. See Unwin, G., in the *Econ. Journal,* vol. x. pp. 394-403.

[2] Ashley, *Economic Organisation of England,* p. 153. See also the useful chapter on the developments in Industrial Technique in Max Weber *General Economic History.*

in general. There was no proletariat, but the workers in every trade were becoming very much alive to the necessity for defending their standards.

We see, in fact, the old and the new economic systems side by side, that of the independent master craftsman, heir of the mediaeval gilds, and the newer factory system ; then, bridging the gulf between them, and typical of the first three-quarters of the eighteenth century, the 'domestic' system, with the capitalist middleman financing production actually carried on in the workers' homes.

In textiles, clothing, boots and shoes, cutlery, and the newer trades springing up, we find this transition stage, and on the Continent also, in the manufacturing industries existing before the use of power machinery ushered in the factory system proper, we see 'domestic' production in full swing.

During the eighteenth century the wool industry was still the most important in the country, but there were considerable manufactures of iron, metal goods, silk, linen, leather, etc., while coal and other minerals were extensively mined. Cotton, too, was becoming a rival to wool, though it did not jump to the commanding position it later attained until the beginning of the following century.

Side by side with these fundamental changes in industry there was a great expansion of foreign trade and a series of trade wars against France and her allies. These left Britain with a great colonial empire, though the same century saw the loss of the North American colonies.

Labour Conditions and Trade Unions

It is not remarkable that the period during which capitalism and imperialism were founded should have witnessed a departure from previous centuries in many directions. Labour conditions were therefore more than usually in a state of flux. The most notable departure from the past was the complete surrender of the code of State regulation of wages and employment that was one of the great achievements of Tudor rule.

During the sixteenth century, by a series of far-reaching measures, the State had set out to regulate wages, industrial training, and employment generally. The code so established fell into disuse ; became, indeed, almost forgotten, after the middle of the eighteenth century. This was not because of the introduction of the factory system, which came later, but because the growing complexity of industry had made the simple procedure laid down by Tudor legislation quite unworkable.[1] The division of labour was proceeding so rapidly that it soon became impossible for the Justices to try to fix rates for specific operations in industrial work.

The old Act itself was only repealed in 1813, long after it had become a dead letter, simply because the wretched conditions accompanying the early years of the factory system impelled the workers to ask, time after time, that this obsolete legislation should again be put into effect.

For the greater part of the eighteenth century, as has already been said, the majority of textile workers and those in other manufacturing trades were working either at home or on the premises of an employer of their own class. The miners and the workers in the heavy metal trades, as well as a minority in the manufacturing trades, were, even early in the century, employed under factory conditions, and the number so employed was being added to all the time, especially after about 1770.

The wages of employed workers averaged about 9s. 6d. a week, ranging from 7s. 1d. in textiles to 13s. 6d. in the cutlery trade. Women's wages varied from 3s. 3d. a week to 6s. 6d., the latter rate being for pottery workers, and the general average was 4s. 7d.[2]

Even in the few cases where wage assessments were made they were not enforced after the middle of the century, and there is ample evidence to show that there was increasing unrest in many trades owing to the low wages and bad working conditions.[3]

Hours of labour were commonly from 14 to 17 daily, even in the coal mines, where, incidentally, there were no safety devices except of the most rudimentary kind.

Boys and girls were freely employed in industry, and even in coal mines and lead mines. Defoe, writing about the middle of the century, recorded that in the clothing district round Halifax there was hardly a single child over four years of age that was not ' earning its own bread.' [4]

[1] For a very late assessment of wages by the Quarter Sessions (1738), see Bland, Brown and Tawney, *English Economic History* (1920), p. 546.

[2] From Arthur Young's *Northern Tour* (1771). See further figures in L. W. Moffit's *England on the Eve of the Industrial Revolution*, ch. ix.

[3] See Hammond, J. L. and B., *Town Labourer, Skilled Labourer*, and Moffit, *op. cit.*

[4] Defoe, *Tour through Great Britain* (1762 ed.).

The earliest attempt to regulate the hours of children's labour
appears to have been a resolution of the Manchester magistrates in
1784, forbidding the nightwork of children and prohibiting a longer
working day than ten hours.[1]   It was not until the very end of the
century that there began to be some agitation for legislation to
protect children, and the first Factory Act, the famous Health and
Morals of Apprentices Act, was not passed until 1802.

Going back to the workers' organisations that sprang out of these
wretched labour conditions we find that the wool workers and the
tailors were among the first to form permanent unions.   In 1720
the master-tailors complained to Parliament that the London and
Westminster tailors, to the number of seven thousand, had formed a
combination to raise wages and shorten hours.[2]   An Act was
promptly passed prohibiting combinations and restraining the
payment or receipt of wages above a stated minimum.   In 1744 the
tailors were proceeded against for flouting the 1720 Act, and a new
law against them was passed in 1767.   Nevertheless, the combination maintained a continuous existence throughout the century.

The wool workers of the West of England, like the tailors, were
reduced to the status of wage-earners by their inability to get the
necessary capital for independent marketing, and they formed a
union very early in the eighteenth century.   We hear of it in 1717,
and in 1718 a Royal Proclamation was issued against the ' lawless
clubs and societies which had illegally presumed to use a common
seal and to act as Bodies Corporate.'   It was all to no purpose,
however, for at many other dates throughout the century we find
complaints against the wool workers' associations.

It should be noted that in Yorkshire it was not until the end of
the century, when the ' domestic system ' of production gave way
to the factory system, that the wool workers in that district established organisations.   Before then they were more or less independent craftsmen, unlike their fellow-workmen in the same industry
in the West of England, who were dependent wage-earners.   The
worsted branch of the wool textile industry was, however, carried
on like the West of England woollen manufacture, and we therefore
find the wool-combers with a union before 1741.

Silk weavers, hosiery workers, and gold beaters were organised

[1] Hutchins and Harrison, *History of Factory Legislation*, p. 9.

[2] Webb, *History of Trade Unionism*, p. 31.   Except where otherwise
stated the succeeding account of trade unionism is based on Webb
(1920 ed.).   See also Galton, F. W., *The Tailoring Trade*.

during the last quarter of the century, and cutlery workers also became active about the same time. Among the other trades that formed unions during the eighteenth century were the hatters, curriers, printers, brush-makers, basket-makers, calico-printers, ship-wrights, farriers, smiths, coachmakers, dyers, carpenters, joiners, bricklayers, cordwainers, and bookbinders. Among the miners, curiously enough, there was no organisation at all, badly though they needed one, for they worked under wretched conditions and they were dependent wage-earners. In 1765 they went on strike to the number of 4000 in Northumberland and Durham, against the ' bonding system,' but even this united action did not result in the formation of a union.[1]

It was the skilled workers, who traditionally had enjoyed not merely relatively high wages, but also protected wages, that immediately set up organisations when the new conditions, placing power in the hands of the employers, led to the abandonment of all pretence of fixing wages by custom. It was the new surging interplay of supply and demand as applied to labour that brought wage standards down, so provoking organised resistance.

Thus, the aim of these early Trade Unions was to preserve the long-standing labour monopoly in their own trades, to restore the old conception of ' customary wages,' and in short to stabilise conditions at the comparatively satisfactory level that had hitherto prevailed. Their method was to seek legislative protection, for that was how the standards had been regulated since Tudor times. Hence there were constant attempts, in this trade to restore the Apprenticeship restrictions of the old law, in another trade to restore the wages assessments by the Justices.

There were appeals to the King or to Parliament, mostly by the West of England woollen workers, in 1719, 1726, 1728, 1748 and 1756, and practically all were successful. Then Parliament turned completely round, being unconsciously under the influence of the new philosophy of competition, and swept away the last relics of State regulation. Adam Smith's *Wealth of Nations* (1776), with its doctrine of freedom of contract, merely made explicit and gave theoretical form to what was already being practised.

Despite the unsympathetic treatment now meted out to the workers, Unions remained isolated from each other and had no conception of the working class as a whole. There *was* no working

[1] See Webb, *The Story of the Durham Miners*, p. 4, and Hammond, *The Skilled Labourer*, p. 12.

class yet, psychologically speaking. There was to each Union merely its own trade, which was being menaced by this new and terrifying law of unlimited competition. Labour was no longer a form of human activity with a conventional remuneration. It was now a commodity, to be bought cheap and sold dear, and each trade saw only its own position under attack. So we may say that while the nineteenth century was the period of development of Trade Unionism, the eighteenth century witnessed only the growth of Trade Unions.

Legal Position of Unions in the Eighteenth Century.

Throughout the whole of the eighteenth century Trade Unions were illegal bodies, as a long series of Acts of Parliament had made it a criminal offence for workmen to combine to change wages, hours, etc.

To understand this we have to go back to the origins of the State regulation of wages that has already been mentioned.

The ravages of the Black Death in the middle of the fourteenth century led to such a shortage of labour that the workers were able to demand much higher wages than had been customary. The craft gilds, already declining in importance and power, were quite unable to control the situation that arose, and the State was forced to intervene.

This it did by passing the Statutes of Labourers [1] which provided for the fixation of wages by the Justices and compelled every able-bodied man and woman under sixty years of age, 'not being a merchant or skilled artificer, nor living on his own land, to serve any one who might require his or her services, at the accustomed or statutory rate of wages.' [2] This law thus covered all workers except the master craftsmen. There followed a long series of Acts strengthening and amplifying this legislation and, most significant for our present purpose, making it an offence to settle wages in any other way. This was natural enough. Having taken over the task of regulating conditions, a task the now decadent gilds were unequal to, the State meant to make it plain that no rival authority would be allowed to function in this sphere. In the 1360 law,

[1] 23 Edw. III (1349) ; cc. 1-8.   25 Edw. III (1351) ; st. II.   34 Edw. III (1360) ; cc. 9-11.

[2] See Jenks, E., *Short History of English Law*, pp. 320 ff., and Slesser, H. H., *Trade Unionism*, ch. i.

confirming and amending the first Statute of Labourers, there was a
clause to ' abolish and render null and void all alliances and covines
of masons and carpenters.' [1] With the same object of prohibiting
combinations to raise wages or otherwise interfere with the State's
functions in regard to labour conditions, dozens of Acts were
passed in succeeding reigns.[2] In 1548, for instance, a very general
Act laid heavier penalties on artificers, workmen or labourers who
should ' conspire, covenant, or promise together, or make any oaths,
that they shall not make or do their work, but at a certain price or
rate, or shall not enterprize or take upon them to finish what
another hath begun, or shall do but a certain work in a day, or shall
not work but at certain hours and times.' [3] The great Elizabethan
Statute of Apprentices (1562-3) [4] consolidated and amended the
previous Acts regulating wages and hours, and instituted the
apprenticeship system for all trades, but it was still a criminal offence
for an employer to offer or for a worker to receive more than the
wage that was customary or fixed by the Quarter Sessions.   There
was therefore no relaxation of the prohibition of combinations to
interfere with these matters.   On the contrary, new legislation was
passed, as time went on, imposing heavier penalties on workmen
who combined, as it was found that societies continued to spring
up in almost every trade, though they were usually short-lived.

As long as the State regulation that this legislation was passed to
maintain was a reality, the combinations that nevertheless existed
were only small and transitory.   As already indicated, it was in the
eighteenth century, when it was no longer a reality, when the notion
of customary rates had begun to crumble under the disintegrating
blast of ' free contract,' and when the number of dependent wage-
earners subject to this new doctrine greatly increased, that really large,
permanent organisations began to appear.   When the State gave up
its function of fixing wages, however, it left intact, and even
strengthened, the laws making combinations illegal, though the
former justification for them had gone.   Thus laws were passed
prohibiting combination among tailors, in 1720-21 ; among wool
workers in 1725-26 ; and in all trades in 1730.   In the succeeding
reign (Geo. III), fifteen or sixteen other Acts were passed with the
same object before 1800.[5] Finally, in 1799-1800, a new general

---

[1] Slesser, *op. cit.*   [2] A list is given in Slesser, *op. cit.*, p. 10.

[3] 2 & 3 Edw. VI, c. 15, s. 1.   See Jenks, *op. cit.*, p. 322.

[4] 5 Eliz. c. 4.   [5] Slesser, *op. cit.*

law was enacted ' to prevent unlawful combinations of workmen.' [1]
The legislation of these two years is usually referred to as ' the
Combination Acts,' since it marked the culmination of the repressive
policy of the preceding centuries, being both more general and more
severe than any law hitherto passed.   The reason for this severity
is to be found in the fears that took hold of the governing classes as a
consequence of the French Revolution ; every society of workmen
was thereupon regarded as a possible centre of revolutionary activity.
For this reason, too, laws to suppress political sedition were used
against Unions, as was the common-law doctrine of ' restraint of
trade.'   The result was that such combinations as did exist were in
the nature of secret societies, and strikes, lockouts, and boycotts were
commonly accompanied by violence and bloodshed on both sides.
Persons convicted were punished with savage and vindictive sentences fit only, even in those times, for the worst criminals.

All this conflict, then, came to a head at the end of the eighteenth
century, when, despite repression, there were a large number of
permanent Unions in existence.

The Industrial Revolution.

The closing years of the eighteenth century and the first quarter
of the nineteenth century were dominated by that extraordinary
growth in the use of machinery, and in the factory system, that is
called the ' Industrial Revolution.'   These great changes, spread out
over more than half a century of time, did indeed alter the face of
England beyond recognition.   It was a period of economic anarchy.
The population increased at a phenomenal rate ; the workers
crowded into the towns, which rapidly became undisciplined collections of ugly factories and uglier houses, the slums of to-day ; productivity increased by leaps and bounds ; prices tumbled, wages
tumbled, and profits soared ; manufacturers saw, and took, their
chance of making fortunes ; the workers and their children sank to
unimaginable depths of degradation as slaves of the new machines,
for there was no controlling authority, at first, to prevent or modify
these conditions.

That, at any rate, is how the period appears to many historians
who look back and try to visualise from contemporary documents

[1] 39 Geo. III (1799), c. 81 ; 39 Geo. III (1800), c. 106.   See Bland,
Brown and Tawney, *op. cit.*, p. 626.

the events of the Industrial Revolution.[1]   More recently, there has arisen a school of writers who deny that conditions were as bad as has been pictured.[2]   They aver that contemporary accounts were often exaggerated and that, in particular, the Report of the Commission on the Factory Bill of 1832 presents a distorted view, as Michael Sadler, who was fighting on behalf of the workers, called evidence that was not typical of the average factory.   However this may be, and allowing for all possible exaggerations, it can be said with certainty that conditions were really deplorable.

The Industrial Revolution was not alone to blame.   The Enclosure movement, which had gone on at an accelerated rate during the latter part of the eighteenth century, contributed to the evil by turning large numbers of workers off the land and leaving them no recourse but to flock into the towns.   The French wars also contributed by making very high taxation necessary, and by dislocating markets, with consequent fluctuations in employment and increases in food prices.

But undoubtedly the ruling motive of the manufacturers, the desire to expand production without limit, was chiefly responsible, for expansion could in general be financed only out of current profits, and hence there was the most powerful incentive to keep the mills running as long as possible each day, to press into service women and young children, and to get the labour as cheaply as possible.   It was not so much the lowness of the wages that caused complaint, however, as the appallingly long hours ; the employment of small children, of six and upwards ; the disgusting housing conditions ; the insanitary and unhealthy factories ; the overdriving ; the sudden degradation of long-established, highly-skilled workmen to the ranks of the unskilled.

These were the effects of the new order which sank into the minds of the workers and left an indelible impress that was to last for a century or more in the traditions of the working-class movement.

At the time, the first result was a series of outbreaks of strikes accompanied by violence.   In many parts of the country the new machines were broken up by infuriated mobs.   When a minimum wage Bill promoted by the weavers in 1808 was defeated in the House of Commons, a strike of cotton and wool workers broke out

[1] See Bland, Brown and Tawney, *op. cit.*, pp. 500-521 ; Hammond, J. L. and B., *The Town Labourer*, etc.

[2] *E.g.*, *An Economic History of Modern Britain* : *The Early Railway Age*, by J. H. Clapham. 1926.

over the whole of Lancashire.   Two years later there was a large-scale strike of Northumberland and Durham miners, and in 1812 of Scottish weavers.

In 1811 the Luddite movement started its campaign of machine-wrecking in the hosiery trade in the Midlands, and this soon spread to other parts of the country, to be met everywhere with savage repression.   The severe unemployment which followed the conclusion of the French wars, in 1815, led to further outbreaks of machine smashing, and in 1818 to widespread strikes in the textile industry.

In 1819 the Peterloo massacre, in which eleven people were killed and hundreds injured by the Yeomanry, in dispersing a perfectly peaceable meeting in Manchester, produced a passion of indignation among the working people, but the Government replied by a series of even more repressive Acts than had hitherto been in force (the Six Acts, as they are called).

In short, there was throughout the period a state of acute unrest among the industrial population, and it almost seemed that England was about to plunge into the bloody revolution the governing classes so desperately feared.

Meanwhile, some attempt was being made to bring about improvements in factory conditions.   Peel's Health and Morals of Apprentices Act of 1802 had accomplished very little because of its limited scope, and in 1815 there was a general enquiry, which was followed by an Act, passed in 1819, prohibiting the employment in factories of children under nine years of age, and imposing other restrictions in regard to children between nine and sixteen.   A further Act of 1825 strengthened this law, but both Acts applied only to cotton mills, and neither was strictly enforced owing to the defects of the inspectorate and the bias of the magistrates.

Partly in revenge for the way in which this Government of manufacturers had treated the landowners, the Tory party then took up the cause of the workers and carried on a great humanitarian campaign in which Lord Shaftesbury, Michael Sadler, and Richard Oastler played a leading part.   A further Act of 1831 reduced the hours of young persons in cotton mills from 72 to 69 a week, and prohibited night work, while in 1842 the employment of women and girls, and of boys under ten, underground in coal mines was forbidden.   In 1844 a new and improved Factory Act was passed, to be followed by others in 1847, 1850 and 1853.   After that there was of course, a long series of Acts increasing the control of the

State over conditions of work. During the first quarter of the century, however, only the faintest beginnings of factory legislation were made. The law of the jungle still operated almost unchecked. It was in this period and in this environment that British Socialism was born.

Trade Union Progress.

Although they remained under the ban of illegality up to 1824, the Unions continued, during the early years of the century, to organise the skilled workers and to carry on their functions of mutual help and agitation for improved conditions. Several of the large strikes that took place have been mentioned. When the Scottish weavers struck, in 1812, the entire strike committee was arrested, just as the employers were preparing to meet them to discuss a settlement. For the ' crime ' of combination the leaders were sentenced to long terms of imprisonment.

Union after union tried to get the old Elizabethan statute put into effect, with its provision for wage fixing, but the only result was that, in 1813-14, the whole of this legislation was repealed (with the exception of a few scraps that were not formally rescinded until 1875).

This marked the final triumph of the new philosophy of Manchesterism, the doctrine of *laissez-faire*. For a long period the whole of English economic life was dominated by the belief in enlightened selfishness as the guide to life. Toynbee, the historian of the Industrial Revolution, satirically expressed this creed in the phrase, ' Man's Self-love is God's Providence.'[1] It was the philosophy of life officially adopted, and it pervaded literature, ethics and religion no less than politics and economics.

Yet, even at this early date, the enactment of the first factory laws showed the dawn of a new conception of life, and very soon a further important step was taken in the repeal of the Combination laws. Mr. and Mrs. Webb have pointed out[2] that before the general Acts of 1799-1800, prohibiting combinations in all trades, such associations had been allowed for the purpose of enforcing the laws. Many examples can be cited of combinations in the eighteenth century being openly allowed to take action for securing wage assessments or for enforcing the apprenticeship provisions of the Elizabethan Act. Before 1799 the suppression of Unions was, as has already been

[1] Toynbee, A., *The Industrial Revolution*, p. 11.

[2] Webb, *History*, ch. ii.

emphasised, only incidental to the State regulation of trade. The 1799-1800 legislation was in a different category. Combinations were now forbidden, not because they sinned against the State's prerogative of regulating trade,—for that was a thing of the past,— but because they sinned against the new doctrine of ' freedom of contract.' Formerly it was to protect the authority of the State that they were suppressed ; now, it was to protect the ' liberty of the individual.'

At the same time this principle was only invoked against workmen. Combinations of employers were nominally prohibited by the 1799-1800 Acts, but in no single case was there a prosecution, although in 1814, to cite one instance, the Sheffield employers openly formed an association for the express purpose of ' restraining trade.'

Doubtless, the fears felt by property owners, lest the example of the French Revolution should be contagious, were partly responsible for the different treatment, but the main reason was that political power was in the hands of those to whose economic interest it was to prevent Trade Union action from raising wages.

Where combinations were prosecuted, the most ferocious punishment followed convictions, the workers concerned being treated as felons. In very many cases, however, they were not prosecuted, either because no one took action, or, in some instances, because the employers themselves accepted and ' recognised ' the Unions. Collective agreements regulating wages were even concluded in the printing trade and in the brushmaking trade in London in 1805, and in the London coopering trade in 1813. There are other instances of the same kind, and many records exist of Unions that maintained an open and unmolested campaign for better conditions, sometimes with the approval of leading employers. It was in the textile trades that combinations were most ruthlessly suppressed, workmen being imprisoned for long periods for the offence of organising. Strikes, too, in all trades were generally followed by prosecutions and heavy sentences, and although it was said in 1823 that the 1800 Act had become a dead letter,[1] it is clear that the result of that legislation, even though it did not succeed in killing trade unionism, was very effectively to prevent the workers from resisting the degradation of their standard of life.

An interesting point to notice is that about this time there appeared to be much more community of feeling among the Unions in different

[1] Webb, *History*, p. 77.

trades than there had been in the eighteenth century. In a number of cases of which records remain, an organisation in one trade would give financial or other help to a Union in another industry when in difficulties.[1]

Repeal of the Combination Acts.

As the fears engendered by the French Revolution began to die away, and the economic situation began to improve with the recovery from the worst effects of the French wars, an agitation arose for the repeal of the repressive legislation of 1799-1800. Political radicalism was becoming a force, and in several quarters independently the demand for repeal was made.

It was Francis Place, the tailor of Charing Cross, who took hold of the campaign, and in co-operation with Joseph Hume, the radical M.P., and McCulloch, the economist, skilfully engineered a Bill through Parliament in 1824, without most of the members of the Government being aware that any such thing was contemplated. The story has often been told of how Place and Hume secured the setting-up of a Committee to consider emigration, the export of machinery, and, as a sideline, the Combination laws ; and of how, the last item being astutely put first, the Committee, ' packed ' by Place and Hume, reported quickly in favour of repeal.[2] When the Bill quietly became law [3] without either debate or division the first real step was taken to emancipate the Unions from their age-long position of outlawry, and a great outburst of Trade Union activity followed. Many new Unions were formed and strikes broke out in every direction. Place tried hard to restrain the leaders, for he saw clearly the danger of too conspicuous activity at the moment. The result could only be to draw the attention of the governing classes to what had occurred, and to alarm them into taking back the freedom just given. So it happened, when their new-found liberty sent many Unions into a frenzy of striking and organising. There was a great cotton stoppage at Glasgow, a shipping strike on the Tyne and Wear, and a host of disputes in many other trades. Place and his colleagues had themselves always taken the view that combinations were solely the creatures of repression, and that if freedom to combine were granted Trade Unionism would die out. The falsity of this notion was soon seen, and the employing class became thoroughly alarmed.

[1] Webb, *History*, p. 91.

[2] Wallas, G., *Life of Francis Place* ; Webb, *History*, p. 96 ff.

[3] 5 Geo. IV, c. 95 (1824).

The Government woke up and another Committee was hastily appointed, 'packed' this time by the enemies of the Unions, who wished to replace Hume's Act by a measure even more drastic than the 1799-1800 law. Again Place employed to the utmost his genius for wire-pulling, and the Unions all over the country, alive at last to the danger that threatened, organised joint bodies for propaganda, sent delegates to influence M.P.'s, prepared monster petitions, and in short made such a stir that the Government had to be content with a much smaller and milder Bill than had been first proposed. The new Act, passed in 1825,[1] was far less favourable to the Unions than the 1824 Act, but still it did maintain the repeal of the 1799-1800 law and thus made it possible for the workers to organise without the taint of illegality.

The Act so circumscribed their activities, however, that while a Union could exist without committing a crime it could hardly act effectively to carry out the purpose of its existence without conflicting at some point with the law. The removal (and in some cases the re-imposition) of embargoes on various forms of Trade Union activity has gone on ever since, but from 1824-25 dates the legal freedom of Trade Unions to exist. It will be clear from what has been said that the State did not create Trade Unionism ; on the contrary, it fought long to deny the workers the right to organise, but it was defeated by the vitality and 'will to live' of the Unions themselves. Many Unions had been formed after 1800, and the 1824-25 legislation led to a further crop of new organisations, including Unions of engineering workers, shipwrights, miners, carpenters and joiners.

The New Unionism of 1829-34.

It is interesting to note that during this early period attempts were made for the first time to set up federations, and even Unions comprising workers in all trades. In addition, the first successful efforts were made to form national Unions, instead of the small local organisations hitherto preferred. The Manchester Steam Engine Makers, for instance, expanded into a national Union about 1825, and the House Carpenters and Joiners established a national Union in 1827. In 1829 the Cotton Spinners tried to form a federal Union covering the British Isles.

Meanwhile, in 1818, an attempt was made to set up a Union for workers in all trades. It had the curious title of 'The Philanthropic

[1] 6 Geo. IV, c. 129 (1825).

Hercules,' but in spite of its name it was such a puny infant that it died as soon as it was born. The same fate befel another attempt in 1826, but the National Association for the Protection of Labour, in 1830, was more successful. This, however, was a federation, leaving each affiliated organisation with complete autonomy. It soon comprised about 150 Unions, mostly in the textile trades, and it ran a weekly journal, *The Voice of the People*. About 1832 it apparently went out of existence. The Builders' Union was the next ambitious project. It included all the various crafts, being the first real 'industrial' Union, in the modern sense of the term, and it lasted until 1834.[1] Elaborate plans were made for a Grand National Gild of Builders to undertake all the building of the country, the foremen to be elected by the workers, and the superintendent by the foremen.[2] The next experiment was the famous Grand National Consolidated Trade Union, of 1834. Robert Owen was its chief recruiter and propagandist.[3] Owen, the father of English socialism, had been preaching co-operative production, and for this, and for his socialist principles in general, he set out to capture the Trade Union movement. The Grand National grew with phenomenal rapidity, about half a million members joining within a few weeks. There was, as Mr. and Mrs. Webb have expressed it, a positive mania for Trade Unionism at this time. From shop assistants to chimney sweeps the workers in every trade crowded into the lodges. The avowed policy of the Grand National was to bring about a general strike, but a series of sectional strikes soon took place, owing largely to the opposition of the employers, who, in many cases, insisted on their employees signing ' the document,' *i.e.* an undertaking to leave or not to join a Union.[4] The governing classes had again taken alarm, and the restrictive effects of the 1825 Act became painfully evident when prosecution after prosecution resulted in convictions and heavy sentences for Trade Unionists. The climax came with the case of the Dorchester Labourers, in 1834. For perfectly peaceable attempts to establish a Union for agricultural workers, at Tolpuddle,

[1] See Postgate, R. W., *The Builders' History*, ch. iii.

[2] See Cole, G. D. H., *Short History of the British Working Class Movement*, vol. i. p. 120 ; and Postgate, *op. cit.*

[3] See Webb, *History*, p. 134 ; for Owen, see Cole, G. D. H., *Robert Owen*.

[4] Such an undertaking has ever since been known in Trade Union history as " the document."

T.U.D. B

in Dorset, with no violence or threats or even secrecy, six workers were arrested and, after a scandalous farce of a trial, were sentenced to seven years' transportation. This monstrous punishment was quickly carried out, whereupon a terrific storm was let loose throughout the country, the Grand National taking the lead in the agitation. In 1836 the remainder of the sentences was remitted, but it was not until 1838 that five of the six returned from Botany Bay, and the sixth did not reach home even then.

In 1834, after a succession of disastrous strikes, the Grand National petered out, and there followed a period of apathy and disillusionment, as far as Trade Union action was concerned.

People turned to the political field for the realisation of their hopes, and the radical reformers came into their own. Already the National Union of the Working Classes, under the influence of William Lovett, had been in the forefront of the Reform Bill agitation of 1831-32, and it was political reform that captured the imagination of working-class leaders for some years to come.

Pause should be made here to look back and note the tremendous change that had come over the scene between 1730 and 1830. The entire character of British industry had altered ; the entire economic and political philosophy of England had undergone a revolution ; the Trade Unions had achieved legal freedom to exist, and had tried to draw together in a spirit of solidarity in large all-inclusive Unions and federations ; a real working-class consciousness had begun to make its appearance, and the foundations of the British socialist movement had been laid.

On the other hand we have to notice the primitive condition of the workers' organisation in 1830 compared with their later development. Unions were still relatively few in number ; they included few workers even in the skilled crafts and practically none outside them ; they had the crudest ideas of organisation and tactics ; there were practically no national Unions ; there was no central organisation at all ; collective bargaining was still a very rare phenomenon ; Trade Unionists were collectively hated and individually despised by the mass of ' respectable citizens.'

A disproportionate amount of space has purposely been given to the origins and early history of the Trade Unions, because it was in those early years and owing to the economic circumstances in which they developed that the organisations assumed forms and took on characteristics that have survived even down to the present day. Their remaining history must be compressed into a very brief space.

The Chartist Period.

Although, after the break-up of the Grand National, political interests took up a large share of the attention of the workers, Trade Union activities, and especially strikes, continued. Arising out of the trial and conviction of the Glasgow Cotton Spinners, for violence and intimidation, in 1838, a further Enquiry into the state of the Combination law was set up by the Government, but it came to nothing. It did, however, lead some of the Unions to overhaul their rules and practices, for it must be confessed that in these early days not only had a good deal of the secret society paraphernalia survived, but violence—on both sides—was by no means uncommon during strikes.

In the Chartist movement itself, from 1837 to 1848, the Unions as a rule took no part, though many of their leaders did. Starting with a fine idealism the movement soon degenerated into a futile squabble. There was really no community of purpose among its leaders, no sense of reality and no organising ability. It flared up into a brief incandescence in 1848, the year of revolutions in Europe, but thereafter flickered into nothingness.[1] This marked the end of what may be called the revolutionary period of Trade Union history.

The New Model.

After 1848 the Unions took on a more businesslike character and devoted themselves to building up their organisations and to evolving practical policies which would bring them immediate gains. The reason for the change was that during the earlier period, from about 1815 to 1850, there was a succession of economic crises in England. For the greater part of that time the workers were in a state of abject poverty and the spirit of unrest and revolt was the natural and inevitable result. From 1850 there was a long period of industrial and commercial expansion and prosperity, which reacted on the Unions to produce a stability and financial strength never known before. This was favourable to the development of sounder methods of organisation and of administrative machinery more adequate to their needs.

[1] For a short account of Chartism see Cole, G. D. H., *Short History of the British Working Class Movement*, vol. i. ; for a detailed study see Hovell, M., *The Chartist Movement* ; West, J., *History of the Chartist Movement*.

The newly-formed Miners' Association of Great Britain and Ireland (1841-48) created a remarkable precedent in 1844 by appointing a full-time solicitor to conduct its legal business, at a salary of £1,000 a year. This 'miners' attorney-general,' as he was called, has given an illuminating account, which should be studied, of the contemporary attitude of the courts towards Trade Unions.[1]

In 1845 the National Association of United Trades was set up as a semi-political, semi-social federation of Unions. In policy it was cautious and practical, demanding machinery for conciliation and arbitration. Most of the big Unions declined to affiliate to it, but a large number of smaller organisations joined, and paid organisers were sent out to bring others into membership. The unfailing hostility of employers to national unions was again aroused and there was a reappearance of the ' document.' After 1851 the National Association ceased to have any influence and it died a natural death about 1860.

It was about this period that many Unions started to issue weekly or monthly trade journals, one of which, the *Flint Glass Makers' Magazine*, maintained an unbroken existence from 1850 onwards.

A further symptom of the new spirit in Trade Unionism was the growth of centralisation. The Ironmoulders, Stonemasons, and other Unions removed the power to strike from the local branches and vested powers in their central executives.

Such developments naturally involved the Unions in difficult problems of finance, administration and business management, and it was from this time that the movement started to evolve its own ' civil service ' of permanent skilled officials.

The most remarkable example of all these changes in Trade Union structure and outlook was the formation in 1851, by a number of Unions of skilled workers in the metal trades, of the Amalgamated Society of Engineers. This event is so important in Trade Union history that the full story should be studied carefully.[2]

After a somewhat doubtful start the new amalgamation found itself with a permanent, regularly-paying membership of 11,000. It was the largest Union in the country, and the most powerful. As Mr. and Mrs. Webb say, ' A trade society which, like the Amalgamated Engineers, could rely on a regular income of £500 a week was without precedent.'[3]

[1] Webb, *History*, p. 183.   [2] Webb, *History*, p. 206 ff.
[3] Webb, *History*, p. 214 n.

A three months' general lockout of the engineering trades, enforced early in 1852 by the newly-formed association of engineering employers, focussed the national attention on the new Union. Much sympathy was aroused among middle-class democrats, but the Union was defeated and in most cases the men on their return were forced to sign the hated ' document ' which once more appeared.

Contrary to anticipation, the Amalgamated Society was not in the least weakened by this defeat. On the contrary, it enjoyed great prestige for many years, and its constitution was copied by many Unions between 1852 and 1889. That constitution set out elaborate rules by which, on the side of friendly benefits, the branches kept the appearance but not the reality of local autonomy. The branches governed themselves, but only in accordance with detailed rules which were made very difficult to alter.

On the trade side centralisation was open and complete, though district committees were established to advise the central executive which, however, kept control in its own hands. There was a high contribution, and this enabled the society to accumulate large funds, which by 1861 amounted to the then enormous total of £73,398.

During the next decade Trade Unions in general flourished and increased in membership and power, and after about 1858 a number of disputes on a larger scale than had for some time been known showed how formidable the newly-strengthened organisations could be.

The greatest of these was the London Builders' strike in 1859-60, over a claim that hours should be reduced to 9 per day. About 24,000 men were involved and the entire Trade Union movement rallied to the Builders' support, chiefly because the employers tried to re-impose ' the document ' and so to destroy the workers' organisations. Not until February 1860 was peace restored, and although the result was a draw, the struggle was not entirely useless, for the London Trades Council arose out of the need then displayed for united action.

During the next few years the Trade Union world was largely under the influence of the ' Junta ' of the five most important leaders and their allies, who combined caution in trade matters with fervour for political reforms.[1]

---

[1] The ' Junta ' consisted of Wm. Allan (Engineers), R. Applegarth (Carpenters), D. Guile (Ironfounders), E. Coulson (London Bricklayers), and G. Odger (Shoemakers).

Trades Councils.

Meanwhile, between 1857 and 1867, Trades Councils were set up in a number of industrial centres. These were voluntary local federations of Trade Union branches, meeting for mutual support in organising and propaganda work. By 1860 they were established in Glasgow, Sheffield, Liverpool and Edinburgh, and London followed in 1861. The Liverpool Trades Guardian Association, set up in 1848, appears to have been the first permanent body of this kind. Temporary organisations of the Trade Union branches in a district had been known much earlier, of course, but they existed only for some emergency, usually a strike.

The London Trades Council, which itself evolved from a Strike Committee, undertook the important, though costly, task of compiling the first Trade Union Directory, and the story of the Council for the following seven or eight years is the story of the Trade Union Movement, for it acted almost as an informal meeting of the secretaries or chief officials of the largest Unions.

It was, however, the Glasgow Trades Council that in 1864 convened the first purely Trade Union Conference for the purpose of discussing a purely working-class grievance,—the iniquitous Master and Servant Acts, under which a breach of contract of employment by workers, (though not by employers), was a criminal offence. The injustice was largely remedied by an Act passed in 1867, directly as a result of the Trade Union agitation.

Meanwhile there was growing up among the more aggressive sections of the Trade Union movement a campaign of opposition to the ' Junta.' It was led by George Potter, the founder of the *Beehive,* a well-known Trade Union weekly journal of the eighteen-sixties.

The Royal Commission of 1867.

The ' Junta ' also came under attack from another quarter and at the moment this was a more serious menace, for it meant nothing more nor less than a renewed attempt by the employers as a class to crush the growing force of Trade Unionism. The immediate excuse was an outbreak of violence in connection with some disputes in Sheffield.

The upshot was the appointment of a Royal Commission in 1867, to investigate not merely the Sheffield outrages but the Trade Union Movement in general. The ' Junta,' alive to the gravity of the situation, formed itself into a private ' cabinet ' of the movement and mobilised a corps of gifted writers, lawyers, etc., in defence of Trade Union rights. Frederic Harrison, Professor Beesley, T. Hughes, M.P., and Henry Crompton were among these friends who gave such valuable help. Frederic Harrison and T. Hughes were members of the Commission, and Applegarth (Secretary of the Carpenters' Union) and William Allan (of the Engineers' Society), were the chief witnesses for the Unions.

The majority report contained recommendations which fell far short of what the employers demanded, and there was, in fact, a distinct revulsion of public opinion in favour of recognising Trade Unionism.

The minority report, signed by T. Hughes, Frederic Harrison and the Earl of Lichfield, proposed to legalise Trade Unions only to the extent of enabling them to protect their funds, while leaving them in other respects purely voluntary associations. A Bill in this sense was drafted by Frederic Harrison and a vigorous campaign was carried on by the ' Junta,' while the Reform Act of 1867, which extended the franchise, helped to give the working-class a potential voting power that was bound to weigh with any government.

Finally in 1871 the Government passed two measures which in the matter of Trade Union status gave the Unions substantially what they asked for, though with some very unpalatable additions in regard to picketing. The Act containing these objectionable provisions was hotly opposed by the workers, the entire movement concentrating for the next four years on its repeal. The imprisonment of seven women in South Wales, in 1871, merely for saying ' Bah ' to a blackleg, was an example of the kind of repression that was still possible. At the General Election in 1874 the Liberal Government was defeated, largely as a consequence of Trade Union propaganda, and for the first time two Trade Unionists, Mr. T. Burt and Mr. A. Macdonald, were elected to the House of Commons, the miners, ironworkers and other unions having started to vote money for parliamentary candidatures. After a further abortive enquiry by a Royal Commission the new Government passed two measures in 1875 and 1876 respectively, conceding the Trade Union demands. More will be said about these Acts in a later paragraph ; here it need only be said that at last both Trade Unions and Collective Bargaining, with its necessary accompaniments, were recognised by the State.

The Miners' Unions.

From about 1858 the Miners had started to build up their powerful organisations, and by 1860 they succeeded in getting the first steps taken to introduce a proper checkweighing system, by which the weights of coal sent up to the surface could be checked by a representative of the men.   Not until 1887 was legislation obtained which placed the appointment of checkweighmen on a satisfactory basis.   This reform had, as Mr. and Mrs. Webb point out, a great influence on mining Trade Unionism, since ' the compulsory levy, upon the whole pit, of the cost of maintaining the agent whom a bare majority could decide to appoint has practically found, for each colliery, a branch secretary free of expense to the Union.' [1]

The Cotton Unions.

The Cotton Unions also consolidated their strength from 1869 onwards, and before long succeeded in obtaining collective agreements covering the entire industry, as well as a Factory Act limiting hours to $56\frac{1}{2}$ weekly for women and children.   The Cotton Unions have always been keenly in favour of legislative regulation of hours of labour, and of course every limitation of the hours of women and children has reacted to the benefit of the men also.

The complexity of the piecework lists in the cotton trade led the Unions to adopt a new type of official, one who knew the economic conditions of the industry and was skilled in the necessary calculations involved in alterations of piece-rates.   The practice was started of appointing officials on the result of competitive examinations, and thus a highly skilled administrative staff has been developed by these organisations.

The Engineering Unions.

In 1871 the Engineering Workers throughout the country scored a great victory by obtaining the 54-hour week.   The Nine Hours League, headed by John Burnett, afterwards Secretary of the Amalgamated Engineers, had carried on a vigorous campaign, and a successful strike on Tyneside, lasting five months, was followed by a general acceptance of the shorter hours by employers in the industry.

This movement was carried on without the backing of the ' Junta ' and it was now that the divergence of policy among the Trade

[1] Webb, *History*, p. 306.

Unions became more marked. The result was that a spirit of sectionalism and internal bickering developed that rendered the Unions powerless to resist the attacks that came with a period of very bad trade after 1875. From 1871 to 1875, indeed, the Trade Union movement was extraordinarily prosperous. Membership increased and new organisations were formed, so that it seemed as though a great revival of working-class activity, similar to that of 1833-34, had been achieved. The revival of 1871-5, however, was different in character from the earlier one. The policy of the Unions was much more practical, much more in accord with the orthodox economics of the time, and not in the least Utopian.

By 1879 the Unions had been forced to the other extreme. Depression and defeat, loss of membership and loss of prestige marked the next few years, for the blight of one of the worst trade slumps that had ever been experienced lay upon the entire nation.

Nevertheless, the larger Unions weathered the storm successfully, their loss of membership proving only temporary, while Trades Councils continued in existence and the Trades Union Congress met annually to discuss the politics of the movement.

The Trades Union Congress indeed was little more than a debating society. First called in 1868, it met every year to talk about every subject under the sun except Trade Union policy and organisation on the industrial field. Its Parliamentary Committee was never an Executive body for the whole movement, but merely a committee for pressing reforms upon Governments and Ministers.

The New Unionism.

About 1885 the revolt against the pedestrian policy of the leaders of the larger Unions began in earnest, Tom Mann and John Burns being the chief rebels. One of the influences chiefly responsible for the quickening of the socialistic spirit animating the new movement was the teaching of Henry George, whose *Progress and Poverty* was amazingly popular in this country among all classes of workers.

On the Eight Hours question the official leaders were quite out of touch with their constitutents. On the question of participation in the International Trade Union Conferences that took place from time to time they were equally behindhand, and it was only at the express commands of Congress that the Parliamentary Committee sent delegates in 1883 and 1886.

The great Dock Strike of 1889, led by Mr. Ben Tillett, marked a turning point in Trade Union history. With their victory, and the organisation by Mr. W. Thorne, and others, of the Gasworkers, a great wave of enthusiasm started for organising all the unskilled workers hitherto hardly touched by any Trade Union. At the same time this propaganda was permeated by socialist philosophy. The ' new Unions ' were more militant and aggressive bodies than the old Unions of skilled workers. Trade Benefits loomed more largely than Friendly Benefits, which in many cases were entirely absent, and benefits altogether were less thought of than a vigorous fighting policy.

The development of a militant socialist policy was fully in accord with the economic conditions of the period. Throughout the years 1850 to 1880 there had been, on the whole, and with periodical depressions, an upward trend in British trade and in the standard of living. By the eighties other countries were beginning to compete effectively, Britain had to fight for her foreign markets, and the rapid expansion of the earlier years was considerably slowed down.

The entire situation began to take on an aspect that is more familiar to us to-day that it was fifty years ago. Socialism began to appear to the workers as something more than a Utopian dream, something, in fact, directly related to their unsatisfactory economic condition and to their even more unsatisfactory prospects. The Trade Unionism that had become stereotyped during the preceding twenty years seemed to the younger members quite inadequate to the newer conceptions of social progress, being concerned more with insurance benefits and arbitration than with the fight to dispossess the property-owning class.

The ' New Unionism ' achieved its success when it captured the Trades Union Congress in 1890, with a programme including the eight hours' day and a series of more or less socialist resolutions.

The stimulus to organisation provided by the dockers' strike, and the ensuing growth of Unions of unskilled workers, reacted on the older Unions, and their membership increased largely. At the same time the stimulus in ideas provided by the new wave of socialist propaganda also permeated the older leaders, and ultimately led to the acceptance by the Trade Union movement generally of socialistic objectives and of independent political representation.

In 1893 the Independent Labour Party was formed, and from that time Keir Hardie's policy was to link up this new, socialist party with the Unions. But though the Trades Union Congress voted funds for the support of independent working-class candidates, there was no official linking-up with the I.L.P. Still, the younger Trade Union leaders were individually associated with the I.L.P., and among Trade Unionists generally the Party had much more influence than had the Social-Democratic Federation, with its strict Marxian basis which never at any time appealed to the British workers.

In 1894 the Trades Union Congress, becoming somewhat scared of the too rapid progress, reformed itself by deciding to exclude from affiliation the Trades Councils, which had originally set up the Congress and had always been affiliated to it. The reason given was that the existing method implied dual representation of workers, first through their national unions, and second through their branches which constituted the Trades Councils. A more potent reason, perhaps, was that the Trades Councils, which incidentally had shared to the full in the revival associated with the New Unionism, were largely dominated by the younger, socialist elements which the Parliamentary Committee of Congress wished to exclude.

Other reforms were also carried with the same object in view. By 1899, however, there was again a socialist majority at Congress, which, by the end of the century, included about a million and a quarter Trade Unionists.

Meanwhile, there had been during the 'nineties a series of important trade disputes in the cotton, shipping, engineering, boot and shoe and coal-mining industries, some of which resulted in the establishment of elaborate machinery for the future settlement of disputes. In Coal Mining and on the Railways, particularly, organisation of the workers made great strides during the last years of the century, though it was not until the new century that the Miners' Federation included the Unions in all the coalfields, and that the Railway Unions were able to secure recognition by the Companies.

The need for greater co-ordination of the Unions for industrial purposes was so evident during these years that in 1899 the Trades Union Congress set up the General Federation of Trade Unions. It is significant that the T.U.C., which in recent years has taken upon itself precisely this function, was in 1899 determined to continue as a debating society, concerning itself largely with political questions.

The General Federation, however, despite the hopes aroused at the time that it would become an effective central co-ordinating body for the entire industrial army, soon degenerated into a mutual insurance organisation, and its strength and importance have continued to dwindle ever since.

Modern Times.

The outstanding feature of the early years of the present century was the development of the Labour Representation Committee from which emerged the Labour Party, as a separate, independent working-class political Party. For the history of this movement, which is somewhat outside the scope of this book, one of the standard histories should be consulted.[1]

Here it is only necessary to say that while the political movement was set on foot by the Unions, and to this day the chief strength of the Labour Party in members and finance lies in the fact that most of the large Unions are affiliated to the Party, they have remained separate organisations, neither possessing any control over the other.

Until 1909 the right of Trade Unions to contribute funds for political candidatures was unquestioned, but in that year a legal decision of great importance decided that such payments were *ultra vires*.[2] Then followed a struggle to obtain legislation reversing this decision, which was, in the existing state of development of the Labour Party, crippling the activities of the workers' political movement. The Act of 1913 partially reversing the Osborne Judgment, and the Act of 1927 re-imposing restrictions, are dealt with in later paragraphs.

A legal blow of another kind was inflicted on the Unions in 1901, by the Taff Vale Judgment,[3] and the propaganda which ensued helped the infant Labour Party enormously. Here again legislation was passed (in 1906) which nullified the effect of the decision ; this also is fully described in later paragraphs.

New Period of Unrest.

With the turn of the century the economic position of Britain definitely appeared to change for the worse. The rate of industrial expansion had slowed down, and now there was a break in the nineteenth century upward trend in real wages.

The result was that by 1908 serious unrest developed throughout industry. The increasing economic pressure made itself felt in

[1] *E.g.* Beer, M., *History of British Socialism* ; Cole, G. D. H., *Short History of the British Working Class Movement*, vol. iii.

[2] Osborne *v.* Amalgamated Society of Railway Servants.

[3] Taff Vale Railway Company *v.* Amalgamated Society of Railway Servants.

demands for higher wages and better conditions, and the Unions began to be influenced by Syndicalist propaganda that was at the same time spreading among the Unions on the Continent, particularly in France and Italy.

In 1907 a national Railway strike was barely averted, but in 1908 there was a national lock-out of woodworkers and a stoppage of cardroom operatives throughout the Cotton industry. In 1909 and 1910 there was a series of strikes in the Coal Mining industry and another serious dispute in the Cotton industry, in 1910. In the same year there was a national lock-out of Boilermakers in the shipyards. Most of these stoppages were not successful from the point of view of the Unions, and there arose a sense of deep disappointment because the ordinary Trade Union methods seemed powerless. At the same time the Labour Party in Parliament, after its initial success in 1906-1909, was beginning to be ignored instead of feared, and it also seemed to be powerless to improve conditions.

Hence a new wave of militancy spread through the Unions. Syndicalism, Industrial Unionism and Guild Socialism in turn became the theme of militant propaganda.

Without necessarily understanding the underlying philosophy of these creeds, the working masses seized on their slogans and their leading ideas with avidity, seeing in them the hope of release from an economic system that appeared to have grown too strong to be dealt with by the ordinary methods of either orthodox Trade Unionism or political democracy. ' The Mines for the Miners ' was the Syndicalist text of the famous South Wales pamphlet, *The Miners' Next Step*, published in 1912.

There was a powerful urge towards amalgamation of Unions, and there were various ' Forward ' movements among the ' rank and file ' workers in many industries.

The *Daily Citizen* was started as the official Labour daily and the militants had the *Herald*, which later became the *Daily Herald* (and later still succeeded the defunct *Citizen* as the official Labour daily).

Meanwhile the tide of strikes had continued, despite a period of comparatively good trade. In 1911 there was a national strike of seamen, followed by sporadic strikes of dockers which were unified and fought through to victory by the Transport Workers' Federation. Then came a strike of all transport workers at Liverpool, which, like the previous disputes, ended in a victory for the Unions. In the following year a determined attempt to smash the transport workers' organisation in London led to a national transport strike, but the weakness of the Federation was shown by the poor response, and the men were beaten.

The Railwaymen won their great victory, including for the first time full recognition, by a national strike involving the stoppage of 145,000 railway workers, in 1911. In 1913 they formed the most important amalgamation that had been achieved for many years, for the National Union of Railwaymen was to serve as a model to the militants of the pre-war years, in much the same way that the Amalgamated Society of Engineers had done to the Trade Union world in 1851. While the latter seemed at the time a triumph of administrative efficiency and centralisation, the National Union of Railwaymen appealed to the progressive workers in 1913 because it appeared to embody the new principle of industrial unionism.

Thus, on the eve of the War, the Trade Union world was again in a state of ferment. Economic conditions were unfavourable, unrest was rampant, new and revolutionary ideas were in the air and were even vitally affecting the organisation and policy of the Unions. It seemed as though the entire movement was in a state of flux, casting around for the solid ground of a new philosophy which would enable it to stand firm amid the perilous buffetings of strange economic forces.

Trade Unionism and the War.

The net effect of the War on Trade Unionism was, somewhat unexpectedly, to give it a standing and strength never before attained or even visualised. That this result was inevitable is seen on reflection. A modern war depends absolutely on the smooth functioning of the industrial machine, for adequate supplies of munitions must be continuously forthcoming in addition to the normal needs of the nation being met. The co-operation, avowed or tacit, of the Trade Unions is therefore essential, at any rate in a country like Britain where a considerable proportion of the workers are organised.

In the initial months of the War unemployment and distress were anticipated on a much larger scale than actually materialised, and to prepare counter measures the Trade Union movement, along with other labour bodies, formed the War Emergency Workers' National Committee, which did much useful work. As the workers joined the fighting forces and the demand for munitions became even more insistent, there was soon a decided shortage of labour. Prices also started to rise steadily. The Unions had voluntarily declared an industrial truce on the outbreak of hostilities, but in face of the rise in the cost of living they were soon compelled to ask for wage increases, and they were able to exert irresistible pressure because of the scarcity of labour. At first the Unions were reluctant to use this new power, and there were many unofficial strikes, called in some cases by 'rank and file' organisations created locally by the workers who felt that their Trade Union machinery was to all intents and purposes helpless for the time being. With a few exceptions the Trades Unions, faced with the position confronting the Government, had, in fact, reluctantly agreed to a suspension of Trade Union workshop practices which might have the effect of limiting production, but only on guarantees being given that the *status quo* would be restored after the War. At the same time a form of compulsory arbitration was agreed to and the Government undertook to limit the employers' profits. In 1915 the first Munitions Act was passed, making these same provisions legally binding. The South Wales miners nevertheless went on strike in the summer of 1915, and proved once for all that compulsion cannot be applied to several hundred thousand workers.

The compulsory arbitration provisions of the Munitions' Act were never popular and there was much friction in their working. There were also more of the unofficial stoppages of work, organised by the 'Workers' Committees,' 'Shop Stewards' Committees,' 'Vigilance Committees,' and similar bodies that developed in many industries, but especially in the munitions trades. These local organisations formed themselves into a National Workers' Committee Movement, which was constantly getting into trouble not only with the Government and the employers but also with the official Trade Union machinery. This movement was strongly socialistic all through, being attracted in the first place to Guild Socialism, and later, as the influence of the Russian Revolution was felt, to more extreme doctrines. With the end of the War these local 'rank and file' bodies and their vague national organisation disappeared, while at the same time the engineering unions incorporated the Shop Steward system into their own Trade Union machinery. The Russian Revolution, however, continued to make a strong sentimental appeal to the British workers.

It was during the War period, mainly through the appeal of Guild Socialist ideas to the 'unofficial' workers' organisations, that the doctrine of 'workers' control' of industry took a firm hold on the labour movement. It became for large numbers of workers the primary goal of the working-class organisations, and in time it permeated the Unions themselves, which, in some cases, added this objective to their formal statement of aims. Although the 'guild' propaganda practically ceased, it is safe to say that the idea of 'workers' control' has remained to this day as one of the chief aims inspiring the Trade Union movement.

The Unions, meanwhile, had been to a large extent absorbed temporarily into the State's administrative machine. For the prosecution of the War and the handling of labour, State regulation on a large scale was needed, and the Unions took their share in this control and regulation. With dramatic suddenness the Trade Union movement found itself not merely recognised by State and employers, but treated with deference and respect, and given large powers in the war-time administration.

A trade unionist was in the War Cabinet; Unions were represented equally with the employers on the Cotton Control Board, the Wool Control Board, and other bodies; the organisation of the workers in Unions was definitely encouraged by the Government, and the Whitley Committee recommended the setting up of Joint Industrial Councils in the well-organised trades, with equal representation of employers and Unions, for the consideration of a wide range of industrial problems.

The effect of War-time conditions on the Unions' power was impressive. Membership and funds increased rapidly until by 1920 the high-water mark was reached with over eight million organised workers, of whom six and a half millions were in the Trades Union Congress.

The huge organisations of miners, railwaymen, and transport workers combined in 1915 to form the Triple Alliance, a loose federation for mutual support in trade movements. Hailed by some as the inspired weapon for the 'social general strike' that had been preached by the Syndicalists, and denounced by others as a grave menace to the State, the Triple Alliance pursued a somewhat uneventful career until the debacle of 1921 which brought about its dissolution.

Up to 1920 the standard of living of the workers was, on the whole, maintained without great difficulty. The Agricultural workers were greatly assisted by the statutory wage boards set up in 1917, and the extension of Trade Boards under the Act of 1918 brought about better conditions in many low-paid, badly organised trades. During 1919-20 there was a spirit of optimism throughout

the industrial world ; everyone was still under the delusion that a
' new world ' was going to emerge from the four years' strife.

Post War.

Then came the disillusionment, with the great post-war depression
starting at the end of 1920.   With deflation came the unprecedented slump in prices, accompanied by an even greater slump in
wages, and by a catastrophic fall in Trade Union membership.
From the end of the War well into the slump, however, the amalgamation movement made great headway among the Unions, and a
number of important fusions took place, among them the formation
of the Amalgamated Engineering Union, the Transport and General
Workers' Union, the National Union of General Workers, the
National Union of Textile Workers, the National Union of Building
Trade Workers and others.   The superior power and efficiency
thus attained enabled these large organisations to cope with the
problems of the depression, despite the fall in membership, far more
vigorously than they could have done at any previous period.

Still, they could not accomplish miracles.   The economic
position of Britain had been seriously assailed.   European and
Asiatic markets for our products had been hopelessly disorganised
as a result of the War.   The world was impoverished, and many
countries, formerly our customers for certain products, had become
self-sufficing, or even rivals to us in the world's markets.

Our economic supremacy, so marked during the period of the
Industrial Revolution and the mid-nineteenth century, had been
effectively challenged in several quarters during the last years of the
century and the pre-war period, and had now, after the War,
definitely gone.

Since the end of the War we have seen an unexampled state of
depression, unemployment, and low wages, in the staple exporting
trades,—the ' unsheltered trades,'—though the so-called sheltered
industries, Transport, Building, and others, have succeeded in maintaining their position.

Coal-mining has, of course, held the centre of the stage, though
Railways and Engineering have each had spectacular stoppages, the
former a strike in 1919, and the latter a lock-out in 1922.   The
Railway strike was mainly notable because the Union defeated the
Government at its own game of publicity, and won over public
opinion, and because the Government afterwards set up for the first
time its machinery for coping with national stoppages in ' essential '

industries. The Engineering lock-out was noteworthy because it settled for the time being, in the employers' favour, their claim to complete control in regard to ' managerial functions.'

Coal, however, has been struggling against economic facts as well as against the most stupid body of employers in the country. After the three months' national stoppage in 1921 there was a period of comparative calm, while a novel wage agreement was tried out under fairly favourable conditions. Those conditions disappeared again in 1925, when a national stoppage was only averted by the nine months' subsidy and the setting up of a Royal Commission.

All the post-war enquiries into the industry had resulted in findings favourable to the miners, or at any rate unfavourable to the owners ; the Sankey Commission of 1919, with its scheme of public ownership ; the Buckmaster Committee of 1924 and the Macmillan Enquiry of 1925. The Samuel Commission of 1925-26 satisfied no one, but the seven months' national stoppage in 1926 accomplished nothing, either for the miners or for the industry. The avoidance of trouble in 1925, by the offer of a subsidy, was due to the solid front presented by the entire Trade Union movement, which was prepared to enforce a national Transport strike in support of the miners.

The National Strike.

In 1926 the miners refused to accept the Report of the Samuel Commission, as did the employers, and a national stoppage was decided upon when drastic wage reductions were announced. A special Trades Union Congress gave the General Council authority to declare a National Strike of Transport, Power, Printing, Iron and Steel, and other industries, in support of the miners. The strike, involving over a million and a half men, lasted nine days and was the one topic of discussion throughout the civilised world, not only for its magnitude and impressive solidarity, but for its orderly and dignified conduct. Partly because of the Government's extraordinary counter-measures, and partly because a settlement considered by the General Council to be reasonable in the circumstances was refused by the Miners' Federation, the strike was called off without its object being achieved.

It was the most notable trial of strength, on the industrial field, that England had ever known, and while it did not for any length of time seriously impair the resources of the movement, even though it was largely a failure, an indirect result was the enactment of a new law in 1927, making such strikes illegal in future and inflicting other disabilities on the Trade Union movement.

It may be useful at this point to survey very briefly the legal position in which Trade Unions have been left by this and earlier legislation since the repeal of the Combination Acts.[1]

Legal Position of Unions ; Modern Times.

From 1824-25 onwards Trade Unions were, as has been said, in a very precarious condition for, although their existence was tolerated, the courts effectively prevented them from carrying on their most necessary activities. The 1825 legislation may have lifted the labourer ' from a status to a contract system,' [2] but it imposed severe penalties for the use of ' violence, threats, intimidation, molestation or obstruction by any person for the purpose of forcing a master to alter his mode of business,' etc.[3] Even where no offence was committed, the law would not intervene to protect a Union's interests. Trade Union funds could therefore be stolen by defaulting officials or withheld by banks, and the Unions had no remedy whatever.

Moreover, about the middle of the nineteenth century the new doctrine of ' common-law conspiracy ' was evolved, according to which, quite independently of the 1825 penalties mentioned above and without any illegal means being used, a combination which ' obstructed ' an employer in his business by persuading men to strike was a conspiracy, and a strike was a criminal offence at common law.[4] That this doctrine should be laid down in 1851 was merely an evidence of the renewed alarm felt by the governing classes in the face of the Trade Union revival then taking place, and to clinch the matter it was embodied in the ' Offences against the Person Act ' of 1861, which refers to ' any unlawful combination or conspiracy to raise the rate of wages.'

The Trade Union Act of 1871, which has already been mentioned on an earlier page, is often called the Trade Unionists' Charter, a title it in some ways deserves, for it undoubtedly marked a great step forward in the legal recognition of the rights of organised labour. It provided that the purposes of a Union should not, merely because they were in restraint of trade, be regarded as criminal,

---

[1] See Slesser and Baker, *Trade Union Law* (Third ed.), and Henderson, A., *Trade Unions and the Law.*   [2] Jenks, *op. cit.* p. 325.

[3] Sir R. Wright, *Law of Criminal Conspiracies,* p. 13.

[4] Jenks, *op. cit.* p. 328 ; Erle, J., in R. *v.* Rowlands (1851), 5 Cox 462.

nor should they render void any agreement or trust. Unions could be registered, and could vest their property in trustees who could sue or be sued on matters affecting the Union's property rights. Thus, the ' common law conspiracy ' doctrine was apparently (but only ' apparently ') abolished and the power to steal Trade Union funds with impunity disappeared. On the other hand the Act expressly denied the Unions the right to incorporation under the Companies Acts, and laid it down that certain agreements made between the Union and its members, or between one Union and another, were not directly enforceable. This is still the position, and, it may be said, it was the position desired in 1871 by the Trade Union movement.

Another law passed in the same year was so reactionary in its effect on Trade Union activities such as picketing and persuasion to strike, that a prolonged agitation led to its replacement by the Conspiracy and Protection of Property Act, 1875. This killed finally the doctrine of ' common-law conspiracy,' which had again been adopted by the courts, despite what was understood to be the intention of the Trade Union Act of 1871. All the old legislation making breach of contract a criminal offence was abolished, except for a few cases where danger to life or property might be caused. Peaceful picketing was also legalised.

The next development was that the courts invented a new offence, or rediscovered and adapted an old one, and applied it to labour disputes. This was incitement to breach of contract,[1] widened into the doctrine of ' civil conspiracy,' which makes it actionable for any combination ' to induce third persons not to enter into the employ of, or supply goods to, the plaintiff, though no actual breach of contract occurs,' provided damage has been suffered.[2] Then came the famous Taff Vale Judgment,[3] in which the House of Lords, reversing the judgment of the Court of Appeal, held that a registered Trade Union could be sued for torts committed on its behalf by its officials. The Taff Vale Railway Company was awarded heavy damages against the Railwaymen's Union (A.S.R.S.), though ' there was no historical authority for such a proposition.' [4] The

---

[1] Temperton v. Russell (1893), 1 Q.B. 715 (C.A.), and other cases cited by Jenks, op. cit. pp. 333-334.

[2] Quinn v. Leathem (1901), A.C. 495. Jenks, op. cit. 334-335.

[3] Taff Vale Railway Company v. Amalgamated Society of Railway Servants (1901), A.C. 426.   [4] Jenks, op. cit. 336.

decision completely upset the status of Unions as everyone thought it had been left by the 1871 Act. At the same time it was in accordance with the general trend of legal development.

In 1906 the Trade Disputes Act was passed reversing the principle of this decision and making it clear that an act done by a combination in pursuance of a trade dispute is not actionable if it would not be actionable without such combination; that inducing a breach of contract is not actionable if done in pursuance of a trade dispute; that peaceful picketing is quite legal, if in pursuance of a trade dispute; and that Trade Unions cannot be sued for the tortious acts of its officials or members.

This drastic measure abolished the new 'civil conspiracy' doctrine and 'incitement to breach of contract' doctrine, as far as disputes were concerned; enlarged the definition of picketing; and nullified the Taff Vale decision. In the main, these benefits have been retained by the Unions, though the 1927 Act limited certain of them.

Then in 1910 a new issue of great importance was raised by the Osborne Judgment,[1] in which the House of Lords held that it was outside the power of a Trade Union to spend its funds on political objects, such as financing the Parliamentary candidature of one of its members or contributing to the support of a member of Parliament.

A Union was declared to be acting *ultra vires* if it put into operation a rule purporting to give such power. As this decision crippled the work of the rapidly growing Labour Party there was a strenuous agitation to secure its reversal. Finally, in 1913, the Trade Union Act [2] was passed which, in addition to authorising the expenditure of a Trade Union's funds on any lawful objects (other than certain specified political objects) authorised by its Rules, provided that funds could be expended on these 'political objects' under certain conditions. These were, in brief, that the members of the Union must on a ballot vote approve of the inclusion of political objects in the Rules of the Union; that the political fund must be kept separate from the other funds of the Union; and that members desiring not to contribute to this fund must be able to 'contract-out' of the obligation to pay, without suffering any loss of benefits or being placed under any disability or disadvantage for so doing.

The Osborne Judgment was therefore only partially reversed by this Act.

[1] Amalgamated Society of Railway Servants *v.* Osborne (1910), A.C. 87. [2] 2 & 3 Geo. V, ch. 30.

In 1927 a further important Act was passed which seriously curtailed the liberties of Trade Unions in regard to political expenditure, strikes, and picketing, and interfered with the freedom of certain classes of labour to organise with their fellow workers in other trades.

The Trade Disputes and Trade Unions Act, 1927,[1] was passed partly as a result of the National Strike in May 1926. Many of its sections were very ambiguously drafted and, at the time of writing, they still remain to be interpreted by the courts. Briefly the Act provided that a sympathetic strike [2] or lockout (and even certain primary strikes) designed or calculated to coerce the Government by inflicting hardship on the community, should be illegal, any person declaring or furthering such a stoppage being guilty of a criminal offence ; that the Trade Disputes Act, 1906, and the Emergency Powers Act, 1920, should not apply to such an illegal strike, though on the other hand no person would be guilty of an offence merely for ceasing work ; that members of Unions should in future have to ' contract-in ' to the obligation to pay political contributions ; that civil servants should not be allowed to join Unions having members outside the Government service or Unions having political objects or connections ; that Local Authorities should not be allowed to make Trade Union membership a condition of employment in their own or their contractors' service ; that breach of contract of service with a local or public authority should be a criminal offence if the probable result would be to cause grave inconvenience to the community ; and that picketing should only be allowed in future under much more stringent conditions.

Meanwhile, the Emergency Powers Act,[3] 1920, had given the Government power to make regulations ' for securing the essentials of life to the community ' in cases of emergency where transport, power supply, food supplies, etc., were threatened. This practically unlimited power was used by the Government during the Coal Stoppage of 1921 and again during the National Strike and Coal Stoppage of 1926. Under its authorisation a great strike-breaking organisation had been set up by the Government.

[1] 17 & 18 Geo. V, ch. 22.

[2] A ' sympathetic ' or ' secondary ' strike is a strike declared, not on account of a dispute in which the strikers are directly concerned, but ' in sympathy ' with other workers engaged in a dispute.

[3] 10 & 11 Geo. V, ch. 55.

The Centralisation of Trade Union Power.

The united action by the Unions in 1926 was possible because, ever since 1920, the Trades Union Congress had also been building up its organisation and its executive body under a new constitution.[1] The Parliamentary Committee had disappeared, and there was now a General Council elected on a system of industrial groups, and possessing much wider powers than had been exercised by the old Committee.

From 1920, in fact, there has proceeded a rapid consolidation and centralisation of power in the hands of the Trades Union Congress and its General Council, which has occupied the role, intended in 1899 for the General Federation of Trade Unions, of a central co-ordinating body, with a properly equipped administrative machine, for the Trade Union Movement as a whole. Every year that has passed has seen an extension of the General Council's work, and its scope and powers have been enlarged since it was first set up.

Both in internal matters of organisation and policy, and in the wider field of the economic interests of the workers generally, it has come to be recognised as the authoritative body entitled to speak on behalf of organised labour, and as such it nominates representatives to Government Commissions and similar bodies. Although it has been given no power to override the autonomy of the Unions or to impose decisions of any kind upon them, its moral authority in the movement is great and continues to grow year by year.

The Trade Union Movement To-day.

Two of the groups represented in the Congress and on the General Council, namely, those for Public Employees and for Non-manual workers, illustrate a comparatively new development in organisation.

Since the beginning of the present century, and more especially since the War, there has been a great growth of Trade Unionism among non-manual workers, or ' black-coated workers,' as they are frequently termed. Post Office workers and other Civil Servants, Railway Clerks, Draughtsmen, Office workers, Municipal employees, Musicians, and Actors are among the groups who have formed

---

[1] See *The Trades Union Congress* and *The General Council of the T.U.C.*, pamphlets published by the Trades Union Congress.

Unions affiliated to the T.U.C. In addition there are many other Unions of technical and professional workers not affiliated, including Teachers, Scientific Workers, Journalists, Bank officials and Accountants. Many of these organisations, (and many of those already mentioned as being affiliated to the T.U.C.), have joined a Federation of Professional Workers, which has a Joint Committee with the General Council of the T.U.C. for the discussion of matters of common interest.

With the Labour Party there has been established joint machinery in the shape of a National Joint Council representing the General Council of the Trades Union Congress, the Executive Committee of the Labour Party, and the Parliamentary Labour Party. In addition the General Council and the Labour Party Executive Committee hold a joint meeting each month, to discuss matters of common interest, and they maintain a joint Library in the common headquarters of the two movements.

The Unions themselves have in recent years set up a great deal of joint machinery, also. Thus, in co-operation with the General Council there is a Trade Boards Advisory Council, to assist the workers' representatives on Trade Boards and promote a common policy ; there is a National Association of Trade Union Approved Societies, in connection with the administration of Health Insurance, and a similar body in connection with the administration of Unemployment Insurance, and both are represented on the General Council's Social Insurance Committee.

In Workers' Education, the Trades Union Congress has encouraged and financed the further education of members of Unions, and for this purpose it operates through the Workers' Educational Association, the National Council of Labour Colleges, and Ruskin College, Oxford.

Individual Unions also have arrangements with one or other of these organisations, directly.

During recent years the General Council has devoted much attention to the organisation of Trades Councils, and many new Councils have been created, all being linked together in a National Conference which appoints representatives to sit with an equal number of General Council representatives on the Trades Councils Consultative Committee.

Finally, the Trades Union Congress and the Labour Party have for some years owned jointly the *Daily Herald*, and the Victoria House Printing Company, which have rendered invaluable service to the Labour movement, by way of propaganda and publicity.

In the international field, the Trades Union Congress has been associated with the International Federation of Trade Unions since this body was re-established after the War. When the International Association of Working Men was founded in 1864 British Trade Unions went to the Conferences and sat with Karl Marx and other continental leaders; indeed the headquarters were located in London. The British movement has retained ever since that time its deep interest in internationalism, and has since the War played a considerable part in promoting international labour activity, a task rendered very difficult by the dissension created by the Moscow 'Red International of Labour Unions.' To this Communist organisation is affiliated the British National Minority Movement, a small minority group which has for several years pursued wrecking tactics inside the Unions and the Trades Councils.

Returning to the international field it is to be noted that many Unions have become affiliated with their own 'Trade Internationals,' *i.e.* international organisations of Unions in a given trade or industry. Thus, there is a Miners' International, to which the Miners' Federation of Great Britain is affiliated. The Trade Internationals work in close co-operation with the International Federation of Trade Unions itself.

In accordance with the Labour clauses of the Versailles Treaty the Trades Union Congress nominates a delegate to the International Labour Organisation of the League of Nations, and close co-operation with the I.L.O. is maintained.

For several years, from 1924 to 1927, the General Council was associated through a joint committee (the Anglo-Russian Advisory Committee) with the Russian Trade Union movement.

This alliance, which was created as a sign of the desire for a sympathetic understanding with the Russian workers, was broken off by the British side in 1927 in consequence of the continuous attacks made by the Russians on the General Council, and their attempts to interfere with the domestic affairs of the Trades Union Congress.

With its increasing complexity of structure, and its many contacts both with foreign movements and with the varied aspects of social and industrial life in Britain, the Trades Union Congress has tended in recent years to formulate its own constructive policy in economic affairs, a policy based largely on the wider experience and knowledge thus gained. It has more and more interested itself—and the same applies to the individual Unions,—in all the problems of industrial management, technique and finance that have become so important to our industrial future. Here, as throughout its history, the movement accords with the economic trend of the age. In a world of changing economic factors, new technological developments, and more complicated industrial organisation, the workers' movement has recognised that it cannot stand still, that it has to adapt its own structure and its own policy to the new conditions.

The simple faith and simpler forms of the Trade Unionism of a hundred years ago, or even of fifty years ago, have been seen to offer a quite inadequate guidance for the needs of to-day. Socialism itself, still firmly adhered to by organised labour, has changed and is changing, just as capitalism has changed and is changing its form. The combine and cartel, electric power and the automatic machine, chemical technology and scientific management, all these things have created a new industrial revolution and have brought in their wake many new problems. In entering into conversations with Lord Melchett's [1] group of employers the General Council of the Trades Union Congress showed its realisation of the changes thus brought about and its determination to take a share in solving the problems and in directing future development.

Here, appropriately enough, this brief sketch may end, with Trade Unionism and its national organisations recognised, accepted, and respected by the employing class and by the State itself. The descendants of those who once treated them with ridicule and contempt, now treat with them on equal terms. That is a great deal, but would anyone say that the destiny of Trade Unionism has finally been fulfilled? Organised labour at least does not believe so, but has a much more splendid vision of its final achievement.

[1] Formerly Sir Alfred Mond.

PART I

VALUE, ASPIRATIONS AND OBJECTS OF TRADE UNIONISM.

THE value and advantages of Trade Unions have, for the workers, a twofold aspect. In the first place the Unions represent in a tangible form all those inner desires and aspirations that have animated every grade and class of labour since the first days of working class history. Born of the poverty and oppression that have accompanied the working of the industrial system, there has been a constant urge impelling the victims to seek and labour for a new system, a promised land where justice and a sufficient livelihood will be assured to all. The Unions have stood as a beacon, pointing the way to its realisation. They have been in truth the symbol of a recurrent hope and faith that out of the present discontents would come a new and better order.

Ever since their foundation they have seemed to offer to the down-trodden worker the only protection against the rapacity and tyranny of the ' boss.' This conception survives as strongly as ever among trade unionists, even though the rigours of the early years of the factory system have been softened, and the language of Holyoake (1)[1] would not seem exaggerated to the worker at the present day.

It is usual for Unions to remind new members of this idealistic side of their movement, and to draw upon history to illustrate the value of organisation, both in connection with these larger aims and in regard to the more practical side, too (2, 3).

The language of an earlier period is often retained even though the Union has become a very modern, scientific

[1] The heavy figures in brackets which are to be found in the commentaries on the Parts refer to the numbered Documents which follow them.

organisation, for there is an emotional value in this evangel-istic expression, as well as a sentimental attachment to it on historical grounds.

For directly propagandist purposes, however, Unions stress much more the practical advantages that come from organisa-tion ; the benefits paid, the wages secured, the reduced hours of work, the legal assistance given, and so on. Every Union has its organisers who are constantly converting workers to trade unionism, and who go out armed with leaflets or pamphlets or posters to secure recruits for the organisation. Every argument that can possibly be used is employed in this propaganda material, and is set out in brief, pithy sentences that the most casual reader may understand. An entire book could be filled with extracts from such leaflets, but the three from which extracts are given are typical (4, 5, 6).

As might be expected, Unions devote special attention to non-unionists, and point out to them, often in very vigorous terms, the real meaning of their abstention (7, 8).

In marked contrast with former denunciations of trade unionism are the present-day opinions held by responsible employers. This point receives fuller treatment in a later section, but the value of Unions in securing the observance of industrial agreements has been well shown by the Industrial Council, which was set up by the Government in 1912 (9).

The objects and aims of trade unionism have also a twofold aspect. The objects of the individual Unions are set out in their Rules, and within these objects so defined the organisa-tions must work. The aims specified in the Rules of a Union are not like the vague provisions of the Constitutions of many countries, which are merely pious declarations ; they are rather to be compared with the Constitution of the United States, outside which not even the Governing Body may step without being pulled up by the courts. Further, the Unions themselves are, according to the famous Osborne judgment, subject, in the same way as Companies and other bodies incorporated under statute, to the doctrine of *ultra vires* (10, 209). The Trade Union Act of 1913, however, while laying it down that in order to be recognised as a trade union a combination must have certain statutory objects, widened the powers which a Union might take for itself, so that at present, apart from restrictions as to political objects, a trade union may embody in its constitution any lawful object it pleases (11).

The traditional purpose of a trade union has been expressed in a well-known definition by Mr. and Mrs. Webb (12), and there are still many Unions that, in theory at any rate, keep within this definition.   The old-established Unions of highly skilled crafts tend to keep to the old-established expression of their objects, and to what many trade unionists would call an ' old fashioned ' policy.   Many of the newer trade unions, General Labour Unions, and even some of the older organisations of skilled craftsmen, have adopted a much more modern and radical statement of their aims.   Unions that came into existence at periods of unrest and social upheaval tended to phrase their objects in socialistic language, while those that were formed in times of peace and prosperity were more likely to adopt the sober language of ' business unionism.' It is impossible to cite more than one or two statements of objects of actual Unions, but instances are given of the objects of an old-established Union of skilled craftsmen in the Printing industry ; a modern amalgamation of old-established organisations of skilled workers in the Engineering industry ; a large modern General Labour Union (very comprehensive statement of objects) ; a Miners' Union and a Union of Government employees, chiefly non-manual workers (13, 14, 15, 16, 17).   In addition there is the statement of objects of an important federation, for such organisations must necessarily differ in this respect from Unions (18).   The objects of the Trades Union Congress, as will be seen, comprise a number of concrete measures as well as the general aims of a federation (19).

Apart from the aims as set out in Rules and Constitutions, it is important to note the more philosophical expressions of the objectives of the movement as a whole.   Nothing is more remarkable, as has been pointed out in the Introduction, than the manner in which the trade union movement has become a convert to Socialism. Remarkable, not because of the fact itself, which is natural enough in view of working-class experience and history, but because of the rapidity with which the change took place. Equally remarkable is the demand during the past fifteen years for 'industrial democracy,' 'workers' control,' 'self-government in industry,'—to use the terms most commonly accepted.

This conception is now to be found embodied in the objects of many Unions (see, for example, the first sentence of the statement of objects in (14); and (2 (a)) in (15); and in one case, at least, the influence of Guild Socialist propaganda is more plainly seen (17). The demand for 'control' is also embodied in the objects of the Trades Union Congress (19).

One has to turn to the more lengthy expositions of trade union aims, however, to find this conception worked out in greater detail. From the enormous mass of literature on the subject a few examples have been selected to illustrate this recent movement among trade unionists (20, 21, 22).

The more subtle advocacy of this same idea has been finely worded by Mr. Tawney (23), while the full-blooded expression of the aims of the I.W.W. has been briefly summarised by the famous American socialist, Eugene Debs (24).

The modern conception of the mission of the T.U.C. has been well put in a recent Presidental address (25). It is not possible, of course, to do justice in the small space available to the great change that has come over the Trade Union Movement of this country in the last twenty years, in regard to the immediate and ultimate aims and objectives of the workers' organisations. Nowhere is this great development more evident than in the changing character and aims of the T.U.C., and the authorities listed below should be studied in this connection.

AUTHORITIES.

The only satisfactory sources for students desiring to make a fuller investigation of the subject dealt with in Part I. of this book are the Rule Books of the Unions, and the periodical Press of the Trade Union movement. The Annual Reports of the T.U.C. are also necessary. As a preliminary to such investigation the student should, of course, study Mr. and Mrs. Webb's *History of Trade Unionism* and *Industrial Democracy* (latest edition of each).[1]

C. M. Lloyd's *Trade Unionism* and G. D. H. Cole's *Organised Labour*, *The World of Labour*, and *Self-Government in Industry* will be found useful, while for the legal side Slesser and Baker's *Trade Union Law* (Third ed.) should be consulted.   B. G. de Montgomery's *British and Continental Labour Policy* and C. W. Pipkin's *The Idea of Social Justice* give useful surveys of the changes in Trade Union and Labour objectives.   For the United States, J. R. Commons and Associates' *History of Labor in the United States* and S. Perlman's *History of Trade Unionism in the United States* are the standard works.   J. M. Budish and G. Soule's *The New Unionism* is especially interesting for its account of the new conception of Trade Union objects and methods in the clothing Unions.

1. Advantages of Trade Unions as seen in 1841.

LECTURE BY G. J. HOLYOAKE, addressed to the ' Trades' Unions ' of Sheffield, 28th Nov., 1841.

The advantages of Trades' Unions will be seen from the remarks made.   Being founded in justice, as we have shown, they must have produced good as no just thing is lost to the world.   They have generated a love of freedom, have knit together the victims of capital, when masters have forgotten honour and justice, and the world compassion and sympathy.   When governments and religion were ranked with the oppressors, Unions were the only barriers between the desolation of capital and machinery, starvation and the poorhouse.

2. The Case for Trade Unions.

PREFACE to the RULE BOOK OF THE AMALGAMATED ENGINEERING UNION, 1926.

United we Stand—Divided we Fall.

The AMALGAMATED ENGINEERING UNION is established to promote the interests of those who follow the trades hereinafter enumerated.

[1] References throughout this book are, unless otherwise stated, to the 1920 edition of Mr. and Mrs. Webb's *History of Trade Unionism* and *Industrial Democracy*.

Objections are sometimes raised against Trade Societies, charges being made that they are monopolies and unjust restrictions; but those who experience the great benefits they confer can fully appreciate their general usefulness. Every artisan following a given occupation has an interest, in common with all those similarly engaged, in forming rules by which that particular trade shall be regulated: the constitution thus set up being available for the assistance of men out of work, for the support of sick, infirm, superannuated, and disabled members, and for giving aid to the families of those who die. Moreover, it is essential for the progress of the worker that he should combine with his fellows; the concentration of means thus enabling him to make his power felt and affording him security against risks to which he would otherwise be exposed.

Such societies as this should contain, if possible, all those engaged in the same calling, or, at all events, the greatest possible number who can be induced to join. For members of a trade working together in large numbers, who by their daily intercourse are made acquainted with each other's circumstances, and who are cognisant of much of the misery which is necessarily attendant on a precarious employment, would be inhuman indeed if they did not unite to relieve the distress of their fellow-workmen, who are often placed in circumstances in which they cannot help themselves. And hence it is that special facilities for membership are now offered to a much larger number of our fellow-workmen. Under this code of rules, apprentices will be admitted at a much earlier period of their apprenticeship; middle-aged men who from pecuniary or other reasons could not previously join us can now do so, as sectional or trade members, only paying a proportional share of contributions; whilst those advanced in years —hitherto entirely neglected, and always the first to suffer in the too-oft recurring disputes between employer and employed—can now become members and receive very substantial assistance when so prevented from following their employment.

We are ready to admit that, whilst in constant employment, our members may be able to obtain the necessaries of life; but there is a fear, and by no means a groundless one, that employment may not be constant. The merest circumstance in the commercial world may influence the condition of thousands of working men; and, when thrown out of employment, all a man's arrangements of a domestic nature are subverted, and his hopes of being enabled by his own frugality to improve his social condition are proved to be only a dream.

The Amalgamated Engineering Union offers a guarantee against most of the evils resulting from this precarious condition. Our primary object is to raise the status of the workmen engaged in the engineering industry, and generally to improve the conditions under which we labour.

These are some of the reasons which have guided us in framing these rules, by which we hope to protect and advance the interests of the members far more effectually, and to confer greater advantages than it is possible to do under sectional unionism.

Our members know the practical value of association, and have manifested their attachment to it. By association we acquire the discipline which allows us to act together, and the patience which enables us to wait for results. Organisation gives to men a special character, and is a source of strength ; it keeps them compact, and concentrates their efforts towards one end, whilst, without it, they are both weak and ineffectual, exercising no influence or control over their own future condition.

We direct your attention, then, to this institution which is the only safeguard of your interests, the only protection of your trade. In return for the many benefits it confers, it behoves us to devote our whole energy to its advancement, and to take every opportunity of making it known and appreciated by those whose interests and duty it is to belong to it. If we do this, we may leave to a future generation not only a trade, but the means of maintaining its best interests, until some more general principle of co-operation shall be acknowledged in society, guaranteeing to every man the full enjoyment of the produce of his labour.

3. The Case for Trade Unions.

NATIONAL UNION OF GENERAL AND MUNICIPAL WORKERS, 1924.

FOREWORD TO RULES.

FELLOW WORKERS,

Trade Unionism has done excellent work in the past, and in it lies the hope of the workers for the future ; that is, the Trade Unionism which clearly recognises that to-day there are only two classes, the producing Working Class, and the possessing Master Class. The interests of these two classes are opposed to each other. The Masters have known this for a long time ; the workers are beginning to see it.

They are beginning to understand that their only hope lies in themselves, that from the Masters as a class they can expect no help, and that divided they fall, united they stand. This is why the Union was formed ; it embraces every kind of labour, and admits all general workers, women as well as men, on an equal footing.

The immediate objects of this Union are the improvement of the material conditions of its members ; the raising them from mere beasts of burden to human beings ; the making brighter and happier the home of every Worker ; the saving of little children from the hard, degrading, bitter life to which they are condemned to-day ; the dividing more equally between all men and women the tears and laughter, the sorrows and the joy, the labours and the leisure of the world.

It is important that all members should understand the necessity for and the aims of this Union ; that they should accept and loyally carry out its rules ; that they should remember that the interests of all workers are one, and a wrong done to any kind of labour is a wrong done to the whole of the Working Class, and that victory or defeat of any portion of the Army of Labour is a gain or a loss to the whole of the Army, which by its organisation and Union is marching steadily and irresistibly forward to its ultimate goal—the Emancipation of the Working Class.

That emancipation can only be brought about by the strenuous and united efforts of the Working Class itself.

WORKERS, UNITE !

4. Value of Trade Unionism to the Workers.

Extract from Organising Leaflet issued by the NAT. UNION OF DIS-TRIBUTIVE AND ALLIED WORKERS.[1]

Tobacco Trade Workers !

DO YOU KNOW that the above Trade Union has more Tobacco Workers in its membership than any other Trade Union in the Kingdom ?

DO YOU KNOW that it was owing to the efforts of Trade Union officials and delegates that you got your improved wages and conditions of labour ?

DO YOU KNOW that as non-unionists you have not been of any assistance to the fighting Union ?

DO YOU KNOW that it costs time, energy and money to do this work for you ?

[1] This and the succeeding organising literature is undated, but was in use shortly before this volume was compiled.

DO YOU KNOW that it is only by *maintaining a strong union* that you can hope to defeat the tactics of *low wage* employers ?

DO YOU KNOW that those who are not with us are against us ?

Join Up Without Delay !

ENTRANCE FEE IS.

5. Value of Trade Unionism to the Workers.

Extract from Organising Leaflet addressed to Women by the NAT. AMAL. UNION OF SHOP ASSISTANTS, WAREHOUSEMEN, ETC.

Why it means so much to her !

A Good Appearance Rightly Adds to One's Self Confidence.

The self confidence which a good appearance fosters is a most important contribution toward success. *It is to a very great extent the measure of other people's confidence in you.*

If you lack a good appearance you are suffering a perpetual handicap. To keep up a good appearance you need

To dress well ;

To get plenty of nourishing food ;

To have money and leisure for congenial recreation.

To live in healthy surroundings.

How can you do this if your wages and working hours do not permit it ?

Low Wages

mean shabby or shoddy clothes.

Low Wages

mean poor and insufficient food. This means a sallow complexion and lack of healthy vigour.

Low Wages and Long Hours Together

mean no opportunity for healthful recreation—no opportunity for choosing or making a happy and healthy environment.

How can a Woman Protect Herself

against low wages and long hours, and make for herself a position worth having and a life worth living ?

You may do this for Yourself

by joining with the thousands of organised

Women who have Learned the Secret

of obtaining and maintaining better conditions, who are helping each other to a higher standard of life through their Trade Union.

6. Value of Trade Unionism to the Workers.

First page of Organising Leaflet issued by the UNION OF POST OFFICE WORKERS.

If, as Ruskin averred, ' there is no wealth but life,' then the Post Office stands convicted as the biggest spendthrift in England. That is the only possible conclusion open to one who has investigated the hardships of the women telephonists in its employ.—Reynolds' News.

Telephone girls do not labour under such adverse conditions as some people would like the public to believe.—P.O. Official.

TELEPHONISTS.

Public Service—and its Reward.

Of all the workers in the Post Office, the Telephonist is probably the object of most criticism—usually uninformed. From the crude jokes in the press, to the impatient caller who has yet to learn how properly to use a 'phone—she puts up with it all cheerfully enough, thanks to her somewhat hardened sense of humour !

The disadvantage of all this is, however, that in the public mind there is created the idea that the Telephonist has a soft job, so that a hard-working woman like Lady Askwith can write to the *Times* complaining of the high wages paid.

The *Union of Post-Office Workers* has taken active steps to place the real facts before the country, and can fairly claim to have caused a change of attitude in the press, particularly as a result of the Telephone Standard Load and the Manchester campaigns.

The work of the Telephonist is intricate and onerous. She frequently works under conditions which discredit the public service. She is still poorly paid. The value of her service to the community, emphasised as it was during the war when she performed air raid duty at great risk and worked for long periods at exceptionally high pressure, has not received that tangible appreciation which it merits.

The Union, the only organisation recognised as representing the Telephonists, has done much to better conditions. Much remains to be done. What is done depends in the long run on the Union receiving the personal support of every Telephonist.

7. Appeal to Non-Unionists.

Extract from Organising Leaflet issued by the NAT. UNION OF
DISTRIBUTIVE AND ALLIED WORKERS.

Has It Ever Struck You

that the Non-Unionist is a source of danger to other workers, as well
as being a real hindrance to his own development as a worker in
the industrial field ?

The Non-Unionist, by his apathy and inaction, practically invites
the Employing Class (which is *powerfully organised*) to do just what
it likes with him.

He *dare not* protest against any injustice, and must often be
content with whatever conditions are imposed.

The Trade Unionist, on the other hand, believes that if it is good
for the employer to join his Federation of Employers, it is good also
for the workers to join a Workers' Organisation.

The Workers' Organisation which has done most good for
employees in your occupation, either by negotiations or (where
interviews are refused) by fighting, is the *National Union of Distributive and Allied Workers* (*N.U.D.A.W.*), and you are hereby
given a hearty invitation to *join up*.

> If the great Trade Union movement
> Is to work for your improvement
>   In the industry in which you are engaged,
> You should rally round our banner,
> In a true and loyal manner,
>   And be eager in the fight that's being waged.

In the N.U.D.A.W. are nearly 100,000 members ready to stand by
each other, financially and morally, in the efforts constantly being
put forth to make life worth living for the wage-earner.

8. Appeal to Non-Unionists.

Extract from Organising Leaflet issued by the NAT. UNION OF
RAILWAYMEN.

To the Non-Unionists Employed by Railway Companies.

THEN.

Before the N.U.R. came into existence, government statistics
disclosed the fact that there were over 100,000 railwaymen—not

boys—receiving £1 or less for a working week of 60 hours.   At that time there was no such thing as a 'Guaranteed Week's' work, and holidays with pay, except for a very small number, was a thing undreamed of.

When the conditions became irksome the method of asking for an advance in wages was by petition, generally signed as a 'round robin' so that the General Manager would not be able to detect the originator of the petition.   And, after all the petitioning, men thought themselves fortunate if they secured another sixpence.

NOW.

To-day, thanks to the N.U.R., thanks to the men who have built up the organisation—very often at great sacrifice—conditions in the Railway world are the envy of the majority of the workers in other industries.

The 10 and 12-hour working day is now only a bad memory. Every man covered by the conciliation machinery now has his guaranteed day and week : he has at least one week's holiday with pay, with his free pass to take him where he *wants to go* on his own system, and, in some cases, other systems also.   And all this has been secured solely by the N.U.R. out of a contribution of 5d. per week.

At present over 400,000 railwaymen are members of the Union. These men recognise that, but for the strength of the N.U.R. the day would rapidly approach when they would sink into the position they were in in 1911 ; and yet, whilst they are combining to resist any encroachments on their conditions of service, whilst they have determined that neither they nor those dependent upon them shall have their standard of life reduced, *you* are still outside the organisation.

YOUR DUTY.

It may be that at one time you held a membership card, and that because of some trivial affair you dropped out.   Or it may be that you think 5d. a week is better in your pocket than in assisting to maintain the only organisation that protects you and those dependent upon you ; but whatever the reason may be, the time has come for you to get inside the organisation ; your mates are *TIRED* of carrying you on their backs ; they are *TIRED* of seeing you hang your head when you see a *MAN* wearing the Union's badge.

Come, pull yourself together ; try to realise that a Man's place is alongside his fellows.   Fill the enclosed form in and take it to the

Branch Secretary—you know who he is—then you will feel that you are playing a Man's part in the great struggle for a proper human existence.

9. Value of Trade Union Organisation in securing Observance of Agreements.

REPORT OF THE INDUSTRIAL COUNCIL ON INDUSTRIAL AGREEMENTS, 1913,   Cd. 6952, p. 7.

The value of efficient organisation on the part of employers and workpeople as a means of securing the due fulfilment of Industrial Agreements is very clearly demonstrated by the experience of the different trades of the country.   Where, as in the Steel trade, the associations of employers and workmen include an overwhelming proportion of the persons engaged in the trade on both sides, it is found that breaches of agreements rarely occur, or, if they do occur, generally occasion no difficulty since they are dealt with by the prompt and efficient action of the Employers' Association or the Trade Union, as the case may be.

In such an industry as the Baking trade, however, where organisation on both sides is imperfect, it appears at present to be the fact that (except in one or two localities where the organisation has been improved) the existence of any agreements that may be arrived at by such part of the employers and workpeople as are organised is constantly imperilled owing to the inability of either side to take effective action in the event of a breach of the agreement occuring.

Between the two extremes exampled by these two trades there are, of course, a large number of intermediate states of organisation, and it is impracticable to divide into two distinct groups the trades in which organisation may be held to be so far perfect as to render any assistance unnecessary, and those in which the organisation is so incomplete that the fulfilment of agreements cannot be secured unless a means is found whereby the existing efforts of the parties may be strengthened.

10. Statutory Objects of a Trade Union.

LORD MACNAGHTEN, IN THE OSBORNE CASE, A.S.R.S. *v.* OSBORNE, 1909, A.C. 87.

It is a broad and general principle that Companies incorporated by Statute for special purposes, and societies, whether incorporated

or not, which owe their constitution and their status to an Act of
Parliament, having their objects and powers defined thereby, cannot
apply their funds to any purpose foreign to the purposes for which
they were established, or embark on any undertaking in which they
were not intended by Parliament to be concerned. . . . This principle is not confined to Corporations created by special Acts of
Parliament.   It applies, I think, with equal force in every case where
a society or association formed for purposes recognised and defined
by an Act of Parliament places itself under the Act, and by so doing
obtains some statutory immunity or privilege.

(LORD ATKINSON, IN THE SAME CASE.)

It is clear in my view that they are, when registered, quasi-
Corporations, resembling much more closely Railway Companies
incorporated by Statute than voluntary associations of individuals
merely bound together by contract, or agreement, express or implied.
And it is plain that, as soon as this character was given to them, and
the rights and privileges they now enjoy were conferred upon them,
it became a matter of necessity to define the purposes and object to
which they were at liberty to devote the funds raised from their
members by enforced contributions.   A definition which permitted
them to do the particular things named, and in addition all things
not in themselves illegal, would be no definition at all, and would
serve no purpose at all.

11. Trade Union—Definition and Powers.

TRADE UNION ACT, 1913 ; 2 & 3 Geo. V, ch. 30.

1.—(1) The fact that a combination has under its constitution
objects or powers other than statutory objects within the meaning of
this Act shall not prevent the combination being a trade union for
the purposes of the Trade Union Acts, 1871 to 1906, so long as the
combination is a trade union as defined by this Act, and, subject to
the provisions of this Act as to the furtherance of political objects,
any such trade union shall have power to apply the funds of the
union for any lawful objects or purposes for the time being authorised
under its constitution.

(2) For the purposes of this Act, the expression ' statutory objects '
means the objects mentioned in section sixteen of the Trade Union
Act Amendment Act, 1876, namely, the regulation of the relations
between workmen and masters, or between workmen and workmen,

or between masters and masters, or the imposing of restrictive conditions on the conduct of any trade or business, and also the provision of benefits to members.

2.—(1) The expression ' trade union ' for the purpose of the Trade Union Acts, 1871 to 1906, and this Act, means any combination, whether temporary or permanent, the principal objects of which are under its constitution statutory objects : Provided that any combination which is for the time being registered as a trade union shall be deemed to be a trade union as defined by this Act so long as it continues to be so registered.

(2) The Registrar of Friendly Societies shall not register any combination as a trade union unless in his opinion, having regard to the constitution of the combination, the principal objects of the combination are statutory objects, and may withdraw the certificate of registration of any such registered trade union if the constitution of the union has been altered in such a manner that, in his opinion, the principal objects of the union are no longer statutory objects, or if in his opinion the principal objects for which the union is actually carried on are not statutory objects.

(3) Any unregistered trade union may, if they think fit, at any time without registering the union apply to the Registrar of Friendly Societies for a certificate that the union is a trade union within the meaning of this Act, and the Registrar, if satisfied, having regard to the constitution of the union and the mode in which the union is being carried on, that the principal objects of the union are statutory objects, and that the union is actually carried on for those objects, shall grant such a certificate, but the Registrar may, on an application made by any person to him for the purpose, withdraw any such certificate if satisfied, after giving the union an opportunity of being heard, that the certificate is no longer justified.

(4) Any person aggrieved by any refusal of the Registrar to register a combination as a trade union, or to give a certificate that an unregistered trade union is a trade union within the meaning of this Act, or by the withdrawal under this section of a certificate of registration, or of a certificate that an unregistered union is a trade union within the meaning of this Act, may appeal to the High Court, or in Scotland to the Court of Session, within the time and in the manner and on the conditions directed by rules of court.

(5) A certificate of the Registrar that a trade union is a trade union within the meaning of this Act shall. so long as it is in force, be conclusive for all purposes.

12. Trade Unions—Definition of Objects.

History of Trade Unionism, BY S. AND B. WEBB, 1920 ed., p. 1.

A Trade Union, as we understand the term, is a continuous association of wage-earners for the purpose of maintaining or improving the conditions of their working lives.

13. Trade Union Objects.

OBJECTS OF THE LONDON SOCIETY OF COMPOSITORS.
(Rule I., subsections 2 and 3, 1925.)

This Society is established to uphold and protect the wages of labour, agreeably to the provisions contained in the London Scale of Prices, and such other prices, customs and usages as belong to the profession, not directly mentioned in the said Scales ; to regulate the number of apprentices and turnovers ; subject thereto, the Society may use all legitimate means to extend the sphere of the Society's operations.

To provide funds for the assistance of unemployed and super-annuated members, insurance of members' clothes and tools against fire, assistance to members desirous of removing or emigrating, payment of sums of money upon the death of members or members' wives, and maintenance of a Reading Room.

Rule LXIII.   Political Fund.

(1) The objects of the London Society of Compositors shall include the furtherance of the political objects to which Section 3 of the Trade Union Act, 1913, applies, that is to say . . .

14. Trade Union Objects.

OBJECTS OF THE AMALGAMATED ENGINEERING UNION.
(Rule 2, 1926.)

2. The objects of the Society shall be :
(i) The control of industry in the interests of the community.
(ii) The organisation of all workers qualified for membership, the development of the most cordial possible relations with other unions in the industry with a view to the bringing into existence of one union for the foundry, engineering and shipbuilding trades, and the obtain-

ing and maintaining of just and proper hours of work, rates of wages, and conditions of labour.

(iii) The settling and negotiation of differences and disputes between the members of the Society and employers by collective bargaining and agreement, withdrawal of labour or otherwise.

(iv) Generally to promote the welfare of the members of the Society.

(v) The provision of benefits to members as follows :

(a) Assistance to members when out of employment or in distressed circumstances, assistance in cases of sickness, accident and disablement, superannuation, assistance for funeral expenses, and for compensation for loss of tools, and such other assistance as may from time to time be decided by the Society, together with all such forms of assistance as are already provided for by these rules.

(b) The provision of legal advice and assistance to members where necessary or expedient.

(c) The provision of grants and endowments to colleges and institutes having for their object independent working-class education.

(vi) The furtherance of political objects as provided by these rules.

(vii) The transaction of insurance business, including insurance under the National Insurance Acts as provided by these rules.

(viii) The extension of co-operative production to assist in altering the competitive system of industry for a co-operative system.

(ix) The establishment or carrying on, or participation, financial or otherwise, directly or otherwise, in the business of printing or publishing of a general newspaper or newspapers, or of books, pamphlets, or publications of any other kind whatsoever in the interests of and with the main purpose of furthering the objects of this Trade Union or of Trade Unionism generally, namely :

The regulation of the relations between workmen and employers or between workmen and workmen, and the provision of benefits to members of Trade Unions, together with such subsidiary purposes as may be calculated to enhance the prosperity of the publications and the business generally.

(x) The furthering of, or participation, financial or otherwise, directly or indirectly, in the work or purpose of any association or federal body, having for its objects the furthering of the interests of Labour, Trade Unionism, or Trade Unionists.

The Society may be affiliated to the International Metal Workers' Federation.

(xi) The furthering of any other purpose, or the participation, financial or otherwise, directly or indirectly, in any other purpose, so far as may be lawful, which is calculated in the opinion of the Society to further the interests of Labour, Trade Unionism, or Trade Unionists.

(xii) The holding, purchase, or leasing, or mortgaging or other dealing with land, including the assistance of members in acquiring houses and real property.

(xiii) In order to achieve the above objects the Society shall have power, in addition to any other powers given them by law or by these rules, to impose such restraints upon the labour of its members or generally to interfere, whether such interference is in restraint of trade or not but so far only as may otherwise be lawful, with the trade or conduct of such industries, businesses, and occupations as may be deemed expedient.

The Society as a constituent part of the Trades Union Congress shall be empowered to take such action by way of a strike as may be determined from time to time by the General Council of the Trades Union Congress, either separately or in conjunction with the National Executive of the Labour Party.

The Society as a constituent part of the Industrial Alliance shall be empowered to take such action as may be deemed necessary to give effect to the constitution, aims, and objects, financial or otherwise, of the said alliance, so long as the union decides to remain a party to such alliance.

(xiv) In particular the Society shall have power to provide funds for maintaining all or some of the benefits from time to time authorised in pursuance of these rules, and for the establishment or maintenance of any undertaking of any kind, financial or otherwise, authorised by the Society, and for any action including collective bargaining, striking, withholding of labour, taking action under the Trade Boards Act, or other statutes either severally, or jointly, or in conference, securing agreements concerning wages or other conditions of the contract of service, whether in defence of its own members, or in support of other workers of allied or other industries, which may, in the opinion of the Society or of its Executive Council, be deemed to be calculated to further the interests of the Society or of the Trade Union movement generally.

15. Trade Union Objects.

OBJECTS OF THE TRANSPORT AND GENERAL WORKERS' UNION.
(Rule 2, 1927.)

Rule 2.—Objects.

1.—The principal objects of the Union are the regulation of the relations between workmen and employers, and between workmen and workmen, and also the provision of benefits to members.

2.—The objects of the Union shall further include :

(*a*) The organisation of all members and other persons qualified for membership, being employees in port, harbour, dock, warehouse, waterside, waterway, road, aerial, and other transport services, and such other workers as may be deemed eligible by the General Executive Council of the Union, and the obtaining and maintaining of just and proper hours of work, rates of wages, and to endeavour by all means in their power to control the industries in which the members are engaged.

(*b*) The settling and negotiating of differences and disputes between the members of the Union and employers, and other Trade Unions and persons, by collective bargaining or agreement, withdrawal of labour, or otherwise.

(*c*) Generally, the power to promote the welfare of the members of the Union in such manner as the General Executive Council from time to time shall deem expedient.

(*d*) The provision of benefits to members as follows :

(i) Assistance to members, or particular classes of members, (1) when out of employment or in distressed circumstances ; (2) in cases of sickness, accident, and disablement ; (3) in old age ; (4) in trade disputes ; (5) for funeral expenses ; (6) upon marriage ; and such other forms of assistance as may from time to time be decided by the Union, or the General Executive Council.

(ii) Legal advice and legal assistance to the Union or its members where, in the opinion of the General Executive Council, it is necessary or expedient.

(iii) Grants and endowments, including scholarships, to members and to the colleges or institutions having among their objects the education of trade unionists.

(*e*) The furtherance of political objects of any kind.

(*f*) The transaction of insurance business, including insurance under the National Health Insurance and the Unemployment Insurance Acts.

(*g*) The extension of co-operative production and distribution.

(*h*) The establishment or carrying on, or participation, financial or otherwise, directly or indirectly, in, the business of printing or publishing of a general newspaper or newspapers, or of books, pamphlets, or publications, or of any other kind of undertaking, industrial or otherwise in the interest of and with the main purpose of furthering the interests of the Union or of trade unionism generally, together with such subsidiary action and purposes as may be calculated to enhance the prosperity of the publications or the business generally, after submission to Delegate Conference or ballot of members.

(*i*) The furtherance of, or participation, financial or otherwise, directly or indirectly, in, the work or purpose of any association or federal body having for its objects the furthering of the interests of labour, trade unionism, or trade unionists, including the securing of a real measure of control in industry and participation by the workers in the management, in the interests of labour and the general community.

(*j*) The furthering of any other action or purpose, or the participation, financial or otherwise, directly or indirectly, in any other purpose, so far as may be lawful, which is calculated, in the opinion of the Union or the General Executive Council, to further the interests of labour, trade unionism, or trade unionists.

(*k*) The provision of opportunities for social intercourse and promotion of sport and social events amongst the members.

3.—In order to achieve the above objects the Union shall have power, in addition to any other powers given them by law or by these rules, to impose such restraints upon the labour of its members, or generally to interfere, whether such interference is in restraint of trade or not, but so far only as may otherwise be lawful, with the trade or conduct of such industries, businesses, and occupations as may be deemed expedient.

4.—The Union shall undertake the employment of the permanent officers of the amalgamated unions.

In the case of the unions which amalgamated in October, 1921, if salaries or conditions have been altered after October 6th, 1920, and prior to the registration of this Union, such alterations shall be taken into consideration and this Union shall **grant** out of its funds, other than those accruing under Part II. of these rules, pensions and/or gratuities to full time officers of this Union and/or of any of the amalgamated unions, and generally honour all obligations of the amalgamated unions or any of them in respect of pensions, grants, etc., to retired officers, which were granted prior to October 6th, 1920.

In the case of unions amalgamating since October, 1921, the conditions, terms, and obligations shall be such as are agreed upon between this Union and the unions desiring amalgamation, and upon ratification shall form an integral part of these rules.

5.—In particular, the Union shall have power to provide funds, by subscription, levy, or otherwise, as the Union or the General Executive Council may direct, for maintaining all or some of the benefits from time to time authorised in pursuance of these rules, and for the establishment or maintenance of any undertaking of any kind, financial or otherwise, authorised by the Union, and for any action, including collective bargaining, striking, withholding of labour, taking action under the Trade Boards Act or other statutes, either severally or jointly, or the securing of agreements concerning wages or other conditions of employment, whether in defence of the members or in support of other workers of allied or other industries, which may, in the opinion of the Union or of the General Executive Council, be deemed to be calculated to further the interests of the Union or of the Trade Union Movement generally. No levy shall be imposed until a vote of members concerned has been taken.

6.—There shall be an Officials' Superannuation Fund, to which the Union shall contribute an amount not less than that contributed by the officials, and the liabilities of the fund shall be guaranteed by the Trade Union Funds of the Union, which may vary its contribution to the fund as and when found to be necessary following an examination of the fund.

7.—For all or any of the above objects the Union and the General Executive Council shall have power (*inter alia*) :

(*a*) To hold, purchase, lease, mortgage, or otherwise deal with land.

(*b*) To erect and furnish such buildings as may be considered necessary or desirable.

(*c*) To raise funds by borrowing money on any real or personal property of the Union, or by levies on its members or any class thereof (subject to proviso in preceding Clause 5).

(*d*) To establish superannuation schemes, contributory or otherwise, for officers and for servants of the Union.

16. Trade Union Objects.

OBJECTS OF DURHAM MINERS' ASSOCIATION.

(Rule 2, 1925.)

Objects.

3.—The objects shall be to raise funds by contributions, levies, fines and donations. *I.*—For the purpose of mutual support. *II.*—To obtain legislative enactments for the more efficient management of mines, whereby the lives and health of miners may be preserved. *III.*—To protect all Lodges and members when unjustly dealt with by their employers or managers in any respect whatever. *IV.*—To provide a weekly allowance for the support of members who may be locked-out or on strike, or laid idle through no fault of their own. *V.*—To seek for no man or lad to be employed more than six hours from bank to bank in one day. *VI.*—To pay a funeral allowance at the death of a member, or of the wife, or child of a member, whether caused by accident or sickness, if subscribed for. *VII.*—To assist all Associations, including Local Federation Boards, that have the same objects, namely, the protection of labour and the granting of benevolent support to members. *VIII.*— Generally to regulate the relations between employers and employed. *IX.*—To become federated with the miners of other counties and countries; but before any action is taken it must be submitted for the approval of Council or County. *X.*—To seek for a living wage for all workers in and about the mines. *XI.*—To promote and financially support Parliamentary Candidates. Each candidate must be a member of the Durham Miners' Association and run solely under the auspices of the National Labour Party, and be subject to its decisions, if elected. *XII.*—To support Education. *XIII.*—To support the Labour Press. *XIV.*—To seek the abolition of capitalism and the substitution of common ownership and control of the means of livelihood.

17. Trade Union Objects.

OBJECTS OF UNION OF POST-OFFICE WORKERS.

(Rule 2, 1925.)

The objects of the Union of Post-Office Workers shall be:

(*a*) The organisation of Post Office Workers into a comprehensive industrial Union, with a view to the Service being ultimately conducted and managed as a National Guild.

(*b*) To regulate the conditions of pay and employment generally between the Government as employer and members of the Union of Post-Office Workers.

(*c*) To encourage the amalgamation of Post Office Associations with similar objects to those of the Union of Post Office Workers into one Union. It shall be competent for the Executive Council to accept any other association as part of the Union of Post-Office Workers on being satisfied that the proper steps have been taken to ascertain the feelings of the members of the Association desirous of joining the Union of Post-Office Workers, but it shall not be competent for the Executive to accept any branch of an association which desires to secede from its parent body, or any individual member or members. The Executive shall at all times have power to submit the question of accepting another association to the annual conference of delegates.

18. Objects of a Federation of Trade Unions.

FEDERATION OF ENGINEERING AND SHIPBUILDING TRADES.
(*Rule* 1, 1924.)

THIS FEDERATION shall consist of trade unions representing the workmen employed in the engineering and shipbuilding industries joined together with a view to finding a policy which will bring about uniform conditions for all workers, and ultimately obtain control of all industries for the benefit of the workers, and shall use its power :

(1) To maintain the right of the combination of labour ;

(2) To promote the principle of collective bargaining by securing the active co-operation of the affiliated trade unions in any attempt by such unions to obtain improved conditions of labour, or to resist any attempt on the part of employers to encroach on existing conditions ;

(3) To mutually support any federated society if individually attacked by employer or bodies of employers, or federations of employers ;

(4) To provide where necessary arbitration or conciliation in trade disputes ;

(5) To improve the general position and status of the workers by securing unity of action amongst the Societies forming the Federation.

19. Objects of the Trades Union Congress.

STANDING ORDERS OF THE T.U.C., 1928.

2.—Objects.

(*a*) The objects of the Congress shall be to promote the interests of all its affiliated organisations and generally to improve the economic and social conditions of the workers.

(*b*) In furtherance of these objects, the General Council shall endeavour to establish the following measures, and such others as the Annual Meeting of Congress may from time to time approve :

1. Public Ownership and control of natural resources and of services—

    (*a*) Nationalisation of land, mines, and minerals.

    (*b*) Nationalisation of railways.

    (*c*) The extension of State and municipal enterprise for the provision of social necessities and services.

    (*d*) Proper provision for the adequate participation of the workers in the control and management of public services and industries.

2. Wages and hours of labour—

    (*a*) A legal maximum working week of 44 hours.

    (*b*) A legal minimum wage for each industry or occupation.

3. Unemployment—

    (*a*) Suitable provision in relation to unemployment, with adequate maintenance of the unemployed.

    (*b*) Establishment of training centres for unemployed juveniles.

    (*c*) Extension of training facilities for adults during periods of industrial depression.

4. Housing—

    Provision for proper and adequate housing accommodation.

5. Education—

    Full educational facilities to be provided by the State from the elementary schools to the universities.

6. Industrial accidents and diseases—

    Adequate maintenance and compensation in respect of all forms of industrial accidents and diseases.

7. Pensions—
    (*a*) Adequate State pensions for all at the age of 60.
    (*b*) Adequate State pensions for widowed mothers and dependent children and mothers whose family breadwinner is incapacitated.

20. The Workers' Desire for Status.

The Waste of Capitalism, published by the TRADES UNION CONGRESS
AND LABOUR PARTY, 1924. P. 100 ff.

No analysis of the present system of production would be complete which omitted the psychological factors, of which the question of ' status ' is one of the most important. What is meant by this oft-used term ?

On the one hand we are told that the worker's claim to status is simply an exhibition of silly snobbishness or pride, and on the other hand we are told that it does not exist except in the minds of a small minority of theorists.

Both these views are, needless to say, wide of the mark. It may be true that the average worker does not go deeply into the philosophy of his feelings and desires nor elaborate them into a theory, but vague and formless though they may be, they exist, and they exercise a profound influence on his work and life. No observer of industrial conditions during the past few years can fail to have noticed this passionate desire, on the part of the younger workers particularly (though the older ones must by no means be excluded from this statement), for a greater share in determining the conditions under which the industrial machine works, for more responsibility, more recognition, more power, as an indispensable factor in production. However expressed this desire has been present, and even where it is unexpressed, its existence can be inferred from its effects, which are, in the brief popular phrase, ' industrial unrest and discontent.' Hence the demand, reduced to a philosophy by theorists, perhaps, but present in the minds of the workers themselves, certainly, for ' workers' control.'

The burden of the worker's complaint is that the industrial system makes him a slave. The status desired is the status of a freeman. The slave status comes about in two quite distinct ways, and we shall do well not to confuse them as they are very often confused. In the first place, craftsmanship is in most industries dying or dead. Human skill and care are for the majority of workers giving way to mechanical power. In fact, we may say that the history of material progress during the last century has been the history of the development of the automatic machine. It may be true, as some industrial psychologists believe, that certain people do not mind the monotony, the absence of personality and responsibility and the lack of all need for initiative, for reasoning and for judgment, involved in all this routine of machine production. The important point is that the great majority of those who are compelled by the system to suffer these things do object to them and, indeed, find them intolerable. No matter what system of industrial and social organisation may be adopted the use of machinery has come to stay. Without it the world could not keep up even the present standard of living, much less raise it to the level we desire.

Is there any solution to this difficulty—that of being tied to machinery ? We think not. The only course, it seems to us, is so to shorten the hours of work, and give the fullest opportunities and means for the enjoyable use of leisure, that the necessary drudgery of machine production shall be undertaken without resentment or injury, and shall be distributed as equally as possible, giving up all idea of having a privileged class which is freed from all distasteful duties.

It is often suggested that a full knowledge of the working of the machine, of the products with which it deals, and of other details of the work will help to convert drudgery into an interesting occupation. We think this is not true of the majority of workers. Any improvement due to such causes is likely to be of very short duration.

It is highly desirable, however, that researches on monotony and fatigue, such as are now being conducted by the Industrial Fatigue Research Board, should be continued and extended. These investigations are watched with keen interest and sympathy by the Labour movement, and much good may be expected to follow the results which have been and will be achieved.

The second kind of slavery to which we have referred is that which results from the subordination of the individual to the organisation, and this is essentially a phenomenon of capitalism. The organisation of each industrial unit has hitherto, particularly since the growth of very large undertakings, been based on the principle of military discipline. The individual worker has become in most cases a mere cog in the machine, a pawn to be moved hither and thither by someone in authority who is carrying out a policy which the subordinate not only does not help to determine, but the very nature and objects of which are kept hidden from him.

The worker goes into the factory, takes his meals, and leaves again at night at fixed and stated times, all to the sound of the siren, the while the exact period of his attendance is accurately and mechanically registered.

He performs his allotted task on the instructions of a foreman, does it by following out a definite, stereotyped set of operations in the determination of which he has had no hand and which may, indeed, violate all his instincts of craftsmanship and good work. If he does anything which is not laid down in the employer's schedule he may be bullied, fined or discharged. There he is, to his own seeming, a feeble unit in the midst of a huge organisation which takes no account of him as a human being—he is merely one of the ' hands '—helpless to affect his environment in the slightest degree.

Is it any wonder the worker does not feel strongly impelled to wear himself out producing more and more profits for the employer ? The wonder is rather that production continues at all, and, in fact, there is no guarantee that it will continue under such conditions. Unrest is growing, not decreasing, and there is likely to be more and more friction and less and less production as time goes on if a remedy is not found. For years this tendency has been reinforced from several directions. On the one hand there has been the ever-increasing specialisation and more minute sub-division of labour with the progress of invention and the development of the automatic machine, so that the organisation itself has become more rigidly organised and disciplined. For economic reasons there has been a huge growth in the trust movement, and we have seen the formation of huge combines, mammoth undertakings which, under present conditions, necessitate a still more mechanical, soulless régime with more authority for those at the top and more ' discipline ' for those at the bottom. Yet, at the same time, there has been an ever-rising level of education for the workers, which has helped to produce the demand for a higher standard of life and a wider conception of the value of human personality and freedom.

The average employee to-day has little or no interest in his work or in producing maximum output partly because the work itself is so often uninteresting drudgery and partly because he sees the organisation, in whose power he is, producing goods the quality and quantity of which someone else has settled, the mode of manufacture of which someone else has settled, under working conditions someone else has settled—all in order to make profits for someone else ! He is not asked to use his own intelligence or judgment, his own craftsmanship or artistic feeling, his own methods or theories. He is not asked to make suggestions about the enterprise as a whole, and in any case he has no fraction of a share in the power of deciding whether any suggestion should be carried into effect. Manufacturing policy, Commercial policy, Financial policy—all are forbidden territories to him. His only share in the enterprise is to be a slave of the owners and do as he is told, on pain of walking the streets as one of the unemployed. For all who believe in human values this is the real indictment of the system.

The sane human being has the desire to create, to use his own intellect and powers to change the material things around him, to affect his environment in the way his own nature dictates. It is these desires and fundamental instincts that the present industrial system frustrates—and in so doing stultifies itself ; for it is part of the irony of things that in putting profits above humanity, the employer is in danger of destroying not only humanity, but also the profits themselves !

To allow free play for initiative and judgment, intelligence and personality, is the only solution. Here, again, we must distinguish between two distinct demands. Does labour claim merely the right to determine the conditions under which it works, that safety and health regulations, arrangements of meal intervals and overtime, and similar questions, should be settled by the workers affected ? Or does it claim also a share in deciding the larger questions of commercial policy, works efficiency, finance, and so on ? The former claim is frequently conceded nowadays, at any rate to the extent of admitting the right of the workers to *some share* in the determination of these factors. Works Councils and, in fact, the entire structure of Whitleyism, serve the purpose of providing the opportunity and the means of settling by mutual agreement a multitude of questions affecting the health and welfare of the workers in such matters as recreation facilities ; works canteens ; the ventilation, lighting and heating of premises ; holidays ; meal reliefs and so on. Such ' joint ' bodies do not concede the workers' claim, for the employers always retain the right of ultimate decision in their own hands. ' Joint Control,' as it is called, is simply (under present conditions) employers' control plus worker's advice—which may or may not be taken. The worker cannot be expected to take any interest in production so long as he is denied the elementary right to determine, in co-operation with his fellow workers, the conditions under which he labours.

But such a sphere is too narrow to satisfy all his legitimate desires. He is dependent not merely for his comfort and his standard of living, but even for his livelihood, upon the wider issues involved in the firm's commercial policy and efficiency. As we have already pointed out, he may be thrown on to the streets because of the foolish acts or short-sighted policy of his employer. His earnings may be curtailed, his labours made unduly onerous, and his health affected because the employer's plant and equipment are out-of-date or the organisation inefficient. Every part of the employer's policy is directly or indirectly of immense consequence to the employee. No solution will, therefore, be satisfactory which does not give the workers a real power of control over *all* the factors necessary to production. Whether they are manual workers or brain workers (to use the current, but very superficial distinction), whether they are craftsmen or labourers, technicians or clerks, they cannot take the desired interest in, and enthusiasm for, their work unless the policy of the undertaking is in part shaped and controlled by themselves.

Labour aims at the extinction of the class of functionless property-owners, but the worker in the factory and workshop is just as determined to get rid of the employer whose ' function ' it is to be an autocrat. Autocracy is as out-of-date in industry as in civil government.

21. Trade Union Demand for Control.

The Greater Unionism, by G. D. H. COLE and W. MELLOR, 1913.   P. 19.

In future, the share of the Trade Unions in the control of industry will inevitably become far greater than it has been in the past. More and more emphasis is being laid upon the rights of the producer, more and more attention is being paid to the conditions under which Labour creates wealth ; more and more it is being realised that the claim of the worker to an enlarged control over his own life cannot be neglected. It is being seen that benevolent legislation from above is no substitute for organised pressure from below ; legislation affecting the conditions of a man's labour can, at the best, only register the efforts of the workers themselves.

22. Trade Union Demand for Control.

Memorandum on the Causes of and Remedies for Labour Unrest, presented by the TRADE UNION REPRESENTATIVES ON THE JOINT COMMITTEE APPOINTED AT THE NATIONAL INDUSTRIAL CONFERENCE held at the Central Hall, London, on February 27th, 1919.   Cmd. 501.

With increasing vehemence Labour is challenging the whole structure of capitalist industry as it now exists.   It is no longer willing to acquiesce in a system under which industry is conducted for the benefit of the few.   It demands a system of industrial control which shall be truly democratic in character.   This is seen on the one hand in the demand for public ownership of vital industries and services and public control of services not nationalised which threaten the public with the danger of monopoly or exploitation.   It is also seen in the increasing demand of the workers in all industries for a real share in industrial control, a demand which the Whitley scheme, in so far as it has been adopted, has done little or nothing to satisfy. This demand is more articulate in some industries than others.   It is seen clearly in the national programmes of the railwaymen and of the miners ; and it is less clearly formulated by the workers in many other industries.   The workers are no longer prepared to acquiesce in a system in which their labour is bought and sold as a commodity in the Labour market.   They are beginning to assert that they have a human right to an equal and democratic partnership in industry ; that they must be treated in future not as ' hands,' or part of the factory equipment, but as human beings with a right to use their abilities by hand and brain in the service not of the few but of the whole community.

The extent to which workers are challenging the whole system of industrial organisation is very much greater to-day than ever before, and unrest proceeds not only from more immediate and special grievances but also, to an increasing extent, from a desire to substitute a democratic system of public ownership and production for use with an increasing element of control by the organised workers themselves for the existing capitalist organisation of industry.

.   .   .   .

The fundamental causes of Labour unrest are to be found rather in the growing determination of Labour to challenge the whole existing structure of capitalist industry than in any of the more special and smaller grievances which come to the surface at any particular time.

These root causes are twofold—the breakdown of the existing capitalist system of industrial organisation, in the sense that the mass of the working class is now firmly convinced that production for private profit is not an equitable basis on which to build, and that a vast extension of public ownership and democratic control of industry is urgently necessary. It is no longer possible for organised Labour to be controlled by force or compulsion of any kind. It has grown too strong to remain within the bounds of the old industrial system, and its unsatisfied demand for the re-organisation of industry on democratic lines is not only the most important but also a constantly growing cause of unrest.

The second primary cause is closely linked with the first. It is that, desiring the creation of a new industrial system which shall gradually but speedily replace the old, the workers can see no indication that either the Government or the employers have realised the necessity for any fundamental change, or that they are prepared even to make a beginning of industrial re-organisation on more democratic principles. . . . It is clear that unless and until the Government is prepared to realise the need for comprehensive reconstruction on a democratic basis, and to formulate a constructive policy leading towards economic democracy, there can be at most no more than a temporary diminution of industrial unrest to be followed inevitably by further waves of constantly growing magnitude.

The changes involved in this reconstruction must, of course, be gradual, but if unrest is to be prevented from assuming dangerous forms an adequate assurance must be given immediately to the workers that the whole problem is being taken courageously in hand. It is not enough merely to tinker with particular grievances or to endeavour to reconstruct the old system by slight adjustments to meet the new demands of Labour. It is essential to question the whole basis on which our industry has been conducted in the past and to endeavour to find, in substitution for the motive of private gain, some other motive which will serve better as the foundation of a democratic system. This motive can be no other than the motive of public service, which at present is seldom invoked save when the workers threaten to stop the process of production by a strike. The motive of public service should be the dominant motive throughout the whole industrial system, and the problem in industry at the present day is that of bringing home to every person engaged in industry the feeling that he is the servant, not of any particular class or person, but of the community as a whole. This cannot be done so long as industry continues to be conducted for private profit, and the widest possible extension of public ownership and democratic control of industry is therefore the first necessary condition of the removal of industrial unrest.

23. Objects of the Workers' Movement.

The Acquisitive Society, by R. H. TAWNEY, 1921.   Pp. 7-8 and p. 139.

As long as men are men, a poor society cannot be too poor to find a right order of life, nor a rich society too rich to have need to seek it. . . . The first principle is that industry should be subordinated to the community in such a way as to render the best service technically possible, that those who render that service faithfully should be honourably paid, and that those who render no service should not be paid at all, because it is of the essence of a function that it should find its meaning in the satisfaction, not of itself, but of the end which it serves.

The second is that its direction and government should be in the hands of persons who are responsible to those who are directed and governed, because it is the condition of economic freedom that men should not be ruled by an authority which they cannot control.

The industrial problem, in fact, is a problem of right, not merely of material misery, and because it is a problem of right it is most acute among those sections of the working classes where material misery is least.   It is a question, first of Function, and secondly of Freedom.

.   .   .   .

The essence of a profession is, as we have suggested, that its members organise themselves for the performance of function.   It is essential, therefore, if industry is to be professionalised, that the abolition of functionless property should not be interpreted to imply a continuance under public ownership of the absence of responsibility on the part of the personnel of industry, which is the normal accompaniment of private ownership working through the wage system.

24. Objects of the Industrial Workers of the World.

An Address delivered at Grand Central Palace, New York, by EUGENE V. DEBS.   10th December, 1905.

The Industrial Workers has been organised for an opposite purpose, and its representatives come in your presence to tell you that there can be no peace between you, the working class, and the capitalist class who exploit you of what you produce ; that as workers, you have economic interests apart from and opposed to their interests, and that you must organise by and for yourselves ; and that if you are intelligent enough to understand these interests, you will sever your relations with the old unions in which you are divided and sub-divided, and join the Industrial Workers, in which all are organised and united upon the basis of the class struggle.

The Industrial Workers is organised, not to conciliate, but to fight the capitalist class.   We have no object in concealing any part of our mission ; we would have it perfectly understood.   We deny that there is anything in common between workingmen and capitalists.   We insist that workingmen must organise to get rid of capitalists and make themselves the masters of the tools with which they work, freely employ themselves, secure to themselves all they produce, and enjoy to the full the fruit of their labours.

The old union movement is not only organised upon the basis of the identity of interests of the exploited and exploiting classes, but it divides instead of uniting the workers, and there are thousands of unions, more or less in conflict, used against one another ; and so long as these countless unions occupy the field there will be no substantial unity of the working class.

25. The Mission and Achievements of Trade Unionism.

PRESIDENT'S ADDRESS TO THE TRADES UNION CONGRESS, 1926.

New problems confront us which are both national and international in character.   They cannot be met merely by demonstrations or resolutions, but must be faced constructively with all the intelligence, the knowledge, and efficiency of organisation we can supply.   They require from us a new conception of the use and purpose of this Congress as an Industrial Parliament of Labour, where industrial and other problems can be threshed out and a constructive programme be evolved for the practical realisation of an economic democracy, parallel to the power of political democracy which has been established in this country.

The founders of this Congress meant it to be a great forum for the discussion of Trade Union problems and policies.   In the earlier days the Congress gave much more attention than it does to-day to the consideration of fundamental principles of economic organisation and industrial development. Without necessarily copying their methods, we need in my opinion to adopt their conception, and the agenda should reflect the working of the Trade Union mind upon the large problems of economic reconstruction and industrial adjustment with which it is the duty of the Trade Unions to concern themselves.

At no time was there a more developing consciousness of the need for change. Everywhere, even among the more enlightened supporters of the existing system, not less than among the representatives of economic radicalism and advocates of change, there is a widening of thought on these questions as to the value of the results achieved by existing methods of production and distribution. An expanding literature is concerned with the causes and consequences of the trade cycle and its correlative problems of unemployment and wage fluctuations. It is being seriously asked whether the existing system provides the right mechanism for the determination of what proportion of the proceeds of industry shall be distributed as spending power. And it is I think a question for the Trade Unions to answer whether the time has not come for us to examine in the light of the new theories, the whole basis and application of the traditional wage policy and methods of determining wages which the Trade Unions have followed.

In my view a scientific wage policy for the unions requires to be thought out in relation to some generally acceptable set of principles for determining the division of the product of industry among those who have a rightful claim upon it. This is especially necessary in regard to nationalised industries. Has not the time arrived for us to consider how we can apply the principle of a living wage, or basic wage, correlated to the index of national production and aiming at the equitable distribution of spending power in relation to family needs and the cost of living ? Inquiry along these lines seems to me to be an indispensable preliminary to any claim we may make for the establishment of a legal minimum wage adjusted to human needs.

However that may be, this Congress with its long tradition of serious and responsible leadership of the organised workers, must strive to secure that our conception of economic and industrial progress does not lag behind our political development.

PART II

THE STRUCTURE OF THE TRADE UNION MOVEMENT.

In studying the structure and organisation of Trade Union-ism, and the relations between its different parts, the origin and development of the movement, as outlined in the Intro-duction, must always be borne in mind. The growth of Trade Unionism in other countries has in most cases followed a very different line, and, as we should expect, the present organisation in those countries displays instructive points of contrast.

Thus, in Germany, the Trade Union movement was the creation of the Social Democratic Party, whereas in Britain the Labour Party was the child of Trade Unionism. We therefore find in Germany a compact organisation of Trade Unions, built up to a large extent on a theoretical, planned basis, while in Britain there is a sprawling, chaotic industrial movement. On the other hand Germany has, owing to its peculiar political and economic history, three separate Trade Union movements ; namely, the ' Free' or Social Demo-cratic Unions ; the ' Christian ' Unions ; and the ' Hirsch Duncker ' or Liberal Unions ; and all these compete in certain industries, whereas in Great Britain there is at any rate only the one movement.

Nevertheless, potent though historical factors are, the needs of the present-day have impressed on the movements in all countries very many characteristics in common. The similarities are even more striking where, as in the case of Britain and the United States, there are certain common origins, while the points of contrast are more conspicuous where, as in the case of Britain and France, both the course of economic development and the present industrial organisation

77

are widely different.   In France, indeed, there has been a
strong Trade Union spirit but a weak organisation.   The
·important principle to note is that structure is the product
both of historical facts and of present needs.

The alarmingly chaotic form of British Trade Union
organisation is part of the heritage which has come down from
the eighteenth and early nineteenth centuries ; it is one of
the penalties of ancient lineage.   It is well, then, to start
with the warning conveyed in (26).

Membership.—While freedom of association is fully
recognised in Britain, there are certain statutory restrictions on membership of Unions, not only as regards the
minimum age, a common enough provision (27), but also
concerning the classes of labour admitted to Unions.   By
recent legislation, civil servants and police may join only
approved types of organisation (28, 29).

The Unions themselves specify in their Rules the classes
of labour admitted to membership.   In some cases a very
wide appeal is made (30), while in others there is a demarcation on craft lines (31).   Good examples of the usual form
of membership Rule are given in (32, 33, 34), but it is quite
impossible to cite, within the limits of space available, anything like a representative selection of such Rules.   Nor is it
possible to deal with the vexed question of overlapping and
' poaching ' of membership, but the reader may be referred to
(66, 68) in this connection.

Government.—It is impracticable, also, to do justice
to the fascinating field of Trade Union government.
Here is a worthy subject for research, for the history and
varying types of Trade Union management mirror for us all
the experiments and theories that political science discusses in
relation to the wider field of national and international
government.   Mr. and Mrs. Webb have, of course, given a
splendid preliminary treatment,[1] but a much fuller study
would be very valuable.   Many are the schemes by which
Unions have tried to work out a system of checks and balances,
for preserving local and individual control while achieving

[1] *Industrial Democracy*, Part I.

centralised strength and efficiency. This ultimate riddle of democracy has tempted Unions to experiment with new forms of constitution, and two of the most recent and interesting types are described in (35, 36), while older varieties will be found in (37, 39).

The ancient form of 'shop' organisation adopted by the Printing Unions is dealt with in (38). The duties of a National Executive are set out in (40), and a typical Rule dealing with the expulsion of members in (41). Two examples of the machinery for hearing complaints and settling disputes between members are shown in (42, 43).

Finance. — The funds of Trade Unions are, of course, derived in the main from the contributions of members and from such investments as may be made. The contributions vary widely, according to the benefits paid, and many Unions have elaborate scales setting out the sums payable and benefits receivable, so that members may choose to pay little and receive little, or to pay substantial amounts weekly or fortnightly, and be entitled, in return, to considerable relief when unemployed, sick, or too old to work. Some Unions have but few benefits of this kind, and a number have no 'friendly' benefits at all, but only 'trade' benefits. These variations naturally affect the rate of contribution. Two Contribution Rules are given in (44, 45) and others will be found in Part III (155, 156). Most Unions have power to raise funds by special levies (46), as well as by regular contributions, but this power is only resorted to in cases of emergency. As a rule an Entrance Fee is also charged, but in general this is of very small amount and it covers the cost of the member's Card and Rule Book.

The financial affairs of Registered Unions are regulated to some extent by law, and in this connection the difficulty that used to be experienced by Unions, before their funds were protected, must be remembered.[1] The provisions regarding Audit, etc., are given in (47), and the duties of the trustees of a Union are set out in (48). For the legal position as to trustees, and as to the Union's property, the reader should

[1] See Introduction, p. 35.

refer to Part IV (219). Ignorant critics have often tried to attack Unions on the score of their so-called Management Expenses, the statistics of which they get from the Returns made to the Chief Registrar. That official himself, however, has dealt with the question in a manner which should be convincing (49).

Organisation.—For twenty years past the great battle that has raged, in this and other countries, concerning the basis of organisation, has been fought on the issue of Industrial *v.* Craft Unionism. Not that these are the only possible forms ; others are mentioned in (50), but it is this particular issue that has aroused the most passionate feeling. The ground is cleared by a few preliminary explanations in (50), and the declarations of the respective advocates of the two systems follow in (51, 52, 53). Some of the most important issues connected with this problem are argued out in the Industrial Court's famous Award 728 (115).

The result of a special Enquiry having been accepted by the Trades Union Congress, one must conclude that, for a time at any rate, the question is settled, as far as the British movement is concerned (54). The German Trade Unions came to a somewhat similar conclusion after an Enquiry of their own, and the American movement has always declined even to toy with the Industrial Unionists' theories, though there have been—and still are—Industrial Unions outside the official machinery of the American Federation of Labour.

To proclaim the impossibility of re-fashioning the entire structure of Trade Unionism, so as to conform to theoretical considerations, is not to deny either the practicability or desirability of taking steps to improve its organisation and centralise its power. Even the amalgamation of Unions, the ' rationalisation ' of the movement, by the formation of large and effective units, has its difficulties, both legal (55), and, far more important, financial and psychological (56). One group of Unions in the Iron and Steel trade adopted a highly ingenious scheme for avoiding the legal difficulties in the days when the law was even more strict, and the general idea of this plan is worth notice (57). The splitting-off of a dissident section of a Union to form a new organisation is one of the deadly sins against Trade Unionism (58).

Although the amalgamation process goes on continuously, many Unions prefer the looser form of association obtained through connection with a Federation. The constitution of a typical Federation is given in (59). This particular body has its local organisation, too, but that is not such a usual feature (60). In powers and scope Federations vary widely, and here it is only possible to cite one example out of many (61, 62). The Triple Alliance was a special form of Federation which, at the time of its formation, seemed to many people to foreshadow an entirely new development of Trade Union power. Clause 8 of its constitution was its weak spot (63). Many other forms of joint machinery between Unions have been devised, both nationally and locally. An interesting example of a local (wartime) joint body is given in (64).

Inter-Union action of many kinds is common, nowadays, but one or two instances only can be given here. Mutual recognition of ' cards,' and agreements for the transfer of members, are important in the Trade Union world, and many Unions have adopted provisions for these purposes (65). Similarly, Unions conclude agreements covering all kinds of questions, including demarcation of membership, joint action in disputes, organisation, etc. (66, 67, 68).

Such questions also cause disputes between Unions, and these are always regrettable if only because of the waste of time and energy involved. If the Unions are affiliated to the T.U.C. they may have the dispute adjudicated upon by the General Council (69), which is thus building up a code of principles governing such cases (70). It is very instructive to study the Reports of the hearings, and the decisions reached (71, 72).

Organisation in the Works. — The organisation of the workers inside the works calls for some notice. Most Unions have their Collectors, Shop Stewards, Walking Delegates, etc., (different names are used in different trades), whose duty it is to collect contributions, to see that workers are fully paid up members of the Union, and so on. In some cases they have the function of looking after the interests of the workers generally, and of adjusting minor differences with the employers. An interesting type of agreement relating to the appointment and powers of Shop Stewards is given in (73). In other industries, also, there are agreements defining the position of these officials, but in many cases the arrangement is quite informal, sometimes being tacitly recognised by the employers and sometimes opposed. An interesting example of Australian recognition of shop stewards is given in (120).

The development of workers' representation within the works is a very difficult and controversial problem. Employers will seldom agree to a direct connection between Unions and such bodies as Works Councils. Yet, without a close connection, the position and even the existence of the Unions may be threatened. With definite hostility to the Unions, on the part of the employers, a system of 'company unionism' is likely to arise, as in so many cases in the United States, where a works organisation is set up as a substitute for Trade Unionism. Even without such hostility, rival organisations and rival loyalties are created. This is the vital problem in the establishment of Works Councils or Committees, a problem in the solution of which Germany has, since the Works Councils Act of 1920, had more experience than any other country.[1] In Britain there has been much less experience though there were many Works Committees set up during the war and early post-war period.[2] A general description of the different types of such bodies is given in (74), while a discussion of the relations between them and the Unions follows in (75).

These Works Committees, of which a number have survived the post-war depression, must be distinguished from Joint Works Councils, such as were recommended by the Whitley Committee. For these, which are also to be found

[1] See Guillebaud, *The Works Council*, Camb. Press, 1928.
[2] See Ministry of Labour *Report on Works Committees*, 1918

in certain trades, the reader should refer to Part IV (233);
the name Works Council should be applied only to such
joint bodies, the term Works Committee being used for the
type of committee consisting of workers alone.

Trades Council. — Very many Trades Councils are
both Trades Councils, (*i.e.* local federations of Trade
Union branches), and also local Labour Parties. Others
are purely industrial bodies. There is no obligation upon
branches of Unions, (as there is in Germany), to affiliate to
Trades Councils, but there has been a great increase in the
number of affiliations since the T.U.C. began an energetic
campaign with the object of bringing the Councils into closer
relations with the Congress. A model constitution has been
drawn up, (omitting the political section, if any), and many
Trades Councils have adopted it (76). The constitution
of a purely industrial Council is given in (77), while the
constitution of the Joint Consultative Committee and the
functions of Trades Councils are given in (78, 79). An
experiment started in 1928 by the General Council, in the
organisation of the unemployed, is shown in (80). The
T.U.C. in 1928, however, decided not to continue with
this form of organisation

Trades Union Congress. — The history of the T.U.C.
has been briefly touched upon in the Introduction. A
sketch of its rise and its ultimate aims appears in (81), and
its constitution follows in (82). The General Council is
broadly described in (83), while (84) shows its detailed
structure, and division into Groups. Its powers are set out
in (85, 86) and it will be remembered that its functions in
connection with Inter-union Disputes have already been
given in (69). Of the more recently acquired powers, that
dealing with industrial disputes, (Standing Order 11), and the
general power of co-ordination on general questions, (86),
are by far the most important. From these it is possible to
see the growth of centralised power in the hands of the T.U.C.
and the commanding position it occupies in the world of
organised labour. In (87) will be found the constitution of
the Trade Boards Advisory Council by which the General

Council, in conjunction with the Unions concerned, seeks to co-ordinate the work of the Union representatives on Trade Boards.

Non-Manual Labour.—A generation ago non-manual workers were scarcely organised at all, and where a beginning had been made they were not associated with the manual workers' Unions. Nowadays that is all changed. Many groups of professional and other non-manual workers have their Trade Unions, some of which are associated with the T.U.C. The great significance of this development is touched on by Mr. Tawney in (88), while (89) sets out the mechanism which links up the Professional Workers' Federation with the T.U.C. A number of Unions are connected with both these bodies, however. Professional Unionism has been especially strong in France, particularly among Civil Servants and Teachers. In Germany, also, there is a strong Federation of Professional Workers' Unions, and a separate one of Civil Service Unions, both of them having close relations with the German General Federation of Trade Unions. In Britain there is no such rigid separation, but since the passing of the Trade Disputes and Trade Unions Act, 1927, the Civil Service Unions have been forced to sever their connection with the T.U.C.

Co-operative Movement.—The relations between the Trade Union movement and the Co-operative movement are necessarily close, and all employees of the latter must be members of a Union (90). Disputes over wages and working conditions arise even here, and the Co-operative Societies and Unions of co-operative employees have erected joint machinery for the adjudication of such matters, the present arrangements being shown in (91).

INTERNATIONAL TRADE UNIONISM.—International relations have always been taken seriously by the British Unions, and at the present time they are maintained chiefly through the T.U.C.'s affiliation to the International Federation of Trade Unions. To this Federation are affiliated the Trade Union Centres of the great majority of the countries having well developed Unions. The main provisions of its Constitution are given in (**92**). Russia, and a few small movements in other countries, are affiliated to the Communist ' Red International of Labour Unions,' and in addition there is a ' Christian ' Trade Union International. Many British Unions are affiliated to their appropriate Trade Internationals, and these in turn are closely associated with the I.F.T.U. itself. The main clauses of the Constitution of a typical Trade International are set out in (**93**).

POLITICAL.

Labour Party. — Apart from the connection between the Trade Union branches and local Labour Parties, in many districts, through the joint Trades Councils, the T.U.C. and the Labour Party have joint machinery nationally. Joint meetings of the General Council and the Party Executive are held regularly, and since 1922 there has been a National Joint Council (**94**). Unions individually affiliate to the Labour Party, but only in respect of their members who have agreed to pay additional political contributions. This question is dealt with in Part III.

AUTHORITIES AND REFERENCES.

On the subject of this Part there is little the student can usefully refer to, except the Rules and the Journals of the Unions themselves, the Reports of the T.U.C., and Webb's *Industrial Democracy*, which is still the only thorough analysis of the structure of the movement.

G. D. H. Cole's *Organised Labour* is useful, though in need of revision. The Report on Organisation in the Annual Report of the T.U.C. for 1927 is extremely important for the survey it gives of the present position, and the preliminary Report in the T.U.C. Annual Report for 1925, (p. 226), is also very informative. The two T.U.C. pamphlets on the *Trades Union Congress* and the *General Council of the Trades Union Congress* are useful, as is *Industrial Negotiations and Agreements,* published by the T.U.C. and Labour Party, though this needs revision. *The Trade Union Movement of Great Britain*, by W. M. Citrine, General Secretary of the Trades Union Congress, is a handy introduction, and the other works in this same series, published by the International Federation of Trade Unions, should be consulted, as they give useful sketches of the foreign Trade Union movements.

For America, the works already mentioned, by Commons and Perlman, will suffice.

---

26. Structure of the British Trade Union Movement.

The Trade Union Movement of Great Britain, by W.M. CITRINE, Gen. Sec. of the T.U.C.   Pub. by the Int. Fed. of Trade Unions, 1926.   P. 27.

As will have been seen from the preceding Chapters, British Trade Unionism presents an extraordinary complexity and absence of uniformity in its structure and methods of organisation.   No single type of Union dominates the field, and every variety of organisation exists, ranging from pure craft unions of a highly localised character to unions which approximate in theory, if not in strict practice, to industrial unions.

British working-class organisation is the creation of centuries, and tradition still plays an important part in influencing the conception of its future development.   It cannot be too strongly emphasised that British Trade Union organisation has not developed according to any preconceived plan applied from a common centre.   Its origins are entirely and strictly economic, and it naturally reflects many different forms of organisation because of the varying stages of development of industry itself.

In this respect it is entirely different from the Trade Union movement in certain of the Continental countries.   There, Trade Unionism drew its inspiration from the Social Democratic Parties, and reflected in the industrial world more or less the social and theoretical conceptions of its founders.

---

27. Membership of Trade Unions—Age.

TRADE UNION ACT (1871) AMENDMENT ACT, 1876;   39 & 40 Vict., ch. 22.

9.—A person under the age of twenty-one, but above the age of sixteen, may be a member of a trade union, unless provision be made in the rules thereof to the contrary, and may, subject to the rules of the trade union, enjoy all the rights of a member except as herein provided, and execute all instruments and give all acquittances necessary to be executed or given under the rules, but shall not be a member of the committee of management, trustee, or treasurer of the trade union.

28. Restriction on Trade Union Membership—Civil Service.

TRADE DISPUTES AND TRADE UNIONS ACT, 1927; 17 & 18 Geo. V, ch. 22.

5.—(1) Amongst the regulations as to the conditions of service in His Majesty's civil establishments there shall be included regulations prohibiting established civil servants from being members, delegates, or representatives of any organisation of which the primary object is to influence or affect the remuneration and conditions of employment of its members, unless the organisation is an organisation of which the membership is confined to persons employed by or under the Crown and is an organisation which complies with such provisions as may be contained in the regulations for securing that it is in all respects independent of, and not affiliated to, any such organisation as aforesaid the membership of which is not confined to persons employed by or under the Crown or any federation comprising such organisations, that its objects do not include political objects, and that it is not associated directly or indirectly with any political party or organisation :

Provided that the regulations made in compliance with the provisions of this section shall not prevent—

(*a*) any person who is at the commencement of this Act an established civil servant from remaining a member of any trade union or organisation not composed wholly or mainly of persons employed by or under the Crown of which he had, at the commencement of this Act, been a member for more than six months, if under the rules thereof there had on the fourth day of April, nineteen hundred and twenty-seven, accrued or begun to accrue to him a right to any future payment during incapacity, or by way of superannuation, or on the death of himself or his wife, or as provision for his children ; or

(*b*) any person employed at the commencement of this Act by or under the Crown who thereafter becomes an established civil servant from remaining, so long as he is not appointed to a position of supervision or management, a member of any trade union or organisation, not composed wholly or mainly of persons employed by or under the Crown, of which he is a member at the date when he so becomes an established civil servant, if under the rules thereof there has at that date accrued, or begun to accrue, to him a right to any future payment during incapacity, or by way of superannuation, or on the death of himself or his wife, or as provision for his children ; or

　　(*c*) a person who in addition to being an established civil servant is, apart from his service as such, also engaged in some other employment or occupation from being a member, delegate, or representative of any trade union or organisation, of which the primary object is to influence or affect the remuneration or conditions of employment of persons engaged in that employment or occupation.

　　(2) Subject as hereinafter provided, any established civil servant who contravenes the regulations made under this section shall be disqualified for being a member of the Civil Service :

Provided that, in the case of a first offence, a civil servant shall forthwith be warned by the head of his department, and the said disqualification shall not take effect if within one month after such warning the civil servant ceases to contravene the said regulations.

　　(3) In this section—

　　(*a*) the expression ' established civil servant ' means a person serving in an established capacity in the permanent service of the Crown, and includes any person who, having been granted a certificate by the Civil Service Commissioners, is serving a probationary period preliminary to establishment ; and

　　(*b*) the expression ' conditions of employment ' means in relation to persons other than persons employed by or under the Crown the conditions of employment of persons employed under a contract of service.

29. Police—Prohibited from joining a Trade Union.

POLICE ACT, 1919 ; 9 & 10 Geo. V, ch. 46.

1.—(1) For the purpose of enabling the members of the police forces of England and Wales to consider and bring to the notice of the police authorities and the Secretary of State all the matters affecting their welfare and efficiency, other than questions of discipline and promotion affecting individuals, there shall be established in accordance with the Schedule to this Act an organisation to be called the Police Federation, which shall act through local and central representative bodies as provided in that schedule.

(2) The Police Federation and every branch thereof shall be entirely independent of and unassociated with any body or person outside the police service.

2.—(1) Subject as aforesaid, it shall not be lawful for a member of a police force to become, or after the expiration of one month from the passing of this Act to be, a member of any trade union, or of any association having for its objects, or one of its objects, to control or influence the pay, pensions, or conditions of service of any police force ; and any member of a police force who contravenes this provision shall be disqualified for continuing to be a member of the force ; and, if any member of a police force continues to act as such after becoming so disqualified, he shall forfeit all pension rights and be disqualified for being thereafter employed in any police force :

Provided that, where a man was a member of a trade union before becoming a constable, he may, with the consent of the chief officer of police, continue to be a member of that union during the time of his service in the police force.

(2) If any question arises whether any body is a trade union or an association to which this section applies, the question shall be determined by the Minister of Labour.

3.—If any person causes, or attempts to cause, or does any act calculated to cause disaffection amongst the members of any police force, or induces, or attempts to induce, or does any act calculated to induce any member of a police force to withhold his services or to commit breaches of discipline, he shall be guilty of a misdemeanour, and shall be liable on conviction on indictment to imprisonment, with or without hard labour, for a term not exceeding two years, or on summary conviction, to imprisonment, with or without hard labour, for a term not exceeding three months, or to a fine not exceeding fifty pounds, or to both such imprisonment and fine, and in either case, if a member of a police force, shall forfeit all pension rights and be disqualified for being a member of any police force : Provided that, where the person convicted of any such offence was a member of a police force and was not sentenced to imprisonment without the option of a fine, the police authority may, if they think fit, pay to him the whole or any part of the rateable deductions which may have been made from his pay.

4.—(1) It shall be lawful for the Secretary of State to make regulations as to the government, mutual aid, pay, allowances, pensions, clothing, expenses and conditions of service of the members of all police forces within England and Wales, and every police authority shall comply with the regulations so made.

(2) A draft of any regulations proposed to be so made as aforesaid shall be submitted to a council, consisting of the joint central committee or a deputation from the joint central committee of the Police Federation and representatives of the chief officers of police and police authorities selected for the purpose by the Secretary of State, after consultation with the County Councils Association and the Association of Municipal Corporations, and before making the regulations the Secretary of State shall consider any representations made by such council.

30. Membership Rule.

AMALGAMATED ENGINEERING UNION, 1926.

Rule 1.—Name, Objects, and Constitution.

1. The Society formed under these rules, hereinafter called ' The Society,' shall be named the Amalgamated Engineering Union. It shall be a registered Trade Union.

The Society shall consist of all male workers engaged in the engineering, shipbuilding, and kindred trades, together with such trades as may be represented by Trade Unions hereinafter amalgamating with the Society.

Sections shall be established covering grades of membership in accordance with the contributions and benefits relating thereto.

31. Membership Rule.

NATIONAL SOCIETY OF BRASS AND METAL MECHANICS, 1927.

Rule 3.—Eligible to Join.

The members of this society shall consist of the following metal mechanics :

(*a*) Casters, moulders, typefounders, getters-down, core-makers, pourers, furnace and ingot men, rollers, breakers-down, casters' helps, plate moulders, machine moulders.

(*b*) Pattern-makers, modellers, chasers, spinners, die-sinkers, engravers, embossers, leaf-beaters, planishers, finishers, turners, vice-hands, fitters, copper braziers, and wrought smiths, metal frame workers, machine hands, general metal mechanics and oxy-acetylene and electric welders, toolmakers.

(c) Burnishers, braziers, bronzers and dippers, polishers, grinders, platers in all materials, and wire wheel makers.

(d) Stampers and piercers, tube and wire workers, die-sinkers.

(e) Electrical, mathematical, nautical, optical, and scientific instrument mechanics in all branches.

(f) Hearth furniture workers, coffin furniture and bedstead mount workers.

(g) Motor and cycle workers.

(h) Needle and fishing tackle workers.

(i) Trimmers, fettlers, and pipe fitters.

(j) Sash and casement makers.

(k) Wireworkers.

32. Membership Rule.

NAT. UNION OF DISTRIBUTIVE AND ALLIED WORKERS, 1924.

22.—Admission of Members and Associates.

SECTION 1.—The qualifications for full membership of the Union shall be as follows :

(a) Without prejudice to the commencing membership of the Union, any person of either sex employed wholly or mainly in any commercial occupation in connection with the retail or wholesale trades shall be eligible for membership. This shall include any employee if engaged at work in connection with any commercial employment and such other allied workers as the members in annual conference may determine.

(b) The Union will be subject in due course to any modifications of constitution or practice as will make it accord with any general plan of trade union re-organisation formulated by an authority set up by or under the assent of the Trades Union Congress, and which is made applicable to all trade union organisations alike.

(c) Applicants must, in accordance with the Trade Union Acts, be not less than sixteen years of age.

(d) Females shall be eligible for membership on the same terms as males.

SECTION 2.—Any person qualified as above shall, subject to the approval of the Executive Council, be eligible as a member of the

Union on payment of an entrance fee of 1s. (or such higher sum as may be determined by the Executive Council or branch committee under bye-laws in any special case) for contribution card and rule book, accompanied by one week's contribution, according to the scale of benefits which the member may select from the Schedule contained in Part II. of these rules.

SECTION 3.—Members of other registered trade unions may, subject to the approval of the Executive Council, be accorded a transfer to this Union, on the scale of contributions and benefits nearest to the one to which they have been contributing in the other Union for at least twelve months at the time of seeking to transfer, and will be entitled to immediate full benefit in accordance with the rules of this Union, providing—

(a) That they are clear on the books of the Union from which they are transferring.

(b) That they comply with the provisions of Section 1 and 6 of this rule.

(c) That they pay a transfer fee of 1s. 6d., or such higher sum as may be determined by the Executive Council in any special case.

SECTION 4. Workers under sixteen years of age qualified by the terms of Section 1 (a) and (b) above may join as associates only on payment of an entrance fee of 1s. for contribution card and rule book, accompanied by one week's contribution in Scale V. On attaining the age of sixteen years male associates must transfer to one of the full membership scales.

SECTION 5.—Each branch committee shall have power to refuse any applicant for membership, but must immediately report such refusal, with the reasons therefor, to the Executive Council. In case of an application being refused, notice of the refusal shall be sent to the applicant within twenty-eight days, and the amount paid by him shall be returned.

SECTION 6.—Any person wishing to become a member of the Union whose health is considered by the branch committee to be unsatisfactory, shall only be allowed to join in the lowest scale. Any member in the lowest scale whose health is considered by the branch committee to be unsatisfactory, shall be refused a transfer to any of the higher scales. In either of the aforesaid cases the persons concerned shall have the right of appeal to the Executive Council, whose decision shall be final.

33. Qualification for Membership.

RAILWAY CLERKS ASSOCIATION RULES. 1928.

2. (*a*) The Association may receive into membership Officers, Agents, Stationmasters, Inspectors, Canvassers, Collectors, and other duly appointed members of the Clerical, Supervisory, Administrative, Professional and Technical Staff in any department of Railway service in the British Isles.

(*b*) Unappointed, supernumerary or temporary Clerical, Supervisory, Administrative, Professional and Technical employees engaged in railway services in the British Isles, and any Clerical, Supervisory, Administrative, Professional, and Technical employees of Railway Carting Agents or of any undertakings carrying on the business of carriers of passengers or goods by land, water or air in the British Isles, or of any undertakings associated with the railway or other undertakings mentioned, may also be accepted, but only at the discretion of the Executive Committee, to whom their applications must in all cases be submitted.

(*c*) The words ' Officers,' ' Agents,' ' Stationmasters,' ' Inspectors,' ' Canvassers,' ' Collectors,' ' Clerical, Supervisory, Administrative, Professional and Technical Staff ' in Clauses (*a*) and (*b*) shall include women engaged in any of those capacities in any such employment as is before-mentioned, and throughout these Rules the words ' he,' ' his,' ' him,' shall be construed as referring to either men or women.

34. Membership Rule.

DURHAM MINERS' ASSOCIATION, 1925.

Constitution.

2.—This Association shall be composed of persons employed in and about the mines in the County of Durham, and may be divided into any number of distinct LODGES, each of which is in the rules referred to as the ' Lodge,' situated in the said County of Durham. Such Lodges may group themselves together as a Federation Board with other Lodges that are affiliated with the Durham County Mining Federation Board.

35. Trade Union Government.

RULES OF THE TRANSPORT AND GENERAL WORKERS' UNION, 1927.

Rule 3.—Constitution and Government.

1.—For the government of the Union there shall be a Biennial Delegate Conference. This Conference shall only consist of elected delegates, President, General and Financial Secretaries, Assistant General Secretary, and National Trade Group Secretaries and heads of departments.

2.—For the general administration of the Union's business and for the government of the Union in the periods between the Biennial Delegate Conferences there shall be a General Executive Council. This Council shall consist of such number of elected members as is provided for in the rules.

3.—For the purpose of administration, the membership of the Union shall be divided according to (*a*) territorial area and (*b*) trade or occupation, or district committee if required.

4.—For the purpose of territorial area administration the British Islands shall be divided into thirteen areas, as follows :—

    (i) London and Home Counties,
    (ii) South of England, including the Channel Islands,
    (iii) West of England,
    (iv) South Wales,
    (v) Midlands,
    (vi) North-West Coast, North Wales, Lancashire, portions of Cheshire, etc.,
    (vii) Scotland,
    (viii) Northern Area, including Northumberland, Cumberland, Westmorland, Durham, parts of North Yorkshire, etc.,
    (ix) North Midlands and Yorkshire,
    (x) East Coast,
    (xi) Ireland,
    (xii) Liverpool,
    (xiii) North Wales,

or such other areas as may from time to time be determined.

5.—The membership shall be divided into six national trade groups, according to the occupation of members of the Union, as follows :

    (*a*) Docks, riverside, wharves (including coal shipping), and warehouses, (*b*) Waterways, including estuaries and canals,

(*c*) Professional, technical, administrative, clerical, and supervisory,

(*d*) Road transport (passenger),

(*e*) Road transport (commercial),

(*f*) General workers, being all other members of the Union, including workers in metal, chemical trades, etc.,

and such other groups as may from time to time be determined.

6.—Each national trade group shall be divided into area trade groups or district committees as the case may be in accordance with the territorial areas, and area trade groups or district committees shall be divided into branches, to one of which every member of the Union shall belong. The territorial area over which each branch shall exercise jurisdiction shall be decided by the General Executive Council, on the recommendation of the area committee.

7.—The division of areas and area trade groups and the allocation of members thereto shall be decided by the General Executive Council, who shall constitute special sub-sections of trade groups as follows : (*a*) for coal shipping, in the case of docks ; (*b*) for metal trades, chemical trades, and flour millers in the case of general workers ; and such other sub-sections as may from time to time seem expedient.

8.—The general policy of the Union shall, subject to the Biennial Delegate Conference, be determined by the General Executive Council, but the policy of every area or trade shall, within the powers delegated to an area or national or area trade group committee by these rules or by the General Executive Council, be determined by such area or national or area trade group committee.

Rule 4.—Delegate Conferences.

1.—The government of the Union and the appointment of its trustees, and the power to make, amend, and revoke the rules of the Union and its constitution, shall be vested in a Biennial Delegate Conference (hereinafter called the Conference), which shall meet in the month of July. Special Conferences may be held as in these rules provided.

.   .   .   .

Rule 5.—General Executive Council.

1. For the general administration of the Union's business there shall be a General Executive Council.

2.—The General Executive Council shall be constituted as follows :

    (*a*) One representative from each territorial area, and

    (*b*) One representative from each national trade group committee.

No person shall represent both an area and a trade group. No permanent full-time officer shall be eligible for nomination.

3.—Each candidate for election to represent an area shall be nominated by a branch within that area. . . . The election shall be by ballot vote of the members within such area, and the voting take place and be completed not later than December 14th, and the elected to take office the following January for two years and hold office for two years only, unless re-elected.

   .   .   .   .

8.—(*a*) The General Executive Council shall transact and overlook the general business of the Union. It shall see that properly prepared quarterly and annual statements of account relating to all financial affairs of the Union are presented at its quarterly meetings, and it may call for the production of any books, vouchers, or documents. It shall have power to direct that special audits or examinations of the books or finances of any branch, area, national or area trade group committee (each of which is hereinafter called ' a local authority ') shall be made by special auditors appointed by the Council.

(*b*) It shall overlook the business of the national trade group and area committees (and district committees set up under the following Clause *c*), and see that they administer the business of the Union properly and according to the rules. It shall require reports to be submitted to it of the work of the national trade group officers and area officers. It shall adjust and decide all differences in questions of administration that arise between branches and area trade group, area, and all other committees.

(*c*) It shall have power to organise any new trade group and to provide for any such new group special conditions and benefits (if necessary or desirable), contributions not being less than those set forth in Schedule 11. ; and to establish a district committee where it shall deem necessary.

(*d*) It shall consider all appeals and resolutions addressed to it from branches, area and national trade groups, and area and all other committees, and decide thereon. It shall decide all questions arising in connection with appeals by members or branches against decisions of area committees concerned in the payment or non-payment of claims for benefit.

9.—The General Executive Council shall appoint all paid officers and permanent officials of the Union (who shall have been financial members for two years) other than the President, General Secretary, Financial Secretary, and Trustees. No new officers shall be appointed by the General Executive Council until after consultation with the national trade group and/or either the area committee or area trade group committee concerned. The General Executive Council shall fix the salaries attached to each official position. It shall have power to dismiss any officer, but such officer shall, by giving notice in writing to the General Secretary within seven days, have a right of appeal to the Appeals Committee, or at his option to the next Ordinary Conference. This right shall not, however, be enjoyed by any official who is dismissed for attempting to disrupt the organisation by advocating, or threatening, secession, or creating a rival organisation. Until the hearing of such appeal the decision of the Council shall be binding.

10.—It shall summon the chief officer of a trade group to attend any meeting at which any matter affecting such trade group is to be discussed.

11.—It shall require reports to be submitted to it of all disputes, and shall take such action with regard thereto as it shall deem fit.

12.—The General Executive Council shall set up the necessary departments for the proper administration of the business of the Union ; allocate officers and prescribe their powers and duties and terms of employment.

13.—(a) The General Executive Council shall decide how the surplus funds of the Union shall be invested, and how such investments shall be varied. Such funds shall be invested in the joint names of the trustees in any of the public stocks or funds or Government securities of the United Kingdom or any British Colony or Dependency, or of any foreign Government or State, or in any securities the interest on which is or shall be guaranteed by Parliament or in bonds with municipal corporations, in the shares or on the security of any other registered society under the Industrial and Provident Societies Acts, or under the Building Societies Act, or of any Company registered under the Companies Act or incorporated by Act of Parliament or by charter, or in, or upon, any mortgage, bond, debenture, or debenture stock, or in freehold or leasehold property in Great Britian, Ireland, and the Channel Islands, or on

T.U.D.   G

mortgage thereof, or in any approved co-operative undertakings. All dividends and interest arising therefrom shall be allocated to the Provident Funds of the Union in such manner as the General Executive Council shall determine.

(*b*) The General Executive Council shall have power to raise or borrow money on any of the properties or securities of the Union by way of mortgage or otherwise in such manner as they shall think fit.

14.—In addition to any express powers in these rules provided, the General Executive Council shall have power generally to carry on the business of the Union, and do such things and authorise such acts, including the payment of moneys, on behalf of the Union as they, in the general interests of the Union, may deem expedient. They shall have power at any time to negotiate on any matters concerning the interests of the members of the Union or the interests of Labour generally, and to conclude agreements with persons and associations not members of the Union. They shall have power to sanction the payment of moneys, authorise payments, make levies, either generally or for particular purposes or districts, and generally within the rules and the standing decisions of the Conference and of the Appeals Committee, to decide the policy of the Union. They shall have power to prepare programmes of action and policy generally, provided that before sanctioning a strike of (*a*) all the members of the Union or (*b*) two or more national trade groups they shall obtain the approval of a Special Delegate Conference and act in accordance with the ballot vote taken in consequence of such approval. No sectional strike shall take place without the sanction of the General Executive Council, and no extension of such a strike to other sections in the Union shall take place without the sanction of the General Executive Council, after consultation with the area and national trade group committees concerned. The General Executive Council alone shall have power to sanction payment of benefit in respect of any strike (other than a strike involving the whole of the members of the Union) and in respect of any lockout. They shall have power to expend moneys on any of the purposes authorised by these rules, or on any other purpose which, in their opinion is expedient in the interests of the Union or its members, including the right to expend moneys on the legal assistance of the members or officers or their dependents, whether in bringing or defending actions or prosecutions in all cases where they may deem fit, and such other legal action as, in their opinion, may be necessary to protect the interests of the Union. They may likewise institute or defend proceedings or authorise the general trustees to institute or defend legal proceedings, against persons who are or who are not members of the Union. They may send delegates or deputations to represent the Union for any purpose they think fit, and shall have power to suspend or expel any member, branch, local authority, or other administrative section of the Union, whether temporarily or permanently, for such reasons and on such terms as they may deem expedient, and their decision, save as herein provided, shall be final and conclusive for all purposes, provided that every member, branch, local authority, or other administrative section shall have the right, within four weeks of the decision of the General Executive Council, to give notice of appeal and to appeal to the Appeals Committee, and the decision of such committee thereon shall be final.

15.—The General Executive Council may delegate to any national or area trade group committee or to any area committee such of their powers as are necessary or expedient and consistent with the powers and duties of such committee as in these rules provided, and may modify or revoke such powers from time to time.

16.—The General Executive Council shall comply with all regulations and instructions of the Ministry relating to the business of the Union under the National Health Insurance Act, or cause such regulations and instructions to be complied with. Except as may be otherwise provided by the National Health Insurance Act, or in these rules, the General Executive Council shall in all things act for and in the name of the Union ; and all acts and orders under the powers delegated to them shall have the like force and effect as the acts and orders of the Union at any general meeting. It shall be the duty of the General Executive Council to keep themselves informed as to the general administration of the Union ; to exercise a general supervision over the keeping of the accounts ; and to verify, from time to time, any cash balances in the hands of the Secretary and other officers.

Rule 6. *National Trade Group Committees.*

1.—For the purpose of conducting the trade group business of the Union there shall be for each trade group, as herein specified, a national committee which shall hold office for the same period as the General Executive Council, as laid down in Rule 5 (3).

2.—Each national trade group committee shall be composed of one or more members from each area trade group committee, and shall be elected by members of the area trade group committee by show of hands. Where a District Committee system operates in place of group committees, the area committee shall determine the method of selecting representatives for the national trade group committees. Only members of the Committee (and/or the branch as the case may be) directly affected by the group concerned shall have the right to nominate and vote.

3.—There shall be six national trade group committees, one for each section or group of members as specified in this rule, namely :

Members performing manual work in and about docks, wharves, riverside, and warehouses.

Members working about waterways.

Members working in a professional, technical, clerical, administrative, or supervisory capacity.

Members working in connection with road transport (passenger).

Members working in connection with road transport (goods and commercial).

Members classified as general workers,

and such other groups as the General Executive Council may hereafter decide.

4.—Each national trade group committee shall transact and overlook for its membership the Union's business as affecting movements relating to pay, hours, and working conditions, and other questions pertaining thereto.

.   .   .   .

Rule 7.—Area Committees.

1.—For the purpose of locally administering the general business of the Union there shall be an area committee for each area which shall hold office for the same period as the General Executive Council as provided in Rule 5 (3).

2.—Area committees shall be composed of representatives of each of the area trade group committees. The members of the area trade group committees shall elect in manner laid down by the General Executive Council delegates to serve on the area committee, on a basis of one representative for every thousand members or part thereof of their group, but no area trade group committee shall be entitled to more than three representatives on the area committee.

.   .   .   .

4.—The powers and duties of the area committee shall include the organisation of groups within the area, the co-ordination of the work of the various area trade groups and sections, the conduct of necessary propaganda, the administration of such business of the Union as affects all sections of the membership in the area, such as general industrial movements, educational work, political administration, etc., the consideration of any dispute arising in the area and reporting thereon to the General Executive Council, with suggestions as to arrangements for the mutual support of respective sections when necessary, and on disputes arising out of the non-payment of benefits.

. . . .

Rule 8.—Area Trade Group Committees.

1.—For the purpose of conducting the trade group business of the Union there shall be an area trade group committee for each of the trade groups in each area, which shall hold office for the same period as the General Executive Council as provided in Rule 5 (3).

. . . .

5.—The area trade group committee shall be consulted upon and advise as to all matters directly affecting the interests of the group.

. . . .

Rule 9.—Branches.

1.—The Union shall be divided into branches, each of which shall consist of not less than fifty members, except by special permission of the General Executive Council. Should the membership of a branch fall below the minimum number of fifty, the members shall be attached to such branch as the General Executive Council, after consultation with the area trade group committee concerned, may direct. A meeting of each branch shall be held either weekly, fortnightly, or at least monthly, and a quarterly meeting shall also be held.

. . . .

3.—Collectors and/or shop stewards may be appointed by a branch subject to the approval of the General Executive Council, whose duty shall be to collect members' contributions, record same in the book provided, and pay in to the branch the actual amounts collected at least once a week.

36. Trade Union Government.

RULES OF THE NATIONAL UNION OF RAILWAYMEN, 1926.

Rule II.—Government of the Union.

1. For the supreme government of the Union there shall be an Annual General Meeting, consisting of eighty representatives, the President, and General Secretaries ; in the absence of the President, or if the office of President shall be vacant, the meeting shall elect a Chairman from amongst the representatives present.

2. The representatives shall each be elected by ballot on the single transferable vote system by the members of branches grouped together in a locality and in such manner as shall as nearly as is possible secure equal representation of all members.

.   .   .   .

3. The Annual or Special General Meeting shall have power :
   (*a*) To amend, rescind or make rules ;
   (*b*) To remove from office any officer ;

.   .   .   .

   (*d*) To expel any member from the Union.
   (*e*) To dissolve any branch of the Union.
   (*f*) To make any levy on the branches or members of the Union.

.   .   .   .

   (*h*) To decide all appeals against the decision of the Executive Committee.
   (*i*) To inaugurate any movement or decree any proceedings in the interests of the Union and its members.

.   .   .   .

   (*m*) It shall govern the Executive Committee.

.   .   .   .

   (*o*) To do all such other things, whether of the kind before specified or otherwise, as may be necessary or desirable in the interests of the Union or its members.

.   .   .   .

Rule III.—General Administration by an Executive Council.

1.—For the general administration of the Union's business and for the government of the Union in the intervals between every two Annual General Meetings, there shall be an Executive Committee consisting of the President, General Secretaries, and twenty-four representatives chosen by the members of the different districts. Each representative must have been a member of the Union for five consecutive years at the date of his nomination, and be, and continue to be, employed on or in connection with a railway.   Should he cease to be so employed for a period of three calendar months he shall be ineligible to continue as a representative. . . .   The Executive Committee shall be divided into four departmental sub-committees comprising the representatives of the departments hereinafter named.

· · · · · · · ·

3. The twenty-four representatives on the Executive Committee shall be chosen by ballot on the single transferable vote system.   The Union shall be formed into six electoral districts for this purpose. Within those districts the various grades shall be divided into four electoral departments.   The electoral departments shall be classified as follows : (1) LOCOMOTIVE department ; (2) TRAFFIC department ; (3) GOODS AND CARTAGE department ; (4) ENGINEERING SHOPS AND PERMANENT WAY.   The Executive Committee shall be chosen from each district triennially, one-third retiring each year ; but should two-thirds of the branches in any particular district be dissatisfied with their representative they shall have power to demand a poll of the members of that district at the expiration of each year. . . .

4. . . . The departmental sub-committees shall meet quarterly if necessary, and prior to the meeting of the Executive Committee. . . .

5. The Executive Committee shall administer the business and affairs of the Union and govern the Union subject to the Annual General Meeting. . . . It shall have power to impose such levies on members and branches as it may consider necessary for the furtherance of the objects and interests of the Union.   It shall interpret the rules of the Union.   It shall decide appeals by branches or members.

· · · · · · · ·

7. Every decision and order of the Executive Committee shall be binding on members and branches, subject to appeal to the next succeeding Annual General Meeting ; and every member of the Union, both present and future, agrees that this clause shall be of full force and effect, and shall form the essential basis of the contract between the Union and its members and every one of them, and that no order or decision of the Executive Committee whatever shall be questioned, reversed, controlled, or suspended except by way of appeal as aforesaid.

· · · · · · · ·

*Rule XIII.—Section 3.   Protection of the Rights and Labour of
     Bodies and Members.*

1. The Executive Committee shall have power to inaugurate and
conduct all trade movements between its members and their employers, and such other movements as in the opinion of the Executive Committee affect the interests of the members of the Union.

2. The method of conducting such movements shall be determined
by the Executive Committee as circumstances warrant.

3. The Executive Committee shall have power to settle disputes
not of a national character that may arise between the members and
their employers.

4. The Executive Committee shall have power to declare strikes,
and to order and direct the members of the Union to withdraw their
labour and to fix the date of such withdrawal, and it shall be the
paramount duty of every member of the Union to conform to such
order and direction.   Failure on the part of any member to comply
with any such order or direction of the Executive Committee shall
be dealt with as laid down in Rule ix, clause 14. . . .

37. Membership and Management.

RULES OF LONDON SOCIETY OF COMPOSITORS, 1925.

II.—Management and Officers.

1. The management of the Society shall be vested in a Committee,
who shall be answerable for their actions to General and Delegate
Meetings of the members.

2. The officers shall consist of Parliamentary Secretary, Treasurer,
Chairman, Secretary, Assistant and Organising Secretary, Financial
Secretary, Assistants, Trustees, and Auditors, all of whom must have
been members of the Society for a period of five consecutive years.

. . . .

IV.—Departments.

The Society shall be divided into the following Departments,
viz. :—

(*a*) THE BOOK DEPARTMENT : To consist of all journeymen
employed in offices where bookwork, jobbing and weekly newspapers are done.   To be under the guidance of these Rules.

(*b*) THE NEWS DEPARTMENT : To consist of all journeymen
employed on daily newspapers.   To be under the guidance of

these Rules, and also the Rules of the News Department.
(LXI., p. 34.)

(c) THE SOCIETY HOUSE AND READING ROOM : For the use of
members of the Book and News Departments only, under the
control of the Committee.

. . . .

VII.—Committee—Constitution.

1. The business of the Society shall be conducted by a Committee,
consisting of twelve members (nine of whom shall be case hands, one
a reader, and two machine operators, of whom one shall be a Lino-
type operator and the other a Monotype operator), who shall, at the
time of nomination, be actually employed in the Book Department,
in possession of the current year's card, and clear on the books ;
have worked at the business not less than five consecutive years as
journeymen in London, and have been members of the Society for
a like period. The News Committee shall also have the right of
sending two representatives, who shall be subject to the same
restrictions as to term of office as other members of the Committee.

2. The Committee shall be elected from the members of the
Society, annually, by ballot.

3. All nominations of Candidates, eligible and willing to serve,
shall be forwarded to the Secretary (on forms prepared for the
purpose) on or before the first Monday in the month of February in
each year, in order that, having been arranged in the order of
seniority of membership, they may be printed ; such nominations
shall be duly signed by the proposer and seconder, and accompanied
by the signature of the Candidate as to his willingness to serve, if
elected.

4. Members holding office in any other capacity in the Society
shall be deemed ineligible for the Committee.

5. The voting papers for the election of the Committee shall be
ready for delivery to chapel[1] officers and members on the second
Monday in February, on application at the Society House, such
papers to be returned to the Secretary, and placed in a ballot-box
prepared for that purpose, on or before half-past eight o'clock in the
evening of the third Monday in the month of February.

[1] The term "chapel" is used in the printing trade to denote the
"shop organisation." It is the administrative unit of the Trade Union
organisation and consists of the workers in the particular office or
"shop."

6. Six scrutineers shall be taken from the Call-Book in like manner as an ordinary call to examine the voting papers, and report the result to the Secretary.   Subject to the provision in Section 1 as to constitution, the twelve Candidates who shall have received the highest number of votes shall serve on the Committee for the ensuing twelve months.

7. Not more than one case hand in any office shall be eligible to serve on the Committee at the same time.   Should more than one be nominated, the whole of the names shall be submitted to the members—the highest in the polling to be elected.   An operator shall not be disqualified from serving for the reason that a case hand working in the same office has also been elected ; or *vice versa*.   In the event, however, of any member of the Committee being employed, subsequent to his election, in the same office as another member of the Board, he shall not vacate his seat in consequence thereof.   If less than twelve duly qualified members are nominated, the Annual General Meeting shall fill up the vacancies from amongst the members present.

8. Should there be an equality of votes for any candidates, in excess of the required number, the names of such candidates shall be submitted to the Annual General Meeting, who shall determine which of the said candidates shall sit on the Committee.

9. The Secretary shall announce the final result of the voting at the Annual General Meeting in each year.

10. Any member of the Committee obtaining employment in a daily paper office shall resign his seat on the Board, if continuing in that employment, at the expiration of one month.

11. The Committee shall meet every Tuesday evening, or oftener, if required, at the Society House, for the transaction of business, at seven o'clock and continue to sit until nine o'clock, if necessary, receiving the sum of 4s. 6d. each for their attendance. For each payment they shall append their signatures in a book kept for that purpose.

12. Should a majority of the members of the Committee be present it shall form a quorum, with power to act.   A record of the attendance of the Committee and all Sub-Committees shall be published.

13. In case any member of the Committee shall die, resign, cease to be a member of the Society, be more than eight weeks in arrear, be out of benefit under any of these rules, discontinue to work at the business, be absent for four successive weeks (except in case of illness), or be removed from office, his seat shall be declared vacant.

Vacancies on the Committee shall be filled by the highest unsuccessful candidates at the previous election who may be eligible and willing to serve ; but if at such election only the required number of candidates were nominated, then, in case of a vacancy arising, it shall be filled up in the same manner as at the annual election.   The Committee shall retire from office on the day of the Annual General Meeting.

14. Any member, having served upon the Committee for two consecutive periods of twelve months, shall not be eligible for re-election until the expiration of·two years.   Any portion of time served through vacancies occurring on the Committee shall not be reckoned as a part of the two consecutive periods of twelve months.

VIII.—Committee—General Powers and Duties.

1. The Committee shall have the general control and management of the Society, consider and decide upon all cases of dispute, answer all questions submitted by Chapels or individual members respecting the prices and customs which may arise in the Book trade ; be authorised, in cases of emergency, to call in all requisite assistance ; and to open and maintain correspondence with the different Typographical Societies, transmitting or receiving any information necessary.

2. They shall, at the first business meeting after their election, appoint such Sub-Committees either then or subsequently, as they may deem expedient.

3. They shall have no power to take, or cause to be taken, a ballot or the members on any matter other than an extension of the Provident Benefit or a grant to another trade society or other body of workers, without having previously caused to be held a Delegate or General Meeting to consider such matter or matters—anything otherwise stated in these rules notwithstanding.

4. On receipt of an application from the Chapel of unemployed members, they shall consider and decide upon the question of taking a ballot for an extension of Provident benefit to members who have exhausted their ordinary benefit.

5. Should application be made to them for pecuniary assistance by any Typographical or other Society, they shall be empowered to grant a sum not exceeding £10, on being satisfied of the emergency of the case, but they shall not vote any extra sum to paid officers without the sanction of a Special General or Delegate Meeting, which they shall have the power to convene for such purpose, and at such time as they may deem expedient.

6. They shall have power to fine (not more than 10s.), suspend, or expel any member acting, or assisting others to act, against the interests of the Society. In cases of suspension, they shall decide whether the suspension shall apply merely in regard to certain benefits, or to loss of membership for the period of suspension, either or both.

7. The decisions given shall be binding upon every Member, subject to appeal to a Delegate or Special General Meeting. Notice of any appeal shall be given to the Committee at least two weeks prior to the holding of such meeting.

8. In the event of a member being summoned before the Committee on any charge, the said member shall be allowed to have one other member with him to assist him in his defence.

IX.—Committee—Power to make Levy.

The minimum capital of the Society (exclusive of the freehold property and the Superannuation Fund) shall be fixed at £4 per member, and in the event of its falling below that amount, the Committee shall be empowered to levy not less than one penny per member weekly until that amount is reached ; but they shall not levy extra subscriptions, nor permit them to be levied, for any other purpose without the sanction of a Special General or Delegate Meeting (subject to the provisions in Rule xxix.).

X.—Committee—Power to Summon Members.

Should any trade dispute or other matter requiring investigation arise in any Chapel, the Committee shall be empowered to summon members to give an explanation. Members neglecting or refusing to attend, after having been summoned by the Secretary, shall be fined 2s., and an order shall be issued to attend the next meeting, which, if also neglected, he or they shall each be fined 2s. 6d., and a final notice shall be sent by the Secretary to the Chapel, stating that if no explanation be given the office will be reported by the Committee to the next Delegate Meeting.

38. Printing ' Chapels.'[1]

RULES OF LONDON SOCIETY OF COMPOSITORS, 1925.

XXIII.—Duties of Chapels.

1. It shall be the duty of each Chapel to appoint one of their members as Collector, to gather the subscriptions from every member

[1] See p. 105, note.

employed in the Office or Chapel, which subscriptions he must pay to the Secretary of the Society weekly, fortnightly, or monthly, according to the decision of the Chapel.

2. Every member employed in an office where a Chapel exists must pay his subscriptions to the Collector, who shall give to the Secretary a list containing the number of the card and the name of each member in alphabetical order when practicable, appending under the respective dates the amount of the weekly subscription according to the scale in Rule v., receiving in return, at the time of payment, a printed form of receipt signed by the Secretary.

3. It shall be the duty of the Chapel to appoint two auditors where the number in Chapel is twenty members or more, and one auditor where the Chapel is under twenty, for the purpose of checking all receipts and payments shown on the Monthly Chapel Sheets, and signing the sheets accordingly.

4. It shall also be the duty of the Father of the Chapel to make a monthly return, on a form provided for that purpose on the back of the Collecting Sheet, of the number of journeymen employed in the office, specifying the number of case compositors (full frame and grass hands) on piece and 'stab respectively, the number of machine compositors and the number and description of machines in use, the number of apprentices and turnovers, and the system under which they work ; also number of hours per man worked in excess of forty-eight per week, together with any special circumstances in the mode of working the office which are contrary to the Scales or customs of the Trade or the Rules of the Society. Chapels failing to comply shall have their names published in the following quarterly business paper, and be fined the sum of 2s. 6d.

5. Only one Chapel shall exist in any office.

6. It shall be the duty of each Chapel to purchase copies of the *London Typographical Journal* to the number of one copy for each six members employed in the office.

39. Trade Union Government.

RULES OF AMALGAMATED ASSOCIATION OF OPERATIVE COTTON SPINNERS AND TWINERS, 1921.

Membership.

3.—The Amalgamation shall consist of an unlimited number of District Associations of Operative Cotton Spinners, Twiners, and

Piecers, and no person shall be admitted a member of the Amalgamation otherwise than through one of the Districts of which the Amalgamation is formed.

Any member of the Amalgamation who is promoted to overlooking may retain his membership, provided he retains his membership of the District Association.

Constitution of Districts.

4.—Each District Association shall include within itself all mills in the locality which, whether from geographical position, similarity of prices, or any other cause it may be found desirable or practicable to govern by the same District Rules, such rules to be in conformity with the rules of the Amalgamation.

Formation of Provinces.

5.—For the better carrying out of the objects of this Amalgamation, districts may form themselves into provinces and be governed by provincial rules, which shall be in accordance with the rules of the Amalgamation.

Government of Districts and Provinces.

6.—Each district or province joining this Amalgamation shall be governed by its own district or provincial rules (always subject to the General Rules of the Amalgamation), and shall have the control and management of its own district or provincial funds.

New Districts and Provinces Joining the Amalgamation.

7.—Any district or province not having joined the Amalgamation, and wishing to do so, shall be allowed, on conditions prescribed by the Executive Council or a Representative Meeting.

Withdrawal of a Mill or Mills from a District or Province.

8.—No mill or mills in connection with this Amalgamation shall be allowed to withdraw from the province or district to which it or they belong, whether for the purpose of acting alone as an isolated province or district of the Amalgamation, or of joining another province or district, without giving such reasons as shall be satisfactory to a General Representative Meeting, duly warned to consider whether such withdrawal is necessary or not.

Legislative Power—How Vested.

9.—The legislative power shall be vested in a Meeting of Representatives from the various provinces and districts included in the Amalgamation.

Representation at General Representative Meetings.

10.—The representation of provinces and districts at General Representative Meetings shall be based upon the number of spinner members, each province or district to be allowed one representative under and up to 200 members ; above 200 and up to 400, two representatives ; above 400 and up to 600, three representatives ; above 600 and up to 800, four representatives ; above 800 and up to 1,000, five representatives ; and one additional representative for every 200 members or fractional part thereof ; such representatives may be either spinners or piecers as the province or district may determine, and each representative shall be allowed third-class railway fares to and from such meeting. The number of representatives present, and the number and names of provinces and districts represented at each meeting shall be published with the minutes of the proceedings.

General Representative Meetings—When Held.

11.—The General Representative Meetings shall be held quarterly, or oftener if necessary, and, unless otherwise decided by the Executive Council or a Representative Meeting, they shall be held on the fourth Saturday in each of the following months : March, June, September, and December, in each year. Business which has not been published on the agenda shall not be entertained, unless such business be considered by the Executive Council to be of great importance, and has transpired in the interval since the publication of the business sheet.

.   .   .   .

Election of President and his Duties.

14.—The President of the Amalgamation shall be elected annually at the March Representative Meetings, and be eligible for re-election. He shall be required to preside over all Executive and Representative Meetings, shall keep order, see that the rules and regulations of the Amalgamation are strictly adhered to at such meetings, and in case of doubt shall assist the Executive or Representatives in expounding the rules of the Amalgamation, for which purpose he shall be allowed to speak for such time and as often as he considers it to be necessary ; but at Representative Meetings he shall not be allowed to vote, except the votes of the Representatives are equal, in which case he shall be allowed to give the casting vote, and for his services shall be allowed such remuneration as a General Representative Meeting may determine.

General Secretary—Mode of Election.

15.—The General Secretary shall be appointed and continue in office so long as he gives satisfaction. In the event of a vacancy occurring in the office of General Secretary, any person who is, or who has been within three years from the time of application, connected with any district or province forming this Amalgamation, either as a member or an officer, shall be eligible for nomination to fill the office of General Secretary. The sole right of electing a permanent General Secretary shall be vested in the Provincial and District Representatives when in meeting assembled, by whom his salary shall be fixed and determined.

40. Government—Duties of Executive.

NAT. SOC. OF BRASS AND METAL MECHANICS, 1927.

Rule 8.   .   .   .   .

Duties of National Executive.

Their duties shall be to consider :

1. Any branch or district council appeal against the decision of the National Executive, and its decision thereon shall be final and binding on the whole society until the rule upon which the decision is based is altered by the consent of the general body of members. Such decision to be in strict conformity to the rules. Also to consider any appeal made by a member expelled by Rule 33, with power to reinstate his membership.

2. The N.E.C. shall obtain the opinion of the members in the area concerned before appointing a full time official in a district of branches or a branch with a membership not exceeding 1,000 members. Such official shall be nominated and balloted for by members in district or branch concerned.

3. To establish and maintain the work of organization, with authority to appoint an organizer or organizers as required by vote of the District. This duty shall be strictly adhered to.

4. To vote all moneys, direct the officers in the due performance of their duties, suspend any officer for fraud, negligence, or incompetence, and transact the ordinary business of this Society.

5. To consider and improve branch by-laws, with power to delete any by-law which it considers to be *ultra vires* of the general rules.

6. To consider all proposed changes in rates of wages or conditions of labour affecting the society.

7. To declare such levies as are required from time to time, such levies to be calculated as contributions, and to remove or reduce the same when in its opinion it is advisable to do so.

8. Notice of appeal to be sent to the general secretary 21 days before the next meeting of the National Executive. The National Executive shall be convened at least once a quarter at fixed dates, or, in case of emergency, at the discretion of the National President and general secretary, who shall give, if possible, not less than six clear days' notice of same.

9. The rent of rooms, halls, printing, railway fares, and deputation pay shall be paid out of the general fund.

10. Members of the National Executive travelling over 200 miles from the branches of which they are members shall receive two days' deputation pay as per rule. If over 100 and less than 200 miles, one day and a half shall be paid. If over 50 miles, one day or any portion of a day, as time and circumstances shall justify. Members who reside in the city, town, or place where the National Executive meet to be paid town deputation as per Rule No. 32.

11. The N.E.C. shall make all arrangements and provide for the due performance of the duties of general secretary in his absence.

12. Should the general fund be reduced below average, 30s. per member (exclusive of superannuation fund), the N.E.C. shall be empowered to declare a levy, which, together with the usual weekly income, shall be sufficient to meet the current demands on the funds. Should the N.E.C. find it necessary to declare a levy for any other particular purpose, they shall not do so without first consulting the branches. Any levy that increases contributions above 50 per cent. should be submitted for approval of the whole of the members before being enforced. All members receiving benefit shall be exempt from levies, also members retaining their membership for superannuation and funeral benefits.

13. The agenda to be carried through in one day if possible.

14. The attendances shall be taken and reported in quarterly or monthly journal on or before the annual day of each year, and forwarded to all branches.

The National Executive shall be invested with full power and authority to carry out Part 2 dealing with the National Health Insurance Acts.

15. In directing and controlling the general secretary and all officers in the proper administration of the State funds.

16. By seeing that the sick committees in no way deviate from the rules and conditions being strictly carried out as required by the Ministry of Health, either as contained in the National Health Insurance Acts or in any regulations which may be hereafter made by the said Ministry.

17. To suspend any officer or committee who fails to comply with Part II. of these rules in the prescribed form of such rules.

18. To require the production of certificates of birth, death, cr marriage, when it is of opinion that such are necessary.

19. And it is hereby empowered in any unforeseen circumstances and condition to act in the interest of the State and the individual members consistent with the National Health Insurance Acts or subsequent amendments thereto.

20. To have full control over the management expenses allowed by the Act aforesaid, and to allocate such proportions to its branches, and in case of objection to be subject only to the approval of the Ministry of Health.

21. And in all matters be the authority responsible to the Ministry.

22. Should the affairs of the society be such as to necessitate a special general meeting of members, the officers and National Executive shall give due notice of such meeting and arrange that all members shall be supplied in printed form with the nature of the business to be brought forward at such special general meeting.

23. No member under 21 years of age shall be a member of the National Executive, or a trustee, treasurer, or secretary of the society, or of any branch thereof.

24. Should an officer of the National Executive refuse to perform his duties to the general satisfaction of the members, or fail to carry out the rules according to Acts of Parliament, the members shall have the power to remove such officer at a special meeting called for the purpose, due notice of the time and place of such meeting to be given to all members.

25. N.E.C. representatives of districts shall be at the disposal of branches at the request of D.C.

26. The National Executive shall at all times strictly adhere to the rules and constitution.

41. Expulsion Rule.

<small>NAT. AMAL. UNION OF SHOP ASSISTANTS, ETC., 1927.</small>

Rule 27.

1. It shall be competent for the Executive Committee to suspend from all Benefits or expel any member from the Union upon proof satisfactory to the Executive Committee being given, that such member has refused to comply with their decision or ruling, or broken the rules for the time being of the Union, or by his conduct has in the opinion of the Executive Committee brought the Union into discredit, or has fraudulently received or misapplied the funds of the Union or the monies of any member entrusted to him for payment to the Union, or has received monies on behalf of the Union and has wilfully withheld or not duly accounted for the same or has knowingly received any benefit from the Union not being entitled thereto, or has practised any fraud on the Union, and on suspension or expulsion of any member who has committed any one or more of the offences aforesaid, he shall refund any monies he may have received as aforesaid, and shall forfeit all contributions paid by him but without prejudice to any liability to prosecution.

All such members shall be supplied with particulars of the charges made against them and have an opportunity of presenting their defence to the Executive Committee.

2. Prosecutions shall be instituted and expulsions effected only by the Executive Committee.

42. Complaints and Supervision.

<small>NATIONAL SOCIETY OF BRASS AND METAL MECHANICS, 1927.</small>

Rule 7.—Duties and Remuneration of National Referee.

The National Referee shall receive complaints from branches against central office or national officers, and place the same before the next N.E.C. meeting. He shall be elected by and from the N.E.C.

.   .   .   .

Rule 22.—Referees.

<small>EACH BRANCH COMMITTEE MUST APPOINT ANNUALLY TWO REFEREES, INCLUDING THE PRESIDENT, TO WHOM THE TRUSTEES MAY COMMUNICATE ON FINANCIAL MATTERS WHENEVER THEY THINK IT DESIRABLE.</small>

They shall examine the branch books, vouchers, membership cards, etc., from time to time, and fully report to branch committee first meeting after such examination. They shall find reliable substitute in event of secretary's illness, as per Rule 20. They shall see that all fines are *strictly* enforced.

Any member who shall have reasonable cause of complaint of laxity of any branch official may appeal to ' members' referee,' who shall have power to lay the complaint before next meeting of committee, such complaint to take precedence on agenda. They shall see that instructions as issued by auditor are duly carried out.

Members' referee shall hold no other office in branch except committee-man.

Every Branch, without exception, must enforce this rule.

43. Disputes and Complaints.

RULES OF DURHAM MINERS' ASSOCIATION, 1925.

Disputes.

101.—Should any dispute arise between a member, or a person who has ceased to be a member, or person claiming through such member or person, or under the rules, and the society, or the committee of management, or any officer of the society, it shall be decided by arbitration. Three Arbitrators shall be elected by the society at the annual general meeting, none of whom shall be directly or indirectly interested in the funds of the society. In each case of dispute the names of the Arbitrators shall be written on pieces of paper and placed in a proper receptacle, and the one whose name is first drawn out by the complaining party, or by someone appointed by him, shall be the Arbitrator to decide on the matter in dispute. In case of a vacancy or vacancies, another Arbitrator or other Arbitrators shall be elected by the Committee to act until the next annual general meeting.

44. Finance.

CONTRIBUTION RULE OF THE NATIONAL UNION OF GENERAL AND MUNICIPAL WORKERS, 1924.

Rule 23.—Membership and Contributions.

. . . .

2. On being accepted as a member of the Union, men shall pay 1s. and women 6d., save where women receive the same wages as

men, when Districts are empowered to receive women under the same conditions as men. These payments include Rule Book, Card of Membership, which shall be uniform throughout the Union, and first week's contribution. The weekly contributions of men shall be 6d. and women 3d.

3. Youths may be accepted as members of the Union on the same terms as women.

45. Finance.

CONTRIBUTION RULE OF THE LONDON SOCIETY OF COMPOSITORS, 1925.

V.—Admission and Subscription.

1. Every compositor working as a journeyman, overseer, store-keeper, reader, or in any other capacity in a fair house, or who may hereafter prove his right so to work, either by indenture or other satisfactory evidence, or by a clear card of membership from a recognised Society, shall be eligible as a member. The rate of subscription shall be as follows :—Members in the General trade, 4s. 6d. per week ; members in the News Department, members employed on Sunday newspapers, members fully employed on the Periodical Scale, and all machine operators, 4s. 9d. per week—of which sums 3s. 6d. per week shall be set apart to meet Superannuation claims. Members of 60 years of age and upwards, who by reason of age or infirmity are unable to earn 20s. per week, shall pay 3d. per week. Any member under 60 years of age who shall satisfy the Committee that he is unable by reason of chronic infirmity to earn 20s. per week, shall likewise pay the sum of 3d. per week ; but in no case shall a member of less than ten consecutive years' membership be entitled to claim under this rule. Unemployed members shall pay 1s. per week, inclusive of any levies ; to be entitled to such reduction they must sign the Call Book as laid down in Rule XLV. Members holding removal cards shall pay 3s. 9d. per week ; out-of-trade members, 4s. per week ; superannuated members on the 1923 scheme 6d., on the old scheme 1d. ; sick members 1d. per week.

2. Every member shall pay, in addition to his weekly subscription, a tax of 3d. upon each hour of overtime worked. The revenue from such tax shall be applied solely to the purposes of the Superannuation Account.

3. Whenever the income of the Superannuation Account fal's below the amount required to meet the current liabilities of the Superannuation benefit, the Committee may take a ballot of the members upon the question of raising the subscription by such sum as shall be deemed sufficient to meet the liability for the ensuing three years or any shorter period, and the extra subscription shall be set off to the credit of the Superannuation Account.

4. Every member shall be furnished with a printed card of membership, on which shall be written his name, number, and date of entry, which card shall be renewable annually to those who are clear upon the Society's books at the close of the year, or failing that, then at such subsequent period as the card may be applied for, in order that all members may be absolutely clear on the books once in each year.

. . . .

46. Finance.

RULES OF DURHAM MINERS' ASSOCIATION, 1925.

General Funds.

35.—The General Funds of this Association shall at no time be reduced below ten thousand pounds. Should at any time the liabilities reduce the funds to a sum verging on this amount, the Committee shall lay the same before the Lodges, for the purpose of all representatives being sent to the ensuing Council meeting prepared to say whether or not a levy shall be laid on the members, or whether the claims in any particular, or all the benefits, shall be reduced until the funds of the Association are sufficiently augmented, so as to allow full benefits in accordance with the rules ; and the Council at all such times shall have power to reduce the allowances or levy the members, as the case may be.

47. Trade Union Funds—Audit, etc.

TRADE UNION ACT, 1871 ; 34 & 35 Vict., ch. 31.

11.—Every treasurer or other officer of a trade union registered under this Act, at such times as by the rules of such trade union he should render such account as herein-after mentioned, or upon being required so to do, shall render to the trustees of the trade union, or to the members of such trade union, at a meeting of the trade union, a just and true account of all moneys received and paid by him since he last rendered the like account, and of the balance then remaining in his hands, and of all bonds or securities of such trade union, which account the said trustees shall cause to be audited by some fit and proper person or persons by them to be appointed ; and such treasurer, if thereunto required, upon the said account being audited, shall forthwith hand over to the said trustees the balance which on such audit appears to be due from him, and shall also, if required, hand over to such trustees all securities and effects, books, papers, and property of the said trade union in his hands or custody ; and if he fail to do so the trustees of the said trade union may sue such treasurer in any competent court for the balance appearing to have been due from him upon the account last rendered by him, and for all the moneys since received by him on account of the said trade union, and for the securities and effects, books, papers, and property in his hands or custody, leaving him to set off in such action the sums, if any, which he may have since paid on account of the said trade union ; and in such action the said trustees shall be entitled to recover their full costs of suit, to be taxed as between attorney and client.

12.—If any officer, member, or other person being or representing himself to be a member of a trade union registered under this Act, or the nominee, executor, administrator, or assignee of a member thereof, or any person whatsoever, by false representation or imposition obtain possession of any moneys, securities, books, papers, or other effects of such trade union, or, having the same in his possession, wilfully withhold or fraudulently misapply the same, or wilfully apply any part of the same to purposes other than those expressed or directed in the rules of such trade union, or any part thereof, the court of summary jurisdiction for the place in which the registered office of the trade union is situate upon a complaint made by any person on behalf of such trade union, or by the registrar, or in Scotland at the instance of the procurator fiscal of the court to which such complaint is competently made, or of the trade union, with his concurrence, may, by summary order, order such officer, member, or other person to deliver up all such moneys, securities, books, papers, or other effects to the trade union, or to repay the amount of money applied improperly, and to pay, if the court think fit, a further sum of money not exceeding twenty pounds, together with costs not exceeding twenty shillings ; and, in default of such delivery of effects, or repayment of such amount of money, or payment of such penalty and costs aforesaid, the said court may order the said person so convicted to be imprisoned, with or without hard labour, for any time not exceeding three months : Provided, that nothing herein contained shall prevent the said trade union, or in Scotland Her Majesty's Advocate, from proceeding by indictment against the said party ; provided also, that no person shall be proceeded against by indictment if a conviction shall have been previously obtained for the same offence under the provisions of this Act.

48. Trustees of Trade Unions.[1]

RULES OF THE NAT. UNION OF DISTRIBUTIVE AND ALLIED WORKERS, 1926.

13.—Trustees.

SECTION 1.—Three members of the Union shall act as trustees. They shall be elected by an Annual or Special Delegate Meeting, and hold office during the will and pleasure of the Union as expressed by the majority of the delegates at an Annual or Special Delegate Meeting.   They shall remain fully qualified members of the Union, and ceasing to be such shall cease to hold the office of trustee.

SECTION 2.—In case of a vacancy occurring, by resignation or otherwise, the Executive Council shall have power to elect another trustee, such trustee to act only until the next delegate meeting.

SECTION 3.—The trustees shall have vested in them all real and personal estate whatsoever belonging to the Union, for the use and benefit of the Union and members thereof, and upon the death or removal of any of such trustees, the real and personal estate so vested in them shall vest in the succeeding trustee or trustees of the Union, without any conveyance or assignment being necessary.

SECTION 4.—The trustees shall, from time to time, as required, and upon the authority of a resolution of the Executive Council, conveyed to them in writing (and which shall be a complete discharge from all liability on the part of the trustees on compliance therewith) :—

(*a*) Invest, re-invest, and vary the investment of the funds of the Union, as may be resolved upon by the Executive Council, in such securities as may be deemed desirable.

(*b*) Pay over to the Executive Council, or to such persons as they may appoint, such sums as may be required for the claims and expenses of the Union from the funds applicable thereto.

SECTION 5.—No trustee shall be liable to make good any deficiency which may arise or happen in the funds, but shall be liable only for those moneys or securities actually received by him.

[1] See also Document 219.

49. Trade Union Finance.

COMMENTS OF CHIEF REGISTRAR ON MANAGEMENT EXPENSES.

Report of Chief Registrar of Friendly Societies on Trade Unions, for
1920.   P. 8.

Management and Other Expenses.

In addition to the ordinary expenses of management, this heading
includes expenditure on organisation and propaganda, checkweighmen's wages (in miners' unions), delegates' expenses, and
expenditure connected with Arbitration and Conciliation Boards
and Industrial Councils. Considerable discussion has recently
taken place upon the alleged extravagant expenditure of Trade
Unions on management. It should be explained that the objects
for which unions are formed include the organisation of the trades as
a whole, and the consideration by means of delegates at conferences
of all matters affecting the trade.   Consequently a large proportion
of the contributions is absorbed in working expenses.   Comparison
of the working expenses of unions is difficult, because of the varying
nature and number of the benefits (apart from trade organisation)
which are assured to members.   For example, in the metals, etc.,
group the average contribution is 1s. 1d. weekly, while in the
agricultural group it is only 2d., but in the former unemployment,
death, superannuation, and other benefits are assured.   These
additional benefits do not involve urgent matters, which must be
dealt with by conferences, and so do not add proportionately to the
expenses of management and organisation.   Thus, in the metals
group, the ratio of management and other expenses to contributions is
only 29 per cent., whilst in the agricultural group the figure is
61 per cent.

Some unions effect no assurances, and in their case the whole of
the income is devoted to management and organisation.   Employers'
associations are in the same position.   Extravagance could not be
charged against them merely because they expend more than 70 per
cent. of their contributions on management and organisation expenses.

In addition, the wide variety of items other than actual expenditure
on management included under the heading (see above) is frequently
overlooked.   Complete details are not available, but a partial
analysis has been made of unions in which the expenditure aggregated
more than £2,000,000, or nearly half the total figure, and it was
found that 41 per cent. was expended in salaries and wages, 5 per

cent. in rent, rates and taxes, and 17 per cent. in stationery, printing, postage, etc.—the three principal items comprised in management expenses. Of other items the heaviest was delegates' fees and travelling expenses—16 per cent.—while legal expenses accounted for 3 per cent., and other miscellaneous expenditure for the remaining 18 per cent.

A comparison is frequently made of the expenditure as incurred before and after the war. In making comparison, account should, of course, be taken of the very great increase in membership. For example, the aggregate expenditure under this heading was nearly four times as much in 1920 as in 1913, but the expenditure per member over the same period showed an increase of only 63 per cent.

50. Types of Trade Union Organisation.

REPORT BY W. M. CITRINE ON TRADE UNION ORGANISATION.
T.U.C. Ann. Rep., 1925. P. 231.

Class or General Unionism.

The underlying principle of this type of organisation is that all workers, irrespective of grade, craft, or occupation, would be in one all-embracing Union. They would sink their craft and sectional prejudices and would aim at a single standard of conditions for all who toil. . . .

Such a Union would have its central executive endowed with executive power corresponding to that of our national centralised Trade Unions. The executive would be representative of the various industrial groups in which the members were engaged. The work of the Union would be departmentalised to conform to those industries, and would be staffed by specialists with a knowledge of the work of their members. In its local or geographical relations, the One Big Union would have its branches in the various areas, each of which would be departmentalised in a similar manner to the national executive. Reaching down from the branches there would be a system of shop stewards representing each of the different types of workers, and these would in turn be organised into workshop committees. . . .

Industrial Unionism.

The general theoretical conception which finds the most ready acceptance is the dividing of the workers into a series of vertical divisions, each representing an industry. There are many conceptions as to what constitutes an industry, and, without a fairly clear definition, any attempt at grouping would result in chaos. The idea of industrial unionism is that of one central organisation directed by a national executive, and organising and controlling the whole of the workers engaged in the processes with which the industry is concerned. It is claimed that the maximum fighting power of the workers could be consolidated in this way. The local organisation of the industrial Union would be its area committee, supplemented by workshop committees. . . . By proper departmentalisation and vertical groupings to suit the sectional needs effective representation could be given to the specialised interests of crafts. . . .

Occupational Unionism.

The conception behind both this type of Unionism and Industrial Unionism is that the control of such large masses of workers places an enormous economic resource in the hands of the Union. It is reasoned that the workers are employed for the production of profits. The object of the Union must therefore be to have the power to withdraw the whole of the labour employed by a given group of employers, so that, not only is profit making prevented, but actual losses, due to the depreciation of capital in the form of plant and machinery and administrative charges, are inflicted to a maximum on the employers. It follows, if this reasoning is accurate, that to make the power of the Union fully felt in conflict with the employers, the Union must have control over the whole of the workers employed by those employers. . . .

Occupational Unionism is distinct from Industrial Unionism in the sense that its divisions traverse horizontally across the field of workers and not vertically, as in the case of Industrial Unionism. . . .

Craft Unionism.

Where workers in a given trade, irrespective of the form of the occupation or industry in which they are employed, are grouped in accordance with their craft identity. . . .

The main distinction between Craft Unionism and the other types . . . is that the crafts are composed solely of skilled workers. There are some exceptions to this rule, and there has been a tendency among certain of the Craft Unions to enrol unskilled and semi-skilled workers. . . .

Federal Unionism.

There are already in existence approximately 90 Federations in the various British industries, and the strength of these varies to a considerable degree. . . . The principal objection to federations is that the form of association is too loose, in so far as it leaves individual Unions with the power to secede if an occasion arises when they disagree profoundly with any action that has or has not been taken by the parent Federation. This is not true of all Federations. . . . Federation need not necessarily be loose at all. . . . Confederation is a development of Federal Unionism. . . . The essential point of the Confederation principle . . . is the creation of a highly centralised Confederation of Unions, to which are transferred practically all the normal industrial negotiating functions.

51. The Case for Industrial Unionism.

From *Self-Government in Industry*, by G. D. H. COLE, 1919,
ch. iii.

There are two main arguments, either in itself sufficient, in favour of Industrial Unionism. But both these arguments hold good only on an initial assumption.

The first argument is that Industrial Unionism provides the stronger force to use against the capitalist. Advocates of Industrial Unionism always point out that against the mass formation of Capitalism a mass formation of Labour is needed, that Craft Unionism has not the strength to combat the vast aggregations of Capital, that it leads essentially to dissension in the workers' ranks, that it enables the employer to play off one set of workers against another, and so to strengthen the capitalist organisation of industry. These arguments are overwhelming in force if, but only if, Trade Unionism is regarded as a class-movement based upon the class-struggle.

If it is not, may not the skilled worker be right to fear alliance with the man further down, and may he not see more hope for himself in holding the unskilled worker under, and thereby preserving his own monopoly of labour ? May he not be right, I mean, if, and only if, there is no class-struggle ? . . .

We must base our Trade Union organisation firmly upon the class-struggle ; we must so organise as to promote the unity of the whole working class. Does not that mean that we must move constantly in the direction of Industrial Unionism? The first argument in favour of Industrial Unionism, then, is this. It alone is consistent with the class struggle; it alone is true to the principle of democracy and fraternity.

The second argument is no less fundamental, and it again rests on an assumption. If the purpose of Trade Unionism is merely protective, if it exists only to maintain or improve the conditions of employment within the wage-system, then there is no case for one form of organisation rather than another. We can decide as expediency may suggest. But if the purpose of Trade Unionsim is a bigger and a finer thing than the mere protection of the material interests of its members; if, in fact, Trade Unionists have set before themselves the positive aim of winning, through their Unions, self-government in industry, there can be no doubt about the right structure.

Clearly, Craft Unions, based on process and not on product, cannot make any effective claim to control industry. Only an Industrial Union, embracing the whole personnel of an industry, can assume control over that industry. . . .

If, then, the workers are to demand control from the State or from the employers, they must build up an organisation capable of assuming control. Clearly, such a body must be 'industrial' in structure. All workers in or about mines must be in the Miners' Union, the whole personnel of the cotton mills must be in the Union of the Cotton Industry. A body consisting of clerks or mechanics or labourers drawn from a number of different industries can never demand or assume control of industry. It can secure recognition, but not control. A Postal Workers' Union or a Railway Union, on the other hand, can both demand and secure producers' control. . . .

The structure of Trade Unionism, then, must be industrial, if it is either to serve its purpose of fighting Capitalism, or to take on its newer and higher function of control. Out of Craft Unionism, however widely its net is spread, can come only bureaucracy tempered by recognition: Industrial Unionism will not only serve as an instrument in the war against the wage-system, but will also prepare the workers, while they are engaged in the struggle, for the period of direct industrial control which awaits them at its end.

52. Industrial Unionism.

From *Industrial Unionism*, published by the BUILDING WORKERS'
INDUSTRIAL UNION, 1914-15.

(Cited by Postgate, *The Builders' History*, 1923, p. 403.)

Industrial Unions must take the place of Trade Unions and be
imbued with the virile determination that they are associations of
workers for overpowering the octopus of capitalism with its attendant
evil, the wage system, and securing the complete control of industry
in the interests of the whole community.   This is the vital difference
to all other isms. . . .

To sum up.

Industrial Unionism means :

(*a*) The organisation of every worker (manual and brain),
corresponding to the industries in which they are employed, thus :

Agricultural Workers' Industrial Union ; Building Workers'
Industrial Union ;   Mining Workers' Industrial Union ;
Transport Workers' Industrial Union, etc., etc.

(*b*) That the Industrial Union shall embrace all workers
actually employed in that industry, regardless of grade, craft,
creed, politics, or sex.

(*c*) That internal organisation shall be of such a character as to
allow complete autonomy for the various Branches, crafts, and
grades to discuss and promote the advance of their particular
interests, consistent with the general policy and effectiveness of the
whole organisation.

(*d*) The Industrial Unions shall be linked up, nationally and
internationally, in a similar way in which the ' triple alliance ' of
Miners, Railway Workers, and Transport Workers are now
linked up, with the avowed object of

(*e*) Securing control of industry, and the abolition of the wages
system.

Society is divided into two classes, the working class and the
employing class—the exploiters and the exploited.   There can be
no peace among the two classes while the employing class own and
control all the means of life, the State, press, and platform . . . The
mistake of the Political Socialist is in the forgetting that the political
government is run in the interests of the capitalist class. . . . The
State is capitalistic in its deepest essence.

53. The Case against Industrial Unionism.

From an article by MR. SIDNEY WEBB, in the *Labour Magazine*, 1923-24,
p. 220.

The producer must regard himself simultaneously as (1) a member
of his craft or specialised vocation, both in his own locality and
throughout the kingdom ; (2) a member alongside workers of other
crafts or vocations of his workshop or factory, mine, or farm ; (3) a
member of the particular capitalist establishment or public service
in which he is engaged ; (4) a member of the industry throughout
the kingdom in which, along with workers in other crafts or vocations, in other establishments or services, in all sorts of localities,
he is co-operating to produce for the community a specific
product.

I doubt whether all these groupings can be united in any one
organisation.   Yet all are necessary to the worker as such.

But some practical solution must be found.   I should be inclined
to look in the direction of (*a*) each Trade Union frankly and cordially recognising the necessity of its members joining with members
of other unions in distinct workshop and establishment organisations,
whether these take the form of shop stewards, shop committees,
canteen committees, works committees, Whitley Councils, or otherwise, with strictly limited functions ; (*b*) each Trade Union conceding
a large measure of autonomy to sectional organisations among its
own members, strictly limited to the specific and peculiar circumstances of separate crafts or vocations ; (*c*) each Trade Union
cordially accepting the necessity of its local branches belonging to
and energetically taking part in the local Trades Councils and
Labour Parties—I should add also the local consumers' co-operative
societies.

If these three principles were accepted and eagerly acted upon by
national executives and delegate conferences, Trade Union dis-
integration might be averted, and further growth promoted.

On the other side, there might well be a ' double card ' arrangement.   The Trade Union might recognise that its members will
frequently be working in establishments, industries, or services with
the affairs of which that Trade Union is not primarily concerned.
There are matters in which the establishment, industry, or service
must act as a whole, irrespective of craft or sectional interests elsewhere.   We should seek to facilitate fluidity so that Trade Unionists

can pass without friction from one establishment, industry, or service to another.

Whether or not I am correctly forecasting the lines of a solution, I venture to emphasise the importance to the Trade Union world of an early decision in the matter. It would be calamitous for British Trade Unionism to fail—essentially through lack of thought and refusal to take counsel together—to bring its organisation up to the level of efficiency of that of the employers. To let British Trade Unionism disintegrate as that of France has done, so that the aims of the past half century are wrested from the workers' grasp, merely because we cannot agree as to how the various producers should be organised would be a disgrace.

And we may incur that disgrace by uncertainty of aim and conflict of purpose. I confess that it seems to me more than ridiculous still further to complicate the problem by trying to devise a form of organisation which will, at one and the same time, serve for the necessary and perpetual function of maintaining and improving the standard of life of the worker, and preventing encroachments on his effective freedom, and also serve as the hypothetical machinery for the future management and control of industry, as the capitalist employer is gradually and increasingly superseded in one service after another by the Socialist commonwealth.

The pursuit of this will-of-the-wisp seems to me to rest on a fallacy from which it is high time that we rid ourselves. The worker or producer has a large part to play in the management and control of the work by which he lives; but he is never going, *as worker or producer*, to *be* that management and control, either individually or jointly. The worker himself would never allow it *in the case of all the other workers, whose products he consumes or whose services he enjoys*. It is, and must be, the community of citizens and consumers, whether in Co-operative Society, Municipality or State, that decides what it wishes to have produced, and when and where, of what kind and quality, and in what quantity. What the producer as producer is concerned with is how he pursues the craft or vocation for which he has deliberately fitted himself, the environment and conditions in which his service to the community is rendered and his working hours are spent, and the improvements and developments which, by taking thought, he can bring to that service.

54. Organisation of Trade Unions.

RECOMMENDATIONS OF THE GENERAL COUNCIL OF THE T.U.C.
ADOPTED BY THE EDINBURGH CONGRESS, 1927.

T.U.C. Annual Report, 1927, p. 99.

ORGANISATION BY INDUSTRY.

At the Hull Congress in 1924 the General Council was instructed to examine the problem of Organisation by Industry, and present a report thereon. Interim reports on the question were submitted to the Scarborough and Bournemouth Congresses, and now the following completed report is submitted. In order that a comprehensive statement may be made it is necessary to incorporate here much of the substance of the interim reports referred to.

Terms of Reference.

The resolution in question, which is of a composite character, and which was drafted from seven separate resolutions and amendments, is as follows :

' This Congress declares—

(*a*) That the time has arrived when the number of Trade Unions should be reduced to an absolute minimum ;

(*b*) That the aim should be as far as possible organisation by industry, with every worker a member of the appropriate organisation ;

(*c*) That it is essential that a united front be formed for improving the standard of life of the workers ;

(*d*) And accordingly instructs the General Council to draw up—

(1) A scheme for organisation by industry, and

(2) A scheme which may secure unity of action without the definite merging of existing unions, by a scientific linking up of same to present a united front.'

.   .   .   .

Interpretation of the Resolution.

Probably no subject has furnished greater opportunities for dogmatism as to the precise form which Trade Union development should take than the recurrent question of industrial organisation, and the Organisation Committee had to apply themselves to a resolution which, whatever the intention of its framers may have been, was ambiguous in phraseology.

T.U.D.   I

It is interesting to note that the resolution was moved by the Miners' Federation and seconded by the A.S.L.E. & F. Quite clearly it is a compromise in wording rather than a compromise in the widely divergent policies of organisation of these two bodies.

The essential points contained in the resolution appear to be

1. A demand for a reduction in the number of unions.
2. Some form of organisation by industry.
3. The attainment of a united front amongst the unions concerned.

The General Council were faced with the task of giving practical expression to the general desire for a more perfect and uniform system of Trade Union organisation, and in the memorandum submitted in 1925 an effort was made to examine the implications of the resolution and the difficulties which stood in the way of their realisation because of the complexities of present-day Trade Union structure.

The Hull resolution, although passed by 2,503,000 votes to 1,428,000, could not be taken as evidence on the part of its supporters of a willingness to adopt without demur any form of organisation which the General Council might devise. The various conceptions of Trade Union organisation have each their respective adherents amongst the unions affiliated to Congress. This was evidenced at the Scarborough Congress by the voting upon a resolution seeking to pledge the General Council to continue its work of amalgamation of existing unions with the ' one big union ' as the ultimate goal. This resolution was defeated by 2,138,000 to 1,787,000. The conception of Trade Union organisation envisaged in this resolution may not necessarily be at variance with the Hull resolution, but the discussion undoubtedly showed that it was regarded by its advocates as an alternative form of organisation.

Evidence of Affiliated Unions.

The General Council appreciated from the commencement the essential need for a thorough examination of the problem, realising that a hastily devised and impractical scheme would be foredoomed to failure. The Council reported to the Scarborough Congress that in its considered judgement, if anything concrete were to be evolved from the Hull resolution, it would be necessary for the General Council to make a thorough investigation into the whole subject of Trade Union organisation. Realising the formidable nature of the task it has proceeded as expeditiously as circumstances have allowed to examine closely the numerous aspects of the problem.

Information has been sought from the unions by a questionnaire to which written replies were requested, whilst verbal evidence has been taken from the principal unions in the following groups : Mining, railways, transport (other than railways), building, engineering, metal trades and general workers.   A vast amount of reliable data has also been collected by the Research Department from rules, reports, and other documents published periodically by affiliated unions.

The investigation has amply justified the view of the General Council, previously expressed, that by such a process alone could the subject be adequately explored.   The ramifications of Trade Union organisation and the differences in conception as to the best form of structure, as indicated by the witnesses and by the information collected, are such that no body of Trade Unionists could have fully appreciated without such investigation.

It was hoped to complete the investigation at a much earlier date, but the disturbed industrial situation has delayed the progress of the work.   Difficulty has also been experienced in obtaining adequate written replies to the questionnaire.   The total number of unions which have sent in any form of reply, other than those cases where verbal evidence has been tendered, is 94 out of 150 to whom the questionnaire was sent.

.   .   .   .

Structure and Lines of Demarcation of Industry.

An examination of the various industries reveals that they are catered for by various types of unions, which may be divided into five general classes :

1. CRAFT organisations ;   2. INDUSTRIAL organisations ;   3. OCCUPATIONAL organisations ;   4. EMPLOYMENTAL organisations ; 5. GENERAL WORKERS' organisations.

Each class of organisation views the demarcation lines of industry from its own standpoint.   Some craft organisations state they are in favour of organisation by industry, the reason for this being that they confine the term ' industry ' to their particular craft.

The divergence of opinion in regard to the boundaries of industry will be realised by the varying contentions as to what determines the boundaries.

The three principal determining factors which are advanced are :
1. The commodity produced or the service rendered.
2. The tool operated.
3. The employer or group of employers.

Those contending that the commodity determines the boundary of industry would argue that all those engaged in the production of cotton materials are in one industry, those producing woollen and worsted materials in another.   If, however, the tool is to be the determining factor the engineers and maintenance men in both these industries might claim that they belonged to the engineering industry and not to either the cotton or the woollen industry.   In the same way, the dyeing and finishing of both classes of goods might be regarded as an industry, and, whilst this contention is not put forward by the unions engaged in dyeing and finishing, in actual practice organisation takes place irrespective of the fact as to whether the commodity dyed is cotton or woollen.

The multiplicity of undertakings controlled by certain companies would lead to chaos were an attempt made generally to apply the conception that the *employer* should determine the boundary of industry, but in the case where this view is most strongly represented there happens to be a more clear cut division than exists in many instances which might be quoted.   The N.U.R. are the strongest adherents to this view, and assert that the railway ' industry ' should not be confined to the actual service of railway transport, but that the whole of the undertakings owned and controlled by the railway companies should be included in the ' industry.'   This contention, however, is strongly contested by craft unions, and no more notable instance can be recorded than that afforded by the railway shops, where an intense struggle has existed between the N.U.R. and the craft unions, and where only recently has it been possible to achieve some measure of agreement.

Were the claim to be pressed in regard to, say, railway printing establishments, the position would probably be strongly contested by the printing unions, whilst if the railway companies were to acquire and control coal mines it is not likely that the Miners' Federation would agree to the railway unions organising the miners employed therein.

GENERAL WORKERS' ORGANISATIONS.—Cutting across the above three methods of industrial demarcation is the view held by the organisations catering for general workers.   In their case no boundaries of industry are recognised.   With nearly one-fifth of the organised workers belonging to these organisations, and the opposition which would in all probability be encountered by adopting one of the other various points of view, it would be useless to recommend any arbitrary lines of demarcation in industry for purposes of organisation. A further obstacle presents itself. Assuming it were possible to define the boundaries of industry there would still remain the difficulty of persuading the majority of unions to conform to these boundaries.

It is unlikely that any union with large groups of members in each of the several industries will countenance a proposal that they should part with the majority of their members, or even relinquish the right of assisting in determining their wages and conditions.

Assuming that a certain union had a membership as follows :

20,000 members in the building trade.
10,000   ,,   ,,   shipbuilding trade,
10,000   ,,   ,,   engineering trade,
 5,000   ,,   ,,   railway shops,
 5,000   ,,   divided amongst five other minor industries,

were that union to be informed of a recommendation that, in place of the present form of organisation, a system of organisation by industry should be introduced under which there was to be one union for the building trade, one for the shipbuilding, one for engineering, and so on, it is likely that such a union would decline to accept the proposal, one of their principal arguments being that their members may be employed in one industry to-day and in another to-morrow.

SCIENCE AND INDUSTRY.—In addition to the difficulties which have been pointed out in connection with the demarcation of industrial boundaries, there must be added the impetus which science is giving to industrial development. That which is a by-product to-day may become a staple industry in a comparatively short space of time. Inventions in connection with the supply of cheap electrical current and the low temperature carbonisation of coal are certain to become commercial propositions in the near future. The continued evolution in machine production will tend further to complicate the classification of industries.

General Schemes Impracticable.

After very careful consideration of the problem, the General Council has been forced to the conclusion that as it is impossible to define any fixed boundaries of industry, it is impracticable to formulate a scheme of 'organisation by industry,' that can be made applicable to all industries.

Dealing with the second part of the Hull resolution, which calls for a scheme of scientific linking without definite merging, the Council has been compelled to recognise the practical difficulties, and though it has tried to solve the problem and has attempted to draft a scheme on the basis of present-day Trade Union organisation in industry, it has been found impossible to make any definite plan, as the General Council has not been empowered to alter the scope of its affiliated unions, which have divergent policies in regard to organisation.

Therefore, the General Council has in this case also come to the conclusion that no general scheme is practicable, though it may be possible for groups of unions which have related industrial interests, and desire closer working, to prepare their own scheme in the light of their own structural, administrative, and industrial circumstances.

Resolutions may be passed, and theoretical contentions advanced, but the fact remains that Trade Union organisation has assumed complex forms which are the growth of generations. Under these circumstances Trade Union organisation will have to be gradually remoulded and its present form *adapted*, rather than *transformed*, to meet the new conditions. *This adaptation is possible only in so far as individual unions express their desire to co-operate or merge with kindred organisations in order to meet the new conditions in the most effective manner.*

55. Trade Unions—Amalgamation.

Trade Union (Amalgamation) Act, 1917; 7 & 8 Geo. V, ch. 24.

1.—(1) Any two or more trade unions may become amalgamated together as one trade union if in the case of each or every such trade union, on a ballot being taken, the votes of at least fifty per cent. of the members entitled to vote thereat are recorded, and of the votes recorded those in favour of the proposal exceed by twenty per cent. or more the votes against the proposal; and, accordingly, section twelve of the Trade Union Act Amendment Act, 1876, shall have effect as if for the words ' by the consent of not less than two thirds of the members of each or every such trade union ' there were substituted the words ' if in the case of each or every such trade union, on a ballot being taken, the votes of at least fifty per cent. of the members entitled to vote thereat are recorded, and of the votes recorded those in favour of the proposal exceed by twenty per cent. or more the votes against the proposal.'

(2) For removing doubts it is hereby declared that the said section twelve applies to the amalgamation of one or more registered trade unions with one or more unregistered trade unions.

56. Amalgamation of Unions.

From REPORT OF THE GENERAL COUNCIL ADOPTED BY THE TRADES UNION CONGRESS, 1927.

T.U.C. Ann. Report, 1927, p. 107 ff.

Obstacles to Amalgamation.

The experience derived from these and other negotiations over a lengthy period of years reveals many difficulties which demonstrate the futility of trying to approach amalgamation except with whole-hearted co-operation from the participating unions.

The General Council agrees that in the majority of cases the most effective method of improving organisation would be by means of amalgamation, but would point out that however desirous it may be to achieve amalgamation amongst its constituent organisations, the real driving force must come from the unions themselves, and no efforts which the Councils may make can accomplish its object if they are met in a reluctant spirit. It is not sufficient for unions to give general acquiescence to the principle of amalgamation and then to break down on the practical details. Nor can any scheme which tends wholly to submerge the identity of important groups of members hope to afford a solution. Where amalgamation has been successful, it has generally been based upon a recognition of the desire for the preservation of the trade identity of various groups of workers, and has created as little change as possible in the powers of self-government in relation to trade matters and benefits.

The principal difficulties which arise in connection with amalgamation may be outlined as follows :

(*a*) LOSS OF TRADE IDENTITY.—The persistent fear of unions upon entering amalgamation negotiations that the membership may be merely absorbed. They fear loss of trade identity, and that adequate representation on the new executive and other bodies, together with adequate functioning facilities, will not be afforded to their particular section or craft. In some cases the lesser unions apprehend that they might not be able to recruit and retain their people in a big general organisation so well as they have done hitherto in their separate societies.

(*b*) CONTRIBUTIONS AND BENEFITS.—The marked difference between the rates of contributions and benefits of kindred unions.

(*c*) FUNDS.—The disinclination of a union to pool its resources with unions of a weaker financial position.

(*d*) POLICY.—Conflicting policy in organisation, in wage policy and in general affairs.

(*e*) OFFICIALS.—The difficulty in connection with placing officials.

Despite these difficulties many notable fusions have taken place within recent years, and there exists to-day a tendency to make strong and consolidated unions.

The General Council therefore wishes to submit certain recommendations for minimising the effect of the principal obstacles which bar the way to more numerous amalgamations, and also in regard to the presentation of amalgamation proposals to the members.

Loss of Trade Identity.

Special provision should be made, where definite craft and occupational interests arise, for the preservation of certain craft or occupational autonomy. In recent years large organisations have found the necessity for grouping together workers with common interests, allowing them to elect a National Committee, and, in addition, permanent officers have been attached to the groups to attend solely to their requirements. In some cases, local and district committees have been set up by the groups, for the consideration of their own peculiar problems. At least part of the executive is elected on a craft or occupational basis. By these means the interests of certain classes of workers have not been submerged and a measure of autonomy has given them responsibility and preservation of identity which is necessary to induce certain sections of workers to link up with a larger organisation.

The General Council would, however, advise that regulations governing working conditions in the respective trades should be distinct from the rules and constitution of the organisation and should be laid down rather as bye-laws for the various sections or trades which may be amalgamated.

Contributions and Benefits on Amalgamation.

A wide divergence in the rates of contributions and benefits may create a critical position in negotiations, but it has been found practicable by slight adjustments to formulate scales of sufficient variety to include all members.   In the event of disagreement on a standard scale of contributions and benefits, it might be possible to confine a standard scale to new entrants and to present members who may elect to join that scale.

This matter is further dealt with in pars. 44, 45, 46.[1]

Officers.

Each union desires that its officers shall lose neither status nor security.   Under these circumstances, it is advisable that provision should be made for security of tenure or for compensation as an alternative.   Arrangements on this principle are always made nowadays where publicly owned concerns are being amalgamated, as in the cases of the London Water Board, the Port of London Authority, the grouping of railways, and the recent merging of electricity undertakings.

Placing of Amalgamation Proposals before Membership.

Instances are so numerous where unions have taken ballots and have not obtained the necessary 50 per cent. vote required by law that the General Council would urge that the presentation of any amalgamation scheme should not be confined to the explanation possible on a ballot paper.

The executives concerned should perfect their own scheme until each is prepared to recommend acceptance, when it would be possible for an intensive campaign to be inaugurated to place before meetings of members the implications of the proposals with a definite recommendation for acceptance.

General Council Assistance.

The General Council is of opinion that on account of the varying conditions which exist, it is impossible to formulate any one scheme of amalgamation which could be made applicable to all groups of unions.   Furthermore, it is felt that any attempt to force a specified system of grouping and to take the initiative in that direction would lead to the reverse of the effect desired.

[1] See Document 159.

Notwithstanding the difficulties described, much of the evidence which has been submitted shows that there is an inherent desire to strengthen the Trade Union Movement, and to this end the General Council will at all times be pleased to render every assistance within its power, by acting as the convener of joint conferences, by appointing a chairman to preside during the subsequent joint negotiations, or even to the extent of drawing up the basis of a scheme to meet the requirements of related unions, in any given case.

Joint Working.

Pending amalgamation, it may be necessary in certain cases to adopt an intermediate stage of closer association by means of joint working arrangements, and the General Council would therefore suggest that concentration upon certain points would facilitate greater co-ordination in the Trade Union Movement. In this connection it feels that greater progress may be made by the adjustment of certain difficulties common to all unions rather than by discussing questions of basic principle, upon which the unions themselves are at variance. It must, of course, be realised that the nature of the joint working arrangements, as well as those of amalgamation, are largely determined by the structure of Trade Union organisation within the groups of trades and occupations concerned.

EMPLOYERS' METHODS.—It is interesting to examine the methods by which the employers consolidate their forces. Although they experience the same difficulties in defining the boundaries of industry as individual units they have in many cases come to arrangements for joint working between firms with related interests. Their agreements on questions of mutual interest have prevented cut-throat competition and eradicated many difficulties they experienced when working without contact.

Undoubtedly to-day many Trade Unions are in competition, and many grades of workers with similar interests have no common channel of approach on questions of wages and working conditions. The possibility of joint working arrangements should, therefore, be considered by unions catering for similar classes of workers, with a view to a common approach being made to employers on questions of wages and working conditions. In addition, this joint working should specifically provide for the elimination of competition for membership.

In this connection it should be mentioned that the varying rates of contributions and benefits tend to create a form of competition between unions. The anomalous position often arises where members of different unions engaged in the same industrial dispute are in receipt of varying rates of dispute pay. In a campaign for new members it is possible that members may join the union with the smallest contributions without having regard to whether the union is the most suitable for the safeguarding of their interests. Contributions and benefits clearly form a subject upon which some common arrangements might be established. This important question is further dealt with in pars. 44, 45, 46.[1]

Methods of Approach.

The chief object of joint working should be in relation to distinct trade purposes, and the General Council is of opinion that, pending amalgamation, the closest possible association must at all times be sought by unions with common wage and industrial interests, based upon the following general principles :

1. A grouping of craft and occupational interests in order to afford adequate expression for all sections of workers concerned.

2. The establishment of a joint body with power to organise united action on industrial matters, without interfering with the autonomy of associated bodies on administrative and other matters peculiar to their own organisations.

3. The provision of financial support in connection with purely trade benefits by means of a common fund contributed by organisations working jointly on trade questions.

4. The recognition of the card of any associated organisation by the other organisation parties to a joint working agreement.

5. The possibility of establishing a greater measure of uniformity in trade contributions and benefits.

. . . .

In connection with the whole question of amalgamation and joint working the General Council recommends that each affiliated union should consider its attitude towards greater consolidation and declare to the General Council in writing :

1. Whether it is prepared to participate in amalgamation negotiations with other unions.

2. The extent to which it is prepared to agree to joint working arrangements with other unions.

3. With which unions, in its opinion, is there the greatest possibility of progress being made in negotiations on either or both of the above questions.

[1] See Document 159.

57. Confederation Scheme of Amalgamation.

BRITISH IRON, STEEL AND KINDRED TRADES ASSOCIATION, 1917.

Clause 1.—Confederation and Central Organisation.

(i) A confederation shall be formed of trade unions in the iron and steel industry, and shall consist of a central organisation to be formed under this agreement (hereinafter called ' the scheme ') and of the societies signatory to this scheme.

(ii) A central organisation shall be formed and called 'The British Iron, Steel and Kindred Trades Association' (hereinafter called "the new association") to be governed and administered in accordance with a code of rules registered under the Trade Union Acts, and the new association shall be party to this scheme.

(iii) In this scheme the expressions ' the confederation ' and ' the affiliating societies ' shall respectively mean and include, where the context permits, the new association and the societies signatory hereto.

Clause 2.—Central Fund and Contribution Thereto.

(i) A central fund shall be created by the payment on the signing hereof of 5s. per member by the affiliating societies other than the new association, such payment to be based upon 90 per cent. of their respective declared memberships less superannuated, honorary, and retired members. This fund shall be controlled and administered by a Central Executive as hereinafter provided.

(ii) The affiliating societies including the new association shall also contribute to the central fund a quarterly amount sufficient to meet the liabilities for salaries expenses of the organising departments, meetings of the Central Executive, and the consultative committee hereinafter provided, assistance in disputes, and all other expenditure of the confederation.

(iii) The Central Executive shall prepare a return each quarter of a year showing the payments made to the central fund and the expenditure incurred, and from this return the Central Executive shall estimate the quarterly amounts to be paid by the affiliating societies to meet the liabilities of the central fund for the ensuing quarter.

(iv) Payment of each such quarterly amount shall be made in full by each of the affiliating societies not later than the expiration of four weeks from a date named by the Central Executive in each quarter and in the event of failure so to pay as aforesaid the society in default shall be liable to pay interest on the amount from time to time remaining unpaid at a rate of not less than 5 per cent. per annum as may be determined by the Central Executive.

Clause 3.—Government of Confederation.

(i) The confederation shall be governed by a Central Executive which shall consist of representatives of the affiliating societies elected according to their respective rules and having representation on the following basis :

(*a*) For the new association the representation shall be on a basis of one representative for every 5,000 members or major portion of 5,000 members in each electoral area, and in respect of each section as provided for in Clause 4 of this scheme.

(*b*) For each of the other affiliating societies representation shall be on the basis of one representative as a minimum and an additional representative for each complete 10,000 members in the Society.

(ii) The Central Executive shall be elected each year in the month of January. It shall meet each quarter or at such other times as may be necessary at the central office of the new association, or at such other place as may from time to time be determined, and the expenses of its members shall be paid from the central fund.

Clause 4.—Election of New Association Representatives on Central Executive.

(i) For the purpose of providing direct executive representation for the different branches of the industry the membership of the new Association shall be arranged in sections as follows :

(*a*) BLASTFURNACE SECTION. Workpeople engaged in the production of pig-iron, including coke-workers, iron-ore miners, etc. ;

(*b*) STEEL MELTING SECTION. Workpeople engaged in Siemens-Martin, Bessemer, and other types of steel melting plants producing steel ingots or castings ;

(*c*) IRON AND STEEL MILL AND FORGE SECTION. Workpeople engaged in section, tube, plate and bar mills and forges ;

(*d*) SHEET AND TINPLATE MILLS SECTION. Workpeople engaged in Staffordshire and Welsh sheet mills and tinplate mills.

(*e*) FINISHING DEPARTMENTS SECTION. Workpeople engaged

in the finishing departments of tinplate works, galvanising works, etc. ;

(*f*) MECHANICS AND STEAM AND ELECTRIC SERVICE SECTION. Workpeople engaged in the driving and manipulation of cranes, engines and machinery driven by steam, hydraulic or electric power, mechanics and other tradesmen engaged in the building or upkeep of plant or machinery, boiler-firemen, etc. ;

(*g*) GENERAL LABOUR SECTION.   All unskilled workmen employed as labourers in or about the iron and steel industry.

(ii) There shall be three electoral areas, viz :—England, Scotland, and Wales, and the branches of each of the three areas shall nominate and elect members on the Central Executive.   The basis of representation to be according to Clause 3, paragraph (i) of this scheme.

Provided that if in neither of the electoral areas or in any two of them the members in any of the sections are not sufficient to entitle them to a representative on the Central Executive the members of that section or sections in the area concerned shall be grouped together, and if the number then obtained is equal to 5000 members, or a major part of 5000 members, they shall be entitled to elect a representative on the Central Executive.

Clause 5.—Consultative Committee.

There shall be a Consultative Committee which shall consist of the General Secretaries of the affiliating societies, and its duty shall be to watch over the general interests of the confederation and to advise the Central Executive thereon.   The members of the Consultative Committee shall be *ex-officio* members of the Central Executive, but without voting power.   They shall meet at the central office of the new association quarterly or at such other times as may be necessary.   They shall not be paid for their services on the Committee but their expenses of attending the meetings shall be paid from the central fund.

Clause 6.—Future Organising Work.

(i) From the date of this scheme coming into force the whole of the work of organising shall be vested in the confederation.   Each of the affiliating societies other than the new association hereby undertakes not to make any new members or to re-enter lapsed members, and in default of carrying out such undertaking the defaulting society shall pay to the funds of the new association a fine of £5 in respect of each such member, and shall transfer such member or members to the new association.

(ii) ' Lapsed ' members shall mean members who have made no payment to the society concerned for a period of 26 weeks, and each of the affiliating societies shall, where necessary, make provision in its existing rules whereby any member who has made no payment to his society for a period of 26 weeks shall be deemed to be a ' lapsed ' member.

(iii) Any dispute arising in respect of this clause shall be referred to the arbitration court established as hereinafter provided, whose decision shall be final and binding.

. . . .

Clause 9.—Trade Disputes—Assistance from Central Fund.

In any case of members of any affiliating society having a dispute with their employers, the matter must be reported to the Central Executive by the society concerned, and if the Central Executive decide to support the members concerned in the dispute the affiliating society shall be entitled to receive from the central fund one-fifth of the total expenditure in strike or lockout benefit paid to the members involved in the dispute during the first 13 weeks.   Provided that in the event of the strike or lockout lasting for a period of more than 13 weeks, the Central Executive shall have power to decide whether or not assistance from the central fund shall be continued beyond such period of 13 weeks.

. . . .

Clause 11.—Members of Affiliating Societies Transferring to the New Association.

(i) It shall be open to individual *bona fide* members of any or either of the affiliating societies to join or transfer to the new association at any time from the date of the scheme becoming operative. On application to transfer, the member or members concerned shall pay up all contributions due to his or their society, and the society shall then grant such members a transfer card.

(ii) For every member of an affiliating society with 52 or more weeks' membership transferring to the new association as before provided, the society concerned shall pay to the new association a sum of £3 as the transfer value of such member, and upon payment of such transfer value in respect of members so transferred the period of membership of the society transferred from shall be regarded as the period of membership of the new association for all purposes under the rules of the new association.   Provided that in respect of members transferred, within a period of 52 weeks from the date of this scheme coming into force, the 5s. paid to the central fund under the terms of Clause 2 shall be regarded as part payment of the transfer value.

.   .   .   .

Clause 14.—Autonomy of Affiliating Societies.

•(i) There shall be no interference with any sliding scale or general wages board agreement between any or either of the affiliating societies and the employers concerned, which is in existence at the date of this scheme coming into force.   Provided that no new sliding scale or general wages board agreement shall be entered into except with the approval of the Central Executive.

(ii) Affiliating societies shall have complete autonomy in their domestic affairs as regards the contributions of their members and administration of their funds, and in all matters outside the province of the Central Executive as provided for in this scheme.

.   .   .   .

Clause 18.—Withdrawals.

In the event of any affiliating society desiring to withdraw from the confederation, the society concerned shall give to the Central Executive not less than three months' notice of its intention, at the same time stating the grounds for withdrawal.   Thereupon the question shall be referred to the arbitration court hereinbefore provided for, and the Central Executive shall be at liberty to place before the said court its grounds for opposing withdrawal.   The withdrawal shall not take place until the decision of the arbitration court has been given, even though the three months' notice may have elapsed.   In the event of withdrawal taking place, the society concerned shall meet its full liabilities to the central fund up to the date of actual withdrawal, and from that date shall cease to have any claim upon the central fund, the Central Executive, the confederation, or any of the affiliating societies or any person or party connected with the confederation.

.   .   .   .

58. ' Break-away ' Unions.

RESOLUTION PASSED BY THE TRADES UNION CONGRESS, 1927.

T.U.C. Ann. Report, 1927, p. 436.

This Congress pledges itself to discourage in every possible way the formation of new Trade Unions, and directs the General

Council to refuse to accept the affiliation of any Trade Union which is composed of members who have broken away from an existing union affiliated to Congress.

59. Constitution and Government of a Federation.

RULES OF NAT. FEDERATION OF BUILDING TRADES OPERATIVES. 1925.

Rule 3.—Constitution.

(*a*) The governing authority shall consist of two Executive members from each National Union affiliated, up to 20,000 paying members, and one for each further 20,000 or part thereof, who shall constitute the Executive Council of the Federation. The Council shall meet quarterly.

(*b*) An Emergency Committee shall be elected from the Executive Council at the annual meeting, and shall consist of the President, Vice-President, and six members. No two members of one trade to be eligible to serve thereon.

(*c*) The Emergency Committee may appoint an Advisory Committee, composed of the President, Secretary, and one or more members resident within reasonable distance of the National Offices.

Such Advisory Committee shall have power to deal with minor business between meetings of the Emergency Committee.

All matters transacted must be submitted to the next Emergency Committee Meeting for confirmation or otherwise.

(*d*) A meeting of the Sub-Committee or Emergency Committee shall be held whenever, in the opinion of the President and Secretary, such business has arisen to necessitate the calling of such meeting, the time and place of meeting to be at the discretion of the President and Secretary. A special meeting, however, shall be called at any time, on the application of not less than three Unions. Copies of the Emergency and Sub-Committee Minutes to be forwarded to members on the Executive, and presented for confirmation to the next full meeting of the Executive Council. Copies of all minutes to be submitted to the E.C. of each affiliated Union for publication in their Monthly Journal.

(*e*) No Union shall appoint a substitute on the Emergency Committee in the place of an elected member.

60. Federation—Local Organisation.

RULES OF NAT. FEDERATION OF BUILDING TRADES OPERATIVES. 1925.

Rule 11.—Local Branches of the Federation.

(*a*) Local branches of the National Federation of Building Trades Operatives may be formed in those localities where there are two or more branches of the National Societies forming the National Federation.

(*b*) Each local branch of the Federation shall have the right to frame local rules for the conduct of their meetings, subject to the consent of the National Executive Council.

(*c*) The local branches of the Federation shall consist of two members from each Union in the district up to 1,000 members, and one for each additional 1,000 or part thereof, subject to a maximum of seven representatives from any one Union, one of whom need not be a member of the Committee or governing authority of each Union in the district. A Union to be allowed to send a deputy in the event of the elected representative being unable to attend. Each delegate present to be entitled to one vote on any question.

. . . .

Rule 12.—Regional Councils.

(*a*) Regional Councils shall be formed by the grouping of Local and Composite Branches within a defined area, *i.e.*, London, Southern, South-Western, Eastern, Midland, South Wales, Yorkshire, North-Western, North-Eastern and Scotland.

(*b*) Each Region shall be divided into not more than seven electoral areas by the grouping of Local and Composite Branches geographically adjacent. Each Local or Composite Branch shall be entitled to nominate one member from their own Branch or one within the defined electoral area for a seat upon the Regional Council. Nominations to be in the hands of the Regional Secretary not later than June 1st of any year. Such officer shall prepare a ballot paper for submission to the branches in the electoral area, and the election shall take place on or before June 30th in any year. Each Local or Composite Branch shall be entitled to one vote and the candidate receiving the highest number of votes shall be declared duly elected.

. . . .

(*d*) The duties of a Regional Council shall be to deal with all matters affecting the Federation within their area, *i.e.*, organising, dealing with trade movements, infringements of rules and trade disputes (subject to the control of the National Executive Council or such Committee or Officer as may be deputed by the said Council). The Regional Council shall cause to be forwarded to the General Office copies of all minutes, circulars and such correspondence pertaining to any notice of grading questions or violations of working rules that in their opinion may lead to a withdrawal of labour.

·   ·   ·   ·   ·   ·   ·   ·

Rule 14.—Composite Branches of the Building Trades.

(*a*) Attached to the Federation there shall be a section known as the Composite Section, and to be called ' The Composite Section of the National Federation of Building Trades Operatives.' It shall be under the direct control of the National Executive Council of the National Federation of Building Trades Operatives and any building trade operatives shall be eligible for membership thereof provided that in the town or district there does not exist a branch of an affiliated Society catering for the applicant.

·   ·   ·   ·   ·   ·   ·   ·

61. Federation—Joint Action.

RULES OF NAT. FEDERATION OF BUILDING TRADES OPERATIVES. 1925.

Rule 13.

(*a*) Joint action should be taken in Regional Districts which desire improved conditions. Any Federated Branch by Special Resolution shall request the Regional District Secretary to call a meeting of the Regional District Council to consider such business. If a trade movement is agreed to by the majority of the Unions represented thereat, the Regional District Secretary shall forward full particulars of the case (duly signed by himself and the Chairman of the Regional District Council) to the Secretary of the National Federation, who shall notify the Executives of the Unions, and they shall, within 21 days of receipt of such advice, notify the National Federation of their decision upon the matter. The National Emergency Committee, on behalf of the National Executive of the Federation, shall have power either to endorse the intended action of the District or refer it to a meeting of the National Executive. It is advisable that all such applications should be lodged at the National Office in the month of January or July.

(*b*) This mode of securing joint action shall not prevent any local branch of the trade affiliated deciding upon a separate trade movement, when wages or conditions are less favourable than kindred Unions in the same locality, or when by so acting they do not come in conflict with the interests of such trades. Before proceeding with such trade movements the sanction of the Local and National Federation to be obtained.

(*c*) The Executive Councils of the Unions concerned will then be entitled to receive amount allowed for members involved, according to rules, when at the end of each month (weekly if preferred), and upon receipt at the National Office of the Federation of the weekly strike sheets, signed by each recipient and duly audited, the Federation will forward to the Executive Council concerned the total amount.

(*d*) All area schemes defining wages to be submitted and endorsed by the E.C. of the National Federation prior to the Regional District Council submitting same to their members for final acceptance or otherwise.

(*e*) In case of lockouts the same plan will be observed upon receipt of satisfactory evidence and reason of such lockout.

62. Federation—Powers over Strikes.

RULES OF NAT. FEDERATION OF BUILDING TRADES OPERATIVES. 1925.

Rule 5.—Benefits.

(*a*) The amount of benefit to be paid shall be 5s. per week per member in dispute, less apprentices.

(*b*) No Society shall enter into a trade dispute affecting another Union or Unions without the sanction of the Executive Council or Emergency Committee being first obtained.

(*c*) The Executive Council or Emergency Committee shall have power to make such inquiries into the conduct of a dispute as they may deem necessary. The power to pay or withhold benefit shall be vested absolutely in the Executive Council.

63. Triple Industrial Alliance: 1915-1921.

COMPRISING THE MINERS' FEDERATION OF GREAT BRITAIN, THE NATIONAL UNION OF RAILWAYMEN, AND THE TRANSPORT WORKERS' FEDERATION.

The Constitution of the Alliance.

1. That matters submitted to this joint body, and upon which action may be taken, should be those of a national character or

vitally affecting a principle which in the opinion of the Executive making the request necessitates combined action.

2. The co-operation of the joint organisation shall not be called upon nor expected unless and until the matter in dispute has been considered by and received the endorsement of the National Executive of the organisation primarily concerned, and each organisation instituting a movement which is likely to involve the other affiliated organisations shall, before any definite steps are taken, submit the whole matter to the joint body for consideration.

3. For the purposes of increasing the efficiency of the movement for combined action, periodical meetings of the three full Executives shall be held at least half-yearly.

4. There shall be appointed a Consultative Committee of six, composed of two members chosen from the Executive Committee of each of the three bodies, whose duty it shall be to meet from time to time, and who shall be empowered to call at any time a special conference of the Executives of the three bodies if in their opinion such conference be necessary.

That a meeting be called on application made by any one of the three bodies.

5. With a view to meeting all management expenses incurred, each affiliated body shall contribute a sum of 10s. per 1000 members per annum, or such sum as may be decided upon from time to time.

6. Simultaneously with these arrangements for united action between the three organisations in question every effort shall proceed among the three sections to create effective and complete control of their respective bodies.

7. Complete autonomy shall be reserved to any one of the three bodies affiliated to take action on their own behalf.

8. That joint action can only be taken when the question at issue has been before the members of the three organisations and decided by such methods as the constitution of each organisation provides, and the conference shall then be called without delay to consider and decide the question of taking action.

9. No obligation shall devolve upon any of the three bodies to take joint action unless the foregoing conditions have been complied with.

64. Joint Committee of Trade Unions.

From MINISTRY OF LABOUR REPORT ON WORKS COMMITTEES, 1918,
p. 97 ff.

PARKGATE WORKS JOINT TRADES COMMITTEE.

I.—Rules for Works Committee.

1. That this organisation be called ' The Parkgate Works Joint Trades Committee.'

2. That the objects of the Committee are :

(*a*) To strengthen Trade Union organisation in the works.

(*b*) To deal with general questions affecting the welfare of all sections in the works.

(*c*) To give assistance to branches in sectional disputes where the branches fail to arrive at a settlement with the firm.

(*d*) To keep a watchful eye on representation on local bodies, and to see that the workmen employed by the firm are not over-looked.

(*e*) To do whatsoever it can to promote a closer union of the different trades represented in the works.

3. That branches be allowed representation as follows : [1]

> Membership of 50—one delegate.
> Membership over 50—two delegates.

4. That the branches be asked to appoint alternative delegates, and forward their names to the Secretary together with the names of the delegates appointed.

5. Any body of trade unionists working in any department, but whose branch is out of the works, may have representation on the same basis as branches.

6. The President and Secretary shall be empowered to call a meeting of the Committee to deal with any matter which arises, or may arise, affecting the welfare of the branches.

7. Any delegate or branch may have a meeting called by giving notice to the Secretary, stating the business they wish to bring before the Committee.

8. That a delegation fee of one shilling per delegate per year be paid to the Committee.

---

[1] With, in addition, the Secretary of each branch, if employed in the works, *ex officio.*

9. That where sectional disputes are dealt with by Committee, deputations to the Management shall consist of two representatives of the Committee and one from the section affected.

10. That the Secretary be *ex officio* member of the Committee.

11. No person allowed to sit on the Committee unless authorised to do so by his branch and certified by the branch secretary.

12. That in the event of any claim being made or dispute which affects the interests of more than one section of the works, such cases shall be dealt with by the Trade Unions concerned and the Joint Trades Committee.

II.

Fourteen trade union branches are represented on the Committee. Seven of the fourteen have no members employed outside the Parkgate Works. The seven are : Four branches of the Iron and Steel Trades Confederation, and a branch each of the Blastfurnacemen, the Enginemen and Cranemen, and the General Labourers. Together these seven branches represent about 1,600 persons in the works. Six of them have three representatives on the Committee ; in each case the secretary of the branch is one of the representatives. The seven trade union branches having only part of their membership within the works are : The Bricklayers, the Amalgamated Society of Engineers, the Blacksmiths, the Moulders, the Boilermakers, the Roll Turners and the Carpenters and Joiners ; together these seven branches represent about 200 persons in the works. Four of them have two representatives, including the secretary in each case, and three one representative on the Committee. Altogether, therefore, the Committee consists of 31 persons including the secretaries of 11 of the 24 branches.

Rule 4, relating to alternative delegates, is stated to be necessary because some men, for example the first hand at a smelting furnace, cannot leave their work at certain times.

The Committee was formed in January, 1916. An attempt to form a Committee had been made in 1913, but, owing to the slight support given to it, this Committee lasted for a few months only. The influences which produced the present Committee were the recognition of common needs and the desire for harmony (*see* Rule 2).

65. Reciprocal Recognition of Trade Union Cards and Transfer Arrangements.

T.U.C. Ann. Rep., 1924, pp. 176-177.

National Union of Railwaymen.

The National Union of Railwaymen has a system of free transfers with a large number of unions. The rule covering such transfers is as follows :

Any person qualified for membership by clause 1 of this rule, who shall produce a fully paid up clearance card from a bona-fide Trade Union, into which he has paid not less than 26 weeks' contributions, shall be accepted as a member of the union free of charge (provided that the said union shall extend the same privilege to the members of this union), and shall be entitled to immediate benefits as provided by Rules 12 and 13, except as otherwise determined by the Executive Committee, but for other benefits he shall stand over the same period as a member who joins in accordance with Clause 3 of this rule, unless otherwise determined by the Executive Committee to meet specific cases.

Typographical Association.

This association has in being a reciprocity scheme with the Printing Machine Managers' Trade Society, the Platen Machine Minders' Society, and the Scottish Typographical Society. In addition the Typographical Association has an agreement with the National Society of Operative Printers and Assistants for the transfer of members of the latter organisation to the Typographical Association when such members are placed in charge of rotary printing machines or are promoted from copyholders to readers.

The clauses in the agreement between the Typographical Association and the National Society of Operative Printers and Assistants having relation to transfers of liabilities are as follows :

(*a*) On the transfer of a member of the N.S.O.P. & A. to the T.A., the latter body agree to halve the usual period of probation provided in their rules, and the former body agree to continue the said member in benefit, under their rules, until such time as the reduced probationary period in the T.A. shall have expired.

(*b*) In branches of the T.A. where supplementary local benefits are provided, members of the N.S.O.P. & A. transferred under this agreement shall be required to pay the minimum entrance fee retained by the branch and to serve the usual probation for supplementary benefits in accordance with the rules of the T.A. branch.

With respect to the Reciprocity Scheme, 1919, agreed upon by the T.A. and the Printing Machine Managers' Trade Society, the following clauses deal with the question of the transfer of members and their liabilities :

(*a*) Any member seeking or obtaining employment in towns within the area of the reciprocating societies shall present his document to the secretary of the society in existence there.   He shall be entitled to receive unemployment benefit or strike allowance (if eligible) in accordance with the provisions of the rules of the association of which he is a member, such weekly sums to be refunded to the society making the payment.

(*b*) Any member of a reciprocating society working in the area of another society shall be admitted as an associate member of the adopted society on payment of 3d. a week.   He shall continue as a full member of his parent society, paying full contributions and receiving full benefits.   Such contributions shall be collected, and the benefits shall be disbursed by the adopted society, in accordance with the terms agreed upon.

(*c*) Any associate member who desires to become a full member of the adopted society may do so subject to the rules and conditions of both societies without the payment of entrance fee.

(*d*) This scheme refers only to the reciprocal payment of unemployed and strike benefit.   Benefits other than these shall be paid direct by the parent society.

(*e*) That accounts under this scheme be settled half-yearly.

(*f*) Disagreements arising out of the scheme to be referred to the Printing and Kindred Trades Federation of the United Kingdom.

66. Inter-Union Agreement.

Agreement between THE RAILWAY CLERKS' ASSOCIATION AND ASSOCIATION OF ENGINEERING AND SHIPBUILDING DRAUGHTSMEN to facilitate the organisation of Railway Draughtsmen.   1924.

1. That members of the Association of Engineering and Shipbuilding Draughtsmen be entered into membership of the Railway Clerks' Association by the payment of a *per capita* fee of 10s. per annum by the A.E. & S.D. to the R.C.A.

2. That the R.C.A., in consultation with the A.E. & S.D., negotiate on behalf of all Railway Draughtsmen. A member of the A.E. & S.D. enrolled in the R.C.A. under Clause I to be a member of the Negotiating Committee dealing with the Railway Authorities respecting Draughtsmen's conditions ; and the A.E. & S.D. to make arrangements to have in attendance at such negotiations a representative of its Executive Committee for the purpose of advising regarding the conditions of Draughtsmen generally in the country.

3. Members of the R.C.A. upon taking up employment as Draughtsmen outside the Railway Service to be transferred to the A.E. & S.D., the R.C.A. to pay a transfer fee of 7s. 6d. in the case of each member so transferred, who will be entered into immediate benefit for Unemployment Benefit and Dispute Pay in the A.E. & S.D.

4. That Draughtsmen members of the R.C.A. may become dual members of the A.E. & S.D. for technical educational purposes upon the payment of a fee of 16s. per annum.

5. That a Joint Advisory Committee be established for the purpose of preventing any undercutting, conducting a joint propaganda campaign, considering matters of policy and programme, and generally to look after the interests of Railway Draughtsmen. The decisions of this Committee to be subject to ratification by the Executive Committees of the two organisations.

6. For the time being this Agreement shall not apply to Ireland.

67. Inter-Union Agreement.

AMAL. TEXTILE WAREHOUSEMEN AND OP. BLEACHERS, DYERS, AND FINISHERS. 1924.

T.U.C. Ann. Report, 1925, p. 188.

The Operative Bleachers, Dyers, and Finishers' Association agree not to attempt organisation work amongst workpeople engaged on various jobs catered for by the Amalgamated Textile Warehousemen who are working in purely textile mills, solely engaged in the spinning and manufacturing of cotton cloth, and to which there is no bleaching, dyeing, or finishing attached.

In cases where at the present time members of the Operative Bleachers, Dyers, and Finishers' Association are working at purely textile mills engaged in any of the occupations catered for by the Amalgamated Textile Warehousemen, it is hereby agreed that the

Amalgamated Textile Warehousemen will recognise the card and membership of the Operative Bleachers, Dyers, and Finishers' Association.

The Operative Bleachers, Dyers, and Finishers' Association and the Amalgamated Textile Warehousemen jointly agree that the decision of the Disputes Sub-Committee of the Trades Union Congress General Council embodied in a report dated 27th May, 1924, with regard to overlapping in the Horwich district, had reference only to the position respecting the two mills in the Horwich area.

It is hereby also jointly agreed between the two associations that, in the event of further questions arising on the question of overlapping and with regard to membership of either of the Associations, a sub-committee of four members from each of the two unions meet to discuss the matter.

68. Inter-Union Agreement.

Nat. Union of Railwaymen ;   Amal. Eng. Union ;   Electrical T.U. ;
United Patternmakers Assn. ;   Nat. Soc. of Coppersmiths, etc. ;
Nat. Union of Foundry Wkrs. ;   United Op. Plumbers, etc. ;
Workers' Union ; Amal. Machine, Engine and Iron Grinders,
etc. ;   Fed. of Engin. and Shipbldg. Trades.   1927.

RAILWAY SHOPMEN.

Agreement with a view to securing Efficient Organisation of Railway Shopmen throughout Great Britain.

1.—Membership.

(*a*) That the membership of the unions, parties to this agreement, catering for shopmen should be regarded as inviolate, and that no member of a union engaged as a railway shopman should be admitted to membership in any other union until after his former union has been consulted and all dues to this union have been met.

(*b*) The membership application form of all the unions concerned in this agreement should contain an inquiry to be answered by the applicant as to whether he is, or has been, a member of any other union, and if so, what his financial relationship is to such union.

(*c*) That for the purpose of providing a uniform method of determining membership, 26 weeks shall constitute the period which should elapse before a man is regarded as having ceased membership in a union.

(*d*) Recognising the respective constitutions of the unions, parties to this agreement, it is agreed that craftsmen, who are not at present members of any union, should be approached to join a union catering for their occupation, it being distinctly understood that the efforts of all unions, parties to this agreement, shall be directed to the elimination of non-unionists. It is also agreed that periodical consultations between local representatives of the said unions shall take place in the various centres with a view to giving effect to this clause.

2.—Subscriptions.

With a view to discouraging the desertions from the unions by the attraction of a cheaper contribution, an endeavour shall be made to secure unification of contribution of each of the unions, parties to this agreement, in so far as Trade Union benefits are concerned.

3.—Benefits.

Each union will be responsible to its members for the payment of benefits in accordance with the rules of the unions concerned.

4.—National Negotiations.

(*a*) It is advisable that all national negotiations affecting the interests of railway shopmen shall be conducted jointly by the unions concerned, parties to this agreement.

(*b*) With respect to purely craft questions each individual union shall have the right of separate negotiations. In the event of national machinery for shopmen being established, each union, party to this agreement, should co-operate to utilise it to the fullest advantage.

5.—Expenses—Local and National Machinery.

The expenses of the local and national machinery shall be met by the unions concerned.

69. Inter-Union Disputes.

Powers of the General Council of the T.U.C.

STANDING ORDERS OF THE T.U.C. 1928.

12.—Disputes between Unions.

(*a*) Where disputes arise, or threaten to arise, between affiliated organisations, the General Council shall use its influence to promote a settlement.

(*b*) Upon application from an affiliated organisation, the General Council shall also have the power to investigate cases of dispute or disagreement between affiliated organisations, whether relating to general industrial questions or demarcation of work.

(*c*) If the parties to a dispute fail to submit the case to the Disputes Committee of the General Council as provided by this Standing Order, it shall not be permissible for such dispute to be raised at the Annual Meeting of Congress.

(*d*) The General Council shall have power to summon the contending organisations to appear before the Disputes Committee of the General Council, and to require such organisations to submit all evidence and information that the Disputes Committee may deem essential to enable them to adjudicate upon the case.

(*e*) If the result of such an inquiry be that the complaining society fails to prove the charge, it shall bear the whole cost of the investigation, including the expenses incurred by the defending society.

(*f*) Should any decision of the General Council in connection with such cases under this section be ignored by any organisation, the Council may at once issue a report to all the unions. If compliance with the decision of the General Council is still refused, the matter shall be reported to Congress to deal with as may be decided upon.

(*g*) If at any time there appears to the General Council to be justification for an investigation into the conduct of any Union, on the grounds that the activities of such Union are detrimental to the interests of the Trade Union Movement, or contrary to the declared principles and policy of the Trades Union Congress, the General Council shall summon such Union to appear before it or its appropriate Committee in order that such activities may be investigated. In the event of the Union refusing to attend, the investigation shall proceed in its absence.

(1) If as the result of such investigation the General Council is convinced that the activities of the Union concerned are detrimental to the interests of the Trade Union Movement, or contrary to the declared principles and policy of the Trades Union Congress, the General Council shall have power

(i) to call upon the Union to cease forthwith such activities, and to undertake not to engage in such activities in future;

(ii) to suspend forthwith the Union from membership of Congress until the next annual Trades Union Congress; and shall submit a report of the case to the next Congress.

(2) Any Union which has been suspended shall have the

right to appeal to Congress, and shall be entitled to appoint
delegates for this purpose in accordance with Standing Orders
Nos. 16 and 17.

(3) Congress shall have the final authority to deal with the
case, whether by way of re-admission, further suspension, or
exclusion from membership of Congress.

70. Inter-Union Disputes.

General Observations made by the DISPUTES COMMITTEE OF THE
GENERAL COUNCIL OF THE T.U.C.

T.U.C. Ann. Report, 1924, p. 156.

The Disputes Committee, in reviewing the work with which they
have had to deal, feel that certain comments may be usefully made
with a view to indicating in broad outline the principal factors which
have emerged from the various disputes.

They have been compelled to treat each case strictly on its merits.
Principally because of the nature of its evolution and the changing
economic conditions, the Trade Union Movement has no clear-
cut method of organisation.

There are three broad types of organisation in existence :

(1) Craft unionism, where workers in a given trade, irrespective
of the form of the occupation, work or industry, in which they are
employed, are grouped in accordance with their craft identity.

(2) Industrial and occupational unionism where the whole of
the workers, skilled, semi-skilled, and unskilled are grouped in
accordance with the industry or occupation in which they are for
the time being employed, irrespective of craft or grade.

(3) General unionism where the workers are organised in
large aggregations irrespective of either craft, industry, or occupation.   In the latter section most of the unskilled workers are found.

The Disputes Committee are not here concerned with a discussion
of the merits of the respective forms of organisation, which, it will be
noticed, are to be discussed under resolutions in Section C of the
Congress Agenda, but they feel obliged to observe that a considerable
number of the disputes with which they have had to deal have been
due to these different conceptions of organisation.

On several occasions the Committee have been asked to assent to
one or other of the above forms of organisation, but they felt unable

to do so, feeling that as Congress has not laid down a decision on these questions the Disputes Committee have no power to decide as to what type of organisation generally should be followed.

Inter-Union Competition.

A considerable number of disputes could be eliminated if something was done to avoid inter-union competition in the sense of unifying contributions and entrance fees. On several occasions cases have come to the notice of the Disputes Committee where two unions catering for exactly the same class of members have had widely differing rates of contributions and entrance fees. The questions of entrance fees and contributions cannot, of course, be divorced from that of benefits, but undoubtedly there is a strong inducement for the indifferent trade unionist to transfer his membership to the Union with the lower contributions.

The Disputes Committee recognise the difficulty of dealing with the situation, but feel it their duty to indicate that it is one of the causes of disputes between Unions.

Main Principles.

Although, because of the reasons stated, the Disputes Committee are not in a position to indicate any definite form of organisation which would have the effect of eliminating a good many of the inter-union disputes, there are certain main principles, which, if followed, would reduce the number of disputes. These are :

(1) The application for membership form of the Unions should contain an inquiry to be answered by the candidate as to whether he is or has been a member of any other Union, and, if so, what his financial relationship to that Union is.

(2) As a general principle, no member of any trade union should be accepted into membership in another without inquiry from the Union concerned.

(3) No member should be allowed to escape his financial obligations by leaving one Union while in arrears and by joining another.

(4) Under no circumstances should a Union accept members from any other Union which is engaged in a trades' dispute. It should be a general understanding that both national and local officials of Trade Unions should refrain from speaking or acting adversely to the interests of any other Union during any period in which the members of the latter Union are participating in

a trades' dispute. Much trouble could be avoided if Unions about to participate in a trades' dispute would take care to inform other unions whose members would be likely to be affected thereby.

The General Council, after giving careful consideration to the above proposals, expressed its concurrence with the observations of the Disputes Committee.

71. Inter-Union Disputes.

Report of Case heard by the DISPUTES COMMITTEE OF THE GENERAL COUNCIL OF THE T.U.C.

T.U.C. Ann. Report, 1924, p. 152.

National Amalgamated Union of Shop Assistants, and National Union of General Workers v. National Drug and Chemical Union. (1923-1924.)

(*a*) On the 22nd October, 1923, Messrs. A. A. H. Findlay (Chairman), W. Kean, and F. Bramley (Secretary of the Disputes Committee), heard certain complaints which had been made by the National Amalgamated Union of Shop Assistants, Warehousemen and Clerks and the National Union of General Workers against the National Drug and Chemical Union in respect of alleged poaching of members by the last-named Union.

(*b*) The complaining Unions asserted that the other organisation had been consistently endeavouring to poach members in the drug and chemical trade, and the same process was now taking place in the heavy chemical trade. The Shop Assistants further claimed that the Drug and Chemical Union was a break-away organisation, the principal members of which had at one time been organised in the National Union of Shop Assistants.

(*c*) In their finding the Disputes Sub-Committee submitted that the charges brought against the National Drug and Chemical Union by the National Union of Shop Assistants having already constituted the subject of an inquiry prior to the first-named Union being admitted to Congress, the Disputes Sub-Committee did not consider it necessary to enter further into the past dispute between those two Societies.

(*d*) The objections raised to the present practice of the Drug and Chemical Union in relation to poaching workers employed in the drug departments of the distributive trade was considered separately, and the charges brought by the National Union of Shop Assistants and the National Union of General Workers were, in the opinion of the Disputes Sub-Committee, substantially proved, as during the proceedings it was made clear that the National Drug and Chemical Union had accepted as members into their organisation members of other Unions affiliated to Congress.

(*e*) The Drug and Chemical Union attempted to justify the admission of members of other unions by stating that they had been duly transferred, but the Disputes Sub-Committee found that they had utilized a transfer form filled in by the applicant member without any official enquiry or arrangement with the Union to which he had belonged.

(*f*) It was suggested that an effort be made between the parties to come to an amicable arrangement about the members who had been taken over by the Drug and Chemical Union, and further to devise a satisfactory form of transfer, to avoid subsequent friction.

(*g*) A further meeting was held on the 7th March, 1924, before Messrs. W. Kean (Chairman), R. T. Jones and W. M. Citrine (Assistant Secretary), when the Shop Assistants and the N.U.G.W. agreed to submit a list of the members alleged to have been taken, together with the date of their last payments to their Unions.   It was also suggested that none of the Unions should accept members of the others employed in the drug and chemical industry except by consultation and agreement with the Unions which the members were leaving.   The Shop Assistants did not accept this second suggestion.

(*h*) Subsequently the National Drug and Chemical Union declined to accept the first proposal, and later intimated that they had decided to disaffiliate from Congress.   Their disaffiliation took place as from the end of April, 1924.

72. Inter-Union Disputes.

Award by DISPUTES COMMITTEE OF THE GENERAL COUNCIL OF THE T.U.C.

T.U.C. Ann. Report, 1926, p. 106.

Amalgamated Engineering Union v. *United Patternmakers' Association* (1925).

(*a*) The A.E.U. wrote on the 27th October, 1925, reporting that correspondence had passed between their Union and the United

Patternmakers' Association, regarding the admission to the U.P.A. of men who had been excluded from the A.E.U. for excessive arrears. Both unions agreed to submit the case of G. R. Johnson as a test case to the Disputes Committee.

(*b*) It appeared from the correspondence that Johnson had been excluded from the U.P.A. for arrears in June, 1918, and had joined the A.E.U. in January, 1920 ; was excluded by the A.E.U. owing 36s. 6d. for arrears in October, 1923 ; was reinstated under promise to pay arrears, and was again excluded owing 70s. 4d. in October, 1924.

(*c*) The case was heard on the 8th December, 1925, by Miss M. Bondfield (in the Chair), J. Beard, J. Davenport, and A. S. Firth (Acting Assistant Secretary), for the Disputes Committee.

(*d*) On behalf of the A.E.U. it was urged that if a man were excluded from an organisation for arrears the fact of his exclusion did not relieve him from his liabilities, and until he had discharged those liabilities no other organisation should be permitted to accept him as a member. They stated that under their rules if an excluded man applied for reinstatement he would be reinstated with his former benefits on paying up his arrears ; but if he applied to become a new member the organisation would forego the arrears, and he would have to pay an entrance fee according to his age, and would have to qualify for benefits. On the other hand, they admitted that he could join a cheaper section than the one to which he had formerly belonged. They refered to Clause 3 of the main principles governing the acceptance of members, passed at the Hull Congress, in support of their view.

(*e*) Reference was made to a case, Amalgamated Engineering Union *v*. West of Scotland Brassturners' Association, heard on the 20th May, 1924, in which the decision was that six members who had been enrolled in the Brassturners' Association while heavily in arrears in the A.E.U. should be required to pay their arrears.

(*f*) On behalf of the United Patternmakers' Association, it was claimed that if a man had been excluded from an organisation all his previous industrial history had been wiped out and he became a non-union man. The U.P.A. strictly carried out the principles passed at the Hull Congress, and they always compelled a man to pay up his arrears to his former union, but in the case where a man had been excluded they considered he had become a non-union man and could join any union he chose.

(g) *The Disputes Sub-Committee decided as follows* :

1. The case of the Amalgamated Engineering Union *v*. West of Scotland Brassturners' Association does not offer a parallel, for the following reasons :

(a) It was a charge of poaching, not concerned exclusively with excluded men, and there was no mention in the report of the case of any of the men having been excluded.

(b) The men were enrolled by the Brassturners' Association, without inquiry being made of the A.E.U., and appeared to have left the A.E.U. because of a grievance.

2. A man who has been definitely excluded from his union must be considered as a non-unionist. In this connection, the Disputes Sub-Committee noted that the A.E.U. had admitted that if the man in question had applied for re-admission, he would be re-admitted as a new member, and they would not in fact attempt to collect the arrears.

3. Therefore, in the judgment of the Disputes Sub-Committee, Clause 3 of the main principles enunciated on Page 157 of the Hull Congress Report does not apply, and

4. The Patternmakers' Association are entitled, equally with the A.E.U., to exercise the right of re-admission according to the provisions contained in their own rules.

73. Shop Stewards and Works Committees.

AGREEMENT IN THE ENGINEERING INDUSTRY AFTER THE 1922 LOCKOUT.

III.—Shop Stewards and Works Committee Agreement.

With a view to amplifying the Provisions for Avoiding Disputes by a recognition of Shop Stewards and the institution of Works Committees, it is agreed as follows :

(*a*) APPOINTMENT OF SHOP STEWARDS.

1. Workers, members of the above-named Trade Unions, employed in a federated establishment, may have representatives appointed from the members of the Unions employed in the establishment to act on their behalf in accordance with the terms of this Agreement.

2. The representatives shall be known as Shop Stewards.

3. The appointment of such Shop Stewards shall be determined by the Trade Unions concerned, and each Trade Union party to this Agreement may have such Shop Stewards.

4. The names of the Shop Stewards and the shop or portion of a shop in which they are employed and the Trade Union to which they belong shall be intimated officially by the Trade Union concerned to the Management on election.

(*b*) APPOINTMENT OF WORKS COMMITTEES.

5. A Works Committee may be set up in each establishment consisting of not more than seven representatives of the Management and not more than seven Shop Stewards, who should be representative of the various classes of workpeople employed in the establishment.

The Shop Stewards for this purpose shall be nominated and elected by ballot of the workpeople, members of the Trade Unions parties to this Agreement, employed in the establishment.

The Shop Stewards elected to the Works Committee shall, subject to re-election, hold office for not more than twelve months.

6. If a question falling to be dealt with by the Works Committee in accordance with the procedure hereinafter laid down arises in a department which has not a Shop Steward on the Works Committee, the Works Committee may, as regards that question, co-opt a Shop Steward from the department concerned. An agenda of the points to be discussed by the Works Committee shall be issued at least three days before the date of the meeting if possible.

(*c*) FUNCTIONS AND PROCEDURE.

7. The Functions of the Shop Stewards and Works Committee, so far as they are concerned with the avoidance of disputes, shall be exercised in accordance with the following procedure :

(*a*) A worker or workers desiring to raise any question in which they are directly concerned shall, in the first instance, discuss the same with their foreman.

(*b*) Failing settlement, the question shall be taken up with the Shop Manager and/or Head Shop Foreman by the appropriate Shop Steward and one of the workers directly concerned.

(*c*) If no settlement is arrived at the question may, at the request of either party, be further considered at a meeting of the Works Committee. At this meeting the O.D.D. may be present, in which event a representative of the Employers' Association shall also be present.

(*d*) Any question arising which affects more than one branch of trade or more than one department of the Works may be referred to the Works Committee.

(*e*) The question may thereafter be referred for further consideration in terms of the ' Provisions for Avoiding Disputes.'

(*f*) No stoppage of work shall take place until the question has been fully dealt with in accordance with this Agreement and with the ' Provisions for Avoiding Disputes.'

(*d*) GENERAL.

8. Shop Stewards shall be subject to the control of the Trade Unions, and shall act in accordance with the Rules and Regulations of the Trade Unions and agreements with employers so far as these affect the relation between employers and workpeople.

9. In connection with this Agreement, Shop Stewards shall be afforded facilities to deal with questions raised in the shop or portion of a shop in which they are employed. Shop Stewards elected to the Works Committee shall be afforded similar facilities in connection with their duties, and in the course of dealing with these questions they may, with the previous consent of the Management, (such consent not to be unreasonably withheld), visit any shop or portion of a shop in the establishment. In all other respects, Shop Stewards shall conform to the same working conditions as their fellow workers.

10. Negotiations under this Agreement may be instituted either by the Management or by the workers concerned.

11. Employers and Shop Stewards and Works Committees shall not be entitled to enter into any agreement inconsistent with agreements between the Federation or Local Associations and the Trade Unions.

12. For the purpose of this Agreement the expression ' establishment ' shall mean the whole establishment or sections thereof according to whether the Management is unified or sub-divided.

13. Any question which may arise out of the operation of this agreement shall be brought before the Executive of the Trade Union concerned, or the Federation, as the case may be.

74. Works Committees.

MINISTRY OF LABOUR REPORT ON WORKS COMMITTEES, 1918, pp. 8, 9.

A distinction must be drawn between ' Works Committees ' and ' Shop Committees.' The former cover the whole of a works (or even, in some cases, the whole of two or three contiguous works) ;

the latter cover a particular department or shop in a works. Among Works Committees it is possible to distinguish three varieties. The first and main variety may be called the ' Industrial Committee.' Such a committee, generally constituted on a Trade Union basis, deals with particular questions affecting the conditions and remuneration of labour in a given works—questions of principle being reserved for the district or national organisations concerned. It is this variety which, being the most important, is often called by the general name of Works Committee. A second variety may be called the ' Welfare Committee.' Such a committee, representing as a rule all the workers in a given works, deals with what may be termed works amenities—ventilation, sanitation, and the like. A third variety, which may be merged with the second, or may be distinct, is the ' Social Union,' or, more exactly, the committee governing the Social Union, where one exists, of the workers employed in the same establishment. Such a committee is concerned with games, recreations, study-circles, picnics and the like.

Apart from these main types there are, of course, local varieties of all sorts. There may be, for instance, a separate ' Mess-room Committee ' ; or, again, there may be a separate ' Women's Committee.' There may be a committee peculiar to a small section of workers (*e.g.*, tool-makers), which handles a large and important area of functions in regard to those workers. Finally, even though there is no regular or standing Works Committees, it may be the case that committees are created *ad hoc* whenever an important question arises in a works, and that these committees are consulted by the management with a view to settling such questions. This indeed is the procedure followed in some of the works where the relations of management and men are most amicable. In some cases the committee so formed consists of the shop stewards of the separate trades.

It may be added that some committees are ' joint,' and embrace representatives of both men and management, meeting together in regular session ; while others (and this is the general rule) are committees of workmen only, but meet the management from time to time (sometimes regularly, and sometimes occasionally ; sometimes directly, and sometimes through their chairman or secretary) to settle grievances and to give or receive information.

Various names have been applied to committees formed during the war, particularly to those formed to deal with such questions as timekeeping. Among the names are ' Workers' Advisory Board,' ' Works' Tribunal,' ' Vigilant Committee,' and ' Works' Council.'

75. Works Committees.
Relations with Trade Unions.

MINISTRY OF LABOUR REPORT ON WORKS COMMITTEES, 1918, p. 37 ff.

Something has already been said in the sections dealing with the constitution, procedure and functions of Works Committees, concerning the relations between such committees and Trade Union organisation. The position is in certain respects somewhat paradoxical; the problem as seen by most Trade Unionists is that of strengthening the Trade Union organisation in the workshop, but, on the one hand, many employers prefer not to deal with the shop stewards in the works but with the outside Trade Union organisation, and, on the other hand, some elements in Trade Unionism prefer that it should stand outside the workshop and handle questions in each works from the outside, while some unionist shop stewards consider that their Works Committees should not be subject to any control of the Trade Unions. The general question of the relation and the relative weight and power of Works Committees and district organisations is one which is likely to be settled gradually in experience and actual working. Here it may be convenient to draw attention to some considerations which appear to affect this general question, particularly as seen in the engineering industry.

The first consideration is that the change in the conditions of working have made necessary the development of new machinery for collective bargaining. Since the questions for which this machinery is required are, to a great extent, peculiar to individual establishments, the collective bargaining, if it is to be done at all, must be carried through in each establishment. At the same time, unless the results are to impair the standard conditions which it is the business of the Unions to uphold, the work must be entrusted to representatives of the Unions. Thus there has come about a natural development in the functions of the shop stewards. Previously they had to see that no encroachments were made on standard conditions; now they may have the more positive duty of participating in the settlement of piece-work prices in terms of these standard conditions.[1]

[1] The appointment by the men of a separate rate fixer, whose business it would be to arrange piece prices with the firm's rate fixer, is a suggested development towards which a movement is being made in one or two firms. In one large establishment, such a duplication is suggested by one of the firm's rate fixers as a very desirable arrangement.

In regard to the changes just mentioned, and in regard also to dilution, the interests of the workpeople belonging to different skilled Unions are more or less the same. This, combined with the natural community in the works, probably accounts for the fact that certain apparent difficulties of representation are, as a rule, easily overcome. The impossibility of so representing different Unions on a Works Committee that satisfaction is secured to all is alleged to be such a difficulty. So far as the skilled trades are concerned—at least in engineering—the difficulty would not appear to be serious. In many cases where even a small minority only of the skilled Unions have *direct* representation there would appear to be no dissatisfaction.

As between the members of skilled and unskilled Unions the position is more difficult. There are several cases of two separate Committees of Shop Stewards—one representing the skilled and the other unskilled and semi-skilled men—in the same works. In other establishments, however, skilled and unskilled men vote for the same committee and act together as members. This would appear to be the most desirable arrangement. The case, however, in which a minority of unskilled men in each department is represented on a Works Committee by a skilled unionist is not exactly on a par with that in which a minority belonging to an unskilled Union is so represented. Apart from the fact that unskilled men are more likely to be distributed through all the departments, so that though in a minority they form a considerable proportion of the total number of employees, there is the further consideration that the similarity of interest and the community of feeling are not so pronounced. In many establishments the difficulty has apparently been surmounted : but in a number of others it is still a serious problem. The problem would appear to be one which cannot be settled by the men in each establishment—though they may provide valuable suggestions— and it must probably be left for the Trade Unions concerned to come to some agreement on the matter. For this reason a certain number of workpeople, both skilled and unskilled, consider that in cases where the difficulty is acute the policy of two committees is the best present working arrangement. The defects of such a system are perhaps too obvious to require particular mention. It may, however, be noted that the system obstructs very considerably that joint consideration of common interests and desires, to find expression for which is one of the main purposes of a Works Committee. It tends instead to concentrate the attention of each committee upon points of divergence of interest.

The coming together into one committee of shop stewards responsible to different Trade Unions raises a number of questions. It is true that the rules by which Unions define the functions of their shop stewards are fairly uniform, and so long as a Works Committee respects the rules of the different Unions there is little fear of overlapping or confusion in functions. The general rule which determines the functions of a Works Committee in relation to Trade Union organisation has already been mentioned. As is said in the case of one Committee, 'The Committee regard questions of general application, relating to rates of wages, hours of work or otherwise, which affect " district conditions," as beyond their jurisdiction. There is no formal rule to this effect; but this limitation of the Committee's power is well understood, and no difficulties have arisen.'

It is thus the rule that general questions of district or national conditions are left to the Trade Unions, while the Works Committee deals with either the detailed application of these general rules within the works or with questions entirely peculiar to the works. On the whole, the information which is available would suggest that the division of jurisdiction is well understood and closely followed. There are, however, certain difficulties.

In the first place there is evidence of uncertainty as to whether or not a Works Committee should undertake certain functions; matters may sometimes seem from one point of view to be 'branch' or 'district' business, and from another to be 'works' business. A tool-room bonus, for instance, may be arranged in a works between a committee and the works manager, and they may agree in regarding it as a works affair, while the local branch (or district committee) of the Union concerned may consider that it is a question of wages which demands their sanction. In view of the variety and complexity of bonus schemes which have been instituted in munitions factories, and of the possible reactions of these upon standard rates, there would appear to be some need for careful definition of a Works Committee's functions in this field.

There is some evidence also of actual conflict of authority. Such cases, however, would appear to have been given an altogether disproportionate prominence in public discussion, to the detriment of those whose main desire is to create a constitutional machinery suited to new and rapidly changing conditions. In a few instances, however, a Works Committee would appear to have been in doubt as to whether it was an independent organisation or one subject to Trade Union control. Thus, a Works Committee wholly composed of Trade Union stewards has made a demand for an advance in wages to which, under an alternative agreement made by the Trade Unions, the workmen represented by it had no claim. In one or two cases representations have been made to Government Departments for advances in wages and improvements in other working conditions in individual works, independently of district or national machinery, though the works in question were known to recognise district standards.

It would appear that the uncertainty as to the real position and powers of a Works Committee in relation to the Trade Unions is, at least in the engineering industry, to some extent due to the fact that the various members of a committee may be responsible to many different Unions. Though, therefore, the Works Committee may aspire to be a unit of government, this is rendered difficult in view of the different and possibly conflicting authorities from which the members obtain their status. One suggested scheme proposes to overcome this particular difficulty so far at least as the Unions of skilled men are concerned. It would bring the committees in the various establishments under the district Engineering Trades Joint Committee, and confine membership of any committee to those organised in the Trade Unions affiliated to the district committee.[1] This question of the relationship of works to district committees is interesting also in view of the proposals contained in the Whitley Report. That Report advocates Joint National and District Councils and Works Committees; and the problem of the relations of the District Council and the Works Committee and their relative functions is one which will need to be investigated when measures are being adopted to institute such Councils.

The need for this consideration of relationships between Works Committees and the district Trade Union organisation would appear to be more necessary in certain industries than in others. It would appear, for instance, that in the iron and steel industry the fact that members in one works commonly form a branch of their Union, and

[1] See p. 135 (of *Report*). In another case where the firm's proposals for a Joint Committee are being considered it is suggested that 'the representatives of the Trade Societies shall be elected and retire in accordance with the rules for the time being of the Joint Committee of Allied Engineering Trades, and shall be subject to its constitution.' In this instance the works in question is the only considerable establishment in the town, and the Trade Unions affiliated to the Allied Engineering Trades include the General Labour Union.

that the secretaries of branches are usually—it may be in virtue of the office they hold—members of the Works Committee, makes the problem of inter-relations less difficult, at least for those Unions which are organised on the basis of works.

A point of procedure may be noticed. It is sometimes the case that a Trade Union official accompanies the representatives of the Works Committee in an interview with the management; or, again, a Trade Union official may attend the deliberations of a Joint Committee if the men so desire.[1]   But this apparently is exceptional; and, as a rule, a Works Committee acts by itself, and refers to Trade Union officials questions which are too large or too difficult to be settled in the works.   It should, however, be noted that many trade unionists are of the opinion that the right of the Trade Union officials to attend committee meetings (or to inspect the minutes of a committee) is a necessary condition of the satisfactory solution of the question of inter-relations.

Two other questions which are involved in this problem of the inter-relations of Works Committees and Trade Unions call for notice.

The first relates to the victimisation of men who show themselves active as shop stewards or as members of a Works Committee.   It is impossible to estimate to what extent such victimisation actually occurs, and this is partly due to the difficulty of defining what victimisation is.   Workmen complain not only of victimisation, but also of the difficulty of bringing the charge home even when (they state) they have no doubt about the facts.   For this reason many of them hold the view that, unless the Works Committee is properly related to and protected by Trade Unions, it cannot hope—in certain establishments at least—to discuss questions before the management with that sense of freedom which is essential to the success of joint deliberations.   In this connection it may be noted that one of two reasons given for the short terms of office of the shop stewards and secretaries of committees in one industry (one and three months respectively) was the fear of victimisation.   The other reason—in this the Works Committee appears to revert to the early forms of conducting the business of Trade Union branches—was stated to be the desire that everyone should take his share of office.

[1] It may also be noted that Officials of the various Unions were members of the workmen's side of the Joint Committee formed in connection with a profit-sharing scheme instituted before the war by a well-known shipbuilding firm in a northern town.

The other question relates to the allegations made by certain Trade Unionists that certain employers—more particularly in one or two industries—are fostering the growth of Works Committees in order to destroy Trade Union influence in their works. The danger, it is said, from the point of view of Trade Unionism is exactly the same as that which is believed to result from profit-sharing, *viz.*, that the workman is detached from his fellows and his power to obtain certain standard conditions is consequently weakened. The further charge has been made, in regard to one or two industries, that the employers were proposing, in the name of the Whitley Report, to form Works Committees without connection with the Unions, and from these committees to build up District and National Councils representative of employers and employed. It must, however, be emphasised that any such action is directly opposed to the proposals of the Whitley Report. These proposals look to the control of Works Committees by National or District Councils which, on the workpeople's side, would be representative of Trade Unions only ; and, in order that Works Committees should be formed on lines satisfactory to the national organisations, the Report proposes that the formation of Works Committees should, as far as possible, follow, and not precede, that of the National and District Councils. A logical application of this order of procedure may be impossible, but wherever individual employers find it desirable to form Works Committees before National or District Councils are instituted, the idea of the Whitley Report may be so far followed that such proposals should be brought before the Trade Unions concerned, and they should be asked to share in the formation of the Works Committee.

76. Trades Councils.

MODEL RULES AND CONSTITUTION FOR THE GUIDANCE OF TRADES COUNCILS. 1926.

The General Council has approved the following Model Rules, Constitution and Standing Orders prepared by the Trades Councils' Joint Consultative Committee for the use of a Trades Council or the Industrial Section of a Trades Council and Labour Party.

Slight adaptation may be required to meet local circumstances.

Name.

    1. The name of the Council shall be ' ————————————.'

Objects.

    2. The objects of the Trades Council shall be :

    (*a*) To promote the interests of all its affiliated organisations, and to secure united action on all questions affecting or likely to affect those interests ;

    (*b*) To help to promote suitable educational, social and sports facilities for adult workers ;

    (*c*) To establish more intimate relations between its affiliated organisations and the Trades Union Congress ;

    (*d*) To improve generally the economic and social conditions of the workers ;

    (*e*) To support and work for the application of the Industrial Workers' Charter, and such objects as the Trades Union Congress may from time to time determine.

In furtherance of these objects, Trades Councils shall co-operate with the local Labour Party where and whenever possible.

Constitution.

    3. The Council shall consist of representatives of Trade Unions or branches of Trade Unions, whose places of meeting are within the area covered by the Council.

The application of any organisation desiring to affiliate shall be submitted to the full Council for its approval or otherwise.

(*a*) REPRESENTATION.

Organisations affiliated to the Council shall be allowed representation on the following basis :

100 members or under, 1 delegate	This scale is merely shown as an example. Where deemed necessary Trades Councils may adhere to their present representation, as it is realised that a uniform scale would make Trades Councils with a large membership unwieldy or stultify the one with a few small unions affiliated.
101 ,, to 250 2 delegates	
251 ,, ,, 500 3 ,,	
One delegate for every additional 250 members.	

(b) GROUPING.

The Council shall be divided into groups catering in the main for the various industries as follows :

GROUP A.

Mining and quarrying.
Railways.
Transport.

GROUP B.

Shipbuilding
Engineering.
Iron and Steel.
Building.

GROUP C.

Cotton.
Other Textiles.
Clothing.
Leather.

GROUP D.

Glass, Pottery, Distribution, etc.
Agriculture.
General Workers.

GROUP E.

Printing and Paper.
Public Employees.
Non-Manual Workers.

GROUP F. (Women's Group).

In addition there shall be a group composed of ———— women representatives of organisations having women members.

This grouping is the one adopted by the Trades Union Congress, and Trades Councils are advised to work, where possible, on similar lines. Local conditions will, however, determine the most suitable grouping, which should be stated here.

Contributions.

4. Each affiliated organisation shall contribute an affiliation fee of ———— per member per annum, payable (annually, half-yearly or quarterly) in advance.

Composition of Industrial Executive.

5. (*a*) The Industrial Executive shall be elected at the Annual Meeting of the Council, and shall be composed of ———— members representing the various groups as may be determined from time to time.

(*b*) Each organisation affiliated to the Council shall be allocated to its appropriate group by the Industrial Executive.

In the event of resignation or death of any member of the Industrial Executive, the group shall be entitled to elect a new representative.

(*c*) If there are two or more unions represented in one group, no union shall be allowed more than one representative on the Executive while any union with over ——— affiliated membership in the same group is without representation.

Nomination of Industrial Executive.

6. (*a*) Each affiliated branch shall have the right to nominate a candidate to represent it in its group on the Industrial Executive.

(*b*) Unions having women members in their organisations, shall, in addition, have the right to nominate one member to represent the Women's Group on the Industrial Executive.

(*c*) A nomination for any group representative may only be made by a branch in that group.

(*d*) All nominated candidates must be delegates to the Council, and nominations for the Executive shall be made at the Council Meeting prior to the Annual Meeting (or sent to the Secretary at least 21 days prior to the Annual Meeting).

Election of the Industrial Executive.

7. The Industrial Executive shall be elected by (ballot) vote at the Annual Meeting of the Council, the necessary number of nominees in each group securing the highest numbers of votes to be declared elected.

Meetings of the Industrial Executive.

8. The Industrial Executive shall conduct the detailed business and report to meetings of the Council.

Any member of the Industrial Executive being absent at three consecutive Executive Meetings shall, unless a satisfactory reason for such absence has been sent to the Secretary, be deemed to have vacated office, and the vacancy shall be filled as provided for in Rule 5 (*b*).

Industrial Executive meetings shall be held on the ——— day in each month. A special meeting of the Industrial Executive may be called in the event of urgent business arising as and when deemed necessary by the President and Secretary.

Group Meetings.

9. In the event of special business arising affecting one or more unions in any particular group, the Secretary may call a meeting of the representatives of unions in that group to consider the question arising.

Minutes of such a meeting shall be submitted to the next meeting of the Council.

Council Meetings.

10. The Annual Meeting of the Council shall take place in the month of ——————— in each year.

The Ordinary General Meetings of the Council shall take place on the first (Thursday) in each month, to commence at ——— p.m., and shall not continue after ——— p.m. unless by special resolution of the Council. Delegates shall register on entry.

Each delegate shall receive from the Secretary not less than ——— clear days' notice of the business to be transacted at such meetings.

A Special Meeting may be called at any time by the Industrial Executive, or in the case of urgency, by the President and Secretary, or upon a written request of ——— delegates. In the latter case the object of the meeting must be clearly stated upon the requisition.

Officers.

11. The Officers of the Council shall be President, Vice-President, Secretary and Treasurer. The Secretary shall remain in office so long as he performs the duties to the satisfaction of the Council, and the President, Vice-President and Treasurer shall be elected at the Annual Meeting.

They shall receive such remuneration as may be decided upon by the Council upon the recommendation of the Industrial Executive. Upon retirement from office, they shall hand over to their successors or to the Industrial Executive all books, cash, keys, papers and other property of the Council.

Duties of Officers.

PRESIDENT.

12. The President shall preside at all meetings of the Council and Committees, and see that the business at meetings and of the Council generally is conducted in a proper manner. At meetings where the President is not in attendance, the Vice-President shall preside ; in the absence of both, the meeting shall elect one of the members present to preside.

SECRETARY.

The Secretary shall attend all meetings of the Council, Industrial Executive and Sub-Committees, keep a correct record of the proceedings and conduct the business of the Council in accordance with the rules. He shall keep a true account of income and expenditure.

He shall receive all moneys due to the Council, and shall pay the same over to the Treasurer without delay. He shall issue to each delegate notice of Council meetings, ———— clear days prior to the meeting except in the case of emergency meetings, when the notice shall be left to the discretion of the President and Secretary. He shall prepare the Annual Report and Balance Sheet, and submit a financial statement whenever requested by the Industrial Executive. Should any delegate be absent from the Council three meetings in succession, the Secretary shall notify his Society of the fact.

All cheques must be signed at least by two of the following officers :

President, Secretary, Treasurer.

TREASURER.

The Treasurer shall keep account of all moneys received from the Secretary, and bank same in the name of the Council.

He shall make such payments as may from time to time be authorised by the Council or the Industrial Executive, and when necessary shall sign cheques for authorised payments.

Auditors.

13. The Council at its Annual Meeting shall appoint two Auditors, whose duty it shall be to audit all accounts and the Annual Financial Statement, certify as to their correctness or otherwise, and report upon their findings at the Annual Meeting of the Council.

Deputations.

14. Any delegate who may be appointed to attend any Conference or transact any business on behalf of the Council, shall be allowed his out-of-pocket expenses, which must not exceed actual third-class railway fare paid, plus an allowance for hotel expenses, etc., of ———— per day when he is called upon to stay overnight, or otherwise a fee of ———— to cover incidental expenses during the day.

Alteration of Rules.

15. No alteration of rule shall take place except as decided at the Annual Meeting, and then only upon a vote of two-thirds of the delegates present voting in favour of the proposed alteration. Three months' notice shall be given to the Secretary of any proposed alteration of rule which it is desired shall be discussed at the Annual Meeting.

NOTES.

In Connection with the Model Rules and Constitution for Trades Councils.

The Model Rules, as submitted by the Trades Councils Joint Consultative Committee, are to govern :

(*a*) Purely Industrial Trades Councils.

(*b*) Industrial Committees of Trades and Labour Councils or Labour Parties.

They may be adapted and embodied in the rules of Trades and Labour Councils having no Industrial Committee, but all such bodies are advised to form an Industrial Committee composed only of Trade Union representatives, who should deal with matters of a purely industrial nature.

Rule 2.—Objects.

The last paragraph, ' In furtherance of these objects, Trades Councils shall co-operate with the local Labour Party where and whenever possible,' refers to the objects contained in the Workers' Charter, and such objects as the Trades Union Congress may from time to time determine.

Rule 3.—Constitution.

(*a*) REPRESENTATION.—As explained in the note at the side of the scale of representation, Trades Councils will have to adopt a suitable scale, having regard to the total affiliated membership and the number of unions attached.

(*b*) GROUPING.—The grouping stated in this rule is that which is adopted for administrative purposes by the General Council. It is suggested that Trades Councils themselves should be organised on similar lines as far as possible. It is recognised that Trades Councils will not be able to set up all these groups because in the majority of districts not more than half the industries will be in existence. The grouping represents a method, by which the Trades Councils may eventually become the local counterparts of the General Council. While the grouping system may not be applicable in detail, the general principle should, however, be observed. There may eventually arise the possibility of ultimate consultation between the groups in local Councils and those of the General Council.

Rule 5.—Composition of Industrial Executive.

This rule is drafted with the idea of obtaining a similarity between the composition of the General Council of the Trades Union Congress and the Executive of a Trades Council or the Industrial Committee of a Trades and Labour Council. Probably no Trades Council will cover the whole of the trades set out under the headings of the various groups.   It may be that some Trades Councils would only cover two or three of the groups set out in the model rules.

The number of representatives of the various groups of the Council will therefore be decided :

(*a*) By the number of Executive members the local Council find from past experience can most efficiently operate ;

(*b*) The number of groups which constitute the Council.

For example, assuming a Trades Council with an Executive Committee of 10 has affiliated unions with the following membership :

200 Railwaymen (GROUP A.)—100 Builders, etc. (GROUP B.)— 500 Agricultural Workers; 100 General Workers; 110 Distributive Workers (GROUP D.)

a suitable representation for the groups would be :

2 for GROUP A.—1 for GROUP B.—7 for GROUP D.

In the case of a Trades Council covering all six groups, the representation would be governed by the number of affiliated members in each group.

Par. (*c*) provides that where two or more unions exist in one group, representation shall not be monopolised by the large unions. As an example take the case given above of the Trades Council composed of three groups where Group D. has seven representatives out of the ten.   The agricultural workers having 500 members would probably obtain, in the ordinary course of events, the whole of the seven representatives for Group D., but in view of this provision the General Workers and Distributive Workers would each be entitled to at least one representative.

Rule 6.—Nomination of Industrial Executive.

(*a*) Each affiliated union may only nominate from its own membership for the Industrial Executive.

(*b*) All Unions having women members may, in addition to their nomination as provided for above, nominate one member, either male or female, as candidate for the election as representative of Group F.

(*d*) Gives alternative methods of nomination—
   (1) Verbally at the meeting prior to the Annual Meeting.
   (2) In writing—as specified in the model rules.

The rules adopted by a Trades Council should specifically state which method is to be adopted.

Rule 7.—*Election of Industrial Executive.*

This rule should state whether voting will take place by ballot or by show of hands.

Rule 8.—*Meetings of Industrial Executive.*

These meetings should take place early in the month. The General Council meets the fourth Tuesday in the month, and in the event of urgent matters arising out of their meeting having to be conveyed to Trades Councils, it is advisable that as little delay as possible should take place. If meetings of the Executive were fixed in the first week of the month this point would be met.

Rule 9.—*Group Meetings.*

Whilst a Trades Council cannot interfere with the autonomy of a local union, correspondence may be received by the Industrial Executive of the Trades Council in connection with a matter affecting one or more unions in any particular group, and under these circumstances it would be in order for them to summon a meeting of that group to discuss the matter in question if deemed necessary, but before doing so the Secretary or Secretaries of the local branches of the Union or Unions concerned should be consulted.

Rules 11, 12 and 13.—*Officers.*

Some Trades Councils have officers other than those stated in the model rules, such as Minute Secretary, Financial Secretary, Registrar, or Trustees. If the local Council desire that these offices should be continued, the necessary provision can be made.

77. Objects and Constitution of the London Trades Council.
(1927).

1. That the Delegates appointed by the Affiliated Societies within the Metropolitan postal area—governed under printed rules, approved by the Executive—be entitled the LONDON TRADES COUNCIL.

2. That the Council shall consist only of Delegates (of either sex) who are legal members of, and duly elected by, *bona fide* Trade Societies, or Branch or Branches of such Societies, and who shall have worked or be working at the trade they represent. That the members of each Society shall elect their Delegates at least once a year, their names and addresses to be forwarded to the Secretary, and their expenses to be paid by the Society or Branch they represent, and not by any outside body of private individuals.

3. (*a*) That the contribution to the Council shall be at the rate of twopence per member per year, *with a minimum* of £1, all subscriptions to be paid quarterly in advance ; the Secretary to communicate to the trades the amount, and when such contributions are due.

(*b*) Local Trades and Labour Councils shall pay the sum of 10s. per year for every 1,000 affiliated members or portion thereof with a minimum of £1.

4. (*a*) That a Delegate Meeting shall be held every month, to which each Society, or Branch thereof, shall be entitled to send one Delegate for every 500 members or portion thereof.

(*b*) A local Trades and Labour Council shall be entitled to send ONE Delegate for every 5,000 or part of 5,000 affiliated members, and every such Delegate shall have worked or be working at the trade he represents.

The Secretary shall issue to all affiliated organisations voting cards in accordance with the amount of affiliation fees paid on the following basis : (a) Trade Union organisations, ONE vote for every 500 members or part thereof.   (b) Trade Councils, ONE vote for every 5,000 members or part thereof.   Election of Committee and Officials shall be by Card Vote.   The Card Vote may be demanded on any motion by three Delegates rising in their places.

5. That the Executive Council shall consist of ten members, the Chairman, Treasurer and the Secretary—who shall be elected by ballot—seven to form a quorum ; five to retire by seniority every six months, at the half-yearly meetings in February and August. *Any member having served two consecutive years on the Executive shall be ineligible for election until a period of one year has elasped.*   All candidates for the Executive shall be nominated at the monthly Delegate Meeting preceding the election, their names to be printed on the agenda for the half-yearly meeting.   If any member leaves the Executive, such retirement shall be notified on the agenda for the following Delegate Meeting.   When the Minutes and business

arising therefrom have been disposed of, the Meeting shall proceed to fill such vacancy by vote of the Delegates, but no trade or industry shall have more than one Delegate on the Executive. Delegates shall not be eligible for election on the Executive until their Societies have been affiliated to the Council for at least six months.

6. That the Executive shall meet on the last Thursday in each month at 7.30 p.m. in the evening, unless ordered otherwise by a new Executive, the members to receive 5s. per sitting for their attendance ; but should any member absent himself (except in case of illness) for more than two ordinary consecutive meetings he shall cease to be a member, his place to be filled as stated in Rule 5.

7. That the duties of the Executive shall be to watch over the general interests of Labour—political and social— both in and out of Parliament and to use their influence in supporting any measure likely to benefit trade unions. They shall investigate cases of appeal made to them by trades in distress, and if, after strict investigation, they consider the cases worthy of support, they shall recommend the trades of London to render such cases every assistance. The Executive shall also have power to furnish credentials to deputations applying under such circumstances, but in no case shall the Executive make levies for any purpose.

8. That should any special circumstances arise demanding the attention of the Executive, the Secretary shall have power to summon their attendance, or if the Executive consider their ordinary meeting night not sufficient for the transaction of business, they shall have power to meet as often as circumstances require. An abstract printed sheet of such Executive Meetings (if by them deemed of sufficient importance) shall be sent to all Societies represented at the Annual General Council Meeting, or to any Society which shall contribute a proportionate share of the expenses.

9. That in cases where the Executive shall consider a question in dispute of great interest to the trades at large, or shall feel themselves not sufficiently powerful to deal with such cases of importance, they shall have power to summon, as soon as possible, a Delegate Meeting of the trades connected or otherwise with the Council to decide such cases of appeal or other business.

10. That the Secretary shall summon a Special Meeting of the Council within ten days of the receipt of a requisition duly signed by Delegates representing ten Societies, stating for what purpose such Meeting is required. The notice convening such special meeting

shall state the business, together with the names of the requisitionists and the Societies they represent.

.   .   .   .

21. That in any agitation or case in which the Council takes part, all monetary transactions shall be under the control of the Executive and finally ratified by the Council.

78. Trades Councils.

RELATION TO THE GENERAL COUNCIL OF THE T.U.C.
Ann. Report of T.U.C., 1924, p. 181.

That a Consultative Committee, consisting of six representatives from the Trades Councils and six from the Trades Union Congress General Council, be appointed.

79. Functions of Trades Councils.

Ann. Report of T.U.C., 1925, p. 213.

1. That local Trades Councils should act through their secretaries as the Labour correspondents for the Trades Union Congress General Council, and forward to the same regular reports of their local proceedings, together with such general information regarding movements amongst the organised workers as may be of value to the Council.

2. To make arrangements whereby the local Trades Councils are informed by the issue of special monthly statements regarding the activities of the Trades Union Congress General Council, and copies of reports, circulars, or other statements issued dealing with general questions of Trade Union policy and activity.

3. The Trades Councils to act as the circulating agencies for all special propaganda publications issued by the Trades Union Congress General Council.

4. When necessary to issue joint statements regarding Trade Union and Labour policy for general circulation, subject to their adoption by the Trades Union Congress General Council.

80. The Unemployed.

SUGGESTED CONSTITUTION for an Unemployed Association. ISSUED BY THE GENERAL COUNCIL OF THE TRADES UNION CONGRESS.[1]

T.U.C. Ann. Report, 1928, p. 111.

Name.

The name of the organisation shall be the ' ——————————
Unemployed Association under the auspices of the ——————————
Trades Council.'

Membership.

Any unemployed person may become a member of the Association by the payment of one penny per week, provided that when employment is secured such member transfers to the appropriate Trade Union covering the industry in which he or she is engaged. Any member more than six weeks in arrears with contributions shall be deemed to have left the Association.

Objects.

To combine in one organisation employed and unemployed persons for combating evils arising from unemployment. To impress on the Government and all local Authorities the need of finding work for those who are workless by Relief Works and any other agency which will meet the need. To obtain for unemployed persons as high a standard of living as possible, and the inauguration of schemes which will prevent degradation of those who are workless and their dependents.

Management.

The management of the organisation shall be vested in an Executive Committee composed of two persons from the following organisations :

From each Branch of Unemployed.
From the Trades Council.
From the Board of Guardians Labour Group.
From the Labour Group of the Local Governing Body.

[1] The T.U.C. held in 1928 decided not to continue with this form of organisation. The scheme is in operation in certain centres.

This committee shall have the right to co-opt any person or persons in an advisory capacity, but such person shall not be allowed to vote. The Executive shall also be empowered to suspend or expel any member who contravenes the rules and/or jeopardises the proper conduct of the Association by his or her action.

The President and Secretary of the Executive shall be elected by the Executive Committee.

The President shall preside over all meetings of the Committee, or in his absence the Committee may elect a member of the Executive to take his place for the time being.

The Secretary shall conduct the business of the Association in accordance with the rules of the Executive Committee. He shall receive all monies for the Association, and keep a record of income and expenditure.

He shall issue monthly to the branches a statement giving full particulars of income and expenditure, such statement to be made up to the end of each calendar month.

Branches.

In localities where more than one branch is opened, each branch of the Association shall elect a Chairman, Secretary and four members to form a branch committee. This Committee shall consider matters arising in their own district, and shall send in their suggestions or complaints to the Executive Committee.

The Branch Secretary shall also take the minutes of the branch meetings and shall be responsible for the collection of contributions from members, and paying in of all amounts so collected to the Secretary of the Executive Committee, weekly. Stewards for the collection of contributions may be appointed by the branch, but such stewards shall hand to the Branch Secretary the amount collected at each meeting.

Finance.

The control of all monies subscribed or collected shall be vested in the Executive, who shall appoint two Trustees. These Trustees shall be responsible for an account being opened in the name of the Association and the Secretary shall bank all monies received, in such account.

All cheques drawn in payment of liabilities of the Association shall bear the signature of two members of the Executive, four members of which shall be authorised to sign such cheques.

Explanatory Notes on Formation of Unemployed Association.

1. The Unemployed Association is to exist for the purpose of organising all unemployed persons, male or female, in a locality.

2. Trade Unionists may enrol, but they must be advised to retain membership of their Trade Union also.

3. Non-unionists should be urged to join the Unemployed Association. They do so on the understanding that when employment is secured they join the appropriate Trade Union.

4. Funds are constituted by means of :
    (*a*) Contributions of 1d. per week per member.
    (*b*) Grants from Trade Unions and Labour Organisations.
    (*c*) Grants from other organisations.
    (*d*) Grants from individual sympathisers.

5. It is essential that a suitable meeting room should be at the disposal of members of the Association. The room should be utilised as a general rendezvous for the unemployed. Newspapers and books should be available, and frequent meetings should be held, addressed by local Members of Parliament, Aldermen, Councillors and other persons who can speak on economic and social or other questions of interest. Endeavours should also be made to run socials and concerts and to cater in every way possible for the welfare of members.

6. An effort should be made to enlist public assistance from all quarters. The help of Religious and Social Organisations may be very useful in securing the use of rooms, either free of cost or at a nominal charge for cleaning. The assistance of anyone who can contribute anything to assist in alleviating the unemployment problem may be sought, irrespective of their opinions on other matters.

7. The Management of the Association is vested in an Executive Committee, provided for in the Constitution, and the Minutes of this Committee should be included in the agenda for each Trades Council meeting.

8. The Constitution provides for the opening of several branches ; this will prove necessary in large industrial centres. Each Branch may appoint two representatives to the Executive Committee.

9. Proper accounts must be kept, and the Association carried on with due regard to the requirements of a properly constituted organisation.

81. Trades Union Congress.

The Story of the Trades Union Congress, published by the T.U.C., 1925.

Over a period of 100 years British Trade Unionism presents a record of continuous growth and expansion. For more than half that period the Trades Union Congress has played an increasingly important part in the development of industrial organisation and policy. Before its advent the Trade Union Movement possessed no central organ to direct its course or to co-ordinate and unify its activities. Its appearance on the scene marks the beginning of a profoundly significant phase of working class history. The results of its work are visible not only in the enormous increase in the power and influence of the organised workers, but in the enhanced authority and prestige of the Trades Union Congress itself. Its right to speak and act in the name of the organised millions of trade unionists is now unchallenged. It has acquired its right of leadership by the exercise of powers vested in it by the affiliated Unions. These powers have been enlarged and extended as the Unions themselves have come to recognise that the furtherance of the aims and interests of the Trade Union Movement as a whole calls for unified leadership and the strongest possible concentration of the Movement's resources. The process has been a gradual one, instinctive rather then conscious in its earlier stages ; but latterly the Trade Unions have been able to discern more clearly the nature of this evolution and the goal to which it tends.

When the Trades Union Congress was founded, two generations ago, it gave little promise of becoming the authoritative and influential body that we know to-day. It was called into being to meet a special emergency, arising from the renewal of attacks upon the right of the working people to combine for the purpose of collective bargaining. Forty years of progress, from the date of the repeal of the Combination Laws in 1824, which swept away no fewer than thirty-four Acts of Parliament, the fruit of five centuries of repressive legislation, had placed the Trade Unions in a strong position. Reorganisation, consolidation and amalgamation of the local trade clubs had brought into existence powerful national Unions of the new type represented by the engineers' society, the carpenters' organisation and other big national bodies. Industrial warfare on a large scale followed the rise of the national unions, whose activities excited the suspicion and hostility not only of the employers but of the Government as well.

Under the pretext of investigating allegations of intimidation and outrage implicating Unions in Sheffield and Manchester, a Royal Commission was appointed in 1867 to inquire into the whole question of Trade Union organisation and method. Although the Trade Union leaders were able, after much difficulty, to place upon the Commission two men (Frederic Harrison and Thomas Hughes) whom they could trust to deal fairly with the Unions, there was only too much reason to fear that the Commission was intended to supply the Government with arguments for the suppression of Trade Unionism, or at any rate to furnish an excuse for the drastic curtailment of the very small amount of liberty enjoyed by the Unions under the existing law. Legal decisions affecting the safety of Trade Union funds also excited great uneasiness among the Trade Union leaders. It was at this critical stage in the development of British Trade Unionism that the Manchester and Salford Trades Council took the initiative in summoning representatives of the entire Trade Union Movement to a national Congress.

.   .   .   .

Ultimate Aims.

More and more as time goes on, Congress will give thought to the problem of making Trade Unionism, which has developed in this country experimentally without conscious direction from a common centre, into a unified and scientifically organised movement. That is the aim of its policy of amalgamation and federation which the General Council has been pursuing among the various Unions covering particular industries and trades. For the fullest possible extension of this policy, as for the strongest possible action in industrial disputes, and for the abolition of wasteful overlapping, sectionalism, and harmful rivalry between Unions, the General Council will, under Congress direction, be responsible. The course of events over a period of nearly sixty years, since Congress was founded, provides the evidence that the Trade Union Movement is not a piece of dead mechanism, but a vital organic force proceeding to still higher forms of organisation in accordance with the laws of its own being.

82. Trades Union Congress. Membership and Finance.

STANDING ORDERS OF THE T.U.C., 1928.

1.—Membership.

(*a*) The Trades Union Congress shall consist of *bona fide* Trade Union organisations affiliated in the manner prescribed in these standing orders.

(*b*) Any *bona fide* Trade Union organisation shall be entitled to make application to become affiliated to the Trades Union Congress, and shall furnish copies of its rules and regulations, together with all such particulars and information as the General Council may require.

(*c*) The General Council shall have full discretion as to the acceptance or rejection of any such application, subject to the decision being submitted to the Annual Meeting of Congress for approval or otherwise.

.   .   .   .

2.—Affiliation Fees.

Each affiliated organisation shall pay the undermentioned fees, based upon the full numerical strength of the society—probationary, free or otherwise :

(*a*) An affiliation fee of 3d. per member per annum, to be paid quarterly at the rate of ¾d. per member.

(*b*) An annual contribution of £1 per 1,000 members towards the expenses of maintaining the International Federation of Trade Unions.

(*c*) A fee of 10s. for each delegate attending the Annual Meeting of Congress.

83. The General Council of the T.U.C.

From *The General Council of the Trades Union Congress ; its Powers, Functions, and Work*, published by the T.U.C., 1925.

Historically, the Trades Union Congress, from its foundation in 1868, right down to the present day, has remained a purely voluntary association of Trade Unions. Within the Congress few organic changes have taken place. Notwithstanding the immense expansion of the Trade Union Movement, the rise of powerful aggregations of Unions of a different type from those which existed when the Congress was founded, and the changed direction of Trade Union policy, the fundamental basis of this voluntary association has not been altered.   Congress remains a deliberative assembly.   The functions it exercises on behalf of its constituent members are still those which it was originally called into being to fulfil.   It proceeds by the parliamentary method of counsel and consent.   Its debates and its decisions are effective only so far as they arise out of a common understanding and express a common will among the constituent Unions.

But, in obedience to an almost unconscious instinct for unity, the Trade Unions which came together in this voluntary association have themselves expressed through Congress their realisation of the need for a representative body which will not only discuss and decide, but will also execute decisions made in the interests of Trade Unionism as a whole.   Congress is a deliberative body which meets normally only once a year and remains in session no more than a single week ; it cannot execute its own decisions.   Nor can it leave to its constituent Unions the responsibility of carrying out individually decisions which involve them collectively.   An executive organ is a necessity.   From its earliest days Congress has had an executive council and a central office, whose functions were to carry out the instructions of Congress, to watch over the interests of Trade Unionism in the intervals between the annual assemblies, and to voice the opinion of the organised trades as occasion required.   Its business also was to organise and prepare the business for each year's Congress, replacing in this respect the local Trades Councils which, at the beginning of the Movement, convened the annual gathering and made themselves responsible for the conduct of its proceedings.

·   ·   ·   ·   ·   ·   ·   ·   ·

Centralised Organisation.

The powers, functions, and work of the General Council are, of course, far wider in their range than those of the old Parliamentary Committee which it has superseded.   The steps by which the Parliamentary Committee developed its authority until the time came for the General Council to inherit that authority and to carry it still further, brought the Congress to a realisation of the fact that they were no longer members of a voluntary association merely, but units of a closely knit and strongly centralised organisation.   Congress has itself assumed a more permanent form, in the sense that it continues to function from day to day through the General Council, which has ceased to be merely an administrative body carrying out a general policy framed by Congress ; the General Council is now an actively functioning organ dealing systematically with the problems of Trade Unionism as they arise, and taking action upon its own initiative in regard to a wide range of questions with which Congress may not have been previously concerned, or in relation to which Congress has only laid down guiding principles for the General Council to observe.

. . . .

From this description it is evident that an effort has been made to approximate the organisation of the central co-ordinating body of the Trade Union Movement more closely to the actual composition and structure of the Movement itself. The advent of the General Council marks a very great stride forward in the direction of a Labour General Staff. That idea has not yet been realised. In the view of many trade unionists, it will not be achieved until Trade Unions assent to the creation of a controlling body sitting in continuous session and devoting its whole time to the tasks of organisation, the co-ordination of effort, and the planning of industrial action on scientific lines.

To this end the development of Congress and the evolution of the General Council steadily tend ; under the stress of events the General Council has been obliged to assume functions and to exercise powers that have not been formally vested in it by Congress, and that tendency is more marked to-day than at any previous stage of Trade Union history. The rise of the Labour Party necessitated the handing over to the political organisation many of the functions and duties which the Congress formerly required the old Parliamentary Committee to discharge ; but this has not meant that the General Council has been shorn of powers and responsibilities. On the contrary, it has been acquiring larger powers and accepting far more onerous responsibilities within its proper sphere.

84. Composition and Election of the General Council of the T.U.C.

STANDING ORDERS OF THE T.U.C., 1928.

4.—Composition of General Council.

(*a*) A General Council shall be elected by Congress, and shall be composed of 32 members, representing 18 Trade Groups as follows :

	REPRESENTATIVES.
Mining and Quarrying - - - -	3
Railways - - - - - -	3
Transport (other than Railways) - -	2
Shipbuilding - - - - - -	1
Engineering, Founding, and Vehicle Building	3
Iron and Steel, and minor Metal Trades -	2
Building, Woodworking, and Furnishing -	2
Printing and Paper - - - - -	1
Cotton - - - - - - -	2
Textiles (other than Cotton) - - -	1
Clothing - - - - - -	1
Leather and Boot and Shoe - - -	1
Glass, Pottery, Chemicals, Food, Drink, Tobacco, Brushmaking, and Distribution -	1
Agriculture - - - - - -	1
Public Employés - - - - -	1
Non-manual Workers - - - -	1
General Workers - - - - -	4
Women Workers - - - - -	2

(*b*) Each organisation affiliated to Congress shall be allocated to its appropriate Group by the General Council, subject to the right of appeal by the unions concerned, such appeals to be considered, and decisions thereon to be given, by the General Council, prior to the issue of the final Agenda of Congress.

(*c*) Members of the General Council shall remain in office until the termination of the next Annual Congress, and shall be eligible for re-election.

(*d*) In the event of death or resignation of any member of the General Council, the candidate who secured the next highest number of votes in the same Group shall be eligible to fill the vacancy.

5.—Qualification for General Council.

(*a*) No candidate shall be eligible for election on the General Council unless he is a delegate (as per Standing Order No. 17) and the society so represented must have contributed towards the payment of the expenses of that Council in accordance with Standing Order No. 3 during the year previous to his or her election.

(*b*) No candidate shall be eligible for election on the General Council who has privately assisted, during the year preceding Congress, in the production of anything made by non-union labour, or by such firms as may be declared unfair by the interested trade society, or who has continued to assist privately in the production of anything made by non-union labour, or by such firms as may be declared unfair by the interested trade society, after such matters have been pointed out to him or her.

6.—Nomination of General Council.

(*a*) Each affiliated union shall have the right to nominate candidates to represent it in its Group on the General Council.

(*b*) Unions including women members in their organisation shall, in addition, have the right to nominate one woman member for the General Council, subject to the provisions of Standing Order No. 5.

(*c*) All nominations for the General Council shall be sent to the Secretary at least twelve weeks prior to the meeting of Congress, and the list of names shall be published on the agenda paper containing the propositions that are to be discussed at Congress. Ballot papers containing the names of such candidates shall be supplied to delegates on the day of election.

7.—Election of General Council.

(*a*) The General Council shall be elected by ballot vote at the Annual Meeting of Congress, the nominees in each Group securing the highest number of votes to be declared elected. Societies shall not be permitted to cast votes on any ballot paper for a number of candidates in excess of the number of persons required to be elected.

(*b*) Canvassing or bartering of votes for any position or purpose shall be strictly forbidden. Any candidate on whose behalf such means are employed shall be held responsible, and upon it being proved to the satisfaction of the General Council, he or she shall be disqualified for election and the society debarred from representation on the General Council or any other position for three years. This notification to be printed at the foot of all ballot papers issued.

(*c*) The ballot papers shall be issued by the Scrutineers, and after being filled up shall then be immediately placed in the box without inspection by the delegates other than those of the society voting.

(*d*) Any delegates found guilty of violating this Standing Order shall at once be reported to Congress, named by the President and expelled.   Such delegate or delegates shall not be eligible to attend Congress again for three years.

9.—*Appointment of Committees.*

(*a*) The General Council at its first meeting after each Congress shall appoint six Group Committees, in general accordance with the following plan :

GROUP A.—8 members :
> Mining and Quarrying, 3 ; Railways, 3 ; Transport, 2.

GROUP B.—8 members :
> Shipbuilding, 1 ; Engineering, 3 ; Iron and Steel, 2 ; Building, 2.

GROUP C.—5 members :
> Cotton, 2 ; Other Textiles, 1 ; Clothing, 1 ; Leather, 1.

GROUP D.—6 members :
> Glass, Pottery, Distribution, etc., 1 ; Agriculture, 1 ; General Workers, 4.

GROUP E.—3 members :
> Printing, 1 ; Public Employés, 1 ; Non-manual Workers, 1.

GROUP F.—5 members :
> 2 women and 3 members appointed by the General Council from organisations having women members.

(*b*) The Group Committee shall cultivate the closest possible contact with federations or other bodies representing the same interests outside the General Council, and the official attached to each Group Committee shall be responsible for collecting and filing of special information regarding the activities of the unions represented by the Group Committees.

(*c*) Each Group Committee shall elect its own Chairman, and shall investigate and submit reports on any matter referred to it by the General Council.   The work and functions of the Group Committees shall be subject to the control of the General Council.

(*d*) Special Committees shall be appointed by the General Council to deal with any questions which may arise from time to time.

85. Powers of the General Council of the T.U.C.

STANDING ORDERS OF THE T.U.C., 1928.

8.—Duties of General Council.

(*a*) The General Council shall transact the business in the periods between each Annual Congress, shall keep a watch on all industrial movements, and shall, where possible, co-ordinate industrial action.

(*b*) It shall watch all legislation affecting labour, and shall initiate such legislation as Congress may direct.

(*c*) It shall endeavour to adjust disputes and differences between affiliated unions.

(*d*) It shall promote common action by the Trade Union Movement on general questions, such as wages and hours of labour, and any matter of general concern that may arise between Trade Unions and Trade Unions, or between employers and Trade Unions, or between the Trade Union Movement and the Government, and shall have power to assist any union which is attacked on any vital question of Trade Union principle.

(*e*) It shall assist Trade Unions in the work of organisation, and shall carry on propaganda with a view to strengthening the Trade Union Movement, and for the attainment of any or all of the above objects.

(*f*) It shall also enter into relations with the Trade Union and Labour Movements in other countries with a view to securing united action.

(*g*) In the event of a legal point arising which in the opinion of the General Council (after consultation with Counsel) should be tested in the House of Lords in the general interest of Trade Unionism, the Council shall be empowered to levy the affiliated societies *pro rata* to provide the necessary expenses. Any society failing to pay the levy shall be reported to Congress.

(*h*) In order that the Trade Union Movement may do everything which lies in its power to prevent future wars, the General Council shall, in the event of there being a danger of an outbreak of war, call a special Congress to decide on industrial action, such Congress to be called, if possible, before war is declared.

(*i*) The General Council shall have power, whenever it deems necessary, to convene a Special Congress to deal with any contingency that may arise.

(*j*) The General Council shall prepare a report of its work for submission to the Annual Meeting of Congress. The report shall contain a list of the General Council meetings with dates, and also names of those members who were present at such meetings. The Standing Orders of Congress and the General Council shall be published with each Annual Report of the proceedings of Congress.

11.—*Industrial Disputes.*

(*a*) It shall be an obligation upon the affiliated unions to keep the General Council informed with regard to matters arising as between the unions and employers, and/or between one union and another, in particular where such matters may involve directly or indirectly large bodies of workers. The General Council shall, if they deem necessary, disseminate the information as soon as possible to all unions in the industry concerned which are affiliated to the Trades Union Congress, and which may be either directly or indirectly affected.

(*b*) The general policy of the Council shall be that unless requested to do so by the affiliated union or unions concerned, the Council shall not intervene so long as there is a prospect of whatever difference may exist on the matters in question being amicably settled by means of the machinery of negotiations existing in the trades affected.

(*c*) In the event, however, of negotiations breaking down and the deadlock being of such a character as to involve directly or indirectly other bodies of workpeople affiliated to the Trades Union Congress in a stoppage of work and/or to imperil standard wages or hours and conditions of employment, the Council may take the initiative by calling representatives of the unions into consultation, and use its influence to effect a just settlement of the difference. In this connection the Council having ascertained all the facts relating to the difference, may tender its considered opinion and advice thereon to the union or unions concerned. Should the union or unions refuse the assistance or advice of the Council, the Council shall duly report to Congress.

(*d*) Where the Council intervenes, as herein provided, and the union or unions concerned accept the assistance and advice of the Council, and where despite the efforts of the Council, the policy of the employers enforces a stoppage of work by strike or lock-out, the Council shall forthwith take steps to organise on behalf of the union or unions concerned all such moral and material support as the circumstances of the dispute may appear to justify.

86. Powers of the General Council on General Questions.

REPORT OF THE GENERAL COUNCIL ADOPTED BY THE TRADES UNION
CONGRESS, 1927.

T.U.C. Ann. Report, 1927, p. 112.

Co-ordination on General Questions.

Effective as Trade Unionism has been and is to-day, it is evident
that its structure is still largely based upon conditions of 30 to 50
years ago. In those days, before the advent of huge capitalist combinations, it was possible for sectional policy more effectively to meet
the position than it is to-day. Changing conditions, new industries,
new processes of production more than ever affect industry as a whole.
Employers have realised this fact and have organised accordingly.
The National Confederation of Employers' Organisations attempts to
deal with all general questions of policy with which their members
are concerned, and the decisions of the Confederation often determine the attitude of affiliated associations and individual employers
in negotiations with Trade Unions ; in fact, it is known that certain
employers on account of pressure from their Confederation have
refused demands to their employees which they might otherwise have
conceded.

As against this effective method of co-ordination on the part of the
employers, the General Council, as the national co-ordinating body
of the Trade Union Movement, has never been empowered to deal
with similar general basic principles for the whole movement. The
position has arisen time after time where individual unions have
found themselves quite unable to move on matters of general principle because the section of employers with which they have been
negotiating have been bound by the decisions of their Confederation.
Under the circumstances the General Council is convinced that this
difficulty will become more marked in the future and believes it will
be impossible to make progress in regard to general questions until
they are dealt with on a much wider basis.

The General Council desires to make it quite clear that these
general questions in no way include technical questions and detailed
application of matters affecting particular trades. Such matters
must at all times be dealt with by the unions themselves.

*The General Council therefore recommends that this necessary
co-ordination should be in the hands of the Trades Union Congress
through the medium of the General Council.*

87. Trade Boards Advisory Council.

STATEMENT OF OBJECTS AND RULES, 1928.

T.U.C. Ann. Report, 1921, p. 153, with amendments.

Objects.

The Trade Boards Advisory Council shall act as the representative and co-ordinating body for the Unions affiliated to the Trades Union Congress and represented on Trade Boards, in the following directions :

(*a*) To secure a common Trade Union Policy regarding the methods adopted by the Government in establishing Trade Boards.

(*b*) To act in consultation with the General Council of the Trades Union Congress on all questions relating to Trade Boards which are of general interest to the Unions affiliated to Congress ; and,

(*c*) To make when necessary joint representations to the Government on behalf of the Trade Unions represented on Trade Boards ; to secure joint consultation between the Unions represented on Trade Boards on all questions relating to Trade Boards' regulations dealing with wages, hours, conditions of employment, or other occupational interests of the members of affiliated societies, and to make joint recommendations on these questions as and when necessary.

Composition of Trade Boards Advisory Council.

1. The Trade Boards Advisory Council shall consist of members appointed by the Executives of the Unions affiliated to the Trades Union Congress, and represented on Trade Boards.

2. Each Union, as qualified above, shall be entitled to appoint one of its members to the Advisory Council.

Where the Union is represented on three or more Trade Boards, it shall have the right to appoint two members.

3. The Annual Meeting of the Advisory Council shall be held during the month of July in each year.

Included in the business of this Meeting shall be the consideration and adoption of the Annual Report and the appointment and election of the Executive Committee in accordance with the following plan :

Election of Executive Committee.

1. Three members of the Executive Committee, one of whom shall be Chairman, shall be appointed by the General Council of the Trades Union Congress.

2. Members of the Executive Committee representing the Advisory Council shall be appointed or elected, as the case may be, as follows :

(*a*) The Executives of those ten Unions concerned having the greatest number of seats on Trade Boards allocated to their members at the time of the appointment shall each appoint one member of the Executive Committee.

Provided that the Executives of those Unions amongst the first ten having more than fifty seats on Trade Boards allocated to them shall each appoint one additional member of the Executive Committee.

The appointments shall be annual, and the retiring members shall be eligible for re-appointment provided that their Unions retain their position amongst the first ten.

(*b*) Those members of the Advisory Council representing the remaining Unions concerned shall elect five members of the Executive Committee annually from persons nominated by the Executives of the Unions. No Executive shall be entitled to make more than one nomination.

Duties of Executive Committee.

1. The Executive Committee shall be responsible for giving effect to the decisions of the Advisory Council, and shall consult with the Trades Union Congress General Council respecting any Trade Boards question affecting Trade Union policy.

2. The Executive shall issue, as may be considered necessary, special reports to the Unions represented by the Advisory Council dealing with special phases of Trade Board activity. It shall supply the Unions with information regarding Trade Boards' awards, and keep the Unions informed of the attitude of the Employers and the Government regarding Trade Boards' policy or regulations, and it shall from time to time submit reports to the General Council of the Trades Union Congress.

3. The Executive shall be the convening body for Advisory Council meetings, and shall convene such meetings additional to the Annual Meeting as and when these may be necessary.

On the request of five Unions for a meeting of the full Council, the same shall be called.

Administrative Department and Finance.

1. The administrative department necessary to give effect to the decisions of the Trade Boards' Advisory Council and Executive Committee shall be supplied by the Trades Union Congress General Council, which shall also appoint the necessary Secretarial Assistants to act for and with the Advisory Council.

2. The Trades Union Congress General Council shall be responsible for the administrative, Official and Office expenses in connection with the work of the Trade Boards Advisory Council, including the expenditure in connection with Advisory Council or Executive Committee meetings. This shall not include travelling or other personal expenses of delegates to Advisory Council or Executive Committee meetings.

3. The administrative department shall be responsible for collecting and filing of Trade Boards awards, special reports dealing with Trade Board policy or activity, and shall supply, as requested, special reports or information to the Unions represented by the Trade Boards Advisory Council.

4. The officials of the Trade Boards department of the General Council, Trades Union Congress, shall act with and on the instruction of the Trade Boards Advisory Council and Executive Committee, subject to a general supervisory control by the Trades Union Congress General Council.

88. Non-manual Workers and Trade Unions.

The Acquisitive Society, by R. H. TAWNEY, 1921, p. 203.

The growth of a class of managers, under-managers, experts, and technicians, who do an ever-increasing part of the scientific and constructive work of industry, but who have no voice in its government, and normally no share in its profits, is one of the most impressive economic developments of the last thirty years. It marks the emergence within the very heart of capitalist industry of a force which, both in status and in economic interest, is allied to the wage earners rather than to the property owners, and the support of which is, nevertheless, vital to the continuance of the existing order.

Almost the most important industrial question of the immediate future is in what direction it will throw its weight.

So far as can be judged at present, the salaried brain-workers appear to be undergoing the same gradual conversion to a cautious and doctrineless trade unionism as took place among the manual workers in the nineteenth century. Mine-managers, under-managers, and surveyors all have their trade unions.

The Railway Clerks' Association, with its 90,000 members, includes stationmasters, inspectors, and other supervisory grades.

Bank officers, insurance officials, pottery managers, technical engineers, not to mention clerks and foremen, are organised in their respective organisations. . . .

From the conversion of industry into a profession those who at present do its intellectual work have as much to gain as the manual workers. For the principle of function, for which we have pleaded as the basis of industrial organisation, supplies the only intelligible standard by which the powers and duties of the different groups engaged in industry can be determined.

89. Non-manual and Professional Workers.

PROFESSIONAL WORKERS JOINT CONSULTATIVE COMMITTEE.

T.U.C. Ann. Report, 1927, p. 153.

The terms of reference of the Joint Consultative Committee are as follows :

1. That a Joint Consultative Committee be formed representing the General Council Trades Union Congress and the National Federation of Professional Workers.

2. That the Joint Committee shall prepare a list of unions and associations, representing professional, technical, and administrative workers, and a survey of ways and means by which such unions could be brought into closer contact.

3. That the Committee shall also prepare suggestions on the best method of convening a general conference of all unions or associations representing professional, technical, administrative, and supervisory workers, also the resolutions most suitable for discussion at such a conference.

90. Trade Unionism and the Co-operative Movement.

T.U.C. Ann. Report, 1926, p. 204.

Co-operative Wholesale Society and Trade Union Membership.

The Co-operative Wholesale Society directors have sought the advice of the General Council on the interpretation of the following resolution passed by the C.W.S. quarterly meeting held on October 4th and 11th, 1924 :

‘ That in the case of all other eligible employés, continuing membership of one or other of the Trade Unions eligible for affiliation to the Trades Union Congress shall be a condition of employment by this Society and dismissal shall follow non-compliance therewith accordingly.’

The difficulties which had arisen affected mainly :

(a) the relationships of foremen in co-operative service to the National Union of Distributive and Allied Workers, and

(b) the organisation of technical workers.

The General Council had some difficulty in interpreting, or attaching to the resolution set forth above any definite meaning.   In communications to the General Council, the C.W.S. directors have used the following forms of words : ‘ eligible for affiliation to the British Trades Union Congress,’ and ‘ recognised for affiliation to the British Trades Union Congress.’

In this connection the General Council have to point out that they are unable to lay down any hard and fast rules with respect to eligibility or recognition.   The practice of the General Council is to take each application for affiliation on its merits, and at times affiliation to the British Trades Union Congress has been sought from unions whose bona-fides could not be questioned, but in view of decisions of Congress that the General Council should devote itself to minimising the number of unions, such applications when opposed by affiliated unions who cater for the same type of worker, have been refused.   In some of these cases amalgamation proposals have been made to the societies seeking affiliation.

The General Council decided that it was unwise at the present time to state conditions either with respect to eligibility or recognition.

In examining the list of unions and societies submitted by the C.W.S. there are two distinct classes :

(a) the professional class which is outside the organised Trade Union Movement, and

(b) the class including clerical workers and foremen, for which unions affiliated to Congress already cater.

With respect to class (a) the General Council informed the C.W.S. directors :

‘ That until there is a recognised change of policy by the official Trade Union Movement as expressed through its Congress, such

workers as are included in, or organised by, the British Association
of Chemists, the Association of Architects, Surveyors, and
Technical Assistants ; the Royal Institute of British Architects ;
the Institute of Mining Engineers, and the National Union of
Scientific Workers who are not catered for at present by unions
affiliated to the Trades Union Congress, the position would be
met by such members continuing to remain members of the
Associations appropriate to their calling.'

With respect to class (b) and with special regard to the National
Amalgamated Society of Foremen and the Amalgamated Managers'
and Foremen's Association of Newcastle-on-Tyne, the General
Council informed the C.W.S. directors that they themselves must
decide whether these unions should be recognised or not.

With respect to the Guild of Insurance Officials, the General
Council informed the C.W.S. directors :

'That while no application for affiliation has been received
from the Guild of Insurance Officials, and whilst its rules appear
to be in conformity with those of a bona fide Trade Union, we
have to say that in our opinion the Guild of Insurance Officials
is a union eligible for membership of Congress, but it does not
necessarily follow that it would be accepted into membership of
Congress.'

With respect to the Bank Officers' Guild the General Council
advised the C.W.S. directors that they would be in order in affording recognition to that society.

91. Disputes between Trade Unions and the Co-operative Movement.

AGREEMENT BETWEEN THE SIGNATORY ORGANISATIONS REPRESENTING
CO-OPERATIVE SOCIETIES AND TRADE UNIONS REPRESENTING
WORKERS EMPLOYED BY SUCH CO-OPERATIVE SOCIETIES.

T.U.C. Ann. Report, 1926, p. 205.

1. In the event of negotiations on matters of wages and/or
general conditions of labour between a co-operative society or any
combination of co-operative societies and a Trade Union, or any
combination of Trade Unions breaking down and failing to produce
agreement, the matters at issue shall, within seven days of the breakdown or non-agreement, be referred to a National Conciliation

Board, and the Board shall meet to deal with the case within 14 days from the date of the reference. No lock-out or strike shall take place unless the matters at issue have been referred to and dealt with by the Board in accordance with the provisions of these rules.

2. The National Conciliation Board shall be composed of twelve representative members—six on the workers' side and six on the employers' side—and an independent chairman.

3. Each Trade Union shall appoint four of its representatives to constitute a workers' panel. Similarly, the Co-operative Union Limited shall appoint four representatives in respect of each of their sections to form an employers' panel. With a view to giving special representation on the employers' panel to the distinctive interests of national co-operative societies or federations, each of these bodies also shall appoint four additional representatives to the employers' panel.

4. From the workers' and employers' panels the representative members of the National Conciliation Board shall be selected as described hereunder.

5. The Trade Union directly party to the prior negotiations which have resulted in breakdown or non-agreement shall, on the case being referred to the National Conciliation Board, have the right to select from the workers' panel the six members required to constitute the workers' side of the Conciliation Board, including in that number, if it so desires, any or all of its own four appointed members of the workers' panel. If there are two or more Trade Unions directly parties to the case they shall, as far as possible in proportion to their respective memberships concerned, share in the selection of the six representatives to form the workers' side of the Conciliation Board : provided that two of the six representatives selected shall be drawn from unions not directly implicated in the matter in dispute. Similar procedure to that prescribed above for a Trade Union or unions shall be followed by the Co-operative Union Limited in respect of their section or sections concerned, or by any other of the employers' organisations signatory to this agreement.

6. The independent chairman shall be drawn in rotation from a panel of six persons, who shall be appointed in a manner to be agreed hereafter. He shall be responsible for the orderly conduct of the proceedings of the Conciliation Board and for the observance of these rules of procedure. He may, if he thinks fit, offer any sug-

gestions or advice to the representative members of the Conciliation Board, but he shall not be allowed to vote on any matters referred to the Board for settlement.   In certain circumstances, however, as outlined in Rule 7 (iii), he will act as an arbitrator.

7. In dealing with any case referred to it the Conciliation Board shall hear and consider any evidence and arguments that may be submitted by the parties to the reference, and endeavour to secure a settlement on one or other of the following lines :

(i) By *unanimous* vote of the twelve representative members of the Conciliation Board.   If a decision can be reached by such a vote the terms of that decision shall constitute an agreement conclusively settling the matters referred to the Board, and be binding on the parties to the reference.

(ii) If a unanimous vote of the twelve representative members of the Conciliation Board cannot be obtained, but there is a *majority on both sides* in favour of terms of settlement, the parties to the reference shall be asked whether or no they will agree to accept a majority decision, and if the reply is in the affirmative (but not otherwise) such majority decision shall be given and shall constitute an agreement conclusively settling the matters referred to the Board and be binding on the parties to the reference.

(iii) If a settlement cannot be secured by the means outlined in (i) and (ii) of this rule, the parties to the reference shall be asked whether or no they will agree to allow the independent chairman to act as arbitrator.   If the parties reply in the affirmative (but not otherwise) the independent chairman shall act as arbitrator and give a conclusive and binding award.

8. A Secretary for each side of the Conciliation Board shall be appointed, who may, or may not, be a member of the Board.

9. The expenses of the employers' representatives at the meetings of the Conciliation Board shall be paid by the Co-operative Union, Limited, and those of the workers' side by the union or unions directly concerned in the reference to the Board.

10. The expenditure in connection with the attendance of the independent chairman and the convening and conducting of the meetings of the Board shall be borne in equal proportions by the Co-operative Union Limited and the union or unions directly concerned in the reference to the Board.

92. International Federation of Trade Unions.

RULES.

Fourth Year Book of the I.F.T.U., 1926.

I.—Composition.

1. The International Federation of Trade Unions shall be composed of the National Trade Union Centres of the various countries, which adopt by their rules the policy and objects of the International Federation of Trade Unions.

2. Only one National Centre from each country may be admitted.

3. The autonomy of the Trade Union movement of each country is guaranteed.

II.—Headquarters.

. . . .

III.—Objects.

5. The objects of the International Federation of Trade Unions shall be :

(*a*) To bring about the unity of the international working class by developing closer relations between the trade unions in all countries.

(*b*) The development of International Trade Secretariats accepting the International Federation of Trade Union's platform.

(*c*) To promote the interests and activities of the Trade Union movement, nationally and internationally.

(*d*) To carry on any activities of general interest to the Trade Unions.

(*e*) To promote the development of International Social Legislation.

(*f*) To promote workers' education.

(*g*) To avert war and combat reaction.

IV.—Methods of Attainment.

6. (*a*) Close co-operation with the affiliated National Centres, and the International Trade Secretariats.

(*b*) Co-operation with other organisations, in so far as such co-operation appears useful in the interests of the Trade Union movement.

(*c*) Giving support to trade union activities in the affiliated countries, as requested by the National Centre concerned.

(*d*) Giving support to trade union activities in countries not yet affiliated.

(*e*) Mediation in cases of dispute within the Trade Union movement.

(*f*) The compilation of statistics.

(*g*) The collection and compilation of information concerning the Trade Union movement and Social Legislation.

(*h*) The publication of a periodical and of other reports of interest to the Trade Union movement.

(*i*) The protection of the workers' interests in immigration and emigration.

(*k*) Propaganda in favour of arbitration and disarmament.

V.—Management.

7. The International Federation of Trade Unions shall be managed by an Executive Committee and a General Council, who shall be obliged to act in accordance with the decisions of the Congresses of the International Federation of Trade Unions.

8. (A). THE EXECUTIVE COMMITTEE.

The executive Committee shall be composed of a President, three vice-presidents, and three Secretaries. . . .

9. (B). THE GENERAL COUNCIL.

The General Council shall be composed of :

(*a*) The members of the Executive Committee.

(*b*) One delegate from each of the groups of countries named hereafter :

.   .   .   .

(*c*) Three representatives of the International Trade Secretariats.

.   .   .   .

12. (C). THE CONGRESS.

The Congress shall consist of the General Council and delegates from the affiliated National Centres. . . .

93. Trade Internationals.

CONSTITUTION OF THE INTERNATIONAL UNION OF ORGANISATIONS COMPRISING THE WORKERS ENGAGED IN FOOD PRODUCING INDUSTRIES, 1924.

I.—Aims and Objects.

1. The International aims to unite the central organisations of the workers in the food producing industries of all countries for the

purpose of cultivating and practising international solidarity and for the more effective protection of their interests.

It aims to achieve these purposes by :

(*a*) Advancing and solidifying the relations between the organisations in the various countries.

(*b*) Mutual exchange of information and understandings concerning important questions upon the economic field as well as the field of protective labour legislation.

(*c*) Assistance to travelling members.

(*d*) Entering into mutual agreements.

(*e*) Keeping away of workers during wage struggles.

(*f*) Financial support during strikes and lockouts of greater dimensions.

II.—*Organisation and Administration of the International Union.*

2. The International Union consists of the national organisations, recognising the existence of the class struggle, who are affiliated with their national central labour body and who recognise the provisions of this constitution. The Union's tasks are to be settled solely by its competent organs. . . .

III.—*The International Congress.*

4. The International Congress, as a rule, takes place every three years, at a place designated by the preceding Congress.

IV.—*International Administration.*

8. The administration of the International Union is composed of representatives of the various national organisations, who are elected by the International Congress.

The number of members is to be 15 delegates and the same number of deputies to be elected by the Congress.

V.—*The International Secretariat.*

B. DUTIES OF AFFILIATED ORGANISATIONS.

12. It is the duty of the national organisations affiliated with the International Union :

(*a*) To report to the Secretariat the holding of their conventions, respecting their decisions, election of their executive officials and the names of the parties authorised to conduct official correspondence.

(*b*) To regularly provide the Secretariat with its official publications and reports in duplicate.

(*c*) To inform the Secretariat as to all important occurrences of interest to the International organisation, especially as it concerns extensive wage movements, working contracts, or mutual agreements entered into with organisations affiliated with the Secretariat, or others.

(*d*) To promptly reply to all inquiries from the Secretariat.

(*e*) To pay the annual dues decided upon by the International Congress promptly at the end of the first six months of each calendar year to the Secretariat.

94. National Joint Council.

T.U.C. Ann. Report, 1921, p. 148.

1.—The National Joint Council.

A National Joint Council shall be appointed, representing the General Council of the Trades Union Congress, the Executive Committee of the Labour Party, and the Parliamentary Party. It shall consist of the Chairman, Secretary, and three other members of each of the three bodies.

2.—Duties of the Council.

The National Joint Council shall :

(*a*) Consider all questions affecting the Labour Movement as a whole, and make provision for taking immediate and united action on all questions of national emergency.

(*b*) Endeavour to secure a common policy and joint action, whether by legislation or otherwise, on all questions affecting the workers as producers, consumers and citizens.

(*c*) Consult, when necessary, a Joint Conference, consisting of the General Council of the Trades Union Congress and the Labour Party Executive, together with a number of Parliamentary Members, which, with the Labour Party Executive, will be equal in number to the numbers of the General Council of the Trades Union Congress.

(*d*) Present an annual report to the Trades Union Congress, and the Labour Party Conference and the Parliamentary Party.

3.—*Officers.*

The Chairman of the General Council of the Trades Union Congress shall be Chairman of the National Joint Council, and the Secretary of the Labour Party shall be the Secretary of the National Joint Council.

4.—*Finance.*

The expenditure incurred by the Council shall be met in equal proportions by the General Council of the Trades Union Congress and the Executive Committee of the Labour Party.

PART III

FUNCTIONS AND METHODS

To attempt to illustrate even a tithe of the multifarious activities of Trade Unions, in the space available, is an impossible task. Nor would it be easy if there were unlimited space, for many of the most important functions and methods of Trade Unions are not recorded in documentary form. One can piece together the result of much research into the practices adopted and the functions silently carried out, as Mr. and Mrs. Webb have so brilliantly done in their *Industrial Democracy*, but the harvest of written records provided by the Unions themselves may, in certain directions, be very small.

Consequently, the documents here presented are merely a selection dealing with some of the more important activities which lend themselves to this treatment. On the other hand, there is for some topics such a wealth of documentary material that justice cannot be done to them in a few short extracts.

Collective Bargaining and Agreements. Collective bargaining is, of course, the chief activity of all Unions, as it is the primary object of such organisations to conclude agreements with employers, to regulate conditions of labour (**95**). Unions may function politically, and in their capacity as citizens the members may use their funds, votes and influence to secure legislation enforcing minimum conditions of employment, and even general social objectives, but their primary function is the organisation of their economic power derived from the possession and collective exercise of the will to work or abstain from working. That power is exercised as truly in the negotiation of agreements as in the conduct of strikes, and frequently far more effectively, which explains why for every dispute over which there is a stoppage of work there are hundreds in which an agreement is negotiated. Strikes are often unavoidable, and, of course, they are very often completely justifiable, from the point of view of results, but the real and continuous exercise of Trade Union power is to be seen far more in the council room than on the picket line.

The desirability of maintaining the system of collective bargaining and agreements is nowadays recognised by practically all British employers of any importance ; this is implicit in many of the documents included in the present collection (101, 211, 212, 213), and it is specifically asserted in (96, 214).

Unions have, generally, specialised officials whose business it is to carry on the skilled work of negotiating. Such officials may, in the early stages of bargaining, be also engaged in other duties, as in the case of shop stewards (73), or the more specialised local representative described in (97, 98). In the later stages it is becoming more usual, in the larger Unions at least, to employ officials for the sole purpose of negotiating, and thus a Trade Union ' civil service ' is being developed for this work and for the necessary administrative tasks (99).

The Agreement itself, when concluded with the employer, is, in this country and in the United States, a ' gentlemen's agreement ' only, (100). It is not legally binding, as such, though its terms may expressly or by implication become the terms of the individual contract of employment. In contrast, the collective agreement in Germany, and elsewhere on the Continent, is a contract the terms of which are legally binding on the individuals concerned, and no employer or worker may enter into a contract of employment which gives less favourable terms to the latter. In U.S.A. more recently there has been a tendency to give a greater degree of legal recognition to collective agreements.[1]

The voluntary nature of agreements in this country is emphasised in (101), as is the fact that in practice such bargains are almost always honoured by both parties, despite the lack of penalties.

[1] *E.g.* Schlesinger *v.* Quinto, 194 N.Y. Supp. 401 (1922).

A number of examples of Collective Agreements are included in the present collection of documents, (*e.g.* **102-106, 112, 113**). Students should refer to the Ministry of Labour's volume of Collective Agreements, which is very comprehensive.[1] From such a collection, or even from the few examples given here, it will be seen that agreements are often very lengthy and detailed documents, covering the entire range of labour conditions and relations. Wages, hours, overtime, holidays, the relations between management and labour, machinery for avoiding disputes, distribution of work, juvenile labour, and many other topics are dealt with in these agreements, which sometimes run to scores of closely printed pages. The piecework lists in the cotton trade or the coal industry, for example, are highly complicated statements which few people outside, and not many inside, the industry in question, could even pretend to understand, so technical are the details.

Some Agreements become famous because of some new principle laid down, as in the mining Agreement of 1921, (**102**), or because of the far-reaching effects on labour relations, as in the York Memorandum, (**113**). A highly interesting Agreement giving the Unions a considerable voice in regulating conditions is shown in (**104**). The present tendency to apply the methods of collective bargaining to the entire field of industry is illustrated in the T.U.C. declaration contained in (**107**) and in the invitation issued by the ' Mond ' group of Employers and accepted by the General Council of the T.U.C. (**108**).

Conciliation and Arbitration.—Very many collective agreements provide for the setting up of machinery for conciliation or arbitration in case of disputes, (**104, 112, 113**). The State itself has long made similar provision in the Conciliation Act of 1896, (**109**), the Railways Act of 1921, (**231**), and elsewhere. The value of conciliation machinery was emphasised by the Industrial Council, set up by the Government, in 1913, (**110**).

Industry as a whole, through the Conferences between the

[1] Last ed., 1910. A new edition will shortly be published.

General Council of the T.U.C. and the 'Mond' group
of Employers, has recently made proposals for additional
machinery for conciliation, (111), but whether this scheme
will be adopted remains to be seen.

Two well-known types of joint organisation for negotiating
and for conciliation are shown in (113), where the Engineering trade's method is described, and (112), which gives the
Building industry's scheme.

The Industrial Courts Act of 1919 provided machinery
for the settlement of, or an enquiry into, a dispute, actual or
apprehended. The appointment and powers of Industrial
Courts are described in (114), while the most famous award
that the Court has so far given is in large part reproduced in
(115). This award is important because it deals with the
difficult and very controversial question of the industry v.
craft basis of wage payment. Industrial Court awards are
not legally binding upon the parties, nor is there any obligation to hold up a strike or lockout pending the Court's report.
In very few cases, so far, has either party refused to abide by
the Court's award. The Industrial Court also acts as the
final appeal tribunal for disputes between Unions of civil
servants and the Government as employer.

Legally binding decisions as to minimum rates of wages,
etc., are made by Trade Boards, in certain low-paid or badly
organised trades, and by the Agricultural Wages Board and
Committees for agricultural workers. The application and
powers of these bodies are set out in (116, 119), and it is to
be noted that in both types there are equal numbers of
workers' representatives, (in practice, Trade Union nominees),
and employers, with several independent members in addition.
In (117, 118), are given the Regulations for a Trade Board
and a specimen Trade Board Order fixing minimum rates, etc.

Compulsory arbitration in industrial disputes has never
found favour in this country, (111), and probably never will,
but in Australia it has long been in operation. An interesting comment of the Commonwealth Arbitration Court on
the value of Trade Unionism is given in (120). The
Canadian ' Lemieux ' Act has aroused much interest in other

countries since it was passed, owing to the provision that a strike or lockout is illegal, in the industries to which the Act applies, pending the Report of the Board of Investigation. Once the Report is issued the parties are free to take any action they please. The important clauses of the Act are given in (121). There have been many stoppages in violation of the Act, but in only a few cases has a prosecution followed.

Strikes and Lockouts.—Great public interest is naturally taken in strikes and lockouts, especially if they are large-scale stoppages, or if they are in ' key ' industries. Actually, as has been observed, stoppages of work are really of much less importance and frequency than one would imagine from a study of the daily press.

Nevertheless, the Trade Union movement will never give up the right to strike, (122), and most Unions have provisions in their Rules for the calling and carrying on of strikes, (123, 35, 36, 37).

Strikes, lockouts, and trade disputes have all been defined by statute in this country, (124), and the mere act of striking is in no case a criminal offence, except where it is both in breach of contract and is likely to lead to danger or grave inconvenience to the community or to cause injury to life or property (125, 126, 127, 128).

Striking, without breach of contract, is in no case a criminal offence, but it is now illegal to declare or instigate or further certain kinds of strikes or lockouts (129). Sympathetic or secondary strikes are lawful, provided they are not otherwise within the definition of illegal strikes, as laid down in (129). The Royal Commission on Trade Disputes, 1906, declared emphatically against the distinction which is made in some countries between primary and secondary strikes, (130), and this view was adopted in the definition of ' trade dispute ' in the Trade Disputes Act of 1906, (124). An example of instructions for a sympathetic strike, (not, however, put into effect), is given in (131) ; this is included here because it was the first case in which the General Council of the T.U.C. took over the direction of an industrial dispute. The general legal position regarding activities in connection with strikes, such as picketing, inducing breach of contract, etc., is illustrated in (132, 133, 134), which must be read together, but of course these extracts do not set out the entire law on the matter. The essential characteristics of the 'secondary boycott' are well summarised in the extract from the judgment in the famous Danbury Hatters' Case in U.S.A. (135).

The use of the powerful weapon of the injunction has not been developed in this country for the purpose of preventing or crippling strikes, as it has been in the United States. A recent Act gives the Attorney-General (the chief law officer of the Government), certain powers, (136), but nothing like the type of injunction which is given in (137) is known in Britain. There is, of course, a bitter controversy in America between the Unions and employers on this matter. Although the Clayton Act apparently safeguarded the Unions, (138), this protection proved quite illusory, and the example already cited shows how comprehensive and far-reaching an injunction can be. It is a fundamental principle in Anglo-American law, however, that the courts will not order the specific performance of a contract of personal employment. This is firmly established in this country, and it was laid down in the United States many years ago, (139), and has been repeatedly affirmed. Thus, although damages may be awarded for breach of contract, no court will issue an injunction to restrain a person from striking, even in breach of contract.

A leading article from a Strike Bulletin, commenting on the settlement of a strike, is of interest, (140). A few of the chief documents in the National Strike of 1926, (usually, but erroneously called the 'General Strike'), are given in (141-150), but many others could be included if the space were available.

The Government's powers and machinery for defeating such large-scale strikes are set out in (151, 152), and these were used in 1926 as well as in earlier disputes. The common Labour view of what is usually termed the 'General Strike' is well expressed in (153).

Benefits.—The range of Trade Union activities is so

extensive that only a few of the main ones can be described here. Mutual Insurance, (154), is one of the oldest functions. Some Unions pay few benefits, and those only of the 'trade' type, (e.g. strike pay), while others have most elaborate scales covering many kinds of insurance, (155-158). The T.U.C. is anxious to reduce the enormous differences in contributions and benefits among Unions catering for similar classes of labour, (159).

The payment of benefits cannot be directly enforced by law, (205), but a recent Act has apparently modified this rule in certain cases, (160).

Political Action.—The present position regarding the party political activities of Trade Unions is indicated in (161, 162), and the model Political Rules issued by the Chief Registrar for the guidance of Unions are set out in (163).

Mr. Winston Churchill bears witness to the value of political action for Trade Unions, in (164), while in (165) Prof. Geldart puts the case for contracting-out of the obligation to pay political contributions, and against the contracting-in method which has since been adopted in the Act of 1927.

One of the innumerable valuable results in the industrial field, of political action, is seen in the Fair Wages Clause, (166).

As explained in the Introduction, the Trade Union movement was responsible for the creation of the Labour Party, and it may be said that since the establishment of the Party the Unions carry on their political work mainly through that organisation. The Unions that are not affiliated to the Party do not normally carry on party political activities, except in the way of moral influence which may be behind some project sponsored by the movement generally.

The Labour Party is still, in the main, the political expression of the Trade Union movement, as will be clear from the constitution of the Party, (167), though the admission of individual members since 1918 is introducing a new element.

Other Activities.—The activities of Unions in placing unemployed members, (168), in informing members of conditions, (169), and in furthering the technical education of their members, (170), are given as examples of what Unions do as part of their normal routine work. A multitude of other functions and activities must remain unmentioned, but it is perhaps worth while to draw attention to a method, very common in the United States and Canada, but very little used in this country and on the Continent, whereby a Union label is attached to goods made by Trade Unionists, and the sale of goods made under ' fair ' conditions is stimulated (171).

The extent of Trade Union participation in so-called managerial functions, and in the control of industry generally, is indicated in Part IV., but one aspect of the question may be dealt with here, as it is part of the recognised Trade Union practice to control, either through collective agreements or by rules and understandings under which the members work, many of the factors affecting the workers in their daily life. The Agreement in the Dyeing trade (104) illustrates this kind of control. The Engineering lockout of 1922 was largely concerned with the Union's claim to a voice in such matters, but on this occasion the employers were victorious (105). Trade Union practices and regulations having the same object were acknowledged as being necessary to the Unions by the Restoration of Pre-War Practices Act, 1918, (172). By this Act employers were legally compelled to allow the restoration of the practices surrendered by the Unions for the period of the War. The Government's recognition of the value of such regulations and customs is indicated in (173). Examples of Trade Union rules imposing restrictions are given in (174, 175), and the attitude of the movement on restriction of output is indicated in (176).

Several examples of Trade Union propaganda have been given in (4-8) and in (177) is a description of a modern publicity campaign on a large scale, conducted by the entire Labour movement. The Educational work of the Trade Unions deserves a volume to itself, but a Report adopted by the T.U.C. must suffice (178).

Policy.—Trade Union policy on some of the outstanding questions of wages, hours, etc., is indicated in succeeding documents. A manifesto against a lowering of the standard of life, (**179**), is followed by a statement of the Trade Union position on Standard Rates, one of the fundamentals of the movement (**180**).

The Living Wage idea is expounded in (**181**), and it has received legislative endorsement in the Agricultural Wages (Regulation) Act, of 1924 (**182**). An eminent Australian judge points out in (**183**) that the conception of a Living Wage is relative to existing economic conditions, and while this is perhaps the general view in this country also, the idea of a basic minimum below which no one should work is firmly implanted in the philosophy of the Labour movement. On piecework, the change in the policy of an important Union that formerly opposed its adoption is shown in the resolution in (**184**), while (**174**) shows the policy of another Union. The relation between piece rates and time rates is dealt with by law, for certain workers, in (**185**), and by collective agreement in (**186**). An old grievance of the workers—rate cutting—is dealt with in (**187**). In some trades collective piecework (**188**) is the rule ; this is illustrated in the agreement in the Dyeing trade (**104**).

Cost-of-living sliding scales are now in operation in many industries. One of the most important is set out in (**112**), and a Labour view of this type of wage-adjustment is given in (**189**), though Trade Union opinion is by no means unanimous on the matter.

A very interesting scheme under which the Union and employers co-operate in the adoption of a system of grading the workers is shown in (**106**).

The broad economic policy of the Trade Union movement as a whole is summarised in two extracts (**190, 191**), while the new wage policy of the American Federation of Labor is indicated in (**192**). A recent expression of opinion by the Industrial Conference between the General Council of the T.U.C. and the Mond Group of Employers, on Rationalisation, is of importance (**193**). Finally, the General Secretary of the T.U.C. expounds his view of the evolution of Trade Union policy (194).

AUTHORITIES AND REFERENCES.

The primary sources of information on the functions and activities of Trade Unionism are the journals and reports of the Unions, Federations, Trades Councils, Trades Union Congress, etc., the daily press, and periodicals dealing with Labour questions.

The files of the *Daily Herald*, the official Labour newspaper, and of the *Labour Magazine*, the *Industrial Review*, the *Labour Year Book*, the *T.U.C. Annual Reports*, and the *Ministry of Labour Gazette*, are indispensable for the purpose. The Government Reports that are important include those of the Royal Commission on Trade Unions, 1869, the Royal Commission on Labour, 1894, (C. 6894, etc.), and the Royal Commission on Trade Disputes, 1906, (Cd. 2825, etc.) ; the Committee on Industry and Trade, vol. ii, entitled Survey of Industrial Relations, 1926 ; the Annual Reports of the Ministry of Labour ; the Ministry of Labour Report on Collective Agreements, 1910 ; the Report of the Industrial Council on Industrial Agreements, 1913, (Cd. 6952) ; the Report of the Provisional Committee of the Industrial Conference, 1919, (Cmd. 501) ; the Reports of the Coal Commissions of 1919, (Sankey), and 1925, (Samuel), and of the Dockers' Court of Enquiry, 1920. In all these cases the Evidence should be studied as well as the Reports, if it is available. The Awards of the Industrial Court are important, and the Reports issued by the Labour Department of the Board of Trade, in pre-war days, on the working of the Conciliation Act, 1896, should be referred to, as should the same Department's Reports, not published since the War, on Strikes and Lockouts.

The only thorough analysis of Trade Union functions and methods is that contained in Webbs' *Industrial Democracy* and *History of Trade Unionism*. Cole's *World of Labour* and *Organised Labour* are useful, and the same author's work, *The Payment of Wages*, is valuable on wage questions. Askwith's *Industrial Problems and Disputes* is interesting on strikes, and there are a number of admirable histories of individual strikes such as *The Dockers' Strike*, by Llewellyn Smith and Vaughan Nash, and *The Great Steel Strike* (U.S.A.), by W. Z. Foster.

The legal aspect of the questions dealt with in this Part is expounded in Slesser and Baker's *Trade Union Law*, (Third Ed.), and

Henderson's *Trade Unions and the Law*. The Reports of the Taff Vale, Osborne, and other leading cases should, of course, be studied. The Report and Appendices of the Royal Commission on Trade Disputes, 1906, are especially important in this connection.

It is impossible to give even a selection of works on all the topics touched upon in this Part, but a useful short bibliography is given in *Trade Unionism* by C. M. Lloyd, which book is in itself an admirable introduction to the more detailed works already mentioned.

Above all, for the activities of the individual Unions, their day-to-day work, and the evolution of their policies, the journals of the Unions and the files of the *Daily Herald* are the only satisfactory sources.

---

95. Collective Bargaining.

Industrial Democracy, by S. AND B. WEBB, 1920 ed., p. 173.

The nature of the Method of Collective Bargaining will be best understood by a series of examples.

In unorganised trades the individual workman, applying for a job, accepts or refuses the terms offered by the employer, without communication with his fellow workmen, and without any other consideration than the exigencies of his own position. For the sale of his labour he makes, with the employer, a strictly individual bargain. But if a group of workmen concert together, and send representatives to conduct the bargaining on behalf of the whole body, the position is at once changed. Instead of the employer making a series of separate contracts with isolated individuals, he meets with a collective will, and settles, in a single agreement, the principles upon which, for the time being, all workmen of a particular group, or class, or grade, will be engaged. . . . The starving man gets his job at the same piecework rate as the workman who could afford to stand out for his usual earnings. The superior craftsman retains all his advantages over his fellows, but without allowing his superiority to be made the means of reducing the weekly wage of the ordinary worker.

This example of the Method of Collective Bargaining is taken from the practice of a ' shop club ' in a relatively unorganised trade. The skilled artisans . . . afford a typical instance of the second stage . . . we find the unions . . . obtaining formal ' working rules,' binding on all the employers and workmen of the town or district. This Collective Bargaining . . . settles, for a specified term, the hours of beginning and ending work, the minimum rate of wages, the payment for overtime, the age and number of apprentices to be taken, the arrangements as to piecework, the holidays to be allowed, the notice to be given by employers and workmen terminating engagements, the accommodation to be provided for meals and the safe custody of tools, and numerous allowances or extra payments for travelling, lodging, ' walking time,' ' grinding money,' etc. These elaborate codes, unalterable except by formal notice from the organisations on either side, thus place on a uniform footing, as regards the hiring of labour, . . . the firm crowded with orders and that standing practically idle. On the other hand, the superior workman retains his freedom to exact higher rates for his special work, whilst the employer of superior business ability, or technical knowledge, and the firm enjoying the best machinery or plant, preserve, it is claimed, every fraction of their advantage over their competitors. . . . Where the product of different towns goes to the same market, we see, in the best organised industries, a still further development . . . The general level of wages . . . is, for instance, settled by . . . national agreements . . . No employer, and no group of workmen, no district association of employers, and no ' province ' of the Trade Union, can propose an advance or accept a special reduction from the established level of earnings. General advances or reductions are negotiated at long intervals, and with great deliberateness, between the national representatives of each party. Thus, we see ruled out, not merely all personal or local exigencies, but also the temporary gluts or contractions of the market, whether in the raw material or in the product. All firms in a district and all districts in the industry being, as far as possible, placed upon an identical footing as to the rate at which they obtain human labour, their competition takes, it is contended, the form of improving the machinery, getting the best and cheapest raw material, and obtaining the most advantageous market for their wares.

96. Collective Bargaining.

REPORT OF THE INDUSTRIAL COUNCIL ON INDUSTRIAL AGREEMENTS 1913. Cd. 6952 ; pp. 9, 16.

The desirability of maintaining the principle of collective bargaining—which has become so important a constituent in the industrial life of this country—cannot be called into question, and we regard it as axiomatic that nothing should be done that would lead to the abandonment of a method of adjusting the relationships between employers and workpeople which has proved so mutually advantageous throughout most of the trades of the country.   We think it undesirable that any proposals should be put forward which might lead to a tendency to refrain from entering into voluntary agreements ; indeed, efforts should, in our opinion, be made to support the continuance of the collective bargain.   Thus there is a danger that the introduction into the terms of agreements of provisions for the enforcement of money penalties or fines may in some instances deter workpeople from entering into agreements which might in other respects have been acceptable to them.

     .   .   .   .

The whole organisation of collective bargaining, of which we have expressed our approval, is based upon the principle of consent. We have found that such collective agreements have been as a rule kept, and we are loth either to interfere with the internal organisation of the Associations on both sides by putting upon them the legal necessity of exercising compulsion upon their members, or to introduce a new principle which might have far-reaching and unexpected effects upon the natural growth of such Associations or upon the spirit with which as a rule they have been carried on.

We have therefore, as will be seen, come to the conclusion that the establishment of a system of monetary penalties is not desirable, and that such penalties as prohibition of assistance to persons in breach should not be made legally obligatory.   We have stated, however, and we wish to give our opinion the maximum degree of emphasis, that where a breach of an agreement has been committed no assistance, financial or otherwise, should be given to the persons in breach by any of the other members of the Associations connected with the agreement.   The language of our Report is intended to express as strongly as possible our adherence to the view that moral influence should in every feasible way be brought to bear in favour of the strict carrying out of agreements, and that, in cases where, by any of the methods to which we have alluded, a breach is found to have been committed, Associations should accept the findings of the tribunal and should exercise to the full the disciplinary powers of their organisation, assisted, as would no doubt be the case, by the force of public opinion.

97. Permanent Officials of Trade Unions.

History of Trade Unionism, by S. AND B. WEBB, 1920 ed., p. 579.

The Trade Official, as we have called him, is largely the result of the prevalence, in certain industries, of a complicated system of piecework remuneration. We have already described how the cotton lists, on the one hand, and the checkweigher clause, on the other, called into existence a specially trained class, which has since been augmented by the adoption of piecework lists in boot and shoe-making and other industries.

The officers of this type are professionals in the art of Collective Bargaining. They spend their lives in intricate calculations on technical details, and in conducting delicate negotiations with the employers or their professional agents. It matters little whether they are the general secretaries of essentially trade societies, such as the federal Unions of Cotton-spinners and Cotton-weavers, or the exclusively trade delegates of societies with friendly benefits, such as the Steel-smelters, the Boilermakers and the Boot and Shoe Operatives. In either case their attention is almost entirely devoted to the earnings of their members. Alert and open-minded, they are keen observers of market prices, employers' profits, the course of international trade, and everything which may affect the gross product of their industry. They are more acutely conscious of incompetency, whether in employer or employed, than they can always express. Supporters of improved processes, new machinery, and ' speeding-up,' they would rather see an antiquated mill closed or an incompetent member discharged, than reduce the Standard Rate.

Nor do they confine themselves exclusively to the money wages of their clients. Among them are to be found the best advocates of legislative regulation of the conditions of employment, and whilst they have during the present century fallen somewhat into the background when wider political issues have come to the fore, the elaboration of the Labour Code . . . has been due, in the main, to their detailed knowledge and untiring pertinacity.

98. Business Agents—Canada.

From 17TH ANN. REP. ON LABOR ORGANISATIONS IN CANADA (for 1927), p. 159.

An important office which has developed with the growth of the trade union movement is that known as business agent. Previous

3]   FUNCTIONS AND METHODS   225

to the creation of this position many trade union matters were referred for attention to committees, the members of which often found it almost impossible to give the time necessary for the work. With a view to overcoming this difficulty certain organisations decided to employ some member as full-time paid representative to attend to the affairs of the union. The present duties of the business agent, who was originally oft-times referred to as the ' walking delegate,' require him, where permissible, to visit the various jobs on which members of his craft are employed to ascertain if all are in good standing with the organisation, and to endeavour to secure applications for membership if there are non-members working. The agent is required to see that the fair wages clauses on government and municipal contracts (where there are such provisions) are observed, and where supposed violations are detected he is empowered to take the necessary steps to bring them to the attention of the proper authorities.

Complaints concerning conditions of employment are referred by the employees to the business agent, it being his duty to adjust difficulties, provided the union considers them of sufficient importance to warrant such action being taken. An important feature of the business agent's duties is that of receiving applications for labor from employers and furnishing the men required so far as may be possible.

Business agents are usually elected annually by the local branches concerned, their salaries being paid from local funds, either from the regular dues or by a weekly or monthly assessment, but in a few instances different methods prevail. In some localities, where a single union is not strong enough to maintain a business agent, two or more local unions of kindred trades sometimes combine to support such an official.

99. Trade Union ' Civil Service.'

Industrial Democracy, by S. AND B. WEBB, 1920 ed., p. 16.

With every increase in the society's membership, with every extension or elaboration of its financial system or trade policy, the position of the salaried official became, accordingly, more and more secure. The general secretaries themselves changed with the development of their office. The work could no longer be efficiently performed by an ordinary artisan, and some preliminary office training became almost indispensable.

The Coalminers, for instance, as we have shown in our description of the Trade Union world, have picked their secretaries to a large extent from a specially trained section, the checkweigh-men.[1]

The Cotton Operatives have even adopted a system of competitive examination among the candidates for their staff appointments.[2]   In other unions any candidate who has not proved his capacity for office work and trade negotiations would stand at a serious disadvantage in the election, where the choice is coming every day to be confined more clearly to the small class of minor officials.

The paramount necessity of efficient administration has co-operated with this permanence in producing a progressive differentiation of an official governing class, more and more marked off by character, training and duties from the bulk of the members.   The annual election of the general secretary by a popular vote, far from leading to frequent rotation of office and equal service by all the members, has, in fact, invariably resulted in permanence of tenure exceeding even that of the English civil servant.

100. Collective Agreements.

REPORT OF THE LABOUR DEPARTMENT OF THE BOARD OF TRADE ON
COLLECTIVE AGREEMENTS, Cd. 5366, 1910, pp. xi-xiii.

The term ' collective agreement ' is applied to those arrangements under which the conditions of employment are governed by the terms of a bargain made between employers and associations of employers and a group of workpeople employed by them, or an organisation of which these workpeople are members, and which represents their interests (as opposed to those cases in which these conditions are arranged between an employer and the different workpeople whom he employs, separately).

The collective bargains here referred to include awards made by arbitrators or an umpire.   In these cases the bargain, instead of being made directly between the parties, is, in effect, made for the parties by a third person or persons acting with their authority, and arranging terms on their behalf.

In some instances the collective bargain is made between a single firm and its employees, or one or more classes of employees.   These are ' shop agreements ' and as a rule affect in each case a compara-

---

[1] *History of Trade Unionism*, p. 291.   [2] *Ibid.*, p. 294.

tively small number of persons. While securing uniformity in conditions of employment as between the different operatives employed by the firm to which it applies, a shop agreement affords no security against undercutting by other firms.

On the other hand, when the agreement regulating industrial conditions is entered into by a number of different firms, and in particular where, as is often the case, the firms bound by a collective agreement comprise the whole or the greater part of the establishments carrying on a given industry, within a wide area, the whole of the workpeople employed by the employers concerned are secured equality of treatment, while each of those employers is, so far as regards all his competitors who are parties to the agreement, protected against the danger of being under-bid by firms obtaining their labour upon easier terms than he himself enjoys.

In this connection it is of interest to note that in some industries the collective agreements which are in force in relation to particular establishments are themselves subordinate to a specific standard, and form an integral part of a general wage scale governing the remuneration of the workpeople in the trade concerned throughout a large area. Thus, in the cotton-spinning industry at Bolton different mills may have different wage lists, but the piece-rates specified in all these lists alike are, by virtue of the agreement between the employers and employed in this trade, required to be such as will yield certain standard weekly earnings, uniform for the whole district, and are adjusted, as occasion may require, by representatives of the two parties, so as to conform to this basis.

The same principle of conformity to a general standard is to be found in the pit lists governing wages in the coal mining industry. . . . Nor, when we are considering the great importance of the part which is played by collective agreements in the regulation of labour conditions in this country, should it escape attention that it is not alone the members of the Trade Unions which are parties to collective agreements whose conditions of employment are determined by these industrial treaties ; for in the majority of cases the conditions there laid down will be found to obtain in practice also in relation to large numbers of non-Unionist workpeople engaged in the trades to which these agreements apply.

101. Collective Agreements.

REPORT OF THE INDUSTRIAL COUNCIL ON INDUSTRIAL AGREEMENTS, 1913.   Cd. 6952 ; p. 4.

It may be of advantage at the outset to consider what might be regarded as a working definition of an industrial agreement.   (It is understood that there is no legal definition of the term.)

An industrial agreement may be described as an arrangement arrived at by employers and workpeople with a view to formulating the general conditions of employment in a particular trade and district.   It is essentially different from (though to a large extent it forms the basis of) the contract of service entered into between an individual employer and an individual workman.   It is, in most cases, arrived at because the employers and workpeople think that a collective agreement is a desirable method of formulating what they have agreed shall be (for the time being, or for some period mentioned in the agreement) the principal terms governing the contracts of service between individual employers and individual workmen.

As a matter of practice, agreements are usually made between Associations of Employers and Associations of Workpeople, and the extent to which these Associations in the various cases cover the whole of the trade concerned differs in almost every instance.

It is to be noted that industrial agreements, considered as contracts between employers and employed, cannot fairly be compared with the ordinary commercial contracts made between individuals or corporate bodies.   In the case of ordinary commercial contracts the persons who enter into the contracts are the principals directly concerned, or at least persons acting under well-defined authority from principals.   Industrial agreements, on the other hand, are frequently made—especially on behalf of the workpeople—by representatives who, by reason of the numbers involved, and the circumstances which surround trade movements, find it difficult to obtain well-defined authority to enter into a settlement, or even to ascertain, beforehand, the exact wishes of those whom they represent. This fact it is necessary to keep clearly in mind in the consideration of the questions now under review.   Notwithstanding these difficulties inherent in dealing with large numbers of workpeople, we find from the evidence that agreements in most cases are well kept.   Although a number of instances of alleged breaches of agreements have been referred to in the course of the Enquiry, the evidence of a considerable majority of the witnesses is to the effect that agreements have, viewed generally, been duly fulfilled by both parties. The breaches that have been mentioned were, with a few exceptions, the result of the action of comparatively few men, or due to exceptional circumstances or to differences and misunderstandings in regard to points of interpretation, and are not, as a rule, countenanced by the respective organisations.

It is recognised by both sides that they are under a strong moral obligation to observe agreements which have been entered into by them or by their representatives on their behalf. The principal exceptions appear to be in trades which are unorganised, or in which on one side or the other the organisation is incomplete or is of recent origin, but we find that where agreements are the outcome of properly organised machinery for dealing with disputes they are, with very few exceptions, loyally observed by both sides. Where agreements have been broken it is frequently found that they were made at times when, owing to the abnormal conditions, great difficulty must have been experienced in arriving at a fair adjustment.

102. Collective Agreement.

TERMS OF SETTLEMENT OF COAL MINING DISPUTE, 1st July, 1921.

1. A National Board shall be constituted forthwith, consisting in equal numbers of persons chosen by the Mining Association of Great Britain and persons chosen by the Miners' Federation of Great Britain.

There shall also be established District Boards, consisting in equal numbers of persons representing owners and workmen in each district.

The National and District Boards shall draw up their own rules of procedure, which shall include a provision for the appointment of an Independent Chairman for each Board.

2. The wages payable in each district shall be expressed in the form of a percentage upon the basis rates prevailing in the district, and shall be periodically adjusted in accordance with the proceeds of the industry as ascertained in such district.

3. The amount of the percentage to be paid in each district during any period shall be determined by the proceeds of the industry in that district during a previous period, as ascertained by returns to be made by the owners, checked by joint test audit of the owners'

books carried out by independent accountants appointed by each side.

4. The sum to be applied in each district to the payment of wages above the standard wages as hereinafter defined shall be a sum equal to 83 per cent. of the surplus of such proceeds remaining after deduction therefrom of the amounts of the following items during the period of ascertainment—

   (*a*) the cost of the standard wages ;
   (*b*) the costs of production other than wages ;
   (*c*) standard profits equivalent to 17 per cent. of the cost of the standard wages ;

and the share of the surplus applicable to wages shall be expressed as a percentage upon the basis rates prevailing in the district.

Provided that if in any period the ascertained proceeds, after deduction of costs other than wages and the cost of the standard wages, prove to have been insufficient to meet the standard profits, the deficiency shall be carried forward as a first charge to be met out of any surplus, ascertained as above, in subsequent periods.

5. If the rates of wages thus determined in any district do not provide a subsistence wage to low paid day wage workers, such additions in the form of allowances per shift worked shall be made for that period to the daily wages of these workers as, in the opinion of the District Board, or, in the event of failure to agree by the parties, in the opinion of the Independent Chairman, may be necessary for the purpose. Such allowances shall be treated as items of cost in the district ascertainments.

6. For the purpose of these periodical adjustments the Units shall be the districts set out in the Schedule hereto, and shall only be varied by the decision of the District Board or Boards concerned, provided that no variation shall take place prior to 1st February, 1922, in the grouping of any district unless it is mutually agreed by the representatives of both sides in the district or districts concerned.

7. The standard wages shall be the district basis rates existing on the 31st of March, 1921, *plus* the district percentages payable in July, 1914 (or the equivalents in any district in which there has been a subsequent merging into new standards), *plus* in the case of piece-workers, the percentage additions which were made consequent upon the reduction of hours from 8 to 7.

8. In no district shall wages be paid at lower rates than standard wages *plus* 20 per cent. thereof.

9. The National Board shall forthwith consider what items of cost are to be included for the purposes of paragraph 4 (b), above, and in the event of agreement not being arrived at by the 31st July, the matter shall be referred to the Independent Chairman for decision.

10. The wages payable by the owners up to the 31st August inclusive shall be based upon the ascertained results of the month of March, and the wages payable during September shall be based upon the ascertained results of the month of July. The periods of ascertainment thereafter shall be decided by the National Board.

11. During the 'temporary period' as hereinafter defined the following special arrangements shall apply in modification of the general scheme set out above :

(a) In calculating the proceeds for March the deduction to be made in respect of costs other than wages shall be the average of such costs during January, February and March.

(b) In any district in which reductions in wages continue to be made after the first ascertainment, no part of the surplus proceeds shall be assigned to profits if and in so far as this would have the effect of reducing the wages below the level in the preceding month.

When in any district there is a break in the continuity of reductions in wages upon the periodical ascertainments, at that point and thereafter the general scheme shall apply fully in regard to owners' surplus profits.

(c) The proviso to paragraph 4 regarding the carrying forward of deficiencies in standard profits shall not apply, but any net losses shall be so carried forward.

(d) The Government will give a grant not exceeding £10,000,000 in subvention of wages.

(e) The subvention shall be available for making such increases to the wages otherwise payable in any district as may be necessary to prevent the reductions below the March rates of wages being greater than the following amounts :

During July, 2s. a shift for persons of 16 years of age and upwards, and 1s. a shift for persons under 16.

During August 2s. 6d. and 1s. 3d. respectively.

During September 3s. and 1s. 6d. respectively, provided that the balance of the subvention is sufficient for this purpose.

(*f*) In any district in which in any month the proceeds available for wages, calculated in accordance with the terms of this settlement, are sufficient to admit of a rate of wages equal to or higher than the rate payable under the maximum reduction for that month the wages payable by the owners shall be calculated not in terms of basis *plus* percentage but on the same basis as during March, less flat rate reductions uniform throughout the district for persons of 16 years of age and upwards and persons under 16 years of age respectively.

(*g*) In any district in which the wages calculated in accordance with the terms of this settlement are less than the wages payable under the maximum reductions aforesaid, the difference shall be met by the owners in that district during September to the extent of the aggregate net profits realised by them on the district ascertainment for July, and during October to the extent of the aggregate net profits realised by them on the district ascertainments for July and August.

(*h*) The expression 'temporary period' means the period from the date of the resumption of work to the 30th September, 1921.

12. The period of duration of this agreement shall be from the date of resumption of work until the 30th September, 1922, and thereafter until terminated by three months' notice on either side.

13. It is agreed as a principle that every man shall be entitled to return to his place when that place is available for him and that men temporarily occupying places during the stoppage shall give way to men working in those places before the stoppage.

It is agreed that on the other hand there shall be no victimisation of men who have been keeping the collieries open, not in the sense that they are to remain at the jobs they filled during the stoppage but that they shall not be prevented from going back to their own jobs or from working subsequently at the colliery.

SCHEDULE REFERRED TO.

Scotland—Northumberland—Durham—South Wales and Monmouth—Yorkshire, Nottinghamshire, Derbyshire, Leicestershire, Cannock Chase and Warwickshire—Lancashire, North Staffordshire and Cheshire—North Wales—South Staffordshire and Salop—Cumberland—Bristol—Forest of Dean—Somerset—Kent.

103. National Working Rules.

IN THE BUILDING INDUSTRY (1926).

1. (*a*) The standard rates of wages shall be those fixed by the Council in accordance with the provisions of Rule 13.

(*b*) The Labourers' rate in any grade shall not be less than 75 per cent. of the standard rate.

2. The working hours shall be 44 hours per week, throughout the year, except that during the period of summer time as determined by Statute the working time shall be extended to 46½ (forty-six and a half) hours per week by adding half an hour to each of the first five working days of the week. Provided that in December and January on work where artificial light can be reasonably supplied the interval of one hour for dinner shall be observed, but in those two months on works where artificial light cannot be reasonably supplied the interval for dinner shall be reduced to half an hour, so that work may terminate during those two months at 4.30 p.m. And provided further that if on any such works where artificial light cannot be reasonably supplied the majority of operatives request that the interval of one hour for dinner may still be maintained throughout December and January, and that the working hours during that period may be consequently reduced to 41½ (forty-one and a half) hours per week, the employer shall be at liberty to arrange accordingly, but nothing shall prevent employers and operatives in any town or area from maintaining by mutual consent the 44 (forty-four) hours week throughout the year.

3. To the undermentioned workmen engaged upon the classes of work specified below, extra wages shall be paid as set out herein :

Timbermen, scaffolders, and well-sinkers, recognised as such - - - - - - -	1d. per hour
Furnace or similar hot work, up to 120° Fahr. -	2d. ,,
Above this temperature, or where special circumstances exist, the local Joint Committee be empowered to arrange special terms.	
Foul or dirty work, such as the repair, replacement, or renewal of main sewers and main sewer manholes, foul and dirty work in chemical works, etc.	1d. ,,
Insulation work when charcoal, silicate of cotton, or powdered cork is used - - - - -	1d. ,,

Detached chimney work and silos, or repair of
church spires—

Above 40 ft. and up to 90 ft. - - -	1d. per hour
Above 90 ft. and up to 150 ft. - - -	2d. ,,
Over 150 ft. - - - - - - -	3d. ,,

Men working in water where watertight boots are
necessary shall be provided with same, and be paid　1d.

Men working in swings and cradles - - -　1d. ,,

Qualified benders and fixers of bars for reinforced
concrete work, on satisfying the Employer that
they have been employed on this description of
work for three months, shall be paid in addition
to the agreed labourers' rate - - - -　1d. ,,
and shall provide themselves with the following tools :

Pliers, chisels, hammers, and hacksaw frames.

When Carpenters are required to re-use materials
for concrete work - - - - - -　1d. ,,

Reconstruction and repair of all firebrick work on
retorts - - - - - - - -　2d. ,,

Reconstruction and repair of all firebrick work on
ovens, other than domestic - - - -　1d. ,,

*The foregoing provisions shall supersede all other existing provisions
for extra wages, subject to any amendment under Rule 13.*

4. Overtime shall be paid at the following rates, namely : First
five days of week :

First two hours, time and a quarter ; second two hours, time and a
half ; afterwards, until starting time next morning, double time.

Time worked between leaving off time on Saturdays and 4 p.m.—
time and a half ; afterwards, until starting time on Monday morning
—double time.

When men start before the usual starting time, they shall be paid
at overtime rates for any time worked beyond the normal day.
Starting time not to be before 6 a.m., and in cases where the Operatives employed are unable to continue at work until the leaving-off
time provided by the working rules, the time worked before the
usual time of starting shall be paid at time and a quarter.

Overtime shall not count until full time for the day has been
made ; this provision not to apply unless the loss of time is through
the workman's own fault.

Christmas Day (in England and Wales) and the first working day of the year in Scotland—double time.

Time worked on public or other holidays, except as aforesaid, provided that such public or other holidays are recognised as holidays for the purposes of the Building Industry in any locality or district by being so defined jointly by the Employers' and Operatives' Organisations of any locality or district and having been confirmed by the appropriate Regional Joint Committee, shall be paid for at time and a half for the period of the normal working day, and at double time thereafter.

Overtime shall not be worked except in cases of urgency, and shall not continue for more than four days consecutively unless by consent of an Overtime Committee appointed by the appropriate local Joint Committee, but in the event of failure to agree, appeal may be made to the Regional Joint Committee. All overtime extending beyond one day, shall be reported immediately to the appropriate Joint Committee. Privilege will be given to the Employers to employ labourers on overtime for the purpose of unloading materials which have not arrived at the job or works in time to be unloaded within the normal working hours.

No departure from the recognised overtime rule shall be allowed on country work which is outside the Area covered by local rules, without sanction of the appropriate Joint Committee. The appropriate Joint Committee shall be that of the district *to* which the men are sent ; in the absence of a Joint Committee in that district, the appropriate Committee shall then be that of the district *from* which the men are sent.

5. The general working conditions shall apply, but separate men from those at work during the day shall be employed, and 3d. per hour above the ordinary rates shall be paid, provided that at least three nights consecutively are worked.

6. (*a*) Walking time shall be allowed and paid for by the Employer at the rate of three miles per hour from an agreed boundary or boundaries, on the outward journey, up to a distance of four miles from such boundary. The men to walk back in their own time, provided that on pay days, if the wages be not paid on the job or place of work, time shall be allowed so that the men can be at the Pay Office at the regular time. All distances between points shall be measured in a straight line.

The agreed boundary or boundaries to mean either :

(i) Defined limits, such as a Borough Boundary or a circle

or circles described about an agreed radius from the centre of the town, or where fares are paid, an agreed tram or 'bus stage.

(ii) A circle described about an agreed radius from the Employers' workshop.

At the option of the Employer the Operatives may be conveyed to and from the job by road or rail or by tram or other conveyance. The expenses of such methods of conveyance to be borne by the Employer and the time travelling therein to the job from the agreed boundary or boundaries to be paid for.

Time spent in walking or travelling, up to a maximum of one hour each way, not to be reckoned as part of the working day, and to be paid for one way at single time rates. Should the normal working day be extended beyond 8 hours, the limit of one hour to be proportionately reduced.

This clause shall not apply to men set on at the job, but a man being finished on one job shall be allowed time and travelling expenses from that job to another job when requested by the Employer.

(b) All men sent to jobs beyond four miles and up to 20 miles from the agreed boundary shall be allowed train fares or be conveyed to and from the job every week ; if more than 20 miles and up to 40 miles every fortnight ; from 40 to 60 miles once a month ; over 60 miles mutual arrangements shall be made between Employer and Operatives before going to the job.

Time travelling to the job at commencement and when returning to the job in accordance with Rule, also time on returning from the job at completion, shall be paid for.

At the option of the Employer, the Operatives may be conveyed to and from the job daily by road or rail, or by tram or by other conveyance, and the time travelling to the job from the agreed boundary shall be paid for.

Time spent in travelling not to be reckoned as part of the working day, and to be paid for at single time rates.

Proper lodging and expenses shall be allowed and paid for by the Employer to all men sent on to jobs necessitating lodging, at the rate of not less than 2s. and not more than 3s. for each night away from home in accordance with Rule, except where, owing to special circumstances, the last-named sum is found to be inadequate, in which eventuality, application may be made to the local Joint Committee for a special rate to be fixed.

The amount of the stipulated allowance to be open to revision by the Council at any Annual Meeting subject to one month's notice from either side.

When men are sent into a higher paid district Employers to pay the higher rate ; if sent into a lower paid district the rate shall be that of the district from which the man is sent.

7. Nothing in the Rules hereinbefore contained shall abrogate any variation of National Rules 1 to 6 inclusive, existing by agreement in any locality at the date of this agreement.

8. The method by which amendments may be made in any provisions of these Working Rules are fully set out in Rules 12 and 13.

9. Any dispute or difference which may arise other than those provided for within the constitution, shall be dealt with under the National Conciliation Scheme, so long as those concerned belong to bodies which are parties to that Scheme, but should that not be the case, the parties to this Agreement hereby agree to enter into immediate negotiation to deal with any dispute, unless the parties on joint appeal avail themselves of the National Conciliation Scheme.

．　　．　　．　　．　　．　　．　　．

104. Collective Agreement.

DYEING TRADE (1914).

An Agreement made the first day of July, 1914, BETWEEN THE BRADFORD DYERS' ASSOCIATION, LIMITED (hereinafter called 'The Association') of the one part and the AMALGAMATED SOCIETY OF DYERS, BLEACHERS, FINISHERS AND KINDRED TRADES, THE NATIONAL SOCIETY OF DYERS AND FINISHERS, and THE NATIONAL UNION OF GAS-WORKERS AND GENERAL LABOURERS OF GREAT BRITAIN AND IRELAND (Trade Unions registered under the Trade Union Acts 1871 to 1906, and hereinafter called 'The Unions') of the other part. WHEREAS the parties hereto have made such arrangements as hereinafter appear for the purpose of defining and regulating the conditions of employment of members of the Unions in the employment of the Association, and of preventing lock-outs and strikes, NOW IT IS HEREBY AGREED as follows—

Engagement of Employees and Terms of Engagement.

1. The Association shall on the engagement of employees first make application to the Unions to supply the employees required.

The Unions shall supply employees with the least possible delay, and if the Unions do not supply employees satisfactory to the Association within 24 hours of receipt of a requisition in writing from the Association, the latter shall be free to engage persons who are not members of the Unions, but such persons shall be required by the Association forthwith to become members of one or other of the Unions.

2. *Any employee ceasing to be a member of any of the Unions shall be required by the Association to resume membership of one or other of the Unions.*

3. Each employee shall give or receive a week's notice for the purpose of terminating his employment (excepting in the case of gross misconduct).

Conditions of Work.

4. The Association shall be entitled to require from its employees work such as can be performed by employees of ordinary health and strength working steadily but without undue physical strain.

5. In any case where an employee is instructed to do anything which he thinks he ought not to be required to do, or which he considers he cannot do properly, *he shall be entitled to lodge a protest with his foreman, and to receive a written acknowledgment of his protest before proceeding with his work*. Upon receipt of such acknowledgment he shall proceed to *follow out his instructions to the best of his ability*. In the event of no agreement being arrived at as to the instructions in respect of which the protest is lodged, the question shall be referred to and settled by the Reference Board.

Collective Piece Work.

6. The Association may at any branch introduce payment by piecework rates. *All piecework shall be based on collective work and collective payment*. By collective piecework is meant work performed by sets or groups of employees.

7. The fixing of rates and the arrangement of sets shall be mutually agreed upon in writing by representatives of the Association and the Unions. Such rates shall be so fixed as to enable a full rated man to earn not less than 7d. per hour. At any branch introducing piecework, *it shall be a condition of the introduction that every employee* (including females) *engaged on productive work shall be paid on a piecework basis within one month from the commencement of the trial.*

8. *No rate or set shall be altered without the consent in writing of the Association and the Union or Unions to which the employees affected belong.*

9. Trials of three calendar months' duration shall precede the final settlement of rates.

10. During the three months' trial, the remuneration of those engaged on the trial shall not be less than the day rates payable under this agreement.

11. If after twelve calendar months from the establishment of the final rates for collective piecework, the employees at any branch so decide they shall have the right upon giving three calendar months' notice in writing, to revert to payment of wages on hourly rates.

12. The rates of employees who on the 20th February, 1913, were engaged on piecework shall as from that date be increased where necessary so as to enable a full rated man to earn not less than 7d. per hour.

13. In addition to the rates of payment fixed upon for piece-workers, *each employee shall, when engaged on night turn, receive 1s. 6d. per night extra, but no other allowance.*

14. There shall as based on the census of 1st January, 1913, be no material displacement of adult labour consequent on or due to the introduction of piecework, but the Association shall have full liberty subject to clauses 7 and 8, to transfer labour between its various branches, and in the meantime any displacement of labour shall so far as possible be that of boys, to help to meet which the engagement of boy labour shall be temporarily stopped. After the adjustment so provided the Association shall be entitled to re-instate boy and other labour on the same basis as hitherto.

15. From and after the 1st July, 1913, no employee shall, unless by mutual agreement between the Union to which he belongs and the Association, be required to work after 12 noon on Saturdays, and an employee on night turn shall not, unless by mutual agreement between the Association and the Union to which he belongs, work more than five nights in any week, and he shall cease work not later than 6 a.m. each day except where work on a continuous process is continued because the day employees are late.

16. Clause 15 shall not apply to cleaning up or to processes necessary to putting the goods into a condition of safety, *e.g.*, drying, which may be carried on until 3 o'clock p.m. on Saturdays. *Piece-workers shall be entitled to extra payment at the rate of $3\frac{1}{2}d$. per hour after 6 p.m. and 12 noon on Saturdays.*

17. The Association may at any time not less than one month after the commencement of a piecework trial elect to demonstrate as to the sufficiency of any rate or rates to enable the men without excessive physical strain to earn not less than 7d. per hour. The demonstration shall be conducted by the workmen engaged on the machine to which the demonstration is to apply, and during such demonstration the employees shall work in the manner directed by the Association. If after such demonstration agreement is not arrived at in regard to the piecework rate or rates, the matter shall be referred to the Reference Board as provided in Clause 18 of this Agreement.

18. If the Association fail to satisfy the representatives of the Union of the sufficiency of any rate or of the fairness of the conditions the question shall be referred to the Reference Board for decision, and if the Association fails to demonstrate that the rate is sufficient or that the conditions are fair (as the case may be) then the Association shall forthwith increase the rate or alter the conditions as the case may require.

Rates of Pay to Employees not engaged on Piecework.

19. The following minimum rates of pay shall be paid to employees not engaged on piecework, and in each instance the same are calculated on the basis of 54 hours per week, and the hourly rate shall be one fifty-fourth of the weekly rate. *Full-rated men shall be entitled to receive not less than 28s. or more than 34s. per week ; Improvers shall receive not less than 20s. but under 28s. per week ; Boys shall receive not less than 11s. but under 20s. per week.* The average rate of wages of each separate group and of the whole shall not be reduced during the existence of this arrangement. The wages of boys and improvers shall be dealt with in the following manner—Boys shall commence at 11s. per week ; they shall be advanced 2s. per week after one year's service, and 1s. per week in each succeeding year, but after attaining 18 years of age they shall become Improvers and their wages shall be 20s. per week. The wages of IMPROVERS shall be advanced, as from 1st July, 1914, from 20s. per week 1s. per week after six months' service in this class, and 1s. per week in each succeeding half-year until they reach the wage of 28s. Advances shall be made on the first pay day in January and July of each year. The ordinary working hours shall be from 6 a.m. to 6 p.m. for the day shift, and from 6 p.m. to 6 a.m. for the

night shift. For employees on the day shift time worked beyond 6 p.m. counts as follows—

Up to 7 *p.m. as time and a quarter* except (*a*) where work on a continuous process is continued because the night employees are late, in which case the day employees time up to 7 p.m. if at the same machine only counts as ordinary time ; and (*b*) in the case of employees who have begun work at 5 a.m. without extra pay who are in all cases entitled to count time worked beyond 6 p.m. as time and a half.

After 12 *noon on Saturdays, and on other days after* 7 *p.m., as time and a half in all cases.* For employees on the night shift time worked beyond 6 a.m. counts as follows—Up to 7 a.m. as time and a quarter, except where work on a continuous process is continued because the day employees are late, in which case the night-workman's time up to 7 a.m. if at the same machine counts as ordinary time. After 7 a.m. as time and a half in all cases. *Every employee on the night shift shall receive* 1s. 6d. *per night extra*, and no other allowance. *No employee on the night shift shall be timed off before* 6 *a.m. except by reason of accident or breakdown.*

No employee shall be allowed to work two successive shifts more than once in any week. Employees who are required to stop temporarily and return the same day shall (if they return at the appointed time) be paid half-pay for the time of stoppage.

GENERAL.

20. Foremen who are engaged solely in the superintendence of work are excluded from this agreement ; the following classes are also excluded—

(*a*) Boys under the age of 14 years.
(*b*) Enginemen.
(*c*) Carters.
(*d*) Vanmen so far as regards piecework.
(*e*) Mechanics, Joiners and their Labourers.
(*f*) Clerks.

Reference Board.

21. For the purpose of determining any dispute between the Association and all or any of the Unions or their members with regard to wages or conditions of employment or any other matter

dealt with by this agreement, except a breach of the provisions of Clause 32, a Reference Board shall be formed. The Reference Board shall consist of 18 members, half of whom shall be appointed by the Association and half by the Unions in such proportions as the Unions shall agree upon.

22. Two Secretaries shall be appointed by the Reference Board, one being a representative of the Association and the other a representative of the Unions, who shall keep proper minutes of the meetings thereof.

23. The Reference Board shall meet at such places as shall be agreed upon and on such occasions as may be specified by seven days' notice in writing to each member of the Board. Meetings may be convened in the following ways—

(*a*) By notice signed by the joint Secretaries. If in the opinion of the joint Secretaries the business is urgent short notice may be given.

(*b*) By notice signed by either of the joint Secretaries and four of the members of the Board.

The notices shall specify the business to be dealt with at the meeting. No business shall be dealt with other than specified in the notice unless a majority of the members present decide that the business is urgent.

24. The members of the Reference Board shall be entitled to elect a chairman either from among or from outside their number. If from among their number he shall be entitled to vote as a member, but shall not be entitled to a casting vote. An outside chairman shall not be entitled to any vote. The chairman shall hold office for such period not exceeding twelve calendar months as he may be appointed, but he may be re-elected from time to time if the Board think fit.

25. Three representatives of the Association and three representatives of the Unions shall form a quorum.

26. The total voting powers of the Association's representatives and the Union's representatives shall be equal irrespective of the numbers present.

27. *In the event of the Reference Board failing to arrive at a decision upon any matter submitted to them, each side shall appoint an Arbitrator to whom the matter in dispute shall be referred.*

28. *All decisions* of the Reference Board and of the Arbitrators so appointed or their Umpire *shall be binding on all parties.* Any such decision may specify the amount not exceeding £1 per man, of

fines, penalties, or damages payable under this agreement by the party at fault.

29. *In the event of any breach by the Association on the one hand, or by any of the Unions or any employee being a member of one of the Unions on the other hand, of any of the provisions herein contained (except the provisions of Clause 32 hereof), or of any decision after that decision has been recorded, of the Reference Board, then and in every such case the Association (if at fault) or the Union (in the case of one of the Unions or any employee being a member of one of the Unions being at fault), shall pay to the Penalty Fund the sum of £1 in respect of each man involved in such breach.*

30. The Penalty Fund shall be in the names of Trustees appointed by the Reference Board.

The Penalty Fund shall be applied to such charitable purposes as may be determined from time to time by the Reference Board.

The Association and the Unions shall deposit the sum of £1,000 each, being a total of £2,000, which shall be invested in the names of the Trustees, each of the said sums being available as security for the payment of any fine, penalty or damages which the party depositing the same may become liable to pay under this Agreement. Upon the determination of this Agreement, the said sums or so much as shall be in existence shall (subject to any unsatisfied claims) be returned to the parties who deposited the same.

31. This Agreement shall remain in force for a period of twelve months from the 20th February, 1913, and shall be deemed to continue beyond that period until determined at any time thereafter by three calendar months' notice in writing from the Association to the Unions, or from the Unions to the Association.

32. *The Association shall not cause or permit any lock-out of its employees during the continuance of this Agreement; nor shall the Unions or any of them advise or induce or support any strike of the employees of the Association during the continuance of this Agreement.*

A strike shall be considered (1) to begin as soon as in consequence of a dispute workmen cease work or tender notices so to do in sufficient numbers to cause a stoppage of any branch and (2) to continue so long as in consequence of such dispute the Union refuses or fails to supply workmen in numbers sufficient to allow normal production to be resumed at such branch.

A lock-out shall be considered (1) to begin as soon as in consequence of a dispute the Association shall terminate the employment or give notice to terminate the employment of workmen in sufficient numbers to cause a stoppage of any branch and (2) *to continue so long as in consequence of such dispute the Association refuses to employ competent members of the Unions in numbers sufficient to allow normal production to be resumed at such branch.*

33. This Agreement shall apply to the following branches of the Association and their employees :

. . . .

34. All previous agreements between the Association and the Unions are hereby cancelled.

105. Trade Unions and Managerial Functions.

AGREEMENT IN THE ENGINEERING INDUSTRY after the 1922 Lockout.

I.—General Principles.

(*a*) The Employers have the right to manage their establishments and the Trade Unions have the right to exercise their functions.

(*b*) In the process of evolution, provision for changes in shop conditions is necessary, but it is not the intention to create any specially favoured class of workpeople.

II.—Procedure for dealing with questions arising.

(1) GENERAL.

(*a*) The procedure of the Provisions for Avoiding Disputes, so far as appropriate, applies to :

(i) General alterations in wages ;

(ii) Alterations in working conditions which are the subject of agreements officially entered into ;

(iii) Alterations in the general working week, but such alterations shall not be given effect to until the appropriate procedure between the Federations and the Trade Union or Unions concerned has been exhausted.

(*b*) Where any alteration in the recognised working conditions other than specified in Clause II., (1) (*a*) hereof, contemplated by the Management will result in one class of workpeople being replaced by another in the establishment, the Management shall, unless the circumstances arising are beyond their control, give the workpeople directly concerned or their representatives in the shop, not less than ten days' intimation of their intention and afford an opportunity for discussion, if discussion is desired, with a deputation of the workpeople concerned and/or their representatives in the shop. Should a discussion not be desired, the instructions of the Management shall be observed, and work shall proceed in accordance therewith. Should a discussion take place and no settlement be reached at the various stages of procedure which are possible within the time available, the Management shall, on the date intimated, give a temporary decision upon which work shall proceed pending the recognised procedure being carried through. The decision shall not be prejudicial to either party in any subsequent discussion which may take place.

(c) Where any class of workpeople is displaced by reason of any act of the Management, consideration shall be given to the case of workpeople so displaced with a view, if practicable, of affording them in the establishment work suitable to their qualifications.

(d) Questions arising which do not result in one class of workpeople being replaced by another in the establishment and on which discussion is desired, shall be dealt with in accordance with the Provisions for Avoiding Disputes, and work shall proceed meantime under the conditions following the act of the Management.

(e) Where a change is made by the Management involving questions of money payments and as a result of negotiations in accordance with the recognised procedure, it is agreed that the claim of the workpeople is established, the decision so arrived at may be made retrospective on the particular claim to a date to be mutually agreed upon, but not beyond the date upon which the question was raised.

(f) Where any local agreement conflicts with the terms of this agreement, the provisions of this agreement shall apply.

(g) Nothing in the foregoing shall affect the usual practice in connection with the termination of employment of individual workpeople.

106. Scheme for Grading Workers (1926).

THE BRASSFOUNDERS' EMPLOYERS' ASSOCIATION IN AGREEMENT WITH
THE NATIONAL SOCIETY OF BRASS AND METAL MECHANICS.

BRASSWORKERS' GRADING SCHEME.

Adopted 14th October, 1910. Revised 3rd December, 1920.
Revised 23rd June, 1913. Revised 17th February, 1926

Definitions.

'Employers' means Private Employer, Firm, or Company.

'Society' means the National Society of Brass and Metal Mechanics.

'Workman' means a Member of the above-named Society.

Conditions.

Qualifications in regard to wages shall be based on ability.

The workman shall be graded, and the grade denoted by different coloured cards, viz.: Brown, Blue, Grey, Red, and Mauve.

The issue of the various Grade Cards shall be in the hands of the Executive of the Society, and they shall be provided with suitable space for the workman's number at his works and in his Society, and for his name and signature.

In view of the complex nature of the Brass Trades, and the constantly varying nature of the work undertaken, it is not possible to enumerate in the following list of qualifications every process or sub-division of the different branches of the trade. It is therefore understood that the qualifications mentioned must, in some cases, serve as 'bases' upon which the workman shall be graded. A workman's general usefulness as a member of the Brass Trades must in such instances receive consideration, apart from his work as a specialist only.

All questions arising relative to *interpretation* shall, in the event of a dispute, be referred to the Board of Conciliation for settlement, or to a joint Sub-Committee appointed for that purpose.

All rates fixed in the following list are, at this date, subject to the Bonus, which now amounts to 21s. 6½d. to each male worker over 21 years of age. To youths between the ages of 18 and 21 years of age the Bonus amounts to 11s. 3½d. per week. Any alteration in these amounts or in the method of dealing with them shall be subject to the recommendations of the National Industrial Courts or any authority recognised by both parties.

All basis rates for castings are inclusive of the pre-war bonus of 20 per cent., or any other existing pre-war bonus.

All day work rates are fixed under similar conditions, and are based on a week of 47 hours.

The employer shall have a right to challenge the qualifications of the holder of any grading card, and require him to submit himself to examination by the Managers of the Municipal Brass Trades' School, in conjunction with a representative nominated by the

Employers' Association, and one by the workman's Society, but in no case shall they be interested parties, and their decision shall be final.

Conditions as to Overtime.

Overtime shall be paid for the first two hours per day at the rate of time and a quarter and afterwards time and a half, in both cases after the normal working hours have been made. Double time to be paid for Sundays and Christmas Day, and for such fixed holidays as are recognised in the district. In any case where a workman loses time for which the employer is responsible such loss of time shall not be taken into account in computing his overtime rates. Payment for night-shifts shall be paid at the rate of time and a quarter.

One Week's Notice

shall be given by either party to terminate engagement, whether the workman is working by day or piecework, such notice to be given at the end of the working week in the respective factories.

C.—Brown Grade.

To all workers 21 years of age, not qualified for D and E Grades. MINIMUM WAGE, 34s. per week.

Present wage, with bonus added in accordance with following agreement.

17th February, 1926.

Memorandum of Agreement between the Brassfounders' Employers' Association and the National Brass and Metal Mechanics, as arranged by their Joint Conciliation Board.

' It is agreed that rates of wages and conditions of labour shall be stabilised for a period of twelve months from this date with the following exception : Those men who, after this date, attain the age of 21 years and who enter Grade C, shall receive the basis wage of 34s. per week plus a bonus of 15s. 6d. until they attain the age of 21½ years, when they shall be entitled to the full bonus of 21s. 6½d.'

D.—(1) Blue Grade.

Twenty-one years of age, with six years' qualification in the trade.

Dressers who turn, screw inside and out or plug and seat, or file flat and square at the vice, or braze.

Dippers who are all round dippers and bronzers, or do art bronzing and colouring, or electro-plating, or have a knowledge of electro-plating and solutions.

Burnishers who are hook or straight burnishers at the vice, or satisfactorily burnish deep thin shell work at the lathe.

Chasers and Repairers who are not qualified for E Grade.

Makers-up who have knowledge and experience of all classes of the trade or branch in which they are employed.

Stampers who undertake all classes of deep or shallow work in all strengths of the metal used.

MINIMUM WAGE, 41s. per week.

Present wage with bonus added, £3 2s. 6½d. per week.

D.—(2) Grey Grade.

Polishers only. Those of average ability who have six years' qualifications in the trade.

MINIMUM WAGE, 43s. per week.

Present wage, with bonus added, £3 4s. 6½d. per week.

E.—(1) Red Grade.

Dressers. Those who have a complete expert knowledge and experience of all classes of lathe or vice work, or work to blue prints or drawings.

Art Bronzers who have an expert knowledge of art bronzing or metal colouring, or electro depositing and solutions.

Pattern Makers or Pattern Chasers.

Chasers and Repairers with expert knowledge of all classes of work.

Burnishers who are experts in all classes of work.

Makers-up who are experts.

Stampers who are experts in all classes of work.

MINIMUM WAGE, 46s. per week.

Present wage, with bonus added, £3 7s. 6½d. per week.

E.—(2) Mauve Grade.

Polishers only. Expert in all processes.

MINIMUM WAGE, 48s. per week.

Present wage, with bonus added, £3 9s. 6½d. per week.

Youths' Wages.

	£	s.	d.			£	s.	d.
18 years of age	-	- 0	18	0				
Bonus - -	-	- 0	11	3½	- - Total	1	9	3½
19 years of age	-	- 1	3	0				
Bonus - -	-	- 0	11	3½	- - Total	1	14	3½
20 years of age	-	- 1	8	0				
Bonus - -	-	- 0	11	3½	- - Total	1	19	3½

Piecework Dressers.

Piecework prices shall be such as to enable a workman of average ability to earn at least 25 per cent. above his basis day work rate, such extra to be in addition to the total earnings on the standard day work rates, including all War Awards.

If C, D, and E graded men, or D and E graded men, are engaged in the same factory doing the same class of work as each other, the prices shall be fixed with regard to the E grade man.

There is no intention to limit the earnings of any pieceworker.

THE BRASSFOUNDERS' EMPLOYERS' ASSOCIATION.

110 EDMUND STREET,
(Corner of Newhall Street),
BIRMINGHAM, *7th December,* 1920.

MESSRS. BRASS AND METAL MECHANICS' SOCIETY,
70 Lionel Street, Birmingham.

Dear Sirs,   PIECEWORKERS.

In reply to your enquiry respecting the position of workers of the above description who fail to earn their daywork rates, I have to inform you that the general practice of the brassfoundry trade in this district is that in cases of this description the daywork rates are paid. This method of payment has been recommended by this Association and there is no desire to depart from it.

Yours faithfully,
J. W. MADELEY, *Director.*

CASTERS' MANUAL.

Daywork Casters.

Principal hand	-	-	-	-	54s. per week of 47 hours.
Moulder	-	-	-	-	42s.	„	„	„
Getter-down	-	-	-	-	35s.	„	„	„

Present wages, with bonus added, are: Principal hand,
£3 15s. 6½d.; Moulder, £3 3s. 6½d.; and Getter-down, £2 16s. 6½d.
per week.

Plumbers, Gas, Steam, Etc., Work.

Weight per mould from	6	to	7	lbs. -	- 17s. 0d. per cwt.
,, ,, ,, over	7	to	8½	lbs. -	- 15s. 9d. ,,
,, ,, ,, ,,	8½	to	9½	lbs. -	- 14s. 0d. ,,
,, ,, ,, ,,	9½	to	10½	lbs. -	- 13s. 6d. ,,
,, ,, ,, ,,	10½	to	12	lbs. -	- 12s. 6d. ,,
,, ,, ,, ,,	12	to	15	lbs. -	- by arrangement.

Strips (if a whole side), 19s. per cwt.

Pot Metal. An extra of 2s. per cwt. above Brass rates.

COCK WORK—WHITE METAL.

| 6 to 7 | lbs. | - | - | 19s. 0d. per cwt. |
| Over 7 ,, 8½ | lbs. | - | - | 17s. 9d. ,, |

This is to apply where there is a continuous output of not less than 72 moulds and not more than one change over from one metal to another takes place during any one week.

For lesser quantities or any other method of working, 20s. per cwt.; if dried, 23s. 6d. per cwt.

Members offered any other system than those in the Clause must report direct to the Secretary of the Branch.

Mill and Forge Brasses, if a full Mould, 7s. 6d. per cwt.

Odd Moulds, 4d. per mould and weight for 12 and under.

Fine Casting—Cabinet, Chandelier, Electric Work and False Cored.

DAY WORK.

| Principal hand | - | - | - | - 60s. per week of 47 hours. |
| Moulder | - | - | - | - 42s. per week of 47 hours. |

Present wages with bonus added are: Principal hand,
£4 1s. 6½d.; *Moulder,* £3 3s. 6½d.

PIECEWORK.

Weight per mould from	1½ to 2	lbs. -	- 8d. per lb.
,, ,, ,, over	2 to 2½	lbs. -	- 54s. per cwt.
,, ,, ,, ,,	2½ to 3	lbs. -	- 45s. ,,
,, ,, ,, ,,	3 to 4	lbs. -	- 38s. ,,
,, ,, ,, ,,	4 lbs. and upwards		32s. ,,

Pin Pattern Work. 7d. per lb. or per piece by mutual agreement.

False Cored Work. Extra to fine work prices by mutual agreement.

Green Work. Under 7 lbs., per mould. - - 31s. per cwt.

| ,, ,, | Over 7 to 8½ lbs. | ,, | - | - 25s. ,, |
| ,, ,, | Over 8½ to 10 lbs. | ,, | - | - 21s. ,, |

Common Cabinet Castings.

From $3\frac{1}{4}$ to $4\frac{1}{4}$ lbs. per mould, 22s. per cwt.

All moulds under $3\frac{1}{4}$ lbs. to be paid for as $3\frac{1}{4}$ lbs.

Over $4\frac{1}{4}$ to $5\frac{1}{4}$ lbs., per mould, 17s. per cwt.

Over $5\frac{1}{4}$ to 7 lbs., per mould, 14s. per cwt.

Jobbing Work to be paid at schedule rate with addition of 2d. per mould for 24 and under, and 1d. per mould for 25 to 72.

Shoes and Plates. 17s. per cwt.

Pulley Bowls—except Chain Wheels. 17s. per cwt.

Odd Moulds. 4d. per mould and weight for 12 and under.

Aluminium. Three times the price at which it should be paid for if in Brass.

Rings, Ventilators, etc. To be paid at scheduled cabinet rates in cases where they can be placed in ordinary moulds. If too large for such or too light to come within weights arranged, rate to be fixed by mutual agreement.

Cored Arms. Extra to fine work by mutual agreement.

Waxes and Plasters. Prices to be arranged by mutual agreement.

Lead and Tin. At scheduled rate for Brass castings, plus 4d. for odd moulds.

Pin Work. 7d. per lb. or per piece by mutual agreement.

Metal Mixing. If poured into ingot from pots under 120 lbs., 1s. 6d. per cwt. If poured into ingot from pots 120 lb. or larger, 1s. 3d. per cwt.

If Scrap exceeds 25 per cent. of total metals weighed out the price of mixing should be paid on the excess weight of Scrap.

Running-down Swarf into ingot from pots under 120 lb., 1s. 9d. per cwt.

Running-down Swarf into ingot from pots 120 lb. or larger 1s. 6d. per cwt.

Running-down Dust into Ingots, 3s. per cwt. on weight delivered.

All patterns taking extra size moulds to be paid an extra rate by agreement, or done day work.

Where higher prices exist they shall not be reduced.

To these prices must be added the War advances of 21s. $6\frac{1}{2}$d. *day workers* ; $2\frac{1}{2}\% + 21s. 6\frac{1}{2}d.$ *pieceworkers.*

All previous lists rescinded.

The agreement with regard to Bonus continues to operate as arranged with the Brassfounders' Employers' Association on February 17th, 1926.

Casters' Waste.

By agreement with the Brassfounders' Employers' Association at a joint meeting of Employers' and Casters' representatives held on the 26th November, 1925, the following was unanimously agreed upon :

' That no tooled castings shall be taken back by the casters as waste.   Edged work not to be considered tooled work.

' Cases of an abnormal amount of faulty castings can be dealt with by representatives of the two Associations if necessary, with a view of determining where the fault lies.'

107. Extension of Collective Bargaining.

PRESIDENT'S ADDRESS TO THE TRADES UNION CONGRESS, 1927.

Nor is it merely in a political sense that we must press forward. Our Trade Unions have not yet reached the limit of their development.   Rather I would say that we are just at the beginning of the constructive period of Trade Unionism.   More and more the workers are aiming at obtaining a share in the control and administration of industry through the Trade Unions.   Training in management and administration is absolutely essential as a preliminary step towards industrial freedom.   Not until the workers fit themselves to deal with the problems of management and the conduct of industry will they be capable of controlling industry.

And here I should like to say this : We all know—employers as well as Trade Unionists—that the vexatious, toilsome, and difficult period through which we are passing is a transitional period.   Much fuller use can be made under these conditions of the machinery for joint consultation and negotiation between employers and employed. We have not reached the limits of possible development in this direction.   It is more than doubtful whether we have seen the fullest possible development of machinery for joint consultation in particular industries.   And practically nothing has yet been done to establish effective machinery of joint conference between the representative organisations entitled to speak for industry as a whole. There are many problems upon which joint discussion would prove of value at the present time.

Such a direct exchange of practical views between representatives of the great organised bodies who have responsibility for the conduct of industry and know its problems at first hand would be of far greater significance than the suggestion which has been made in certain quarters for a spectacular national conference under Government or other auspices to discuss a vague aspiration towards ' industrial peace.'   Discussion on these lines would bring both sides face to face with the hard realities of the present economic situation, and might yield useful results in showing how far and upon what terms co-operation is possible in a common endeavour to improve the efficiency of industry and to raise the workers' standard of life.   It is important that our movement should frame a clear-cut and coherent policy on practical lines.   We should not be deterred by allegations that in entering into such discussions we are surrendering some essential principle of Trade Unionism.   On the contrary, they will lead to a much clearer understanding on the part of our own organised movement of the immediate practical objectives at which we ought to aim and for which we are entitled to use the influence and power with which this Congress is invested.

108. Industrial Conferences.

Invitation addressed to the General Council of the T.U.C. by SIR A. MOND'S GROUP OF REPRESENTATIVE EMPLOYERS, 23rd November, 1927.

Dear Sir,—As there appears to us, after investigation, to be no single existing organisation of employers which can take the initiative in inviting discussions to cover the entire field of industrial reorganisation and industrial relations, we desire, as a representative group of employers, to extend to the General Council of the Trades Union Congress an invitation to meet us to consider questions relating to these matters.

The movement towards industrial co-operation has recently received a great accession of strength and there seems to be general agreement that a useful purpose would be served by a consideration of certain fundamental factors in industrial reorganisation and industrial relations with the view to the formulation of definite and concrete proposals applicable to and to be determined in detail by the various industries concerned.

We realise that industrial reconstruction can be undertaken only in conjunction with and with the co-operation of those entitled and empowered to speak for organised Labour.   The necessity of every action being taken to achieve the fullest and speediest measures of industrial reconstruction, therefore, impels us to seek the immediate co-operation of those who are as vitally interested in the subject as ourselves. We believe that the common interests which bind us are more powerful than the apparently divergent interests which seem to separate.

The prosperity of industry can in our view be fully attained only by full and frank recognition of facts as they exist and an equally full and frank determination to increase the competitive power of British industries in the world's markets, coupled with free discussion of the essentials upon which that can be based. That can be achieved most usefully by direct negotiation with the twin objects of the restoration of industrial prosperity and the corresponding improvement in the standard of living of the population.

If this is agreed, we would proceed to enumerate the topics which might serve as a basis for our discussions. We hope that you will agree that a useful purpose could be served by representatives of your Council entering into discussion with this object in view.

Yours faithfully.

[The letter was signed by Sir Alfred Mond (now Lord Melchett) and twenty other Employers.]

109. Conciliation Boards.

CONCILIATION ACT, 1896 ; 59 & 60 Vict., ch. 30.

1.—(1.) Any board established either before or after the passing of this Act, which is constituted for the purpose of settling disputes between employers and workmen by conciliation or arbitration, or any association or body authorised by an agreement in writing made between employers and workmen to deal with such disputes (in this Act referred to as a conciliation board), may apply to the Board of Trade for registration under this Act.

(2.) The application must be accompanied by copies of the constitution, byelaws, and regulations of the conciliation board, with such other information as the Board of Trade may reasonably require.

(3.) The Board of Trade shall keep a register of conciliation boards, and enter therein with respect to each registered board its name and principal office, and such other particulars as the Board of Trade may think expedient, and any registered conciliation board shall be entitled to have its name removed from the register on sending to the Board of Trade a written application to that effect.

(4.) Every registered conciliation board shall furnish such returns, reports of its proceedings, and other documents as the Board of Trade may reasonably require.

(5.) The Board of Trade may, on being satisfied that a registered concilation board has ceased to exist or to act, remove its name from the register.

(6.) Subject to any agreement to the contrary, proceedings for conciliation before a registered conciliation board shall be conducted in accordance with the regulations of the board in that behalf.

2.—(1.) Where a difference exists or is apprehended between an employer, or any class of employers, and workmen, or between different classes of workmen, the Board of Trade may, if they think fit, exercise all or any of the following powers, namely,—

(*a*) inquire into the causes and circumstances of the difference ;

(*b*) take such steps as to the Board may seem expedient for the purpose of enabling the parties to the difference to meet together, by themselves or their representatives, under the presidency of a chairman mutually agreed upon or nominated by the Board of Trade or by some other person or body, with a view to the amicable settlement of the difference ;

(*c*) on the application of employers or workmen interested, and after taking into consideration the existence and adequacy of means available for conciliation in the district or trade and the circumstances of the case, appoint a person or persons to act as conciliator or as a board of conciliation ;

(*d*) on the application of both parties to the difference, appoint an arbitrator.

(2.) If any person is so appointed to act as conciliator, he shall inquire into the causes and circumstances of the difference by communication with the parties, and otherwise shall endeavour to bring about a settlement of the difference, and shall report his proceedings to the Board of Trade.

(3.) If a settlement of the difference is effected either by conciliation or by arbitration, a memorandum of the terms thereof shall be drawn up and signed by the parties or their representatives, and a copy thereof shall be delivered to and kept by the Board of Trade.

3. The Arbitration Act, 1889, shall not apply to the settlement by arbitration of any difference or dispute to which this Act applies, but any such arbitration proceedings shall be conducted in accordance with such of the provisions of the said Act, or such of the regulations of any conciliation board, or under other rules or regulations, as may be mutually agreed upon by the parties to the difference or dispute.

4. If it appears to the Board of Trade that in any district or trade adequate means do not exist for having disputes submitted to a conciliation board for the district or trade, they may appoint any person or persons to inquire into the conditions of the district or trade, and to confer with employers and employed, and, if the Board of Trade think fit, with any local authority or body, as to the expediency of establishing a conciliation board for the district or trade.

5. The Board of Trade shall from time to time present to Parliament a report of their proceedings under this Act.

6. The expenses incurred by the Board of Trade in the execution of this Act shall be defrayed out of moneys provided by Parliament.

7. The Masters and Workmen Arbitration Act, 1824, and the Councils of Conciliation Act, 1867, and the Arbitration (Masters and Workmen) Act, 1872, are hereby repealed.

8. This Act may be cited as the Conciliation Act, 1896.

110. Conciliation Boards, etc.

REPORT OF THE INDUSTRIAL COUNCIL ON INDUSTRIAL AGREEMENTS, 1913. Cd. 6952, p. 5.

The extent to which some form of conciliatory machinery exists in connection with the various industries of this country is a marked feature of the industrial life of the community, and the success which has attended the operations of the various Voluntary Boards of Conciliation and Arbitration points to the desirability of the continued maintenance of this form of adjusting trade disputes. The basis of these Conciliation Boards and Joint Committees is mutual consent, and their value in the past has depended upon the loyal acceptance, on the part of the constituents on both sides, of the decisions arrived at in accordance with the procedure of the Boards. This acceptance is purely voluntary, depending solely upon the sense of moral obligation. So far as has been shown by the evidence which we have heard, loyal acceptance of the decisions of the Conciliation Boards has been the rule in all the trades concerned, and it would appear inexpedient to attempt to substitute for these voluntary forms of machinery some alternative method based upon principles other than that of mutual consent. . . .

Where there exists in any trade a recognised form of conciliatory machinery for the adjustment of disputes agreed by both sides to come within the Conciliation Scheme, we consider that it is unnecessary that there should be any intervention on the part of the community (acting through a Government Department or otherwise) until the existing procedure has been exhausted, but in order that the interests of the community may be adequately safeguarded we couple with this opinion the view that it is desirable that before a cessation of work takes place there should be a period of time (after the existing procedure has been exhausted) sufficient to admit of (*a*) the further consideration of the position by the parties, and (*b*) the opportunity of the introduction into the discussion of some authority representing the interests of the community.

We consider that it is an essential part of a Conciliation Board or Joint Committee that there should be attached to it some authority to which, in the event of a deadlock, the parties may appeal for a recommendation as to a settlement. We do not view with favour the establishment of ' compulsory ' arbitration, but we do regard it of great importance that the Conciliation Board or Joint Committee should possess a means of arriving at finality. We think that before there is a reversion to the method of strike or lockout, it is important that there should be a pronouncement upon the question at issue by some independent body, or by some impartial individual, and that with this object in view the question in dispute should be thoroughly debated by a body representative of those whose interests are concerned, presided over (at some stage or other, but not necessarily the first) by an independent person invested with the power of recommending a decision, should he fail to reconcile the two sides of the Board or the Joint Committee.

111. Conciliation Machinery.

Scheme adopted by THE CONFERENCE ON INDUSTRIAL REORGANISATION AND INDUSTRIAL RELATIONS, 4th July, 1928.

The Prevention of Disputes.

A.—PREAMBLE.

Successful as the machinery for negotiation between Employers and Workers has been in avoiding the outbreak of industrial disputes, it is felt that there are various ways in which the existing machinery for negotiation might be improved or strengthened. The historical review on conciliation and arbitration in industrial disputes given in the Survey of Industrial Relations by the Balfour Committee demonstrates the great amount of anxious thought which has been given in this country during the last 40 years towards evolving machinery for the avoidance of strikes and lockouts.   In no industrial country has so much been done, and it is only fair to say that the existing machinery has, on the whole, been successful in dealing with the great majority of disputes.   On the other hand, this does not blind us to the fact that during the last few years the existing machinery has failed to deal with certain disputes of a serious magnitude.

The main problem would, therefore, appear to be to find means of avoiding the outbreak of disputes which have failed to be settled by the ordinary negotiating machinery in the industries concerned. From the outset it is agreed that :

(i) Nothing should be done to interfere with the beneficial work which is being carried on by existing joint machinery.

(ii) Wherever possible the existing joint machinery should be improved or strengthened.

(iii) The application of the element of compulsion would be unacceptable and undesirable.

This Conference is convinced that the most valuable and helpful element towards seeking a means of preventing disputes lies in the main objective of the Conference—the strengthening of good relations between organisations on both sides and their recognition of joint industrial responsibility.   This Conference believes that a broader acceptation of the responsibility of industry as a whole for the avoidance of stoppages of work should be developed.

To enable this to be done under the best auspices it is felt that Joint Conciliation Boards should be formed, composed equally of representative Trade Union leaders and of employers representative of industry.

B.—ELECTIVE BODIES.

In view of the proposal to establish a National Industrial Council, consisting of the General Council of the Trades Union Congress on the one side and an equal number of representatives of employers to be nominated by the Federation of British Industries and the National Confederation of Employers' Organisations on the other, it is agreed that the elective bodies to a Joint Standing Committee to appoint Joint Conciliation Boards should be as follows :

(i) That the Joint Standing Committee should consist of ten

representatives of the workers and ten representatives of the employers.

(ii) That the ten representatives of the workers should be nominated by the General Council members of the National Industrial Council.

(iii) That the ten representatives of the employers should be nominated by the representatives of the National Confederation of Employers' Organisations on the National Industrial Council.

The Joint Conciliation Boards should be at liberty to discuss and consider in relation to industrial disputes all questions of any character relating to the industry under consideration.

It is understood that the members nominated to the Joint Standing Committee and the Joint Conciliation Boards would be as representative on the one side of employers as on the other side of the workers, and should be equal in number.

C.—RECOMMENDATIONS.

Accordingly it is recommended that :

1. A Standing Committee of the National Industrial Council nominated as to half its members by the General Council representatives of the National Industrial Council and as to half by the National Confederation of Employers' Organisations representatives of the National Industrial Council should be set up to act as the elective and executive authority for the provision of Joint Conciliation Boards for industrial disputes.

2. The Joint Standing Committee should lay down the detailed nature of the Joint Conciliation Boards, their procedure and functions, but that in doing this they should be guided by the following considerations :

(a) When a dispute has failed to be settled within an industry, on the application of either party the Joint Standing Committee would make available a Joint Conciliation Board to investigate and report upon the matters tending towards a dispute.

In order to facilitate investigation it is desirable that both parties should arrange that on an application made to the Joint Standing Committee no stoppage of work or alteration in conditions should take place pending the report of the Joint Conciliation Board.

(b) The report of the Joint Conciliation Board should be reported to the parties and to the Joint Standing Committee before publication.

(c) The personnel of the Joint Conciliation Boards should not be permanent. The Joint Standing Committee should appoint in each particular case referred to a Joint Conciliation Board, the most suitable representatives to deal with the particular industry or matter tending towards dispute.

(d) The Joint Standing Committee should have authority to reject application for reference to the Joint Conciliation Board if, in their opinion, the dispute was not of such a nature as should be referred.

(e) The Joint Standing Committee should also fix a time limit for the stages of reference, hearing, and report to a Joint Conciliation Board so that the matters in dispute should be reviewed promptly and reported upon without undue delay.

112. National Joint Council for the Building Industry.

CONSTITUTION OF THE COUNCIL (1926).

MEMORANDUM OF AGREEMENT *between the Employers' and Operatives' National Associations and Federations connected with the Building Trades in England, Wales, and Scotland, who are signatories to this Agreement in regard to the Regulation of Wages and Hours of Work, and of such other matters involving money payments as are set forth in the Rules and Regulations hereto.*

1. It is agreed that as and from the date of this Agreement the rates of Wages of Workmen employed in the Building Industry, the Hours of Labour, and such other matters as are mentioned in the Rules hereto, except as hereinafter expressly provided in Rule 13, shall be determined on a National basis, anything to the contrary contained in any Local or Area Agreement notwithstanding ; but that conditions of employment other than those mentioned herein shall be determined on a Local or Area basis, as heretofore, unless and until otherwise agreed.

2. Pursuant to the terms of Clause 1 hereof, the Parties hereto jointly and severally declare that unless and until this Agreement is terminated in the manner hereinafter provided they will not permit, endorse, sanction, or otherwise condone any claim for or agreement for any variation except as aforesaid of any of the matters mentioned in the Rules hereto, having for its object the determination of any of those matters on any other than a National basis, and will respectively use all means in their power to prevent or nullify any such claim or agreement for any such variation.

3. It is further agreed that, in order to carry out this Agreement according to its true intent and meaning, a National Joint Council shall be appointed and the following Rules and Regulations shall be observed during the currency of the Agreement.

RULES

Of the National Joint Council for the Building Industry, hereinafter referred to as the Council.

1. (*a*) The Council shall consist of not more than forty Members, half of whom shall be Employers' Representatives and half Workmen's Representatives appointed annually by and apportioned among the parties affiliated to the Council in such manner as the respective sides shall from time to time agree, to take office at each Annual Meeting.

(*b*) All Members of the Council shall retire annually, but be eligible for reappointment. The annual appointment of the Members of the Council shall be notified to the Clerk not later than the 1st of March in each year.

(*c*) Casual vacancies occurring during the year shall be filled by the body which appointed the Member whose place has become vacant.

2. The duties of the Council shall be :

(*a*) To deal, in accordance with the Rules and Regulations hereinafter provided, with the following matters :

     (i) Rates of Wages and/or Grading.
     (ii) Working Hours.
     (iii) Extra Wages.
     (iv) Overtime.
     (v) Night Gangs.
     (vi) Walking, Travelling and Lodging Allowances.

(*b*) To interpret its own decisions as and when necessary.

(*c*) To provide for such references to the constituent bodies as may be necessary in the case of a decision or decisions involving a constitutional amendment, or any other question which the Council wishes to refer to the members of the constituent bodies for approval or otherwise.

(*d*) To give binding decisions in cases involving variations of the National Working Rules.

(*e*) To make such further provisions by way of rule or regulation as may appear necessary from time to time, and (*f*) Generally to do all things necessary to the furtherance or attainment of the foregoing objects or any of them.

3. (*a*) The Statutory Meeting of the Council shall be held in the second week of January. The Annual Meeting shall be held in March. Other meetings may be held at such other times as the Council, or in its default the Chairman, may appoint.

(*b*) A special meeting shall be held upon a requisition signed by any ten members of the Council. Such requisition must state the business for which the meeting is to be held, and no other business shall be transacted at such meeting.

(*c*) Except as provided in Rule (12 *c*) at least seven days' notice shall be given of meetings of the Council.

4. The Officers of the Council shall consist of a Chairman and Vice-Chairman elected from among the members of the Council, together with joint Secretaries and a Clerk. The Clerk's duties and remuneration shall be fixed by the Council.

5. (*a*) The expenses incurred by the Council shall be borne as to one-half by the bodies represented on the Employers' side and one-half by those represented on the Workmen's side, and each side shall distribute the share it has to bear among the constituent bodies thereof as may be agreed among them from time to time.

(*b*) The Employers' and Operatives' sides respectively shall pay the expenses of their representatives on the Council.

(*c*) An estimate of the probable expenses of the Council for the ensuing year shall be presented at the Annual Meeting thereof, and after approval by the Council shall become due and payable by the respective constituent bodies in accordance with their respective shares distributed as aforesaid.

. . . .

8. Except the Council by a three-fourth's majority on each side decide otherwise, the voting shall be by ballot, each side voting separately. Any decision to be binding must be carried by a majority of votes on each side of those present and voting. The Chairman shall have one vote only as a Member of the Council.

. . . .

11. (*a*) The Council shall not deal with disputes except such as are concerned with the interpretation of its own decisions. The Council's decision thereon shall be final and binding.

(*b*) Notice of any such dispute shall be given to the Joint Secre-taries, and the dispute shall be considered by the Council at its next meeting, and in any case within twenty-one days of receipt of such notice, and the Council's decision, if any, shall be forthwith communicated to the parties concerned.

(c) If the Council fails to reach a decision, it shall consider whether the dispute shall be referred to Arbitration under Rule 14, and in the event of failure to refer to Arbitration the parties concerned shall be informed forthwith. Should the dispute be referred to Arbitration, the parties concerned shall be likewise informed.

.   .   .   .

13. The following provisions shall govern 'Variation Amendments' of rates of wages and/or grading, working hours, extra wages, overtime, night gangs, and walking, travelling, and lodging allowances.

(a) Decisions of the Council upon any question of variation arising under this Rule shall be final and binding.

(b) The Council shall at each Statutory Meeting review the wages payments for the time being in force under the National Working Rules, and make such Variation Amendments thereof as may appear to the Council just and equitable, subject to the conditions that :

(i) For the purposes of this Agreement the following scale of grade rates hereinafter referred to as 'Standard Rates' are assumed, except as hereinafter provided, to correspond to a cost-of-living index figure of 78 points above pre-war level as per the figures published in the *Ministry of Labour Gazette*.

Grade Classification.	Standard Rate.	Labourers' Rate.
A	1s. 8d.	1s. 3¼d.
A1	1s. 7½d.	1s. 2¾d.
A2	1s. 7d.	1s. 2½d.
A3	1s. 6½d.	1s. 2d.
B	1s. 6d.	1s. 1¾d.
B1	1s. 5½d.	1s. 1¼d.
B2	1s. 5d.	1s. 1d.
B3	1s. 4½d.	1s. 0½d.
C	1s. 4d.	1s. 0¼d.
C1	1s. 3½d.	11¾d.

Should the Ministry of Labour index figures of the cost of living, published monthly during the antecedent period January to December inclusive, show there has been an average variation in the cost of living of not less than 6·5 (6½) points, the Council shall give a decision making a Variation Amendment of the rates of wages of a halfpenny per hour in respect of each complete average variation of not less than 6·5 (6½) points, to take effect on and from the first day of February next ensuing, and such a Variation Amendment shall be final and binding.

(ii) The standard rates for London shall be the ' A ' grade rate for the time being in operation, plus 1½d. per hour, within the area covered by the 12 mile radius, and the ' A ' grade rate plus 1d. per hour within the area covered by the 12-15 mile radius.

Should the Council deem it necessary to provide for other exceptional rates applicable to any of the foregoing Standard Rates, it may do so upon application from or through the appropriate Regional Joint Committee, as provided for in the Regulations herein, providing always that any such exceptional rate shall be authorised in respect of a defined district and for a limited prescribed period not exceeding twelve months, and that at the termination of such period such district shall revert to its previous position in the aforesaid scale of standard rates unless the Council upon a fresh application shall decide otherwise.

(iii) The differential rates existing in some districts are not affected by the fixing of the foregoing standard rates.

Where it may be agreed by a Regional Joint Committee or an Area Joint Committee, as provided for in the Regulations herein, that some differential rate of wages should be adopted, such proposals before becoming operative must be submitted to the National Joint Council as provided and such proposals and action arising thereout-of shall, anything to the contrary notwithstanding, be regarded as a variation amendment.

(c) It shall be permissible, by complying with the regulations, for any district to show cause why its standard rate classification should be varied.   For the purpose of dealing with such applications nationally after they have been regionally dealt with, the Council may appoint a Commission and delegate thereto powers in regard to receiving applications, taking evidence and making recommendations to the Council as to the decisions which should be given, and the reports and recommendations of such Commission shall be dealt with ordinarily at a Statutory Meeting in the first instance and thereafter at any subsequent meeting.   An application for a standard rate to be allocated to a town or district not previously classified may be dealt with at any time, and a recommendation thereon by the said Commission shall be accepted by the Parties as a provisional standard rate to be submitted to the Council for confirmation or otherwise at the first meeting thereafter.

(*d*) Questions of grading shall be dealt with by the Council on their merits prior to dealing with any question as to whether any variation is required under sub-section (*b*) hereof.

(*e*) Where a Regional Joint Committee is of opinion that some variation of Clauses 2 to 6 inclusive of the National Working Rules is desirable so far as that Region is concerned, it shall be competent for such Committee to propose such variation of the said Clauses or any of them to meet Regional circumstances in the manner provided by the regulations herein.

(*f*) Either side (Employer or Operative) in any area desiring to initiate a variation under this agreement shall first submit its proposal or proposals, in writing, to its own appropriate Regional body, which shall consider them and forward them to its appropriate National body together with its own observations thereon, for the consent or otherwise of such National body to the initiation of such variation, and no proposal or proposals shall be communicated to any other party to this agreement, unless and until such National consent is first had and obtained.

Either side (Employer or Operative) in any region desiring to initiate a variation under this Agreement shall first submit its proposal or proposals in writing to its appropriate National body for its consent to initiate such variation or otherwise, and no proposal or proposals shall be communicated to any other party to this Agreement unless and until such National consent is first had and obtained.

(*g*) Failing Agreement by the National Joint Council to any proposed variation of National Working Rules 1 to 6 inclusive and pending any other action that may be adopted under this Agreement such Rules shall continue to apply.

(*h*) Any Variation Amendment made by the Council shall continue in force until further amended by the Council in accordance with the preceding clauses, and shall apply to all grades and all sections of the Industry similarly, unless otherwise expressly decided by the Council.

In the event of proposals for Variation Amendment resulting in deadlock in the Council, a solution of the deadlock may be sought either under Clause 14 or Clause 15 hereof.

14. After the procedure for arriving at a decision on any matter before the Council has been carried out in accordance with this

Constitution and Rules without a settlement having resulted therefrom, it shall be competent for the purpose of more effectually attaining the objects of the Council, provided that a majority of each side of the Council is in favour of such a course, to refer the matter to the Industrial Arbitration Court or to call in an Arbitrator or Arbitrators with power to decide the matter, and where this is done the decision of such Court or of such Arbitrator or Arbitrators shall be final and binding. In the event of such a reference, the costs, if any, shall be borne in equal shares by the Employers and Operatives, unless left to the discretion of the referee or referees by mutual consent of the Council.

15. Pending the completion of the procedure set out in the foregoing Rules, no stoppage of work shall take place on any pretext whatever, but in the event of a deadlock ensuing, it shall be the duty of the Council to appoint a Committee to examine the position with a view of ascertaining upon what terms the question at issue might be settled. The Committee shall have full powers of conference with the Executives of the adherent bodies, and shall report to the Council within one month from the date of appointment. Failing a settlement, either by agreement or by reference to arbitration, the Council shall report to the adherent bodies that the matter has proved incapable of settlement, whereupon either Party shall be at liberty to take any action it may deem expedient on the expiry of 14 days' notice duly given.

16. Any National body desiring to become affiliated to this Council shall make application in writing to the Joint Secretaries, who shall cause the application to be laid before the Council, which, before deciding thereon, shall invite the observations of the then Parties hereto, and shall consider and deal with the application.

17. Every Party to this Agreement shall notify the Clerk in the event of any local Association becoming affiliated to its National adherent body (either directly or through a Regional branch) within 14 days of such affiliation being agreed upon.

18. Any Party desiring to retire from this Agreement may do so on giving notice in writing on or before September 29th in any year, to expire at the Annual Meeting in the following year, but shall remain liable for any undischarged share of the expenses due from it in respect of the maintenance of the Council.

Regulations governing Procedure in regard to matters to be submitted
to the Council.

. . . .

9. Regional Joint Committees serve as connecting links between the Council and the localities, and shall comply with the following regulations :

(*a*) The total membership of a Regional Joint Committee shall not exceed thirty, viz., fifteen employers and fifteen operatives ; provided always that only representatives of organisations directly affiliated to the Council shall be eligible.

(*b*) Where representation of the Industry on the Operatives' side is not adequately met by Operatives who are members of the National Federation of Building Trades Operatives the membership shall comprise one representative of each Operatives' Trade Association which is directly affiliated to the Council, the balance of the representation on the Operatives' side to be allotted on an industrial basis by the National Federation of Building Trades Operatives.

Representation on the Employers' side to be agreed upon between the parties concerned in each Region, that is, between the Employer bodies who, through their National Associations, are attached to the Council.

Should the Parties in any Region fail to agree as to the proper representation of the various Employer bodies, or any of them, the matter shall be referred to a Standing Committee, appointed by, and representative of, the Employer bodies attached to the Council, who shall take evidence and give a decision. In assessing the value of any claim the Standing Committee shall regard the representation on the Council of any body concerned as relevant.

(*c*) (i) Where the Regional Joint Committees decide to deal as a Regional unit with variation amendments as provided in Rule 13 of the Rules of the Council, the Regional Joint Committees will initiate proposals for such variations, and submit same to the National Joint Council for approval or otherwise.

(ii) Where it is arranged that such matters be dealt with as area units by Joint Area Committees the Regional Joint Committees will consider the variations initiated by the Joint Area Committees, and submit them to the National Joint Council for approval or otherwise as they may recommend.

10. Area Joint Committees may be appointed by the Regional Joint Committees who will, in that case, define in detail the repre-

sentation and functions thereof which shall be consistent with those relating to the Regional Joint Committees. Such Area Joint Committees will serve as connecting links between the Regional Joint Committee and the individual members so far as the application of the working rules is concerned, and be responsible for carrying out the working rule agreement applicable to their respective areas, and will initiate proposals for variation amendments and submit same to the Regional Joint Committees.

11. If any variation amendment initiated at an Area Joint Committee by any party to this Agreement fails to secure agreement, the initiating party shall have right of appeal to the Regional Joint Committee.

If such variation amendment secures agreement it shall be sent forward to the Regional Joint Committee as a recommended variation.

In either event any party to this Agreement in any other Area, within the Region concerned, objecting thereto shall be entitled to intervene and be heard before the Regional Joint Committee and have its objection considered.

If there is a failure to agree on the Regional Joint Committee, appeal shall be by the initiating party, where the variation amendment proposal from the area is not a recommended variation, or by the Area Joint Committee, where it is a variation recommended by such Committee to the National Joint Council.

If agreement is reached at the Regional Joint Committee the variation amendment shall go forward to the National Joint Council as a recommended variation.

In any event any party to this Agreement in any other Region objecting thereto shall be entitled to intervene before the National Joint Council and have its objection considered.

Decisions by the National Joint Council shall be final, but the fact that a proposal for variation has failed to secure approval shall not debar it from being reinitiated by complying with the regulations as to initiation.

(*d*) All notices respecting regrading and variation applications to be sent, in the first instance, during October in any year, to the Secretary of the Federation (Operative or Employer) covering the Regional Area concerned, for transmission, if approved by his Committee, to the Secretary of the Federation representing the other side, who shall have fourteen days in which to issue a counter-notice. An application for the standard rate of the district to be applied to a section of the Industry in which hitherto the Operatives have not received the standard rate, is a regrading application for the section of the Industry concerned, and must be dealt with accordingly.

(*e*) When dealing with grading or regrading applications in respect of towns or districts in which the Employers and/or Operatives are not affiliated to a National body adherent to the Council, a representative or representatives of the local Employers and/or Operatives shall be invited to appear before the Regional Joint Committee, and, if necessary, before the Grading Commission.

(*f*) Any application for regrading or variation under Rule 13*b* (ii and iii) must, *inter alia*, give definite answers in writing to the following questions :

(i) How does the cost of living in the applicant town or district compare with the cost of living in Grade A towns ?

In this connexion information should be given as to the average rent, including rates, of pre-war built houses occupied by Building Trades' Operatives.

(ii) What is the average wage rate per hour and per week agreed, or currently paid, in the applicant town or district to workmen in—

(*a*) The Building Trade ?
(*b*) Any other industry or industries carried on in the applicant town or district ?

(iii) What is the population of the applicant town or district ?
(iv) What are the local facilities for the transit of workmen ?
(v) What is the demand in the applicant town or district for—

(*a*) Building Trade Craftsmen's services ?
(*b*) Building Trade Labourer's services ?

(vi) State whether the applicant town or district is mainly—

(*a*) Industrial.   (*b*) Residential.   (*c*) Agricultural.

(vii) What is the geographical situation of the applicant town or district relative to other towns and to other adjacent Regional Areas ?

(viii) To what extent is the Building Trade organised in the applicant town or district—

(*a*) As to the Employers ?
(*b*) As to the Operatives ?

(ix) To what extent was the Building Trade organised in the applicant town or district in 1914—

(*a*) As to the Employers ?
(*b*) As to the Operatives ?

(x) What was the agreed rate of wages for Building Trades Craftsmen, in the applicant town or district, in 1914 ?

(xi) What number of hours constituted the normal working week in 1914 ?

(xii) Is there anything in the health conditions of the applicant locality which detrimentally affects the earnings of labour ?—and if so, what ?

(xiii) Give any additional particulars which, in your opinion, will assist the Council in coming to a decision.

12. It shall be competent for duly appointed representatives or officials of the Region concerned and likewise of the National body or bodies concerned to be present and participate in the proceedings connected with the initiation of a variation in an Area or Region and at any subsequent proceedings relating thereto, but they shall have no vote.

113. Machinery for Settling Disputes.

YORK MEMORANDUM.

Memo. of Special Conference between the Engineering Employers' Federation and the Amalgamated Society of Engineers held within Station Hotel, York, on 17th April, 1914.

Referring to the termination by the society of the agreement of 1st October, 1907, and the premium bonus agreement, the representatives of the society agree to forthwith recommend their members to authorise their Executive Council to enter into negotiations with the Federation with the view to arriving at an agreement in substitution of the agreement of 1907 and the premium bonus agreement, and both parties agree that meantime the following provisions for avoiding disputes shall be observed :

When a question arises an endeavour shall be made by the management and the workmen directly concerned to settle the same in the works or at the place where the question has arisen.   Failing settlement, deputations of workmen, who may be accompanied by their organising district delegate (in which event a representative of the employers' association shall also be present) shall be received by the employers by appointment without unreasonable delay for the mutual discussion of any question in the settlement of which both parties are directly concerned.   In the event of no settlement being arrived at, it shall be competent for either party to bring the question before a local conference to be held between the local association and the local representatives of the society.

In the event of either party desiring to raise any question a local conference for this purpose may be arranged by application to the secretary of the local association or to the local representative of the society.

Local conferences shall be held within seven working days unless otherwise mutually agreed upon from the receipt of the application by the secretary of the local association, or the representative of the society.

Failing settlement at a local conference of any question brought before it, it shall be competent for either party to refer the matter to a Central Conference, which, if thought desirable, may make a joint recommendation to the constituent bodies.

Central Conferences shall be held on the second Friday of each month, at which questions referred to Central Conference prior to 14 days of that date shall be taken.

Until the procedure provided above has been carried through, there shall be no stoppage of work, either of a partial or a general character.

114. Industrial Courts and Enquiries.

INDUSTRIAL COURTS ACT, 1919, 9 & 10 Geo V., ch. 69.

Part I.—Industrial Courts.

1.—(1) For the purpose of the settlement of trade disputes in manner provided by this Act, there shall be a standing Industrial Court, consisting of persons to be appointed by the Minister of Labour (in this Act referred to as ' the Minister '), of whom some shall be independent persons, some shall be persons representing employers, and some shall be persons representing workmen, and in addition one or more women.

(2) A member of the Industrial Court shall hold office for such term as may be fixed by the Minister at the time of his appointment.

(3) For the purpose of dealing with any matter which may be referred to it, the Court shall be constituted of such of the members of the Court as the president may direct.

(4) The president of the Court, and the chairman of any division of the Court, shall be such person, being one of the independent persons aforesaid, as the Minister may by order, given either generally or specially, direct.

2.—(1) Any trade dispute as defined by this Act, whether existing or apprehended, may be reported to the Minister by or on behalf of either of the parties to the dispute, and the Minister shall thereupon take the matter into his consideration and take such steps as seem to him expedient for promoting a settlement thereof.

(2) Where a trade dispute exists or is apprehended, the Minister may, subject as hereinafter provided, if he thinks fit and if both parties consent, either—

(*a*) refer the matter for settlement to the Industrial Court ; or

(*b*) refer the matter for settlement to the arbitration of one or more persons appointed by him ; or

(*c*) refer the matter for settlement to a board of arbitration consisting of one or more persons nominated by or on behalf of the employers concerned and an equal number of persons nominated by or on behalf of the workmen concerned, and an independent chairman nominated by the Minister, and, for the purpose of facilitating the nomination of persons to act as members of a board of arbitration, the Minister of Labour shall constitute panels of persons appearing to him suitable so to act, and women shall be included in the panels.

(3) The Minister may refer to the Industrial Court for advice any matter relating to or arising out of a trade dispute, or trade disputes in general or trade disputes of any class, or any other matter which in his opinion ought to be so referred.

(4) If there are existing in any trade or industry any arrangements for settlement by conciliation or arbitration of disputes in such trade or industry, or any branch thereof, made in pursuance of an agreement between organisations of employers and organisations of workmen representative respectively of substantial proportions of the employers and workmen engaged in that trade or industry, the Minister shall not, unless with the consent of both parties to the dispute, and unless and until there has been a failure to obtain a settlement by means of those arrangements, refer the matter for settlement or advice in accordance with the foregoing provisions of this section.

3.—(1) The Minister may make, or authorise the Industrial Court to make, rules regulating the procedure of that Court, and those rules may, amongst other things, provide for references in certain cases to a single member of the Court, and provide for enabling the Court to sit in two or more divisions, and to sit with assessors, who may be men or women, for enabling the Court or any division of the Court to act notwithstanding any vacancy in their number, and for enabling questions as to the interpretation of any award to be settled without any fresh report or reference.

(2) The Minister may make rules regulating the procedure to be followed in cases where matters are referred for settlement to the arbitration of one or more persons appointed by the Minister.

(3) The Arbitration Act, 1889, shall not apply to any reference to the Industrial Court, or to any reference to arbitration under this Act.

(4) Where the members of the Industrial Court are unable to agree as to their award, the matter shall be decided by the chairman acting with the full powers of an umpire.

(5) Where any trade dispute referred to the Industrial Court involves questions as to wages, or as to hours of work, or otherwise as to the terms or conditions of or affecting employment which are regulated by any Act other than this Act, the court shall not make any award which is inconsistent with the provision of that Act.

Part II.—Courts of Inquiry.

4.—(1) Where any trade dispute exists or is apprehended, the Minister may, whether or not the dispute is reported to him under Part I. of this Act, inquire into the causes and circumstances of the dispute, and, if he thinks fit, refer any matters appearing to him to be connected with or relevant to the dispute to a court of inquiry appointed by him for the purpose of such reference, and the court shall, either in public or in private, at their discretion, inquire into the matters referred to them and report thereon to the Minister.

(2) A court of inquiry for the purposes of this Part of this Act (in this Act referred to as ' a court of inquiry ') shall consist of a chairman and such other persons as the Minister thinks fit to appoint, or may, if the Minister thinks fit, consist of one person appointed by the Minister.

(3) A court of inquiry may act notwithstanding any vacancy in their number.

(4) The Minister may make rules regulating the procedure of any court of inquiry, including rules as to summoning of witnesses, quorum, and the appointment of committees and enabling the court to call for such documents as the court may determine to be relevant to the subject matter of the inquiry.

(5) A court of inquiry may, if and to such extent as may be authorised by rules made under this section, by order require any

person who appears to the court to have any knowledge of the subject-matter of the inquiry to furnish, in writing or otherwise, such particulars in relation thereto as the court may require, and, where necessary, to attend before the court and give evidence on oath, and the court may administer or authorise any person to administer an oath for that purpose.

5.—(1) A court of inquiry may, if it thinks fit, make interim reports.

(2) Any report of a court of inquiry, and any minority report, shall be laid as soon as may be before both Houses of Parliament.

(3) The Minister may, whether before or after any such report has been laid before Parliament, publish or cause to be published from time to time, in such manner as he thinks fit, any information obtained or conclusions arrived at by the court as the result or in the course of their inquiry :

Provided that there shall not be included in any report or publication made or authorised by the court or the Minister any information obtained by the court in the course of their inquiry as to any trade union or as to any individual business (whether carried on by a person, firm, or company) which is not available otherwise than through evidence given at the inquiry, except with the consent of the secretary of the trade union or of the person, firm, or company in question, nor shall any individual member of the court or any person concerned in the inquiry, without such consent, disclose any such information.

. . . .

Part IV.—General.

7. Any expenses incurred by the Minister in carrying this Act into operation, including the expenses of the Industrial Court and of any court of inquiry, shall be paid out of moneys provided by Parliament.

8. For the purposes of this Act :

The expression ' trade dispute ' means any dispute or difference between employers and workmen, or between workmen and workmen connected with the employment or non-employment, or the terms of the employment or with the conditions of labour of any person :

The expression ' workman ' means any person who has entered into or works under a contract with an employer whether the contract be by way of manual labour, clerical work, or otherwise, be expressed or implied, oral or in writing, and whether it be a contract of service or of apprenticeship or a contract personally to execute any work or labour.

9. Provision shall be made by rules under this Act with respect to the cases in which persons may appear by counsel or solicitor on proceedings under this Act before the Industrial Court, before an arbitrator or before a court of inquiry, and except as provided by those rules no person shall be entitled to appear on any such proceedings by counsel or solicitor.

10. This Act shall not apply to persons in the naval, military, or air services of the Crown, but otherwise shall apply to workmen employed by or under the Crown in the same manner as if they were employed by or under a private person.

11. In the case of a trade dispute in the industry of agriculture, steps to be taken under this Act by the Minister of Labour shall be taken in conjunction with the Board of Agriculture and Fisheries.

12.—(1) In the application of this Act to Scotland a reference to an oversman shall be substituted for any reference to an umpire, and a reference to the Board of Agriculture for Scotland shall be substituted for any reference to the Board of Agriculture and Fisheries.

.   .   .   .

13. The Minister shall from time to time present to Parliament a report of his proceedings under this Act.

14. This Act may be cited as the Industrial Courts Act, 1919.

115. Industrial Court.

AWARD No. 728, 8th July, 1922, RAILWAY SHOPMEN.

THE INDUSTRIAL COURT.

(728.) RAILWAY SHOPMEN—ENGLAND AND WALES.
(Rates of Pay—Railway Rates—District Rates—Shops, Running Sheds and Depots—Conditions of Service.)

Parties :

The following Railway Companies, namely :

Alexandra Docks Railway—Barry Railway—Cardiff Railway—Great Eastern Railway—Great Western Railway—Hull and Barnsley Railway—London and North Western Railway—Lancashire and Yorkshire Railway (now amalgamated with the L. and

N.W. Railway)—London and South Western Railway—Maryport and Carlisle Railway—Midland Railway—North Eastern Railway—North Staffordshire Railway—Rhymney Railway—South Eastern and Chatham Railway—Taff Vale Railway and National Union of Railwaymen—Federation of Engineering and Shipbuilding Trades, comprising :

Associated Blacksmiths' and Ironworkers' Society of Great Britain and Ireland—United Society of Boilermakers and Iron and Steel Shipbuilders—National Society of Brass Workers and Metal Mechanics—London Society of Amalgamated Brass Workers—London United Brass Founders' Society—National Union of Sheet Metal Workers and Braziers—National Society of Coppersmiths, Braziers and Metal Workers—Dock, Wharf, Riverside and General Workers' Union of Great Britain and Ireland—National Amalgamated Union of Enginemen, Firemen, Mechanics, Motormen and Electrical Workers—Electrical Trades Union—Amalgamated Society of Farriers and Blacksmiths—National Amalgamated Furnishing Trades Association—National Union of General Workers—National Union of Operative Heating and Domestic Engineers—General Iron Fitters' Association—Iron, Steel and Metal Dressers' Trade Society—National Amalgamated Union of Labour—National Union of Stove, Grate, Fender and General Light Metal Workers—Birmingham Operative Tinplate, Sheet Metal Workers' and Braziers' Society—National Amalgamated Society of Operative House and Ship Painters and Decorators—United Patternmakers' Association—United Operative Plumbers' and Domestic Engineers' Association of Great Britain and Ireland—Amalgamated Society of Railway Vehicle Builders, Wheelwrights, Carpenters and Mechanics—Ship Constructors' and Shipwrights' Association—Amalgamated Union of Upholsterers—National Union of Vehicle Builders—Amalgamated Wheelwrights', Smiths' and Kindred Trades Union—Amalgamated Society of Woodcutting Machinists of Great Britain and Ireland—Amalgamated Society of Woodworkers.

National Federation of Building Trades Operatives—National Federation of General Workers, comprising :

National Union of General Workers—National Amalgamated Union of Labour—Workers' Union.

Terms of Reference.

To determine the rates of pay and conditions of employment applicable to the various classes of men employed in the several departments of the railway shops or in connection therewith, on the understanding that the rates of pay and conditions of employment so awarded shall be applied as from the date determined by the Court alike to present staff and to future entrants.

1. The matter was referred under the Industrial Courts Act, 1919, by the Minister of Labour to the Industrial Court for settlement. Representatives of the parties were heard by the Court on 21st and 22nd February, 1922.

2. Voluminous documents were put in by the parties in support of their respective cases, and much time has been occupied in sifting the evidence, both verbal and written, which was submitted. About 600 workshops, running sheds and depots throughout England and Wales have been considered, involving questions with respect to some 1,500 different classes of workpeople and the rates of pay and conditions of about 110,000 men.

3. The case is one of an extremely complex character. The employees concerned belong to the class known generally as railway shopmen, who may be described broadly as those manual workers employed by railway companies who are not employed immediately and directly in the working of traffic. The work done by railway companies incidentally to their main purpose of providing transport is many-sided in character and of great extent. Not only do the building and maintenance of locomotives and rolling stock give rise to an enormous amount of mechanical engineering and coach work, but the upkeep or construction of stations, signals, telegraphs, tunnels, bridges, docks and ferries necessitates the employment of many classes of workpeople associated with many other trades and industries. Insofar as they are represented by the Unions who are parties to the proceedings, it is the workers concerned in these varied activities of the railway companies whose wages and conditions of service are brought under review in the present case. The parties agreed that the workpeople to be included in these proceedings are those engaged in the railway carriage and wagon departments, running sheds, mechanical and civil engineering departments, signal and telegraph departments, and docks and marine departments of the sixteen railway companies who are parties ; or put in another way, they include those employees who are now in receipt of a war wage of 33s. 6d. a week and were formerly in receipt of the $12\frac{1}{2}$ per cent. or $7\frac{1}{2}$ per cent. bonus, excepting employees in the stores department and the hotels department, the steel smelting and rolling mill staffs and all women and juvenile workers. The number employed on the shop staff by the sixteen railway companies who are parties represents about 75 per cent. of the total of the shop staff employed by the railway companies in England and Wales. The wages of the employees concerned consist in the main in the

case of time or day workers of base rates and a war wage or bonus amounting to 33s. 6d. per week. Piece workers received their piece work earnings and (if not included in the piece price) a war advance or bonus of $17\frac{1}{2}$ per cent. on earnings and a further war wage or bonus of 26s. 6d. per week.

4. The origin of the present differences is to be found in the requests which were made to the railway companies in and prior to the year 1914 and have since been repeated from time to time by several trade unions for payment of ' district rates,' that is to say, the rates agreed upon or recognised by organised employers and workers in particular trades and industries in particular localities.

5. On 7th April, 1920, at a time when the railways were working under Government control, a letter was sent to the Federation of Engineering and Shipbuilding Trades, and also to the National Union of Railwaymen, by the Negotiating Committee of General Managers which was then acting for the Ministry of Transport. In the letter it was stated that ' the railway companies generally would be prepared to concede the principle of district rates to the men employed in their various shops on the clear understanding that the men would be debarred from any railway privileges except, perhaps, such privileges as they obtain to-day under the privilege ticket arrangement.' A committee representing the National Union of Railwaymen and the craft unions (enumerated on the first page of this Decision) was set up which discussed with representatives of the companies various questions involved. At a meeting of such Joint Committee on 5th November, 1920, certain ' Heads of Arrangements ' were adopted, in which it was recorded :

' 1. The Craft Unions and the National Union of Railwaymen assented to the principle of grouping places at which Railway Shopmen are employed and fixing Railway Rates for the different classes of railway shopmen in each group.

. . . .

' 4. The group Railway Rates for the principal classes of Shop Employees to be based, generally, on the prevailing district rates as agreed between the Employers' and Workmen's Associations in each particular group of places.

' 5. Group Railway Rates to be agreed by the parties hereto for any class of Shopmen peculiar to Railway employment, and for whom, therefore, there is no recognised " District Rate."

' 6. Group Railway Rates, either more or less than the recognised District Rates, to be similarly agreed for any class of Shopmen whose work differs materially in character from that of like graded men in non-railway shops.

'7. Differential Group Railway Rates to be similarly agreed for Railway men with common designations, but whose work differs materially in character, *e.g.*, Carpenters in Carriage Shops compared with rough Carpenters in the Civil Engineering Department employed out on the line.

'8. Any Railway Rates for a class of Shopmen fixed under this arrangement to rise or fall with any national rise or fall in the recognised rates in non-railway shops that occurs in any particular group as the result of agreement between the Employers' and Workmen's Associations, or of arbitration proceedings, or otherwise. Any such alteration in Railway Rates to be agreed between the parties hereto before being adopted.'

.   .   .   .   .   .

Protracted negotiations between all the parties concerned followed this provisional agreement, and differences were revealed upon which it was found that no agreement was possible. The matters at issue come before the Court unprejudiced by any proposals or admissions made by any of the parties in the course of the proceedings prior to the hearing.

Rates of Pay.

6. The request for district rates, reiterated before the Court, indicates the demand now put forward by the National Federation of Engineering and Shipbuilding Trades, the National Federation of Building Trades, and certain of the constituent unions of the National Federation of General Workers.

7. The claim for district rates is based on the contention that insofar as the railway companies employ men who are members of a particular craft or calling, they should pay the rates of wages which are recognised by other employers in that trade. For example, it is contended that to men employed in the engineering grades the rates recognised in the engineering trade should be paid, while the men employed in coach-making or in house-building should receive the rates respectively recognised in the carriage and wagon trade and the building trade.

8. Certain railway companies in England and Wales have conceded to craftsmen, or to certain classes of craftsmen, the principle of the district rate of wages; but where this has been done it has

been sometimes accompanied by the deduction of a 'differential,' that is, a sum considered to represent wholly or in part the value of certain privileges enjoyed by a railway worker over and above those common to his fellow workers in the employment of outside firms. Further reference to these railway privileges will be made below. Differences have also existed in regard to the rates paid in the various parts of the same line. While some companies have applied to some sections of workers, but not to all, a 'line rate' which operates uniformly and in disregard of local circumstances throughout all the shops and depots on the line, others have paid to the men employed in the different centres rates of wages determined, to a greater or lesser degree, by local conditions.

9. For these reasons, among others, the rates of wages paid by railway companies to men of the same description in different centres show considerable variation. Moreover, the differences in rates do not rest upon any clearly defined and agreed principle, but result largely from accidental causes. All parties are agreed that rates and conditions should, so far as possible, now be brought into conformity with a general plan.

10. While the claim of the National Federation of Engineering and Shipbuilding Trades, the National Federation of Building Trades Operatives, and certain constituent unions of the National Federation of General Workers, was for district rates, the claim of the National Union of Railwaymen, supported to some extent by the Workers' Union, was that the Court should fix rates applicable to Railway Shopmen as such, and without necessary or exclusive regard to district rates for similar classes of workmen employed by other concerns. The argument of the National Union of Railwaymen was that the manufacturing and maintenance work carried on by railway companies was incidental to and in some respects inseparable from the business of transport ; and that if anomalous differences between the rates of men employed in the various branches of railway work were to be avoided, the railways must be looked to as an indivisible whole, and some degree of standardisation attempted.

11. In some respects the submission of the railway companies was intermediate between that of the National Federation of Engineering and Shipbuilding Trades and the National Union of Railwaymen. Subject to their claim for a wage 'differential' for railway privileges, and subject also to the special consideration and treatment of some exceptional cases, they were prepared to follow generally the district rates as regards fitters in the mechanical engin-

eering trade, and to some extent as regards labourers. As regards all other classes, the rates were to be determined, speaking generally, in the case of skilled workers, by reference to the fitter's rate and, in the case of so-called semi-skilled and unskilled workers, by reference to the labourer's rate ; so that the rates of any class of skilled, semi-skilled or unskilled workers, wherever employed, should always bear the same relationship to the rates of all other grades of workers.

12. The three sets of claims, broadly outlined above, involved much detail. The claim to district rates, though simple in idea, gives rise to many difficulties. Principal among these is the fact that for many classes of workers at many places district rates do not exist, or are not generally recognised ; so that, to deal with the present position merely by declaring in favour of district rates, would be to leave untouched very large numbers of employees. There is also the further though less serious difficulty that in some places, and as regards some trades, the rate generally recognised as the district rate is related to a class of work which though nominally the same, is in fact different from railway work ; and the district rate is, therefore, either by excess or deficiency, inappropriate to railway employees. It has also to be borne in mind that district rates are determined by employers and workpeople outside the railway industry ; and to concede the claim for district rates would be to bind the railway companies and the railway employees to the observance of decisions to which they were not parties, and which may have been brought about by conditions not applicable to railways. Moreover, movements in wages do not occur in all trades simultaneously, or by the same amounts ; and the payment of district rates would involve a position in which some workers employed in a railway workshop would be liable to suffer reductions or enjoy advances in wages at a time when no similar reductions or advances applied to their fellow workers in the same establishment. Such a condition is not unknown in large establishments employing numerous classes of workers ; it obtains to some extent in railway shops at the present time ; and is in some degree inevitable. But its general inconvenience is so manifest that serious reflection is required before a change is made which would intensify difficulties of this kind rather than diminish them.

13. The proposals of the National Union of Railwaymen aim at achieving a high degree of uniformity. It was proposed by the Union that the various workshops, depots and out-stations on each railway should be divided into not more than three groups, the basis

of division being (*a*) the situation of the establishment, and (*b*) the character of the work performed.   London and district (10 miles from Charing Cross) was to form one group.   Such places as Birmingham, Derby, Eastleigh, Manchester, Swindon, Newcastle and York were to be included in the second, while the third group was to comprise the remainder.   The actual allocation of the various workshops, depots and out-stations was to be left as a matter to be agreed between the railway companies and the other parties concerned.   It was proposed that the rates of wages (plus war wage and bonus) as paid in the London district in January, 1922, should be taken as the basis for the London district or Group I.   The rates in Group II were to be not more than 2s., and Group III not more than 4s. below those of men in Group I.   The employees themselves, with the exception of a few to be dealt with specially, were to be grouped into eight grades, the rate of the lowest class being 14s. below that of the highest.   The rates as thus arranged were to be subject to variation with movements in the cost of living, provided, however, that they did not fall below certain specified figures, for example, 69s. a week in the highest grade and 55s. in the lowest. The principles of a sliding scale and of a ' stop ' rate are similar to those obtaining in the case of those classes of railway employees, known as the Conciliation Grades, who are concerned with the working of traffic.

The general features and conception of the scheme are attractive from the point of view of securing uniformity and order in a vast and complex system.   The Court, however, are concerned with the question of its immediate practicability ; and it appears to them that, whatever future developments may bring, it would be impolitic to attempt in one stage to achieve so large a measure of unification as is involved in the scheme.

14. The companies' proposals were also put before the Court in great detail.   The companies rejected the proposal to institute a sliding scale, but in other respects adopted in part the proposals made by the various Unions.   They were, however, more elaborate and took greater cognisance of the existing position.   The number of groups into which it is proposed that the railway shops should be classified was seven, and the number of grades of workpeople sixteen. Because of a lack of uniformity in the relationship between craftsmen's and labourers' rates, the grouping of shops for the purpose of craftsmen's rates did not correspond with the grouping for the purpose of the rates of labourers and the classes regarded by the com-

panies as semi-skilled. The companies submitted a list of some 200 different occupations with the grading proposed for each under the general scheme. It was averred that the actual number of craft and grade names of groups of workpeople at present is some 1,400 or 1,500 ; but the companies stated that they would be able, by reclassification, to include this larger number within the 200 classes proposed. As in the case of the National Union of Railwaymen's proposals, a few occupations fell outside the general scheme, and were to be dealt with specially.

15. The issues involved in the case are as difficult as they are important. Between the proposals of the companies and those of the National Union of Railwaymen the difference is largely one of degree. Both aim at a measure of standardisation. Between these two sets of proposals and those of the National Federation of Engineering and Shipbuilding Trades, however, the difference is more fundamental, and involves the question whether, so far as their manufacturing and maintenance work is concerned, the railways are to be regarded as being engaged in a large number of different industries, and whether they should observe the rates pertaining to each. The Court have given this question the thought and consideration its importance merits. So vast an organisation as the railways of England and Wales must, as regards the employment it affords, present special and peculiar features. On the traffic side this fact is obvious and well recognised ; and the great majority of all the employees of railway companies are in receipt of wages on the basis of their being railway workers, without direct reference to the rates of pay obtaining in other industries. It appears to the Court that the principle, thus recognised, of regarding railway service as an industry in itself is a sound one, and that the principle should be applied to the manufacturing side of the companies' activities. The manufacturing and maintenance work undertaken by railway companies is of such great extent and so closely connected with the main business of transport that it cannot properly be regarded as something subordinate to it. It is bound up with the whole question of the prosperity and success of railway enterprise, and cannot in practice be divorced from the other functions of the companies. In the running sheds, and on the permanent way, much work is done which illustrates how, at certain points, the line of division between the ' conciliation ' and the ' shop ' grades is, and must of necessity be, almost arbitrary in character. It has also to be noted that the manufacturing work of the companies is non-competitive in the

sense that the products are not made for sale but are used for the companies' own purposes.

16. The Court have, therefore, reached the conclusion that railway service should be regarded by them as being a distinct industry to which special conditions attach, and that the Court's Decision should not impose on the companies and the employees an obligation to adopt or follow the rates of wages agreed upon or recognised by employers and workers in other industries employing similar classes of labour. In other words the Court have decided to proceed upon the basis of determining railway rates for the various classes of workpeople before them, and not to award district rates as such.

17. While, in the Court's view, the proper course is to regard the railway service as an industry in itself, it is manifest that where it draws upon supplies of labour of a kind required in other industries, the rates of wages paid by the railway companies cannot, without inconvenient consequences, differ too widely from the rates obtainable by the men elsewhere. But to say that the rates within and without the railway service should be generally similar, is not to require that they should be absolutely identical, or that they should always move in unison. In determining the rates to be paid to railway shopmen, the Court have kept in view, among other factors, the district rates of the various classes of workmen, where such district rates exist. But, for the reasons already set out, they have not regarded such district rates as binding upon them and as predetermining their decision.

.   .   .   .

General Uniformity of Wages.

21. The result of the evidence shows a necessity of introducing into the railway system, so far as the shop staff is concerned, a principle or method of dealing with wages which will bring to an end the practice of fixing wages on the basis of merely local or temporary conditions, without reference to the rates of men of like skill and occupation employed in the railway service in other parts of the country. During the war the railways became virtually one organism. The period of Government control has ceased, but the experience has shown how closely inter-related are the interests of the various lines. The Railways Act of 1921, providing as it does for the grouping of lines in large amalgamations, points to the development of railways as a unified system. As regards the ' conciliation ' grades the employees' wages and conditions of service

have already been brought under a scheme operating upon and observed by all lines.

22. The advantages of general uniformity or standardisation in the case of the shopmen are readily comprehended. Progress in the direction of standardisation must, however, be regulated to some extent by time and experience. In connection with the case the Court were furnished with particulars of the present wages of all the men employed in the grades now concerned by the railway companies. The rates at present paid show a variation much wider than can be explained on economic grounds ; and it has become clear that, for practical reasons, a limit must be set upon what, at this stage, should be done in the matter of getting rid of those differences and disparities which appear unwarrantable. The Court have endeavoured, therefore, so to frame their decision that a substantial advance shall be made towards standardisation without, however, necessitating changes in rates of wages greater than should be loyally accepted by the side on whom, in any particular case, the burden may fall.

.   .   .   .

Future Changes in Rates of Wages.

30. All parties are concerned in the manner in which future alterations in rates of wages shall be made. To decide in favour of district rates would be to imply that, as those rates changed from time to time, the rates of the railway employees would also change. The National Union of Railwaymen, as already stated, desired that the rates determined by the Court should be subject to a sliding scale based on the cost of living as are the rates applied to the ' conciliation ' grades. The companies' view was that the rates fixed on the principles desired by them should vary automatically with national variations in the outside engineering trade.

31. The reasons that have impelled the Court to arrive at a conclusion adverse to the granting of district rates must be again invoked. So long as the railway service is regarded as a separate industry, subject to its own conditions of prosperity and depression, it appears to be undesirable that alterations in rates of wages brought about in other industries, by the conditions of those industries, should automatically result in exactly similar changes on the railways.

At the same time, the effect of demand and supply in the case of particular kinds of labour cannot be ignored, and general movements of wages in outside trades, or in those akin to railways in their manufacturing aspect, must probably be reflected in some degree in the rates of the railway shopmen. The mechanical regulation of wages by reference to a cost of living sliding scale does not, therefore, appear to the Court to be very appropriate to the circumstances.

32. The Court have accordingly arrived at the conclusion and express it as their Decision that general changes in the rates of wages now determined, including the war wage or bonus of 26s. 6d. a week, shall be the subject of previous negotiation between the parties as occasion arises, when all the relevant factors can be taken into account.

33. In this connection, the Court entertain the hope that the parties will find it possible to set up some machinery for negotiation by which industrial questions affecting the companies and the employees either of a national or a local character may be considered without undue delay. Some railway centres appear already to have joint committees, representative of the various Trade Unions and classes of men affected, by which the consideration of matters by the companies and the men is much facilitated. The extension of this system to centres where it does not already obtain appears to the Court much to be desired.

. . . .

G. T. Reid,
Secretary,
5, Old Palace Yard, S.W.1.
8th July, 1922.

William W. Mackenzie,
President.
J. McKie Bryce.
F. S. Button.

116. Trade Boards.

Trades to which the Acts apply.

Trade Boards Act, 1918 ; 8 & 9 Geo. V., ch. 32.

1.—(1) The Trade Boards Act, 1909, (in this Act referred to as 'the principal Act') shall apply to the trades specified in the Schedule to that Act and to any other trades to which it has been applied by a provisional order made under section one of that Act by the Minister of Labour (in this Act referred to as 'a special order').

(2) The Minister of Labour (in this Act referred to as 'the Minister') may make a special order applying the principal Act to any specified trade to which it does not at the time apply if he is of the opinion that no adequate machinery exists for the effective

regulation of wages throughout the trade, and that accordingly, having regard to the rates of wages prevailing in the trade, or any part of the trade, it is expedient that the principal Act should apply to that trade.

. . . .

Constitution and Proceedings.

TRADE BOARDS ACT, 1909 ; 9 Edw. VII., ch. 22.

11.—(1) The Board of Trade may make regulations with respect to the constitution of Trade Boards which shall consist of members representing employers and members representing workers, (in this Act referred to as representative members), in equal proportions and of the appointed members. Any such regulations may be made so as to apply generally to the constitution of all Trade Boards, or specially to the constitution of any particular Trade Board or any particular class of Trade Boards.

(2) Women shall be eligible as members of Trade Boards as well as men.

(3) The representative members shall be elected or nominated or partly elected and partly nominated as may be provided by the regulations, and in framing the regulations the representation of home workers on Trade Boards shall be provided for in all trades in which a considerable proportion of home workers are engaged.

(4) The Chairman of a Trade Board shall be such one of the members as the Board of Trade may appoint, and the secretary of the Trade Board shall be appointed by the Board of Trade.

. . . .

(6) In order to constitute a meeting of a Trade Board, at least one-third of the whole number of the representative members and at least one appointed member must be present.

. . . . . .

12.—(1) A Trade Board may establish district trade committees consisting partly of members of the Trade Board and partly of persons not being members of the Trade Board but representing employers or workers engaged in the trade and constituted in accordance with regulations made for the purpose . . . and acting for such area as the Trade Board may determine.

(2) Provision shall be made by the regulations for at least one appointed member acting as a member of each district trade committee, and for the equal representation of local employers and local

workers on the committee, and for the representation of home-
workers thereon in the case of any trade in which a considerable
proportion of home-workers are engaged in the district, and also for
the appointment of a standing sub-committee to consider applications for special minimum piece-rates and complaints made to the
Trade Board under this Act, and for the reference of any applications or complaints to that sub-committee.

(3) A Trade Board may refer to a district trade committee for
their report and recommendations any matter which they think it
expedient so to refer.

. . . .

13.—(1) The Board of Trade [1] may appoint such number of
persons (including women) as they think fit to be appointed members
of Trade Boards.

(2) Such of the appointed members of Trade Boards shall act on
each Trade Board or district trade committee as may be directed by
the Board of Trade,[1] and, in the case of a Trade Board for a trade in
which women are largely employed, at least one of the appointed
members acting shall be a woman :

Provided that the number of appointed members acting on the
same Trade Board, or the same district trade committee, at the
same time, shall be less than half the total number of members
representing employers and members representing workers.

General Powers.

TRADE BOARDS ACT, 1918; 8 & 9 Geo. V., ch. 32.

10. A Trade Board for any trade may, if they think it expedient
so to do, make a recommendation to any Government Department
with reference to the industrial conditions of the trade, and the
Department to whom the recommendation is made shall forthwith
take it into consideration.

TRADE BOARDS ACT, 1909; 9 Edw. VII., ch. 22.

3. A Trade Board shall consider, as occasion requires, any matter
referred to them by a Secretary of State, the Board of Trade, or any
other Government department, with reference to the industrial
conditions of the trade, and shall make a report upon the matter to
the department by whom the question has been referred.

[1] The Ministry of Labour now perform this duty.

Power to fix Wages.

TRADE BOARDS ACT, 1918 ; 8 & 9 Geo. V., ch. 32.

3.—(1) . . . .

Every Trade Board shall, subject to the provisions of this section, fix a minimum rate of wages for time-work in their trade (in this Act referred to as ' a general minimum time-rate ') and may also fix for their trade—

(*a*) A general minimum rate of wages for piece-work (in this Act referred to as ' a general minimum piece-rate ') ;

(*b*) A minimum time-rate (which shall not be higher than the general minimum time-rate) to apply in the case of workers employed on piece-work for the purpose of securing to such workers a minimum rate of remuneration on a time-work basis (in this Act referred to as ' a guaranteed time-rate ') ;

(*c*) A minimum rate (whether a time-rate or a piece-rate) to apply, in substitution for the minimum rate which would otherwise be applicable, in respect of hours worked by a worker in any week or on any day in excess of the number of hours declared by the Trade Board to be the normal number of hours of work per week or for that day in the trade (in this Act referred to as ' an overtime rate ') ;

Any of the minimum rates aforesaid may be fixed so as to apply universally to the trade or so as to apply to any special process in the work of the trade, or to any special area, or to any class of workers in the trade, or to any class of workers in any special process or in any special area. . . . .

6.— . . . . A Trade Board may fix a piece-work basis time-rate in any case . . . . and a piece-work basis time-rate may be higher or lower than the general minimum time-rate.

. . . .

117. Trade Boards.

STATUTORY RULES AND ORDERS, 1919, No. 2216.

REGULATIONS, *dated November* 20*th*, 1919, *made by the Minister of Labour, under section* 11 *of the Trade Boards Act,* 1919 (9 *Edw.* 7, *c.* 22), *with respect to the Constitution and Proceedings of the Trade Board for the Hat, Cap and Millinery Trade* (*England and Wales*).

The Minister of Labour is pleased, in pursuance of his powers under Section 11 of the Trade Boards Act, 1919, and of every other power him hereunto enabling, to make the annexed Regulations :

1. A Trade Board shall be established in England and Wales for the Hat, Cap and Millinery Trade, as specified in the Trade Boards (Hat, Cap and Millinery) Order, 1919, that is to say, the making from any material of men's, women's or children's headgear, or the trimming thereof; including :

Warehousing, packing or other operations incidental to or appertaining to the making or trimming of men's, women's or children's headgear ;

but excluding :

1. The casting and making of solid metal helmets ;
2. The making of rubberised or oilskin headgear where carried on in association with or in conjunction with the making of other rubberised or oilskin articles ;
3. The making of nurses' or servants' caps, chefs' caps, hospital ward caps, or similar articles ;
4. The making of field bonnets, sun bonnets, boudoir caps, or infants' millinery where carried on in association with or in conjunction with the making of dresses, non-tailored skirts, wraps, blouses, blouse-robes, jumpers, sports coats, neckwear, tea-gowns, dressing gowns, dressing jackets, pyjamas, underclothing, underskirts, aprons, overalls, nurses' and servants' caps, juvenile clothing, baby linen or similar articles ;
5. The making of fur hats, where made in association with or in conjunction with the manufacture of furs or furriers' skins into garments, rugs or similar articles ;
6. The making of knitted headgear and the making of headgear from knitted fabrics where carried on in association with or in conjunction with the manufacture of the knitted fabrics ;
7. Warehousing, and packing of men's, women's or children's headgear and other similar operations carried on in shops mainly engaged in the retail distribution of articles of any description that are not made or trimmed on the premises.

2. The Board shall consist of not less than 59 and not more than 67 persons, of whom 3 shall be appointed members and the remainder representative members. The representative members shall be members representing employers and workers, respectively, in equal proportions.

3. The Chairman and Deputy Chairman shall be appointed by

the Minister of Labour from among the members of the Trade
Board, and each of them shall (provided that he continues to be a
member of the Trade Board) hold office for a period of two years,
but shall be eligible for re-appointment.

4. The appointed members shall be such of the appointed members of Trade Boards as may be directed by the Minister of Labour
to act on the Trade Board provided that not more than three shall
act on the Trade Board at any one time, and that at least one shall be
a woman.   The term of office of an appointed member shall be two
years.

5. The selection and appointment of representative members
shall be as follows, due regard being paid to the representation of
the various branches of the trade and of the various districts in which
the trade is carried on :

(a) Twenty-six members representing employers in the trade,
who are not habitually engaged in sub-contracting, shall be chosen
by the Minister of Labour after considering names supplied by
such employers.

Two members representing employers in the trade, who are
habitually engaged in sub-contracting, shall be chosen by the
Minister of Labour after considering names supplied by such
employers.

(b) Twenty-eight members representing workers in the trade
shall be chosen by the Minister of Labour after considering
names supplied by such workers.

6. The Minister of Labour may, if he thinks it necessary in order
to secure proper representation of any class or classes of employers or
workers, after giving the Trade Board an opportunity to be heard,
appoint additional representative members to serve upon the Trade
Board for a period not exceeding two years.   The number of such
additional representative members shall always be an even number,
not exceeding eight in all.   Half shall be representatives of employers and half shall be representatives of workers.

7. Any member representing employers who ceases to be an
employer and becomes a worker at the trade shall vacate his seat.
Any member representing workers who becomes an employer in the
trade shall vacate his seat.   The question of fact shall in each case be
determined by the Minister of Labour.

8. Any member who, in the opinion of the Minister of Labour,
fails without reasonable cause to attend one-half of the total number
of meetings in a calendar year shall vacate his seat.

9. If, in the opinion of the Minister of Labour, any member shall be incapable of acting as a member of the Trade Board, the Minister of Labour may determine his appointment, and he shall thereupon vacate his seat.

10. At the end of one year from the date of the establishment of the Trade Board the members representing employers and the members representing workers shall retire from the Board.

11. At the end of two years from the date of the establishment of the Trade Board fourteen representative members to be chosen by lot from among the members representing employers and fourteen representative members to be chosen by lot from among the members representing workers (in each case excluding additional representative members appointed under paragraph 6 of these Regulations) shall retire from the Trade Board.

12. Subject to the provisions of paragraphs 6, 7, 8, 9, 10 and 11, the term of office of a representative member shall be two years, provided that—

(*a*) a member appointed to fill a casual vacancy shall sit for the unexpired portion of the term of office of his predecessor; and

(*b*) a seat rendered vacant by effluxion of time shall be temporarily occupied by the retiring member until a successor is appointed.

13. Any person vacating his seat on the Trade Board under any of the preceding paragraphs or for any other reason shall be eligible for re-appointment as a member of the Trade Board.

14. A vacancy among members shall be filled in the same manner as in the case of the original appointment to the vacated seat.

15. Every member of the Trade Board shall have one vote. If at any meeting of the Board the numbers of members present representing employers and workers, respectively, are unequal, it shall be open to the side which is in the majority to arrange that one or more of its members shall refrain from voting, so as to preserve equality. Failing such an arrangement, the Chairman, or in his absence the Deputy Chairman, may, if he thinks it desirable, adjourn the voting on any question to another meeting of the Board.

16. The Trade Board shall continue in existence until dissolved by order of the Minister of Labour.

17. The Trade Board may be known under the short title of ' The Hat, Cap and Millinery Trade Board (England and Wales).'

18. Any question upon the construction or interpretation of these Regulations shall, in the event of dispute, be referred to the Minister of Labour for decision.

Dated this 20th day of November, 1919.

R. S. Horne,
Minister of Labour.

118. Trade Board Order, 1928.

HAT, CAP, AND MILLINERY TRADE BOARD—ENGLAND AND WALES.

Whereas the Minister of Labour has received notification from the Trade Board established under the Trade Boards Acts, 1909 and 1918, for the *Hat, Cap and Millinery* trade in *England and Wales*, that the said Board has, in pursuance of the powers vested in it by the said Acts, varied General Minimum Time Rates, Piece-Work Basis Time Rates and Overtime Rates for certain classes of Male Workers and General Minimum Time Rates and Overtime Rates for certain classes of Female Workers in the said trade, and the rates as varied are set out in italics in the Schedule to this Order ;

And whereas the Minister of Labour, having taken the matter into consideration, is of opinion that the variations of rates so made as aforesaid should be confirmed ;

Now, therefore, the Minister of Labour in pursuance of the powers vested in him by Section 4 of the Trade Boards Act, 1918, and of every other power him hereunto enabling, hereby confirms the said variations of rates so made, and he specifies the *Twenty-third* day of *January*, 1928, as the date from which the same shall become effective.

Given under the Official Seal of the Minister of Labour this Sixteenth day of January in the year One thousand nine hundred and twenty-eight.

H. J. Wilson,
Secretary of the Ministry of Labour.

_____

The Minimum Rates as varied and confirmed by this Order become effective as from the 23rd January, 1928, and are printed in italics in the Schedule below. Minimum Rates which remain in force without alteration are printed in ordinary type.

Schedule.

—

PART I.

GENERAL MINIMUM TIME-RATES FOR MALE AND FEMALE WORKERS.

MALE WORKERS.

MALE WORKERS of 22 years of age or over.

PARAGRAPH (1).

Male workers employed in any section of the Trade other than the Felt Hat Section, as :—

		Per hour	
		s.	*d.*
(i)	*Cutters as defined in Paragraph (16) of this Schedule*	1	5
(ii)	*Blockers, Body Makers, or Finishers as defined in Paragraph (17) of this Schedule* - - -	1	5
(iii)	*Stiffeners as defined in Paragraph (18) of this Schedule* - - - - - - -	1	5
(iv)	*Shapers as defined in Paragraph (19) of this Schedule* - - - - - -	1	5

PARAGRAPH (2).

Male workers employed in the Felt Hat (Wool) section of the Trade on any of the following operations, namely :—

Proofing (Head man only) ; Dyeing (Head man only) ; Blocking (Coning not to be included if the operation is preparatory to Blocking) ; Pressing ; Finishing ; Curling ; Flanging ; Cutting ; Ironing and Paring ; Velouring ;
and who have had not less than three years' experience after the age of 19 on one or more of such operations - - - **1 5**

PARAGRAPH (3).

Male workers employed in the Felt Hat (Fur) section of the Trade on any of the following operations, namely :—

Forming ; Hardening ; Planking ; Proofing (Head man only) ; Dyeing (Head man only) ; Blocking ; Pressing ; Finishing ; Brushing ; Curling and Steaming ; Flanging ; Cutting ; Ironing and Paring ; Trimming ; Velouring ;
and who have not less than three years' experience after the age of 19 on one or more of such operations - - - **1 5**

PARAGRAPH (4).   Per hour

   All male workers other than those for whom minimum   s. d.
rates provided in Paragraphs (1), (2) and (3) above   - 1 1

MALE WORKERS under 22 years of age.

PARAGRAPH (5).   d.

Male Workers of 21 and under 22 years of age	-	11
,,	,,	20	,,	21	,,	-	-	9
,,	,,	19	,,	20	,,	-	-	8
,,	,,	8	,,	19	,,	-	-	6½
,,	,,	17	,,	18	,,	-	-	5½
,,	,,	16	,,	17	,,	-	-	4½
,,	,,	15	,,	16	,,	-	-	3½
,,	,, under 15 years of age	-	-	-	2½

PARAGRAPH (6).

   Workers commencing employment in the Hat, Cap, and Millinery Trade for the first time at or over the age of 19 may serve their first period of six months of employment at 7d. per hour, and their second period of six months at 8d. per hour. On the expiration of one year's employment in the Trade these workers shall receive the rate applicable to their age.

FEMALE WORKERS.

PARAGRAPH (7).   Per hour.

FEMALE WORKERS other than Learners :   d.
   (a) Workers other than Home-workers   -   -   7
   (b) Home-workers (as defined in Paragraph (20) of this
        Schedule) -   -   -   -   -   7

PARAGRAPH (8).

FEMALE LEARNERS :

   (as defined in Paragraph (21) of this Schedule and provided the conditions specified therein are complied with) :

	Per hour.		Per week of 48 hours.	
	d.		s.	d.
During 1st year of employment	- 1½	i.e.	6	0
,, 2nd ,, ,,	- 3	,,	12	0
,, 3rd ,, ,,	- 4½	,,	18	0
,, 4th ,, ,,	- 6	,,	25	0

PARAGRAPH (9).

The General Minimum Time Rates for Learners set out in Paragraph (8) are subject to the following conditions :—

(*a*) The advances shall become due on the completion of each 12 months' employment in the trade.

(*b*) A learner shall cease to be a learner and be entitled to the full General Minimum Time-Rate applicable to female workers other than learners upon completion of 4 years' employment in the trade.

(*c*) If the conditions set out in Paragraph (21) of this Schedule are not complied with, the General Minimum Time-Rate applicable is that for female workers other than learners set out in Paragraph (7).

(*d*) *A female worker who enters or has entered the trade for the first time at 18 years of age or over, shall be deemed, for the purposes of the application of the Minimum Rates of Wages fixed by the Trade Board, and the calculation of the period of learnership, to have completed one year's employment as a learner.*

PART II.
PIECE-WORK BASIS TIME-RATES

PARAGRAPH (10).

MALE WORKERS :

	Per hour.	
	s.	d.
(*a*) *Male Workers of the classes specified in Paragraphs (1), (2) and (3) of this Schedule* - - -	1	6½
(*b*) All other Male Workers - - - - -	1	2½

PARAGRAPH (11).

FEMALE WORKERS :

(*a*) All Female Workers other than Home-workers -	8
(*b*) Home-workers (as defined in Paragraph (20) of this Schedule) - - - - - -	8

Note.—In the case of all Workers employed on Piece-work, each Piece-Rate paid shall be such as would yield, in the circumstances of the case, to an ORDINARY WORKER of the class in question, not less than the Piece-Work Basis Time-Rate appropriate to the class.

PART III.

OVERTIME RATES FOR MALE AND FEMALE WORKERS OF ALL AGES.

PARAGRAPH (12).

In accordance with Section 3 (1) (c) of the Trade Boards Act, 1918, the Trade Board have declared the NORMAL NUMBER OF HOURS OF WORK in the Trade to be as follows :

> In any week (exclusive of Sunday and Customary Public and Statutory Holidays) -   -   -   - 48
> On any day other than Saturday -   -   -   - 9
>> Provided that all time worked by a worker on Sundays and Customary Public and Statutory Holidays and time worked on Saturday (subject to the provisions set out below) shall be regarded as Overtime.

The Minimum Rates for Overtime in respect of time worked by a worker of the classes specified in Parts I and II of this Schedule in excess of the declared normal number of hours so far as it is lawful under the Factory and Workshop Acts, and any other legislation governing employment, for the worker to work during such time, shall be as follows :—

FOR WORKERS EMPLOYED ON TIME-WORK :

PARAGRAPH (13).

A.—ON ANY DAY other than Saturday, Sunday and Customary Public and Statutory Holidays :

(i) During the FIRST TWO HOURS OF OVERTIME, One-and-a-Quarter Times the General Minimum Time-Rate otherwise applicable, i.e., TIME-AND-A-QUARTER.

(ii) For OVERTIME, AFTER THE FIRST TWO HOURS OF OVERTIME, One-and-a-Half Times the General Minimum Time-Rate otherwise applicable, i.e., TIME-AND-A-HALF.

Provided that where it is the established practice of an employer only to require attendance on five days a week, the Overtime Rates specified in sub-paragraphs A (i) and A (ii) of this Paragraph shall not be payable on any day (other than Saturday, Sunday and Customary Public and Statutory Holidays) until the time worked exceeds $9\frac{1}{2}$ hours and $11\frac{1}{2}$ hours respectively.

B.—On Saturday in respect of :

(i) That class of worker who customarily attends on six days a week :

For all Overtime worked after the first five hours One-and-a-Half Times the General Minimum Time-Rate otherwise applicable, *i.e.*, TIME-AND-A-HALF.

Note.—During the first five hours worked on Saturday the Minimum Rate applicable for this class of worker is the appropriate General Minimum Time-Rate set out in Part I of this Schedule.

(ii) That class of worker who customarily attends on five days a week :

(*a*) During the first two hours of Overtime, that is to say, during the first two hours worked on Saturday, One-and-a-Quarter Times the General Minimum Time-Rate otherwise applicable, *i.e.*, TIME-AND-A-QUARTER.

(*b*) For Overtime after the first two hours of Overtime One-and-a-Half Times the General Minimum Time-Rate otherwise applicable, *i.e.*, TIME-AND-A-HALF.

Provided that if Saturday is one of the days on which a worker of this class customarily attends for work, the day of the week on which he does not customarily attend (not being a Sunday) shall be substituted for Saturday for the purpose of the application of the Overtime Rates set out in Sub-paragraph B (ii) of this Paragraph.

C.—On Sunday and Customary Public and Statutory Holidays :

For all time worked, so far as it is lawful under the Factory and Workshops Acts, and any other legislation governing employment, for the worker to work during such time, Twice the General Minimum Time-Rate otherwise applicable, *i.e.*, DOUBLE TIME.

Note.—The Overtime Rates set out in Sub-Paragraphs A, B and C of this Paragraph are payable as provided above, in respect of all Overtime worked on any day, notwithstanding that the number of hours worked in the week does not exceed 48.

D.—For all time worked in any week in excess of 48 hours, One-and-a-Quarter Times the General Minimum Time-Rate otherwise applicable, *i.e.*, TIME AND-A-QUARTER, except in so far as higher Overtime Rates are payable under the provisions of Sub-paragraphs A (ii), B (i), B (ii) (*b*), and C of this Paragraph.

Provided that where it is the established practice of an employer to require attendance only on alternate Saturdays, the Overtime Rate shall not be payable in the week in which attendance on Saturday is required until 50 hours have been worked.

FOR WORKERS EMPLOYED ON PIECE-WORK:

PARAGRAPH (14).

All Workers employed on Piece-Work shall receive in respect of all Overtime worked, IN ADDITION TO PIECE-RATES, each of which would yield, in the circumstances of the case, to an Ordinary Worker not less than the Piece-Work Basis Time-Rate applicable:

(*a*) AN AMOUNT EQUAL TO ONE-QUARTER OF THE APPROPRIATE PIECE-WORK BASIS TIME-RATE.

(*b*) AN AMOUNT EQUAL TO ONE-HALF OF THE APPROPRIATE PIECE-WORK BASIS TIME-RATE, or

(*c*) AN AMOUNT EQUAL TO THE FULL APPROPRIATE PIECE-WORK BASIS TIME-RATE,

according as the Overtime Rate which would have been payable under the provisions of Paragraph (13), if the worker had been employed on Time-Work, were:

(*a*) TIME-AND-A-QUARTER.

(*b*) TIME-AND-A-HALF, or

(*c*) DOUBLE-TIME, respectively.

PARAGRAPH (15).

In the application of the Overtime Rates set out in this Part of this Schedule the following provisions apply:

(*a*) In the case of workers who customarily attend on six days a week, any other day, not being Sunday, may be substituted for Saturday as the weekly short day, and in such case the provisions of Paragraphs (12), (13) and (14) above shall apply in like manner as if in such provisions ' Saturday ' were substituted for such short day, and such short day were substituted for ' Saturday.'

(*b*) Where it is, or may become, the established practice of an employer to require attendance on Sunday instead of Saturday, the Minimum Rates for Overtime shall apply to workers in like manner as if in the provisions of this Schedule as to Overtime the word ' Saturday ' were substituted for ' Sunday ' and the word ' Sunday ' for ' Saturday.'

PART IV.

DEFINITIONS.

For the purpose of the application of the minimum rates of wages set out in this Schedule the following definitions apply :

PARAGRAPH (16).

A CUTTER is a male person who is employed in a section of the Trade, other than the Silk Hat Section, in marking in and/or cutting any kind of material, and has been mainly employed in marking in and/or cutting for not less than 3 years after the age of 19.

Provided that this definition shall not include the cutting of cloth or other textile materials for the Stitchers of Hat Leathers.

PARAGRAPH (17).

A BLOCKER, BODY MAKER, or FINISHER is a male person who is employed in :

(i) covering, pulling-on and/or blocking hats or caps ; or
(ii) blocking straws, hoods or shapes, of any materials ; or
(iii) making shapes by means of a gas block ;
and has been mainly employed in such pulling-on and/or blocking or making for not less than 3 years after the age of 19.

PARAGRAPH (18).

A STIFFENER is a male person who is employed in stiffening and has been mainly employed in stiffening for not less than 3 years after the age of 19.

PARAGRAPH (19).

A SHAPER is a male person who is employed in putting into shape by hand work the brim part of any hat or helmet which is made on a body or foundation of any material, and has been so employed for not less than 3 years after the age of 19.

PARAGRAPH (20).

A HOMEWORKER is a worker who works in her own home or in any place not under the control or management of the employer.

PARAGRAPH (21).

A FEMALE LEARNER is a worker who :

(*a*) is employed during the whole or a substantial part of her time in learning any branch or process of the trade specified in

Paragraph (22) of this Schedule by an employer who provides the learner with reasonable facilities for such learning, and

(*b*) has received a certificate in accordance with rules from time to time laid down by the Trade Board, and held subject to compliance with conditions specified in this Section, or has made application for such certificate which has been duly acknowledged and is still under consideration. Provided that the certification of a learner may be cancelled if the other conditions of learnership are not complied with.

Provided that an employer may employ a female learner on her first employment without a certificate for a probation period not exceeding four weeks, but in the event of such learner being continued thereafter at her employment the probation period shall be included in her period of learnership.

PART V.

GENERAL.

APPLICABILITY OF MINIMUM RATES.

Paragraph (22).

The above Minimum Rates of Wages apply to all workers in England and Wales in respect of all time during which they are employed in any branch of the trade specified in the Trade Boards (Hat, Cap and Millinery) Order, 1919, that is to say :

The making from any material of men's, women's or children's headgear, or the trimming thereof ;

Including :

Warehousing, packing or other operations incidental to or appertaining to the making or trimming of men's, women's or children's headgear ;

But excluding :

(1) The casting and making of solid metal helmets ;

(2) The making of rubberised or oilskin headgear where carried on in association with or in conjunction with the making of other rubberised or oilskin articles ;

(3) The making of nurses' or servants' caps, chefs' caps, hospital ward caps, or similar articles ;

(4) The making of field bonnets, sun-bonnets, boudoir caps, or infants' millinery where carried on in association with or in conjunction with the making of dresses, non-tailored skirts, wraps,

blouses, blouse-robes, jumpers, sports coats, neckwear, tea-gowns, dressing gowns, dressing jackets, pyjamas, underclothing, under-skirts, aprons, overalls, nurses' and servants' caps, juvenile clothing, baby linen or similar articles ;

(5) The making of fur hats, where made in association with or in conjunction with the manufacture of furs or furriers' skins into garments, rugs, or similar articles ;

(6) The making of knitted headgear and the making of head-gear from knitted fabrics where carried on in association with or in conjunction with the manufacture of the knitted fabrics ;

(7) Warehousing and packing of men's, women's and children's headgear and other similar operations carried on in shops mainly engaged in the retail distribution of articles of any description that are not made or trimmed on the premises.

DEDUCTIONS.

PARAGRAPH (23).

The Minimum Rates of Wages set out in this Schedule must be paid clear of all deductions other than deductions under the National Insurance Act, 1911, as amended by any subsequent enactments or deductions authorised by any Act to be made from wages in respect of contributions to any superannuation or other provident fund.

PAYMENT OF HIGHER RATES.

PARAGRAPH (24).

The above rates are minimum rates and do not prevent the pay-ment of higher rates of wages.

NOTE.—*The employment of women, young persons and children is subject to the provisions of the Factory and Workshop Acts ; the Employment of Women, Young Persons and Children Act, 1920 ; the Education Acts, and the Shop Acts.*

119. Agricultural Wages Board and Committees.

AGRICULTURAL WAGES (REGULATION) ACT, 1924 ; 14 & 15 Geo. V., ch. 37.

1.—(1) Subject to the provisions of this Act, the Minister of Agriculture and Fisheries (in this Act referred to as the Minister) shall, as soon as may be, establish an agricultural wages committee for each county in England and Wales, and an Agricultural Wages Board for England and Wales.

(2) An agricultural wages committee and the Agricultural Wages Board shall respectively be constituted in accordance with the provisions of the First Schedule to this Act and shall be established by order made by the Minister.

(3) The Minister may, if he thinks it expedient, establish one agricultural wages committee for two or more counties instead of a separate committee for each county should resolutions in favour of such combination be passed by the representative members of the committees for the several counties, and thereupon that committee shall be the agricultural wages committee for the combined counties.

.   .   .   .

2.—(1) Subject to the provisions of this Act, agricultural wages committees shall fix minimum rates of wages for workers employed in agriculture for time work, and may also, if and so far as they think it necessary or expedient, fix minimum rates of wages for workers employed in agriculture for piece work.

(2) Any such minimum rates may be fixed by a committee so as to apply universally to all workers employed in agriculture in the county for which the committee act, or to any special class of workers so employed, or to any special area in the county, or to any special class in a special area, subject in each case to any exceptions which may be made by the committee for employment of any special character, and so as to vary according as the employment is for a day, week, month, or other period, or according to the number of working hours, or the conditions of the employment, or so as to provide for a differential rate in the case of overtime.

In the exercise of their powers under this subsection a committee shall, so far as is reasonably practicable, secure a weekly half-holiday for workers.

(3) If, on an application in that behalf, a committee are satisfied that any worker employed or desiring to be employed on time work to which a minimum rate fixed under this Act is applicable is so affected by any physical injury or mental deficiency, or any infirmity due to age or to any other cause, that he is incapable of earning that minimum rate, the committee shall grant to the worker a permit exempting, as from the date of the application, or from any later date specified in the permit, the employment of the worker from the provisions of this Act requiring wages to be paid at not less than the minimum rate, subject to such conditions as may be specified in the permit, including if the committee think fit, a condition as to the wages to be paid to the worker ; and, while the permit has

effect, an employer shall not be liable to any legal proceedings under this Act for paying wages to the worker at a rate less than the minimum rate if the conditions specified in the permit are complied with. If an application for a permit is not disposed of within twenty-one days after the day on which it is received, then the employer of the worker to whom the application relates shall not be liable to any legal proceedings under this Act for paying wages to the worker at a rate less than the minimum rate during the interval between the expiration of the said period and the date on which the application is ultimately disposed of.

. . . .

(5) A committee may, if they think it expedient, cancel or vary any minimum rate fixed under this Act.

(6) Before fixing, cancelling or varying any minimum rate, the committee shall give such notice as may be prescribed of the rate which they propose to fix or of their proposal to cancel the rate or of the proposed variation of the rate as the case may be, and of the manner in which and the time within which objections to the proposal may be lodged, not being less than fourteen days from the date of the notice, and shall consider any objections to the proposal which may be lodged within the time mentioned in the notice.

Where the proposal is modified in consequence of any objection so lodged, notice of the modified proposal need not be given except where in the opinion of the Agricultural Wages Board the proposal has been altered so materially that a fresh notice ought to be given.

3.—(1) Where a committee have fixed any minimum rate of wages or have cancelled or varied any such rate, they shall forthwith send in the prescribed manner to the Agricultural Wages Board notification of their decision.

(2) The Agricultural Wages Board, on receipt of such notification, shall as soon as practicable make such order as may be necessary for the purpose of carrying out the decision of the committee.

(3) The Board shall, as soon as may be after they have made an order under this section, send notification thereof to the committee concerned, and give notice of the making of the order and the contents thereof in the prescribed manner.

(4) Any such minimum rate or the cancellation or variation thereof shall become effective from the date specified in that behalf in the order.

The date to be specified shall be a date subsequent to the date of the order and where, as respects any employer who pays wages at intervals not exceeding seven days, the date so specified does not correspond with the beginning of the period for which wages are paid by that employer, the rate, or the cancellation or variation thereof, shall become effective as from the beginning of the next such period following the date specified in the order.

.   .   .   .

5. If an agricultural wages committee

(*a*) do not, within two months after the committee are established and a chairman is appointed, fix and notify to the Agricultural Wages Board a minimum rate of wages which they are required to fix under this Act ; or

(*b*) fail to fix and notify to the Agricultural Wages Board a minimum rate of wages in substitution for any such rate as aforesaid which, by cancellation or otherwise, has ceased to operate ; or

(*c*) by a resolution of the representative members of the committee request the Agricultural Wages Board to fix, cancel, or vary a minimum rate of wages ;

the Agricultural Wages Board may, after giving the prescribed notices, by order fix, cancel or vary the rate as the case requires, and for that purpose shall have and may exercise all the powers of the committee.

6. The Minister may direct an agricultural wages committee to reconsider any minimum rate which has been fixed by them, and thereupon the committee shall reconsider the same and notify to the Minister the result of their reconsideration.

7.—(1) Where any minimum rate of wages has been made effective by an order of the Agricultural Wages Board under this Act, any person who employs a worker in agriculture shall, in cases to which the minimum rate is applicable, pay wages to the worker at a rate not less than the minimum rate, and, if he fails to do so, shall be liable on summary conviction in respect of each offence to a fine not exceeding twenty pounds and to a fine not exceeding one pound for each day on which the offence is continued after conviction.

(2) In any proceedings against a person under this section it shall lie with that person to prove that he has paid wages at not less than the minimum rate.

.   .   .   .

(10) Any agreement for the payment of wages in contravention of this Act, or for abstaining to exercise any right of enforcing the payment of wages in accordance with this Act, shall be void.

. . . .

8.—(1) The Minister shall, in addition to any special power to make regulations given to him under this Act, have power to make regulations for the following purposes—

(*a*) for requiring the wages committees by order to define the benefits or advantages (not being benefits or advantages prohibited by law) which may be reckoned as payment of wages in lieu of payment in cash and the value at which they are to be reckoned, and for enabling the committees by order to limit or prohibit the reckoning of benefits or advantages as payment of wages in lieu of cash, and for enabling the committees on the application of any employer or worker, to determine any question which may arise as to the value of any such benefits or advantages, or generally as to any contract of employment so far as the application of this Act thereto is concerned ;

(*b*) for requiring the agricultural wages committees by order to define, for the purposes of any differential rate for overtime, the employment which is to be treated as overtime employment ;

. . . .

14. Nothing in this Act shall prejudice the operation of any agreement or custom for the payment of wages at a rate higher than the minimum rate fixed under this Act.

FIRST SCHEDULE.

CONSTITUTION AND PROCEEDINGS OF AGRICULTURAL WAGES COMMITTEES AND THE AGRICULTURAL WAGES BOARD.

AGRICULTURAL WAGES COMMITTEES.

1. An agricultural wages committee shall consist of members representing employers and members representing workers in agriculture in the county for which the committee act (in this Act referred to as representative members), in equal proportions, of two impartial members appointed by the Minister and of a chairman.

2. The representative members shall be either nominated or elected as may be provided by regulations made under this schedule, and shall be nominated or elected in the manner prescribed by such regulations.

AGRICULTURAL WAGES BOARD.

7. The Agricultural Wages Board shall consist of members representing employers and members representing workers in agriculture (in this Act referred to as representative members) in equal proportions together with such number of members (in this Act referred to as appointed members) as the Minister may think fit to appoint, but so that the number of appointed members shall not exceed one-quarter of the total number of members of the Board when fully constituted.

8. The representative members shall be either nominated or elected as may be provided by regulations made under this schedule, and shall be nominated or elected in the manner prescribed by such regulations.

9. The chairman of the Board shall be such one of the appointed members as the Minister may nominate. At every meeting of the Board the chairman if present shall preside, and, if he is absent, such appointed member as the members then present choose shall preside.

10. At least one member of the Board shall be a woman.

11. The Board may, in accordance with regulations under this Schedule, appoint one or more committees consisting of members representing employers and members representing workers in agriculture in equal proportions and of one or more appointed members, and may refer to any such committee for report and recommendations any matter which they think it expedient so to refer, and may also, if they think fit, delegate to any such committee any of their powers and duties under this Act, other than any power or duty to fix, cancel, or vary minimum rates of wages.

120. Australian Arbitration Award (Commonwealth Court).

FEDERATED MOULDERS (METALS) UNION OF AUSTRALIA AND THE ADELAIDE STEAMSHIP COMPANY LIMITED, AND OTHERS, 20 C.A.R. 890.

Variation of above award—Application to Broken Hill Proprietary Co., Ltd. (23 C.A.R. 7, 1926).

On the 30th December, 1925, the Broken Hill Proprietary Company Limited lodged an application to vary the award in the above matter by deleting clause 16 (e) of the award and inserting in lieu thereof a clause to the effect that the applicant company should only be bound by the award as to wages and the quarterly adjustment of wages and should as to all other conditions of employment be bound by the New South Wales State Arbitration Court award.

The application came on for hearing before Deputy President Sir John Quick in Melbourne on the 19th February, 1926 :

A. Burgess for the Broken Hill Pty. Coy. Ltd.

L. Morgan for the Federated Moulders (Metals) Union.

On the 19th February, 1926, Deputy President Sir John Quick delivered the following judgment :

Of course there is no doubt as to the granting of the proposed variation asked for in this summons, because it after all merely makes an alteration in dates and descriptions in order to bring it into line with the amendment of State laws.   But the most important part, it seems to me, not only provides for the re-enactment of the old State law, but it also provides for the recognition of the shop stewards in the following clause :

' The company will give recognition to any delegate appointed by and from among the employees for the particular shop or department where he is employed, and he shall be allowed the time to interview the company or its representatives in working hours in case of any dispute affecting employees in his shop or department.'

That is a recognition of an important principle which has been long advocated by registered organisations, and which has been frequently discussed in this court before me and, I think, other members of the court, and hitherto the employers have very strenuously and strongly objected to any clause of the kind.   Generally speaking, the court has recognised the force of the objection, feeling that it was founded upon the right of the employers to carry on their business without the intervention of any trade union officials.   I think this variation, embodying as it does, a direct and expressed recognition of shop stewards by such a great employer of labour as the Broken Hill Propty. Company, will mark a considerable change in the attitude of the employers of Australia—a change which is of a very desirable character.   As far as my own personal views are concerned I have never seen the grounds for the strong objections hitherto urged by employers.   I think the Broken Hill Propty. Coy. recognise, as no doubt other great employers will come to recognise, the value of the pacific authority of union officials in either anticipating a settlement or actually helping to settle industrial disputes arising in these large industrial establishments.   I think that trade officials of trusted and proved character and experience will help largely in preventing the development of industrial disputes. Their powers of intervention in waiting on the employers and making representations as to possible differences will help to prevent the growth, expansion, or aggravation of these difficulties. I think it ought to be one of the functions of a trade union to have the authority which is now being recognised by this great company. I hope that other employers will see the wisdom and importance of recognising the same principle.

If the great Broken Hill Propty. Coy. find that it is not inconsistent with their proprietary right as employers of labour in such a big enterprise, involving 4000 hands, I see no reason why employers on a smaller scale should not find the same thing.

The time has come when I think unions should be trusted more in the future than they have been in the past. I think their powers for securing and maintaining industrial peace are very great, and I believe that grants of power such as this will help to give them a greater status, and make them more valuable instrumentalities in the preservation of industrial peace. I hope, when such powers are granted, that they will be wisely used in the interests of the men themselves and the industry on which the men are dependent for their daily labour, as well as in the interests of the employers who have such great risks and responsibilities. I have the greatest amount of pleasure in granting this variation, coupled with this recognition of shop stewards.

121. Canadian Industrial Disputes Investigation Act.

6 & 7 Edw. VII., ch. 20 [1907], as amended by [1910] ch. 29 ; [1918] ch. 27 ; [1920] ch. 29 ; and [1925] ch. 14.

2A. This Act shall apply to the following disputes only :
(i) Any dispute in relation to employment upon or in connection with any work, undertaking or business which is within the legislative authority of the Parliament of Canada, including but not so as to restrict the generality of the foregoing :

(*a*) works, undertakings or business operated or carried on for or in connection with navigation and shipping, whether inland or maritime ;

(*b*) lines of steam or other ships, railways, canals, telegraphs and other works and undertakings connecting any province with any other or others of the provinces, or extending beyond the limits of the province ;

(*c*) lines of steamships between a province and any British or foreign country ;

(*d*) ferries between any province and any British or foreign country, or between two provinces ;

(*e*) works, undertakings or business belonging to, carried on or operated by aliens, including foreign corporations immigrating into Canada to carry on business ;

(*f*) such works as, although wholly situate within the province, have been or may be declared by the Parliament of Canada to be for the general advantage of Canada, or for the advantage of two or more of the provinces ;

(*g*) works, undertakings or business of any company or corporation incorporated by or under the authority of the Parliament of Canada.

(ii) Any dispute which is not within the exclusive legislative authority of any provincial legislature to regulate in the manner provided by this Act.

(iii) Any dispute which the Governor in Council may by reason of any real or apprehended national emergency declare to be subject to the provisions of this Act.

(iv) Any dispute which is within the exclusive legislative jurisdiction of any province and which by the legislation of the province is made subject to the provisions of this Act.

. . . .

56. It shall be unlawful for any employer to declare or cause a lockout, or for any employee to go on strike, on account of any dispute prior to or during a reference of such dispute to a Board of Conciliation and Investigation under the provisions of this Act, or prior to or during a reference under the provisions concerning railway disputes in the Conciliation and Labour Act : Provided that nothing in this Act shall prohibit the suspension or discontinuance of any industry or of the working of any persons therein for any cause not constituting a lockout or strike : Provided also that, except where the parties have entered into an agreement under section 62 of this Act, nothing in this Act shall be held to restrain any employer from declaring a lockout, or any employee from going on strike in respect of any dispute which has been duly referred to a Board and which has been dealt with under section 24 or 25 of this Act, or in

respect of any dispute which has been the subject of a reference under the provisions concerning railways disputes in the Conciliation and Labour Act.

57. Employers and employees shall give at least thirty days' notice of an intended or desired change affecting conditions of employment with respect to wages or hours ; and in the event of such intended or desired change resulting in a dispute, it shall be unlawful for the employer to make effective a proposed change in wages or hours or for the employees to go on strike, until the dispute has been finally dealt with by a Board, and a copy of its report has been delivered through the Registrar to both the parties affected ; the application for the appointment of a Board shall be made by the employers or employees proposing the change in wages or in hours ; neither of those parties shall alter the conditions of employment with respect to wages or hours, or on account of the dispute do or be concerned in doing directly or indirectly, anything in the nature of a lockout or strike, or a suspension or discontinuance of employment or work, but the relationship of employer and employee shall continue uninterrupted by the dispute, or anything arising out of the dispute ; but if, in the opinion of the Board, either party uses this or any other provision of this Act for the purpose of unjustly maintaining a given condition of affairs through delay, and the Board so reports to the Minister, such party shall be guilty of an offence, and liable to the same penalties as are imposed for a violation of the next preceding section.

58. Any employer declaring or causing a lockout or making effective a change in wages or hours contrary to the provisions of this Act shall be liable to a fine of not less than one hundred dollars, nor more than one thousand dollars for each day or part of a day that such lockout or change exists.

59. Any employee who goes on strike contrary to the provisions of this Act shall be liable to a fine of not less than ten dollars nor more than fifty dollars, for each day or part of a day that such employee is on strike.

60. Any person who incites, encourages or aids in any manner any employer to declare or continue a lockout, or any employee to go or continue on strike contrary to the provisions of this Act, shall be guilty of an offence and liable to a fine of not less than fifty dollars nor more than one thousand dollars.

122. The Right to Strike.

RESOLUTIONS PASSED BY THE TRADES UNION CONGRESS, 1924.

T.U.C. Ann. Report, 1924, pp. 487, 338.

' *That this Congress reaffirms its determined opposition to compulsory arbitration, and again declares that under no circumstances will it permit any interference with the right to strike.*'

.   .   .   .

' *That this Trades Union Congress hereby reaffirms the vital and constitutional right of Trade Unions to assist each other by direct industrial action or by moral support in any strike or lock-out which may arise.*'

123. Procedure in Trade Disputes.

RULES OF AMALGAMATED ASSOCIATION OF OPERATIVE COTTON SPINNERS AND TWINERS, 1921.

Disputes—Mode of Procedure.

24.—SECTION 1.—A general cessation of work on the part of our members in furtherance of a demand for an increase, or opposition to a reduction, in the rate of wages, or from any other cause, shall not be resorted to except with the consent of at least four-fifths of the members of the Amalgamation who take part in the vote as per this rule.   To ascertain this, the following method of procedure must be adopted.

SECTION 2.—The E.C. shall call a Representative Meeting, and should the representatives, by a majority of two-thirds or more, decide in favour of submitting the question in dispute to a ballot of the members, then a vote shall be taken as provided for in this rule ;. but should there not be two-thirds of the delegates present in favour of sending the question to the members, then the matter shall be dropped.

SECTION 3.—Each district must provide itself with a ballot box, but the voting papers shall be supplied from the General Office and the voting shall take place on a day and time fixed by the Representative Meeting.

SECTION 4.—The ballot shall be by envelope vote.   Each district shall make due provision by the proper distribution of the envelopes (each containing a voting paper duly stamped with the district seal) to each member in the several mills, and the shopman shall be responsible for the proper collection of the same at the mill.   When the members have voted and sealed their envelopes, such shopmen shall attend the same day at the appointed hour to put the envelopes into the district ballot box.

SECTION 5.—Each district or branch secretary shall be empowered to supply any member who is fully financial with an envelope and voting paper (who may on the day of the poll be absent through any cause whatever from the mill where he is employed), and such secretary shall duly collect and deposit the said envelopes the same day at the appointed hour in the ballot box.

SECTION 6.—At the conclusion of the poll the boxes shall be opened in the presence of the persons previously appointed by the Local Committee to count the votes, and after the counting is completed a full return of the votes recorded, and how they were recorded, shall be sent by post the same evening to the General Office. The voting papers must be kept for six months after the vote is taken, and each district shall have supplied to it a printed copy of the result, with a detailed vote of each district.

SECTION 7.—Should it be found that four-fifths of the members voting are in favour of a stoppage, their decision shall be acted upon ; but if less than four-fifths of the members voting record their votes for a stoppage, then the men shall remain at work.

SECTION 8.—In disputes at individual firms the same course of procedure shall be gone through, with the difference that only the men who will be stopped shall be required to vote, and the Local Committee shall act as managers of the business, and count the votes.

SECTION 9.—At any time whilst the dispute is in progress the Executive Council of the Amalgamation may, if they deem it desirable, order a fresh vote to be taken in either general or individual disputes, either for the purpose of ascertaining whether the views of the members have changed, or submitting to them any fresh points that may have arisen since the previous vote was taken.

.   .   .   .

Method of Procedure in Individual Disputes and Penalty for Leaving Work without Authority.

30.—Should a dispute arise between an individual firm and their workpeople which they cannot arrange to their mutual satisfaction, it shall be the duty of such operatives to bring the question in dispute before the Local Committee, who shall take such means in accordance with general law as may appear to them desirable to secure its amicable settlement ; but should they fail in their endeavours to accomplish it, they shall then refer the matter to the General Secretary of the Amalgamation, who shall take action in accordance with Section 9 of Rule 16.   Failing to effect a settlement, he will bring the question in dispute before the Executive Council, who shall take such action upon it as may appear to them desirable, and, if found necessary, call a Representative Meeting, whose decision shall be binding upon all its members ; but in no case whatsoever shall any member of the Amalgamation be allowed any support from its funds who shall leave work without authority from the Representatives in meeting assembled or the Executive Council.

124. Strikes and Lockouts—Definitions.

Trade Disputes and Trade Unions Act, 1927 ; 17 & 18 Geo. V., ch. 22.

8.—(2) For the purposes of this Act—

(a) the expression ' strike ' means the cessation of work by a body of persons employed in any trade or industry acting in combination, or a concerted refusal, or a refusal under a common understanding of any number of persons who are, or have been so employed, to continue to work or to accept employment ;

(b) the expression ' lock-out ' means the closing of a place of employment or the suspension of work, or the refusal by an employer to continue to employ any number of persons employed by him in consequence of a dispute, done with a view to compelling those persons, or to aid another employer in compelling persons employed by him, to accept terms or conditions of or affecting employment.

Trade Disputes Act, 1906 ; 6 Edw. VII., ch. 47.

5.—(3) In this Act and in the Conspiracy and Protection of Property Act, 1875, the expression ' trade dispute ' means any dispute between employers and workmen, or between workmen and workmen, which is connected with the employment or non-employment or the terms of the employment, or with the conditions of labour, of any person, and the expression ' workmen ' means all persons employed in trade or industry, whether or not in the employment of the employer with whom a trade dispute arises.

125. Breach of Contract a Criminal Offence in Certain Cases. Seamen.

MERCHANT SHIPPING ACT, 1894 ; 57 & 58 Vict. ch. 60.

221. If a seaman lawfully engaged, or an apprentice to the sea service, commits any of the following offences he shall be liable to be punished summarily as follows :

(*a*) If he deserts from his ship he shall be guilty of the offence of desertion and be liable to forfeit all or any part of the effects he leaves on board, and of the wages which he has then earned . . . and also, except in the United Kingdom, he shall be liable to imprisonment for any period not exceeding twelve weeks with or without hard labour.

(*b*) If he neglects, or refuses without reasonable cause, to join his ship, or to proceed to sea in his ship, or is absent without leave at any time within twenty-four hours of the ship's sailing from a port . . . or is absent without leave and without sufficient reason from his ship or from his duty, he shall, if the offence does not amount to desertion . . . be guilty of the offence of absence without leave, and be liable to forfeit out of his wages a sum not exceeding two days' pay . . . and also, except in the United Kingdom, he shall be liable to imprisonment for any period not exceeding ten weeks with or without hard labour.

.   .   .   .

225.—(1) If a seaman lawfully engaged or an apprentice to the sea service commits any of the following offences, in this Act referred to as offences against discipline, he shall be liable to be punished summarily as follows ; (that is to say),

(*a*) If he quits the ship without leave after her arrival at her port of delivery, and before she is placed in security, he shall be liable to forfeit out of his wages a sum not exceeding one month's pay :

(*b*) If he is guilty of wilful disobedience to any lawful command, he shall be liable to imprisonment for a period not exceeding four weeks, and also, at the discretion of the court, to forfeit out of his wages a sum not exceeding two days' pay :

(*c*) If he is guilty of continued wilful disobedience to lawful commands or continued wilful neglect of duty, he shall be liable to imprisonment for a period not exceeding twelve weeks, and also, at the discretion of the court, to forfeit for every twenty-four hours' continuance of disobedience or neglect, either a sum not exceeding six days' pay, or any expenses properly incurred in hiring a substitute.

. . . .

(*e*) If he combines with any of the crew to disobey lawful commands, or to neglect duty, or to impede the navigation of the ship or the progress of the voyage, he shall be liable to imprisonment for a period not exceeding twelve weeks.

. . . .

236.—(1) If a person by any means whatever persuades or attempts to persuade a seaman or apprentice to neglect or refuse to join or proceed to sea in or to desert from his ship, or otherwise to absent himself from his duty, he shall for each offence in respect of each seaman or apprentice be liable to a fine not exceeding ten pounds.

(2) If a person wilfully harbours or secretes a seaman or apprentice who has wilfully neglected or refused to join, or has deserted from his ship, knowing or having reason to believe the seaman or apprentice to have so done, he shall for every seaman or apprentice so harboured or secreted be liable to a fine not exceeding twenty pounds.

126. Breach of Contract a Criminal Offence in Certain Cases. Gas and Water; Injury to Life or Property.

Conspiracy and Protection of Property Act, 1875; 38 & 39 Vict. ch. 86.

4. Where a person employed by a municipal authority or by any company or contractor upon whom is imposed by Act of Parliament the duty, or who have otherwise assumed the duty of supplying any city, borough, town, or place, or any part thereof, with gas or water, wilfully and maliciously breaks a contract of service with that authority or company or contractor, knowing or having reasonable cause to believe that the probable consequences of his so doing, either alone or in combination with others, will be to deprive the inhabitants of that city, borough, town, place, or part, wholly or to a great extent of their supply of gas or water, he shall on conviction thereof by a court of summary jurisdiction or on indictment as hereinafter mentioned, be liable either to pay a penalty not exceeding twenty pounds or to be imprisoned for a term not exceeding three months, with or without hard labour.

Every such municipal authority, company, or contractor as is mentioned in this section shall cause to be posted up, at the gasworks or waterworks, as the case may be, belonging to such authority or company or contractor, a printed copy of this section in some conspicuous place where the same may be conveniently read by the persons employed, and as often as such copy becomes defaced, obliterated, or destroyed, shall cause it to be renewed with all reasonable despatch.

If any municipal authority or company or contractor make default in complying with the provisions of this section in relation to such notice as aforesaid, they or he shall incur on summary conviction a penalty not exceeding five pounds for every day during which such default continues, and every person who unlawfully injures, defaces, or covers up any notice so posted up as aforesaid in pursuance of this Act, shall be liable on summary conviction to a penalty not exceeding forty shillings.

5. Where any person wilfully and maliciously breaks a contract of service or of hiring, knowing or having reasonable cause to believe that the probable consequences of his so doing, either alone or in combination with others, will be to endanger human life, or cause serious bodily injury, or to expose valuable property whether real or personal to destruction or serious injury, he shall on conviction thereof by a court of summary jurisdiction, or on indictment as herein-after mentioned, be liable either to pay a penalty not exceeding twenty pounds, or to be imprisoned for a term not exceeding three months, with or without hard labour.

127. Breach of Contract a Criminal Offence in Certain Cases. Electricity.

ELECTRICITY (SUPPLY) ACT, 1919; 9 & 10 Geo. V., ch. 100.

31. Section four of the Conspiracy and Protection of Property Act, 1875, (which relates to breaches of contract by persons employed in the supply of gas or water), shall extend to persons employed by a joint electricity authority or by any authorised undertakers in like manner as it applies to persons mentioned in that section, with the substitution of references to electricity for the references to gas or water.

128. Breach of Contract a Criminal Offence in Certain Cases. Public Authorities.

TRADE DISPUTES AND TRADE UNIONS ACT, 1927; 17 & 18 Geo. V., ch. 22.

6.—(4) There shall be added to section five of the Conspiracy, and Protection of Property Act, 1875, the following provision, that is to say :

' If any person employed by a local or other public authority wilfully breaks a contract of service with that authority, knowing or having reasonable cause to believe that the probable consequence of his so doing, either alone or in combination with others, will be to cause injury or danger or grave inconvenience to the community, he shall be liable, on summary conviction, to a fine not exceeding ten pounds or to imprisonment for a term not exceeding three months.'

129. Illegal Strikes.

TRADE DISPUTES AND TRADE UNIONS ACT, 1927; 17 & 18 Geo. V., ch. 22.

1.—(1) It is hereby declared—

(*a*) that any strike is illegal if it—

(i) has any object other than or in addition to the furtherance of a trade dispute within the trade or industry in which the strikers are engaged ; and

(ii) is a strike designed or calculated to coerce the Government either directly or by inflicting hardship upon the community ; and

(*b*) that any lock-out is illegal if it—

(i) has any object other than or in addition to the furtherance of a trade dispute within the trade or industry in which the employers locking-out are engaged ; and

(ii) is a lock-out designed or calculated to coerce the Government either directly or by inflicting hardship upon the community :

and it is further declared that it is illegal to commence, or continue, or to apply any sums in furtherance or support of, any such illegal strike or lockout.

For the purposes of the foregoing provisions—

(*a*) a trade dispute shall not be deemed to be within a trade or industry unless it is a dispute between employers and workmen, or between workmen and workmen, in that trade or industry, which is connected with the employment or non-employment or the terms of the employment, or with the conditions of labour, of persons in that trade or industry ; and

(*b*) without prejudice to the generality of the expression ' trade or industry ' workmen shall be deemed to be within the same trade or industry if their wages or conditions of employment are determined in accordance with the conclusions of the same joint industrial council, conciliation board or other similar body, or in accordance with agreements made with the same employer or group of employers.

(2) If any person declares, instigates, incites others to take part in or otherwise acts in furtherance of a strike or lock-out, declared by this Act to be illegal, he shall be liable on summary conviction to a fine not exceeding ten pounds or to imprisonment for a term not exceeding three months, or on conviction on indictment to imprisonment for a term not exceeding two years :

Provided that no person shall be deemed to have committed an offence under this section or at common law by reason only of his having ceased work or refused to continue to work or to accept employment.

(3) Where any person is charged before any court with an offence under this section, no further proceedings in respect thereof shall be taken against him without the consent of the Attorney-General except such as the court may think necessary by remand (whether in custody or on bail) or otherwise to secure the safe custody of the person charged, but this subsection shall not apply to Scotland, or to any prosecution instituted by or on behalf of the Director of Public Prosecutions.

(4) The provisions of the Trade Disputes Act, 1906, shall not, nor shall the second proviso to subsection (1) of section two of the Emergency Powers Act, 1920, apply to any act done in contemplation or furtherance of a strike or lock-out which is by this Act declared to be illegal, and any such act shall not be deemed for the purposes of any enactment to be done in contemplation or furtherance of a trade dispute :

Provided that no person shall be deemed to have committed an offence under any regulations made under the Emergency Powers

Act, 1920, by reason only of his having ceased work or having refused to continue to work or to accept employment.

. . . . . .

8.—(2) (c) a strike or lockout shall not be deemed to be calculated to coerce the Government unless such coercion ought reasonably to be expected as a consequence thereof.

130. Sympathetic or Secondary Strikes.

REPORT OF THE ROYAL COMMISSION ON TRADE DISPUTES AND TRADE COMBINATIONS, 1906. Cd. 2825, p. 15.

We are of the opinion that the Act of 1875 should be made to extend to so-called secondary strikes, and we state this with greater confidence because the majority of those examined by us, whose evidence was of the greatest weight, agreed that there was no valid reason for drawing a distinction between secondary and other strikes.

131. Sympathetic Strike.

NOTICE OF PROPOSED SYMPATHETIC STOPPAGE OF COAL TRANSPORT, 1925.

T.U.C. Ann. Report, 1925, p. 179.

Lock-out of Coal Miners, Aug. 1, 1925.

OFFICIAL STOPPAGE OF THE MOVEMENT OF COAL.

Official Instructions to all Railway and Transport Workers as agreed unanimously by a Joint Conference of the National Union of Railwaymen, Associated Society of Locomotive Engineers and Firemen, Railway Clerks' Association, and the Transport and General Workers' Union Executives, and approved by the General Council of the Trades Union Congress.

Railways.

1. Wagons containing coal must not be attached to any train after midnight on Friday, July 31st, and after this time wagons of coal must not be supplied to any industrial or commercial concerns, or be put on the tip roads at docks for the coaling of ships.
2. All coal *en route* at midnight on Friday to be worked forward to the next siding suitable for storing it.
3. Any coal either in wagons or stock at a depot may be utilized

at that depot for the purpose of coaling engines for passenger and goods trains, but must not be moved from that depot to another.

Docks, Wharves, Etc.

COAL EXPORTS.

All Tippers and Trimmers will cease work at the end of the 2nd shift on July 31st.

COAL IMPORTS.

On no account may import coal be handled from July 31st.

GENERAL.

A general stoppage of men handling coal on other classes of tonnage on Friday midnight.

Waterways and Locks.

All men on canals, waterways, etc., engaged in carrying coal will cease Friday midnight, with the exception of men who have coal *en route*, who will be allowed to take it to destination and tie up. *Safety men for pumping, etc., will be permitted to work for safety purposes only.*

Road Transport.

All men engaged in delivering coal to commercial and industrial concerns will cease Friday night, July 31st. Men delivering for domestic purposes will cease at 12 noon, Saturday, August 1st.

Local Committees.

For the purpose of carrying out these instructions the members of the organizations herein concerned shall, from each district, establish small sub-committees so as to co-ordinate policy in giving effect to same.

132. Trade Disputes—Conspiracy and Intimidation ; Picketing.

CONSPIRACY AND PROTECTION OF PROPERTY ACT, 1875 ; 38 & 39 Vict., ch. 86.

3.—An agreement or combination by two or more persons to do or procure to be done any act in contemplation or furtherance of a trade dispute between employers and workmen shall not be indictable as a conspiracy if such act committed by one person would not be punishable as a crime.

T.U.D.   X

Nothing in this section shall exempt from punishment any persons guilty of a conspiracy for which a punishment is awarded by any Act of Parliament.

Nothing in this section shall affect the law relating to riot, unlawful assembly, breach of the peace, or sedition, or any offence against the State or the Sovereign.

A crime for the purposes of this section means an offence punishable on indictment, or an offence which is punishable on summary conviction, and for the commission of which the offender is liable under the statute making the offence punishable to be imprisoned either absolutely or at the discretion of the court as an alternative for some other punishment.

Where a person is convicted of any such agreement or combination as aforesaid to do or procure to be done an act which is punishable only on summary conviction, and is sentenced to imprisonment, the imprisonment shall not exceed three months, or such longer time, if any, as may have been prescribed by the statute for the punishment of the said act when committed by one person.

. . . .

7.—Every person who, with a view to compel any other person to abstain from doing or to do any act which such other person has a legal right to do or abstain from doing, wrongfully and without legal authority,—

    1. Uses violence to or intimidates such other person or his wife or children, or injures his property ; or,

    2. Persistently follows such other person about from place to place ; or,

    3. Hides any tools, clothes, or other property owned or used by such other person, or deprives him of or hinders him in the use thereof ; or,

    4. Watches or besets the house or other place where such other person resides, or works, or carries on business, or happens to be, or the approach to such house or place ; or,

    5. Follows such other person with two or more other persons in a disorderly manner in or through any street or road,

shall, on conviction thereof by a court of summary jurisdiction, or on indictment as herein-after mentioned, be liable either to pay a penalty not exceeding twenty pounds, or to be imprisoned for a term not exceeding three months, with or without hard labour.

133. Strikes and Trade Union Activities.

TRADE DISPUTES ACT, 1906 ; 6 Edw. VII., ch. 47.

1.—The following paragraph shall be added as a new paragraph after the first paragraph of section three of the Conspiracy and Protection of Property Act, 1875 :

' An act done in pursuance of an agreement or combination by two or more persons shall, if done in contemplation or furtherance of a trade dispute, not be actionable unless the act, if done without any such agreement or combination, would be actionable.'

2.—(1) It shall be lawful for one or more persons, acting on their own behalf or on behalf of a trade union or of an individual employer or firm in contemplation or furtherance of a trade dispute, to attend at or near a house or place where a person resides or works or carries on business or happens to be, if they so attend merely for the purpose of peacefully obtaining or communicating information, or of peacefully persuading any person to work or abstain from working.

(2) Section seven of the Conspiracy and Protection of Property Act, 1875, is hereby repealed from ' attending at or near ' to the end of the section.[1]

3.—An act done by a person in contemplation or furtherance of a trade dispute shall not be actionable on the ground only that it induces some other person to break a contract of employment or that it is an interference with the trade, business, or employment of some other person, or with the right of some other person to dispose of his capital or his labour as he wills.

134. Picketing—Restrictions on.

TRADE DISPUTES AND TRADE UNIONS ACT, 1927 ; 17 & 18 Geo. V., ch. 22.

3.—(1) It is hereby declared that it is unlawful for one or more persons (whether acting on their own behalf or on behalf of a trade union or of an individual employer or firm, and notwithstanding that they may be acting in contemplation or furtherance of a trade dispute) to attend at or near a house or place where a person resides or works or carries on business or happens to be, for the purpose of obtaining or communicating information or of persuading or inducing

---

[1] This part has accordingly been omitted from Sec. 7 in the preceding Document. (ED.)

any person to work or to abstain from working, if they so attend in such numbers or otherwise in such manner as to be calculated to intimidate any person in that house or place, or to obstruct the approach thereto or egress therefrom, or to lead to a breach of the peace ; and attending at or near any house or place in such numbers or in such manner as is by this subsection declared to be unlawful shall be deemed to be a watching or besetting of that house or place within the meaning of section seven of the Conspiracy, and Protection of Property Act, 1875.

(2) In this section the expression ' to intimidate ' means to cause in the mind of a person a reasonable apprehension of injury to him or to any member of his family or to any of his dependants or of violence or damage to any person or property, and the expression ' injury ' includes injury to a person in respect of his business, occupation, employment or other source of income, and includes any actionable wrong.

(3) In section seven of the Conspiracy, and Protection of Property Act, 1875, the expression ' intimidate ' shall be construed as having the same meaning as in this section.

(4) Notwithstanding anything in any Act, it shall not be lawful for one or more persons, for the purpose of inducing any person to work or to abstain from working, to watch or beset a house or place where a person resides or the approach to such a house or place, and any person who acts in contravention of this subsection shall be liable on summary conviction to a fine not exceeding twenty pounds or to imprisonment for a term not exceeding three months.

135. The Boycott.

THE DANBURY HATTERS CASE.

Lawlor v. Loewe ; U.S. Supreme Court, 1915.   235 U.S. 522.

MR. JUSTICE HOLMES delivered the opinion of the Court :

This is an action under the Act of July 2nd, 1890, chap. 647, sec. 7, 26, Stat. at L. 209, 210, Comp. Stat. 1913, sec. 8820, 8829, for a combination and conspiracy in restraint of commerce among the states, specifically directed against the plaintiffs (defendants in error), among others, and effectively carried out with the infliction of great damage. . . .

The substance of the charge is that the plaintiffs were hat manufacturers who employed non-union labor ; that the defendants were members of the UNITED HATTERS OF NORTH AMERICA and also of

THE AMERICAN FEDERATION OF LABOR ; that in pursuance of a general scheme to unionise the labor employed by manufacturers of fur hats (a purpose previously made effective against all but a few manufacturers), the defendants and other members of the United Hatters caused the American Federation of Labor to declare a boycott against the plaintiffs and against all hats sold by the plaintiffs to dealers in other states, and against dealers who should deal in them ; and that they carried out their plan with such success that they have restrained or destroyed the plaintiffs commerce with other states.

The case now has been tried, the plaintiffs have got a verdict, and the judgement of the district court has been affirmed by the circuit court of appeals. . . .

It requires more than the blindness of justice not to see that many branches of the United Hatters and the Federation of Labor, to both of which the defendants belonged, in pursuance of a plan emanating from headquarters, made use of such lists and of the primary and secondary boycott in their effort to subdue the plaintiffs to their demands.   The union label was used, and a strike of the plaintiff's employees was ordered, and carried out to the same end, and the purpose to break up the plaintiff's commerce affected the quality of the acts.   *Loewe* v. *Lawlor*, *208 U.S. 274, 299.*   We agree with the circuit court of appeals that a combination and conspiracy forbidden by the statute was proved, and the question is narrowed to the responsibility of the defendants for what was done by the sanction and procurement of the societies above named.

136. Injunctions—Power of Attorney-General.

TRADE DISPUTES AND TRADE UNIONS ACT, 1927 ;   17 & 18 Geo. V. ch. 22.

7. Without prejudice to the right of any person having a sufficient interest in the relief sought to sue or apply for an injunction to restrain any application of the funds of a trade union in contravention of the provisions of this Act, an injunction restraining any application of the funds of a trade union in contravention of the provisions of section one of this Act may be granted at the suit or upon the application of the Attorney-General.

In the application of this section to Scotland, there shall be substituted therein for references to an injunction references to an interdict, and for the reference to the Attorney-General a reference to the Lord Advocate.

137. Injunction in U.S.A.

District Court of the United States for the Northern District of Illinois, 1st Sept., 1922 ; INJUNCTION AGAINST RAILWAY EMPLOYEES' DEPT. OF THE A.F. OF L.

Therefore, because of the great and irreparable damage that is daily being inflicted upon the people of the United States, it is, without notice to the defendants, ordered by the court :

1. That said defendants and each of them and each and all of their attorneys, servants, agents, associates, members, employees and all persons acting in aid of or in conjunction with them, be temporarily enjoined and restrained from—

(*a*) In any manner interfering with, hindering or obstructing said railway companies, or any of them, their agents, servants or employees in the operation of their respective railroads and systems of transportation or the performance of their public duties and obligations in the transportation of passengers and property in interstate commerce and the carriage of mail, and from in any manner interfering with, hindering or obstructing the agents, servants and employees of said railway companies or any of them engaged in the inspection, repair, operation and use of trains, locomotives, cars and other equipment of said railway companies or any of them, and from preventing or attempting to prevent any person or persons from freely entering into or continuing in the employment of said railway companies or any of them for the inspection and repair of locomotives and cars or otherwise ;

(*b*) In any manner combining, conspiring, confederating, agreeing and arranging with each other or with any other person or persons, organisations or associations to injure, interfere with or hinder said railway companies or any of them in the conduct of their lawful business of transportation of passengers and property in interstate commerce and the carriage of the mail ; or to injure, interfere with, hinder or annoy any employee of said railway companies or any of them in connection with the performance of their duties as such employees or while going to or returning from the premises of said railway companies in connection with their said employment, or at any time or place, by displays of force or numbers the making of threats, intimidation, acts of violence, opprobrious epithets, jeers, suggestions of danger, taunts, entreaties, or other unlawful acts or conduct towards any employee or employees or officers of said railway companies or any of them or towards persons desirous of or contemplating entering into such employment ;

(c) Loitering or being unnecessarily in the vicinity of the points and places of ingress or egress of the employees of said railway companies, to and from such premises, in connection with their said employment ; or aiding, abetting, directing or encouraging any person or persons, organisation or association, by letters, telegrams, telephone, word of mouth, or otherwise to do any of the acts aforesaid ; trespassing, entering or going upon the premises of the said railway companies, or any of them, to do any of the acts aforesaid, or for any other purpose whatsoever, at any place or in the vicinity of any place where the employees of said companies or any of them are engaged in inspecting, overhauling, or repairing locomotives, cars, or other equipment, or where such employees customarily perform such duties or at any other place on the premises of said railway companies, or any of them, except where the public generally are invited to come to transact business with said railway companies as common carriers of passengers and property in interstate commerce ;

(d) Inducing or attempting to induce by the use of threats, violent or abusive language, opprobrious epithets, physical violence or threats thereof, intimidations, display of numbers or force, jeers, entreaties, argument, persuasion, rewards, or otherwise, any person or persons to abandon the employment of said railway companies, or any of them, or to refrain from entering such employment ;

(e) Engaging, directing, or encouraging others to engage in the practice commonly known as picketing, that is to say, assembling or causing to be assembled numbers of the members of said Federated Shop Crafts or others in sympathy with them in proximity with them of said railway companies, or any of them, at or in the vicinity where the employees thereof are required to work and perform their duties, or at or near the places of ingress or egress thereto or therefrom, and by threats, persuasion, jeers, violent or abusive language, violence or threats of violence, taunts, entreaties, or argument, or in any other way prevent or attempt to prevent any of the employees of said railway companies or any of them from entering upon or continuing in their duties as such employees, or so to prevent or attempt to prevent, any person or persons from entering or continuing in the employment of said railway companies, or any of them, and from aiding, abetting, ordering, assisting, directing or encouraging in any way any person or persons in the commission of any of said acts ;

(f) Congregating upon or directing, aiding or encouraging the congregating upon, or maintaining at or near any of the yards, shops, depots, terminals, tracks, waylands, roadbeds or premises of said railway companies, or any of them, any guards, pickets or persons to perform any act of guarding, picketing or patrolling any such yards, shops, depots, terminals, or other premises of said railway companies, or any of them ; and in any manner threaten, intimidate, by suggestions of danger or personal violence towards any servant or employee of said companies, or any of them, or towards contemplating the entering of such employment ; or aiding, encouraging, directing, or causing any other person or persons so to do ;

(*g*) Doing or causing or in any manner conspiring, combining, directing, commanding or encouraging the doing or causing the doing by any person or persons of any injury or bodily harm, to any of the servants, agents, or employees of said railway companies, or any of them ; going singly or collectively to the homes, abodes, or places of residence of any employee of the said railway companies, or any of them, for the purpose of intimidating, threatening, or coercing such employee or member of his family, or in any manner by violence or threats of violence, or otherwise, directed towards any said employee or member of his family, induce or attempt to induce such employee to refuse to perform his duties as an employee of said railway companies, or any of them ; from so attempting to prevent any person or persons from entering the employ of either of said railway companies, and from aiding, encouraging, directing, commanding, or causing any person or persons so to do ;

(*h*) In any manner directly or indirectly hindering, obstructing or impeding the operation of any of the trains of said railway companies, or any of them, in the movement, and transportation of passengers and property in interstate commerce or in the carriage of the mail, or in the performance of any other duty as common carriers, and from aiding, abetting, causing, encouraging, or directing any person or persons, association or organisation to do or cause to be done any of the matters or things aforesaid ;

(*i*) In any manner by letters, printed or other circulars, telegrams, telephones, word of mouth, oral persuasion, or suggestion, or through interviews to be published in newspapers or otherwise in any manner whatsoever, encourage, direct or command any person, whether a member of any or either of said labor organisations or associations defendants herein, or otherwise, to abandon the employment of said railway companies, or any of them, or to refrain from entering the service of said railway companies or either of them.

2. The said defendants . . . and each of them, as officers as aforesaid and as individuals, be restrained and enjoined from—

(*a*) Issuing any instructions, requests, public statements or suggestions in any way to any defendant herein or to any official or members of any said labor organisations constituting the said Federated Shop Crafts, or to any official or member of any system federation thereof with reference to their conduct or the acts they shall perform subsequent to the abandonment of the employment of said railway companies by the members of the said Federated Shop Crafts, or for the purpose of or to induce any such officials or members or any other persons whomsoever to do or say anything for the purpose or intended or calculated to cause any employee of said railway companies or any of them to abandon the employment thereof, or to cause any persons to refrain from entering the employment thereof, to perform duties in aid of the movement and transportation of passengers and property in interstate commerce and the carriage of the mails ;

(*b*) Using, causing, or consenting to the use of any of the funds or moneys of said labor organisations in aid of or to promote or encourage the doing of any of the matters or things hereinbefore complained of.

138. Injunctions—U.S.A.

Sec. 20 of the Clayton Act of 15th Oct., 1914 ; 38 Stat. L. c. 323.

20. That no restraining order or injunction shall be granted by any court of the United States, or a judge or the judges thereof, in any case between an employer and employees, or between persons employed and persons seeking employment, involving, or growing out of, a dispute concerning terms or conditions of employment, unless necessary to prevent irreparable injury to property, or to a property right, of the party making the application, for which injury there is no adequate remedy at law, and such property or property right must be described with particularity in the application, which must be in writing and sworn to by the applicant or by his agent or attorney.

And no such restraining order or injunction shall prohibit any person or persons, whether singly or in concert, from terminating any relation of employment, or from ceasing to perform any work or labor, or from recommending, advising, or persuading others by peaceful means so to do ; or from attending at any place where any such person or persons may lawfully be, for the purpose of peacefully obtaining or communicating information, or from peacefully persuading any person to work or to abstain from working ; or from ceasing to patronize or to employ any party to such dispute, or from recommending, advising, or persuading others by peaceful and lawful means so to do ; or from paying or giving to, or withholding from, any person engaged in such dispute, any strike benefits or other moneys or things of value ; or from peaceably assembling in a lawful manner, and for lawful purposes ; or from doing any act or thing which might lawfully be done in the absence of such dispute by any party thereto ; nor shall any of the acts specified in this paragraph be considered or held to be violations of any law of the United States.

139. Injunctions and their Limitations (U.S.A.).

ARTHUR *v.* OAKES (1894) 63 Fed. 310.

Judgment by Circuit Justice Harlan.

The questions before us relate to the power of a court of equity, having custody by receivers of the railroad and other property of a corporation, to enjoin combinations, conspiracies, or acts upon the part of the receivers' employees and their associates in labor organisations, which, if not restrained, would do irreparable mischief to such property, and prevent the receivers from discharging the duties imposed by law upon the corporation. . . .

It was contended that the circuit court exceeded its powers when it enjoined the employees of the receivers ' from combining and conspiring to quit, with or without notice, the service of said receivers, with the object and intent of crippling the property in their custody, or embarrassing the operation of said railroad, and from so quitting the service of said receivers, with or without notice, as to cripple the property, or prevent or hinder the operation of said railroad.'

This clause embodies two distinct propositions,—one, relating to combinations and conspiracies to quit the service of the receivers with the object and intent of crippling the property or embarrassing the operation of the railroad in their charge ; the other, having no reference to combinations and conspiracies to quit, or to the object and intent of any quitting, but only to employees ' so quitting ' as to cripple the property or prevent or hinder the operation of the railroad.

Considering these propositions in their inverse order, we remark that the injunction against employees so quitting as to cripple the property or prevent or hinder the operation of the railroad was equivalent to a command by the court that they should remain in the active employment of the receivers, and perform the services appropriate to their respective positions until they could withdraw without crippling the property or preventing or hindering the operation of the railroad. The time when they could quit without violating the injunction is not otherwise indicated by the order of the court.

Under what circumstances may the employees of the receivers, of right, quit the service in which they are engaged? Much of the argument of counsel was directed to this question. We shall not attempt to lay down any general rule applicable to every case that may arise between employer and employees. If an employee quits without cause, and in violation of an express contract to serve for a stated time, then his quitting would not be of right, and he would be liable for any damages resulting from a breach of his agreement, and perhaps, in some states of case, to criminal prosecution for loss of life or limb by passengers or others, directly resulting from abandoning his post at a time when care and watchfulness were required upon his part in the discharge of a duty he had undertaken to perform. And it may be assumed for the purposes of this discussion that he would be liable in like manner where the contract of service, by necessary implication arising out of the nature of the circumstances of the employment, required him not to quit the service of his employer suddenly, and without reasonable notice of his intention to do so.

But the vital question remains whether a court of equity will, under any circumstances, by injunction, prevent one individual from quitting the personal service of another? An affirmative answer to this question is not, we think, justified by any authority to which our attention has been called or of which we are aware. It would be an invasion of one's natural liberty to compel him to work for or to remain in the personal service of another. One who is placed under such constraint is in a condition of involuntary servitude,—a condition which the supreme law of the land declares shall not exist within the United States, or in any place subject to their jurisdiction. . . .

The rule is, we think, without exception that equity will not compel the actual affirmative performance by an employee of merely personal services, any more than it will compel an employer to retain in his personal service one who, no matter for what cause, is not acceptable to him for service of that character. The right of an employee engaged to perform personal service to quit that service rests upon the same basis as the right of his employer to discharge him from further personal service.   If the quitting in the one case or the discharging in the other is in violation of the contract between the parties, the one injured by the breach has his action for damages ; and a court of equity will not, indirectly or negatively, by means of an injunction restraining the violation of the contract, compel the affirmative performance from day to day or the affirmative acceptance of merely personal services.   Relief of that character has always been regarded as impracticable.

. . . The result of these views is that the court below should have eliminated from the writ of injunction the words, ' and from so quitting the service of the said receivers, with or without notice, as to cripple the property or prevent or hinder the operation of said railroad.'

140. A Strike Settlement.

LEADING ARTICLE FROM *The Workers' Bulletin*, a strike journal issued during the Belfast strike of 1919.   Issue of 11th February, 1919.

MIDNIGHT, FEBRUARY 10TH.

The beginning of the end has come.   The men's delegates have agreed to submit the terms set out below to be decided by a ballot. In doing this they take up the attitude of leaving the decision to the free vote of the men themselves,—they neither recommend acceptance nor advise refusal.   This is as it should be.   The workers now have their fate in their own hands, and it is for them to say whether this offer meets with their approval or otherwise.   Let every man use his own judgment.   In these columns we have consistently supported the view that the National settlement will be on a 44 hours basis, and for that reason we have never wavered in our belief that the ultimate goal would be victory.   We have no reason to alter this view.   All the information in our possession strengthens this position, and we venture to predict that possibly before the result of the ballot is known there will be a movement on the part of the Government to establish a 44 hour week.   It is a pity to allow the Welsh wizard to gain cheap fame by coming on the scene and, with a wave of his hand, sweeping away difficulties that do not exist. The ' 44 ' is assured, and it is only a question of to-day or next week.

What we do regret is that the Belfast employers did not rise to the occasion and show some statesmanship.   They have preferred to play their selfish class game and d—— the consequences.   We shall see if it was worth while.   Meantime there is no cause for despondency.   The ' 44 ' is coming and you are only asked to decide by your vote whether it will come sooner or later.

LATER.

We learn that the Federation has decided that, before taking the ballot, a Conference with the city employers must be held to ensure that a settlement will be binding on all parties.   There are attempts being made to stampede the men and to break down their unity and solidarity.   We would give the warning that it is *all or none*, and that the Federation are going to stand by all the workers, and not merely a section of them.

The delegates have played their part, and they look to the workers to support them in their determination that the men in the city shops shall work the same hours as their comrades in the shipyards.   The challenge has been thrown down that the delegates are afraid to trust the rank and file.   This challenge they have now taken up, and the responsibility is thrown on the workers themselves to show where they stand.   If the men are prepared to fight the issue out *now*, let them say so on the ballot paper, and the delegates will continue the fight in their name.   It is for the workers to decide.

The Terms.

' On condition of the men resuming work on the terms in operation on the 25th January, we undertake to call a National Conference of Engineering and Shipbuilding Trades to consider the hours question within thirty days from resumption of work.   We also undertake to recommend to that Conference a shorter working week than 47 hours, as in our opinion a working week better suited for working on the one-break system under the conditions prevailing in Belfast could be arranged, and failing a settlement by such a Conference we, as Belfast employers, will arrive at a settlement with our own men as early as possible,—in any case within 21 days after National Conference.

The Conference referred to is to include representatives of Belfast employers and workmen.'

————

Every movement for increased wages, shorter hours, or improved working conditions has been met with the cry that industries would be ruined and foreign competition would drive us out of the market. The little ' white slaves ' of Victorian England were freed, and no calamity followed. Factory Act after Factory Act came, and still Great Britain held her markets. Locally Trade Boards have been set up, which have doubled, and in some cases trebled, the starvation wage of the sweated workers in certain branches of the linen and other industries. Every time it is suggested that an industry must pay a living wage to its workers employers hold up their hands in holy horror, and declare the country is going to be ruined. The Americans have long ago discovered that low-wage labour does not even PAY, apart altogether from the social and moral aspects of the matter.

The U.S.A., with a scale of wages far above ours, has been forging ahead. The same line of argument applies to shorter hours. It is notorious that excessive hours of labour lower the total output. War conditions have brought investigations into the question of industrial fatigue, and the instinct of the worker in demanding a 44 hour week is shown to be sound by the reports published in Government Blue Books.

When the ' 44 ' has been won, the Belfast workers will continue to build better ships than all the world, and the city will be all the richer in the knowledge that justice has been done to those whose brain and muscle have made our city what it is.

141. The National Strike of 1926.

PRESIDENT'S ADDRESS TO THE TRADES UNION CONGRESS, 1926.

T.U.C. Ann. Report, 1926, p. 70.

The National Strike.

In view of the considerations which arise from the National Strike of May last, it is necessary I should deal with certain of the more important aspects of what is in many respects the most significant development in our history since this Congress was founded in 1868. Those who took part in that Congress could hardly have foreseen such a demonstration of working-class solidarity. They had not then obtained the first charter of Trade Union rights ; they could not have foretold the political development of the organised movement, nor could they have calculated the various stages of growth and expansion through which it would pass before it reached such a climax of power and ordered action and discipline as was displayed during those days of May, 1926.

When the representatives of the unions were called together in

1868, Trade Unionism was facing a situation not unlike the one that confronts us to-day. They were then, as we are now, exposed both to deliberate misrepresentation and to the bitter hostility and suspicion of sections of the public who were profoundly ignorant of the methods, motives and aims of the Trade Unions.

The founders of this Congress met the situation not by hysterical denunciations or sensational threats, but by a calm discussion of Trade Union principles and policy. That has been the tradition of our Congress, and one which we must not depart from to-day. Having nothing secret or sinister in our methods or aims, nor any purpose to serve which we cannot openly avow, we continue to believe with the pioneers of our movement, that suspicion, hostility and fear will yield to reason and plain argument. The common-sense of the British people, the resources of loyalty and devotion in the masses we represent at this Congress, can be relied upon to defeat the reactionary forces that are conspiring to shackle and destroy this Congress with all the achievements of the movement it represents.

The stoppage of the principal transport and other industries of this country in May last has been termed a general strike, a term which has been deliberately misused by our adversaries to justify the false assertion that its purpose was to hold up the life of the country—but that is an aspect of the case to which I shall refer later. I want to consider as briefly as I can the causes that produced the national strike, to show its justification, the issues it raises and to emphasise what is to be learned from that inspiring and convincing manifestation of unity, loyalty and determination on the part of our movement.

As to the causes, they are such that I would urge those who now form the Government of the country, the Press which claims to express and to mould public opinion, and in particular the employers of the country, to try to understand them. It is necessary that the fundamental character of the causes of that stoppage and its implications shall be understood and appreciated if similar crises are to be avoided in future.

The Prime Minister, in one of those moments of apparent escape from the influence of his diehard and reactionary colleagues, approached the question with some degree of understanding in saying that he realised that sympathy for the miners was the dominant motive underlying the action of the Trade Unions, and had his colleagues in the Government and the general body of employers been able to show even that much appreciation of the mind of the workers in the national strike, it would be better for the country.

It will be fatal to the future welfare of this country and destructive of all our hopes of peaceable progress, if that great and spontaneous demonstration of working-class solidarity, so generous in its readiness to run risks and make sacrifices on behalf of others, so inspiring as a revelation of the true spirit of Trade Union brotherhood, is regarded as the outcome of a sort of evil conspiracy of a few agitators meeting at Eccleston Square.[1] It has been so misinterpreted. Nothing can be more dangerous than to proceed upon an assumption so false and so perverse.

On a previous occasion when the workers showed the same impressive unanimity in making common cause, when from field and factory, workshop and mine they poured into the trenches in France and Flanders, regardless of risks or sacrifices for what they believed to be a righteous cause, their action evoked a different response from other classes.

The promises and the assurances of social and economic reconstruction made in those days of national crisis, have not been honoured. On the contrary, with a reversion to unrestricted private enterprise and control, has come a continuous downward movement of wages ; a steady pressure upon the standards of working-class life ; a drastic curtailment of an already inadequate programme of national expenditure on essential social services, education, health, everything that contributes to the building up of a progressive civilisation. All this, that the bondholder may receive the uttermost farthing, and that the money-monger may continue to exact usury and levy toll upon productive enterprise.

Political enfranchisement and a generation or two of compulsory education have brought about a profound change in the workers' views concerning their status in industry and their conditions under the existing system, and their protest against their position has grown stronger and stronger under the influence of the increasingly serious problem of unemployment, with its dire effects upon their social and economic life.

No one with any intelligent understanding of the collective mind of the working-class of this country could fail to realise that, given the set of circumstances as they existed on May 1st, a stoppage of a national character was inevitable. The choice lay between action by a controlled and disciplined movement, or industrial chaos and disorder. Certainly the representatives of the Government have no occasion to be under any misapprehension as to the outcome of the

[1] Then the Headquarters of the Trades Union Congress. (ED.)

mid-night breakdown on the 30th April of the sincere and arduous efforts of the General Council of this Congress to find a peaceable way out of the difficulty, and of the failure of the Government to respond to the appeal of the Council's representatives to make that possible.

I pause here to remind the British public that of all the organised bodies in this country, the workers' organisation, and later representatives of the Christian Churches alone, have earnestly attempted by mediatory efforts to find a means of honourable settlement.

The mining dispute, important as it was in its immediate effect, was but the climax to something that goes much deeper than that event. The strike reflected the growing discontent of the workers with the whole structure and policy of the industrial system, and their determination to resist the traditional idea, that bad trade can be made good, economic vitality and progress attained, and industry placed in a healthy condition, by the mere expedient of degrading the standard of life of the working people.

.   .   .   .

The supreme lesson of the national strike is the clear evidence it adduced as showing that the Trade Union Movement retains belief in the essential rightness of democratic methods. All that could be done in the way of provocation by the agents of the Government to goad our people into acts of violence and disorder was resorted to. The ostentatious display of military force with all its modern devices of slaughter, the flaming manifestoes of Mr. Winston Churchill in the Government strike organ, the truculent manifestations of class feeling by the volunteer strike-breakers—none of it caused our people to turn aside from the declared objective and limited purpose of the stoppage. It was not the unions but the Government which endeavoured to convert an industrial struggle into a political conflict, and sought to make party capital out of it. Nothing but the restraint, forbearance and good sense of our members prevented the agents of the Government fomenting a revolutionary temper and plunging the country into conditions of civil war. The dignified contempt with which all this was received by our people is itself a repudiation of the boastful claim by our opponents that this unnecessary display of force affected the continuance or otherwise of the stoppage.

From the attacks that have been made, it is evident that while the implications of the national strike are seen from opposite points of view by the extremists of reaction and the extremists of revolution, there is a curious similarity in the view taken by both, of the possibilities inherent in that weapon. Both envisage it as an attack upon the constitutional institutions of the country. By the one we are charged with using the strike to that end, and by the other we are abused for having failed to do so.

Let us examine the implications of these points of view. Having regard to the position the Trade Union Movement has reached, and in anticipation of the struggle which appears to be impending for the maintenance of Trade Union rights and liberties, it is imperative that we should have a clear understanding of the purpose we want this Congress to serve, the policy we want the Congress to pursue and the goal we seek to attain.

That I venture to assert is not expressed by any of those who find their inspiration and authority from sources outside our movement, and can see in the events of last May nothing but an occasion for converting the legitimate Trade Union right to strike into the means for a revolutionary upheaval.

Our critics at both extremes are guilty of fundamental error. The British working people have set themselves to achieve their aims by the method of democracy which means in politics the parliamentary system, and in economic life a system of collective Trade Union effort, that has been pursued as a manifestation of the commonsense and practical spirit of our people.

We have had a Labour Government, the symbol of our victory in that long-drawn-out political conflict of last century, when the people—the working people—won the right to vote. What is more to my present purpose, we have our deeply rooted Trade Union Movement, powerful, efficient, well-organised, the instrument by which the working people have begun to secure and will, I am convinced, ultimately accomplish industrial and economic freedom. It is not a question of altering our fundamental aim or the direction of our efforts and our thoughts, but rather one of a continued strengthening and broadening of our ranks to embrace all who accept our principles and have a conviction of the justice of our cause and sympathy with our ideals.

When the unions combined their forces last May they were not invoking any new principle of industrial action, but simply asserting more effectively on a larger scale the traditional Trade Union refusal to accept dictated terms of employment whether from the employers or the Government. As a means of resisting such settlements in industrial disputes the weapon used by the unions last May will not be left unused, when it is sought to enforce upon any section of the workers terms which have not been made the subject of negotiation and collective agreement.

With the modern developments of capitalist economy and joint stock operations it is not possible to tell where the economic interest of the employer begins or where it ends. In the ramification of those interests he may be employing workpeople in a score of different trades. The policy he pursues as an employer affects the common interests of the workers in those trades.

If the basic Trade Union principle that ' an injury to one is the concern of all ' is to have any significance—and a Trade Union is under an obligation to utilise its entire resources if necessary to protect a single unit of its membership from injustice—then it must be equally recognised that with an organised movement an attempt to impose unjust conditions on any section or part must be met with the combined resistance from the whole movement. That position must be accepted if under modern conditions Trade Unionism is to remain an effective medium for the defence of working-class interests. Moreover, while no intelligent person would deliberately and unnecessarily advocate the strike, so long as the only power in the economic system the worker has is the right to withhold his labour, he must, if needs be, exercise that right along with and on behalf of his fellows, or surrender his manhood.

In our consideration of this question, however, a matter of vital importance arises. If, on the principle stated, it is right that the whole movement may be required to rally to the defence of any part, if a common effort, a common sacrifice is required, it must also be accepted as equally fundamental that the interest of no part of the movement is superior to the interest of the whole.

142. National Strike, 1926.

GOVERNMENT'S DECISION TO BREAK OFF NEGOTIATIONS,
3rd May, 1926.

Mining Dispute ; National Strike. T.U.C. 1927, p. 11.

' His Majesty's Government believe that no solution of the difficulties in the coal industry which is both practicable and honourable to all concerned can be reached except by sincere acceptance of the Report of the Commission. In the expression " acceptance of the report " is included both the reorganisation of the industry which should be put in hand immediately, and pending the results of the reorganisation being attained such interim adjustment of wages or hours of work as will make it economically possible to carry on the industry in the meantime. If the miners or the Trade Union Committee on their behalf were prepared to say plainly that they accept this proposal the Government would have been ready to resume the negotiations and to continue the subsidy for a fortnight.

' But since the discussions which have taken place between Ministers and members of the Trade Union Committee it has come to the knowledge of the Government not only that specific instructions have been sent (under the authority of the Executives of the Trade Unions represented at the Conference convened by the General Council of the Trades Union Congress) directing their members in several of the most vital industries and services of the country to carry out a general strike on Tuesday next, but that overt acts have already taken place, including gross interference with the freedom of the Press. Such action involves a challenge to the constitutional rights and freedom of the nation.

' His Majesty's Government, therefore, before it can continue negotiations must require from the Trade Union Committee both the repudiation of the actions referred to that have already taken place, and an immediate and unconditional withdrawal of the instructions for a general strike.'

143. National Strike, 1926.

LETTER FROM THE GENERAL COUNCIL OF THE T.U.C. TO THE PRIME MINISTER in reply to the Government's decision to break off negotiations. 3rd May, 1926.

Mining Dispute ; National Strike. T.U.C. 1927, p. 12.

' Dear Sir,—Your letter of the 3rd inst. announcing the Government's decision to terminate the discussions which had been resumed on Saturday night was received by the General Council with surprise and regret. The negotiations which had taken place between the Industrial Committee of the General Council and representatives of the Cabinet had been adjourned for a brief period in order to allow the Industrial Committee to confer with the full General Council and representatives of the Miners' Federation who were on your premises, in order to advance the efforts which the Industrial Committee had persistently been making to accomplish a speedy and honourable settlement of the mining dispute.

'The Trade Union representatives were astounded to learn that without any warning the renewed conversations which it was hoped might pave the way to the opening up of full and unfettered negotiations had been abruptly terminated by the Government for the reasons stated in your communication. The first reason given is, that specific instructions have been sent under the authority of Trade Unions represented at the Conference convened by the General Council of the Trades Union Congress directing their members in several industries and services to cease work. We are directed to remind you that it is nothing unusual for workmen to cease work in defence of their interests as wage earners, and that the specific reason for the decision in this case is to secure for the mineworkers the same right from the employers as is insisted upon by employers from workers—namely, that negotiations shall be conducted free from the atmosphere of strike or lock-out. This is a principle which Governments have held to be cardinal in the conduct of negotiations.

'With regard to the second reason, that overt acts had already taken place, including gross interference with the freedom of the Press, it is regretted that no specific information is contained in your letter. The General Council had no knowledge of any such acts having occurred and the decisions taken by it definitely forbid any such independent and unauthorised action. The Council is not aware of the circumstances under which the alleged acts have taken place. It cannot accept any responsibility for them, and is taking prompt measures to prevent any acts of indiscipline. The Council regrets that it was not given an opportunity to investigate and deal with the alleged incidents before the Government made them an excuse for breaking off the peace discussions which were proceeding.

'The public will judge the nature of the Government's intentions by its precipitate and calamitous decision in this matter, and will deplore with the General Council that the sincere work which the Council has been engaged in to obtain an honourable settlement has been wrecked by the Government's unprecedented ultimatum.

'Yours faithfully,

(Signed) 'ARTHUR PUGH (Chairman),

'WALTER M. CITRINE (Acting Secretary).'

144. National Strike, 1926.

INSTRUCTIONS TO TRADE UNIONS.

Labour Year Book, 1927, p. 104.

TRADES UNION CONGRESS GENERAL COUNCIL.

THE MINING SITUATION.

PROPOSALS FOR CO-ORDINATED ACTION OF TRADE UNIONS.

[It should be understood that memoranda giving detailed instructions will be issued as required.]

1. Scope.

The Trades Union Congress General Council and the Miners' Federation of Great Britain having been unable to obtain a satisfactory settlement of the matters in dispute in the coalmining industry, and the Government and the mineowners having forced a lock-out, the General Council, in view of the need for co-ordinated action on the part of affiliated unions in defence of the policy laid down by the General Council of the Trades Union Congress, directs as follows :

Trades and Undertakings to Cease Work.

Except as hereinafter provided, the following trades and undertakings shall cease work as and when required by the General Council :—

TRANSPORT, including all affiliated unions connected with Transport, i.e., railways, sea transport, docks, wharves, harbours, canals, road transport, railway repair shops and contractors for railways, and all unions connected with the maintenance of, or equipment, manufacturing, repairs, and groundsmen employed in connection with air transport.

PRINTING TRADES, including the Press.

Productive Industries.

(*a*) IRON AND STEEL.

(*b*) METAL AND HEAVY CHEMICALS GROUP.—Including all metal workers and other workers who are engaged, or may be engaged, in installing alternative plant to take the place of coal.

BUILDING TRADE.—All workers engaged on building, except such as are employed definitely on housing and hospital work, together with all workers engaged in the supply of equipment to the building industry, shall cease work.

ELECTRICITY AND GAS.—The General Council recommend that the Trade Unions connected with the supply of electricity and gas shall co-operate with the object of ceasing to supply power. The Council request that the Executives of the Trade Unions concerned shall meet at once with a view to formulating common policy.

SANITARY SERVICES.—The General Council direct that sanitary services be continued.

HEALTH AND FOOD SERVICES.—The General Council recommend that there should be no interference in regard to these, and that the Trade Unions concerned should do everything in their power to organise the distribution of milk and food to the whole of the population.

With regard to hospitals, clinics, convalescent homes, sanatoria, infant welfare centres, maternity homes, nursing homes, schools, the General Council direct that affiliated unions take every opportunity to ensure that food, milk, medical and surgical supplies shall be efficiently provided.

2. Trade Union Discipline.

(a) The General Council direct that, in the event of Trade Unionists being called upon to cease work, the Trade Unions concerned shall take steps to keep a daily register to account for every one of their members. It should be made known that any workers called upon to cease work should not leave their own district, and by following another occupation, or the same occupation in another district, blackleg their fellow workers.

(b) The General Council recommend that the actual calling out of the workers should be left to the unions, and the instructions should only be issued by the accredited representatives of the unions participating in the dispute.

3. Trades Councils.

The work of the Trades Councils, in conjunction with the local officers of the Trade Unions actually participating in the dispute, shall be to assist in carrying out the foregoing provisions, and they shall be charged with the responsibility of organising the Trade Unionists in dispute in the most effective manner for the preservation of peace and order.

4. Incitement to Disorder and Spies.

A strong warning must be issued to all localities that any person found inciting the workers to attack property, or inciting the workers to riot, must be dealt with immediately. It should be pointed out that the opponents will in all probability employ persons to act as spies and others to use violent language in order to incite the workers to disorder.

5. *Trade Union Agreements.*

The General Council further direct that the Executives of the Unions concerned shall definitely declare that in the event of any action being taken and Trade Union agreements being placed in jeopardy, it be definitely agreed that there will be no general resumption of work until those agreements are fully recognised.

6. *Procedure.*

(*a*) These proposals shall be immediately considered by the Executives of the Trade Unions concerned in the stoppage, who will at once report as to whether they will place their powers in the hands of the General Council and carry out the instructions which the General Council may issue from time to time concerning the necessary action and conduct of the dispute.

(*b*) And, further, that the Executives of all other affiliated unions are asked to report at once as to whether they will place their powers in the hands of the General Council and carry out the instructions of the General Council from time to time, both regarding the conduct of the dispute and financial assistance.

A. PUGH, Chairman.

April 30th, 1926.   WALTER M. CITRINE, Acting Secretary.

145. T.U.C. Policy and Control in the National Strike, 1926.

LETTERS SENT TO THE PRIME MINISTER.

National Strike; Special Conference: Report. T.U.C. 1927, p. 37.

To the Right Hon. Stanley Baldwin, M.P.,   May 1st, 1926.
10, Downing Street, Whitehall, S.W. 1.
DEAR SIR,

MINING LOCK-OUT : ESSENTIAL FOODSTUFFS.

I am directed to inform you that in the event of the strike of unions affiliated to the Trades Union Congress taking place in support of the miners who have been locked out, the General Council is prepared to enter into arrangements for the distribution of essential foodstuffs.

Should the Government desire to discuss the matter with the General Council they are available for that purpose. The General Council will be glad to learn your wishes in this respect.

Yours faithfully,

WALTER M. CITRINE (Acting Secretary).

May 1st, 1926.

To the Right Hon. Stanley Baldwin, M.P.,
 10, Downing Street, Whitehall, S.W. 1.

DEAR SIR,

MINING LOCK-OUT.

I have to advise you that the Executive Committees of the Trade Unions affiliated to the Trades Union Congress, including the Miners' Federation of Great Britain, have decided to hand over to the General Council of the Trades Union Congress the conduct of the dispute, and the negotiations in connection therewith will be undertaken by the General Council.

I am directed to say that the General Council will hold themselves available at any moment should the Government desire to discuss the matter further.

Yours faithfully,

WALTER M. CITRINE (Acting Secretary).

146. National Strike, 1926.

GENERAL COUNCIL'S POLICY IN REGARD TO ORDERLY CONDUCT.

The British Worker, 5th May, 1926, and other dates.

MESSAGE TO ALL WORKERS.

The General Council of the Trades Union Congress wishes to emphasise the fact that this is an industrial dispute. It expects every member taking part to be exemplary in his conduct and not to give any opportunity for police interference. The outbreak of any disturbances would be very damaging to the prospects of a successful termination to the dispute.

The Council asks pickets especially to avoid obstruction and to confine themselves strictly to their legitimate duties.

147. National Strike, 1926.

GENERAL COUNCIL'S POLICY CONSTITUTIONAL.

The British Worker, 9th May, 1926, p. 4.

The General Council does NOT challenge the Constitution.
It is not seeking to substitute unconstitutional government.
Nor is it desirous of undermining our Parliamentary institutions.
The sole aim of the Council is to secure for the miners a decent standard of life.
The Council is engaged in an Industrial dispute.
In any settlement, the only issue to be decided will be an industrial issue, not political, not constitutional.
There is no Constitutional crisis.

148. National Strike, 1926.

GENERAL COUNCIL'S MESSAGE AT THE CLOSE OF THE FIRST DAY.

The British Worker, 5th May, 1926, p. 1.

The workers' response has exceeded all expectations. The first day of the General Strike is over. They have manifested their determination and unity to the whole world. They have resolved that the attempt of the mineowners to starve three million men, women and children into submission shall not succeed.

All the essential industries and all the transport services have been brought to a standstill. The only exception is that the distribution of milk and food has been permitted to continue. The Trades Union General Council is not making war on the people. It is anxious that the ordinary members of the public shall not be penalised for the unpatriotic conduct of the mineowners and the Government.

Never have the workers responded with greater enthusiasm to the call of their leaders. The only difficulty that the General Council is experiencing, in fact, is in persuading those workers in the second line of defence to continue at work until the withdrawal of their labour may be needed.

The conduct of the trade unionists, too, constitutes a credit to the whole movement. Despite the presence of armed police and the military, the workers have preserved a quiet orderliness and dignity, which the General Council urges them to maintain, even in the face of the temptation and provocation which the Government is placing in their path.

To the unemployed, also, the General Council would address an earnest appeal. In the present fight there are two sides only—the workers on the one hand and those who are against them on the other.

Every unemployed man or woman who ' blacklegs ' on any job offered by employers or the authorities is merely helping to bring down the standard of living for the workers as a whole, and to create a resultant situation in which the number of unemployed must be greater than ever.

The General Council is confident that the unemployed will realise how closely their interests are involved in a successful issue to the greatest battle ever fought by the workers of the country in the defence of the right to live by work.

149. National Strike, 1926.

THE STRIKE HEADQUARTERS ORGANISATION.

ARTICLE IN *The British Worker*, 11th May, 1926, p. 3.

Eccleston Square, where the offices of the T.U.C. are situated, has been transferred from a sleepy residential square into one of the busiest spots in the country.

Every few minutes despatch riders are arriving or departing, bringing and taking news, instructions and information to the different areas. Cars with deputations, officials, members of committees and volunteers, are also going to and fro in continual procession.

Everything is quiet and orderly, everyone doing his or her job without confusion or complaint.

All this organisation has been developed since the first actual day of the strike. Volunteers have poured in, offering their services, their cars, cycles, and motor-cycles.

Within the building the General Council, the supreme body of the control of all phases of the strike, conducts its business with the same methodical precision and coolness.

For convenience and administration, the General Council has been organised into various committees. Most important of these from the point of view of the strike is what is known as the ' Strike Organisation Committee.' Mr. Ernest Bevin and Mr. A. A. Purcell, M.P., are in charge of this committee, and they deal with all questions from the areas and with strike conduct policy.

The reports that are continually arriving from all parts of the country are first handled by an Intelligence Department, which prepares from them a bird's-eye view of the whole situation for the information of the full General Council.

Closely linked with Intelligence is the Publicity Department, which prepares from the reports summaries for the frequent 'Bulletins' that are issued; also matter for use in the BRITISH WORKER, and for reference and propaganda purposes.

The transport section works in close conjunction with these two sections, and, in addition to handling the incoming and outgoing despatches and communications, is responsible for the transport of staff, officials, and others on strike business.

The hundreds of people who are continually arriving for advice, assistance and instruction, are sorted out by an Interviewing Committee. Often this committee is able to deal with the questions raised; if not, the visitors are sent to the appropriate committee or official.

Last, but perhaps the most important, is the Negotiating Committee, presided over by the Chairman of the Council, Mr. Arthur Pugh. This committee deals with the questions of high policy that arise; its work is carried on in consultation with the Miners' Federation Executive and the full body of the General Council.

150. National Strike, 1926.

THE 'SAMUEL MEMORANDUM,' on which the General Council of the T.U.C. ended the National Strike.

Mining Dispute ; National Strike, T.U.C. 1927, p. 22.

1. The negotiations upon the conditions of the coal industry should be resumed, the subsidy being renewed for such reasonable period as may be required for that purpose.

2. Any negotiations are unlikely to be successful unless they provide for means of settling disputes in the industry other than conferences between the mineowners and the miners alone. A National Wages Board should, therefore, be established which would include representatives of those two parties with a neutral element and an independent chairman. The proposals in this direction tentatively made in the Report of the Royal Commission should be pressed and the powers of the proposed Board enlarged.

3. The parties to the Board should be entitled to raise before it

any points they consider relevant to the issue under discussion, and the Board should be required to take such points into consideration.

4. There should be no revision of the previous wage rates unless there are sufficient assurances that the measures of reorganisation proposed by the Commission will be effectively adopted. A committee should be established, as proposed by the Prime Minister, on which representatives of the men should be included, whose duty it should be to co-operate with the Government in the preparation of the legislative and administrative measures that are required. The same committee, or alternatively the National Wages Board, should assure itself that the necessary steps so far as they relate to matters within the industry are not being neglected or unduly postponed.

5. After these points have been agreed and the Mines National Wages Board has considered every practicable means of meeting such immediate financial difficulties as exist, it may if that course is found to be absolutely necessary, proceed to the preparation of a wage agreement.

6. Any such agreement should :—

(i) If practicable be on simpler lines than those hitherto followed.

(ii) Not adversely affect in any way the wages of the lowest paid men.

(iii) Fix reasonable figures below which the wage of no class of labour for a normal customary week's work, should be reduced in any circumstances.

(iv) In the event of any new adjustments being made, should provide for the revision of such adjustments by the Wages Board from time to time if the facts warrant that course.

7. Measures should be adopted to prevent the recruitment of new workers over the age of 18 years into the industry if unemployed miners are available.

8. Workers who are displaced as a consequence of the closing of uneconomic colleries should be provided for by :

(a) The transfer of such men as may be mobile with the Government assistance that may be required as recommended in the Report of the Royal Commission.

(b) The maintenance for such period as may be fixed of those who cannot be so transferred and for whom alternative employment cannot be found ; this maintenance to comprise an addition to the existing rate of unemployment pay under the Unemployment Insurance Act of such amount as may be agreed. A contribution should be made by the Treasury to cover the additional sums so disbursed.

(*c*) The rapid construction of new houses to accommodate transferred workers. The Trades Union Congress will facilitate this by consultation and co-operation with all those who are concerned.

151. Disputes in Essential Industries—Government Measures.

EMERGENCY POWERS ACT, 1920, 10 & 11 Geo. V., ch. 55.

1.—(1) If at any time it appears to His Majesty that any action has been taken or is immediately threatened by any persons or body of persons of such a nature and on so extensive a scale as to be calculated, by interfering with the supply and distribution of food, water, fuel, or light, or with the means of locomotion, to deprive the community, or any substantial portion of the community, of the essentials of life, His Majesty may, by proclamation (hereinafter referred to as a proclamation of emergency), declare that a state of emergency exists.

No such proclamation shall be in force for more than one month, without prejudice to the issue of another proclamation at or before the end of that period.

(2) Where a proclamation of emergency has been made, the occasion thereof shall forthwith be communicated to Parliament, and, if Parliament is then separated by such adjournment or prorogation as will not expire within five days, a proclamation shall be issued for the meeting of Parliament within five days, and Parliament shall accordingly meet and sit upon the day appointed by that proclamation, and shall continue to sit and act in like manner as if it had stood adjourned or prorogued to the same day.

2.—(1) Where a proclamation of emergency has been made, and so long as the proclamation is in force, it shall be lawful for His Majesty in Council, by Order, to make regulations for securing the essentials of life to the community, and those regulations may confer or impose on a Secretary of State or other Government department, or any other persons in His Majesty's service or acting on His Majesty's behalf, such powers and duties as His Majesty may deem necessary for the preservation of the peace, for securing and regulating the supply and distribution of food, water, fuel, light, and other necessities, for maintaining the means of transit or locomotion, and for any other purposes essential to the public safety and the life of the community, and may make such provisions incidental to the powers aforesaid as may appear to His Majesty to be required for making the exercise of those powers effective :

Provided that nothing in this Act shall be construed to authorise the making of any regulations imposing any form of compulsory military service or industrial conscription :

Provided also that no such regulation shall make it an offence for any person or persons to take part in a strike, or peacefully to persuade any other person or persons to take part in a strike.

(2) Any regulations so made shall be laid before Parliament as soon as may be after they are made, and shall not continue in force after the expiration of seven days from the time when they are so laid unless a resolution is passed by both Houses providing for the continuance thereof.

(3) The regulations may provide for the trial, by courts of summary jurisdiction, of persons guilty of offences against the regulations ; so, however, that the maximum penalty which may be inflicted for any offence against any such regulations shall be imprisonment with or without hard labour for a term of three months, or a fine of one hundred pounds, or both such imprisonment and fine, together with the forfeiture of any goods or money in respect of which the offence has been committed : Provided that no such regulations shall alter any existing procedure in criminal cases, or confer any right to punish by fine or imprisonment without trial.

(4) The regulations so made shall have effect as if enacted in this Act, but may be added to, altered, or revoked by resolution of both Houses of Parliament or by regulations made in like manner and subject to the like provisions as the original regulations ; and regulations made under this section shall not be deemed to be statutory rules within the meaning of section one of the Rules Publication Act, 1893.

(5) The expiry or revocation of any regulations so made shall not be deemed to have affected the previous operation thereof, or the validity of any action taken thereunder, or any penalty or punishment incurred in respect of any contravention or failure to comply therewith, or any proceeding or remedy in respect of any such punishment or penalty.

3.—(1) This Act may be cited as the Emergency Powers Act, 1920.

(2) This Act shall not apply to Ireland.

152. Government's Anti-strike Organisation.

MINISTRY OF HEALTH CIRCULAR 636, England and Wales, 1925.

To   MINISTRY OF HEALTH,
  Town Councils.   WHITEHALL, S.W. I,
  Metropolitan Borough Councils.   20TH NOVEMBER, 1925.
  Urban District Councils.
  Rural District Councils.

Sir,

I AM directed by the Minister of Health to refer to the Circular Letter which was sent to Local Authorities in May 1922 (see Appendix (A)), in which it was stated that it would be for Local Authorities to make such arrangements for the maintenance of local services as might be thought to be required in the event of need arising.

The events of recent years have shown that an industrial dispute may be so extended as to interfere seriously with communications, the conveyance of food and of other necessities, the supply of light and power and the health and means of livelihood of the population at large.   While it is desirable that Government authorities, whether central or local, should keep aloof from any industrial dispute so far as it affects only the employers and the employed in the industry concerned, it is essential that other members of the community should be protected from the dangers and inconveniences of such a situation as is here indicated.   This protection can best be supplied by decentralised organisation designed to secure the maintenance of services essential to the well-being of the community.

Should such an emergency occur it is to their Local Authorities that the people will naturally turn for help in the difficulties which they may have to meet, and in order that any action initiated locally may harmonise with the national measures which the Government consider it desirable to take they think it necessary now to communicate to Local Authorities the following outline of the organisation which would be brought into operation by the Government to deal with essential services which are not purely local in character. This outline will, if it be necessary, be supplemented by further details in a later communication.   By 'emergency' is meant a state of affairs necessitating the issue of a Proclamation under the Emergency Powers Act, 1920, as a preliminary to the issue of Regulations 'for securing the essentials of life to the country.'

The organisation which the Government propose is designed to supplement and to assist in an emergency the normal methods of communication, supply and distribution and to give to all those who can help an opportunity of doing so in the manner most required. It is not intended that the Government should substitute new machinery for that ordinarily existing to meet the essential needs of the community.

1. A Minister will in such an emergency act as Civil Commissioner on behalf of the Government in each of ten Divisions covering the whole of England and Wales. He will be assisted by a staff consisting mainly of representatives of the Departments of Government concerned and dealing with the following subjects : Transport ; Food ; Postal Services ; Coal. It will be the duty of the Civil Commissioner and his staff during the emergency to keep in touch with the Local Authorities in each Division and to be available for consultation by them ; and he will be empowered if necessary to give decisions on behalf of the Government.

The towns in which Civil Commissioners will be stationed and the general outlines of the areas of the Divisions for which they will act are set out in Appendix (B).

The Officers who will act as the Chief Assistants to the Civil Commissioners and those who will act as Technical Representatives for the services mentioned have been appointed, and these Officers will, as requisite, put themselves in touch with representatives of Local Authorities, and provide them with such information as may be practicable in regard to details of the organisation.

2. Each Division is divided into suitable areas for administering essential national services and, if considered necessary, for recruiting volunteers for those purposes. In each area there will on an emergency be a local Food Officer, a local Road Officer and a Haulage Committee and a Coal Emergency Officer, besides representatives (where required) for other essential services. There will also be a Chairman selected by the Government to convene and preside over a Volunteer Service Committee in each area for the recruitment of volunteers to assist in maintaining essential national services.

In any town in which the Chairman of the Committee might consider it necessary to open a recruiting centre, it is earnestly hoped that it would be found practicable for the Local Authority concerned to combine with him in making the centre available for recruiting both for national and for local purposes, allocating by arrangement volunteers to local and national services in accordance with their qualifications and the needs of the occasion. Local Authorities are not expected to take any action so far as national services are concerned, unless and until approached by the Chairman.

3. On an emergency arising reliance will be placed to the utmost extent upon normal channels for the supply and distribution of food, and to this end the Divisional Food Representative upon the Civil Commissioner's staff will arrange for consultation with the principal traders as to the stocks of essential food-stuffs in their possession or in transit. In the event of any shortage or delay in the supply of essential food-stuffs to the Division, the Food Representative will be in possession of information as to alternative sources of supply and the means to make them available.

Local distribution and local shortages not affecting national supplies will ordinarily be dealt with by the local Food Officer.

4. Road Transport will be dealt with on similar lines. The Road Commissioner upon the Civil Commissioner's staff will be assisted by Road Officers and Haulage Committees in each of the areas comprised in the Division, who will endeavour by voluntary arrangement to promote the economical use of existing vehicles and where necessary the diversion of vehicles from less to more important services. Road Commissioners and Road Officers will be furnished with powers to this end should the exercise of such powers prove necessary.

5. In an emergency full directions will be sent as to the supply and distribution of coal. These directions may, if necessary, limit the supply of coal obtainable for any household or business, and may also place upon Local Authorities responsibilities for regulating the consumption of gas and electricity within their districts. They would probably necessitate in most cases the allocation of a particular officer or officers by the Local Authority during the period that they were in force.

The Local Authority will have the assistance of a Coal Emergency Officer and of a Committee of Traders within their own district.

6. The maintenance of law and order and the protection of persons and property from violence may be one of the most important services. The organisation of the necessary arrangements and the control of the Police and Special Constabulary rest with the Police Authorities and the Chief Constables, but the Local Authorities might co-operate, for instance, in securing able-bodied citizens of good character to serve as Special Constables. The arrangements

for the enrolment of Special Constables will be made by the Police, and any men who come forward as Special Constables, or who offer their services in a general capacity and appear most suited for service as Special Constables should be referred to the Police Station or other place of enrolment appointed for the purpose.

7. While it is impossible to draw any hard and fast line of demarcation between national and local services which is universally applicable the position may be broadly defined as follows : Local Authorities are expected to undertake responsibility for the maintenance of local public utility services ; in addition they are asked to co-operate with the national organisation in regard to local transport and the local distribution of coal. In the absence of further directions they are not expected to undertake responsibility for the local distribution of food nor are they asked to accept responsibility for shipping, railway or postal communications, or docks and harbours except where the Local Authority are also the Port Authority.

8. It will be realised that in an emergency the burden upon national resources must in any event be considerable and responsibility could not be accepted by the Government for expenditure incurred by Local Authorities in meeting local needs. Where, however, a joint recruiting station is established, the expenditure incurred would have to be allocated between the Government and the Local Authority concerned. Precise instructions on this point would be issued to Chairmen of Volunteer Service Committees.

I am, Sir,

Your obedient Servant,

W. A. ROBINSON.

Appendix (A).   *Circular* 312.
                              (*England and Wales.*)

MINISTRY OF HEALTH,
WHITEHALL, S.W. 1,
MAY 23, 1922.

Sir,

I AM directed to refer to the ' Memorandum for the Guidance of Local Authorities,' which was issued in April of last year, and to state that His Majesty's Government have decided that the Memorandum is to be regarded as withdrawn from the present date, and that it will be for Local Authorities to make such arrangements for maintenance of local services as may be thought to be required in the event of need arising. The copies of the memorandum sent to you should be destroyed forthwith as the financial and other provisions will not be applicable on any future occasion.

I am, Sir,

The Clerk
   to the Local Authority.

Your obedient Servant,
   W. A. Robinson, *Secretary.*

Appendix (B).

Divisional Headquarters.	Area of Division.
London	London, Middlesex, Herts, Essex, Kent, Sussex, Surrey.
Reading	Berks, Oxfordshire, Bucks, Hants, Isle of Wight, Wilts.
Bristol	Gloucestershire, Somerset, Dorset, Devon, Cornwall.
Cardiff	Glamorgan, Carmarthen, Pembroke, Cardigan, Radnor, Brecon, Monmouthshire.
Liverpool	Lancashire, Cheshire, Denbighshire, Montgomeryshire, Merioneth, Carnarvonshire, Anglesey, Flintshire, Cumberland, Westmorland.
Newcastle-on-Tyne	Northumberland, Durham.
Leeds	Yorkshire.
Nottingham	Notts, Lincolnshire, Rutland, Leicestershire, Northants, Derbyshire.
Birmingham	Warwickshire, Worcestershire, Herefordshire, Salop, Staffordshire.
Cambridge	Cambridgeshire, Beds, Hunts, Norfolk, Suffolk.

153. The Social General Strike.

The World of Labour, by G. D. H. Cole, 3rd ed., p. 203.

On the whole the social General Strike may be dismissed as a rather barren contribution of the theorists to economic propaganda. It is Anarchist in its origin, and has throughout the unpractical and Utopian character of Anarchistic ideas in a very marked degree.

To that small minority which is always dreaming of the great to-morrow that never comes it will continue to appeal as a dramatic representation of the recovery by the disinherited of the birthright they have lost ; in revolutionary countries it may even, in combination with political causes and forces, play a part in actual revolutions ;

but in countries like England painfully afflicted with the art of compromise and muddling through, ideas gain more by being turned into business propositions than by being artistically and dramatically expressed.

The idea behind the General Strike is sound enough, and in a romance like *News from Nowhere* there is no reason for objecting to its use ; but the main business of the friends of Labour to-day is to convince the workers, and that, in Great Britain at any rate, they will never succeed in doing by means of such imaginative conceptions as the General Strike.

For the unimaginative, mysticism is merely mystification ; the General Strike is the General Strike and nothing more.

It does not, for the average worker, symbolise the class-struggle and the final triumph of democracy ; it is merely ' a fool's idea of running a revolution.' If it is to be received in that spirit, the less we hear of it on this side of the Channel the better. England will never breed the wilder revolutionaries in any numbers, just as it has never bred Anarchists. It may import them ; but, on the whole, imported ideas do not pay. If we are to have a gospel of revolt, we must create it for ourselves, out of the materials in our hands.

154. Mutual Insurance.

Industrial Democracy, by S. AND B. WEBB, 1920 ed., p. 152.

By the phrase ' Mutual Insurance,' as one of the Methods of Trade Unionism, we understand . . . the provision of a fund by common subscription to ensure against casualties ; to provide maintenance, that is to say, in cases in which a member is deprived of his livelihood by causes over which neither he nor the union has any control. This obviously covers the ' benevolent' or friendly society side of Trade Unionism, such as the provision of sick pay, accident benefit, and superannuation allowance, together with ' burial money.'. . . But it includes also what are often termed ' trade ' benefits ; grants for replacing tools lost by theft or fire, and ' out of work ' pay, from the old-fashioned ' tramping card ' to the modern ' donation ' given when a member loses his employment.

. . . On the other hand our definition excludes all expenditure incurred by the union as a consequence of action voluntarily undertaken by it, such as the cost of trade negotiations, the " victim pay " accorded to members dismissed for agitation, and the maintenance of men on strike.

155. Contributions

NAT. SOCIETY OF BRASS

Section.	Weekly Contributions.	Unemployment.	Sick Pay.
A I. 21 to 40 years. — Section A. Members in this Section receive 10s. Dividend each year.	1s. 4d. per week.	12s. for 13 weeks. 9s. for 13 weeks. Afterwards Retention Benefit as per rule 37.	11s. for 10 weeks. 5s. for 13 weeks. 2s. 6d. for 52 weeks.
A II. 18 to 21 years. — 10s. annual Dividend.	1s. per week.	8s. for 13 weeks. 6s. for 13 weeks. Retention Benefit as per rule 37.	9s. for 10 weeks. 4s. 6d. for 13 weeks. 2s. 3d. for 52 weeks.
A III. 16 to 18 years. — 5s. annual Dividend.	6d. per week.	4s. for 13 weeks. 3s. for 13 weeks. Retention Benefit as per rule 37.	4s. 6d. for 10 weeks. 2s. 3d. for 13 weeks. 1s. 2d. for 52 weeks.
GENERAL SECTION. B I. — 21 years and upwards.	1s.	12s. for 13 weeks. 9s. for 13 weeks. Afterwards Retention Benefit as per rule 37.	5s. for 10 weeks. 2s. for 52 weeks.
GENERAL MEMBERS. B II. — Over 18 and under 21 years.	8d.	8s. for 13 weeks. 6s. for 13 weeks. Retention Benefit as per rule 37.	4s. per wk. for 10 wks. 1s. 6d. wk. for 52 wks.
B III. — Over 16 and under 18 years.	4d.	4s. for 13 weeks. 3s. for 13 weeks. Retention Benefit as per rule 37.	2s. per wk. for 10 wks. 9d. per wk. for 52 wks.
C or TRADE SECTION.	9d.	10s. for 13 weeks. 7s. for 13 weeks. Afterwards Retention Benefit as per rule 37.	—

Retention Benefit.—Retention of membership is member's contribution paid if out of work, after provided the member attends on out-of-work pay day to have his contribution entered.
Funeral Benefit.—Members under 40 years of age in all sections are entitled to Double Rule 41, or Treble if 2d. extra is paid in accordance with Scale, Rule 41.
There is no entrance fee in any section. Legal Assistance given in all approved cases.
Benevolent Fund to assist members in need.

nd Benefits.

ND METAL MECHANICS, 1927.

Section.		Superannuation.	Dispute Pay.	Funeral.
A I. 1 to 40 ears.	Section A. Members in this Section receive 10s. Dividend each year.	Per week. 5s. after 20 years. 6s. after 25 years. 7s. after 30 years. 8s. after 35 years. 10s. after 40 years. At 60 years of age ; Moulders and Pol- ishers, 55 years of age.	Per week. 20s. for 13 weeks. 15s. for 13 weeks. 10s. for 13 weeks. Afterwards Retention Benefit as per rule 37.	Death of Member, £10. Member's Wife, £5. Each Member's Child under 16 years of age, £1, as per Scale see rule 41.
A II. 18 to 21 years.	10s. annual Dividend.	—	13s. 6d. for 13 weeks. 10s. for 13 weeks. 7s. for 13 weeks.	Death of Member, £10. Member's Wife, £5. Each Member's Child under 16 years of age, £1, as per Scale, see rule 41.
A III. 16 to 18 years.	5s. annual Dividend.	—	7s. for 13 weeks. 5s. for 13 weeks. 3s. 6d. for 13 weeks.	
GENERAL SECTION. B I. 21 years and upwards.		Per week. 5s. after 20 years. 6s. after 25 years. 7s. after 30 years. 8s. after 35 years. 10s. after 40 years. At 60 years of age ; Moulders and Pol- ishers, 55 years of age.	Per week. 20s. for 13 weeks. 15s. for 13 weeks. 10s. for 13 weeks. Afterwards Retention Benefit as per rule 37.	Death of Member, £10. Member's Wife, £5. Each Member's Child under 16 years of age, £1, as per Scale, see rule 41.
GENERAL MEMBERS. B II. Over 18 and under 21 years.		—	Per week. 13s. 4d. for 13 weeks. 10s. for 13 weeks.	Death of Member, as per scale, £10. Member's Wife, £5. Each Member's Child under 16 years of age, £1, as per Scale, see rule 41.
B III. Over 16 and under 18 years.		—	6s. 8d. for 13 weeks. 5s. for 13 weeks.	
C or TRADE SECTION		—	15s. for 10 weeks. 12s. for 10 weeks. 8s. for 10 weeks. Afterwards Retention Benefit as per rule 37.	Death of Member, £10. Member's Wife, £5. Each Member's Child under 16 years of age, £1, as per Scale, see rule 41.

exhaustion of out-of-work benefit, for a period not exceeding 26 weeks, and 1s. a week,

Funeral Benefits by the payment of an extra Penny per week in accordance with Scale,

156. Benefits.

NATIONAL UNION OF DISTRIBUTIVE AND ALLIED WORKERS, 1924.

SCHEDULE OF SCALES OF CONTRIBUTIONS AND BENEFITS.

Scale.	Weekly Contribution at 16 years of age and upwards.	Weekly Benefit when out of Employment, 10 weeks.	Weekly Benefit during Sickness or Temporary Disablement, 10 weeks.	Funeral Benefit on Death of Member.	Permanent Disablement and Distress Benefits. Disablement through Accident or Infirmity. Total.	Partial	Total Disablement through Illness.	Distress Grant.	Dispute and Victimisation Benefit. During Unemployment through a Strike sanctioned by the Executive Council, or through Lock-out, or Victimisation due to action by or on behalf of the Union. 16 to 20 Years. Per Week.	21 Years and over. Per Week.	Trade Protection and Legal Aid.
I.	1s. 4d.	15s.	15s.	£12	£100	£50	£10	Up to £10	12s.	24s.	Members in all Scales are advised legally on matters relating to Employment, such as Workmen's Compensation, Truck, etc., and are protected regarding Wages, Hours, Overtime, Holidays, etc.
II.	1s.	10s.	10s.	£8	£100	£50	£10	Up to £10	12s.	24s.	
III.	8d.	5s.	5s.	£4	£100	£50	£10	Up to £10	12s.	24s.	
IV.	6d.	...	...	£4	...	...	...	...	12s.	24s.	
V.	Weekly Contribution, 3d	FOR ASSOCIATES.—All persons under 16 years of age, and also for Females 16 years of age and upwards.							All Ages per week, 6s.		

157. Benefits.

SCHEDULE II. OF TRANSPORT AND GENERAL WORKERS' UNION RULES, 1927.

(*d*) *Legal.*

Legal assistance (subject to the discretion of the General Executive Council) may be given to members on matters arising out of their employment.

(*e*) *Dispute Benefit.*

Members having paid twenty-six weekly trade union contributions involved in a dispute taking place with the sanction of or by the instructions of the General Executive Council, or which has been given recognition by the General Executive Council or by any Delegate Conference, or involved in any lockout, shall be entitled to benefit as follows :

If the weekly contribution is 6d. or more, the benefit will be 20s. per week, and 2s. per week for each child under fourteen years of age, provided that in the event of both parents being so entitled one benefit only shall be payable in respect of each child,

If the weekly contribution is 3d. or 4d., then the benefit will be 12s. per week,

If the weekly contribution is 2d., then the benefit will be 8s. per week,

always providing that should members be paid dispute benefit from another trade union by virtue of their membership with that trade union, the General Executive Council shall, if it so decide, withhold payment of this benefit.

(*f*) *Victimisation Benefit.*

Claims for victimisation benefit shall only be allowed if the General Executive Council is satisfied that the member claiming has been victimised as a result of his or her trade union activities or has been victimised by reason of his or her participation in a strike or lock-out officially recognised by the General Executive Council. The assistance granted to victimised members shall be determined by the General Executive Council.

(*g*) *Accident Benefit.*

1.—Any member with nine months' membership, having made thirty-nine weekly payments at one of the rates set out in Schedule

V., and not disentitled to benefit by reason of Schedule II. (*c*), who whilst at work meets with an accident which incapacitates him from following his employment, provided that such accident was not the result of drunkenness, disorderly or improper conduct, or through exposing himself to unnecessary risks, shall be entitled to the benefit for accident set out in Schedule V., after which his accident allowance shall cease, but should he declare off the accident allowance before the sixteen weeks have expired and afterwards declare on for another accident within two years, he shall be placed in receipt of the same weekly allowance as when he declared off the accident allowance, and all previous weeks' allowances shall be counted as part of a continued accident.   A member having received the sixteen weeks' accident allowance shall not be entitled to any further accident allowance until two years have elapsed from the time of receiving the last payment, and then only in the event of a new accident.   Any member claiming the accident allowance shall send to his branch secretary a doctor's certificate, along with a declaring-on note in the form printed at the end of Schedule IV.   Accident allowance will date from the day of receiving the doctor's certificate and declaring-on note, except where the accident is of a character necessitating the removal of the injured member to hospital or where there are circumstances which preclude the accident being speedily reported to the branch secretary or official of the Union when payment of benefit shall date from the day following date of accident.   Claims received by the branch secretary after 4 o'clock will date from the following day.

2.—A doctor's certificate must be sent to the secretary every fortnight so long as the member is on accident allowance, and any member neglecting to do so will forfeit the accident allowance until such time as the certificate arrives.

3.—Any member suspected of malingering shall be reported to the branch or the area secretary, who shall have power to appoint a physician or surgeon, and two members of his branch, to investigate his case and give a certificate as to his accident, the expenses to be borne by the Union.   Any member making a false declaration of accident, or certified to be malingering, shall refund all moneys received in such case, and shall forfeit all benefits for 13 weeks, and if detected a second time he shall be expelled from the Union.

4.—If any member before sending in his declaring-off note be detected doing any kind of work he shall be fined £1.

(*h*) *Funeral Benefit.*

On the death of any member of not less than nine months' membership, having made 39 weekly payments, and being in compliance, in accordance with Schedule II. (*c*), funeral benefits as follow shall be paid to his nominee or to the person or persons whom the General Executive Council shall in their absolute and final discretion consider entitled to it :

For members paying full contributions £5, rising £1 for every additional consecutive year of full benefit after the first year, with maximum of £10, providing always that in the case of all new members joining or transferring after the 1st January, 1928, who are 50 years of age or over, the benefit shall be limited to £5.

For like members paying 4d. per week, £3, rising by 10s. for every additional consecutive year of full benefit after the first year, with a maximum of £5.

For like members paying 3d. per week and 2d. quarterage, £3, rising by 10s. for every additional consecutive year of full benefit after the first year, with a maximum of £5.

For like members paying 2d. per week and 1d. quarterage, £3.

Female members leaving industry may qualify for funeral benefit by continuing to contribute 1s. 1d. quarterly, in advance.

(*i*) *Marriage Dowry.*

Women members who have contributed continuously on a scale not less than 4d. per week for a period of three years from 1st January, 1928, and who are not disentitled to benefit by reason of Schedule II. (*c*) shall be entitled to a grant of £2 on marriage.

158. Benefits.

AMALGAMATED ENGINEERING UNION SCALES OF BENEFIT, 1926

SCHEDULE.

TABLE OF CONTRIBUTIONS AND BENEFITS.

Section.	Weekly Contributions.	Weekly Contribution and Entrance Fee Combined. For First Six Months.	Benefits. Unemployment.	State Unemployment.
1	1s. 6d.	Men not exceeding 22 years of age 1s. 8d., plus 1d. per week for each additional year up to 45. (Men over 40 not accepted, unless rejoining.)	Under five years member and over one year:— First 14 weeks, 10s. per week. Next 20 weeks, 8s. ,, Next 18 weeks, 6s. ,, Five years member and under ten years:— First 14 weeks, 10s. per week. Next 30 weeks, 8s. ,, Next 34 weeks, 6s. ,, Ten years member and over:— First 14 weeks, 10s. per week. Next 30 weeks, 8s. ,, Continuous, 6s. ,,	State benefit to the full extent allowed by statutory regulations.

Benefits—(Contd.)

Sick.	State Sick.	Superannuation.	Accident.	Tools.	Funeral.
Under five years member:— First 20 weeks, 10s. per wk. Next 32 weeks, 5s. „ Five years member and under ten years:— First 26 weeks, 10s. per wk. Next 78 weeks, 5s. „ Ten years member and over:— First 26 weeks, 10s. per wk. Continuous after above, 5s. per week.	Members on Health Insurance Section who are approved through the Society will receive the full State benefit allowed by statute in addition to Trade Union benefit.	If 25 years a member and 55 years of age or over, 7s. per wk. If 30 years a member and 55 years of age or over, 8s. per wk. If 35 years a member and 55 years of age or over, 9s. per wk. If 40 years a member and 55 years of age or over, 10s. per wk.	A free member permanently disabled from working or any of the trades covered by the membership of the union is entitled to a maximum of £100. Legal assistance shall be paid at discretion of the E.C.	Entitled to benefit for loss of tools, but not to exceed £10.	£12; or £5 for wife, leaving £7 for member. (Between six and twelve months' membership, £5.

TABLE OF CONTRIBUTIONS AND BENEFITS—Contd.

Section.	Weekly Contributions.	Weekly Contribution and Entrance Fee Combined. *For First Six Months.*	Benefits. *Unemployment.*	*State Unemployment.*
2	1s.	Men not exceeding 22 years of age 1s. 2d., plus 1d. per week for each additional year up to 45. (Men over 40 not accepted, unless rejoining.)	First 14 weeks, 10s. per week. Next 10 weeks, 5s. " Next 6 weeks, 2s. 6d. "	State benefit to the full extent allowed by statutory regulations.
3	6d.	Men not exceeding 22 to not exceeding 28, 8d. Men exceeding 28 to not exceeding 35, 9d. Men exceeding 35 to not exceeding 40, 10d. Men over 40, 11d.	First 8 weeks, 8s. per week. Next 8 weeks, 5s. " When on dispute the 5s. is paid for a total period of 44 weeks.	State benefit to the full extent allowed by statutory regulations.
4	3d.	Youths not more than two years in the shops, 3d. After two years, 4d.	—	—

Sick.	State Sick.	Superannuation.	Accident.	Tools.	Funeral.
2 Less than ten years member:— First 14 weeks, 8s. per wk. Next 10 weeks, 4s. ,, Next 6 weeks, 2s. 6d. ,, Ten years member and over:— First 14 weeks, 10s. per wk. Next 10 weeks, 5s. ,, Next 6 weeks, 2s. 6d. ,,	Members on Health Insurance Section who are approved through the Society will receive the full State benefit allowed by statute in addition to Trade Union benefit.	If 25 years a member and 55 years of age or over, 4s. per wk. If 30 years a member and 55 years of age or over, 5s. per wk. If 35 years a member and 55 years of age or over, 6s. per wk. If 40 years a member and 55 years of age or over, 7s. per wk.	A free member permanently disabled from working at any of the trades covered by the membership of the union is entitled to a maximum of £60. Legal assistance shall be paid at discretion of E.C.	Entitled to benefit for loss of tools, but not to exceed £6.	£8 ; or £3 for wife, leaving £5 for member. (Between six and twelve months' membership £3.)
3 —	Members on Health Insurance Section who are approved through the Society will receive the full State benefit allowed by statute.	—	Legal assistance only.	Entitled to benefit for loss of tools, but not to exceed £6.	£5 ; £2 10s. over 55 years of age on admission.
4 First 26 weeks, 5s. per wk. Next 52 weeks, 2s. 6d. ,,	Members on Health Insurance Section who are approved through the Society will receive the full State benefit allowed by statute in addition to Trade Union benefit.	—	Legal assistance only.	Entitled to benefit for loss of tools, but not to exceed £5.	£5

TABLE OF CONTRIBUTIONS AND BENEFITS—Contd.

Section.	Weekly Contributions.	Weekly Contribution and Entrance Fee Combined.	Benefits.	
			Unemployment.	State Unemployment.
5	9d.	1s. per week for first 10 weeks, irrespective of age.	5s. per week for 15 weeks in any period of 52 weeks.	State benefit to the full extent allowed by statutory regulations.
			Dispute benefit of 10s. per week for 8 weeks, inclusive of the 5s. donation benefit, and contingent benefit in accordance with Rule 28, subject to the dispute being endorsed by the Executive Council, and Legal assistance.	
5ᴬ	6d.	—	Dispute benefit of 10s. per week for 8 weeks, subject to the dispute being endorsed by the Executive Council, and Legal assistance.	—

Benefits—(Contd.)

	Sick	State Sick.	Superannuation.	Accident.	Tools.	Funeral.
5 (Industrial Section)	—	Members on Health Insurance Section who are approved through the Society will receive the full State benefit allowed by statute.	—	Legal assistance only.	—	—
5ᴬ (Industrial Section)	—	Members on Health Insurance Section who are approved through the Society will receive the full State benefit allowed by statute.	—	Legal assistance only.	—	—

159. Contributions and Benefits.

FROM THE REPORT OF THE GENERAL COUNCIL TO THE TRADES UNION
    CONGRESS, 1927, adopted by Congress.   *T.U.C. Ann. Report,*
    1927, p. 110 ff.

CONTRIBUTIONS AND BENEFITS.

Reference has already been made to this subject, and it has been
shown that rates of contributions and benefits always become a
serious question when amalgamation proposals are under consideration.

The matter has therefore been closely surveyed, and this has
entailed the exploration of masses of detail, which show that at
present there is no real measure of uniformity.

The variation in contributions is almost wholly determined by the
benefits which are payable.   It is not possible to set out detailed
comparisons of benefits in the space of this report, but some idea is
given in the summary of evidence in the appendix.

The statement has been made by certain unions that the low rates
of contributions payable in contemporary unions create a form of
unfair competition, and that in some instances part of this variation
is accounted for by the fact that one union has to bear the expense for
all negotiating machinery, the results of which are shared by the
other unions.   Where this exists it has been likened to the action of
a non-unionist who is prepared to accept the advantages fought for by
Trade Unions without having contributed towards them.

Possible Adjustments.

The General Council realises that it is impracticable to suggest
that there should be a standard rate for contributions and benefits
throughout the whole Trade Union Movement, largely on account
of the fact that the demands upon the funds of different classes of
unions vary as the result of many causes.   Certain types of unions
cater for industries with less risk of unemployment than others,
whilst some have administrative and negotiating machinery so complex as to demand a slightly higher management contribution, whilst
in certain cases special trade benefits, such as tool insurance, are
necessary.   The General Council is of opinion, however, that in
closely related unions a greater measure of similarity in scales of
contributions and benefits would remove many practical difficulties
in regard to amalgamation, tend to reduce undesirable competition

for members, and in time of industrial dispute, assure a similar measure of support to all those directly concerned.

An important point in connection with negotiating is, of course, that negotiators should feel that they have not only a well-organised membership behind them, but that there are adequate fighting funds which can be utilised in a struggle to maintain or improve wages and working conditions. The result of even a short strike upon the finances of a union is sufficient evidence in support of the claim that contributions should be sufficient, not only to enable a Trade Union to withstand attacks upon the standard of life of its members, but also to ensure that when the struggle is over a rapid recovery of its financial position is possible.

Provident Benefits.

Turning to the question of provident benefits, it is difficult to compile information which would reveal the percentage of lapsed members in those unions with low contributions as compared with that in unions where contributions are comparatively high, with correspondingly high benefits, but it is well-known that a member contributing for special benefits is loath to lose his title to those benefits by allowing his membership to lapse.

Generally speaking, it may be assumed that provident benefits are an important factor in preventing great fluctuations in membership. By this, the General Council would not infer that the provision of provident benefits is the most important function of Trade Unionism, but rather that benefits which are a form of insurance materially assist in maintaining a state of organisation necessary for efficient Trade Union action, and, furthermore, in their own interests Trade Unionists are usually prepared to pay a contribution which is adequate to provide assistance for sickness, death, and certain other benefits.

The question of contributions and benefits has already been referred to as one of the obstacles which have been encountered in bringing schemes of amalgamation to fruition. The opinion of the General Council has also been expressed that one of the most practical approaches to the problem of reducing the number of unions would be to obtain a greater degree of uniformity in this direction.

160. Legal Enforcement of Trade Union Benefits in certain Cases.

TRADE DISPUTES AND TRADE UNIONS ACT, 1927 ; 17 & 18 Geo. V., ch. 22.

2.—(1) No person refusing to take part or to continue to take part in any strike or lock-out which is by this Act declared to be illegal, shall be, by reason of such refusal or by reason of any action taken by him under this section, subject to expulsion from any trade union or society, or to any fine or penalty, or to deprivation of any right or benefit to which he or his legal personal representatives would otherwise be entitled, or liable to be placed in any respect either directly or indirectly under any disability or at any disadvantage as compared with other members of the union or society, anything to the contrary in the rules of a trade union or society notwithstanding.

161. Trade Unions—Political Objects.

TRADE UNION ACT, 1913 ; 2 & 3 Geo. V., ch. 30.

3.—(1) The funds of a trade union shall not be applied, either directly or in conjunction with any other trade union, association, or body, or otherwise indirectly, in the furtherance of the political objects to which this section applies (without prejudice to the furtherance of any other political objects), unless the furtherance of those objects has been approved as an object of the union by a resolution for the time being in force passed by a ballot of the members of the union taken in accordance with this Act for the purpose by a majority of the members voting ; and where such a resolution is in force, unless rules, to be approved, whether the union is registered or not, by the Registrar of Friendly Societies, are in force providing—

(a) That any payments in the furtherance of those objects are to be made out of a separate fund (in this Act referred to as the political fund of the union), . . . and

(b) That a member who is exempt from the obligation to contribute to the political fund of the union shall not be excluded from any benefits of the union, or placed in any respect either directly or indirectly under any disability or at any disadvantage as compared with other members of the union (except in relation to the control or management of the political fund) by reason of his being so exempt, and that contribution to the political fund of the union shall not be made a condition for admission to the union.

(2) If any member of a trade union alleges that he is aggrieved by a breach of any rule made in pursuance of this section, he may complain to the Registrar of Friendly Societies, and the Registrar of Friendly Societies, after giving the complainant and any representative of the union an opportunity of being heard, may, if he considers that such a breach has been committed, make such order for remedying the breach as he thinks just under the circumstances ; and any such order of the Registrar shall be binding and conclusive on all parties without appeal and shall not be removable into any court of law or restrainable by injunction, and on being recorded in the county court, may be enforced as if it had been an order of the county court. In the application of this provision to Scotland the sheriff court shall be substituted for the county court, and ' interdict ' shall be substituted for ' injunction.'

(3) The political objects to which this section applies are the expenditure of money—

(a) on the payment of any expenses incurred either directly or indirectly by a candidate or prospective candidate for election to Parliament or to any public office, before, during, or after the election in connexion with his candidature or election ; or

(b) on the holding of any meeting or the distribution of any literature or documents in support of any such candidate or prospective candidate ; or

(c) on the maintenance of any person who is a member of Parliament or who holds a public office ; or

(d) in connection with the registration of electors or the selection of a candidate for Parliament or any public office ; or

(e) on the holding of political meetings of any kind, or on the distribution of political literature or political documents of any kind, unless the main purpose of the meetings or of the distribution of the literature or documents is the furtherance of statutory objects within the meaning of this Act.

The expression ' public office ' in this section means the office of member of any county, county borough, district, or parish council, or board of guardians, or of any public body who have power to raise money, either directly or indirectly, by means of a rate.

(4) A resolution under this section approving political objects as an object of the union shall take effect as if it were a rule of the union and may be rescinded in the same manner and subject to the same provisions as such a rule.

(5) The provisions of this Act as to the application of the funds of a union for political purposes shall apply to a union which is in whole or in part an association or combination of other unions as if the individual members of the component unions were members of that union and not the unions ; but nothing in this Act shall prevent any such component union from collecting from any of their members who are not exempt on behalf of the association or combination any contributions to the political fund of the association or combination.

4.—(1) A ballot for the purposes of this Act shall be taken in accordance with rules of the union to be approved for the purpose, whether the union is registered or not, by the Registrar of Friendly Societies, but the Registrar of Friendly Societies shall not approve any such rules unless he is satisfied that every member has an equal right, and, if reasonably possible, a fair opportunity of voting, and that the secrecy of the ballot is properly secured.

162. Trade Unions' Political Funds.

TRADE DISPUTES AND TRADE UNIONS ACT, 1927; 17 & 18 Geo. V., ch. 22.

4.—(1) It shall not be lawful to require any member of a trade union to make any contribution to the political fund of a trade union unless he has at some time after the commencement of this Act and before he is first after the thirty-first day of December, nineteen hundred and twenty-seven, required to make such a contribution delivered at the head office or some branch office of the trade union, notice in writing in the form set out in the First Schedule to this Act of his willingness to contribute to that fund and has not withdrawn the notice in manner hereinafter provided ; and every member of a trade union who has not delivered such a notice as aforesaid, or who, having delivered such a notice, has withdrawn it in manner hereinafter provided, shall be deemed for the purposes of the Trade Union Act, 1913, to be a member who is exempt from the obligation to contribute to the political fund of the union, and references in that Act to a member who is so exempt shall be construed accordingly :

Provided that, if at any time a member of a trade union who has delivered such a notice as aforesaid gives notice of withdrawal thereof, delivered at the head office or at any branch office of the trade union, he shall be deemed for the purposes of this subsection to have withdrawn the notice as from the first day of January next after the delivery of the notice of withdrawal.

For the purposes of this subsection, a notice may be delivered personally or by any authorised agent and any notice shall be deemed to have been delivered at the head or a branch office of a trade union if it has been sent by post properly addressed to that office.

(2) All contributions to the political fund of a trade union from members of the trade union who are liable to contribute to that fund shall be levied and made separately from any contributions to the other funds of the trade union and no assets of the trade union, other than the amount raised by such a separate levy as aforesaid, shall be carried to that fund, and no assets of a trade union other than those forming part of the political fund shall be directly or indirectly applied or charged in furtherance of any political object to which section three of the Trade Union Act, 1913, applies; and any charge in contravention of this subsection shall be void.

(3) All rules of a trade union made and approved in accordance with the requirements of section three of the Trade Union Act, 1913, shall be amended so as to conform to the requirements of this Act, and as so amended shall be approved by the Registrar of Friendly Societies (in this Act referred to as ' the Registrar ') within six months after the commencement of this Act or within such further time as the Registrar may in special circumstances allow, and if the rules of any trade union are not so amended and approved as aforesaid they shall be deemed not to comply with the requirements of the said section.

(4) Notwithstanding anything in this Act, until the thirty-first day of December, nineteen hundred and twenty-seven, it shall be lawful to require any member of a trade union to contribute to the political fund of the trade union as if this Act had not been passed.

(5) If the Registrar is satisfied, and certifies, that rules for the purpose of complying with the provisions of this section, or for the purposes of the Trade Union Act, 1913, as amended by this Act, which require approval by the Registrar have been approved by a majority of the members of a trade union voting for the purpose, by the executive or other governing body of such a trade union, or by a majority of delegates of such a trade union voting at a meeting called for the purpose, the Registrar may approve those rules and those rules shall thereupon have effect as rules of the union notwithstanding

that the provisions of the rules of the union as to the alteration of rules or the making of new rules have not been complied with.

(6) Section sixteen of the Trade Union Act, 1871 (which provides for the transmission to the Registrar of annual returns by registered trade unions), shall apply to every unregistered trade union so far as respects the receipts, funds, effects, expenditure, assets and liabilities of the political fund thereof.

First Schedule.

FORM OF POLITICAL FUND CONTRIBUTION NOTICE.

Name of Trade Union...

Name of member's branch (if any)....................................

POLITICAL FUND (CONTRIBUTION NOTICE).

I HEREBY give notice that I am willing, and agree, to contribute to the Political Fund of the
Union and I understand that I shall, in consequence, be liable to contribute to that Fund and shall continue to be so liable unless I deliver at the head office, or some branch office, of the Union a written notice of withdrawal : I also understand that after delivering such a notice of withdrawal I shall still continue to be liable to contribute to the political fund until the next following first day of January.

A..................B...................

Address.....................................

Membership number (if any)............

............day of........................19......

163. Political Rules.

MODEL RULES ISSUED BY THE CHIEF REGISTRAR, 1927.

Rules for Political Fund.

1. The objects of the Trade Union shall include the furtherance of the political objects to which Section 3 of the Trade Union Act, 1913, applies, that is to say, the expenditure of money—
   (*a*) on the payment of any expenses incurred either directly or indirectly by a candidate or prospective candidate for election to

Parliament or to any public office, before, during, or after the election in connection with his candidature or election ; or

(*b*) on the holding of any meeting or the distribution of any literature or documents in support of any such candidate or prospective candidate ; or

(*c*) on the maintenance of any person who is a member of Parliament or who holds a public office ; or

(*d*) in connection with the registration of electors or the selection of a candidate for Parliament or any public office ; or

(*e*) on the holding of political meetings of any kind, or on the distribution of political literature or political documents of any kind, unless the main purpose of the meetings or of the distribution of the literature or documents is the furtherance of statutory objects within the meaning of the Act, that is to say, the regulation of the relations between workmen and masters, or between workmen and workmen, or between masters and masters, or the imposing of restrictive conditions on the conduct of any trade or business, and also the provision of benefits to members.

The expression 'public office' in this rule means the office of member of any county, county borough, district, or parish council, or board of guardians, or of any public body who have power to raise money, either directly or indirectly, by means of a rate.

2. Any payments in the furtherance of such political objects shall be made out of a separate fund (hereinafter called the political fund of the union).

No assets of the union, other than the amount raised by the separate levy provided in Rule 7, shall be carried to the political fund of the union, and no assets of the union other than those forming part of the political fund of the union shall be directly or indirectly applied or charged in furtherance of any such political objects as aforesaid ; and any charge in contravention of this provision shall be void.

3. No member of the union shall be required to make any contribution to the political fund of the union unless he has delivered, as provided in Rule 6, at the head office or some branch of the union notice in writing, in the form set out in Rule 4, of his willingness to contribute to that fund, and has not withdrawn the notice in manner provided in Rule 5. Every member of the union who has not delivered such a notice or who, having delivered such a notice, has withdrawn it in manner provided in Rule 5, is to be deemed for the

purpose of these rules to be a member who is exempt from the obligation to contribute to the political fund of the union.

4. The form of notice of willingness to contribute to the political
fund of the union is as follows :

FORM OF POLITICAL FUND CONTRIBUTION NOTICE.

Name of Trade Union...

Name of member's branch (if any)....................................

POLITICAL FUND (CONTRIBUTION NOTICE).

I HEREBY give notice that I am willing, and agree, to contribute to
the Political Fund of the
Union and I understand that I shall, in consequence, be liable to
contribute to that Fund and shall continue to be so liable unless I
deliver at the head office, or some branch office, of the Union a
written notice of withdrawal ; I also understand that after delivering
such a notice of withdrawal I shall still continue to be liable to contribute to the political fund until the next following first day of
January.

A.................B..................

Address.......................................

Membership number (if any)............

............day of.........................19......

5. If at any time a member of the union, who has delivered such
a notice as is provided for in Rules 3 and 4, gives notice of withdrawal thereof, delivered, as provided in Rule 6, at the head office
or at any branch office of the union, he shall be deemed to have
withdrawn the notice as from the first day of January next after
the delivery of the notice of withdrawal.

6. The notices referred to in Rules 3, 4 and 5 may be delivered
personally by the member or by any authorised agent of the member,
and any notice shall be deemed to have been delivered at the head
or a branch office of the union if it has been sent by post properly
addressed to that office.

7. All contributions to the political fund of the union from
members of the union who are liable to contribute to that fund
shall be levied and made separately from any contributions to the
other funds of the union.

The contribution to the political fund of the union shall be the sum of   d. payable [annually] [quarterly] [monthly] [weekly] on

8. A member who is exempt from the obligation to contribute to the political fund of the union shall not be excluded from any benefits of the union, or placed in any respect either directly or indirectly under any disability or disadvantage as compared with other members of the union (except in relation to the control or management of the political fund of the union) by reason of his being so exempt.

9. Contribution to the political fund of the union shall not be made a condition for admission to the union.

10. If any member alleges that he is aggrieved by a breach of any of these rules for the political fund of the union, he may complain to the Chief Registrar of Friendly Societies, and the Chief Registrar, after giving the complainant and any representative of the union an opportunity of being heard, may, if he considers that such a breach has been committed, make such order for remedying the breach as he thinks just in the circumstances ; and any such order of the Chief Registrar shall be binding and conclusive on all parties without appeal and shall not be removable into any court of law or restrainable by injunction, and on being recorded in the county court, may be enforced as if it had been an order of the county court.

11. The executive committee shall cause to be printed, as soon as practicable after the approval and registration of these rules for the political fund of the union, a number of copies thereof having at the end copies of the certificates of approval and registration sufficient for the members of the union, and a further number for new members, and shall send to the secretary of each branch a number of copies sufficient for the members of the branch.   The secretary of each branch shall take steps to secure that every member of the branch, so far as practicable, receives a copy of these rules, and shall supply a copy to any member at his request.   A copy thereof shall also be supplied forthwith to every new member on his admission to the union.

The provisions of this rule shall apply to the present alteration and any subsequent alterations of the rules for the political fund of the union.

12. A return in respect to the political fund of the union shall be transmitted by the union to the Chief Registrar of Friendly Societies before the first day of June in every year prepared and made up to such date and in such form and comprising such particulars as

the Chief Registrar may from time to time require, and every member of the union shall be entitled to receive a copy of such return, on application to the treasurer or secretary of the union, without making any payment for the same.

Signatures of three members of the executive body of the trade union.

1...

2...

3...

164. Political Activities of Trade Unions.

Mr. Winston Churchill in the House of Commons.   Parl. Deb., 30th May, 1911.

I should have no hesitation in saying that it is quite impossible to prevent trade unions from entering the political field.   The sphere of industrial and political activity is often indistinguishable, always overlaps, and representation in Parliament is absolutely necessary to trade unions, even if they confine themselves to the most purely industrial forms of action, and the moment you touch representation you reach the very heart and centre of political life, because the disputes as to representation raise every question of general politics and party politics which can be imagined. . . . In the great majority of cases workmen do not feel injured even if their very small contributions are taken to support trade union politics with which they do not agree.   They do not in the great majority of cases object.   Many of them do not think very much about it.   Very few workmen, luckily for them, are cursed with logical or theological subtleties of mind. They do not mind, in practice and as a general rule in the great majority of cases, paying for their union politics, which they regard as advancing the interests of their class, then voting for a different political party which they regard as advancing political affairs upon another road at the same time.   There is a great deal more sense and deep reason and sagacity in that lack of logical subtlety than might appear upon the surface. . . . It is not good for trade unions that they should be brought in contact with the courts, and it is not good for the courts.   The courts hold justly a high and, I think, unequalled prominence in the respect of the world in criminal cases, and in civil cases between man and man, no doubt, they deserve and command the respect and admiration of all classes in the community, but where class issues are involved, it is impossible to pretend that the courts command the same degree of general confidence. On the contrary, they do not, and a very large number of our population have been led to the opinion that they are, unconsciously no doubt, biassed. . . . We know perfectly well that the trade union movement ought to develop, ought not to be stereotyped, ought to have power to enter a new field and to make new experiments. . . . We wish to set the trade unions free to develop their efforts, to build up in this country a minimum standard of life and labour, and to secure the happiness of the people.

165. Conscientious Objection to Political Contributions.

The Osborne Judgment and After, by W. M. GELDART, p. 41.

The conclusion would seem to be that if trade unions are to be allowed to take part in politics there must be a conscience clause for the conscientious objector. What are the proper limits of conscientious objection may be difficult as an abstract question ; it is not usually difficult to settle in practice. . . . Now the dissentient trade unionist is entitled to demand not only that he shall not be compelled to subscribe to a fund which is to be devoted solely to political purposes of which he disapproves, but also that specific sums shall not be taken for the like purpose out of the general funds to which he contributes. . . .

On the other hand, he cannot reasonably make a point of conscience of the fact that the union has a policy of which he may disapprove, and backs that policy with all the influence at its command. . . . To allow a conscience clause for the dissenting unionist is not the same thing in principle as to make the payment a purely voluntary one. Vaccination was not made optional when relief was given to the conscientious objector.

Some evidence of conscientious objection must be given before the plea can be allowed. So the union which decides to raise a political fund may fairly ask that those who refuse to contribute shall definitely state that they object. Mere indifference coupled with a willingness to throw a common burden on others has no right to masquerade as conscience.

It may be suggested that if the conscientious objector is to be allowed to stand out it would be simpler that trade unions should give up definitely any attempt at political action in their corporate capacity, and that those of their members who desire political action should form distinct societies for the purpose. That this is a desirable course is a view held not only by those who stand apart from the political party with which trade unions are at present identified, but by some, I believe, who would claim to be not the least advanced in the ranks of that party.

Now if the majority, or even an active and considerable minority, hold that this is the better course there is an end of the matter : trade unions as such will cease from political activity as soon as there ceases to be a largely preponderant opinion among trade unionists in its favour. The question is one for trade unionists themselves to settle. But if there is an overwhelming feeling, as there seems likely to be for some time to come, among trade unionists in favour of corporate political action, there are two reasons which make it desirable that the law should openly allow them such action. In the first place, the political society which took over the political work of trade unions would probably be formed on the basis of the union organisation : every union would have its counterpart in a corresponding political society consisting substantially of the same members and staffed largely by the same officers. The political society would in fact, but not in name, be merely the trade union acting in another capacity, and questions might arise at every turn which of the nominally distinct bodies was concerned.

In the second place, if there is any danger of unfair pressure being put on dissentients, it would seem that the danger is far less where the dissentient's position is openly recognised and legally protected than it would be if political activity subject to the conscience clause was allowed to trade unions.

166. Fair Wages Clause.

CLAUSE INSERTED IN GOVERNMENT CONTRACTS, AND FURTHER CLAUSES INSERTED AS RECOMMENDED BY THE FAIR WAGES ADVISORY COMMITTEE.

The Fair Wages Clause, T.U.C. and Labour Party, 1923, p. 3.

1. The contractor shall in the execution of his contract observe and fulfil the obligation upon contractors specified in the resolution passed by the House of Commons on the 10th March, 1909, namely :

' The contractor shall, under the penalty of a fine or otherwise, pay rates of wages and observe hours of labour not less favourable than those commonly recognised by employers and trade societies (or in the absence of such recognised wages and hours, those which in practice prevail amongst good employers) in the trade in the district where the work is carried out. Where there are no such wages and hours recognised or prevailing in the district, those recognised or prevailing in the nearest district in which the general industrial circumstances are similar shall be adopted.

Further, the conditions of employment generally accepted in the district in the trade concerned shall be taken into account in considering how far the terms of the Fair Wages Clause are being observed. The contractor shall be prohibited from transferring or assigning, directly or indirectly, to any person or persons whatever, any portion of his contract without the written permission of the Department. Sub-letting other than that which may be customary in the trade concerned shall be prohibited.

The contractor shall be responsible for the observance of the Fair Wages Clause by the sub-contractor.'

2. EXHIBITION OF NOTICE AT WORKS. The contractor shall cause the preceding condition to be prominently exhibited, for the information of his workpeople, on the premises where work is being executed under the contract. In trades where it is the practice the contractor shall also cause to be exhibited, or have available for inspection, a copy of any signed agreement determining the rates of wages and hours of labour commonly recognised by employers and trade socieites in the district.

3. INSPECTION OF WAGES BOOKS, ETC. The contractor shall keep proper wages books and time sheets showing the wages paid and so far as practicable the time worked by the workpeople in his employ in and about the execution of the contract, and such wages books and time sheets shall be produced whenever required for the inspection of an officer authorised by the Department.

4. FACTORY CLAUSE. (For inclusion in contracts in certain trades.) All work executed under the contract shall be carried out at the contractor's own factory or workshop at .... or other place approved by the Department, and no work under the contract shall be done in the homes of the workpeople.

5. DIRECT PAYMENT OF WAGES. (For inclusion in contracts in certain trades.) All wages earned by workers engaged on work under the contract shall be paid directly to them and not through a foreman or others supervising or taking part in the operations on which the workers are engaged.

167. Labour Party.

Constitution and Standing Orders, 1927.

Labour Party Ann. Rep., 1927, p. 275.

1.—Name.

The Labour Party.

2.—Membership.

The Labour Party shall consist of all its affiliated organisations,[1] together with those men and women who are individual members of a local Labour Party, who subscribe to the Constitution and Programme of the Party, and who, if eligible for Trade Union membership, are Trade Unionists.

3.—Party Objects.

NATIONAL.

(*a*) To organise and maintain in Parliament and in the country a Political Labour Party, and to ensure the establishment of a Constituency Labour Party in every County Constituency and every Parliamentary Borough, with suitable divisional organisation in the separate constituencies of Divided Boroughs ;

(*b*) To co-operate with the General Council of the Trades Union Congress, or other Kindred Organisations, in joint political or other action in harmony with the Party Constitution and Standing Orders ;

(*c*) To give effect as far as may be practicable to the principles from time to time approved by the Party Conference ;

(*d*) To secure for the producers by hand or by brain the full fruits of their industry, and the most equitable distribution thereof that may be possible, upon the basis of the common ownership of the means of production and the best obtainable system of popular administration and control of each industry or service ;

(*e*) Generally to promote the Political, Social, and Economic Emancipation of the People, and more particularly of those who depend directly upon their own exertions by hand or by brain for the means of life.

INTER-DOMINION.

(*f*) To co-operate with the Labour and Socialist organisations in the Dominions and the Dependencies with a view to promoting the purposes of the Party and to take common action for the promotion

[1] Trade Unions, Socialist Societies, Co-operative Societies, Trades Councils, and Local Labour Parties.

of a higher standard of social and economic life for the working population of the respective countries.

(*g*) To co-operate with the Labour and Socialist organisations in other countries and to assist in organising a Federation of Nations for the maintenance of Freedom and Peace, for the establishment of suitable machinery for the adjustment and settlement of International Disputes by Conciliation or Judicial Arbitration, and for such International Legislation as may be practicable.

4.—Party Programme.

(*a*) It shall be the duty of the Party Conference to decide, from time to time, what specific proposals of legislative, financial, or administrative reform shall receive the general support of the Party, and be promoted, as occasion may present itself, by the National Executive and the Parliamentary Labour Party : provided that no such proposal shall be made definitely part of the General Programme of the Party unless it has been adopted by the Conference by a majority of not less than two-thirds of the votes recorded on a card vote.

(*b*) It shall be the duty of the National Executive and the Parliamentary Labour Party, prior to every General Election, to define the principal issues of that Election which in their judgment should be made the Special Party Programme for that particular Election Campaign, which shall be issued as a manifesto by the Executive to all constituencies where a Labour Candidate is standing.

(*c*) It shall be the duty of every Parliamentary representative of the Party to be guided by the decision of the meetings of such Parliamentary representatives, with a view to giving effect to the decisions of the Party Conference as to the General Programme of the Party.

5.—The Party Conference.

1. The work of the Party shall be under the direction and control of the Party Conference, which shall itself be subject to the Constitution and Standing Orders of the Party.   The Party Conference shall meet regularly once in each year, and also at such other times as it may be convened by the National Executive.

2. The Party Conference shall be constituted as follows :

(*a*) Trade Unions and other societies affiliated to the Party may send one delegate for each 1,000 members on which fees are paid.

(*b*) Constituency Labour Party delegates may be either men or women resident or having a place of business in the constituency they represent, and shall be appointed as follows :—

In Borough and County Constituencies returning one Member to Parliament, the Constituency Labour Party may appoint one delegate.

In undivided Boroughs returning two Members, two delegates may be appointed.

In divided Boroughs one delegate may be appointed for each separate constituency within the area. The Constituency Labour Party within the constituency shall nominate and the Central Labour Party of the Divided Borough shall appoint the delegates. In addition to such delegates the Central Labour Party in each Divided Borough may appoint one delegate.

An additional woman delegate may be appointed for each constituency in which the number of affiliated and individual women members exceeds 500.

(*c*) Trades Councils under Section 8, clause *c*, shall be entitled to one delegate.

(*d*) The members of the National Executive, including the Treasurer, the Members of the Parliamentary Labour Party, and the duly-sanctioned Parliamentary Candidates shall be *ex-officio* members of the Party Conference, but shall, unless delegates, have no right to vote.

6.—*The National Executive.*

(*a*) There shall be a National Executive of the Party consisting of twenty-three members (including the Treasurer), elected by the Party Conference at its regular Annual Meeting, in such proportion and under such conditions as may be set out in the Standing Orders for the time being in force, and this National Executive shall, subject to the control and directions of the Party Conference, be the Administrative Authority of the Party.

(*b*) The National Executive shall be responsible for the conduct of the general work of the Party. The National Executive shall take steps to ensure that the Party is represented by a properly constituted organisation in each constituency in which this is found practicable ; it shall give effect to the decisions of the Party Conference ; and it shall interpret the Constitution and Standing Orders and Rules of the Party in all cases of dispute subject to an appeal to the next regular Annual Meeting of the Party Conference by the organisation or person concerned.

(*c*) The National Executive shall confer with the Parliamentary Labour Party at the opening of each Parliamentary Session, and also at any other time when the National Executive or the Parliamentary Party may desire such conference on any matters relating to the work and progress of the Party, or to the efforts necessary to give effect to the General Programme of the Party.

7.—*Parliamentary Candidatures.*

(*a*) The National Executive shall co-operate with the Constituency Labour Party in any constituency with a view to nominating a Labour Candidate at any Parliamentary General or By-Election. Before any Parliamentary Candidate can be regarded as finally adopted for a constituency as a candidate of the Labour Party, his candidature must be sanctioned by the National Executive.

(*b*) Candidates approved by the National Executive shall appear before their constituencies under the designation of 'Labour Candidate' only. At any General Election they shall include in their Election Addresses and give prominence in their campaigns to the issues for that Election as defined by the National Executive from the General Party Programme. If they are elected they shall act in harmony with the Constitution and Standing Orders of the Party in seeking to discharge the responsibilities established by Parliamentary practice.

8.—*Affiliation Fees.*

1. Trade Unions, Socialist Societies, Co-operative Societies, and other organisations directly affiliated to the Party (but not being affiliated Constituency Labour Parties or Trades Councils) shall pay 3d. per member per annum to the Central Party Funds with a minimum of 30s.

The membership of a Trade Union for the purpose of this clause shall be those members contributing to the political fund of the Union established under the Trade Union Act, 1913.

2. The affiliation of Trades Councils will be subject to the following conditions :

(*a*) Where Constituency Labour Parties and Trades Councils at present exist in the same area every effort must be made to amalgamate these bodies, retaining in one organisation the industrial and political functions, and incorporating the constitution and rules for the Constituency Labour Parties in the rules of the amalgamated body.

(*b*) Where no Constituency Labour Party is in existence and the

Trades Council is discharging the political functions, such Trades Council shall be eligible for affiliation as a Constituency Labour Party, providing that its rules and title be extended so as to include Constituency Labour Party functions.

(*c*) Where a Constituency Labour Party and a Trades Council exist in the same area, the Trades Council shall be eligible to be affiliated to the Constituency Labour Party, but not to the National Party except in such cases where the Trades Council was affiliated to the National Party prior to November 1, 1917. In these cases the Executive Committee shall have power to continue national affiliation on such conditions as may be deemed necessary.

(*d*) Trades Councils included under Section (*c*) shall pay an annual affiliation fee of 30s.

3. Constituency Labour Parties must charge individually enrolled members, male a minimum of 1s. per annum, female 6d. per annum ; and 2d. per member so collected must be remitted to the Central Office, with a minimum of 30s. as the affiliation fee of such Constituency Labour Party.

4. In addition to these payments, a delegation fee of 10s. to the Party Conference or any Special Conference may be charged.

9.—*Condition of Eligibility of Delegates from Constituent Bodies to either Constituency or Local Labour Parties or to any National or Local Conference of the Labour Party*.

Every person nominated to serve as a delegate shall individually accept the Constitution and principles of the Labour Party.

STANDING ORDERS.

1.—Annual Conference.

. . . .

4. Persons eligible as delegates must be paying *bona fide* members, or paid permanent officials of the organisation sending them.

5. No delegate to the Conference shall represent more than one Society, and no Member of Parliament who has not joined the Parliamentary Labour Party is eligible as a delegate.

6. Every person nominated to serve as a delegate shall individually accept the Constitution and principles of the Labour Party.

7. Members of affiliated organisations claiming exemption from political contributions under the Trade Union Act, 1913, shall not be entitled to act as delegates.

. . . . . .

3.—*Voting*.

Voting at the Party Conference shall be by Cards issued as follows :

Trade Unions and other affiliated societies shall receive one Voting Card for each 1,000 members or fraction thereof paid for.

Trades Councils affiliated under Section 8, Clause *c*, shall receive one Voting Card.

Every Constituency Labour Party shall receive one Voting Card for each delegate sent in respect of each Parliamentary Constituency within its area.

Central Labour Parties in Divided Boroughs shall receive one Voting Card.

4.—*National Executive*.

1. The National Executive shall be elected by the Annual Conference, as a whole, and shall consist, apart from the Treasurer, of (*a*) 13 representatives of the affiliated organisations ; (*b*) five representatives of the Constituency Labour Parties ; and (*c*) four women. The Executive shall be elected by ballot vote on the card basis from three lists of nominations confined to delegates appointed to attend the Annual Conference.

2. Each affiliated national organisation shall be entitled to nominate one candidate for LIST A ; and two candidates if the membership exceeds 500,000. Each candidate must be a *bona fide* member of the organisation by which he or she is nominated.

3. Each Parliamentary Constituency organisation, through its Constituency Labour Party or Trades Council, may nominate one candidate for LIST B, and the candidate so nominated must be resident or have his or her place of business within the area of the nominating Constituency Labour Party.

4. Each affiliated organisation shall be entitled to nominate one woman candidate for LIST C, and two candidates if the membership exceeds 500,000, whether such nominees are or are not members of the nominating organisation.

5. The National Executive shall elect its own Chairman and Vice-Chairman at its first meeting each year and shall see that all its officers and members conform to the Constitution and Standing Orders of the Party.

6. No member of the General Council of the Trades Union Congress is eligible for nomination to the National Executive.

7. The consent of candidates must be secured before their nomination for office.

8. The National Executive shall present to the Annual Conference a Report covering the work and progress of the Party during its year of office, together with the Financial Statement and Accounts duly audited, which shall be in the hands of the Local Parties and affiliated organisations at least 14 days before the opening of the Annual Conference.

. . . .

Conference Decisions re Non-affiliated Political Parties.

At the 24th and 25th Annual Conferences held in London and Liverpool in 1924 and 1925, the following Resolutions were passed :

1. That the application for affiliation from the Communist Party be refused.

2. That no member of the Communist Party shall be eligible for endorsement as a Labour Candidate for Parliament or any Local Authority.

3. (*a*) No member of the Communist Party shall be eligible to become a member of any Individual Section of any Affiliated Local Labour Party, or be entitled to remain a member.

(*b*) The National Executive also desires to intimate to the Conference that in its opinion affiliated Trade Unions can only act consistently with the decisions of the Annual Conference in its relation to the Communists by appealing to their members, when electing Delegates to National or Local Labour Party Conferences or meetings, to refrain from nominating or electing known members of non-affiliated Political Parties, including the Communists.

168. Placing of Unemployed Members.

RULES OF THE LONDON SOCIETY OF COMPOSITORS, 1925.

XLV.—Call-Book Regulations.

The Call-Book, in which unemployed compositors holding clear cards of membership, and not more than eight weeks in arrear, as well as those holding temporary working cards, may insert their names in numerical order, subject to the following rules, shall remain open from 8.30 a.m. till 1 p.m. from Monday till Friday, and from 8.30 a.m. till 12 noon on Saturday :

(*a*) The Call-Book shall be placed in the Society House. All members, on becoming unemployed, shall place their names therein in order of arrival, and the book shall remain open for signatures from 8.30 a.m. till 1 p.m. each day, Saturdays 12 noon.

(*b*) Each day, from first signing till procuring employment, each member shall place his initial in the column for that day opposite his name.

(*c*) All names not crossed off by each Tuesday shall be copied in exact order by the assistant, for use the following week.

(*d*) Any member writing another member's name in the book shall forfeit his own position, as well as that of the member for whom he signs.

(*e*) No member intoxicated on the premises shall be entitled to any benefit from the Call or Unemployed Claim Books for that day.

(*f*) No member shall be allowed to sign the book whilst in work, or while not in a position to accept work.

XLVI.—*Rules Governing Calls.*

The following shall be the regulations governing members who have signed the Call-Book :

(*a*) All calls for workmen received at the Society House shall state for what class of work the men are required, and shall be given to the members first on the list who are able to accept such calls. The calls shall be made at 11.45 a.m., 3.30 p.m., and 5 p.m. each day. In cases of urgency, the Secretary shall exercise his discretion as to the time of giving the call.

(*b*) Any member whose name appears on the Call-Book must accept whatever appropriate call may come to his name in numerical order, or have his name erased from the Call and Unemployed Claim Books for the day.

(*c*) Employers, Overseers, or their agents may choose workmen from the list, irrespective of the position in which their names appear on the book ; but the members so chosen may, if they think fit, refuse such employment, unless of those present they are first in order on the book.

(*d*) Any member obtaining employment by a call or calls from the Society House, when such work amounts to 13s., shall, on its completion, place his name at the bottom of the list.

(*e*) Any member obtaining employment through personal application or otherwise (not being a call from the book), shall not lose his position therein, unless employed or having work to go to the following morning.

(*f*) Should any member, after having obtained a call, forfeit such call by neglect or irregularity, he shall be suspended from all the privileges of membership for one month.

(*g*) All members sent from the Society House shall bear a document signed by the Secretary, certifying the bearer or bearers to be the members attending in obedience to the call, unless the person applying for workmen shall accompany the members sent ; but no call shall be transferred to another member except with the approval of the Secretary.

(*h*) Should any officer be proved to have given calls to members of the Society except from the Call-Book, he shall be immediately suspended by the Committee, and dealt with as they think fit.

(*i*) No member of the Society in receipt of strike pay shall take precedence of calls at the Society House.

(*k*) Any member intercepting, in the street or elsewhere, a messenger with a call that is intended for the Secretary, shall be dealt with by the Committee as they may determine.

(*l*) All calls shall be filed by the Assistant, with the name of the member or members sent, the time, and the nature of the call responded to.   Such record shall be kept at least twelve months, and shall be accessible to any member or members, upon application to the Committee.

169. The Service of Statistics.

From *The Association of Engineering and Shipbuilding Draughtsmen, Its Structure and Work*, 1928, p. 11.

In the early days of the Association, soon after its foundation in Glasgow, it became evident that it was necessary to collect and classify all ascertainable information of conditions of employment for drawing offices throughout the country.   The necessity for the compilation of these particulars, and their dissemination amongst members, was all the greater since there were no standard conditions agreed upon between draughtsmen and their employers for hours worked, payment for overtime, payment for and duration of holidays, payment during sickness, and rates of salaries.   The possession of this information enabled the draughtsmen to know what to expect when moving from one post to another.

The provision, therefore, of a service of A.E.S.D. statistics would have been a natural consequence, even if there had not been still more weighty reasons for the collection of data.   The most important of these reasons is obviously that collective bargaining with employers (the Association's chief function) would be very difficult without such statistics. Another advantage of almost equal importance, however, is to be found in the ability to provide up-to-date wage information for members who are in touch with prospective employers. The practice of consultation of the A.E.S.D. by members has been growing gradually until it is now no uncommon thing for ten to twenty letters or telegrams to be received in the course of a day at Headquarters, and it is found that about five-sixths of these can be answered, on the average, from Statistics Schedules. In order to facilitate matters, special postcards can be had on application, either to Branch Secretaries or to the General Secretary. These postcards, which are addressed in front to A.E.S.D. Headquarters, only require the filling in of the name and address of the firm and the name and address of the member. The usual procedure at Headquarters is to deal with this type of communication before any other, the replies being sent off immediately.

The value of these replies to individuals is very clear. Enquirers are thus put in a position to obtain proper rates of salary, and other conditions, besides being safeguarded against taking a job with a firm known to be a bad employer, or even with some firm with which the Association may be in dispute.

As mentioned above, often in the past it has been a common assumption that so long as increase in salary was got when changing employment other things could be taken for granted. It is apparent, however, as a result of the Association's investigations, that it is also highly desirable to have a knowledge of the firm's reputation, the holidays given, the staff conditions, and whether or not there is payment for overtime. Apart from these very important particulars it does not follow that because a member is getting a larger salary by going to another office he is obtaining as much as he should obtain in comparison with similar men already employed at the firm concerned. The A.E.S.D. statistics service can safeguard this and it helps to prevent inadvertent undercutting with inevitable loss to the individual and possibly also to his fellow members and future office colleagues.

The next step in Association policy in regard to the Service of Statistics depended on the result of a ballot of members which was taken on the question of obligatory consultation of the Association before taking situations. The result of the ballot was in favour of such consultation, and the consequent policy whereby all members write Headquarters before taking a post is now in successful operation.

170. Technical Interests of Trade Unions.

From *The Association of Engineering and Shipbuilding Draughtsmen, Its Structure and Work*, 1928, p. 16.

From eight to twelve original pamphlets, ranging from about 40 to 80 well-illustrated pages, dealing with engineering or shipbuilding subjects, written mainly by A.E.S.D. members, are published each session. Of these over 120,000 have been sold during the past eight years, at the extremely cheap price of 1s. per copy, to members.

A prominent employer has expressed himself as of the opinion that the A.E.S.D. pamphlets are 'the best technical publications on the market.' A further development has also been made by the publication of two high-class text-books, and a new series, consisting of data sheets, sold at the very cheap rate of 2d. These data sheets, like the pamphlets, contain charts and other information directly useful to the members in their work. Loose covers are also on sale for convenient keeping of both pamphlets and data sheets.

Works visits have become a valued Association activity at many branches. Parties are organised by the local technical committees for inspecting interesting engineering and other establishments, ranging from a ship to a wireless broadcasting station. On many occasions the popularity is so great that the numbers attending have to be limited and tickets balloted for.

A considerable number of branches have a syllabus of lectures which are mainly technical, but also contain lectures of a general cultural or educational type.

The A.E.S.D. technical activities may be described as, in essence, practical papers by the men on the jobs, *directly* usable, and related to everyday technical requirements of all—from the junior to the highest skilled senior draughtsman or designer.

All branches get grants in aid of technical work, based on the sales of A.E.S.D. pamphlets in their area. Part of the funds of the A.E.S.D. are also available for expenses of lectures, visits, etc.

171. The Trade Union Label.

AMERICAN FEDERATION OF LABOR PROCEEDINGS, 1905, p. 26.

The issuance of a label by our unions is at once a declaration of our earnest desire to serve all our people best, and a guarantee that the article it adorns is the product of labor under the most sanitary and comparatively fairer conditions than otherwise obtained.

It is an appeal to the sympathy and co-operation of our fellows to be helpful in the work for material, moral and social improvement of all our people.   In no more tangible way can a sympathetic public render effective service to their brothers and sisters of toil than by demanding the union label.   There is no duty which our fellow workers, and particularly our fellow unionists, should more cordially and consistently adhere to than the demand for the union label and the union card.

Because of the good it does and can do, because of its effectiveness as a potent factor in our life's work as individuals and in our organised capacity, we should, in our national conventions, international unions, state, central, and local bodies, propagate the work of creating a healthier and more general demand and insistence for the insignia of honest, sanitary, and fair conditions of labor, the union label.

172. Trade Union Practices.

RESTORATION OF PRE-WAR PRACTICES ACT, 1919 ; 9 & 10 Geo. V.,
ch. 42.

1.—(1) Where, in any establishment to which this Act applies, any rule, practice or custom obtaining before the war in any industry or branch of an industry (hereinafter referred to as a trade practice) has, during and in consequence of, the present war, been departed from, the owner of that establishment shall be under an obligation, at the expiration of two months from the passing of this Act, to restore or permit the restoration of the trade practice so previously obtaining, and for one year after such restoration is effected, or if it has been effected before the date of the passing of this Act for one year after that date, to maintain or permit the continuance of the trade practice.

(2) Where any industry or branch of industry, which before the war was not carried on in an establishment, commenced to be carried on in the establishment during the war and continues to be carried on therein after the termination thereof, or where the establishment is one which commenced to be worked after the beginning of war, the owner of the establishment shall be under the obligation, at the expiration of two months from the passing of this Act, to introduce or permit the introduction of, and for one year after such introduction is effected, or if it has been effected before

the date of the passing of this Act for one year after that date, to maintain or permit the continuance of, such trade practices as obtained before the war in other establishments where that industry or branch was carried on under circumstances most nearly analogous to those of the establishment in question.

173. Trade Union Practices.

Temporary Surrender during the War and their Recognition by the Government

E. S. MONTAGU, MINISTER OF MUNITIONS, IN THE HOUSE OF COMMONS, PARL. DEB., 15th August, 1916.

But the cessation of disputes and the postponement of the reforms which slowly emerged from the clash of conflicting interests do not exhaust the full measure of the sacrifices which organised Labour has made.   The Trade Unions place on one side the whole armour of Trade Union regulations upon which they had hitherto relied.   For the weapons slowly forged during long years of struggle—rules and customs relating to hours of labour, overtime, the right of entrance to trades, demarcation of industry, the regulation of boy labour, and the exclusion of women from certain classes of occupations—all these, directly or indirectly, might have tended to reduce the output during the War.   The Government asked Labour to put all these on one side.   It was a great deal to ask.   I doubt if any community has ever been asked for greater sacrifices ; but with a loyalty and statesmanship which cannot be over-estimated, the request was readily granted.   The Trade Unions required, and they were right to require, a scrupulous record and recognition of what they were conceding.   It was promised to them as a right, but they will receive more—not only the restoration of the system they temporarily abandoned, but the gratitude of the army, and of the nation, and they will, I trust, place the nation still further in their debt by playing an important part in devising some system which will reconcile in the future conflicting industrial interests.

174. ' Trade Practices.'

RULES OF NAT. SOC. OF BRASS AND METAL MECHANICS, 1927.

Rule 30.—Instructions to Members, which will be strictly enforced.

CLAUSE I.—A member wishing to leave one manufactory to go to another with the intention of improving his position, should first seek the advice of the secretary or emergency committee, and if such member acts according to the advice given he shall, if he be legally discharged from such manufactory, receive such benefit as he may be entitled to.

CLAUSE 2.—All workmen leaving situations are recommended to give every information to their fellow-members about to take their places in an honourable manner.

CLAUSE 3.—Members are strongly advised not to take any situation advertised until enquiries have been made of the secretary or shop steward.

CLAUSE 4.—All members on attaining the age of 21 must receive not less than the minimum rate of the district, including the conditions of such district.

CLAUSE 5.—No member in the polishing trade shall be allowed to employ women as polishers.

CLAUSE 6.—All men employed in factories shall be paid direct from office, under-hand labour shall be abolished, and members should co-operate to end the system.

CLAUSE 7.—Where members under 18 years of age are required to work piecework they shall be paid the full man's piecework price.

CLAUSE 8.—Members shall only be allowed to contract on a payment by result system, and employ under-hands, on the following conditions : That the district rates shall be guaranteed ; and, after the time rates have been deducted from the earnings of the team, any surplus balance shall be shared, *pro rata*, direct through the office.

CLAUSE 9.—When once a piece price is fixed or bonus agreed upon, the same shall not be reduced without change of method of production. *No member to introduce the piecework system into a time-work shop.* Where piece-work system is adopted, prices to be fixed by a committee of workmen, and when once a piece-work price is fixed or bonus agreed upon the same shall not be reduced without change of method of production.

CLAUSE 10.—Change of address must be notified as per Rule 49.

CLAUSE 11.—All accidents shall be reported to the society so that members may receive advice in their claim for compensation.

CLAUSE 12.—Any member of this society being in the militia, army reserve, territorial corps or special constabulary, meeting with an accident while pursuing those duties, shall not have any claim upon this society's funds, excepting in case of death, or what they are entitled to under the National Health Insurance Acts. (*See Part II. of these Rules.*)

CLAUSE 13.—The Society on no account shall be used for capitalistic military purposes.

175. Overtime and Nightshift Rules.

RULES OF NAT. SOC. OF BRASS AND METAL MECHANICS, 1927.

Rule 34.—Overtime.

Except where better conditions prevail, which shall still be recognized, subject to sanction of N.E.C., members called upon to work overtime shall insist on receiving as follows :—

OVERTIME ON DAYSHIFT.

(*a*) A full day shall be worked before overtime is reckoned, with the following exceptions, viz.:—Time lost through sickness certified to the satisfaction of the employers ; lying off on account of working all the previous night ; absence with leave or enforced idleness.

(*b*) Where works are on short time no overtime shall be paid for work done between the full time starting hour and the full time stopping hour, but work beyond these limits shall be paid for as overtime provided the full shortened day has been worked.

(*c*) A workman working through his meal hour shall be paid at overtime rate unless an equivalent period is allowed.

(*d*) Overtime worked either before or after the normal working hours shall be paid at the rate of time and half except in the case of work done between midnight and the commencement of the following day shift by a workman who continues working until after midnight, in which case it shall be paid at double time.

(*e*) In the event of a workman being called upon to return to work after having ceased work and gone home for the day, overtime shall commence and be paid for from the time of restarting at the rate payable for that hour as though he had worked continuously.

(*f*) A workman sent home between midnight and 2 a.m. shall be paid double time for the hours worked after midnight and receive an allowance of time and half for working hours between the time when he is sent home and 6 a.m.

(*g*) A workman sent home after 2 a.m. shall be paid double time for the hours worked after midnight and receive an allowance of double time for working hours between the time he is sent home and 6 a.m.

(*h*) All hours worked between 12 midnight Saturday and 12 midnight Sunday shall be paid double time.

(*i*) Payment for overtime shall be calculated on dayshift rates.

NIGHTSHIFT.

(*a*) Nightshift is where men, other than dayshift men, work throughout the night for not less than three consecutive nights.

(*b*) A full nightshift week shall consist of 47 working hours worked on five nights with one or two breaks for meals, each night, to be mutually arranged. Time lost through sickness certified to the satisfaction of the employers ; lying off on account of working all the previous day ; absence with leave or enforced idleness shall not be taken into account.

(*c*) Nightshift shall be paid at the rate of time and a third for all hours worked. Hours worked after the full night has been worked shall be paid at the rate of time and two-thirds.

(*d*) Nightshift men shall receive double time for all hours worked between Saturday midnight and Sunday midnight. Work done on Saturday other than above, and on Monday morning until the day-shift starting hour, shall be paid time and two-thirds.

(*e*) Dayshift men who have worked during the day beyond the mid-day meal hour and are required to go on nightshift the same night shall be paid overtime rates for the night's work. Dayshift men who have been notified that they have to go on nightshift the same night and are allowed home before the mid-day meal hour that day shall be paid nightshift rates.

(*f*) Payment for nightshift and for overtime on nightshift shall be calculated on dayshift rates.

176. Trade Unions and Restriction of Output.

The Waste of Capitalism, published by THE TRADES UNION CONGRESS
AND THE LABOUR PARTY, 1924, p. 94.

Two of the most frequent and most bitter charges which employers make against workers are that labour deliberately restricts output by ca' canny methods, Trade Union rules and restrictions, and other means, and that labour opposes the introduction of labour-saving machinery.

One of the most frequent and most weighty charges which the workers bring against capitalism is that there is no security of employment, but, on the contrary, the perpetual menace of unemployment, bringing poverty and ruin in its train. We shall see that these charges and counter charges have a great deal to do with each other.

First of all, what are the facts ? As regards the introduction of labour-saving machinery, we have shown elsewhere that the opposition to, or neglect of, such machinery comes in almost every industry from the employers' side. We are all aware that in the past the workers have frequently opposed the displacement of labour by new machinery, but in modern times their organisations adopt no such policy. It is impossible to maintain that such opposition is, or has for many years been, generally adopted by labour, though naturally it is possible to find isolated instances here and there just as it is easy to find a similar attitude taken up by individual employers.

.   .   .   .

As a matter of fact, there is a good deal of confusion in the use of the term ' restriction of output by Trade Union rules and customs.' When employers use the phrase they generally mean that certain Trade Union requirements do, in fact, lead to lower production than would otherwise be possible. This will be readily admitted, but the point is that these rules or customs have not been devised for the express purpose of restricting production ; they are merely necessary safeguards against the various methods by which the workers' standard of life and of working conditions may be lowered, and they have been proved by much bitter experience to be absolutely essential. Such safeguarding of the workers' standard is one of the primary reasons for the existence of Trade Unions. The rules and customs of these organisations only restrict production in the same sense that the laws of the land were thought to restrict it by hygienic standards, maximum hours, etc. We now know that such standards tend in the long run to increase production (though we should still consider them necessary if they did not), and the same is, we claim, true of Trade Union standards. When the workers deny that there is general restriction on their part they mean that there is no deliberate, conscious restriction. When such deliberate restriction does occur in isolated cases it is due to the fear of unemployment or lower wages resulting from unlimited output, *i.e.*, to the position of insecurity in which the worker is placed under the present system.

The economists and the employers have frequently drawn attention to this ' fallacy ' of the working man's supposition that labour-saving machinery or unlimited output can result in unemployment It is no fallacy, however, except when long views are taken. The worker cannot afford to take long views.   If he is thrown out of work because fewer men are needed, on the introduction of a new machine, or because, output having been unlimited, the job is finished, there is no consolation in the reflection that ultimately there will be a greater demand for labour as a result of the increase in production and lower costs.   The Iron and Steel Trades Departmental Committee admitted this in the following words :—' The distribution of labour is often seriously affected by the introduction of new processes, appliances and machinery, and doubtless hardship, even if of a temporary nature, often results by reason of the supersession of labour by machinery.   In consequence, there has been a marked tendency to insist upon the retention of as large a number of men as possible when new machinery has been introduced, thus making for an uneconomical distribution of labour.   The Committee believe that the expansion of the scope of associations of workmen and employers would give the means of devising better expedients for the re-distribution of labour which has become superfluous than are possible at the present time.'   This is the policy pursued by the Unions : not to resist the progress of invention, an utterly futile and unnecessary course, but to ensure that the introduction of labour-saving methods shall be so arranged that the workers do not suffer.   If the interests of the labour concerned are safeguarded, no opposition to labour-saving is offered by the Trade Union Movement.   Individual workers or groups, however, somewhat naturally adopt the other course if there is any doubt as to their security of employment, and they cannot be blamed for so doing. The remedy is obvious—security of employment must be guaranteed in all cases, and at wages and under conditions not less favourable than those previously enjoyed.

. . . .

Unless such security is guaranteed, either by pledges having reference to this particular matter, or preferably by general schemes for preventing unemployment or providing full wages during such periods of unemployment as cannot be avoided, it is idle to expect that these forms of restriction of output can be eliminated. . . . What we can say is that security of employment, with maintenance of standards, is an essential without which no other changes will suffice to remove the suspicions and fears which are now present in the minds of the workers.

177. Organisation of Trade Union Campaign.

NATIONAL CAMPAIGN AGAINST TRADE DISPUTES AND TRADE UNIONS
BILL, 1927. *T.U.C. Ann. Rep.*, 1927, p. 251.

Organisation of Campaign.—Machinery.

In considering the provisions necessary for the conduct of the campaign it was felt that in order to carry the agitation to all parts of the country it was advisable to work on the basis of the National Labour Party's constituency machinery already in existence.

The country was therefore divided into nine regions as follows :—

1. North Eastern.—2. North Western.—3. Midlands.—
4. Eastern Counties.—5. Home and Southern Counties.—
6. South Western.—7. London.—8. Wales.—9. Scotland.

Political regional and local officers were already at the disposal of the Labour Party, and it was felt that these officers should be supplemented by industrial officers. Nine industrial regional officers were therefore appointed, who were in each case full-time officials of an affiliated Trade Union.

To secure the services of industrial district and local officers it was necessary to communicate with the affiliated unions asking for the names and addresses of full-time officials whose services could be placed at the disposal of the General Council for full-time or part-time service during the period of the campaign. The unions were asked to accept responsibility for the salaries of the officials whose services were utilised, the General Council being responsible for travelling and incidental expenses. In response to this appeal 247 offers were received, the majority of which were for part-time service. The names and addresses of these officials were sent to the appropriate industrial regional officers for their assistance in erecting the necessary district and local machinery, and also as speakers.

Within a short space of time 52 districts were set up, and progress was soon made in the organisation of local machinery.

. . . .

The duties of the officers responsible to the National Trade Union Defence Committee were as follows :

REGIONAL INDUSTRIAL AND POLITICAL OFFICERS.

(*a*) To set up the district machinery and assist in appointing the district industrial and political officers.

(*b*) To act in the closest co-operation for the general supervision of the machinery in their districts.

(*c*) To act in an advisory capacity to the National Committee, and as travelling officers of the National Trade Union Defence Committee under the control of the national officers.

DISTRICT INDUSTRIAL OFFICERS.

(*a*) Compiling a list of industrial speakers for Trade Union branch, club, and workgate meetings.

(*b*) The development and organisation of these meetings.

(*c*) Consultation with Trade Union branch and district officers in order to pay special attention to isolated Trade Union branches and factories, in order to ensure that the campaign was carried into every part of the district.

DISTRICT POLITICAL OFFICERS.

(*a*) Compiling a list of local speakers and arranging their services.

(*b*) Allotment of national speakers drafted into the district.

(*c*) Supervision of constituency organisations in the planning of meetings in connection with (*a*) and (*b*).

LOCAL OFFICERS.

The local officers who, in most cases though not all, were the secretaries of the local Trades Councils and the Divisional or Borough Labour Parties, were responsible for the actual conduct of the campaign in the localities.

Preliminary Conferences.

The first step which was taken after the appointment of regional officers was the calling of Conferences in 44 centres. Delegates invited to attend these Conferences were—

(*a*) representatives of Trade Union branches and District Committees ;

(*b*) representatives of local Divisional and Borough Labour Parties ;

(*c*) representatives of local governing bodies.

The Conferences in the main were held in the afternoon of the first or second Saturdays or Sundays after May Day, and were attended by two national speakers (one industrial and one political) together with a legal adviser. The purpose of the Conferences was to explain the Trade Disputes and Trade Unions Bill and its implications, and also the proposed methods of conducting the campaign.

.   .   .   .

As district and local officers were appointed local speakers' panels were compiled and the campaign proper was launched. The meetings which were held may be divided into two categories :

1. Public meetings.
2. Trade Union branch and workshop gate meetings.

Special attention was paid to country districts adjacent to the various localities, and arrangements were made by the National Committee to provide for the expenses of local speakers to these districts where the locality was itself unable to shoulder the burden. Reports show that this work was so comprehensive in character that villages were visited which had not been touched in any previous national campaign, and which were in some cases neglected even in times of a General Election.

Local Speakers.

It is impossible to state the number of meetings which have been held, but the speakers' panels which were compiled by the district officers are evidence of the extent to which local speakers assisted in the campaign, and their sustained efforts are worthy of the highest praise.

National Speakers.

In addition, national speakers were booked by the district officers through headquarters. The total number of such bookings was 650, covering a total of 1,150 meetings and demonstrations.

Demonstrations.

On June 26th monster demonstrations were held in many centres throughout the country in protest against the Trade Disputes and Trade Unions Bill, which had just passed the Third Reading. These demonstrations, though affected by the weather, aroused tremendous interest. The one which was held in Hyde Park illustrates what was done in the other centres on a smaller scale. For the Hyde Park demonstration the whole Industrial, Labour and Co-operative Movements united to make the occasion stand out in history. The main procession, including bands, decorated co-operative vehicles, scores of Trade Union banners, and many thousands of marchers, was the largest which has been held in the history of the Labour Movement. In addition to the main procession, the largest procession which has been known in West London marched independently to the park. Twelve platforms, from which the leaders of each section of the movement spoke, were surrounded by the huge crowds. At 5 o'clock a bugle sounded, speeches ceased, and the Trade Union Covenant was read. The bugle sounding a second time was the signal for tens of thousands of workers to raise their right hands pledging themselves to stand by the Trade Union Covenant. This scene was very impressive, and will long be remembered by those who attended.

General.

Reports which have been received from regional, district, and local officers and speakers show that the campaign exceeded anything which the movement has previously attempted, both in respect to the number of meetings held and the extent to which the campaign penetrated into villages and hamlets throughout the country. In fact, it may be truly said that the campaign was carried into the homes of the people.

178. Educational Activities.

EXTRACTS FROM REPORT OF THE TRADE UNION EDUCATION ENQUIRY COMMITTEE, 1921.

(Subsequently adopted by the Trades Union Congress.)

Since the inauguration of Ruskin College in 1899, trade union interest in the education of the workers has surely though slowly developed. The National Union of Railwaymen and the South Wales Miners' Federation have made themselves jointly responsible for the Labour College, an increasing number of unions are providing scholarships to the Labour College and Ruskin College, and affiliation to the W.E.A., the Plebs League, or the Scottish Labour College has become a fairly common practice.

These activities, however, express on the whole little more than a perfunctory regard for what is undoubtedly the most urgent problem of the working class movement, viz., the education of the worker.

Apart from the Iron and Steel Trades Confederation, to whose educational activities we make reference elsewhere in our report, no trade union has yet devised a way by which interest in education may be stimulated amongst its members and a demand—varying from single lectures to full-time courses of study—provided for and an educational enthusiasm and tradition developed within the trade union movement generally under conditions adequately controlled by the trade unions themselves.

How to make provision for what is undoubtedly a very varied demand, under conditions that will enlist the interest and confidence of the trade union movement as a whole, while at the same time complying with such State regulations as will make it possible for public funds to be used to meet costs of tuition, presents a series of problems which have as yet only been partially worked out.   Sufficient, however, has been accomplished to indicate the lines along which further extensive developments are, in our opinion, possible.

The importance of doing so has been expressed by Mr. Arthur Pugh, chairman of the W.E.T.U.C., at its conference held on October 16, and we venture to submit the following extract from his address :

It may be thought that the many difficulties facing the trade union movement make it inopportune to ask it to consider educational problems.   Yet those who hold positions of responsibility know that the very circumstances that make it appear inopportune only throw into bold relief the pressing need for courageously facing them.

.   .   .   .

The Necessity for Education.

The progress of working class organisation and outlook foreshadows the approach of fundamental changes in our social and industrial relations and gives education a new meaning to trade unionists.   It is therefore becoming more urgent that, so far as possible, trade unionists, but more especially those holding positions of responsibility in executive, district, and branch organisations, should be men and women having a wide range of knowledge germane to economic and political problems, and such trained capacity as will enable them not only to understand the immediate results of decisions and actions but also to foresee possible ultimate results.

Apart from these general considerations, the increasing activities of trade unions have called into existence a series of educational problems which can only be satisfactorily dealt with by trade unions accepting responsibility for the provision of suitable facilities.

A brief comparison between the activities of trade union branches and district organisations thirty years ago with those that obtain to-day will illustrate this striking change.   Trade union government involves an ever-increasing responsibility.   The administration of trade union rules and regulations has become more intricate and difficult, and each new amalgamation and federation increases these complexities.

Branch records require to be kept with greater accuracy than appeared to be necessary at the beginning of the period we are considering. Friendly benefit and unemployed benefit require to be administered, not only in compliance with the rules of the union, but also with the regulations governing the administration of the National Health Insurance and Unemployment Acts. In view of the equipment in secretarial staff and machinery of the modern employers' organisation, not only a practical and technical knowledge of the trade or industry, but mental alertness and trained minds are more and more essential if trade unions are to hold their own in negotiations around the conference table or before the arbitration court in dealing with thousands of matters affecting their members' standard of life. Vital questions of policy and principle tend to shift more and more from national executives to branch and district committees, and executive officers require to rely to an increasing extent on branch and district officers for such interpretation of their decisions as will maintain harmony and unity within the union.

The success of both trade negotiations and strikes is to-day a far truer measure of the intelligent loyalty of the members and the tact and trained judgment of branch and district officers than it was three decades ago. In addition, a greatly increased complexity in business organisations, necessitating a corresponding growth in the industrial and political activities of trade unions, both local and national, during the last twenty years, is one of the most significant developments of the century.

All this clearly points to the need for a corresponding development in educational activities. Many negotiations and strikes that have failed would have succeeded, and much other useful work might have been accomplished by the trade unions, if only a small portion of the money that has been spent in these struggles had been devoted to training the latent mental capacity of the men engaged in them.

The power, prestige, and influence of trade unionism rests on the mental calibre of its membership.

We have received memoranda from a number of representatives of national trade unions dealing with the educational needs of their respective organisations. The perusal of these proves conclusively that the subjects of study in which trade union members are interested are very diversified, that the demand is scattered, the standard of educational attainment aimed at is very varied, and that there exists a very extensive latent desire for education which has not yet been stimulated.

Diversity of Subjects of Study.

The subjects of study desired by trade union members cover the whole field of social science and many other subjects which are not usually included in this category, such as literature, music, and art. Usually working-class students begin by requesting facilities for the study of trade union history, industrial history, problems of industrial control, and economics.   These, however, only cover a small part of the wide range of subjects now being studied by trade union students. The following list of actual subjects studied, although far from complete, illustrates the diversified interests of trade union students :

Trade Union History and Problems	International Problems
Co-operative History and Problems	Psychology
Industrial History	Biology
Political History	Social Psychology
History of Social Movements	Sociology
Problems of Reconstruction	Philosophy
Industrial Administration	Literature
Local Government	Music
Economic Theory	Art
Political Theory	

Scattered Character of the Demand.

The difficulties in the way of making provision for such diversity of interests are increased by the fact that the demand in any given area is so scattered.   Undoubtedly the desire for educational opportunities in the aggregate is very great, but the actual number of students in any given area is as yet comparatively small.

Varied Standards of Attainment.

The standards of attainment aimed at are almost as varied as the subjects studied.   A rapidly increasing number of trade unionists attend educational lectures on subjects of interest to trade unions and the working-class movement generally, but only a percentage of these are prepared to undertake serious study.   Amongst those who do, the time which they are willing to devote to study varies from a few hours' reading at home, or attendance at Study Circles, to attendance at Three-Year Courses in Tutorial Classes, or residence for a period of years at the Labour College (London) or Ruskin College (Oxford).

The Extent of the Latent Demand.

Although trade union students attending classes and colleges now number several thousands, the number who are members of any one trade union, apart from the miners, railwaymen, and iron and steel workers, is in no case numerous. It may, therefore, be thought that if the number of active students who are members of one organisation represent the extent of the demand within that union, it is hardly justified in expending large sums in making provision for a demand that probably does not exist. We are of opinion, however, that, encouraging as has been the increase in the number of trade union students within recent years, it represents only a small portion of those who can be induced to enrol themselves as students if suitable methods are devised and right conditions provided.

The majority of working men and women leave school before they have acquired the reading, much less the study, habit. On leaving school new interests enter into their lives that take up all their spare time for periods from six to twenty or more years. Usually it is only when confronted with the more serious problems of life, or through interest in the aims and objects of their respective organisations, that the desire for study is awakened. For many reasons (one of the most important being their doubt as to their capacity to undertake study) they do not seek opportunities. This latent desire requires to be stimulated. Interest requires to be awakened. Help is needed to overcome early difficulties and the natural hesitancy associated with such an effort. The number of trade unionists who are in this position and who can be induced to avail themselves of educational opportunities suited to their needs and interests is undoubtedly very large, if they are assisted in the right way.

Varied Types of Colleges, Classes, etc., used to stimulate and provide for the demand.

The task of stimulating and providing for this scattered and varied demand for opportunities to study a very large number of subjects has, for the most part, been left to the Labour College (with which is associated the Plebs League), Ruskin College, and the W.E.A. In addition to these the Co-operative Movement conducts extensive educational activities for its own members.

The central authority for co-operative education is the Central Education Committee of the Co-operative Union. For the year 1913-14 the total number of students (junior and adult) attending classes under the supervision of the Central Education Committee was 21,953. Of these the number of adult students attending classes on non-vocational subjects has been given as 1,553.

A number of trades councils, local labour parties, and socialist organisations also organise classes and educational lectures under the auspices of their respective organisations.   The following illustrates how varied are the types of colleges, classes, etc., used to stimulate interest and provide facilities :

1.—RUSKIN COLLEGE.
    (*a*) Tuition in residence.
    (*b*) Tuition by correspondence.

2.—THE LABOUR COLLEGE AND PLEBS LEAGUE.
    (*a*) Tuition in residence.
    (*b*) External classes, lectures, and tuition by correspond-
        ence.

3.—THE WORKERS' EDUCATIONAL ASSOCIATION.
    (*a*) Short full-time courses, varying from one to four weeks
        in residence at Holybrook House.
    (*b*) Summer schools at Bangor, Oxford, Saltburn, Canter-
        bury, Cambridge, Repton, Shipham, and elsewhere.
    (*c*) Week-end schools.
  External
    (*a*) Tutorial three-year classes.
    (*b*) One-year classes.
    (*c*) Study circles, single lectures, courses of lectures.

4.—THE SCOTTISH LABOUR COLLEGE.
    Tuition in day and evening classes.
    Tuition by correspondence.

5.—Special summer schools, week-end schools, and short full-time courses organised by the W.E.T.U.C., Workers' Union, National Federation of Women Workers, and other trade unions.

Working Class Colleges and Educational Organisations.

The working class colleges and educational organisations which are primarily concerned with providing the varied educational facilities for trade unionists are :
    Ruskin College.
    The Labour College, with which is associated the Plebs League.
    The W.E.A. (Workers' Educational Association).
    The Scottish Labour College.

    .   .   .   .

The foregoing classification of the types of colleges, classes, schools, etc., used to stimulate interest and provide facilities represents a series of educational organisations and classes varying in method, standard of work, duration of study period, and subjects studied.

Financial Problems.

The diversified character of both the demand and the varied types of colleges, classes, etc., required to provide for it makes it clear that no one trade union can hope to meet adequately the varied needs of its members. The costs involved in organisation alone would amount to more than any union is yet prepared to expend. It is therefore necessary to consider how far it is possible to devise methods by which trade unions can use the services of the working class organisations and colleges that exist under conditions that will enable them to control policy, finance, and the kind of education provided for their members, and at the same time permit of public funds being used to meet the costs of tuition.

.   .   .   .

The aims and objects of trade unions are regarded by their members as both practical and idealistic. Their activities can therefore be summarised under two main headings :

1. Securing for the wage earners the best possible conditions under the existing system.

2. Entirely changing the industrial system by establishing in industry and society such democratic conditions and relations as will satisfy the legitimate aspirations of the working class.

From the standpoint of the former we hold that just as public funds are available to equip men and women to become experts in capitalist industry, so also should public funds be available to equip members of trade unions to become more efficient members of their respective organisations, for the reason that industrial progress is as dependent on the efficiency of trade unionism as on the efficiency of capitalist experts.

With reference to the second object we also submit that public funds should be available for the education of the members of trade unions. The numerical strength of our trade unions is such that, given a common purpose, it can, if it chooses to use the means at its disposal, entirely change the system.

The right of trade unions as a recognised part of the social and industrial system to use their power, influence, and prestige to effect a revolution in a constitutional way—*i.e.*, by consent—is not chal-

lenged.   If the right of trade unions to effect vast changes in a constitutional way is conceded, then we submit that public funds should
be available to equip trade unions for the task, as only by such means
can social and industrial changes that are now inevitable be effected
in a peaceable, constitutional way.

Moreover, the Board of Education, local education authorities,
and universities are no more than trustees of public money to be used
in the provision of education.   As such, their primary function should
be confined to satisfying themselves that the standard of education
attained by the students is such as justifies the payment of grant aid.

Neither Governments, universities, nor local authorities ought to
interfere with the social outlook of the classes, the books or authorities
consulted, or the opinions held by the students.

We know, however, that, despite the reasonableness of this claim,
there are education authorities and universities which are not prepared to concede it.   For this reason trade unions must retain for
themselves the right, so far as is necessary, to make educational
provision for their members independent of either universities or
local education authorities.   But to establish as a principle that trade
union funds can only be used in assisting to provide education,
independent of universities and local authorities, would either
impose a strain on the financial resources of trade unions which they
would find it impossible to bear or prevent trade unions from providing education for other than a comparatively small number of
their members.

For these reasons we recommend for your special consideration
the scheme adopted by the Iron and Steel Trades Confederation.

The Workers' Educational Trade Union Committee.

*The W.E.T.U.C. consists of a central committee and seven divisional
committees, which operate over all parts of England, Scotland and Wales
in which there are branches of the Iron and Steel Trades Confederation.   Each of these committees consists of representatives of the Confederation and the W.E.A., the Confederation in each case having the
majority representation.   The practice is for a member of the Confederation to be appointed as chairman and for the W.E.A. district
secretary to be appointed as organising secretary.   Each divisional
committee is responsible for organising the educational activities of the
Confederation within its own division.   They submit to the central
committee schemes of work, with estimates of cost, for which, if approved,
the costs are met from funds provided by the Confederation.*

By this method the Confederation has established an organisation which enables it to utilise the services of all educational organisations and institutions. It is thus able to organise and make provision for the most varied demands of its members in all parts of the country, while public funds are made available to meet the cost of tuition of those of its members attending classes complying with the Board of Education regulations. It retains control over finance, policy, and the kind of education provided for its members. It has avoided the heavy costs and dislocation of trade union business involved in building up an educational organisation of its own by using the W.E.A. organisation for this purpose, while retaining complete control over its own educational machinery.

. . . .

This remarkable development of educational activity amongst the members of one trade union is indicative of the possibilities in the scheme.

The constitution of the W.E.T.U.C. provides for other trade unions participating in the scheme under such conditions as will enable them to meet the needs of their members in an effective and economical way. Each union can determine the amount it desires to spend, the way in which it shall be spent, retaining control over its own finance and the kind of education provided. The constitution provides the means whereby trade union educational activities may be co-ordinated while leaving to each union complete freedom to decide its own educational programme.

By this means it practises ' control' as understood by the W.E.A., and ' independence' as understood by the Labour College, husbanding its funds to meet the cost of organisation, the provision of lectures, courses of lectures, week-end schools, etc., for which no public funds are available.

The financial advantage of this method to trade unions will be considerably increased in the near future. A recent report by the Government Committee on Adult Education strongly recommends that :

(a) Universities and local authorities should devote a considerable proportion of their revenue to the provision of adult education.

(b) Classes of adult students should be regarded as self-governing bodies, with the right to select their own subjects and the determining voice in the selection of their tutor.

In view, however, of the policy of economy on which the Government and local authorities have embarked there appears little likeli-

hood of these important recommendations being given effect to in
the near future, unless trade unionists (locally and nationally) bring
effective pressure to bear on the Treasury and local authorities.

.   .   .   .

Recommendations.

We therefore recommend :

(1) *The endorsement of the organisation set up by the Iron and
Steel Trades Confederation as an experiment which offers the basis of a
scheme providing the best and most economical means of :*

(a) *Co-ordinating the educational activities of trade unions.*

(b) *Enabling trade unions to meet the varied n eds of their
members by utilising the services of Universities, Ruskin College,
The Labour College, The Scottish Labour College, and the Workers'
Educational Association.*

(c) *Providing conditions that permit of trade unions supplement-
ing the activities of these bodies in any way they may deem necessary
in the interest of their members.*

(d) *Retaining control over finance, policy, and the education
provided.*

(2) *That educational institutions or organisations supported by
trade union funds must provide for adequate working-class control.*

(3) *That the rules of each trade union should provide for a portion
of its funds being available for educational purposes.*

(4) *That while each trade union must be free to make such arrangements as it believes to be in the best interests of its members as a whole,
the following general principles should govern any educational scheme
in which trade union funds are being expended :*

(a) *The scheme should be of such a character as will enable the
trade union to retain control over its own expenditure and the
education provided for its members.*

(b) *Classes attended by trade union students should be regarded as
self-governing bodies,* i.e., *the students to have the right to select their
own subject and the final voice in the appointment of the tutor, such
classes to come under the auspices of a* bona-fide *working class
organisation.*

(c) *That educational schemes approved by trade unions should, so
far as possible, aim at providing for the varied needs of their
members.*

(d) *That, apart from those colleges and classes which prefer not
to use public funds to meet the costs of tuition, public grants in aid*

of education should be utilised as far as possible—subject to the provisos contained in these recommendations—in meeting the costs of tuition.

(5) That the Parliamentary Committee of the Trades Union Congress be requested to make representation to the Board of Education as to :

(a) The importance of universities and local education authorities giving effect to the recommendations of the Committee on Adult Education.

(b) Establishing an Adult Education Fund to be administered by the Board working in conjunction with voluntary bodies concerned in adult working-class education. This fund to be devoted to assisting the educational work of organisations undertaking the provision of facilities which are ineligible for ordinary State grants and for pioneer work.

(c) Providing adequate maintenance for lads following the sea who are desirous of pursuing a continuous course of study.

(6) That trades councils make representation to their local education authorities with a view to their giving effect to the recommendations of the Committee on Adult Education.

179. Wages and Hours.

Trade Union Attitude to Attacks on Labour Standards.

Manifesto issued by the General Council of the T.U.C., 1923.
T.U.C. Ann. Rep., p. 160.

THE ATTACK ON LABOUR STANDARDS.

The Trades Union Congress General Council on the Defence.

The Trades Union Congress General Council, as representing the Trade Union movement, have received and considered reports from the organisations affiliated to Congress relating to the attempts by employers' associations to degrade labour standards by reducing wages and increasing the hours of labour.

The reports clearly indicate that many employers of labour, having forced substantial reductions in wages, are attempting to follow up these successes by a further attack on the most vital condition of employment, namely, the normal working-day or week.

Trade Union Standards in Danger.

The Trades Union Congress General Council view with alarm this attempt to deprive the organised workers of the principal advantage secured by over 60 years' Trade Union effort and sacrifice, and declare that this attempt must be met by determined and united resistance on the part of the Trade Union movement. The retention of a reasonable working day or week is a matter of vital concern for the workers, as representing the most important achievement of industrial organisation. The increase of leisure secured for the workers is a matter of importance as providing opportunities for education, physical development, and the possession of greater opportunities to devote some portion of their lives to the duties of citizenship and the responsibilities of domestic life.

The Workers' Share in Industrial Progress.

The reduction in the normal working day or week also represents, to a great extent, the workers' share in the achievements of modern industry. During the last 150 years industrial conditions have been revolutionised. Labour-saving devices have been introduced, steam and electric power have been developed, and the increased productive capacity of industry, following innumerable inventions and scientific discoveries, has enabled those who work by hand and brain to increase enormously their output.

We claim that these achievements should naturally lead to a reduction in the hours of labour, thus securing a reasonable standard of comfort for those employed in the productive and distributive undertakings of the country. If machine and electric power are to be labour-saving, it must not be at the expense of those who labour. If increased production is to make life easier for the workers, and improve their physical and mental capacity, then such improvement must be secured by reducing the normal working day or week. Otherwise the achievements of modern science, the triumphs of industrial invention, and the increased productivity of industry, will mean the exclusion of the workers from the natural advantages which should follow this kind of progress.

Conditions of Modern Industry.

We also call attention to the fact that the conditions of modern industrial development, such as the specialisation of industry and the subdivision of labour, tend to limit the opportunity for mental development in connection with industrial occupations. This tendency will seriously limit the mental development of the worker unless compensating opportunities are provided by restricting the hours of labour. The shorter working day or week will enable the worker to secure educational development if the changes in industrial life, which now limit the opportunity inside the factory, are utilised to increase the leisure time and opportunity for mental development at the end of the working day. We claim for the workers a share in the triumphs of civilisation and industrial progress. That share can only be obtained by a reduction in the hours of labour. Deprived of this valuable advantage, the workers will be unable to participate in any real sense in the achievements of modern industry.

In view of the foregoing, we must resist the extension of the normal working day or week even if it be demonstrated that such a change would increase the output of the worker. After careful and scientific investigation by impartial authorities it is on record that an increase in the hours of labour does not necessarily mean increased output per unit employed in industry. In several industries substantial reductions in the hours of labour have been effected without any serious reduction in output, and in certain cases output has been increased as the normal working day or week has been restricted.

Accumulated evidence also indicates that excessive hours of labour limit the efficiency, reduce the physique, and paralyse the mental capacity of the worker. These factors tend to limit the productive capacity of the worker apart from the psychological causes which operate when the worker suffers from an injustice created by the intolerable condition of excessive hours.

Trade Revival and Industrial Unrest.

The Trades Union Congress General Council, representing those who suffer from trade depression and who would gain by a trade revival, have also to warn the employers and the community generally regarding the dangers involved in further attacks on labour standards. The belief exists amongst organised workers that employers are determined to utilise the present slump for the purpose of degrading conditions of employment to the lowest possible point. The action of certain Employers' Federations fully justifies the impression that they consider the reduction of labour standards the line of least resistance as a means of cutting down expenditure and reducing the cost of production.

As one group of employers secures success others follow, and the low standards obtained in one industry are quoted in other industries as a reason why the worker should submit to reductions without protest. The conditions of labour in foreign countries are also being quoted to demonstrate to the British worker why his standard of life should be reduced.

Organised Labour will not adopt a policy which will hinder a revival of trade, but we cannot accept a degradation of the conditions of employment as a means for securing trade success, nor will the workers agree that trade prosperity secured by degrading their conditions of life and labour is in any way a success.

We are satisfied that attacks on Labour standards develop a serious state of Labour unrest and revolt.   A trade revival without industrial peace is impossible, and industrial peace is out of the question if attacks are made on organised Labour for the purpose of securing extensions of the normal working day or week.

United Resistance.

Accepting the responsibility for defending Labour standards, the Trades Union Congress General Council will encourage resistance to all attempts which may be made to degrade the conditions of Labour, and will use all the power at their disposal for the purpose of securing a united and determined stand against any effort which may be made by an employers' combination, however powerful, to resist the opportunities of the workers by extending either the normal working day or week.

180. The Standard Rate.

Industrial Democracy, by S. AND B. WEBB, 1920 ed., p. 279.

Among Trade Union Regulations there is one which stands out as practically universal, namely, the insistence on payment according to some definite standard, uniform in its application.   Even so rudimentary a form of combination as the ' shop club ' requires that all its members shall receive, as a minimum, the rate agreed upon with the foreman for the particular job.

The organised local or national Union carries the principle further, and insists on a Standard Rate of payment for all its members in the town or district.   The Standard Rate, it should be observed, is only a minimum, never a maximum. . . . In fact, though there are certain seeming exceptions with which we shall deal separately, we know of no case in which a Trade Union forbids or discourages its members from receiving a higher rate of remuneration, for the work actually performed, than the common Standard Rate fixed for the whole body.

But although the Standard Rate is a minimum, not a maximum,

the establishment of this minimum necessarily results in a nearer approximation to equality of rates than would otherwise prevail. . . .

This conception of a Standard Rate is, as we need hardly explain, an indispensable requisite of Collective Bargaining.   Without some common measure, applicable to all the workmen concerned, no general treaty with regard to wages would be possible.   But the use of a definite standard of measurement is not merely an adjunct of the Method of Collective Bargaining.   It is required for any wholesale determination of wages upon broad principles.

The most autocratic and unfettered employer spontaneously adopts Standard Rates for classes of workmen. . . . This conception of a constant standard of measurement the Trade Union seeks to extend from establishments to districts, and from districts to the whole area of the Trade within the kingdom.

181. The Principle of the National Minimum.

Mrs. Webb's Minority Report of the War Cabinet Committee
on Women in Industry (1919).   Cmd. 135, p. 274.

I think it impossible to avoid the conclusion that the prescription, and the resolute enforcement throughout the whole community, of minimum conditions of service, form an indispensable basis of any decent social order.   The case for what has been called the National Minimum appears to me to have been now fully demonstrated.   We have to assume that it is one of the primary duties of the Legislature and the Executive Government to provide for the prescription ; for the periodical adjustment ; for the adaptation to particular circumstances of localities and industries ; and for the systematic enforcement of such a national minimum, which should include, at least, the fundamental requirements of leisure, sanitation, education, and subsistence. . . .

The national minimum cannot be other than the basic minimum, below which, in the judgment of the community for the time being, it is nationally inexpedient to allow any human being to descend. It has nothing to do with the proper or desirable remuneration of labour, or with the share of the national income to which any or all of the sections of the wage-earning population may reasonably aspire.   Moreover, it includes no provision for the cost of acquiring skill or proficiency, or for any standard of life in excess of the national minimum, or other expenses which the performance of special duties or the fulfilment of particular functions may involve.   In fact, in any organised and civilised society, the continued existence of persons receiving no more than the national minimum, equipped with no more than universal training, possessing no specialised skill, and fulfilling no specific function, ought to become steadily more exceptional.

182. The Living Wage.

AGRICULTURAL WAGES (REGULATION) ACT, 1924; 14 & 15 Geo. V., ch. 37.

2.—(4) In fixing minimum rates a committee shall, so far as practicable, secure for able-bodied men such wages as in the opinion of the committee are adequate to promote efficiency and to enable a man in an ordinary case to maintain himself and his family in accordance with such standard of comfort as may be reasonable in relation to the nature of his occupation.

183. The Living Wage—Relativity of the Conception.

JUSTICE BROWN, IN THE PLUMBERS' CASE; S. Australian Industrial Reports, vol. i., 1916-18, p. 122.

The statutory definition of the living wage is a wage adequate to meet the normal and reasonable needs of the worker. In other words, the conception is ethical rather than economic. The Court has not to determine the value of the services rendered, but to determine what is necessary to meet normal and relative needs. It should be obvious that in the interpretation of reasonable needs the Court cannot be wholly indifferent to the national income. The reasonable needs of the worker in a community where national income is high are greater than the reasonable needs of the worker in a community where the national income is low.

184. Piecework.

RESOLUTION ADOPTED BY NATIONAL COMMITTEE MEETING OF THE AMALGAMATED ENGINEERING UNION, 1928.

Recognising that 75 per cent. of our membership are working on some system of payment by results, we, as a union, should recognise same, and negotiate for a National Agreement of Control.

185. Piece Rates—Relation to Time Rates.

AGRICULTURAL WAGES (REGULATION) ACT, 1924; 14 & 15 Geo. V., ch. 37.

4. Any worker employed in agriculture in any county on piece work for which no minimum piece rate has been fixed or any person authorised by such a worker may complain to the agricultural wages committee for the county that the piece rate of wages paid to the worker for that work is such a rate as would yield in the circumstances of the case to an ordinary worker a less amount of wages than the minimum rate for time work applicable in the case of that worker, and the committee may, on any such complaint after giving the employer an opportunity of making such representations as he thinks desirable, direct that the employer shall pay to the worker such additional sum by way of wages for any piece work done by him at that piece rate at any time within fourteen days before the date of complaint and before the decision of the committee thereon as in their opinion represents the difference between the amount which would have been paid if the work had been done by an ordinary worker at the minimum rate for time work and the amount actually received by the worker by whom, or on whose behalf, the complaint is made, and any sum so directed to be paid may be recovered by or on behalf of the worker from the employer summarily as a civil debt.

186. Piecework Agreement.

Memorandum of Conference between the Engineering and the National Employers' Federations and the Amalgamated Society of Engineers, Steam Engine Makers' Society, United Machine Workers' Association, Toolmakers' Society, Electrical Trades Union, Smiths and Strikers' Society, Brassfounders' Society, Amalgamated Instrument Makers' Trade Society, and Brassworkers' Society, held at Central Hall, Central Buildings, London, on 1st April, 1919.

Question Discussed.—Piecework.

Where, by reason of the introduction of the 47-hour week, a workman is not able to earn on piecework his previous remuneration on the same job the employer will undertake to recommend that suitable adjustments shall be made on the piecework price for that job.

It is agreed that piecework prices should be such as will enable a workman of average ability to earn at least $33\frac{1}{3}$ per cent. over present time rates (excluding war bonuses). Piecework prices once established shall not be altered unless the means or method of manufacture is changed.

Meantime it is agreed that where prices are such that on account of the reduction in hours the workman of average ability is unable to earn $33\frac{1}{3}$ per cent., the necessary adjustment should be made.

187. Piece-Rates—Notice against Cutting.

OFFICIAL NOTICE ISSUED TO WORKERS AT GOVERNMENT ORDNANCE FACTORY, WOOLWICH.

Piecework Earnings.

In order to remove any misapprehension which may exist, it is notified that no reductions are made in 'rate fixed' piecework prices unless changes are made in the method of production. When that takes place the prices are fixed having regard to such changes of method.

This, of course, does not apply to temporary or 'job' prices. The above has been the unaltered practice before the war, and will be so continued both during and after the war, without regard being paid to any special efforts which may now be made to expedite output.

No limitation has been or will be imposed on the earnings of pieceworkers.

(Signed)   H. F. DONALDSON,
Chief Superintendent of Ordnance
7th August, 1915.   *Factories.*

188. Collective Piecework.

Report of the Board of Trade (Labour Department) on Collective Agreements between Employers and Workpeople, 1910. Cd. 5366, p. xvi.

With respect to payment by results, it should be remarked that in many instances the work paid for is performed by a group of men working together. In the case of some piecework groups the members of the gang are all employed directly by one and the same employer; but in other cases the chief member of the group is a sub-employer, that is to say, a man who agrees with the principal

employer to get the work done for him with the assistance of workmen whom this 'sub-contractor' employs for this purpose.
Instances of sub-contract work are to be found among coal-hewers in
some districts, puddlers, and sheet millmen, among workmen of
certain classes employed in the shipbuilding industry, *e.g.*, angle-
smiths and platers, among cotton spinners and weavers, timber
porters, and a considerable number of other classes of workpeople.

Division of Piece-work among Group.

In those cases in which an employer gets work done by a number
of workpeople working together as a piece-work group, the methods
adopted in relation to the division of the piece-price are very various.

In some trades the lump piece-price paid for the labour of the
group is divided equally among all the members of the gang ; this
is the practice among, *e.g.*, corn porters in London.

In other trades the total amount received for the work is divided
between the workmen in certain fixed proportions, these proportions
being in some trades laid down in precise terms by the agreements
between employers and employed under which wages are regulated
in the industry. . . .

In some instances the arrangement made in relation to the division
of the lump sum paid for the performance of a piece-work job
carried out by a group of workmen is that the subordinate members
of the group shall receive out of this sum fixed rates of time-wages,
but shall not have any further claim, while the whole of the balance
remaining after deducting the time-wages of these assistants goes to
the principal member or members of the group.

This is the case, for example, in the shipbuilding industry in
relation to angle-smiths and platers.   It is of interest to observe
that in the instances just referred to, as in other similar cases (in
which workmen remunerated by piece-wages are assisted by helpers
paid by time-wages), the rate of time-wages paid to these assistants
will frequently be found to be higher than the ordinary rate paid for
the work concerned to men either working single-handed on time-
wages or assisting leading men employed on time-wages.

The reason is that in cases of this nature the helpers are expected
to work at 'piece-work speed' ; and since accordingly they do
more work per hour, they claim and receive a higher rate of pay per
hour than they would be entitled to if working under circumstances
not requiring them to put forth special exertion.

189. Cost-of-Living Sliding Scales.

From *Industrial Negotiations and Agreements*, pub. by the TRADES UNION CONGRESS AND LABOUR PARTY, 1922, p. 44.

The Cost of Living Sliding Scale is merely a piece of machinery for maintaining the purchasing power of money wages, leaving the workers' organisations free to concentrate on the improvement of real wages. In the past Labour has had to expend its energies and funds on two quite different objects, which, however, became mixed up with each other, the distinction finally being lost in the general objective of ' higher wages.' ' Higher wages ' really mean two distinct propositions ; first, higher money wages in order to maintain real wages, and, second, higher real wages in order to improve the standard of living. The failure to distinguish between real wages and money wages has over and over again led the workers in the wrong direction, and the fact that a Cost of Living Sliding Scale does once and for all sweep out of the way the source of this confusion is the strongest argument in its favour. There is an end to all the fighting to keep money wages rising as prices rise, and all the efforts of Labour can be concentrated on raising real wages and so improving the standard of life of the workers.

It may, however, be objected that this view assumes a continual rise in prices, and that while the advantages are obvious in such a case, the position is reversed when prices are falling. It may be said that in a period of falling prices the absence of a Cost of Living Sliding Scale would mean a continuous improvement in real wages while the operation of a scale would merely maintain them at the same level.

Actually there is little force in this objection, because, without a scale, wages do, in fact, fall when prices fall and rise when prices rise. There is always a tendency for wages to lag behind prices, but the lag is generally greater when prices are rising than when they are falling. This results in a loss to the wage earner if the movement is unregulated, whereas a Cost of Living Sliding Scale ensures an equitable adjustment throughout. Even if this were not the case, and the lag were equal in both cases, it has to be remembered that normally the workers' organisations expend much time, energy and money in forcing up money wages as rapidly as possible during periods of rising prices and in resisting unfair wage reductions during periods of falling prices. All this is saved by the operation of a Sliding Scale, and Unions can work with the single aim of securing basic increases, that is to say, of improving real wages.

What of the other objections mentioned ?   It will be noticed that they apply only to the particular scales now in operation.   It is true that the Ministry of Labour Index Number of Cost of Living is not satisfactory, and does not command universal confidence, but it will not always be so.   It is quite certain that when conditions are normal a new inquiry will be undertaken, and a Cost of Living Index established which it is to be hoped will be accepted on all sides.

The provision that only the lower paid workers are fully recompensed for higher cost of living is again no necessary part of a Sliding Scale.   It happens to be a feature of the scales now in existence, because the conditions at the time they were set up were abnormal. It was claimed, whether rightly or wrongly we need not stop to inquire, that other classes had been forced to accept temporarily a lower standard of living in consequence of the war, and that the better paid ranks among the workers should bear their share of the burden, this being accomplished by means of the specially devised Sliding Scales.   Certainly no one would, from the workers' point of view, accept such a provision in normal times.   All Sliding Scales based on cost of living must, if they are to receive consideration at all, provide for wage increases proportional to cost of living increases for all workers, and not merely for the lowest paid.

A similar reply is to be made to the objection that increases in real wages cannot easily be obtained.   This was so during the war period, but there is no reason why it should be so in normal times. On the contrary, it should be laid down and clearly understood at the outset that any Sliding Scale adopted is agreed to quite without prejudice to claims for higher real wages.   In ordinary times claims for basic increases would really be more easily made if Sliding Scales were in force, because the issue would be much more simple and the argument would not be obscured by irrelevant references to the cost of living.   The workers have nothing to lose by insisting always that discussion shall centre upon real wages rather than money wages, and once it became habitual, as it soon would, to think in terms of real wages it would be no more difficult than it is now to press for increases.   Under the present system we find that wherever wages rise the workers are largely robbed of the incresae by a rise in prices.   Under a Sliding Scale they would be automatically and immediately recompensed for any such rise in the cost of living.

To the final objection that professional and other classes have no Sliding Scales the answer is that many of them wish they had, for no section has been so hard hit (relatively speaking) by the high cost of living.

190. Trade Union Policy.

REPORT OF GENERAL COUNCIL OF THE T.U.C. ON THE MOND-TURNER CONFERENCES. *T.U.C. Ann. Rep.*, 1928, p. 209.

Ever since the war and the economic dislocation which, in the absence of constructive measures on the part of the Government was an inevitable consequence, it has been clear that Britain's industrial position is a very serious one.

The severe and widespread unemployment, the decline in the standard of living of certain sections of the working class, the situation of the coal industry, and the grave position of the iron and steel, shipbuilding and engineering, cotton, and other industries, are all factors in the experience of the past seven years that must be of great concern to the Trade Union Movement.

Whatever beliefs may be held as to the immediate tactics or wider policy of the movement, all those whose duty it is to promote the interests of the workers must regard the situation with grave anxiety and with the earnest desire to examine the problems relating to these distressing conditions with a view to finding immediate relief. The Council is fully convinced that any elected body which at such a time failed to explore any and every means which has for its object the improvement of the conditions of those it represents would be unworthy to hold office.

Broadly speaking, there were three possible lines of policy open to the Trade Union Movement. The first was to say, frankly, that the unions will do everything possible to bring the industrial machine to a standstill, to ensure by all possible means the breakdown of the entire system, in the hope of creating a revolutionary situation on the assumption that this might be turned to the advantage of the workers and to the abolition of capitalism. That policy the Trade Union Movement has decisively rejected as futile, certain to fail, and sure to lead to bloodshed and misery.

The second course was one of standing aside and telling employers to get on with their own job, while the unions would pursue the policy of fighting sectionally for improvements. The objections to this course are that it is entirely inconsistent with the modern demand for a completely altered status of the workers in industry, and that it is a futile policy, a confession of failure, for unions to say they are going to take no hand in the momentous changes that are taking place in the economic life of the nation.

The third course is for the Trade Union Movement to say boldly that not only is it concerned with the prosperity of industry, but that it is going to have a voice as to the way industry is carried on, so that it can influence the new developments that are taking place. The ultimate policy of the movement can find more use for an efficient industry than for a derelict one, and the unions can use their power to promote and guide the scientific reorganisation of industry as well as to obtain material advantages from that reorganisation.

Faced with the situation that now prevails in this country, the Council has taken the view that the third course was the only one it was possible to take if the Trade Union Movement was to endure as a living, constructive force. That policy affords the best hope of raising the status, security, and standard of living of the workers whom the Council represents. At all events, a very grave responsibility would have been taken by anyone who refused to consider the possibilities of such a course, or who neglected to take any opportunity that offered of pursuing it.

191. Economic Policy of the Trade Union Movement.

PRESIDENT'S ADDRESS TO THE TRADES UNION CONGRESS, 1926.
T.U.C. Ann. Rep., 1926, p. 76.

It has been the historic task of Trade Unionism to raise the standard of working-class life. In the days before State systems of social insurance, compensation for accident, and organised public care of widows and orphans and aged people, it was the Trade Unions that looked after the victims of a soulless industrialism ; it was the unions which inculcated thrift ; it was the unions which built up that magnificent system of trade and friendly benefits which protected the workers and their dependents from the worst ravages of capitalist economy under which human labour was treated as a commodity and under the operation of which the life of a man was of no more value than the working life of a machine, easily scrapped and as easily replaced. It was in those circumstances that the Trade Unions shouldered the enormous burden of a self-supporting system of insurance against unemployment, inadequate as it was to the needs of the case, and it was the persistent agitation of the unions which created a conscious public opinion as to the responsibility of the State towards the victims of our industrial system.   There is not a worker in this country to-day, whether a Trade Unionist or not, but has reaped material advantage from Trade Union efforts.   There is not a contribution paid to Trade Union funds but has brought its hundredfold returns in the protection afforded and in the improved standards of wages, hours and conditions of labour, and in the many other ways which Trade Union organisation has secured.

There is no institution in the country comparable to the Trade Union Movement with its network of machinery covering the whole field of industry, its expert staffs with first-hand technical and practical experience, its administrative and organising functions— the whole of it in operation from day to day in the interests of the working people.   The general public, impressed only with the incidents arising from industrial disputes, has no conception of the thousands of questions arising daily with which the unions have to deal, and upon the satisfactory handling of which the wheels of industry are kept in motion.   All the various Acts of Parliament relating to factory regulation and conditions, workmen's compensation, employers' liability, health and unemployment provisions, contracts of service—all that concerns the working life of the country comes within the scope of Trade Union activities, to an even greater extent than is true of the administrative departments of the Government.   The services rendered by the unions in the constant supervision of these matters, in the protection afforded to the workers in countless ways the public never hears of, in the diversity of the responsibilities which the unions undertake on behalf of the workers, have no parallel in any other form of organised service, and if they were suspended for a single week the result would be confusion and disorganisation and conflict throughout the whole range of industry.

The workers' organisation has grown in strength and influence decade by decade, and generation after generation, because it has accepted such responsibilities and fulfilled these obligations on behalf of the working people.

Is it anti-social to seek to imbue the workers with a true sense of their value in the economic life of the country ; to develop their capacity to exercise functions in the control of industry, even if it means the supersession of a system based upon the principle of

' every man for himself and the devil take the hindmost,' by one of organised national control and co-operative effort ?

Are the foundations of society threatened when the organised workers range themselves unitedly to resist the policy of attacking their standard of life as a too ready alternative to the more enlightened policy of reducing costs by the most economic use of national resources, by the fullest application of science and invention and the elimination of wasteful methods of production and distribution ? On the contrary, it is a matter of vital importance that these objectives of Trade Union policy shall be kept in view and be steadily pursued, not alone in the interests of the working people, but of the entire community which lives by their labour, their skill, their punctual and faithful discharge of economic functions.

192. Wage Policy.

RESOLUTION ADOPTED BY THE ANNUAL CONVENTION OF THE AMERICAN
FEDERATION OF LABOR, 1925. Proc. 1925, p. 271.

We hold that the best interests of the wage-earners, as well as those of the whole social group, are served, in increasing production in quality as well as in quantity, by high wage standards which assure the sustained purchasing power to the workers and, therefore, higher national standards for the environment in which they live, and means to enjoy cultured opportunities. We declare that wage reductions produce industrial and social unrest, and low wages are not conducive to low production costs. We urge upon wage-earners everywhere that we oppose all wage reductions, and we urge upon managements the elimination of waste in production in order that selling prices may be lower and wages higher.

To this end we recommend co-operation in the study of waste in production, which the assay of the Federated American Engineering Societies, covering important industries, has shown to be 50 per cent. attributable to management, and only 25 per cent. attributable to labor, with 25 per cent. attributable to other sources. . . . Social inequality, industrial instability and injustice must increase unless the workers' real wages—the purchasing power of their wages—coupled with a continuing reduction in the number of hours making up the working day, are progressed in proportion to man's increasing power of production.

193. Rationalisation.

RESOLUTION ADOPTED BY THE INDUSTRIAL CONFERENCE BETWEEN THE
GENERAL COUNCIL OF THE T.U.C. AND THE "MOND" GROUP
OF EMPLOYERS, 4th July, 1928.

The tendency towards a rational organisation of industry and
trade including the grouping of individual units within an industry
into larger units is recognised, and this tendency should be welcomed
and encouraged in so far as it leads to improvements in the efficiency
of industrial production, services, and distribution, and to the
raising of the standard of living of the people.

This Conference endorses the following Resolutions on Rationalisation adopted by the World Economic Conference held at Geneva in
May, 1927, which understood by rationalisation—' the methods of
technique and of organisation designed to secure the minimum waste
of either effort or material.   It includes the scientific organisation of
labour, standardisation both of material and of products, simplifica-
tion of processes and improvements in the system of transport and
marketing.'

The resolutions adopted were :

" The (World Economic) Conference considers that one of
the principal means of increasing output, improving conditions of
labour, and reducing costs of production is to be found in the
rational organisation of production and distribution.

The (World Economic) Conference considers that such
rationalisation aims simultaneously :

1. At securing the maximum efficiency of labour with the
minimum of effort ;

2. At facilitating by a reduction in the variety of patterns
(where such variety offers no obvious advantage), the design,
manufacture, use, and replacement of standardised parts ;

3. At avoiding waste of raw materials and power ;

4. At simplifying the distribution of goods ;

5. At avoiding in distribution unnecessary transport, burden-
some financial charges, and the useless interposition of middlemen ;

Its judicious and constant application is calculated to secure—

(1) To the community greater stability and a higher standard
in the conditions of life ;

(2) To the consumer lower prices and goods more carefully
adapted to general requirements ;

(3) To the various classes of producers higher and steadier remuneration to be equitably distributed among them.

It must be applied with the care which is necessary in order, while at the same time continuing the process of rationalisation, not to injure the legitimate interests of the workers ; and suitable measures should be provided for cases where during the first stage of its realisation it may result in loss of employment or more arduous work.

It requires, further, so far as regards the organisation of labour in the strict sense of the term the co-operation of employees, and the assistance of trade and industrial organisations and of scientific and technical experts."

It is recognised that certain measures of rationalisation may tend to displace labour or to modify in undesirable ways the conditions of work, and that safeguards are therefore necessary to ensure that the interests of the workers do not suffer by the adoption of such measures. It is therefore agreed that schemes for providing such safeguards should be considered as part of the general question of the Displacement of Labour.

Recognising the necessity for adaptability and elasticity in industry it is suggested that the Trade Unions and employers concerned should consider the advisability of making provisions for testing variations from existing practices or rules on agreed experimental bases with proper safeguards against an extension of such conditions being claimed by or imposed upon the industry beyond the agreed limits.

194. Trade Union Policy.

The Next Step in Industrial Relations, by W. M. CITRINE, Gen. Sec. of the Trades Union Congress. Manchester Guardian Supp., 30th Nov., 1927, p. 8.

It is sometimes suggested that the spokesmen of the trade union movement in encouraging discussion of the place and functions of the unions in relation to new conditions in industry are initiating a fresh departure in policy and are abandoning their supposedly traditional attitude of hostility to the employers. On the one hand, we are told that employers welcome recent declarations of representative trade unionists as evidence of an altered disposition on the part of the unions in dealing with the problem of industrial relations. On the other hand, these declarations have been interpreted by some trade union advocates of continuous and uncompromising warfare with employers as a craven plea for peace at any price, and as a traitorous betrayal of the workers by their 'leaders.' It seems to me, therefore, to be necessary at the outset to clear away the misapprehensions that exist regarding the significance to be attached to these utterances.

Trade unionism has reached the end of a definite stage in its evolution. It has established a virtually unchallenged control of the organised power of the workers. It has by no means reached the limits of expansion in numbers and influence. It has certainly not seen the end of possible developments in its structure and organisation. Neither has the process of consolidation and closer co-ordination which has been going on under the guidance of the Trades Union Congress General Council come to a standstill. But it has already attained a position of great authority. It has become a power in the land, with a growing consciousness of purpose, to which increased responsibilities and obligations cannot fail to be attached. The position that trade unionism has already attained as an established institution, and the functions it is capable of exercising in the economic life of the country are the outcome of a more or less unplanned development of union organisation. And the next stage in the evolution of trade unionism depends in no small measure upon a general recognition of the changes taking place in industry and of the part which the workers' organisations are qualified to play in the promotion of efficiency, economy, and scientific development in the productive system.

In turning their minds in this direction the trade unions are not contemplating any new departure in fundamental policy. They are, on the contrary, pursuing logically and consistently the line of policy they have pursued from their earliest days. It is a travesty of industrial history to represent the unions as carrying on an incessant conflict with employers with the object of making the present system unworkable. It is almost entirely due to the action of the unions that machinery for the settlement of industrial disputes through joint consultation and negotiation has been set up in practically all trades and industries. By far the larger proportion of disputes arising in industry from year to year are settled by these means. And history attests the fact that the main object of the unions has been in the past to get the best out of the existing system, to defend the workers' standards against the attacks of employers, to improve those standards wherever possible, and to meet the dictatorship of irresponsible capitalist groups by the organisation of social and economic power among the workers.

Owing to the circumstances surrounding the birth of the unions and to the economic environment in which they have developed, they have necessarily been forced to follow hitherto a hand-to-mouth policy, meeting each concrete issue as it arose without any very comprehensive plan in mind. But there has been a steady growth of conscious purpose among the unions and an equally marked tendency towards the concentration of authority in the hands of a central body representative of the whole organised movement. The most important manifestation of this tendency is to be seen in the powers reposed in the General Council of the Trades Union Congress, entitling that body not only to intervene in industrial disputes in which some vital question of principle affecting the unions as a whole is involved, but also empowering the General Council to undertake negotiations on general basic principles and to co-ordinate the policy of the unions on general questions. Vested with these powers, it is clearly within the province of the General Council to formulate its ideas in a concrete and practical form for the guidance of the organised movement in the immediate future.

What conception of trade union aims is likely to guide the representatives of the organised movement in framing the general policy ? This is the question which raises as a clear-cut issue the meaning of recent declarations regarding the possibility of establishing better industrial relations, with the object of improving conditions in industry and securing a steadily rising standard of life. It is conceivable, but in the last degree unlikely, that the unions may say it is not their aim to increase the efficiency of industry : to do so, in the opinion of some trade unionists, is merely to postpone the inevitable breakdown of the existing system, and they consider the plain duty of the unions is to hasten that collapse and to organise the workers so that they can take advantage of it when it comes. Alternatively, the unions may say their aim should be to keep up the defensive struggle for the maintenance of existing standards and to improve them as opportunity offers, but to accept no responsibility at all for any effort that can be made to improve the organisation of industry on the present basis of private ownership. A third possibility is that the unions should actively participate in a concerted effort to raise industry to its highest efficiency by developing the most scientific methods of production, eliminating waste and harmful restrictions, removing causes of friction and avoidable conflict, and promoting the largest possible output so as to provide a rising standard of life and continuously improving conditions of employment.

The third of these alternatives is the one that the trade unions are most likely to consider as a practical possibility. An obstructive or merely negative attitude is unthinkable, if only because it cannot arrest the profound and far-reaching changes that are taking place in the organisation and control of industry, but would effectually silence the unions' claim to a share in the responsibility of guiding economic developments. The approach to a new industrial order is not by way of a social explosion, but by a planned reconstruction in which the unions will assume a larger share of control in directing industrial changes. Within the last quarter of a century there have been vast changes in technology, in methods of management, enlargement of the scale of production, finance, and organisation. Scientific research, psychological investigation, and enlightened common sense have been applied in working out the principles of a more efficient, economical, and humane system of production. What is called in a convenient phrase ' the rationalisation of industry ' is proceeding at a rapid pace in the highly industrialised communities. Standardised products, simplified processes, scientific planning of workshops, labour-saving machinery, improved technique of management are its guiding principles. Not only do the unions claim to be consulted about their application to the concrete problems of industrial organisation, but they have a positive contribution to make in developing them over the whole field of production. The degree of organisation they have achieved among the workers gives them the power to assume much more important functions than those they have hitherto discharged. It is in respect of these wider economic functions which the unions are capable of undertaking that a decided forward step can now be taken in the direction of an effective relationship which will ensure greater stability and harmony in industry.

Trade union functions in the past have been somewhat restricted. They have been concerned mainly, apart from their trade and friendly benefits aspect, with the regulation of relations between employers and employed in the limited field of negotiation on questions of wages, working hours, and conditions of employment. The joint machinery of consultation and conference—works committees, industrial councils, and the like—serves a useful purpose in bringing questions of wages, hours, and conditions to an agreed settlement and reducing friction and conflict.   A multitude of disputes are disposed of by these means before they reach the point of causing stoppages of work.   There is still ample scope for extending this machinery on both a local and a national scale.   But this aspect of trade unionism appertains to what I may call the politics of industry, and the union functions which require to be enlarged lie more in the economic sphere.   No planned and systematic attempt has been made to secure the co-operation of the unions in the field of industrial administration.   And it is in this field that both employers and trade unions are most concerned to come to an understanding.

Under the conditions of fierce international competition for markets which now prevails the organisers of industry have to strain every nerve to raise the level of efficiency, to cut costs of production, and to abolish waste in every branch of their enterprise.   The trusts, cartels, and combinations of capital which diminish internecine competition, price-fixing, and delimitation of markets, the measures taken to secure control of supplies of raw material are all evidence of the adaptations now taking place ; and they affect the interests of the wage-earners in the most material way.   The wage-earners are, in fact, affected by every development of industrial organisation which aims at increasing efficiency, reducing costs, and eliminating waste.   But they are especially and vitally concerned with those developments when they are carried out at their expense. Employers are only too prone to believe that efficiency and economy are synonymous with lower wages, longer hours, speeding-up, and such forms of ' scientific management ' as those which bring the worker down to the level of an automaton whose every movement is regulated by a standard procedure based on motion studies and time studies.

There is an inevitable psychological reaction to the imposition of such systems as ' Taylorism ' autocratically introduced without consultation with the workers' representatives.   The opposition to new processes, labour-saving machinery, and changes in workshop practices has been greatly exaggerated, and where it is encountered it is undoubtedly due to ruthless exploitation of methods which from the standpoint of the individual worker offer him in immediate results only insecurity and unemployment.

As long as the workers are allowed to remain under the impression that they have little to gain either materially or in status by the introduction of methods and measures designed to promote greater efficiency and economy, but, on the contrary, may even suffer by their adoption, progress is rendered difficult. One important function of the trade unions, if their assistance is to be secured, must be the maintenance of such safeguards as will ensure the fullest advantage being taken of all the improvements in methods and technique that can be devised with the hearty goodwill of the workers. The possibilities of such co-operation producing a very real advance in the scientific organisation of production are numerous, but are practically unexplored.

As a first step, therefore, it appears to me to be necessary for representatives of the organised employers and of the unions to seek a mutual understanding regarding the extension of union responsibility in matters of industrial administration. How best can this be done ? It is astounding that despite the development of machinery of negotiation there is yet no joint body able to speak authoritatively on behalf of employers and the workers as a whole. On the employers' side there exists the National Confederation of Employers' Organisations ; on the side of the unions there is the Trades Union Congress General Council. Is it unreasonable to suggest that regular periodical meetings of these bodies should take place in the form of, say, a National Industrial Council ? Such a joint body would not be expected to deal with the many detailed questions peculiar to separate industries. Its work would be confined to the discussion of those questions which are of common interest to all industries, and to those with which it is beyond the power of any individual industry adequately to deal. It would play an important part in co-ordinating the activities of the various industries instead of allowing each to proceed almost without relation to the others. I conceive such a national industrial council not as an alternative but as a necessary corollary to the development of industrial councils for each industry ; and when I speak of industrial councils I mean bodies with a much wider conception of their obligations than the adjustment of wages disputes only.

The machinery suggested above would therefore take the form of—

    1. A National Industrial Council, and,
    2. Councils for each separate industry.

It might be suggested that such a National Industrial Council would be best composed of representatives elected from the employers and workers in each of the separate industries. Without excluding the possibility of ultimate development in that direction, the unwieldiness of such a body, because of large numerical representation, would make the project, in the initial stages at all events, practically impossible.

It may be found that no basis of confidence and goodwill exists upon which such a relationship can rest. It is unfortunately true that suspicion and antagonism vitiate the relations of the employers and the unions at the present time. They must be removed before anything useful can be accomplished. But the best way of removing them is to face candidly and in a matter-of-fact spirit the question whether the discipline and loyalty of the organised workers can be put to no other use than warfare, or may be used for the furtherance of constructive aims to the common advantage.

Discussion on these lines, after initial decisions on the broad question of policy have been taken, should lead the parties to the formulation of a practical programme. In general terms, I am convinced that the co-operation of the trade unions can be secured for the realisation of a maximum of efficiency in the employment of labour, the reduction of costs of production, and the elimination of waste in all branches of production and distribution, provided that adequate guarantees are given to ensure security of employment and an equitable share in the gains resulting from increased productivity and economies achieved as the process of ' rationalisation ' goes on. The nature of these guarantees requires to be very carefully considered, for security of employment and adequate wages are of paramount importance to the workers. How far the methods of wage determination, the system of unemployment insurance, and existing practices in respect of the employment and dismissal of workers will be modified as the functions of the trade unions are enlarged constitutes one of the most interesting aspects of the discussion.

A wide field of fruitful negotiation, with numerous possibilities of mutual agreement, lies in the application of the principles of scientific management as that term is now understood, embodying not merely the methods of ' Taylorism ' but the results of research into industrial fatigue, the physical and psychological conditions under which work is carried on, and the proper planning and layout of work. A great body of evidence is available to show that immense economies in effort and production costs can be obtained by giving attention to these matters and securing the active interest and co-operation of the workers. It lies with the unions to invoke that interest and to guide their co-operation, as well as to safeguard them from such ruthless exploitation as that which marked the introduction of 'Taylorism' in its cruder stages.

Inevitably consideration must be given to the allegation that production is restricted by 'ca' canny' methods, demarcation, and trade union rules and customs. It is a reciprocal responsibility which the trade unions will not be afraid to face when their place and functions in the sphere of industrial administration have been properly defined. With it goes the question of responsibility for reducing the amount of avoidable 'absenteeism' and diminishing the losses resulting from accidents, sickness, and related causes. On all these matters the unions have a positive contribution to make, as they have also on questions of labour 'turnover,' piecework, apprenticeship, systematic overtime, and other problems.

Profit-sharing and schemes of co-partnership which admit employees as shareholders in the concerns that employ them may be worthy of exploitation as another field wherein the functions of the trade unions can be extended. To profit-sharing and employee-shareholding schemes on an individualistic basis there are valid objections from the union point of view, but it is possible to conceive them in operation on a collectivist basis with the union acting as steward and trustee. It lies with the union, too, to assume responsibility for such representation of the workers on works committees, joint councils, and boards of management as will follow the development of what I have called 'the politics of industry,' meaning the extension of the principle of joint conference on matters of commercial policy as well as of industrial administration and regulation of wages and working conditions.

Thus the field of inquiry and negotiation appears to be very wide, once the idea of enlarging the functions of the trade unions is admitted and a basis of mutual confidence can be established. I have endeavoured to show how the responsibilities of the unions can be developed and more stable relations may be brought about. I will say nothing about the alternative, if no progress is possible on this path, except to prophesy that it opens a vista of increasing disorder, instability, and conflict.

PART IV

THE STATUS OF TRADE UNIONS

THE status of Trade Unions, their present and future place in the State and in industry, is a matter of peculiar interest to jurists and political scientists, but it is by no means an academic question, devoid of practical importance. On the contrary, the actual powers and functions of Trade Unions will be enlarged or crippled according to the predominant views in the community at large on this problem.

The Unions have in the past been harassed far more for their potentialities than for their actual practices, and the attitude of the community towards them is in general influenced by the uneasy sense that they are foreign bodies in the public eye, rebellious groups that do not fit into the orthodox framework of society.

The ceaseless pressure of economic events may, as at the present day, drive Governments and industrialists into an acceptance and recognition of Trade Unionism, according to it a status higher than it has ever had before, but every reminder that the workers' organisations are independent groups sends the State into a new frenzy of restrictive legislation. The stages through which Trade Unionism has passed have been briefly outlined in the Introduction. Unions are now perfectly lawful organisations. Freedom of Association is fully recognised by the law of this country (195).

Legal Status.—It is not possible here to set out in full the legal status of Unions, as very difficult and doubtful points of law are involved. Broadly speaking, Trade Unions are lawful bodies but they do not possess corporate status. They are, at most, quasi-corporations (10). In England it is laid down by statute that the mere fact of a Union's being in restraint of trade does not make it unlawful (195), and, in the United States, Unions are expressly ruled out of the

439

purview of the anti-trust laws, which are aimed against combinations in restraint of trade (196), though this statutory freedom has been ingeniously whittled down by the courts.[1] Unions are not allowed in this country to become incorporated, (197), but certain American States allow incorporation, as does a Federal Act of 1886 (198). Many Continental countries allow, and some compel, Trade Unions to acquire legal personality.

In Anglo-American law the trend of development has been in the direction of treating Unions as corporate bodies, even though in theory they are not so. This tendency was arrested to a great extent, in this country, by the passing of the Trade Disputes Act of 1906, which definitely freed Unions from the liability to be sued for torts committed by them or on their behalf (199). This freedom does not extend to illegal strikes, however, (200). On occasion, Unions have been allowed to act as corporate bodies, with power to sue, even in Great Britain, (201), but generally they may neither sue nor be sued, except in the cases above mentioned. The Taff Vale judgment, the principle of which was reversed by the Act of 1906, indicated the point reached in the development of legal theory on this matter in 1901 (202). This is the attitude that has been consistently upheld since in the United States, (203), where Unions are now, in general, treated as corporations even when they are not legally incorporated. In Britain, the unique status devised by the framers of the Trade Union Act of 1871 still remains, (204), and a Union's agreements on such matters as benefits, contributions, etc., are not in general directly enforceable (205). The view of the Royal Commission of 1906, on the legal status of Unions, is given in (206).

Through trustees, the property of a Union can be protected and used, (207), and a Union may now spend its funds on any lawful object authorised under its constitution, (11), subject to certain restrictions regarding political expenditure (161, 162).

[1] See, for example, Duplex Printing Press Co. *v.* Deering, 1921. 254 U.S. 443.

The law will protect the rights of members of Unions in certain limited ways only. It will, for example, order the re-instatement of a member who has been expelled otherwise than in accordance with the Rules of the Union, or even, in the case of a member expelled for non-participation in an illegal strike, where the Rules permit, (160, 200). The courts will not in general, however, directly enforce a member's claim to benefits, or a Union's claim to contributions, even though an agreement between the parties is broken by the refusal to pay. Nor will an agreement between a Union and an Employers' Association be generally enforced, nor any other agreement of the kinds mentioned in (205). These statements are subject to certain qualifications, and for a full exposition the reader is referred to a text-book of Trade Union Law.[1] The agreements already mentioned will be enforceable, for instance, in the case of associations not unlawful at common law. As the majority of Unions have objects in restraint of trade, however, this exception is not very important.

The status of Trade Unions would be enormously enhanced if membership of a Union were to be compulsory in all industries. Unions naturally try to achieve this by the use of their own power, and in many cases they refuse to allow their members to work with non-unionists (208). This is the cause of an appreciable proportion of the strikes that take place, and the result is often to bring about the complete unionisation of the firm concerned. Many agreements nowadays provide that workers shall be members of their appropriate union (e.g. 104, 106). This pressure that Unions exert on non-unionists is precisely analogous to the exercise in a similar way of the much greater power possessed by the medical and legal professions, and indeed by all vocational organisations from the mediaeval gilds onwards. Employers' Associations act in the same way ; it is inevitable, as Mr. Baldwin pointed out in his famous ' Peace in our Time ' speech (209).

On the other hand, workers have in the past often had to

[1] See Slesser and Baker, *Trade Union Law* (1927).

sign ' the document,' pledging themselves not to join or remain in a Union. This is seldom heard of in these days, in this country, though it is not altogether unknown. It is very common in the United States, where it is known as the ' yellow dog ' contract. A more modern form of ' the document,' in the shape of an agreement to work with non-unionists, is shown in (210), but this is not often encountered, either, in this country.

Many employers, while not prepared to employ only trade unionists, are quite willing to express publicly their preference for employees who are organised. This is found in the Electrical Supply, Transport, and other industries (211, 212).

On the recognition of Trade Unions and the desirability of both employers and workers being organised, there is now, in this country, general agreement among all employers of any importance. This is well expressed in the declaration by the Industrial Conference of 1919 (213), and, as will be seen later, it is emphatically affirmed in the Whitley Reports (232-234). The Conference of the Trades Union Congress General Council and the Mond Group of Employers has more recently laid it down even more clearly (214).

While employers in general are free to make trade unionism a condition of employment, for their employees, Local and Public Authorities are, since 1927, prohibited from enforcing such a condition and from giving preferential treatment to trade unionists. At the same time the prohibition applies equally in the other direction; such Authorities may not discriminate against trade unionists or make non-unionism a condition of employment. This provision applies also to contractors doing work for a Local or Public Authority (215).

Apart from this, there are no legal limitations other than those previously mentioned for civil servants and for police (28, 29). In all other cases employers are free to make either unionism or non-unionism a condition of employment, without qualification, and to dismiss a worker for belonging or for not belonging to a Union. Dismissal of or discrimination against a worker for his trade union membership or activities is termed Victimisation, and is very bitterly resented by all Trade Unionists. Most Unions have special Rules for Victimisation Benefit (*e.g.* **157**). During the War, Victimisation was forbidden by law, in munition works, (**216**), but that was a temporary provision only. Most responsible employers now denounce the practice, and the Conference of the Trades Union Congress General Council and the Mond Group of Employers has recently issued an emphatic statement on the subject (**217**).

In America the legal position is similar to that obtaining in this country, but without restrictions on Public Authorities, except that non-membership of a Union may, and membership of a Union may not, be made a condition of employment in certain cases.

A Kansas law prohibiting employers from making non-membership of a Union a condition of employment has been declared unconstitutional and void (**218**). Many other decisions have been given to the same effect.

As regards other countries, we may note that membership of a Union recognised by the State is practically compulsory in Soviet Russia and in Italy; such bodies alone are allowed to speak and act for the workers. In Germany, France, Belgium, Czecho-Slovakia, and also in Australia under a federal law, dismissal on account of membership of a Union is illegal.

Registration.—Trade Unions may be registered or not, as they please. Registration in accordance with the Act of 1871, (**219**), gives certain privileges, but they are not considerable and many Unions do not trouble to register. In some respects Registered Unions may even be at a disadvantage as compared with unregistered Unions, since in cases where section 4 of the Act of 1906 does not operate, the former may be sued, whereas it is doubtful whether unregistered Unions may be.

Trade Unions and the State Administration.—In modern times the State has attempted to bring the Trade Unions into closer relation with the machinery of public administration. In Great Britain, the Unions themselves are in theory seldom recognised for this purpose, though in practice their co-operation is sought. For example, section 4 of the Mining Industry Act, 1920, **(220)**, provides that four members of the Coal Advisory Committee shall be representative of the workers in and about the coal mines, and three others representative of the workers in other industries. Trade Unions are not mentioned, but it is the Unions that nominate the mineworkers' representatives and the Trades Union Congress that nominates the representatives of workers in other industries. In the administration of the Miners' Welfare Fund, however, the Union is specifically mentioned **(220)**, and Trade Unions were officially recognised in the appointments to War Pensions Committees, **(221)**. In the case of Trade Boards, **(116)**, it is the Unions that in practice appoint the workers' members, and in the appointment of the Port of London Authority, **(222)**, it is the Unions that are consulted, while Union participation is an integral part of the Bristol Dockers' Registration Scheme, **(223)**. So with many other appointments to Governmental Commissions, Boards, etc., both advisory and administrative **(224)**. The Court of Enquiry into the Transport Dispute 1920, recommended the general adoption of the practice for Port Authorities **(225)**.

The Unions have also participated more directly in public administration in connection with Unemployemnt and Health Insurance. A number of Unions have taken advantage of the provision, which has been in operation since compulsory Unemployment Insurance was inaugurated for certain trades in 1911, whereby under certain conditions the Union machinery may be substituted for the State machinery, the Union acting as the State's agent in the administration of the scheme. This arrangement is shown in **(226)**, and is explained by the Ministry of Labour in **(227)**. It is especially interesting because Trade Unions are, in practice, the only organisations that are able to enter into such arrangements.

In the case of Health Insurance, on the other hand, the Trade Union is only one among many types of organisation that may and do set up ' Approved Societies ' for the administration of the scheme.

Trade Unions and Industrial Administration.—The Cotton Control Board provided one of the most interesting examples of Trade Union participation in industrial administration during the War period, (228), and Wool Control was another instance. These War experiments disappeared, however, with the coming of Peace.

At the present time the Unions are recognised in certain cases as the appropriate bodies to appoint representatives for various functions in the conduct of industry. In the Coal and Railway industries the workers are given certain powers by statute. Checkweighers perform important duties in the coal mines, and while they are appointed by the workers, they are, in practice, Union officials (229). The mineworkers may also appoint inspectors, a power that is frequently exercised (230).

In the case of the Railway National Wages Board set up under the Railways Act, 1921, both the Railway Unions and the Trades Union Congress, as such, are recognised for the appointment of representatives (231).

In industries not regulated by statute the participation of the workers in some instances is to a certain extent secured—in theory at least—by Joint Industrial Councils, Joint Works Councils, etc. The Whitley Reports (232, 233) were the outcome of wartime conditions and of the workers' claim for self-government in industry. They were accepted by the Government, and it was announced that the Councils set up under the scheme would be regarded by the Government as the authoritative bodies in the trades concerned, (234); it was further definitely laid down that the Councils were to be based on representation through Trade Unions and employers' associations only (232, 235).

Most Whitley Councils that were established soon degenerated into ordinary negotiating bodies, confined to wages, hours, etc., though a few have done something to live up to the ideals set by the Whitley Committee (236).

The Joint Committee and Boards proposed by the Government in 1920, for the Coal Industry, failed to materialise, owing to the miners' opposition and their refusal to operate this part of the Act (237).

The most ambitious example of post-war proposals for the reconstruction of industry on democratic lines was the famous Foster Report, relevant extracts from which are given in (238).

A recent type of scheme proposed by Labour for the workers' participation in the control of industry is to be found in the Coal and Power scheme presented by the Miners, the Trades Union Congress, and the Labour Party to the Samuel Commission in 1925 (239).

Pluralism.—The demands and schemes for workers' control or joint control have been powerfully reinforced by the development of pluralist doctrines concerning the personality of voluntary associations and the denial of State sovereignty. It was F. W. Maitland, one of the greatest British jurists, who laid the foundations of this theory as far as English thought was concerned. A group of brilliant writers, largely Labour in sympathies,—H. J. Laski and G. D. H. Cole, for example,—have applied the doctrine to industrial problems, stressing the rights of vocational groups such as Trade Unions. Geldart has well expressed the doctrine, also, and has pointed out that if the Taff Vale judgment was in accord with it, the Osborne judgment was as clearly opposed to it (240). Mr. and Mrs. Webb agree with this attitude, (241), though they have not travelled as far along the pluralist road as have Mr. Cole (242), and Professor Laski, (243).

Projects for Industrial Parliaments evolve naturally from this type of speculation. Germany and France have their National Economic Councils, but opinions differ as to their success, so far. Mr. and Mrs. Webb oppose the idea of a vocational Parliament dealing with general questions, but this is seldom proposed nowadays, (244). In this country the Industrial Conference of 1919 put forward an ambitious scheme, (245), and a more practical proposal has more recently been made by the Industrial Conference between the

General Council of the Trades Union Congress and the Mond group of Employers (**246**).

An eloquent philosophic statement of the pluralist position by Prof. Laski closes this section (**247**).

AUTHORITIES AND REFERENCES.

For the legal side of the subject dealt with in this Part, students should consult Slesser and Baker's *Trade Union Law* (Third Edition). A more condensed account is given in Henderson's *Trade Unions and the Law*. Prof. E. Jenks' *Short History of English Law* is also valuable. It is necessary for the serious student to read the Reports of the principal legal cases, as well as the text-books. For other countries the International Labour Office's *Freedom of Association* should be read, and the same Office's very useful annual, *International Survey of Legal Decisions on Labour Law* should be studied. For the United States, mention may be made of the annual volume of Legal Decisions affecting Labor, issued by the United States Bureau of Labor Statistics, and the judgments of the U.S. Supreme Court,—especially the dissenting judgments,—in Labor cases, are of unique interest and value. Ellingwood and Coombs' *The Government and Labor* gives a useful selection of judgments and other first-hand material. The Appendix on Freedom of Association contained in A. V. Dicey's *Law and Opinion* is illuminating and suggestive.

On Trade Union participation in State and industrial administration, some of the volumes in the Carnegie Foundation's Economic and Social History of the World War are useful, notably *The Cotton Control Board*, by H. D. Henderson, and Mr. Cole's *Trade Unionism and Munitions, Workshop Organisation*, and *Labour in the Coal Mining Industry*.

Slesser and Henderson's *Industrial Law* is useful for certain statutory provisions.

On the industrial side, the Ministry of Labour Reports on Joint Industrial Councils and Works Committees are valuable, and here, as elsewhere, Webbs' *Industrial Democracy* and *History of Trade Unionism* are indispensable. *The Frontier of Control* by C. Goodrich, is interesting though now largely out-of-date. The Reports and Evidence of the Sankey Commission (1919) and of the Shaw Enquiry (1920), are a mine of suggestion and information for the Coal and Transport industries, respectively. For workers' control in general, Mr. Cole's *Self Government in Industry*, *The World of Labour* and *Guild Socialism Re-stated* are worth reading, and the thesis there worked out should be compared with Webbs' *Constitution for a Socialist Commonwealth*.

For Pluralist ideas the reader should turn to Maitland's Introduction to Gierke's *Political Theories of the Middle Age*, and to Maitland's *Collected Papers*, vol. iii., especially the papers on Moral Personality and Legal Personality, and the Unincorporate Body. These give the lawyer's views, and for the political aspect Cole's *Social Theory* is useful. Above all, Laski's *Authority in the Modern State*, *The Foundations of Sovereignty*, and *A Grammar of Politics* should be studied.

---

195. Trade Unions not Unlawful.

TRADE UNION ACT, 1871 ; 34 & 35 Vict., ch. 31.

2. The purposes of any trade union shall not, by reason merely that they are in restraint of trade, be deemed to be unlawful, so as to render any member of such trade union liable to criminal prosecution for conspiracy or otherwise.

3. The purposes of any trade union shall not, by reason merely that they are in restraint of trade, be unlawful so as to render void or voidable any agreement or trust.

196. Freedom of Association—U.S.A.

SECTION 6 OF THE CLAYTON ACT OF 15TH OCTOBER, 1914 ; 38 Stat. L. c. 323.

Sec. 6. That the labor of a human being is not a commodity or article of commerce. Nothing contained in the anti-trust laws shall be construed to forbid the existence and operation of labor, agricultural, or horticultural organisations, instituted for the purpose of mutual help, and not having capital stock or conducted for profit, or to forbid or restrain individual members of such organisations from lawfully carrying out the legitimate objects thereof ; nor shall such organisations, or the members thereof, be held or construed to be illegal combinations or conspiracies in restraint of trade, under the anti-trust laws.

197. Trade Unions cannot be incorporated under the Companies Acts, etc.

TRADE UNION ACT, 1871 ; 34 & 35 Vict., ch. 31.

5. The following Acts, that is to say,

(1) The Friendly Societies Acts, 1855 and 1858, and the Acts amending the same ;

(2) The Industrial and Provident Societies Act, 1867, and any Act amending the same ; and

(3) The Companies Acts, 1862 and 1867,

shall not apply to any trade union, and the registration of any trade union under any of the said Acts shall be void, and the deposit of the rules of any trade union made under the Friendly Societies Acts, 1855 and 1858, and the Acts amending the same, before the passing of this Act, shall cease to be of any effect.

TRADE UNION ACT (1871) AMENDMENT ACT, 1876 ; 39 & 40 Vict., ch. 22.

7. Whereas by the ' Life Assurance Companies Act, 1870 ' it is provided that the said Act shall not apply to societies registered under the Acts relating to Friendly Societies : The said Act (or the amending Acts) shall not apply nor be deemed to have applied to trade unions registered or to be registered under the principal Act.

COMPANIES (CONSOLIDATION) ACT, 1908 ; 8 Edw. VII., ch. 69.

294. Nothing in this Act shall affect the provisions of section five of the Trade Union Act, 1871, except that the reference in that section to the Companies Acts, 1862 and 1867, shall be read as a reference to this Act.

198. Incorporation of Trade Unions—U.S.A.

FEDERAL ACT OF 29TH JUNE, 1886 ; 24 Stat. L. 86.

1. The term ' National Trade Union,' in the meaning of this Act, shall signify any association of working people having two or more branches in the States or Territories of the United States for the purpose of aiding its members to become more skilful and efficient workers, the promotion of their general intelligence, the elevation of their character, the regulation of their wages and their hours and conditions of labor, the protection of their individual

rights in the prosecution of their trade or trades, the raising of funds for the benefit of sick, disabled, or unemployed members, of the families of deceased members, or for such other object or objects for which working people may lawfully combine, having in view their mutual protection or benefit.

2. National Trade Unions shall, upon filing their articles of incorporation in the office of the recorder of the District of Columbia, become a corporation under the technical name by which said National Trade Union desires to be known to the trade ; and shall have the right to sue and be sued, to implead and be impleaded, to grant and receive, in its corporate or technical name, property, real, personal, and mixed, and to use said property, and the proceeds and income thereof, for the objects of said corporation as in its charter defined : *Provided,* That each union may hold only so much real estate as may be required for the immediate purposes of its incorporation.

3. An incorporated National Trade Union shall have power to make and establish such constitution, rules, and by-laws as it may deem proper to carry out its lawful objects, and the same to alter, amend, add to, or repeal at pleasure.

4. An incorporated National Trade Union shall have power to define the duties and powers of all its officers, and prescribe their mode of election and term of office, to establish branches and sub-unions in any Territory of the United States.

5. The headquarters of an incorporated National Trade Union shall be located in the District of Columbia.

199. Freedom of Trade Union from Liability to be Sued.

TRADE DISPUTES ACT, 1906 ; 6 Edw. VII., ch. 47.

4.—(1) An action against a trade union, whether of workmen or masters, or against any members or officials thereof on behalf of themselves and all other members of the trade union in respect of any tortious act alleged to have been committed by or on behalf of the trade union, shall not be entertained by any court.

(2) Nothing in this section shall affect the liability of the trustees of a trade union to be sued in the events provided for by the Trades Union Act, 1871, section nine, except in respect of any tortious act committed by or on behalf of the union in contemplation or in furtherance of a trade dispute.

200. Suability of Trade Unions in Certain Cases.

TRADE DISPUTES AND TRADE UNIONS ACT, 1927 ; 17 & 18 Geo. V.,
ch. 22.

2.—(2) No provisions of the Trade Union Acts, 1871 to 1917,
limiting the proceedings which may be entertained by any court,
and nothing in the rules of a trade union or society requiring the
settlement of disputes in any manner shall apply to any proceeding
for enforcing any right or exemption secured by this section, and in
any such proceeding the court may, in lieu of ordering a person who
has been expelled from membership of a trade union or society to be
restored to membership, order that he be paid out of the funds of the
trade union or society such sum by way of compensation or damages
as the court thinks just.

201. Power to Sue in Certain Cases.

RESTORATION OF PRE-WAR PRACTICES ACT, 1919 ; 9 & 10 Geo. V.,
ch. 42.

2.—(3) Proceedings against an employer for an offence under
this Act may be instituted by or on behalf of any worker affected or
by or on behalf of a trade union or federation of trade unions, and
any party to any such proceedings may appear and be represented
by an official of the trade union or federation of trade unions, or of
the federation of employers, to which he belongs.

202. Status of Trade Unions.

TAFF VALE RAILWAY CO. *v.* AMALGAMATED SOCIETY OF RAILWAY
SERVANTS, A.C. (1901), 436 ; per Lord MacNaghten.

Has the legislature authorised the creation of numerous bodies of
men capable of owning great wealth and of acting by agents with
absolutely no responsibility for the wrongs they may do to other
persons by the use of that wealth and the employment of those
agents ?   I cannot find anything in the Acts of 1871 and 1876 to
warrant or suggest such a notion.   Nothing of the sort was contemplated by the minority of the members of the Royal Commission
on Trade Unions whose views found acceptance with the legislature.
Paragraph 4 of their Report said it should be provided that except so
far as combinations are thereby exempted from criminal prosecution

nothing should affect . . . the liability of every person to be sued by law or in equity in respect of any damage which may have been occasioned to any other person through the act or default of the person so sued.

If the liability of every person was to be preserved, it follows that it was intended by the strongest advocates of trade unionism that persons should be liable for concerted as well as for individual action, and for this purpose it seems to me that it cannot matter in the least whether the persons acting in concert be combined together in a trade union or collected and united under any other form of association.

If trade unions are not above the law, how are these bodies to be sued ?   I have no doubt whatever that a trade union, whether registered or unregistered, could be sued in a representative action if the persons selected as defendants be persons who, from their position, may be taken fairly to represent the body. . . . May a registered trade union be sued in and by its registered name ?   I cannot see any difficulty of such a suit.   It is quite true that a registered trade union is not a corporation, but it has a registered name and a registered office.   The registered name is nothing more than a collective name for all the members.   The registered office is the place where it carries on business.   A partnership firm which is not a corporation, nor, I suppose, a legal entity, may now be sued in the firm's name.   The Act of Parliament actually provides for a registered trade union being sued in certain cases for penalites, by its registered name, as a trade union, and does not say that the cases specified are the only cases in which it may be so sued.

I see nothing contrary to principle or contrary to the provisions of the Trade Union Acts in holding that a trade union may be sued by its registered name.

203. Liability of Trade Unions to be Sued.—U.S.A.

United Mine Workers *v.* Coronado Coal Co.   U.S. Supreme Court, 1922.   259 U.S. 344.

Chief Justice Taft said, in part :
There are five principal questions pressed by the plaintiffs.

.   .   .   .

The second is that the United Mine Workers of America, District No. 21 United Mine Workers of America, and the local unions made defendants, are unincorporated associations and not subject to suit, and therefore should have been dismissed from the case.

. . . .

In every way the union acts as a business entity, distinct from its members. No organised corporation has greater unity of action, and in none is more power centred in the governing executive bodies. Undoubtedly, at common law, an unincorporated association of persons was not recognised as having any other character than a partnership in whatever was done, and it could only sue or be sued in the name of its members, and their liability had to be enforced against each member. . . .

But the growth and necessities of these great labor organisations have brought affirmative legal recognition of their existence and usefulness and provisions for their protection, which their members have found necessary. Their right to maintain strikes, when they do not violate law or the rights of others, has been declared. The embezzlement of funds by their officers has been especially denounced as a crime. The so-called union label, which is a quasi-trademark to indicate the origin of manufactured product in union labor, has been protected against pirating and deceptive use by the statutes of most of the states, and in many states authority to sue to enjoin its use has been conferred on unions. They have been given distinct and separate representation and the right to appear to represent union interests in statutory arbitrations, and before official labor boards . . . out of the very necessities of the existing conditions and the utter impossibility of doing justice otherwise, the suable character of such an organisation as this has come to be recognised in some jurisdictions, and many suits for and against labor unions are reported in which no question has been raised as to the right to treat them in their closely united action and functions as artificial persons, capable of suing and being sued. It would be unfortunate if an organisation with as great power as this International Union has in the raising of large funds, and in directing the conduct of 400,000 members in carrying on, in a wide territory, industrial controversies and strikes, out of which so much unlawful injury to private rights is possible, could assemble its assets to be used therein free from liabilities for injuries by torts committed in the course of such strikes. . . .

Our conclusion as to the suability of the defendants is confirmed in the case at bar by the words of Sections 7 and 8 of the Anti-trust Law. The persons who may be sued under Sec. 7 include

' corporations and associations existing under or authorised by the laws of either the United States, the laws of any of the Territories, the laws of any State, or the laws of any foreign country.' (*July* 2, 1890, 26 *Stat. L.* 210.)

This language is very broad, and the words, given their natural significance, certainly include labor unions like these.

(The judgment of the court below, against the union, was, however reversed on other grounds.)

204. Status of Trade Unions.

FREDERIC HARRISON, at the Royal Commission on Trade Unions, 1869. MINORITY REPORT.

Trade Unions are essentially clubs and not trading companies, and we think that the degree of regulation possible in the case of the latter is not possible in the case of the former. All questions of crime apart, the objects at which they aim, the rights which they claim, and the liabilities which they incur are for the most part, it seems to us, such as courts of law should neither enforce, nor modify, nor annul. They should rest entirely on consent.

205. Trade Union Agreements not Directly Enforceable.

TRADE UNION ACT, 1871 ; 34 & 35 Vict., ch. 31.

4. Nothing in this Act shall enable any court to entertain any legal proceeding instituted with the object of directly enforcing or recovering damages for the breach of any of the following agreements, namely,

1. Any agreement between members of a trade union as such, concerning the conditions on which any members for the time being of such trade union shall or shall not sell their goods, transact business, employ, or be employed :

2. Any agreement for the payment by any person of any subscription or penalty to a trade union :

3. Any agreement for the application of the funds of a trade union,—

    (*a*) To provide benefits to members ; or,

    (*b*) To furnish contributions to any employer or workman not a member of such trade union, in consideration of such employer or workman acting in conformity with the rules or resolutions of such trade union ; or,

(c) To discharge any fine imposed upon any person by sentence of a court of justice ; or,

4. Any agreement made between one trade union and another ; or,

5. Any bond to secure the performance of any of the above-mentioned agreements.

But nothing in this section shall be deemed to constitute any of the above-mentioned agreements unlawful.

206. Status of Trade Unions.

ROYAL COMMISSION ON TRADE DISPUTES, ETC., 1906 ; Report, Cd. 2825, Para. 33.

Trade Unions, which originally were looked upon as illegal combinations, have made out their claim to enfranchisement and existence.   But having done so they cannot put their claims higher than to say that they are institutions which are beneficial to the community as a whole.   But so are many other institutions—banks, railways, insurance companies, and so on.   It may have been right to provide, as has been done, that the Courts shall not have power directly to enforce agreements between Trade Unions and their members in the same manner as they can in the case of shareholders and policy holders in the institutions above mentioned.   But when Trade Unions come in contact by reason of their own actions with outsiders, and *ex hypothesi*, wrong those outsiders, there can be no more reason that they should be beyond the reach of the law than any other individual, partnership or institution.   Such a claim has indeed in former times been made by the spiritual as against the civil authority, and has been consistently disallowed.   What was denied to religion ought not in our judgment to be conceded to Trade Unionism.

207. Actions by or against Registered Trade Unions in Respect of Property.

TRADE UNION ACT, 1871 ; 34 & 35 Vict., ch. 31.

9. The trustees of any trade union registered under this Act or any other officer of such trade union who may be authorised so to

do by the rules thereof, are hereby empowered to bring or defend, or cause to be brought or defended, any action, suit, prosecution, or complaint in any court of law or equity, touching or concerning the property, right, or claim to property of the trade union ; and shall and may, in all cases concerning the real or personal property of such trade union, sue and be sued, plead and be impleaded, in any court of law or equity, in their proper names, without other description than the title of their office ; and no such action, suit, prosecution, or complaint shall be discontinued or shall abate by the death or removal from office of such persons or any of them, but the same shall and may be proceeded in by their successor or successors as if such death, resignation, or removal had not taken place ; and such successors shall pay or receive the like costs as if the action, suit, prosecution, or complaint had been commenced in their names for the benefit of or to be reimbursed from the funds of such trade union, and the summons to be issued to such trustee or other officer may be served by leaving the same at the registered office of the trade union.

10. A trustee of any trade union registered under this Act shall not be liable to make good any deficiency which may arise or happen in the funds of such trade union, but shall be liable only for the moneys which shall be actually received by him on account of such trade union.

208. Non-Unionists.

RULES OF NAT. SOC. OF BRASS AND METAL MECHANICS, 1927.

Rule 33.

CLAUSE 1.—*A member who is a journeyman, foreman, charge-hand, or piece-worker, shall not have under his control or supervision, or employ any person above the age of 18 who is not a member of this society, or trade unionist, and to whom he does not pay the minimum rate of the district. Should he violate this rule he shall be summoned before the committee. If he refuses to appear he shall be fined 2s. 6d. for non-attendance. If he persistently refuses to appear the committee shall have the power to expel him from the society subject to appeal to the national executive.*

CLAUSE 2.—A member recommending a *non-unionist* to a vacant situation, when it is proved that he knew of a member on the funds who would suit such a vacancy, shall be fined 5s.

A member of this society behaving unfairly in any way to another, or upbraiding him for any relief he may at any time have received, or any pay he may have been allowed for services rendered, or in any unjust way taking advantage of his fellow-members, by giving information to any non-members of the active part taken in the interest of this society by a fellow-member, or of any number of members meeting for the purpose of criticizing or denouncing the future policy or the internal business of this society to any non-member, be fined the sum of 5s. for the first offence, and for the second offence shall be suspended from all benefits for three months.

209. The Prime Minister on Trade Unions and Employers' Associations.

MR. BALDWIN in the House of Commons. PARL. DEB., 6TH MARCH, 1925.

Now, if you look at an employers' organisation for a moment—and we will assume that it has come into being to protect the industry in the world market—we cannot lose sight of the fact that in that organisation, just as much as in the men's organisation, the mere fact of organising involves a certain amount of sacrifice of personal liberty. That cannot be helped. Everybody knows that perfectly well, both employers and employees.

To a certain extent both these organisations must on one side be uneconomic. A trade union is uneconomic in one sense of the word when it restricts output, and when it levels down the work to a lower level. It is an association for the protection of the weaker men, which has often proved uneconomic. Exactly the same thing happens in the employers' organisation. Primarily it is protective, but in effect it is very often uneconomic, because it keeps in existence works which, if left to the process of competition, would be squeezed out, and whose prolonged existence is really only a weakness to the country. It has also another very curious effect, not at all dissimilar from that of the trade union reaction, which shows that both those organisations are instinct with English traditions.

The workmen's organisation is formed to see that under the conditions a workman cannot get his living in a particular trade unless he belong to that union. An employers' organisation is formed in that particular trade for the protection of the trade, and it has the result of effectively preventing any new man starting in that trade. . . . The whole tradition of our country has been to let Englishmen develop their own associations in their own way, and with that I agree. But there are limits to that. . . . As these associations come along and become more powerful, on whichever side they are, there may come a time when not only they may injure their own members—about which probably there would be a good deal of argument—but when they may directly injure the State. It is at that moment any Government should say that, whatever freedom and latitude in that field may be left to any kind of association in this free country, nothing shall be done which shall injure the State, which is the concern of all of us and far greater than all of us or of our interests. . . .

There are few men fitted to judge, to settle and to arrange the problem that distracts the country to-day, between employers and employed. There are few men qualified to intervene who have not themselves been right through the mill, who themselves know exactly the points where the shoe pinches, who know exactly what can be conceded and what cannot, who can make their reasons plain ; and I hope that we shall always find such men trying to steer their respective ships side by side, instead of making for head-on collisions. . . .

Although I know that there are those who work for different ends from most of us in this House, yet there are many in all ranks and all parties who will re-echo my prayer : ' Give peace in our time, O Lord.'

210. ' The Document '—Modern Form.　London Builders— 1914.

The Builders' History, by R. W. POSTGATE, p. 416.

...........................1914.

To Messrs..

I agree, if employed by you, to peacefully work with my fellow-employees (engaged either in your direct employment or in that of any sub-contractor) whether they are members of a trade society or not, and I agree that I will not quit your employment because any of your employees is or is not a member of any trade society ; and I also agree that if I commit any breach of this agreement I shall be subject to a fine of twenty shillings, and I agree that the amount of such fine may be deducted from any wages which may be due to me.

Witness...................... 　　Name...................................
　　　　　　　　　　　　　　　Address.............................

211. Trade Unionism Preferred by Employers.

Notice posted by the LONDON GENERAL OMNIBUS CO., at its Garages
throughout London. 1927.

While there is no obligation on the part of any employee to
belong to a Trade Union, the Company find it mutually convenient
to have some organisation to represent the staff collectively on their
behalf. The Company therefore recognise the Transport Workers'
Federation for drivers and conductors and inside staff (other than
craftsmen).

212. Trade Unionism Preferred by Employers.

Resolution passed unanimously by Employers' and Employees' repre-
    sentatives at a JOINT MEETING OF THE LONDON DISTRICT COUNCIL
    NO. 10, (GREATER LONDON AREA), held on the 11th June, 1924, and
    subsequently passed by the NATIONAL JOINT INDUSTRIAL COUNCIL
    for the SUPPLY SECTION OF THE ELECTRICAL INDUSTRY.

The Employers' Side of the Council desire, in conjunction with
the Trade Union Side, to remind all concerned that the No. 10
Council, as at present constituted, is based on the principle of
organised employers and employees. Negotiations, therefore,
between the Employers' Side of this Council and individual employees
would be an impossibility.   The Employers and Trade Unions are
in regular contact in negotiation of wages, conduct of arbitrations,
settlement of local disputes, etc., and are responsible for the administrative expenses incurred.

The Council desire that publicity should be given to this statement,
because both sides in their experience are confident that the interests of
employers and employees in this Area are best served by individuals
joining their respective organisations with the object of maintaining
a representative and authoritative Council for the settlement of all
such questions by agreement, if possible, instead of resorting to force.

213. Trade Union Recognition.

REPORT OF THE PROVISIONAL JOINT COMMITTEE OF THE INDUSTRIAL
        CONFERENCE, 1919. Cmd. 501, p. 10.

On the subject of methods of negotiation between employers and
workpeople the Committee recognised the importance of establishing an understanding on the question of ' recognition.'   Their
opinion is as follows :

(*a*) The basis of negotiation between employers and workpeople should, as is presently the case in the chief industries of the country, be the full and frank acceptance of the employers' organisations on the one hand, and trade unions on the other, as the recognised organisations to speak and act on behalf of their members.

(*b*) The members should accept the jurisdiction of their respective organisations.

(*c*) The employers' organisations and the trade unions should enter into negotiations for the purpose of the establishment of machinery or revision, if necessary, of existing machinery, for the avoidance of disputes, and the machinery should provide, where in any question at issue there are more than one employers' organisation or trade union representing the same class of employers or workpeople, a representative method of negotiation, so that settlements arrived at will cover all parties concerned.   The machinery should also contain provisions for the protection of the employers' interests where members of trade unions of workpeople are engaged in positions of trust or confidentiality, provided the right of such employees to join or remain members of any trade union is not thereby affected.

214. Trade Union Recognition.

Resolution agreed upon by the INDUSTRIAL CONFERENCE OF THE GENERAL COUNCIL OF THE TRADES UNION CONGRESS and the 'MOND' GROUP OF EMPLOYERS, on 4th July, 1928.

It is agreed that the two main aspects of Trade Union recognition are, (*a*) recognition on questions of general policy and fundamental principle affecting industry as a whole, and (*b*) recognition on matters affecting individual industries.   Taking the first, it is recognised that the Trades Union Congress representing as it does the affiliated Trade Unions is the most effective organisation and is the only body which possesses the authority, and can exercise such authority, through its General Council, to discuss and negotiate on all questions relating to the entire field of industrial reorganisation and the industrial relations necessary thereto.

As regards individual industries it is agreed that the most effective co-operation can best be obtained by deliberation and negotiation with the accredited representatives of affiliated Unions or of Unions recognised by the General Council of the Trades Union Congress as bona fide Trade Unions.

It is recognised that industry in this country in the last generation has benefitted by the progressive increase in the volume of negotiations which have taken place between employers and representatives of Trade Unions and by an enormous growth of joint machinery for such negotiations in varying forms, namely Industrial Councils, Conciliation Boards, Conferences, etc. It may be stated that it is now the usual practice of employers to negotiate on all questions of working conditions, including wages, hours and other matters relating to the trade or industry, with the Executives and officials of the appropriate affiliated Unions or of other bona fide Trade Unions as already defined.

This practice and method of procedure has in our experience proved to be so beneficial that in our view it should be encouraged and extended.

It is therefore considered that it is definitely in the interests of all concerned in industry that full recognition should be given to affiliated Unions or other bona fide Trade Unions as already defined, as the appropriate and established machinery for the discussion and negotiation of all questions of working conditions including wages and hours, and other matters of common interest in the trade or industry concerned.

We further consider that negotiations between employers and workmen are facilitated by workmen being members of an affiliated Union or other bona fide Trade Union as already defined, and also by employers likewise being organised.

215. Compulsory Trade Unionism Forbidden for Local Authority Employees.

TRADE DISPUTES AND TRADE UNIONS ACT, 1927; 17 & 18 Geo. V., ch. 22.

6.—(1) It shall not be lawful for any local or other public authority to make it a condition of the employment or continuance in employment of any person that he shall or shall not be a member of a trade union, or to impose any condition upon persons employed by the authority whereby employees who are or who are not members of a trade union are liable to be placed in any respect either directly or indirectly under any disability or disadvantage as compared with other employees.

(2) It shall not be lawful for any local or other public authority to make it a condition of any contract made or proposed to be made

with the authority, or of the consideration or acceptance of any tender in connection with such a contract, that any person to be employed by any party to the contract shall or shall not be a member of a trade union.

(3) Any condition imposed in contravention of this section shall be void.

216. Victimisation Forbidden.

MUNITIONS OF WAR ACT, 1917 ; 7 & 8 Geo. V., ch. 45.

9. No workman employed on or in connection with munitions work shall be discharged on the ground that he has joined or is a member of a trade union, or that he has taken part in any trade dispute, and if any employer discharges a workman on any such ground he shall be guilty of an offence triable by a munitions tribunal of the second class, under the Munitions of War Act, 1915, and shall be liable to a fine not exceeding ten pounds, and the tribunal may order that the whole or any part of the fine imposed shall be paid as compensation to the workman : Provided that nothing in this section shall prejudice any right of action for wrongful dismissal that the workman may have against his employer.

217. Victimisation.

Resolution agreed upon by the INDUSTRIAL CONFERENCE OF THE GENERAL COUNCIL OF THE TRADES UNION CONGRESS and the ' MOND ' GROUP OF EMPLOYERS, on 4th July, 1928.

The principle of Trade Union recognition having been agreed upon, it is realised that such organisations have social responsibilities as well as duties to their members. With the purpose of securing increased national prosperity and improved industrial relations, it is felt that everything possible should be done to avoid any causes of friction which militate or might militate against these objects.

Among the causes of friction and unrest is what is generally described as victimisation as applied either to workmen or employers.

It is agreed that it is most undesirable that any workman should be dismissed or otherwise penalised on account of his membership of a Union, on account of his official position in a union or on account of any legitimate Trade Union activities, or activities recognised at present or in the future by the parties concerned or allowed by agreement between the parties.

It is recognised that misunderstanding exists upon consequences which it is claimed followed the great dispute of 1926. Without expressing any view upon the events of 1926 and their consequences, we consider, on account of the vital importance of improved industrial relations, that where workmen are being penalised for any part they played in those events, whether justified or not, such action is to be deprecated. For the sake of a better understanding in the future in the industrial world we hope efforts will be made to restore the pre-1926 position.

We are further of opinion that where a prima facie case is established that a workman has been dismissed or otherwise penalised for his membership of a Trade Union or for activities as previously defined, some appeal machinery should be provided for the investigation and review of such a case. At such an appeal the parties should be entitled to be represented by the Trade Union or employers' organisation respectively.

218. Non-Membership of Union as Condition of Employment.—U.S.A.

COPPAGE v. KANSAS, 19 5. 236 U.S. 1.

Section 1 of a Kansas statute of 1903 reads as follows :
' That it shall be unlawful for any individual or member of any firm, or any agent, officer, or employee of any company or corporation, to coerce, require, demand or influence any person or persons to enter into any agreement, either written or verbal, not to join or become or remain a member of any labor organisation or association, as a condition of such person or persons securing employment, or continuing in the employment of such individual, firm or corporation.'

This Act was declared unconstitutional and void by the U.S. Supreme Court in the above case. Mr. Justice Pitney said, in part :—
Laying aside, therefore, as immaterial for present purposes so much of the statute as indicates a purpose to repress coercive practices, what possible relation has the residue of the Act to the public health, safety, morals, or general welfare ? None is suggested and we are unable to conceive of any. The Act, as the construction given to it by the state court shows, is intended to deprive employers of a part of their liberty of contract, to the corresponding advantage of the employed and the upholding of the labor organisations.

But no attempt is made, or could reasonably be made, to sustain the purpose to strengthen these voluntary organisations, any more than other voluntary associations of persons, as a legitimate object for the exercise of the police power.   They are not public institutions, charged by law with public or governmental duties, such as would render the maintenance of their membership a matter of direct concern to the general welfare.   If they were, a different question would be presented.

As to the interest of the employed it is said by the Kansas Supreme Court to be a matter of common knowledge that ' employees, as a rule, are not financially able to be as independent in making contracts for the sale of their labor as are employers in making a contract of purchase thereof.'   No doubt, wherever the right of private property exists, there must and will be inequalities of fortune ; and thus it naturally happens that parties negotiating about a contract are not equally unhampered by circumstances.   This applies to all contracts, and not merely to that between employer and employee. Indeed, a little reflection will show that wherever the right of private property and the right of free contract co-exist, each party, when contracting, is inevitably more or less influenced by the question whether he has much property, or little, or none ; for the contract is made to the very end that each may gain something that he needs or desires more urgently than that which he proposes to give in exchange.   And, since it is self-evident that, unless all things are held in common, some persons must have more property than others, it is from the nature of things impossible to uphold freedom of contract and the right of private property without at the same time recognising as legitimate those inequalities of fortune that are the necessary result of the exercise of those rights.   But the 14th Amendment, in declaring that a state shall not ' deprive any person of life, liberty, or property without due process of law ' gives to each of these an equal sanction ; it recognises ' liberty ' and ' property ' as co-existent human rights, and debars the states from any unwarranted interference with either.   (Holmes, Day, and Hughes, J. J., dissented.)

219. Registration of Trade Unions.

TRADE UNION ACT, 1871 ;   34 & 35 Vict., ch. 31.

6. Any seven or more members of a trade union may by subscribing their names to the rules of the union, and otherwise complying with the provisions of this Act with respect to registry, register such trade union under this Act, provided that if any one of the purposes of such trade union be unlawful such registration shall be void.

7. It shall be lawful for any trade union registered under this Act to purchase or take upon lease in the names of the trustees for the time being of such union any land not exceeding one acre, and to sell, exchange, mortgage, or let the same, and no purchaser, assignee, mortgagee, or tenant shall be bound to inquire whether the trustees have authority for any sale, exchange, mortgage, or letting, and the receipt of the trustees shall be a discharge for the money arising therefrom ; and for the purpose of this section every branch of a trade union shall be considered a distinct union.

8. All real and personal estate whatsoever belonging to any trade union registered under this Act shall be vested in the trustees for the time being of the trade union appointed as provided by this Act, for the use and benefit of such trade union and the members thereof, and the real or personal estate of any branch of a trade union shall be vested in the trustees of such branch, and be under the control of such trustees, their respective executors or administrators, according to their respective claims and interests, and upon the death or removal of any such trustees the same shall vest in the succeeding trustees for the same estate and interest as the former trustees had therein, and subject to the same trusts, without any conveyance or assignment whatsoever, save and except in the case of stocks and securities in the public funds of Great Britain and Ireland, which shall be transferred into the names of such new trustees ; and in all actions, or suits, or indictments, or summary proceedings before any court of summary jurisdiction, touching or concerning any such property, the same shall be stated to be the property of the person or persons for the time being holding the said office of trustee, in their proper names, as trustees of such trade union, without any further description.

. . . .

13. With respect to the registry, under this Act, of a trade union, and of the rules thereof, the following provisions shall have effect :

(1) An application to register the trade union and printed copies of the rules, together with a list of the title and names of the officers, shall be sent to the registrar under this Act :

(2) The registrar, upon being satisfied that the trade union has complied with the regulations respecting registry in force under this Act, shall register such trade union and such rules :

(3) No trade union shall be registered under a name identical with that by which any other existing trade union has been registered, or so nearly resembling such name as to be likely to deceive the members or the public :

(4) Where a trade union applying to be registered has been in operation for more than a year before the date of such application, there shall be delivered to the registrar before the registry thereof a general statement of the receipts, funds, effects, and expenditure of such trade union in the same form, and showing the same particulars as if it were the annual general statement required as herein-after mentioned to be transmitted annually to the registrar :

(5) The registrar upon registering such trade union shall issue a certificate of registry, which certificate, unless proved to have been withdrawn or cancelled, shall be conclusive evidence that the regulations of this Act with respect to registry have been complied with :

(6) One of Her Majesty's Principal Secretaries of State may from time to time make regulations respecting registry under this Act, and respecting the seal (if any) to be used for the purpose of such registry, and the forms to be used for such registry, and the inspection of documents kept by the registrar under this Act, and respecting the fees, if any, to be paid on registry, not exceeding the fees specified in the second schedule to this Act, and generally for carrying this Act into effect.

14. With respect to the rules of a trade union registered under this Act, the following provisions shall have effect :

(1) The rules of every such trade union shall contain provisions in respect of the several matters mentioned in the first schedule to this Act :

(2) A copy of the rules shall be delivered by the trade union to every person on demand on payment of a sum not exceeding one shilling.

15. Every trade union registered under this Act shall have a registered office to which all communications and notices may be addressed ; if any trade union under this Act is in operation for seven days without having such an office, such trade union and every officer thereof shall each incur a penalty not exceeding five pounds for every day during which it is so in operation.

Notice of the situation of such registered office, and of any change therein, shall be given to the registrar and recorded by him : until such notice is given the trade union shall not be deemed to have complied with the provisions of this Act.

16. A general statement of the receipts, funds, effects, and expenditure of every trade union registered under this Act shall be transmitted to the registrar before the first day of June in every year, and shall show fully the assets and liabilities at the date, and the receipts and expenditure during the year preceding the date to which it is made out, of the trade union ; and shall show separately the expenditure in respect of the several objects of the trade union, and shall be prepared and made out up to such date, in such form, and shall comprise such particulars, as the registrar may from time to time require ; and every member of, and depositor in, any such trade union shall be entitled to receive, on application to the treasurer or secretary of that trade union, a copy of such general statement, without making any payment for the same.

Together with such general statement there shall be sent to the registrar a copy of all alterations of rules and new rules and changes of officers made by the trade union during the year preceding the date up to which the general statement is made out, and a copy of the rules of the trade union as they exist at that date.

Every trade union which fails to comply with or acts in contravention of this section, and also every officer of the trade union so failing, shall each be liable to a penalty not exceeding five pounds for each offence.

Every person who wilfully makes or orders to be made any false entry in or any omission from any such general statement, or in or from the return of such copies of rules or alterations of rules, shall be liable to a penalty not exceeding fifty pounds for each offence.

.   .   .   .

FIRST SCHEDULE.

Of Matters to be provided for by the Rules of Trade Unions Registered under this Act.

1. The name of the trade union and place of meeting for the business of the trade union.

2. The whole of the objects for which the trade union is to be established, the purposes for which the funds thereof shall be applicable, and the conditions under which any member may become entitled to any benefit assured thereby, and the fines and forfeitures to be imposed on any member of such trade union.

3. The manner of making, altering, amending, and rescinding rules.

4. A provision for the appointment and removal of a general committee of management, of a trustee or trustees, treasurer, and other officers.

5. A provision for the investment of the funds, and for an annual or periodical audit of accounts.

6. The inspection of the books and names of members of the trade union by every person having an interest in the funds of the trade union.

TRADE UNION ACT (1871) AMENDMENT ACT, 1876 ; 39 & 40 Vict., ch. 22.

3. Whereas by section eight of the principal Act it is enacted that ' the real or personal estate of any branch of a trade union shall be vested in the trustees of such branch : ' The said section shall be read and construed as if immediately after the herein-before recited words there were inserted the words ' or of the trustees of the trade union, if the rules of the trade union so provide.'

4. When any person, being or having been a trustee of a trade union or of any branch of a trade union, and whether appointed before or after the legal establishment thereof, in whose name any stock belonging to such union or branch transferable at the Bank of England or Bank of Ireland is standing, either jointly with another or others, or solely, is absent from Great Britain or Ireland respectively, or becomes bankrupt, or files any petition, or executes any deed for liquidation of his affairs by assignment or arrangement, or for composition with his creditors, or becomes a lunatic, or is dead, or has been removed from his office of trustee, or if it be unknown whether such person is living or dead, the registrar, on application in writing from the secretary and three members of the union or branch, and on proof satisfactory to him, may direct the transfer of the stock into the names of any other persons as trustees for the union or branch ; and such transfer shall be made by the surviving or continuing trustees, and if there be no such trustee, or if such trustees refuse or be unable to make such transfer, and the registrar so direct, then by the Accountant-General or Deputy or Assistant Accountant-General of the Bank of England or Bank of Ireland, as the case may be ; and the Governors and Companies of the Bank of England and Bank of Ireland respectively are hereby indemnified for anything done by them or any of their officers in pursuance of this provision

against any claim or demand of any person injuriously affected thereby.

.   .   .   .

6. Trade unions carrying or intending to carry on business in more than one country shall be registered in the country in which their registered office is situate ; but copies of the rules of such unions, and of all amendments of the same, shall, when registered, be sent to the registrar of each of the other countries, to be recorded by him, and until such rules be so recorded the union shall not be entitled to any of the privileges of this Act or the principal Act, in the country in which such rules have not been recorded, and until such amendments of rules be recorded the same shall not take effect in such country.

In this section ' country ' means England, Scotland, or Ireland.

8. No certificate of registration of a trade union shall be withdrawn or cancelled otherwise than by the chief registrar of Friendly Societies, or in the case of trade unions registered and doing business exclusively in Scotland or Ireland, by the assistant registrar for Scotland or Ireland, and in the following cases :

(1) At the request of the trade union to be evidenced in such manner as such chief or assistant registrar shall from time to time direct :

(2) On proof to his satisfaction that a certificate of registration has been obtained by fraud or mistake, or that the registration of the trade union has become void under section six of the Trade Union Act, 1871, or that such trade union has wilfully and after notice from a registrar whom it may concern, violated any of the provisions of the Trade Union Acts, or has ceased to exist.

Not less than two months previous notice in writing, specifying briefly the ground of any proposed withdrawal or cancelling of certificate (unless where the same is shown to have become void as aforesaid, in which case it shall be the duty of the chief or assistant registrar to cancel the same forthwith) shall be given by the chief or assistant registrar to a trade union before the certificate of registration of the same can be withdrawn or cancelled (except at its request).

A trade union whose certificate of registration has been withdrawn or cancelled shall, from the time of such withdrawal or cancelling, absolutely cease to enjoy as such the privileges of a registered trade union, but without prejudice to any liability actually incurred by such trade union, which may be enforced against the same as if such withdrawal or cancelling had not taken place.

220. Workers' Representation on Advisory Committees and Miners' Welfare Fund.

PROVISION CONTAINED IN THE MINING INDUSTRY ACT, 1920; 10 & 11 Geo. V., ch. 50.

4.—(1) The Board of Trade shall appoint committees for the purpose of giving the Board advice and assistance on matters connected with their powers and duties under this Act relating to coal and the coal industry and to the metalliferous mining industry respectively, and may appoint one or more other committees for the purpose of giving the Board advice and assistance on matters connected with any of their other powers and duties relating to mines and the mining industry, and in appointing members of any committee hereinbefore referred to the Board of Trade shall act after consultation with the various interests concerned.

(2) The Board of Trade shall refer to an advisory committee for advice any question relating to the powers and duties of the Board relating to mines and the mining industry which appears to the Board of such a nature as to make such reference desirable, and shall take into consideration any representations thereon which may be made to the Board by any such committee.

(3) The advisory committee on coal and the coal industry shall consist of a chairman and twenty-four other persons, of whom—

Four shall be representative of owners of coal mines ; four shall be representative of workers in or about coal mines ; three shall be representatives of employers in other industries ; three shall be representative of workers in other industries ; one shall be a mining engineer ; two shall be agents or managers or under-managers of coal mines holding first class certificates ; one shall be a coal exporter ; one shall be a coal factor or coal merchant ; one shall be a person with experience of commerce other than the production or distribution of coal ; one shall be a person with experience in co-operative trading ; three shall be persons with expert knowledge of medical or other science.

.   .   .   .

20.—(1) There shall be constituted a fund to be applied for such purposes connected with the social well-being, recreation, and conditions of living of workers in or about coal mines and with mining education and research as the Board of Trade, after consultation with any Government Department concerned, may approve.

(2) The owners of every coal mine shall, before the thirty-first day of March, nineteen hundred and twenty-one, and before the same day in each of the subsequent five years, pay into the said fund a sum equal to one penny a ton of the output of the mine during the previous calendar year, and the sums so payable in respect of any mine shall be defrayed as part of the working expenses of the mine and shall be recoverable either as a debt due to the Crown or by the Board of Trade summarily as a civil debt :

Provided that in the case of the first payment the amount shall be calculated with reference to the output during the six calendar months ending the thirty-first day of December, nineteen hundred and twenty.

(3) The duty of allocating the money from time to time standing to the credit of the said fund to the several purposes aforesaid shall be vested in a committee consisting of five persons, appointed by the Board of Trade, of whom one shall be appointed by the Board of Trade after consultation with the Mining Association of Great Britain, and another after consultation with the Miners' Federation of Great Britain. The committee shall have the assistance of three assessors appointed by the Minister of Health, the Board of Education and the Secretary for Scotland respectively ; the assessors shall have the right of attending meetings of the committee and of taking part in the deliberations thereof, but not of voting ; and different persons may be appointed by the above-mentioned departments to act as assessors in relation to different matters :

Provided that the Committee shall take into consideration any scheme submitted by a district committee, and that before allocating any money for a local purpose they shall consult with the district committee (if any) concerned ; and that the Committee shall allocate for the benefit of the several districts mentioned in Part I. of the Second Schedule to this Act sums equal to four-fifths of the contributions from the owners of coal mines in those districts respectively.

(4) The committee may invite a local authority to submit a scheme for any of the purposes to which the fund may be applied, and, if such scheme be approved by the committee, they may make such grants in aid to the said local authority out of the fund and upon such conditions as may seem to them desirable :

Provided that in no case shall any grant be made out of the fund for the building or repairing of dwelling-houses.

221. Workers' Representation on War Pensions Committees, etc.

NAVAL AND MILITARY WAR PENSIONS, ETC., ACT, 1915, 5 & 6 Geo. V., ch. 83.

1.—(1) For the purposes herein-after mentioned relating to pensions and grants and allowances made in respect of the present war to officers and men in the naval and military services of His Majesty and their wives, widows, children and other dependants, and the care of officers and men disabled in consequence of the present war there shall be constituted a Statutory Committee of the Royal Patriotic Fund Corporation (hereinafter referred to as the Corporation) consisting of twenty-seven members, appointed as herein-after mentioned.

(2) Of the said twenty-seven members—

twelve (of whom one shall be chairman and one vice-chairman and some shall be women and not less than two shall be representatives of labour) shall be appointed by His Majesty;

.   .   .   .

2.—(1) For the purpose of assisting the Statutory Committee in the execution of their duties, a local committee shall be established for every county and county borough, and for every borough and urban district having a population of not less than fifty thousand the council of which so desires, and for any other borough or urban district for which the Statutory Committee, on the application of the council thereof, considers it desirable that, having regard to the special circumstances of the case, a separate local committee should be established.

(2) The constitution of a local committee shall be such as may be determined by a scheme framed by the council of the county or borough or urban district and approved by the Statutory Committee; so, however, that every such scheme shall provide—

.   .   .   .

(c) for the inclusion of women and representatives of labour among the members of the local committee.

.   .   .   .

CIRCULAR ISSUED TO COUNTIES, COUNTY BOROUGHS, ETC., BY THE
STATUTORY COMMITTEE, 19th February, 1916, p. 4.

As regards Labour, the representatives of which, it is suggested,
shall be not less than one-fifth of the total number of members of
the Local Committee, it is unnecessary to point out that what is
sought for in connection with its representatives by means of recommendations from appropriate organisations or bodies is not merely
the presence on the Committee of persons who are cognizant of
working class conditions or who themselves belong to the manual
working class, but the representation on the Committee of working
class opinion and the cordial and continued co-operation of working
class organisations in the work of the Committee.   It is with this
object that the Model Scheme suggests that appropriate organisations may recommend representatives for appointment.   In addition
to the Local Trades Councils in which the local Trade Unions are
usually combined, there are often large and powerful branches of
national Trade Unions which have contributed many men to the
Services.   The difficult case of unorganised labour, which in some
parts of the $\left\{\begin{array}{l} \text{County} \\ \text{Borough} \end{array}\right\}$ may comprise a large proportion of workers,
should be specially considered by the Council.   In such cases, and
where there is a doubt as to what working class organisations exist
in the locality or as to the number of persons they respectively represent, information may with advantage be sought from the Secretary
to the Parliamentary Trades Union Congress.[1]

.   .   .   .

It may be of value that there should be included amongst the
members of the Committee some women representatives of the wives
or widows of the rank and file.   In case of difficulty in carrying out
this suggestion, information may usefully be sought from the Secretary of the Joint Committee of Women's Organisations at 34 Meck-
lenburg Square, London, W.C.   These organisations include the
four national organisations of women of the manual working class,
which have branches in many parts of the Kingdom, viz. :

The Women's Co-operative Guild, The Women's Trade
Union League, The Railway Women's Guild, and The Women's
Labour League.

[1] *i.e.* Parliamentary Committee of the T.U.C., now the General
Council of the T.U.C.   (ED.)

222. Port of London Authority.

PORT OF LONDON ACT, 1908 ; 8 Edw. VII., ch. 68.

1.—(1) An authority (in this Act referred to as the Port Authority) shall be established for the purpose of administering, preserving, and improving the port of London and otherwise for the purposes of this Act.

. . . .

(3) The Port Authority shall consist of a chairman and vice-chairman and other members elected and appointed in manner provided by this Act.

. . . .

(5) Subject to the provisions of this section, the number of elected members shall be eighteen. . . .

(6) Subject to the provisions of this section, the number of appointed members shall be ten, appointed as follows : . . . By the Board of Trade—2. . . . By the London County Council (not being members of the Council)—2.

. . . .

(7) With a view to providing for the representation of labour on the Port Authority, one of the members of the Port Authority appointed by the Board of Trade shall be appointed by the Board after consultation with such organisations representative of labour as the Board think best qualified to advise them upon the matter, and one of the members of the Port Authority appointed by the London County Council shall be appointed by the council after consultation with such organisations representative of labour as the council think best qualified to advise them upon the matter.

223. Trade Unions and Transport Registration Scheme.

BRISTOL DOCKS SCHEME, 1919.

TRANSPORT WORKERS COURT OF ENQUIRY, 1920. Cmd. 937, p. 58.

Registration.

1. There shall be a complete Registration Scheme for all general labour in or about the Docks divided into :

(*a*) All Dock Labour.

(*b*) All Carters, Warehousemen, and permanent Loaders.

The term ' general labour ' does not include members of Engineering and other Craft Trades, and the permanent administrative Staffs of Employers.

Men to be Registered.

2. All men at present holding Record Books to be registered. No other men to be registered except those men who previously were employed on the Docks, and are now being demobilised from H.M. Forces.

Date Operative.

3. The scheme shall come into operation on March 31st, 1919, and all men under the Scheme to be members of the Dockers' Union.

Registration by Tally.

4. Registration to be by means of a metal Tally. Tallies to be of two varieties, viz. :

(*a*) All Dock Labour (round and square, marked ' D ').
(*b*) All Carters, Warehousemen, and Permanent Loaders (oval and triangular, marked ' C ').

Tallies are not interchangeable. Carters' Tallies will not be accepted for employment as Dock Labourers, or *vice versa*, except when there is a shortage of labour in one section, and a surplus of labour in the other, and only when this shortage is certified by the Labour Advisor. The Tally number issued to a man shall be retained by him during the whole of his service, and the same number shall be entered on his Union Card. Tallies to be exchanged quarterly at the Dockers' Union Offices.

Each quarter's Tallies will be of distinct shape to ensure that they are exchanged quarterly.

The change of Record Books for Tallies will be made during the last week of the present quarter. . . .

No Engagement without Tally.

5. No man shall be engaged who is not in possession of the official Tally.

Retention of Tallies.

6. The Tally must be collected by the Employer or his representative upon a man's engagement and retained until the termination.

. . . .

13. In case additional men are required at any time in the port, no man shall be admitted without the consent of the Port Labour

Committee, and in the event of more men being required, applications would be considered by the Port Labour Committee, or Sub-Committee thereof, provision to be made that such Committee meets at regular intervals.

EXAMINATION OF THE GENERAL MANAGER AND SECRETARY OF THE BRISTOL DOCKS, BY THE COURT OF ENQUIRY. Cmd. 936, p. 205.

Q. The Port Labour Committee now consists of representatives of the employers and of the men ?

A. And of the Ministry of Labour.

Q. How many of each ?   I think the names are given on the last page, page 4.

A. I am the Chairman.   There are five representatives of different classes of employers and five representatives of the Dockers' Union.   The Secretary is an official of the Ministry of Labour. The Divisional Labour Ministry Official is also a member and comes very often.

Q. Does this Committee issue the Tallies to the men ?

A. This Committee issues the tallies through the Dockers' Union Offices to the men.

Q. Who really has the control of the issuing of the tallies ?

A. The control of the issuing of the tallies to the casuals is done entirely by the Union officials.

Q. The rules provide, I think, for a sufficient number of tallies being issued in order to meet the demands at the docks ?

A. Yes, and perhaps it would be convenient here if I explain that we meet temporary demands for an increase of labour by the issue of temporary tallies, the numbers being fixed in negotiation between my office and representatives of the Union.

224. Railway Rates Tribunal.

RAILWAYS ACT, 1921 ; 11 & 12 Geo. V., ch. 55.

20.—(1) There shall be established a court styled the Railway Rates Tribunal (in this Act referred to as the ' rates tribunal '), consisting of three permanent members, with power to add to their number as hereinafter provided, and the rates tribunal shall be a court of record and have an official seal which shall be judicially noticed, and the rates tribunal may act notwithstanding any vacancy in their number.

24.—(1) There shall be constituted two panels, the one (hereinafter referred to as the general panel) consisting of thirty-six persons, twenty-two being nominated by the President of the Board of Trade after consultation with such bodies as he may consider to be most representative of trading interests, twelve being nominated by the Minister of Labour after consultation with such bodies as he may consider most representative of the interests of labour and of passengers upon the railways, and two being nominated by the Minister of Agriculture and Fisheries after consultation with such bodies as he may consider most representative of agricultural and horticultural interests, and the other (hereinafter referred to as the railway panel) consisting of eleven persons nominated by the Minister after consultation with the Railway Companies' Association, and one person nominated by the Minister to represent railways and light railway companies not parties to the Railway Companies' Association.

(2) A member of a panel shall hold office for such term, not exceeding three years from the date of his appointment, as may be determined at the time of appointment, and then retire, but shall be eligible for reappointment.

.   .   .   .

(4) Whenever for the purposes of any particular case or proceeding the rates tribunal either upon application by any of the parties or otherwise so request, or the Minister thinks it expedient, there shall be added to the rates tribunal two additional members nominated by the Minister from the panels, one selected from the general panel and one from the railway panel.

In selecting a member from the general panel, regard shall be had to the particular class of case or proceeding to be heard, so that, as nearly as may be, the person so selected shall be conversant with and have knowledge of the technicalities that may arise in such particular case or proceeding.

(5) Any person appointed under the provisions of this section shall, for the purposes of any proceedings in respect of which he may be so appointed, be a member of the rates tribunal and shall, subject to the provisions of this Part of this Act and to the general rules made thereunder, exercise all the powers and functions of a permanent member of the rates tribunal.

225. Labour Representation on Port Authorities.

REPORT OF THE TRANSPORT WORKERS' COURT OF ENQUIRY, 1920.
H.C. 55 of 1920, para. 27.

27. But there is—and it is a serious matter—a defect. The port authorities and employers are engaged in daily contact with enormous bodies of men, and with a system, to which they cannot be blind, under which the fringe of unemployment is great and under-employment is greater. In the opinion of the Court the organisation of all the ports in the Kingdom would be strengthened by the admission of, or an increase in, the direct representation of labour on the governing bodies. It appears to the Court manifest that the labour situation might be ameliorated, conditions of labour might undergo advantageous reform, and loss of output might be avoided, if the direct representation here recommended in principle were introduced. The extent and manner of such representation would be for the national council to determine.

226. Participation by Trade Unions in the Administration of National Unemployment Insurance Scheme.

UNEMPLOYMENT INSURANCE ACT, 1920 ; 10 & 11 Geo. V., ch. 30.

17.—(1) Subject as hereinafter provided, the Minister may, on the application of any society approved under the National Insurance Act, 1911, or body ancillary thereto, or any other association of employed persons (other than any such society, body, or association being an industrial assurance company or a collecting society, or a separate section of such company or society, or a society organised by such company or society solely or jointly with other bodies), being a society or other association the rules of which provide for payments to its members, or any class thereof, while unemployed, make an arrangement with the society or other association that, in lieu of paying unemployment benefit under this Act to persons who prove that they are members of the society or other association, there shall be repaid periodically to the society or other association out of the unemployment fund such sum as appears to be, as nearly as may be, equivalent to the aggregate amount which those persons would have received during that period by way of unemployment benefit under this Act if no such arrangement had been made :

Provided that the Minister shall not make or continue an arrangement with a society or other association under this section—

(a) .   .   .   .

(b) Unless the society or association has such a system of ascertaining the wages and conditions prevailing in every employment within the meaning of this Act in which its members are engaged and of obtaining from employers notification of vacancies for employment and giving notice thereof to its members when unemployed as is in the opinion of the Minister reasonably effective for securing that unemployed persons competent to undertake the particular class of work required shall, with all practicable speed, be brought into communication with employers having vacancies to fill.

.   .   .   .

(6) The Minister may, with the consent of the Treasury, and subject to such conditions and otherwise as the Minister may prescribe, pay to any society or other association with which an arrangement under this section is in force by way of contribution towards the administrative expenses of the society or other association in connection with the arrangement such sum, not exceeding in any year an amount calculated at the rate of one shilling for each week of the aggregate number of weeks of unemployment in respect of which a repayment is made to the society or other association under this section, as he thinks fit, and any sum so paid shall be treated as part of the expenses incurred by the Minister in carrying this Act into effect.

227. Trade Union's Part in Administration of Unemployment Insurance.

MINISTRY OF LABOUR REPORT ON NATIONAL UNEMPLOYMENT INSURANCE, 1923, p. 137 ff.

In order to be qualified to make an arrangement an association or society must pay out-of-work benefit from its own funds on a certain scale, and must :

(a) have an effective system for obtaining from employers notification of vacancies, and for placing its unemployed members quickly in such suitable vacancies as may be available, and

(b) have an effective system of ascertaining wages and conditions in employments in which its members are engaged.

The associations with which arrangements were made under

the earlier scheme were trade unions which already, in most cases, made out-of-work payments under their own rules from their own private funds, and had, therefore, experience in dealing with the problems relating to the test of unemployment, willingness to work, etc., which arise in the course of administration. . . .

Further, the trade unions were in general organised on a craft or industrial basis and possessed detailed knowledge of the different varieties of skill and experience required for different jobs . . . in many cases the trade union was a recognised link between the employer who desired workpeople and the industrial workers who required work. . . .

The nature of the evidence of unemployment which associations having arrangements are required to obtain from their unemployed members naturally follows in general the lines laid down for direct claimants. That method, which was itself for the most part, copied from the general practice of the trade unions covering workers in the trades insured under the Act of 1911, is, . . . the requirement of the attendance of the claimant, in general daily, during ordinary working hours, in order to sign an unemployed register or vacant book as evidence of his unemployment.   This method is appropriate to the circumstances of most industries, but it is not the only method in use by trade unions which have experience in the matter of out-of-work payments.   In making arrangements, therefore, the Department have regard to the special circumstances of different trades or industries and have admitted certain variations.

228. Trade Unions in Industrial Administration.

WAR-TIME—THE COTTON CONTROL BOARD, (1917-1919)

From *The Cotton Control Board*, by H. D. HENDERSON (Secretary to the Board), 1922, pp. 7, 8, 12, 13, 28, 33, 34.

The Cotton Control Board was unique among war controls in the degree to which it assumed the character and elicited the response of a representative trade organ.   Technically it might be a sub-ordinate branch of the Government, amenable to its authority. But it was quite otherwise that the members of the Board conceived the relationship.   It was to the various interests of which they were the representatives that they held themselves responsible.   . . . the

Control Board wielded its powers and issued its decrees with the sovereign freedom of a Dominion legislature.

．　　．　　．　　．　　．　　．　　．　　．

The Cotton Control Board was originally composed as follows. . . . Apart from the Chairman himself, there were eight representatives of the industry proper : four of the employers and four of the operatives. . . . The remaining four members represented the interests of the merchants and of the Government. . . . Within a few weeks . . . the employers . . . obtained two additional members, and the equal balance between employers and operatives was upset.

．　　．　　．　　．　　．　　．　　．　　．

The Board's arrangements for the payment of unemployment benefits were of the simplest kind. It was out of the question to create an immense administrative organisation with offices and staff in each locality. The organisation of the trade unions was well adapted for the purpose. The Board decided accordingly to devolve upon the trade unions the task of paying out the benefits to all operatives, unionists and non-unionists alike. A scale of payments was issued by the Board, and certain rules were laid down as to the circumstances which entitled operatives to claim these payments. For the rest, the Board's part in the work was confined to the remission of cheques to the unions either in advance or in repayment of sums already spent.

In the working of this system the union officials enjoyed a wide discretion.

To the trade union officials the whole arrangement was peculiarly agreeable. Without any encroachment upon their own carefully accumulated funds, they had all the pleasure of paying out to their members benefits upon an unprecedentedly generous scale, with a satisfying sense that it was in a large measure their scheme and that credit was due to them. When it came to paying a non-unionist, the pleasure was heightened for most by the excellent opportunity afforded for a little homily. For their trouble they received small but welcome allowances from the Central Board proportioned to the number of workpeople whom they paid. They enjoyed, as we have already seen, a wide and congenial discretion in the interpretation of doubtful points of detail. . . . The Board placed implicit confidence in the unions and in their officials, trusted them to pay out its money in accordance with the spirit as well as with the letter of its rules, and deemed it unnecessary to exercise any supervision to see that they actually did so . . . as the result, it may be confidently hazarded that the proportion of wrongful payments under the Control Board's scheme was not a fraction of that which occurred under the Government Out-of-Work Donation scheme, with all its provisions for repeated signings-on at the Labour Exchange and the rest of its elaborate machinery.

229. Checkweighers in Coal Mines.

COAL MINES REGULATION ACT, 1887 ; 50 & 51 Vict., c. 58.

13. (1) The persons who are employed in a mine and are paid according to the weight of the mineral gotten by them, may, at their own cost, station a person (in this Act referred to as a ' checkweigher ') at each place appointed for the weighing of the mineral, and at each place appointed for determining the deductions in order that he may on behalf of the persons by whom he is so stationed take a correct account of the weight of the mineral or determine correctly the deductions as the case may be.

(2) A checkweigher shall have every facility afforded to him for enabling him to fulfil the duties for which he is stationed, including facilities for examining and testing the weighing machine and checking the tareing of tubs and trams where necessary ; and if at any time proper facilities are not afforded to a checkweigher as required by this section, the owner, agent and manager of the mine shall each be guilty of an offence against this Act, unless he proves that he had taken all reasonable means to enforce to the best of his power the requirements of this section.

(3) A checkweigher shall not be authorised in any way to impede or interrupt the working of the mine, or to interfere with the weighing, or with any of the workmen, or with the management of the mine.

.   .   .   .

(8) If the person appointed by the owner, agent or manager to weigh the mineral impedes or interrupts the checkweigher in the proper discharge of his duties, or improperly interferes with or alters the weighing machine or the tare in order to prevent a correct account being taken of the weighing and tareing, he shall be guilty of an offence against this Act.

14.—(1) Where a ' checkweigher ' has been appointed by the majority, ascertained by ballot, of the persons employed in a mine who are paid according to the weight of the mineral gotten by them, and has acted as such, he may recover from any person for the time being employed at such mine and so paid his proportion of the checkweigher's wages or recompense, notwithstanding that any of the persons by whom the checkweigher was appointed may have left the mine or others have entered the same since the checkweigher's appointment, any rule of law or equity to the contrary notwithstanding.

.   .   .   .

COAL MINES (CHECK WEIGHER) ACT, 1894 ; 57 & 58 Vict., c. 52.

1. If the owner, agent or manager of any mine, or any person employed by or acting under the instructions of any owner, agent or manager, interferes with the appointment of a check weigher, or refuses to afford proper facilities for the holding of any meeting for the purpose of making such appointment, in any case in which the persons entitled to make the appointment do not possess or are unable to obtain a suitable meeting place, or attempts, whether by threats, bribes, promises, notice of dismissal, or otherwise howsoever, to exercise improper influence in respect of such appointment, or to induce the persons entitled to appoint a check weigher, or any of them, not to re-appoint a check weigher, or to vote for or against any particular person or class of persons in the appointment of a check weigher, such owner, agent or manager shall be guilty of an offence against the Coal Mines Regulation Act, 1872.

COAL MINES (WEIGHING OF MINERALS) ACT, 1905 ; 5 Edw. VII., c. 9.

1.—(2) A statutory declaration, made by the person who presided at a meeting for the purpose of appointing a check weigher or deputy check weigher, to the effect that he presided at that meeting, and that the person named in the declaration was duly appointed check weigher or deputy check weigher, as the case may be, by that meeting, shall be forthwith delivered to the owner, agent or manager of the mine, and shall be *prima facie* evidence of that appointment.

.   .   .   .

(5) Where a check weigher or deputy check weigher is appointed by a majority, ascertained by ballot, of the persons employed at the mine, and paid according to the mineral gotten, he shall not be removed by the persons employed in the mine except by a majority, ascertained by ballot, of the persons employed and paid as aforesaid at the time of the removal.

.   .   .   .

3. All persons who are entitled, by the principal Act or this Act, to appoint a check weigher or deputy check weigher shall have due notice given to them of the intention to appoint a check weigher or deputy check weigher, by a notice posted at the pithead or otherwise, specifying the time and place of the meeting, and have the same facilities given to each of them for the purpose of recording their votes, either by ballot or otherwise, in such appointment.

230. Inspections on behalf of Workmen.

COAL MINES ACT, 1911 ; 1 & 2 Geo. V., c. 50.

16.—(1) The workmen employed in a mine may, at their own cost, appoint two of their number or any two persons, not being mining engineers, who are or who have been practical working miners and have had not less than five years' experience of underground work, to inspect the mine, and the persons so appointed shall be allowed once at least in every month, accompanied, if the owner, agent or manager of the mine thinks fit, by himself or one or more officials of the mine, to go to every part of the mine, and to inspect the shafts, roads, levels, workings, air-ways, ventilating apparatus, old workings and machinery, and shall, where an accident has occurred in a mine of which notice is required under this Act to be be given, be allowed to go together with any person acting as legal adviser to the workmen, or with a mining or electrical engineer selected by the workmen, accompanied as aforesaid, to the place where the accident occurred, and to make such inspection as may be necessary for ascertaining the cause of the accident. . . .

(2) Every facility shall be afforded by the owner, agent and manager and all persons in the mine for the purpose of the inspection and the manager shall on demand produce to the persons appointed the certificates of all firemen, examiners or deputies employed in the mine, and the persons appointed shall, except where the inspection is an inspection for the purpose of ascertaining the cause of an accident, forthwith make and sign a full and accurate report of the result of the inspection in a book to be kept at the mine for the purpose ; and the owner, agent or manager shall forthwith cause a true copy of the report to be sent to the inspector of the division.

231. Railway Wages Boards.

RAILWAYS ACT, 1921; 11 & 12 Geo. V., ch. 55.

PART IV.

WAGES AND CONDITIONS OF SERVICE.

62. As from the date when railways of which possession was taken under the Regulation of the Forces Act, 1871, and retained under the Ministry of Transport Act, 1919, cease to be in possession of the Minister, and until otherwise determined by twelve months' notice on either side (such notice not to be given before the first day of January, nineteen hundred and twenty-three), all questions relating to rates of pay, hours of duty or other conditions of service of employees to whom this Part of this Act applies shall, in default of agreement between the railway companies and the railway trade unions, be referred to the Central Wages Board, or, on appeal, the National Wages Board, as reconstituted under this Act.

63.—(1) Arrangements shall be made for establishing for each railway company affected one or more councils, consisting of officers of the railway company and representatives of the men employed by the company elected by those men.

(2) The constitution and functions of any such council shall be such as may be determined by schemes made in manner hereinafter appearing, it being understood that the functions of the council shall generally be such as are mentioned in paragraph (16) of the Report of the Reconstruction Committee on the Relations between Employers and Employed, dated the eighth day of March, nineteen hundred and seventeen.

64.—(1) As from the passing of this Act, the Central Wages Board and the National Wages Board shall be reconstituted in the following manner :

(a) the Central Wages Board shall be composed of eight representatives of the railway companies and eight representatives of the railway employees. The railway companies' representatives shall be appointed by the railway companies. The employees' representatives shall be appointed by the railway trade unions, four by the National Union of Railwaymen, two by the Associated Society of Locomotive Engineers and Firemen, and two by the Railway Clerks' Association ;

(b) the National Wages Board shall be composed of six representatives of the railway companies, who shall be appointed by the railway companies, six representatives of the railway employees (two of whom shall be appointed by the National Union of Railwaymen, two by the Associatied Society of Locomotive Engineers and Firemen, and two by the Railway Clerks' Association), and four representatives of the users of railways, with an independent chairman nominated by the Minister of Labour. The four representatives of the users of railways shall be nominated as follows :

One by the Parliamentary Committee of the Trades Union Congress ; one by the Co-operative Union ; one by the Association of British Chambers of Commerce ; and one by the Federation of British Industries.

(2) Nothing in the constitution of either such Board shall be held to prejudice the right of any party to a reference to the Board to raise any point they may consider relevant to the issue, and any point raised shall be taken into consideration by the Board.

65. For the purpose of giving effect to the foregoing provisions of this Part of this Act, and in particular for the purpose of defining the constitution and functions of such councils as aforesaid, schemes shall be made and may, from time to time, be varied by a committee consisting of six representatives of the General Managers' Committee of the Railway Clearing House and six representatives of the National Union of Railwaymen, the Associated Society of Locomotive Engineers and Firemen, and the Railway Clerks' Association.

Such schemes may be determined by twelve months' notice by either side of such committee, but such notice shall not be given before the first day of January, nineteen hundred and twenty-three.

66.—(1) The employees to whom this Part of this Act applies are those employed by the railway companies hereinafter mentioned and the Railway Clearing House in the grades of employees included in the several national agreements referred to in the Seventh Schedule to this Act (other than employees who, in accordance with the classification for the time being in force, are in the special class), and such other grades of employees as the parties to such schemes as aforesaid may hereafter agree to include in the schemes.

(2) The railway companies hereinbefore referred to are, until the amalgamation schemes come into operation, the railway companies mentioned in the second and third columns of the First Schedule to this Act of whose undertakings the Minister was in possession on the fifteenth day of August, nineteen hundred and twenty-one, including, as respects any railways jointly owned or worked by two or more

such companies, a joint committee of those companies, and after those schemes come into operation the amalgamated companies, including, as respects any railways jointly owned or worked by two or more of those companies, a joint committee of those companies.

232. The Whitley Report.

REPORT OF THE RECONSTRUCTION COMMITTEE ON RELATIONS BETWEEN EMPLOYERS AND EMPLOYED. 19 7.

To the Right Honourable D. Lloyd George, M.P., Prime Minister.

SIR,

We have the honour to submit the following Interim Report on Joint Standing Industrial Councils.

2. The terms of reference to the Sub-Committee are :

' (i) To make and consider suggestions for securing a permanent improvement in the relations between employers and workmen.

(ii) To recommend means for securing that industrial conditions affecting the relations between employers and workmen shall be systematically reviewed by those concerned, with a view to improving conditions in the future.'

. . . .

5.

In the interests of the community it is vital that after the war the co-operation of all classes, established during the war, should continue, and more especially with regard to the relations between employers and employed.   For securing improvement in the latter, it is essential that any proposals put forward should offer to workpeople the means of attaining improved conditions of employment and a higher standard of comfort generally, and involve the enlistment of their active and continuous co-operation in the promotion of industry.

To this end, the establishment for each industry of an organisation, representative of employers and workpeople, to have as its object the regular consideration of matters affecting the progress and wellbeing of the trade from the point of view of all those engaged in it, so far as this is consistent with the general interest of the community, appears to us necessary.

. . . .

7. With a view to providing means for carrying out the policy outlined above, we recommend that His Majesty's Government

should propose without delay to the various associations of employers and employed the formation of Joint Standing Industrial Councils in the several industries, where they do not already exist, composed of representatives of employers and employed, regard being paid to the various sections of the industry and the various classes of labour engaged.

.   .   .   .

13. In the well-organised industries, one of the first questions to be considered should be the establishment of local and works organisations to supplement and make more effective the work of the central bodies. It is not enough to secure co-operation at the centre between the national organisations ; it is equally necessary to enlist the activity and support of employers and employed in the districts and in individual establishments. The National Industrial Council should not be regarded as complete in itself; what is needed is a triple organisation—in the workshops, the districts, and nationally. Moreover, it is essential that the organisation at each of these three stages should proceed on a common principle, and that the greatest measure of common action between them should be secured.

14. With this end in view, we are of opinion that the following proposals should be laid before the National Industrial Councils :

(a) That District Councils, representative of the Trade Unions and of the Employers' Association in the industry, should be created, or developed out of the existing machinery for negotiation in the various trades.

(b) That Works Committees, representative of the management and of the workers employed, should be instituted in particular works to act in close co-operation with the district and national machinery.

As it is of the highest importance that the scheme making provision for these Committees should be such as to secure the support of the Trade Unions and Employers' Associations concerned, its design should be a matter for agreement between these organisations.

Just as regular meetings and continuity of co-operation are essential in the case of the National Industrial Councils, so they seem to be necessary in the case of the district and works organisations. The object is to secure co-operation by granting to workpeople a greater share in the consideration of matters affecting their industry, and this can only be achieved by keeping employers and workpeople in constant touch.

15. The respective functions of Works Committees, District Councils, and National Councils will no doubt require to be determined separately in accordance with the varying conditions of different industries. Care will need to be taken in each case to delimit accurately their respective functions, in order to avoid overlapping and resulting friction. For instance, where conditions of employment are determined by national agreements, the District Councils or Works Committees should not be allowed to contract out of conditions so laid down, nor, where conditions are determined by local agreements, should such power be allowed to Works Committees.

16. Among the questions with which it is suggested that the National Councils should deal or allocate to District Councils or Works Committees the following may be selected for special mention :

(i) The better utilisation of the practical knowledge and experience of the workpeople.

(ii) Means for securing to the workpeople a greater share in and responsibility for the determination and observance of the conditions under which their work is carried on.

(iii) The settlement of the general principles governing the conditions of employment, including the methods of fixing, paying, and readjusting wages, having regard to the need for securing to the workpeople a share in the increased prosperity of the industry.

(iv) The establishment of regular methods of negotiation for issues arising between employers and workpeople, with a view both to the prevention of differences, and to their better adjustment when they appear.

(v) Means of ensuring to the workpeople the greatest possible security of earnings and employment, without undue restriction upon change of occupation or employer.

(vi) Methods of fixing and adjusting earnings, piecework prices, etc., and of dealing with the many difficulties which arise with regard to the method and amount of payment apart from the fixing of general standard rates, which are already covered by paragraph (iii).

(vii) Technical education and training.

(viii) Industrial research and the full utilisation of its results.

(ix) The provision of facilities for the full consideration and utilisation of inventions and improvements designed by workpeople, and for the adequate safeguarding of the rights of the designers of such improvements.

(x) Improvements of processes, machinery and organisation and appropriate questions relating to management and the examination of industrial experiments, with special reference to co-operation in carrying new ideas into effect and full consideration of the workpeople's point of view in relation to them.

(xi) Proposed legislation affecting the industry.

17. The methods by which the functions of the proposed Councils should be correlated to those of joint bodies in the different districts, and in the various works within the district, must necessarily vary according to the trade.   It may, therefore, be the best policy to leave it to the trades themselves to formulate schemes suitable to their special circumstances, it being understood that it is essential to secure in each industry the fullest measure of co-operation between employers and employed, both generally, through the National Councils, and specifically, through district Committees and workshop Committees :

.   .   .   .

21. It appears to us that it may be desirable at some later stage for the State to give the sanction of law to agreements made by the Councils, but the initiative in this direction should come from the Councils themselves.

.   .   .   .

23. It may be desirable to state here our considered opinion that an essential condition of securing a permanent improvement in the relations between employers and employed is that there should be adequate organisation on the part of both employers and workpeople. The proposals outlined for joint co-operation throughout the several industries depend for their ultimate success upon there being such organisation on both sides ; and such organisation is necessary also to provide means whereby the arrangements and agreements made for the industry may be effectively carried out.

24. We have thought it well to refrain from making suggestions or offering opinions with regard to such matters as profit-sharing, co-partnership, or particular systems of wages, etc.   It would be impracticable for us to make any useful general recommendations on such matters, having regard to the varying conditions in different trades.   We are convinced, moreover, that a permanent improvement in the relations between employers and employed must be founded upon something other than a cash basis.   What is wanted is that the workpeople should have a greater opportunity of participating in the discussion about the adjustment of those parts of industry by which they are most affected.

.   .   .   .

26. We venture to hope that representative men in each industry, with pride in their calling and care for its place as a contributor to the national well-being, will come together in the manner here suggested, and apply themselves to promoting industrial harmony and efficiency and removing the obstacles that have hitherto stood in the way.

[Signed by Mr. J. H. Whitley and twelve others, 8th March, 1917.   in addition to the Secretaries.]

APPENDIX.

The following questions were addressed by the Reconstruction Committee to the Sub-Committee on the Relations between Employers and Employed in order to make clear certain points which appeared to call for further elucidation. The answers given are subjoined.

Q. 1. *In what classes of Industries does the Interim Report propose that Industrial Councils shall be established ?   What basis of classification has the Sub-Committee in view ?*

A. 1. It has been suggested that, for the purpose of considering the establishment of Industrial Councils, or other bodies designed to assist in the improvement of relations between employers and employed, the various industries should be grouped into three classes—(*a*) industries in which organisation on the part of employers and employed is sufficiently developed to render the Councils representative ; (*b*) industries in which either as regards employers and employed, or both, the degree of organisation, though considerable, is less marked than in (*a*) and is insufficient to be regarded as representative ; and (*c*) industries in which organisation is so imperfect, either as regards employers or employed, or both, that no Associations can be said adequately to represent those engaged in the trade.

It will be clear that an analysis of industries will show a number which are on the border lines between these groups, and special consideration will have to be given to such trades.   So far as groups (*a*) and (*c*) are concerned, a fairly large number of trades can readily be assigned to them ; group (*b*) is necessarily more indeterminate.

For trades in group (*a*) the Committee have proposed the establishment of Joint Standing Industrial Councils in the several trades. In dealing with the various industries it may be necessary to consider specially the case of parts of industries in group (*a*) where organisation is not fully developed.

.   .   .   .

Q. 3. It is understood that membership of the Councils is to be confined to representatives elected by Employers' Associations and Trade Unions ? What is the view of the Sub-Committee regarding the entry of new organisations established after the Councils have been set up ?

A. 3. It is intended that the Councils should be composed only of representatives of Trade Unions and Employers' Associations, and that new organisations should be admitted only with the approval of the particular side of the Council of which the organisation would form a part.

233. Works Committees.

REPORT OF THE WHITLEY COMMITTEE, 1917.

COMMITTEE ON RELATIONS BETWEEN EMPLOYERS AND EMPLOYED.

Supplementary Report on Works Committees.

To the Right Honourable D. Lloyd George, M.P., Prime Minister.
SIR,

In our first and second Reports we have referred to the establishment of Works Committees,[1] representative of the management and of the workpeople, and appointed from within the works, as an essential part of the scheme of organisation suggested to secure improved relations between employers and employed. The purpose of the present Report is to deal more fully with the proposal to institute such Committees.

2. Better relations between employers and their workpeople can best be arrived at by granting to the latter a greater share in the consideration of matters with which they are concerned. In every industry there are certain questions, such as rates of wages and hours of work, which should be settled by District or National agreement, and with any matter so settled no Works Committee should be allowed to interfere ; but there are also many questions closely affecting daily life and comfort in, and the success of, the business, and affecting in no small degree efficiency of working, which are peculiar to the individual workshop or factory. The purpose of a Works Committee is to establish and maintain a system of co-operation in all these workshop matters.

[1] In the use of the term 'Works Committees' in this Report it is not intended to use the word 'works' in a technical sense ; in such an industry as the Coal Trade, for example, the term 'Pit Committees' would probably be the term used in adopting the scheme.

3. We have throughout our recommendations proceeded upon the assumption that the greatest success is likely to be achieved by leaving to the representative bodies of employers and employed in each industry the maximum degree of freedom to settle for themselves the precise form of Council or Committee which should be adopted, having regard in each case to the particular circumstances of the trade ; and, in accordance with this principle, we refrain from indicating any definite form of constitution for the Works Committees. Our proposals as a whole assume the existence of organisations of both employers and employed and a frank and full recognition of such organisations. Works Committees established otherwise than in accordance with these principles could not be regarded as a part of the scheme we have recommended, and might indeed be a hindrance to the development of the new relations in industry to which we look forward. We think the aim should be the complete and coherent organisation of the trade on both sides, and Works Committees will be of value in so far as they contribute to such a result.

4. We are of opinion that the complete success of Works Committees necessarily depends largely upon the degree and efficiency of organisation in the trade, and upon the extent to which the Committees can be linked up, through organisations that we have in mind, with the remainder of the scheme which we are proposing, viz., the District and National Councils. We think it important to state that the success of the Works Committees would be very seriously interfered with if the idea existed that such Committees were used, or likely to be used, by employers in opposition to Trade Unionism. It is strongly felt that the setting up of Works Committees without the co-operation of the Trade Unions and the Employers' Associations in the trade or branch of trade concerned would stand in the way of the improved industrial relationships which in these Reports we are endeavouring to further.

5. In an industry where the workpeople are unorganised, or only very partially organised, there is a danger that Works Committees may be used, or thought to be used, in opposition to Trade Unionism. It is important that such fears should be guarded against in the initiation of any scheme. We look upon successful Works Committees as the broad base of the Industrial Structure which we have recommended, and as the means of enlisting the interest of the workers in the success both of the industry to which they are attached and of the workshop or factory where so much of their life is spent. These

Committees should not, in constitution or methods of working, discourage Trade Organisations.

6. Works Committees, in our opinion, should have regular meetings at fixed times, and, as a general rule, not less frequently than once a fortnight. They should always keep in the forefront the idea of constructive co-operation in the improvement of the industry to which they belong. Suggestions of all kinds tending to improvement should be frankly welcomed and freely discussed. Practical proposals should be examined from all points of view. There is an undeveloped asset of constructive ability—valuable alike to the industry and to the State—awaiting the means of realisation ; problems, old and new, will find their solution in a frank partnership of knowledge, experience and goodwill. Works Committees would fail in their main purpose if they existed only to smooth over grievances.

7. We recognise that, from time to time, matters will arise which the management or the workmen consider to be questions they cannot discuss in these joint meetings. When this occurs, we anticipate that nothing but good will come from the friendly statement of the reasons why the reservation is made.

8. We regard the successful development and utilisation of Works Committees in any business on the basis recommended in this Report as of equal importance with its commercial and scientific efficiency ; and we think that in every case one of the partners or directors, or some other responsible representative of the management, would be well advised to devote a substantial part of his time and thought to the good working and development of such a committee.

9. There has been some experience, both before the war and during the war, of the benefits of Works Committees, and we think it should be recommended most strongly to employers and employed that, in connection with the scheme for the establishment of National and District Industrial Councils, they should examine this experience with a view to the institution of Works Committees on proper lines, in works where the conditions render their formation practicable. We have recommended that the Ministry of Labour should prepare a summary of the experience available with reference to Works Committees, both before and during the war, including information as to any rules or reports relating to such Committees, and should issue a memorandum thereon for the guidance of employers and workpeople generally, and we understand that such a memorandum is now in course of preparation.

10. In order to ensure uniform and common principles of action, it is essential that where National and District Industrial Councils exist the Works Committees should be in close touch with them, and the scheme for linking up Works Committees with the Councils should be considered and determined by the National Councils.

11. We have considered it better not to attempt to indicate any specific form of Works Committees. Industrial establishments show such infinite variation in size, number of persons employed, multiplicity of departments, and other conditions, that the particular form of Works Committees must necessarily be adapted to the circumstances of each case. It would, therefore, be impossible to formulate any satisfactory scheme which does not provide a large measure of elasticity.

We are confident that the nature of the particular organisation necessary for the various cases will be settled without difficulty by the exercise of goodwill on both sides.

[Signed by Mr. J. H. Whitley and fourteen others, in addition to the Secretaries.][1]

18th October, 1917.

234. Official Recognition of Joint Industrial Councils (Whitley Councils).

EXTRACT FROM LETTER ADDRESSED BY THE MINISTER OF LABOUR TO THE LEADING EMPLOYERS' ASSOCIATIONS AND TRADE UNIONS, regarding the Report of the Whitley Committee, 20th October, 1917.

In order, therefore, that the Councils may be able to fulfil the duties which they will be asked to undertake, and that they may have the requisite status for doing so, the Government desire it to be understood that the Councils will be recognised as the official standing Consultative Committees to the Government on all future questions affecting the industries which they represent, and that they will be the normal channel through which the opinion and experience of

[1] Sir G. J. Carter and Mr. Smillie were unable to attend any of the meetings at which this Report was considered and they therefore do not sign it. Sir G. J. Carter has intimated that in his view, in accordance with the principles indicated in paragraphs 3, 4 and 5 of the Report, it is important that Works Committees should not deal with matters which ought to be directly dealt with by the firms concerned or their respective Associations in conjunction with the recognised representatives of the Trade Unions whose members are affected.

an industry will be sought on all questions with which the industry is concerned. It will be seen, therefore, that it is intended that Industrial Councils should play a definite and permanent part in the economic life of the country, and the Government feels that it can rely on both employers and workmen to co-operate in order to make that part a worthy one.

235. Joint Industrial Councils (Whitley Councils) to be based on Trade Unions and Employers' Associations.

EXTRACT FROM LETTER ADDRESSED BY THE MINISTER OF LABOUR TO THE LEADING EMPLOYERS' ASSOCIATIONS AND TRADE UNIONS, regarding the Report of the Whitley Committee, 20th October, 1917.

Thirdly, it should be made clear that representation on the Industrial Councils is intended to be on the basis of existing organisations among employers and workmen concerned in each industry, although it will, of course, be open to the Councils, when formed, to grant representation to any new bodies which may come into existence and which may be entitled to representation. The authority, and consequently the usefulness of the Councils will depend entirely on the extent to which they represent the different interests and enjoy the whole-hearted support of the existing organisations, and it is therefore desirable that representation should be determined on as broad a basis as possible.

236. ' A Success of Whitleyism.'

A Success of Whitleyism, by L. H. GREEN, Secretary of the Joint Industrial Council for the Flour Milling Industry. *Manchester Guardian Supp.*, 30th November, 1927, p. 22.

Whitley Councils, like other forms of organisation in a democratic country, depend primarily on the goodwill of their constituent elements if they are to function satisfactorily. That is why the general strike of last year was the most stringent test that could have been applied. The fact of the strike was proof of the bankruptcy of goodwill on a national scale on both sides, for a time at any rate. Was there sufficient good-will, industry by industry, to withstand the shock ?

The writer approaches this question as one who for nine years has been secretary of an employers' federation in one of our basic industries, and who has at the same time been the secretary of both

sides of the Whitley Council for that industry.   His work has therefore necessarily brought him into close touch with other organisations both of employers and of workpeople.

The outstanding point of difference between a Whitley Council
and other joint committees of employers and of workpeople is that
these other bodies are either *ad hoc* bodies, summoned to meet from
time to time as discussion of some temporarily burning topic becomes
necessary, or are dependent, as in the case of trade boards, upon the
casting vote of a chairman who is not connected with the industry.
The Whitley Council, on the other hand, consists wholly of employers
directly connected with the particular industry, on the one hand, and
of the elected representatives of the workpeople on the other.   The
chairman is elected alternately from each of the two sides ; he has no
casting vote because there are only two votes, one for each of the
two sides.   A decision by the Council, therefore, is a decision
thoroughly representative of the industry.

Moreover, this is no *ad hoc* body which meets only for purposes of
conciliation in times of stringency.   It does not meet to consider
methods of making the stable fast after the steed has escaped.   It
meets regularly to decide matters not only of urgency arising out of
questions of wages and hours, but to discuss those wider and equally
important matters concerning conditions of work which are comprised under such headings as welfare, safety, and education.   It is
the mutual confidence engendered by frequent meeting that matters,
for men who, by constant association, have experience of each other's
integrity, build up an atmosphere of trust, and do not approach the
problems of industry in the huckstering spirit of the market-place or
in the pedantic spirit of a legal tribunal.

To the industry, therefore, with which the writer is connected,
accustomed to deal with its problems in this essentially English
fashion, the general strike came as a great shock, not merely owing to
the dislocation of business, but even more perhaps because it suggested the bankruptcy of that confidence upon which our dealings
had been based.   It is true that the dislocation of business was not so
serious as in most industries, it is true that there were instances of
workpeople who balloted upon the instructions to strike received
f om their headquarters, and decided that they preferred the constitutional method of giving a week's notice to terminate their engagements, but, speaking generally, it seemed doubtful for a time whether
our Whitley Council would weather the storm.

It was at that point that the value of including non-contentious matter within the Council's scope became apparent.   Two years earlier the Council had set up a committee to deal with technical education in the industry, and to this Committee were added the representatives of the educational authorities concerned, principals of technical institutes, teachers, the City and Guilds of London, and the Board of Education.   During the months immediately following the general strike this Committee quietly continued its work, thus maintaining active liaison between the two sides.   At the same time the Employers' Federation set up a special committee to investigate the work of the Whitley Council during the preceding seven years and to make suggestions for the future.   The following quotation from the report issued by that Committee is of interest :

' The principal complaint is concerned with the violation of the national agreements in the general strike.   The Committee shares to the full the resentment caused by this breach of trust.   At the same time it should be stated that, although the upheaval was national in its scope, approximately two-thirds of the men in the industry remained loyal to the agreements.   A similar breach of agreement took place in every organised industry included in the strike, whether there was a Whitley Council in operation, or some other form of joint machinery.

' Although the employees' leaders followed the instruction of the Trades Union Congress Committee apparently without protest in calling men out in breach of their agreements, the Committee thinks that this action taken in exceptional circumstances should not be allowed to destroy the work of the previous seven years, but rather that the spirit of loyalty to their employers shown by the majority of the workpeople and the continuance in those cases of the national agreements should be recognised by a continuance of joint relations.'

The Committee agree that the continuance of these joint relations is best secured by the maintenance and extension of the Whitley organisation.   Incidentally we may say that the report of the Committee was unanimous, as was also its acceptance by the whole industry.

The important point in this decision is the recommendation of extension.   Having decided that the Whitley form of organised joint relationship through the medium of the national council, the district council, and the works committee had justified itself and should be maintained, the Committee reread the original Whitley Report, and it seemed to them that their Joint Council, successful though it had been, was only a very partial realisation of the kind of council that the Whitley Report envisaged.   Except for the recent inclusion of technical education within its scope, the Council had been little more than a piece of conciliation machinery.   That, even so, it had survived the shock of the general strike was evidence that the foundations had been well and truly laid.   It was time now to turn back to the original recommendations of the Whitley Committee that each such joint council should ' have as its object the regular consideration of matters affecting the progress and well-being of the trade from the point of view of all those engaged in it, so far as this is consistent with the general interest of the community.'

Early this year, then, a resumption of the joint meetings, for purposes other than technical education, was made.   The first point of agreement was in the nature of a concession by the employers, who agreed to stabilise the existing rate of wages for one year at least ; the second point was in the nature of a concession by the workpeople, who agreed to a greater measure of elasticity in the working of the two-shift system ;   the third point was in the nature of a concession by both sides, for it involved a definite limitation of the amount of overtime which could be worked.

The way was then clear for the extension of the Council's activities, and in this connection the leader of the workpeople's representatives made a striking statement.   He said :

' Labour represents a great constructive brain ;   hitherto that constructive brain has not been made sufficient use of ;   in fact, it has been driven to using its fighting psychology in order to get anywhere.

' It lies largely with the managerial side to decide in future whether the constructive brain of the workers is to be used for industry as a whole or whether it is to develop its fighting capacity—in order to maintain its decent standard of wages and conditions.'

A joint committee was set up to inquire into the working of the Factory Acts in the particular industry ;   so far it has concentrated on the safeguarding of machinery and the prevention of accidents. But other questions such as the provision of protective clothing, of adequate lavatory and messroom accommodation come also within its scope, and ultimately it may well function as a standing committee competent to advise the Home Office, if its advice be sought, in regard to technical matters arising out of accidents.   Another joint committee has been set up to inquire into the allegation that a certain kind of disease is prevalent amongst the workpeople employed in the industry.   The Technical Education Committee has extended its work to include a scheme providing for the recruitment of labour into the industry on a scientific basis instead of on the haphazard methods now employed.

It is not claimed that these activities exhaust the potentialities of the Whitley organisation, but it is claimed that they are a step in the right direction, and that ' peace in industry ' is only to be obtained by each trade following some such methods and making the fullest use of the best available brains both on the employing side and amongst the workpeople. This does not exclude the need of a national organisation on both sides to give a lead in matters of general policy.

It will be well at this point to refer briefly to a practical and fundamental difficulty. It is stated at the beginning of the Whitley Report that the recommendations refer to those industries ' in which there exist representative organisations on both sides '—that is to say, industries where the employers and the workpeople are so organised that the decision of the joint body is the decision of the whole trade, and that the necessary sanctions therefore exist for putting those decisions into effect.

Speaking generally, trade unions are closely organised and their members are accustomed to obey orders ; on the other hand, most employers' organisations are voluntary bodies, membership of which can be terminated at six or twelve months' notice, and the members, being employers, are individualists, and do not readily subordinate their private views or interests. An employer, for instance, who is dissatisfied with a decision of the Whitley Council may hand in his notice of resignation from his federation and be automatically freed thereby from observing the national agreements. On the other hand, it is unlikely that his workpeople will resign from their union, and as long as the union is a party to any agreement made by the Whitley Council its members will expect the provisions of all such agreements to be carried out.

Two courses are open to the employer : if the union is strong he will be compelled to observe the national agreements though escaping all share in the expenditure, whether of time or of money, for which his federation is liable ; if the union is weak he can ignore those agreements, cut wages, and worsen the conditions of labour.

Stated quite crudely, therefore, at the present time the ultimate sanction of Whitley Council agreements lies in the ability of the union to enforce them. That is both illogical and unfair.

It is to the credit of employers in general that their word in these matters is their bond, but there is always a minority temperamentally

so constituted that they refuse to join an organisation though ready
to reap all the advantages that such an organisation brings them, or
mentally domiciled in the nineteenth century, when strikes and lockouts were regarded as necessary evils.   This minority of unreasonable or reactionary employers has been so powerful as to put certain
Whitley Councils out of action altogether and seriously to hamper
the work of others.   The Association of Joint Industrial Councils,
therefore, has drafted a bill to secure statutory authority for those
Whitley Councils that desire to possess it.   The bill leaves each
Council free to apply or not to apply for this statutory authority, and
provides that it should be applicable only to those decisions which
the Council concerned wishes to be enforced in this way.

Such a bill is in accordance with the Report of the Whitley
Committee itself, which says : ' It appears to us that it may be
desirable at some later stage for the State to give the sanction of law
to agreements made by the Councils.'

.   .   .   .

Perhaps the strongest argument in favour of the Whitley method
of organisation is that in the 54 industries which possess these joint
councils, employing 3,000,000 workpeople, hardly any strike or
lock-out (apart from the general strike) has taken place on a national
or even on a large scale during the whole of the post-war period—a
period of exceptional difficulty in industrial relations.

237. Joint Councils, etc., in the Coal Industry.

PROVISIONS CONTAINED IN THE MINING INDUSTRY ACT, 1920, 10 & 11
Geo. V., ch. 50, but never operated.

PART II.

REGULATION OF COAL MINES.

7. The Board of Trade shall by regulations provide for the
constitution—

(a) of a pit committee for every coal mine where a resolution
in favour thereof is passed by a majority (to be ascertained by
ballot in accordance with the said regulations) of the workers
employed in or about the mine, except that it shall not be necessary to constitute a pit committee for any mine which is a small
mine within the meaning of the Coal Mines Act, 1911 ;

(b) of a district committee for each of the districts mentioned
in Part I of the Second Schedule to this Act ;

(*c*) of an area board for each of the areas mentioned in Part II of that schedule ;

(*d*) of a National Board ;

having such functions as may, subject to the provisions of this Act, be prescribed by the regulations, and the procedure and meetings of the several committees and boards shall be such as may be prescribed by the regulations :

Provided that—(i) where a district is co-extensive with an area, the district committee shall perform the functions of the area board as well as of the district committee ; (ii) districts and areas may be varied by order of the Board of Trade after consultation with the National Board and with the consent of the district committees or area boards affected ; (iii) where a mine situate in one district has, for industrial purposes, been customarily dealt with as if it were a mine situate in an adjoining district, that mine shall, for the purposes of this Part of the Act, if the owner and the workers employed in or about the mine so agree, be treated as being situate in such adjoining district.

8.—(1) A pit committee shall not exceed ten in number and shall consist of representatives of the owners and management of the mine appointed by the owners and of workers employed in or about the mine selected by ballot of the workers in accordance with the regulations from amongst their own number, so however that the representatives of the workers shall constitute half of the number of the pit committee.

(2) The functions of a pit committee shall be to discuss and make recommendations with respect to—

(*a*) the safety, health, and welfare of the workers in connexion with their work at the mine ;

(*b*) the maintenance and increase of output ;

(*c*) reports made on an inspection under section sixteen of the Coal Mines Act, 1911, which reports shall be referred to the committee by the manager ;

(*d*) disputes arising in connection with the mine including disputes as to wages ;

(*e*) any other questions and matters relating to the mine which may be prescribed by the regulations.

(3) In the case of a mine for which a pit committee is established the management of the accommodation and facilities for taking baths and drying clothes provided under section seventy-seven of the Coal Mines Act, 1911, shall be under the control of the pit committee

instead of that of a committee established in accordance with sub-section (5) of that section.

(4) The regulations shall provide for matters which cannot be satisfactorily disposed of by the pit committee being referred to the district committee, or, in the case of questions to which the Coal Mines Act, 1911, applies, to the inspector of the division.

(5) For enabling a pit committee to exercise their functions under paragraphs (a) and (b) of subsection (2) of this section, the committee shall be entitled to be furnished by the manager of the mine with such relevant information as may be necessary for the purpose, and may appoint two of their members, one being a person concerned in the management of the mine and one being a worker, to make periodical inspections of the mine or any part thereof and to report the result of their inspections to the committee, and the persons so appointed shall have all such facilities for the purpose of making inspections as persons appointed to make inspections under section sixteen of the Coal Mines Act, 1911, and that section shall apply accordingly.

(6) Any recommendations of the pit committee made on any report under section sixteen of the Coal Mines Act, 1911, which has been referred to the committee, and on any other matters to which that Act relates, shall be sent to the inspector of the division by the manager.

9.—(1) A district committee shall consist of representatives of the owners and management of the coal mines in the district appointed by the owners in accordance with the regulations constituting the committee, and an equal number of representatives of workers employed in or about such mines elected by the workers in accordance with those regulations.

(2) A district committee shall take into consideration—

(a) questions affecting the district of the same nature as those which may be the subject of discussion and recommendations by a pit committee ;

(b) any questions which may be referred to them by a pit committee ;

(c) any questions which may be referred to them by the area board, or the Board of Trade ;

and, if the matter is one proper to be dealt with by the area board rather than by the district committee, they shall refer the matter to the area board, and in any other case they shall deal with the matter themselves and make such recommendations as they think fit, and, if their recommendations are not complied with, they may forward them with a report on the matter to the Board of Trade.

10.—(1) An area board shall consist of representatives of the owners and management of the coal mines in the area nominated in accordance with the regulations constituting the board by the representatives of the owners and management who are members of the various district committees within the area, and an equal number of representatives of workers employed in or about such mines so nominated by the representatives of workers who are members of the district committees within the area.

(2) The area board shall take into consideration—

(a) questions affecting the area of the same nature as those which may be the subject of consideration by a district committee ;

(b) any questions which may be referred to them by a district committee ;

(c) any questions which may be referred to them by the National Board or the Board of Trade,

and, if the matter is one proper to be dealt with by the National Board rather than by the area board, in that it raises any question affecting more than one area, they shall refer the matter to the National Board, and in any other case they shall deal with the matter themselves, and make such recommendations as they think fit, and, if their recommendations are not complied with, they may forward them with a report on the matter to the Board of Trade.

(3) An area board shall formulate, at such intervals and on such principles as may be prescribed by the National Board, schemes for adjusting the remuneration of the workers within the area, having regard among other considerations to the profits of the industry within the area, and any such scheme when formulated shall be submitted to the National Board for their approval, and, if approved by that Board, shall be referred to the Board of Trade, and for the purposes of this subsection the owners of mines in the area shall furnish to accountants appointed by the area board such information as they may require in order that they may ascertain for the information of the area board particulars of the output, cost of production, proceeds and profits in the area as a whole :

Provided that no such scheme shall be formulated during the period of the operation of the Coal Mines (Emergency) Act, 1920, or, if the Board of Trade so direct, whilst an order made by the Board of Trade under Part I of this Act as to the distribution of profits is in force.

(4) The accountant so appointed as aforesaid shall not include in his report or disclose information with respect to any particular undertaking, and, if he does so, he shall be guilty of an offence and liable on summary conviction to a fine not exceeding fifty pounds.

11. The Board of Trade may by regulations provide for district committees or area boards determining any questions and exercising any powers which before the passing of this Act can be determined or exercised by a conciliation board or by a joint district board constituted under the Coal Mines (Minimum Wage) Act, 1912 ; and the regulations may provide for the appointment of an independent chairman, with a casting vote, to preside at meeetings of any district committee or area board when determining any such question or exercising any such power, and may add to or alter the districts mentioned in the Schedule to the Coal Mines (Minimum Wage) Act, 1912 :

Provided that the regulations shall not provide for the appointment of such an independent chairman when the committee or board acts as a conciliation board except in pursuance of an agreement to that effect.

12.—(1) The National Board shall consist of such number of members as may be prescribed by the regulations, of whom one-half shall be representatives of the owners and management of coal mines throughout the United Kingdom, and one-half shall be representatives of workers employed in or about such mines.

(2) The National Board shall take into consideration—

(a) questions, including wages questions, affecting the coal mining industry as a whole ;

(b) any questions which may be referred to them by an area board ;

(c) any questions which may be referred to them by the Board of Trade ;

and may make recommendations in respect thereof, and may, in any case when their recommendations are not complied with, or in any other case where they think fit, forward their recommendations with a report on the matter to the Board of Trade.

(3) The National Board shall also determine, subject to the approval of the Board of Trade, the principles on which schemes by area boards under this Part of this Act for adjusting the remuneration of workers are to be framed, and shall consider all such schemes when submitted to them for their approval.

13. Where any recommendations made by a district committee or area board or by the National Board, or any scheme made by an area board and approved by the National Board, have been forwarded or referred to the Board of Trade as aforesaid, the Board of Trade shall take such recommendations or scheme into consideration, and may, if they think fit, give directions requiring any person engaged in the coal mining industry to comply therewith, and it shall be the duty of every person to whom those directions apply to comply therewith, and if any such person fails to do so he shall be guilty of an offence against the Coal Mines Act, 1911 :

Provided that, where the recommendations relate to matters within the scope of the authority of some other Government department, the Board of Trade before giving any such directions as aforesaid shall obtain the approval of that other department.

14. For the purpose of the foregoing provisions of this Part of this Act, the expression ' recommendation ' means a recommendation approved by a majority of the representatives of the owners and management present at the meeting at which the recommendation was passed, and by a majority of the representatives of the workers so present.

15. There shall be paid to the members of pit committees such fees for attendance at meetings thereof as may be prescribed by the regulations, and such payments, together with any expenses incurred in accordance with the regulations by such committees in the discharge of their functions, shall be payable by the owner of the mine as part of the working expenses of the mine.

.   .   .   .

17. If at the expiration of one year from the passing of this Act it appears to the Board of Trade that the scheme of this Part of the Act has been rendered abortive by reason of the failure on the part of those entitled to appoint representatives as members of the pit and district committees, area boards, and the National Board to avail themselves of such right, the Board of Trade shall issue a report of the circumstances, and that report shall be laid before Parliament, and at the expiration of thirty days during the session of Parliament from the date when it is so laid all the provisions of this Part of this Act shall cease to have effect unless in the meantime a resolution to the contrary is passed by both Houses of Parliament.

238. The Foster Report on Organised Public Service in the Building Trade.

INTERIM REPORT OF A COMMITTEE APPOINTED BY THE INDUSTRIAL
COUNCIL FOR THE BUILDING INDUSTRY, 1919.

1. This Committee was appointed to consider the question of Scientific Management and Reduction of Costs with a view to enabling the Building Industry to render the most efficient service possible.

2. The terms 'Scientific Management' and 'Reduction of Costs' do not at first sight suggest any very far-reaching enquiry, but we decided unanimously at our first meeting that if we were to do any really useful work we must review the whole structure of the building industry in order to bring forward recommendations that would be of real service.

3. Although in the fabric of our industrial order, the material and the human sides are so intimately interwoven that it is impossible completely to separate them, we found it useful to set up two sub-committees to specialise respectively on the twin subjects of production and distribution of the product. The recommendations of these two groups have been reviewed by the full committee and are combined in the document we now present.

4. As our investigation proceeded, we became more and more impressed with the immense possibilities lying latent in the new system of industrial self-government implied in the constitution of our Industrial Council, and we believe that, given the vision, the faith and the courage, our industry will be enabled to lead the way in the industrial and social re-adjustments that are imminent.

We have glimpsed the possibility of the whole Building Industry of Great Britain being welded together into one great self-governing democracy of organised public service, uniting a full measure of free initiative and enterprise with all the best that applied science and research can render. The whole trend of modern industrial development is already setting in this direction. We have now much valuable experience of control by the State, by the municipality, by the co-operative organisations of consumers, by the joint-stock company, and by individual private enterprise. Most of these forms of control offer advantages, but each of them presents serious defects.

5. We believe that the great task of our Industrial Council is to develop an entirely new system of industrial control by the members

of the industry, itself,—the actual producers, whether by hand or
brain,—and to bring them into co-operation with the State as the
central representative of the community whom they are organised
to serve.   Nothing short of this will produce the full development of
the ' team spirit ' in industry, which is the key to the whole problem
of production ; nothing short of this is worthy of the high ideals for
which our Industrial Council stands.   But such a reconstruction of
our industrial fabric cannot be achieved in a day.   There are many
problems that require patient experiment, and experience must be
purchased in the school of trial and error.   Our hope for the future
lies in the liberation and right direction of men's true generous
qualities of goodwill, enthusiasm, and adventure.   They must be
our constant guide, and no fear of risks that seem to be involved
must allow us to deny them.

6. The recommendations that we now bring forward are therefore based upon their immediate availability, and are designed to
lay the foundation of an industrial system which, while giving full
play to individual enterprise and complete freedom from the be-
numbing hand of bureaucracy, shall yet tend to develop that sense of
comradeship and solidarity that is so essential for efficient service.

We believe that they will be much improved by full discussion
and frank criticism in the Council, and we submit them in the belief
that if our industry will give a clear and courageous lead in the
direction we have tried to indicate, its example will be of the greatest
possible service to our country at this critical time of transition.

The Problem Stated.

7. It became clear at a very early stage that there are four main
factors that tend to the restriction of output.   They are :

(*a*) The fear of unemployment.

(*b*) The disinclination of the operatives to make unrestricted
profit for private employers.

(*c*) The lack of interest in the industry evidenced by operatives
owing to their non-participation in control.

(*d*) Inefficiency, both managerial and operative.

8. We begin, then, with the question of employment.

In a report such as this it seems unnecessary to elaborate the well-
known seasonal difficulties with which our industry is confronted.
We therefore immediately proceed to indicate the lines of remedy.

The Regularisation of Demand.

9. The aim we have in view is the development of the highest

possible efficiency in a well-organised building service. To this end we consider it essential that the whole productive capacity of the industry should be continuously engaged and absorbed, and that a regular flow of contracts should replace the old haphazard alternations of congestion and stagnation.

It is well known that the proportion of public to private work is very considerable, and that it is well within the powers of public authorities to speed up or to delay contracts.

We therefore recommend :

(*a*) That the Industrial Council shall set up a permanent Committee entitled The Building Trades Central Employment Committee, with the necessary clerical staff.

(*b*) That each Regional Council shall similarly set up a Building Trades Regional Employment Committee.

(*c*) That each Local or Area Council shall similarly set up a Building Trades Area Employment Committee.

(*d*) That each Committee shall consist of an equal number of employers and operatives with one architect appointed by the local professional Association of Architects or by the R.I.B.A., as may be most appropriate.

10. The first duty of these Committees would be to regularise the demand for building,

(*a*) At the approach of slack periods, by accelerating new building enterprises, both public and private, with the co-operation of architects and local authorities.

(*b*) Conversely, at periods of congestion, by advising building owners to postpone the construction of such works as are not of an urgent character.

11. Except when modified by special arrangements we recommend that the Central, Regional, and Area Employment Committees should co-operate with the appropriate State, county or district authorities.

Although we propose that these Committees should consist of producers only, we contemplate the fullest possible co-operation with the Government and local authorities at every stage, not only because they are important customers, themselves, but also because they are the duly elected representatives of the consuming public.

12. We recognise that such a scheme would involve some measure of restraint upon individual employers and realise that the small non-federated employer would be an obstacle to its ordered working,

but we are convinced that combined pressure by members of the Building Trades' Parliament or its constituents should eventually overcome this obstacle. Such spreading over of work from year to year and season to season will not of itself solve the whole problem of providing a steady stream of work.

The Decasualisation of Labour.

13. We recommend that the second main function of the Local Employment Committee shall be the decasualisation of labour, and the difficulty of providing employment during wet and bad seasons has yet to be faced. We feel that a certain amount of investigation is still needed in this direction and venture to suggest that the Building Trades' Parliament should approach the representatives of other industries and public authorities with a view to investigating the possibility of ' dove-tailing ' or seasonal interchange of labour.

There would appear to be a large volume of national and private work which could be undertaken when the industry itself could not usefully employ all its available labour, for example :

(*a*) Afforestation.

(*b*) Roadmaking.

(*c*) The preparation of sites for housing schemes.

(*d*) Demolition of insanitary or condemned areas in preparation for improvements.

14. The question of the method of paying men so engaged in other occupations in bad seasons will be considered later in relation to the scheme we are recommending for the provision of unemployment pay.

15. When all other methods of providing steady and adequate employment for the operatives have been exhausted, then the industry is faced with the question of its responsibility towards its employees during possible periods of unemployment. We are convinced that the overhanging fear of unemployment must be finally removed before the operative can be expected whole-heartedly to give of his best. Considerations of humanity and efficiency alike, therefore, demand that provision shall be made by the industry itself adequately to maintain the operative and his family during any period of unemployment arising from causes outside his control.

This accomplished, we believe that the whole atmosphere of industry will experience a great and vitalising change, and that efficiency of production will be much increased.

16. We accordingly suggest that termination of employment

upon any job should be subject to one week's notice instead of one hour (except in the case of a strike or lockout) and that the local Employment Committee should be immediately notified of such approaching terminations and also of all vacancies occurring.

The machinery for filling vacancies already exists in the trade union organisation and should be developed to the greatest possible extent, in order to supplement the State Employment Exchanges, so far as the building industry is concerned.

Unemployment Pay.

17. We further recommend that in cases of unavoidable unemployment, the maintenance of its unemployed members shall be undertaken by the industry through its Employment Committees, and that the necessary revenue should be raised by means of a fixed percentage on the wages bills, and paid weekly to the Employment Committee by each employer on the joint certificate of himself and a shop steward or other accredited trade union representative.

18. The amount of the percentage charge necessary to raise funds for the maintenance of members unavoidably unemployed will naturally depend upon the amount of the State subsidy for the purpose, and also upon the efficiency of the Employment Committees in the matter of :

(*a*) Regularisation of demand, and

(*b*) Decasualisation of labour,

but it is already evident from past experience that the percentage will certainly be small, and that a charge of 5 per cent. would probably be more than ample. An estimate of the revenue required for the coming year should be laid before the Industrial Council annually and the rate of percentage fixed accordingly.

19. While the collection of this revenue should be carried out by the Employment Committees, the payments should be made by periodical refund to the trade unions, who would thus become an important integral part of the official machinery and would distribute the unemployment pay in accordance with the regulations prescribed by the Industrial Council and its Committees.

20. Every duly registered member when prevented, for a period to be fixed, from working at the proper craft at the full standard rates of the district, should be entitled to unemployment pay, whether the cause be sickness, accident, shortage of work, or stress of weather. In all cases the amount would be inclusive of any benefit under the State and Trade Union Schemes.

21. We further recommend that every registered member should be entitled to one week's summer holiday pay per annum, and at the same scale and from the same fund as the unemployment pay.

22. For purpose of this scheme ' Members of the Industry ' would be trade unionists engaged therein, including the clerical, technical, and managerial staffs, who register with the Employment Committees for participation.

. . . .

27. We frankly recognise here that we are again faced with the fundamental difficulty that there still exist in the industry large numbers of small non-federated employers, and on the other hand operatives who are not trade unionists. Nevertheless, we feel that the benefits of such a scheme will have a very material effect in inducing employers and operatives to come into their respective associations.

The Wages of Management.

28. At this point it is necessary to state that the first question discussed by the Committee was the possibility of the adoption by individual firms of some scheme of profit-sharing or co-partnership which would abolish the second factor limiting output.

It immediately became clear, however, that such schemes secure no backing, either by the trade union representatives or by the majority of the operatives. All such methods of payment are strictly forbidden in the rules of most trade unions in the industry. Hitherto the reasons of this objection have been :

(i) The fear of increased unemployment.

(ii) The fear of disintegrating influences being introduced among the workers, thus weakening the authority of the trade unions.

(iii) The difficulty of applying most methods of payment by results to the peculiar conditions of the building industry.

29. But it was found that the trade unions involved would be prepared to reconsider their attitude if the surplus earnings of the industry went not to individuals but to some common service controlled by the industry as a whole.

30. This brought us immediately to the consideration of the wages of management. Here we were immediately faced with the peculiarly difficult organisation of the building industry. . . . Thus, in any attempt to fix some scale of remuneration for the different

types of management we are at once faced with the difficulty of the proper determination of an adequate salary.

31. In parenthesis, we would here like to remark that no opposition to an adequate remuneration is likely to be offered by the trade unions who may discuss this scheme.

.   .   .   .

The Hiring of Capital.

34. It will already have become evident that the whole conception of organised public service that we are developing demands the acceptance of three main principles as an essential preliminary to that increase of efficiency without which the cost to the community cannot be reduced.

(a) Regular rates of pay to the operatives that will ensure a real and satisfactory standard of comfort.

(b) Salaries to owner-managers commensurate with their ability.

(c) A regular rate of interest for the hire of capital.

35. These established, the whole atmosphere will be clarified, the interdependence of the different sections will be better understood and the ' team spirit ' will rapidly develop.

.   .   .   .

Conditions of Entry into the Industry.

42. It is obvious that the important improvements we have outlined will tend to make service in the industry more attractive, and while the interests of this public service emphatically demand the enrolment of every member who can be trained and utilised in the building industry, we fully recognise that indiscriminate enrolment must be prevented by careful regulation.

43. We therefore recommend that the development of the industry should be kept under constant review by the Employment Committees, and that these Committees should periodically notify the trade unions as to the number of new members that may apply for registration under the employment scheme, after a suitable trade test or evidence of previous service in the industry. . . .

44. In anticipation of such periodical notifications we further recommend that the trade unions should establish waiting lists and that the periods of waiting should be utilised for technical training, approved by the Building Trades' Parliament.

.   .   .   .

54. The bulk of the evidence led us to the following additional recommendations :

(*a*) That there should be more inducement to the most talented operatives to increase their efficiency, and to undertake positions of greater responsibility.   .   .   .   .

Works Committees.

55. We realise that no uniform arrangements or recommendations beyond a minimum can be made, as local conditions vary so considerably, nor can we presume to advise the individual employer how to organise any particular operation.   But we realise very strongly the value of useful suggestions by the operatives.   We therefore recommend that this can be best utilised by the establishment of Works Committees upon which management and labour may interchange their specialist knowledge and discuss questions of mutual interest. Other benefits would undoubtedly accrue.   The value of joint organisation would be brought more nearly home to the whole of the employers and operatives alike, and thus the work of the Building Trades Industrial Council would be more keenly and nearly appreciated in all localities and workshops.

Conclusion.

In summing up the conclusions that we have reached, we would again lay special emphasis upon the keynote of our work : the development of the ' team spirit ' in industry which we believe to be the only real solution of the whole problem of production.

This analogy of the athletic team conveys our meaning more accurately than any other form of words we can devise—implying, as it does, a fundamental basis of loyalty, enthusiasm, and efficiency for a common aim.

It sounds across the whole industrial arena the trumpet call of a new idea—the conception of our industry as a great self-governing democracy of organised public service.

We have endeavoured, we hope successfully, to outline the true foundation for such a consummation, namely :

Freedom and security for initiative and enterprise.

Complete removal of the fear of unemployment.

Salaries to management commensurate with ability.

Hire of capital at the market rate of good securities.

Provision of common services controlled by the whole industry, and financed from its surplus earnings.

We have not hesitated to make great demands, for the emergency and the opportunity are also great, and this is no time for dalliance.

We believe that the spectacle of organised management and labour uniting their constructive energies upon a bold scheme of reorganisation and advance will transform the whole atmosphere of our industrial life, and that the force of a great example is the only thing that will lead the way to the commonwealth that all men of goodwill desire.

[Signed by four representatives of the employers
and seven representatives of the Unions.]

239. Trade Unions and Nationalisation.

SCHEME FOR THE GOVERNMENT OF A NATIONALISED COAL INDUSTRY, presented by THE MINERS' FEDERATION OF GREAT BRITAIN, THE TRADES UNION CONGRESS and the LABOUR PARTY, to the Royal Commission on the Coal Industry, 1925.

The Power and Transport Commission.

A Power and Transport Commission should be established, which would take the place of the present Electricity Commission. This Commission should consist of six full-time Commissioners representing expert knowledge on (*a*) coal, (*b*) electricity, (*c*) gas, (*d*) transport, (*e*) commercial questions, (*f*) labour questions, together with a chairman. The Commission should be attached to the Board of Trade, and the President of the Board should be answerable for its work in Parliament.

The Power and Transport Commission would have the duty of dealing with the development of power (including coal) and transport. In this connection its functions would be :

(*a*) To survey the problems of power and transport development as regards both needs and possibilities.

(*b*) To undertake and administer the interconnection of generating stations and the trunk line transmission of power.

(*c*) To lay down conditions governing power and transport undertakings, both public and private.

(*d*) To co-operate with the Department of Industrial and Scientific Research in the promotion of research into power production and coal by-products and kindred questions.

(e) To undertake or to arrange for the commercial application of the results of research into power and transport problems.[1]

In addition to exercising these functions, the Power and Transport Commission would form (as explained below) the final authority determining the larger questions of policy relating to the coal industry.

The National Coal and Power Production Council.

A National Coal and Power Production Council should be established. This body would consist of an equal number of executive and administrative officials and of miners and by-product workers, say twelve in all, elected by their respective organisations, largely from the Provincial Councils, and, say, two representatives of the Power and Transport Commission, together with the Chief Officers of the Central Coal Administration and the Chief Inspector of Mines, in an advisory capacity.

The Council would be presided over by the Secretary for Mines or his deputy.

[1] It may be convenient to amplify these proposals. At the present time power production and distribution and the treatment of coal are in the hands of both public and private undertakings. It is not proposed at the present juncture that these should necessarily be nationalised. New coal treatment and power production plants will be established by the reorganised coal industry, and will, of course, be publicly owned. The chief transport services are privately owned, and any suggestion for their reorganisation would not be relevant to the present inquiry. It will, however, be necessary to give the Power and Transport Commission powers to utilise railway track for transmission lines and to require electrification of railways if they think fit, subject, of course, to Parliamentary powers being acquired for this purpose. It will, moreover, be necessary to arm the Commission with authority to prohibit the establishment of new power and coal distillation undertakings, or to permit them, subject to the fulfilment of such conditions as the Commission may require, or to take over existing enterprises which can be most economically worked in conjunction with the nationalised coal industry. It may also be pointed out that the Commission would be concerned with hydroelectric schemes as well as with coal utilisation schemes. Broadly speaking, it seems to us that the generation, transmission, and local distribution of power should be dealt with as separate functions. So far as the nationalised coal industry is concerned its attention would be confined to the generation of power. The intercommunication of generating stations and the trunk line transmission of power would be carried on under the auspices of the Power and Transport Commission. Local distribution would be a matter for Local Authorities.

The Coal and Power Production Council would require to meet not less than once a fortnight and would be responsible for the organisation and conduct of the industry in much the same way as a board of directors is responsible for the conduct of a company. The Coal and Power Production Council would, subject to what has already been stated with regard to the duties of the Power and Transport Commission and subject also to the consultation with the Consumers' Council referred to below, be charged with the duty of supervising all the internal affairs of the industry, of securing the use of the most efficient methods of producing and treating coal, and of seeing that material of the necessary quantity and kind was provided. The duties of the Coal and Power Production Council would be defined by statute.

As regards total output and kind of output, type of plant for treatment, research, etc., it should act in conjunction with the Power and Transport Commission, with whom the final decision in these matters would rest. Capital expenditure, if in excess of a certain figure, would require the sanction of the latter body.

Provincial Councils.

Provincial Councils should be established in such areas as the Coal and Power Production Council, in consultation with the Power and Transport Commission, might determine. These Councils should consist of a Chairman and Vice-Chairman appointed by the Coal and Power Production Council, six representatives of the manual and manipulative workers, six representatives of the technical and administrative workers, together with the Chief Officers of the area and the District Inspector of Mines in an advisory capacity.

The Councils should discharge such functions as the Coal and Power Production Council might from time to time devolve upon them. These functions might properly include the supervision of the conduct and administration of the industry in the district, but not capital expenditure except below a sum to be determined by the Coal and Power Production Council. All other questions of capital expenditure would be matters for the Coal and Power Production Council acting with the sanction of the Power and Transport Commission.

The appointment of the Chief Officers in the district should be made by the Provincial Council, subject to the approval of the Coal and Power Production Council.

Pit and Works Committee.

Pit or Works Committees should be established at each mine, consisting of (*a*) the manager, under-manager, and commercial manager ; (*b*) two members nominated by the Provincial Council ; (*c*) four members elected by the employés in the mine or power works.

These Committees should meet at least once a fortnight, and their functions should be to advise the management as to (*a*) safety, health, etc. ; (*b*) output and matters relating thereto, *e.g.*, questions of equipment. The final responsibility for the conduct of the mines or works would rest with the manager, subject to the decisions of the Provincial Council.

Relations between Central and Local Administration.

The relations between the central and local administration of the industry would, no doubt, need to be adjusted from time to time on the basis of experience. The view taken in this scheme is that, within the framework of a national system, there should be as much freedom as possible for each coalfield, in order to make proper allowance for the different circumstances prevailing in different areas, and to avoid the disadvantages of a too stereotyped central direction. The activities of the Provincial Councils, however, would need to be in harmony with the general policy of the Coal and Power Production Council.

The Consumers' Council.

A Consumers' Council should be established, consisting of representatives of employers and workers in the coal and power using industries, Local Authorities, Co-operative Societies, and the body responsible for the export trade, together with a Secretariat, to be maintained out of moneys provided by Parliament. The Consumers' Council would be presided over by the Secretary for Mines or his deputy.

It would consider all matters common to consumers, including prices, transport rates and methods, and methods of distribution. It would also advise the Power and Transport Commission regarding changes in demand and the needs of coal and power users.

The Coal and Power Production Council and the Consumers' Council would meet from time to time for the negotiation of prices and wages and the consideration of questions affecting coal and power supply, as is explained below.

It might be found desirable to set up committees of users of other by-products to determine prices by negotiation with the Coal and Power Production Council.

The Determination of Wages and Prices.

Whilst it is hoped that there would be regular consultation between the two Councils on all questions of common interest, the most important problems which would arise would be those relating to wages and prices. With regard to wage questions it is proposed that applications for modifications in wages should first come before the Coal and Power Production Council. This body, however, should not have power to arrive at any decision. It should communicate the fact that an application has been received to the Consumers' Council, and a joint session of an equal number of members from each of the two Councils should then be held at which the case should be stated by the representatives of the workers concerned. In the event of a majority of the representatives of the two Councils in joint session agreeing that a change should be made, they should have power to effect it.

If, as a result of the joint discussion, no settlement could be reached, the question might then be referred by the two Councils to a specially constituted court with a personnel and terms of reference agreed upon by the parties concerned. Such a court would report upon the facts of the case and make recommendations for a settlement which would, in general, no doubt, be acceptable as terms of settlement or as a basis for further negotiations.

As regards the determination of prices, it is proposed that this should be systematised by the organisation of producers (sellers) and consumers (buyers) and carried on with a full knowlege of all the relevant facts as regards costs of production.

Proposed price changes should be discussed between the Production Council and the Consumers' Council on the basis of ascertained costs. Should it happen that no compromise is reached, then the prices in question should be determined by the President of the Board of Trade, or by an independent tribunal set up by him.

Internal Distribution.

To develop the productive side of the coal industry, and to leave as it is the existing system of distribution, where it is generally held that considerable economies are possible, would be unfair to the reorganised coal industry, as well as to the consumers of coal.

It is necessary, in our opinion, to effect at least two changes :

(*a*) The transport of coal in trucks of which nearly one-half belong to more than 1,000 separate companies and individuals, each of whom reserves his own trucks for his own use, should be brought to an end.   Irrespective of its ownership, the rolling stock needed to move coal should be available for all coal.   The authority responsible for the conduct of the industry, in our scheme the Coal and Power Production Council, should be given the necessary powers to require this change to be made, and to deal with analogous questions such as the size of trucks.

(*b*) It would be the duty of the Coal and Power Production Council, through its Coal Sales Branch, to secure that household coal was distributed to the consumer more economically than at present. It is suggested that the machinery to be used for this purpose should consist, in general, of Local Authorities, which are in many cases already large purchasers of coal for gas and electricity works, for schools and other public buildings.   The Local Authority would act through a Coal Distribution Committee, to which might be added representatives of domestic and industrial producers.

The Export Trade.

With a view to securing the best terms in foreign markets, it is desirable, in our opinion, that a single authority should be established for the purpose of handling the export trade in coal.   It is suggested, therefore, that the conduct of the export trade should either be placed in the hands of a Coal Export Commission, consisting of, say, three Commissioners with knowledge of the coal export trade, or, alternatively, that it should be vested in a Public Utility Corporation consisting in the main of existing coal exporters, *i.e.*, a joint stock company operating under a definite limitation of the rate of dividend payable and such other regulations as the State might wish to impose.

The Export Commission (or Corporation as the case may be) should be separated from and independent of the coal industry, but it should form part of the Coal and Power Consumers' Council referred to above.   In the event of an Export Commission being established the President of the Board of Trade should be answerable to Parliament for its activities.   If the proposal of a Public Utility Corporation were adopted the responsibility of the State would be less direct.

The export body would purchase coal from the coal industry at prices negotiated with the coal industry and would carry on foreign trade in coal.

240. Real Personality of Groups.

The Osborne Judgment and After, by W. M. GELDART, pp. 19, 21.

One consideration of a more general character should be added which will serve to differentiate trade unions from other classes of associations and incorporated bodies.　The conception of a body of members as a real being which can be truly said to have a personality is one fast gaining ground among students of jurisprudence and political science, and is displacing the old view that the personality of such a body is a mere fiction of the law.

. . . .

Independently of its scientific formulation, the English Courts for some years past have been tending in the same direction in a number of decisions which only receive their full meaning by reference to some such doctrine.

. . . .

A trade union is neither one of the organs of the State nor is it a body whose aims are limited to the promotion of the pecuniary and individual interests of its members.　Even in the days of small unions there was a wider outlook than mere self-advancement.

The relation of a workman to his union was always one of soli-darity, for which we should look in vain in the case of the shareholders of a company.　Far more is this true at the present day.　The policy of the great federations, the policy of trade unions assembled in a general congress, must more and more be determined by con-siderations broader than those which affect exclusively the workmen of any one trade or the members of trade unions.　The way in which trade unions have promoted and contributed to higher education among the working classes is only one instance of this broadening outlook.　In these circumstances we shall see something inappro-priate in a policy which would narrowly define for the future what shall and what shall not be the lawful purposes that a trade union may pursue.

241. Corporate Status of Groups.

History of Trade Unionism, by S. AND B. WEBB, 1920 ed., p. 611.

Now, the subject of corporations is one of those in which there had been, among the past generations of English lawyers, a silent and almost unselfconscious development of doctrine, of which, in

Germany, Gierke has been the great inspirer, and Maitland, in this country, the brilliant exponent.

Our English law long rigidly refused to admit that a corporate entity could arise of itself, without some formal and legally authoritative act of outside power. How, it was asked, without some definite act of creation by a superior, could the *persona ficta* come into existence ? How, otherwise (as Madox quaintly puts it), could this mere ' society of mortal men ' become something ' immortal, invisible and incorporeal ' ? As a matter of fact associations or social entities of all sorts always did arise, without the intervention of the lawyers, and nowadays they arise with amazing ease, without any act of creation by a superior ; and when the English lawyers refused to recognise them as existing, it was they who were irrational, and the common law itself that was at fault. Nowadays we live in a world of social entities of all sorts and of every degree of informality, corporate entities that to the old-fashioned lawyers are still legally non-existent as such—clubs and committees of every possible kind ; groups and circles, societies and associations for every conceivable purpose ; unions and combinations and trusts in every trade and profession ; schools and colleges and ' University Extension Classes,' often existing and spending and acting most energetically as entities, having a common purse and a single will, in practice even perpetual succession and (if they desire such a futile luxury) a common seal, without any sort of formal incorporation.

Gradually, English lawyers (whom we need not suspect of reading Gierke, or even, for that matter, Maitland), were unconsciously imbibing the legally heterodox view that a corporate entity is anything which acts as such ; and so far from making it impossible for the *persona ficta* to come into existence without a formal act of creation, they had been, by little alterations of procedure and imperceptible changes in legal principles, sometimes by harmless little dodges and fictions of the Courts themselves, coming near to the practical result of putting every association, which is, in fact, a social entity, however informal in its constitution and however ' spontaneous ' in its origin, in the same position as a *persona ficta*, for the purpose of suing and of being sued, as if it had been created by a formal instrument of incorporation.

.   .   .   .

Now this development of legal doctrine to fit the circumstances of modern social life is, when one comes to think of it, only common sense. If twenty old ladies in the workhouse club together to pro-

vide themselves with a special pot of tea, and agree that one among
them shall be the treasurer of their painfully hoarded pennies as a
common fund, they do, in fact, create a social entity just as real in its
way as the Governor and Company of the Bank of England. . . .
And considering that Trade Unions were now in fact social entities,
often having behind them more than a hundred years of ' perpetual
succession ' ; counting sometimes over a hundred thousand members
moving by a single will ; and occasionally accumulating in a common
purse as much as half a million of money, the Law Lords might well
think it absurd and irrational of Parliament to have decided in 1871-6,
and again in 1906, to regard them as unincorporated groups of
persons, having, in a corporate capacity, no legally enforceable
obligations and hardly any legally enforceable rights.

242. The State and Voluntary Associations.

Self-Government in Industry, by G. D. H. COLE, 1919, ch. v.

The Osborne decision, which rendered illegal the use of Trade
Union funds for political purposes, was based upon a totally wrong
conception of the nature of Trade Unionism. . . . The real principle
at issue was greatly more important than the important special
point involved. The judges, in giving their decision, were really
affirming their view that Trade Union rights are purely the creation
of statute law and that Trade Unions themselves are artificial bodies
created by statute to perform certain functions. Some opponents
of the Osborne decision, on the other hand, expressed the view that a
Trade Union is not a creature of statute law, but a natural form of
human association, and therefore capable of growth and the assumption of new purposes.

In short, there was really, on the one side, the view that all the
rights and powers of other forms of association are derived from the
State, and, on the other side, the view that these rights and powers
belong to such associations by virtue of their nature and the purposes
for which they exist.

Let us now try to apply the view which we have taken of the
State's real nature to this particular case. Trade Unions are
associations based on the ' vocational ' principle. They seek to
group together in one association all those persons who are co-operating in making a particular kind of thing or rendering a particular
kind of service. In the common phrase, they are associations of
' producers,' using ' production ' in the widest sense. The State,

on the other hand, we have decided to regard as an association of
' users ' or ' enjoyers,' of ' consumers,' in the common phrase.   If
this view is right, we cannot regard Trade Unions as deriving their
rights, including the right to exist, from the State.   Associations of
producers and consumers alike may be said, in a sense, to derive
these rights from the community ; but we cannot conceive of an
association of producers deriving its right to exist from an association
of users.

Our view, then, of the nature and rights of vocational and other
forms of association is profoundly modified by the view we have
taken of the nature of the State.   We now see such associations as
natural expressions and instruments of the purposes which certain
groups of individuals have in common, just as we see the State, both
in national and in local government, as the natural expression and
instrument of other purposes which the same individuals have in
common when they are grouped in another way.   Similarly, our
whole view of the relation of the State to other forms of association
is profoundly modified, and we come to see the State, not as the
' divine ' and universally sovereign representative of the community,
but as one among a number of forms of association in which men are
grouped according to the purposes which they have in common.
Men produce in common, and all sorts of association, from the
mediaeval guild to the modern trust and the modern Trade Union
spring from their need to co-operate in production.

243. The Future Organisation of Industry.

The State in the New Social Order, Fabian Tract No. 200, by HAROLD J.
LASKI, 1922.

Second only in importance to education, and in large part dependent upon it, is the growth of industrial self-government.   It
has become intolerable that the mass of men should be the mechanical recipients of orders they are compelled to execute without
scrutiny.   It has become finally clear that the release of individuality
—after all, the ultimate purpose of the state—is utterly impossible
so long as the control of industry is confided to a small number of
men whose decisions need not take account of the wills of those who
work under them.   It may be admitted that the transformation of
industrial control presents immense difficulties.   The mass of the
workers has not been trained to work that is instinct with responsibility.   The capitalist régime has sought not the men who think but

the men who obey. It has subordinated to the acquisitive impulse whatever spirit there is of service and creativeness in those who are subject to its dominion. It has obscured the processes by which it governs. It has so divorced the actual work of production from the business of direction as to leave the industrial pattern unintelligible to those whose lives are dependent upon its right arrangement. So complex have its mechanisms become that no single formula—guild socialism, consumers' co-operation, the multiplication of small peasant proprietorship—has any but a limited application. In the discovery, therefore, of institutions which enable the industrial worker to be something more than a tender of machines it is inevitable that there should be hazardous experiment; and the corollary of experiment is failure. But that feeling of unfreedom which Mr. Justice Sankey discovered among the miners, which interferes with the quantity and quality of their work, is typical of labour as a whole. It demands, as is now recognised, channels of response which will minimise its intensity.

.　　.　　.　　.　　.　　.　　.　　.

Equality of opportunity will undoubtedly multiply the number of citizens fit for political function. But the two important possibilities it opens are, first, that the state becomes informed by a common purpose, and, second, that it is enabled to utilise the reservoir of talent that, with the present disparity, is bound to remain largely undiscovered.

Nor does this doctrine involve the abolition of property as such. It simply limits the rights of ownership by insisting that they shall be conditioned by the performance of service. It must, of course, further limit those rights by organising social institutions in such a fashion that they leave each citizen who desires the sense of freedom in their working to perform, where he has the capacity, responsible functions. It involves, that is to say, the democratisation of industrial control, and the decentralisation of political control. It means for the mines such a form of organisation as that, for instance, which Mr. Justice Sankey has depicted. There, at least, in pit, in district, and in the industry as a whole, the abolition of private ownership would remove barriers which now stand in the path of service and achievement. The miner who could convince his fellows that he was competent to direct their labours could test his powers in an increasingly wider field.

.　　.　　.　　.　　.　　.　　.　　.

But when we pass from functions . . . which concern men as citizens rather than men as producers, analysis makes it obvious that the simple formulae of representative government do not apply. What we need, then, is to take the services that have to be performed and devise institutions for their government. We have so to devise them that we may secure to each function the rights without which citizenship is impossible, and, within the boundaries of that limiting principle, to free the general legislative assembly from the task of intimate and incessant supervision. It is not, in any case, fit for such a task ; for, as Mill long ago pointed out, a popular assembly is in its nature unfitted to administer or dictate in detail to those who control administration. Here it becomes necessary to depart from the narrowly geographical habit of our political thinking. We must learn to think of railways and mines, cotton and agriculture, as areas of government just as real as London and Lancashire. They are relatively unified functions which need, just as much as geographical units, organs of administration. Clearly, of course, it is easier to give a simple form of institutionalism to an industry like mining, which is susceptible of immediate nationalisation, than to an industry like cotton-spinning, in which the formulae of nationalisation are far more dubious. But, granted the conference of powers to a representative assembly for the cotton industry, granted, also, the principles of citizenship within which it must work, it is not difficult to imagine mechanisms through which a constitutional system of government might work there. As with the mines, it is necessary to give representation in such a functional assembly to interests which need special protection—the consumer, the technician, allied industries in a special sense related to cotton. It is necessary, also, to use such associations as the trade unions and the employers' federations as the basis upon which selections of personnel must be made. Nor should any barriers be put in the way of joint consultation between industry and industry. Whether a national economic council is implied in such a scheme as this it is very difficult to say. The problem of its constitution is extraordinarily complex ; and the solution of general industrial questions is, as a rule, really the solution of problems of citizenship which come within the scope of Parliament. Their administration is almost always a special problem of a particular function, and is better left to the function for settlement. When the German Economic Council has had a longer life we shall be better able to judge the possibilities it involves.

It may be useful at this stage to indicate the institutional pattern implied in a social philosophy of this kind. We visualise a Parliament with the taxing power, which lays down fundamental rules, and administers, through the Cabinet, the matters of general citizenship. Below it would be territorial and functional institutions. The one would be concerned with the normal subject matter of local government ; and, under the revised areas of control, they would possess that greater complex of powers characteristic of the first-class German municipality, rather than the narrow delegation inherent in the British system. Each industry would possess an industrial council in which management and labour, technicians and the representatives of allied industries, together with the representatives of the public, would take their place. Such a council would have as its business the application to the industry it controlled of the minimum basis of civilisation we have suggested as now fundamental. It would consider all questions affecting industrial relations within its scope of reference. It would issue decrees, perhaps of the nature of provisional orders, where it was desired to go beyond the principles of the national minimum. It would undertake research ; and it would have a special costings and audit department of which the task would be to secure complete publicity upon the details of the business process within the trade. It is possible, also, that a National Industrial Council would be required ; but it is doubtful whether it is possible to build it, and uncertain whether the questions it would seek to resolve are not, in fact, problems with which the ordinary Parliament is better able to deal.

244. A Vocational Parliament in the Socialist Commonwealth ?

A Constitution for the Socialist Commonwealth of Great Britian, by S. AND B. WEBB, 1920, p. 309 ff.

There remains the question whether, in the reorganisation of the vocational world herein adumbrated as part of the Socialist Commonwealth, there is any place or function for a national assembly of vocational representatives. Frankly, we do not see that there is. So far as experience affords any guide, there is the very smallest indication in Great Britain of the practicability of such an assembly, or of any possible function that it could perform. There is, as has already been mentioned, at present no sign, in any country, of any common national assembly of representatives of the brain-working professions even among those employed at salaries. Among the manual workers, even with the common bond of resistance to the capitalist employer, the Trades Union Congress, after more than half a century of existence, cannot be said to have manifested any very intense corporate life ; or—apart from the purely political issues, not affecting the trades or the Trade Unions, as such, which are now dealt with by the conferences of the Labour Party—to have discovered any purpose that it can serve other than that of defending the institution of Trade Unionism against attack [1] . . . without making intolerably large an assembly that will have to represent something like 20,000,000 active producers, no vocation numbering fewer than 30,000 members could, on any arithmetical basis, claim as much as a single representative, whilst the miners and agriculturalists would want as many as thirty apiece.

What is more important is, however, the consideration that, even if a National Assembly could be formed by election from all the several vocations among which the twenty million producers would be divided, there would be, as it seems to us, no interest that the representatives would, as members of their several vocations, have in common. *To have interests in common, even when there is disagreement about them, appears to be indispensable for any effective assembly.*

. . . .

That is not to say that there cannot be any room, in the reorganisation of the vocational world, for general assemblies on a vocational basis. Whilst there seem no place and no function in the Socialist Commonwealth for a national assembly professing to formulate a General Will of all the several vocations as such—a national assembly which would represent, if not exactly the same aggregate of individuals, at any rate precisely the same aggregate of families as the members elected by the adult citizens in geographical constituencies —there is no need to deprecate assemblies of delegates of various vocational associations, any more than those of delegates of the membership of a single association, for dealing with any matters in which they feel that they have, as representatives of distinctive vocations, any common interests. The most important type of such an assembly might be one representing a number of distinct vocations that felt themselves allied to each other, and separated from the rest of the community, in respect of some distinctive common needs in vocational education, or in their conditions of employment, or in their terms of service.

[1] See *History of Trade Unionism*, by S. and B. Webb.

245. Industrial Parliament Project.

RECOMMENDATIONS OF THE PROVISIONAL JOINT COMMITTEE OF THE INDUSTRIAL CONFERENCE, 1919.   Cmd. 501, p. 12.

The considered views of the Committee are as follows :

Preamble.

A National Industrial Council should not supersede any of the existing agencies for dealing with industrial questions.   Its object would be to supplement and co-ordinate the existing sectional machinery by bringing together the knowledge and experience of all sections, and focussing them upon the problems that affect industrial relations as a whole.   Its functions therefore would be advisory.

Such a Council would have to be large in order to give due representation to all the industrial interests concerned ; at the same time it should be as small as is consistent with an adequate representative basis.   Since in any case it would be too large for the transaction of detailed business, a Standing Committee, large enough to ensure that it will not be unrepresentative, will be needed.   The Council must be elected, not nominated, otherwise its authority will not be adequate to the proper discharge of its functions.   The method of election must be determined by each side for itself, subject to two conditions : first, that the members must be representative of organisations, not of individual employers or workpeople ; and, second, that the organisations concerned adopt such a method of election or appointment that their nominees can be regarded as fully representative.

In order that the Council may have the necessary independent status and authority if it is to promote industrial peace, the Government should recognise it as the official consultative authority to the Government upon industrial relations, and should make it the normal channel through which the opinion and experience of industry will be sought on all questions with which industry as a whole is concerned.

In addition to advising the Government the Council should, when it thought fit, issue statements on industrial questions or disputes for the guidance of public opinion.

Objects.

To secure the largest possible measure of joint action between the representative organisations of employers and workpeople, and to be the normal channel through which the opinion and experience of industry will be sought by the Government on all questions affecting industry as a whole.

It will be open to the Council to take action that falls within the scope of its general definition. Among its more specific objects will be :

(*a*) The consideration of general questions affecting industrial relations.

(*b*) The consideration of measures for joint or several action to anticipate and avoid threatened disputes.

(*c*) The consideration of actual disputes involving general questions.

(*d*) The consideration of legislative proposals affecting industrial relations.

(*e*) To advise the Government on industrial questions and on the general industrial situation.

(*f*) To issue statements for the guidance of public opinion on industrial issues.

CONSTITUTION.

I. The Council.

1. The Council shall consist of four hundred members fully representative of and duly accredited by the Employers' organisations and the Trade Unions, to be elected as to one half by the Employers' organisations, and as to one half by the Trade Unions.

2. Subject to the conditions stated in Clause 1, the method of election and allocation of representatives shall be determined by each side for itself.

     .   .   .   .

3. Members of the Council shall retire annually, and shall be eligible for re-election by the organisations which they represent. Casual vacancies may be filled by the side in which the vacancy occurs, any member so appointed to sit until the end of the current year.

4. The Council shall meet at least twice a year, and in addition as often as the Standing Committee hereafter referred to deem to be necessary.

5. The Minister of Labour for the time being shall be President of the Council and shall, when possible, preside at its meetings. There shall be three Vice-Presidents, one appointed by the Government to be Chairman of the Standing Committee hereafter referred

to, one elected by and from the Employers' representatives on the Council, one elected by and from the Trade Unions' representatives. In the absence of the President the Chairman of the Standing Committee shall preside, in his absence one of the other Vice-Presidents.

The Chairman of the Committee shall be a whole-time officer, and shall have associated with him two secretaries, one appointed by the Employers' representatives on the Council, one appointed by the Trade Unions' representatives.

6. *Voting.*—The two sides of the Council shall vote separately, and no resolution shall be declared carried unless approved by a majority of those present on each side. Each side shall determine for itself the method of voting.

7. *Finance.*—The expenses of the Council, subject to sanction by the Treasury, shall be borne by the Government.

8. The Council shall be empowered to make Standing Orders for the conduct of its business.

II. *The Standing Committee.*

1. There shall be a Standing Committee of the Council, consisting of 25 members elected by and from the employers' representatives on the Council, and 25 members elected by and from the trade union representatives.

2. The method of election of members shall be determined by each side of the Council for itself.

3. The Standing Committee shall be empowered to take such action as it deems to be necessary to carry out the objects of the Council. It shall consider any questions referred to it by the Council or the Government, and shall report to the Council its decisions.

4. The Standing Committee shall be empowered to appoint an Emergency Committee and such Sub-Committees as may be necessary.

5. The Standing Committee shall be empowered to co-opt representatives of any trade not directly represented upon it for the consideration of any question affecting that trade.

6. The Standing Committee shall meet as often as may be necessary, and at least once a month.

7. The Government shall appoint a Chairman to the Standing Committee, who shall preside at its meetings, but shall have no vote. There shall be two Vice-Chairmen, one elected by and from the

employers' representatives on the Committee, and one by and from the trade union representatives. In the absence of the Chairman the Vice-Chairmen shall preside in turn.

8. The Standing Committee, with the consent of the Treasury, shall be empowered to appoint such secretaries and other officers as may be necessary for the conduct of its business.

9. The Standing Committee shall be empowered to make Standing Orders for the conduct of its business.

10. Finance.—The expenses of the Standing Committee shall, subject to sanction by the Treasury, be borne by the Government.

246. National Industrial Council.

RESOLUTION AGREED UPON BY THE INDUSTRIAL CONFERENCE OF THE GENERAL COUNCIL OF THE TRADES UNION CONGRESS AND THE 'MOND' GROUP OF EMPLOYERS, 4th July, 1928.

It is agreed that it is desirable for the continuous improvement of Industrial Reorganisation and Industrial Relations that a National Industrial Council should be formed, and it is recommended that the necessary steps for its formation should be taken immediately.

It is recommended that the composition of the National Industrial Council should be as follows :

(*A*) The representatives of the workers should be the members of the General Council of the Trades Union Congress.

(*B*) An equal number of representatives of the employers should be nominated by the Federation of British Industries and the National Confederation of Employers' Organisations.

It is agreed that the three main functions of the National Industrial Council should be :

1. To hold regular meetings once a quarter for general consultation on the widest questions concerning industry and industrial progress.

2. To establish a Standing Joint Committee for the appointment of Joint Conciliation Boards, as set out in detail in the Agreed Resolution on the Prevention of Disputes.

3. To establish and direct machinery for continuous investigation into industrial problems.

247. Pluralism and Voluntary Groups.

Authority in the Modern State, by H. J. LASKI, 1919, pp. 56 ff.

Freedom of thought, then, the modern state must regard as absolute ; and that means freedom of thought whether on the part of the individual or of a social group. Nothing is more stupid than for the state to regard the individual and itself as the only entities of which account must be taken, or to suggest that other groups live by its good pleasure. That is to make the easy mistake of thinking that the activities of man in his relation to government exhaust his nature. It is a fatal error. The societies of men are spontaneous. They may well conflict with the state ; but they will only ultimately suffer suppression if the need they supply is, in some equally adequate form, answered by the state itself. And it is tolerably clear that there are many such interests the state cannot serve. The growth of religious differences, for example, makes the state-adoption of any religious system a matter of doubtful expediency ; and that means, as has been before insisted, that the internal relations of churches will in fact deny state-interference. A Society like the Presbyterian Church, which recognises only the headship of Christ, will resist to the uttermost any external attempt at the definition of its life ; and experience seems to suggest that the state will lose far more than it can gain by the effort.

Where the fellowship is economic in nature the problem is, indeed, far more complex ; for the modern state is, at every turn, an economic organisation. But, even here, the impossibility of absorption is shown by the tragic history of such things as the Combination Acts. The state may well exact responsibility for the thought such fellowships may have where it seeks translation into action ; but it will establish its exaction only where the individual, himself judging between conflicting claims, is driven to feel that the effort of the state is more valid than the other.

. . . .

This theory of internal limitation upon the action of authority is essentially a pragmatic one. It admits that any system which failed in practice to secure what is largely termed the end of social life would be inadequate. It is sufficiently alive to the importance of stability to seek to place the fundamental notions of each age beyond the temptation of malicious enterprise. It is such notions that we have termed rights. It is such notions we have denied the power, at least in theory, of governments to traverse.

For we say that their realisation is essential to the end of the state ; and government is itself only a means to that end.

The state, in fact, must limit its instruments by the law of its own being. Sovereignty, in such an aspect, can never belong to the government if we term it the supreme power to do what is thought necessary. Government, it is clear, will have a power to will. But that will may come into conflict with other wills ; and the test of the allegiance it should win is the degree in which it is thought to be more in harmony than its antagonists with the end of social life.

And this, it is clear also, envisages a pluralistic conception of society. It denies the oneness of society and the state. It insists that nothing is known of the state purpose until it is declared ; and it refuses, for obvious reasons, to make *a priori* observations about its content. It sees man as a being who wishes to realise himself as a member of society. It refers back each action upon which judgment is to be passed to the conscience of the individual. It insists that the supreme arbiter of the event is the totality of such consciences. It does not deny that the individual is influenced by the thousand associations with which he is in contact ; but it is unable to perceive that he is absorbed by them. It sees society as one only in purpose ; but it urges that this purpose has, in fact, been differently interpreted, and is capable of realisation by more than a single method. In such an analysis the state is only one among many forms of human association. It is not necessarily any more in harmony with the end of society than a church or a trade union or a freemason's lodge. They have, it is true, relations which the state controls ; but that does not make them inferior to the state. The assumption of inferiority, indeed, is a fallacy that comes from comparing different immediate purposes. Moral inferiority in purpose as between a church and state there can hardly be ; legal inferiority is either an illegitimate postulation of Austinian sovereignty, or else the result of a false identification of state and society. . . .

The state, as we have seen, is in reality the reflexion of what a dominant group or class in a community believes to be political good. And, in the main, it is reasonably clear that political good is to-day, for the most part defined in economic terms. It mirrors within itself, that is to say, the economic structure of society. It is relatively unimportant in what fashion we organise the institutions of the state.

Practically they will reflect the economic system ; practically, also, they will protect it. The opinion of the state, at least in its legislative expression, will largely reproduce the opinion of those who hold the keys of economic power. There is, indeed, no part of the community of which economic power is unable to influence the opinions. Not that it will be an absolute control that is exerted by it. The English statute-book bears striking testimony to the results of the conflict between the holders of economic power and those who desire its possession ; and, often enough, there has been generous co-operation behind the effected change. But the fundamental truth remains that the simple weapons of politics are alone powerless to effect any basic redistribution of economic strength. . . .

Mr. Osborne's dislike of a labour party with a political programme did not prove a general truth that the historic lines of party-division in England represent a satisfactory alignment of economic power to the working-man. It did not prove that there was, in fact, a possible harmony of interest between trade unions of which the dominant purpose was the control of industry in the interests of democratization and employers who deny the utility of such control. . . . The trade union is concerned with the business of production ; the state is, above all, concerned with the general regularity of the supply for consumption. What, then, the trade union is compelled to deny is the subordination of the function he fulfils as a producer to his interest in the supply of his needs. . . .

To admit the trade union to an effective place in government, to insist that it is fundamental in the direction of production, is to make the worker count in the world. He may be then, also, a tender of machines ; but where his trade union is making decisions in which his own will is a part he is something more than a tender of machines. His very experience on this side of government will make him more valuable in his quality as citizen.

SHORT BIBLIOGRAPHY

HISTORICAL

General

BEER, MAX. *The History of British Socialism.* (Bell.) New edition in preparation.

COLE, G. D. H. *A Short History of the British Working Class Movement.* (Labour Publishing Co.) 3 vols. 1925, 1926, 1927. 6s. each.

HAMMOND, J. L. & B. *The Village Labourer.* (Longmans, Green.) 1927. 6s.

    The Town Labourer. (Longmans, Green.) 1925. 6s. 6d.

    The Skilled Labourer. (Longmans, Green.) 1920. 12s. 6d.

    The Rise of Modern Industry. (Methuen.) 1925. 10s. 6d.

HOWELL, G. *Labour Legislation, Labour Movements and Labour Leaders.* (Benn.) 1902. 2 vols. 7s. and 2s. 6d.

TRADES UNION CONGRESS. *The Story of the T.U.C.* (T.U.C.) 1925. 2d.

WEBB, S. & B. *History of Trade Unionism.* (Longmans, Green.) 1920. 21s.

Special

COLE, G. D. H. *Robert Owen.* (Benn.) 1925. 15s.

COLE, G. D. H., and ARNOT, R. P. *Trade Unionism on the Railways.* (Fabian Society and Students' Bookshops Ltd.) 1s.

COLE, G. D. H. *Trade Unionism and Munitions.* (Oxford University Press.) 1923. 7s. 6d.

    Workshop Organisation. (Oxford University Press.) 1923. 7s. 6d.

    Labour in the Coal-Mining Industry. (Oxford University Press.) 1923. 7s. 6d.

EDWARDS, NESS. *History of the South Wales Miners.* (Labour Publishing Co.) 1926. 2s. 6d.

ORTON, W. A. *Labour in Transition. A Survey of British Industrial History since 1914.* (Allan.) 1924. 5s.

POSTGATE, R. W. *The Builders' History*. (Labour Publishing Co.) 1923. 5s. 6d.

SELLEY, E. *Village Trade Unions in Two Centuries*. (Allen & Unwin.) 1919. 4s. 6d. and 3s.

WALLAS, G. *Life of Francis Place*. (Allen & Unwin.) 4th edition. 1925. 7s. 6d.

WEBB, S. *The Story of the Durham Miners*. (Fabian Soc. and Lab. Pub. Co.) 1922. 5s. and 2s. 6d.

DESCRIPTIVE

APPLETON, W. A. *Trade Unions, Their Past, Present and Future*. (Allan.) 1925. 3s. 6d.

CITRINE, W. M. *The Trade Union Movement of Great Britain*. (International Federation of Trade Unions.) 1926. 1s. 6d.

COLE, G. D. H. *The World of Labour*. (Macmillan.) 1928. 6s.
   Organised Labour. (Labour Publishing Co.) 1924. 6s.
   Self-Government in Industry. (Macmillan.) 1928. 5s.

DRAKE, B. *Women in Trade Unions*. (Labour Publishing Co.) 1920. 8s. 6d. and 6s.

GOODRICH, CARTER. *The Frontier of Control*. (Bell.) 1921. 7s. 6d.

LLOYD, C. M. *Trade Unionism*. (Black.) 1928. 3rd edition. 5s.

TRADES UNION CONGRESS. *Annual Report*. (T.U.C.) 3s.
   The General Council of the T.U.C. Its Powers, Functions and Work. (T.U.C.) 1925. 2d.

WEBB, S. & B. *Industrial Democracy*. (Longmans, Green.) 1920. 21s.

LEGAL

HENDERSON, A. *Trade Unions and the Law*. (Benn.) 1927. 8s. 6d. and 6s.

SLESSER, SIR H. H., and BAKER, C. *Trade Union Law*. (Nisbet.) 1927. 21s.

SLESSER, SIR H. H., and HENDERSON, A. *Industrial Law*. (Benn.) 1924. 70s.

TILLYARD, PROFESSOR F. *Industrial Law*. (Black.) 1928. 2nd edition. 15s.

REFERENCE

19th Abstract of Labour Statistics. (H.M. Stationery Office.) 1928. Cmd. 3140. 4s.

Annual Report of Chief Registrar of Friendly Societies on Trade Unions. (H.M. Stationery Office.) 1926 issue. 3s.

Directory of Employers' Associations, Trade Unions, etc. (H.M. Stationery Office.) 1925. 3s.

International Federation of Trade Unions Year Book. Annually (I.F.T.U.) 10s.

Labour Year Book. Annually. (Trades Union Congress and Labour Party.) 5s. and 3s. 6d.

FOREIGN

ATKINSON, M. A. Trade Unionism in Australia. (Sydney : W.E.A. London : Students' Bookshops Ltd.) 1915. 1s. 6d.

COMMONS, J. R., AND ASSOCIATES. History of Labour in the United States. (Macmillan.) 2 vols. 1921. 36s.

GITSHAM, E., and TREMBATH, J. F. Labour Organisation in South Africa. (Durban : E.P. and Commercial Printing Co., Ltd. London : Students' Bookshops Ltd.) 1926. 5s. and 1s. 8d.

INTERNATIONAL FEDERATION OF TRADE UNIONS. C. MERTENS. Trade Union Movement in Belgium. (I.F.T.U.) 1925. 1s. 1d. post free.

SIGFRID HANSSON. Trade Union Movement of Sweden. (I.F.T.U.) 1927. 10d. post free.

SASSENBACH, J. Twenty-five Years of International Trade Unionism. 1926. 1s. 6d.

SEIDEL, R. The Trade Union Movement of Germany. 1928. 1s. 6d.

INTERNATIONAL LABOUR OFFICE. The Trade Union Movement in Soviet Russia. (King.) 1927. 4s.

LEVINE, L. Syndicalism in France : A Study in Revolutionary Syndicalism. (King.) 9s.

PERLMAN, S. A. History of Trade Unionism in the United States. (Macmillan.) 1923. 8s. 6d.

SAPOSS, D. Readings in Trade Unionism. (New York : Doran.) 1926. 10s.

(See also International Federation of Trade Unions Year Book. (I.F.T.U. 10s. Labour Year Book. (Trades Union Congress and Labour Party.) 5s. and 3s. 6d.)

PERIODICALS

Industrial Review.   (Trades Union Congress.)   2d. per month.

Labour Magazine.   (Trades Union Congress and Labour Party.)   6d. per month.

Ministry of Labour Gazette.   (H.M. Stationery Office.)   6d. per month.

(Many Trade Union Journals, of which a full list will be found in the *Labour Year Book*.)

INDEX

All references are to Pages.

PRINTED IN GREAT BRITAIN BY ROBERT MACLEHOSE AND CO. LTD.
THE UNIVERSITY PRESS, GLASGOW.